Encyclopedia of Counseling

Encyclopedia of Counseling

Cross-Cultural Counseling

VOLUME 3

Editor-in-Chief
Frederick T. L. Leong
Michigan State University

Senior Editor
Madonna G. Constantine
Teachers College, Columbia University

Associate Editor
Roger L. Worthington
University of Missouri–Columbia

SAGE

Los Angeles • London • New Delhi • Singapore

A SAGE Reference Publication

Copyright © 2008 by SAGE Publications, Inc.

All rights reserved. No part of this book may be reproduced or utilized in any form or by any means, electronic or mechanical, including photocopying, recording, or by any information storage and retrieval system, without permission in writing from the publisher.

For information:

SAGE Publications, Inc.
2455 Teller Road
Thousand Oaks, California 91320
E-mail: order@sagepub.com

SAGE Publications Ltd.
1 Oliver's Yard
55 City Road
London EC1Y 1SP
United Kingdom

SAGE Publications India Pvt. Ltd.
B 1/I 1 Mohan Cooperative Industrial Area
Mathura Road, New Delhi 110 044
India

SAGE Publications Asia-Pacific Pte. Ltd.
33 Pekin Street #02-01
Far East Square
Singapore 048763

Printed in the United States of America.

Library of Congress Cataloging-in-Publication Data

Encyclopedia of counseling/Frederick T. L. Leong, general editor
    v. cm.
"A SAGE reference publication."
Includes bibliographical references and index.
    Contents: v. 1. Changes and challenges for counseling in the 21st century, A-Z/editor, Elizabeth M. Altmaier—v. 2. Personal and emotional counseling, A-Z/editor, Howard E.A. Tinsley—v. 3. Cross-cultural counseling, A-Z/editor, Madonna G. Constantine—v. 4. Career counseling, A-Z / editor, W. Bruce Walsh.
IISBN 978-1-4129-0928-0 (cloth : alk. paper)
    1. Counseling—Encyclopedias. I. Leong, Frederick T. L. II. Altmaier, Elizabeth M.

BF636.54.E53 2008
158'.303—dc22
                                                              2007045854

This book is printed on acid-free paper.

08 09 10 11 12 10 9 8 7 6 5 4 3 2 1

Publisher/Acquiring Editor:	Rolf A. Janke
Developmental Editors:	Sara Tauber, Carole Maurer
Reference Systems Manager:	Leticia Gutierrez
Production Editor:	Tracy Buyan
Copy Editor:	Colleen Brennan
Typesetter:	C&M Digitals (P) Ltd.
Proofreader:	Andrea Martin
Indexer:	Julie Sherman Grayson
Cover Designer:	Michelle Kenny
Marketing Manager:	Amberlyn Erzinger

Contents

Editorial Board, *vi*

List of Entries, *vii*

Reader's Guide, *xi*

About the Editors, *xix*

Contributors, *xxi*

Entries

Volume 3, Cross-Cultural Counseling: A–Z

941–1390

Editorial Board

Editor-in-Chief

Frederick T. L. Leong, Ph.D.
Michigan State University

Volume 3 Editors

Senior Editor

Madonna G. Constantine, Ph.D.
Teachers College, Columbia University

Associate Editor

Roger L. Worthington, Ph.D.
University of Missouri–Columbia

Advisory Board Members

Patricia Arredondo, Ed.D.
Arizona State University

Charles J. Gelso, Ph.D.
University of Maryland

P. Paul Heppner, Ph.D.
University of Missouri–Columbia

Francis G. Lu, M.D.
University of California, San Francisco

Paula S. Nurius, Ph.D.
University of Washington

Derald Wing Sue, Ph.D.
Teachers College, Columbia University

List of Entries

Volume 3

Acculturation
Acculturative Stress
Achievement Gap
Adaptation
Adoption, Transracial. *See* Transracial Adoption
Affirmative Action
African Americans
Afrocentricity/Afrocentrism
Alaska Natives
Allocentrism
American Indians
American Jews
Antisemitism
Arab Americans
Arredondo, Patricia
Asian American Psychological Association
Asian Americans
Assimilation
Association of Black Psychologists
Atkinson, Donald Ray

Barriers to Cross-Cultural Counseling
Bernal, Martha E.
Bias
Bicultural
Bilingual Counseling
Bilingualism
Biracial
Black English
Black Psychology
Black Racial Identity Development
Bureau of Indian Affairs

Casas, Jesús Manuel
Certificate of Degree of Indian Blood
Change Agent

Civil Rights
Clark, Kenneth Bancroft
Clark, Mamie Phipps
Classism
Collectivism
Colonialism
Color-Blind Racial Ideology
Communication
Confucianism
Constantine, Madonna G.
Critical Race Theory
Cross, William E., Jr.
Cross-Cultural Psychology
Cross-Cultural Training
Cultural Accommodation and Negotiation
Cultural Encapsulation
Cultural Equivalence
Cultural Mistrust
Cultural Paranoia
Cultural Relativism
Cultural Values
Culture
Culture-Bound Syndromes
Culture-Free Testing
Culture Shock

Deficit Hypothesis
Demographics, United States
Discrimination
Diversity
Drapetomania

Empowerment
Enculturation
Espiritismo
Ethnic Cleansing
Ethnic Identity
Ethnicity

Ethnic Minority
Ethnic Pride
Ethnocentrism
Etic–Emic Distinction
Eurocentrism

Familismo
Fatalism
Filial Piety

Healthy Paranoia
Helms, Janet E.
Help-Seeking Behavior
High-Context Communication
Hispanics, Hispanic Americans. *See* Latinos

Identity
Identity Development
Idiocentrism
Immigrants
Indian Health Service
Indigenous Healing
Individualism
Intelligence Tests
Interracial Comfort
Interracial Marriage
Ivey, Allen E.: Counseling Theory and Skills Training

Kwanzaa

LaFromboise, Teresa Davis
Latinos
Learned Helplessness
Leong, Frederick T. L.
Locus of Control
Loss of Face
Low-Context Communication

Machismo
Marianismo
Marsella, Anthony J.
Model Minority Myth
Monocultural
Multicultural Counseling
Multicultural Counseling Competence
Multiculturalism
Multicultural Personality
Multicultural Psychology
Multiracial Families

National Association for the Advancement of Colored People
Nationalism
National Latina/o Psychological Association

Oppression
Organizational Diversity
Orthogonal Cultural Identification Theory

Pacific Islanders
Pedersen, Paul Bodholdt
Personal Space
Pluralism
Political Correctness
Poverty
Power and Powerlessness
Prejudice

Race
Racial Identity
Racial Microaggressions
Racial Pride
Racism
Refugees
Religion/Religious Belief Systems
Reversed Racism

Santería
Second Culture Acquisition
Sexism
Social Identity Theory
Social Justice
Society for the Psychological Study of Ethnic Minority Issues
Society of Indian Psychologists
Socioeconomic Status
Sojourner
Spirituality
Stereotype
Stereotype Threat
Sue, Derald Wing: Contributions to Multicultural Psychology and Counseling
Sue, Stanley

Third World
Tokenism
Translation Methods
Transracial Adoption
Trimble, Joseph E.

Universalism

Visible Racial/Ethnic Groups
Vontress, Clemmont Eyvind

White, Joseph L.
White Americans

White Privilege
White Racial Identity Development
Worldview

Xenophobia

Reader's Guide

This list is provided to assist readers in locating entries on related topics. Some entry titles appear in more than one category.

Assessment, Testing, and Research Methods

Academic Achievement (Vol. 2)
Academic Achievement, Nature and Use of (Vol. 4)
Achievement, Aptitude, and Ability Tests (Vol. 4)
Adaptive Behavior Testing (Vol. 2)
Adult Career Concerns Inventory (Vol. 4)
Affect (Mood States), Assessment of (Vol. 2)
Armed Services Vocational Aptitude Battery (Vol. 4)
Assessment (Vol. 4)
Behavioral Observation Methods, Assessment (Vol. 1)
Behavior Assessment System for Children, Second Edition (Vol. 1)
Behavior Rating Scales (Vol. 1)
Biodata (Vol. 4)
Campbell Interest and Skill Survey (Vol. 4)
Card Sorts (Vol. 4)
Career Attitudes and Strategies Inventory (Vol. 4)
Career Barriers Inventory (Vol. 4)
Career Beliefs Inventory (Vol. 4)
Career Decision-Making Difficulties Questionnaire (Vol. 4)
Career Decision Scale (Vol. 4)
Career Decision Self-Efficacy Scale (Vol. 4)
Career Development Inventory (Vol. 4)
Career Factors Inventory (Vol. 4)
Career Mastery Inventory (Vol. 4)
Career Maturity Inventory (Vol. 4)
Career Occupational Preference System (Vol. 4)
Career Planning Survey (Vol. 4)
Career Services Model (Vol. 4)
Career Style Interview (Vol. 4)
Career Thoughts Inventory (Vol. 4)
Career Transitions Inventory (Vol. 4)
Clinical Interview as an Assessment Technique (Vol. 2)
Cognition/Intelligence, Assessment of (Vol. 2)
Cognitive Information Processing Model (Vol. 4)
College Student Experiences Questionnaire (Vol. 4)
Common Factors Model (Vol. 2)
Community-Based Action Research (Vol. 1)
Computer-Assisted Testing (Vol. 2)
Conners' Rating Scales—Revised (Vol. 1)
Continuous Performance Tests (Vol. 1)
Culture-Free Testing (Vol. 3)
DISCOVER (Vol. 4)
Employee Aptitude Survey (Vol. 4)
Environmental Assessment Technique (Vol. 4)
Expressed, Manifest, Tested, and Inventoried Interests (Vol. 4)
Functional Behavioral Assessment (Vol. 1)
General Aptitude Test Battery (Vol. 4)
Hall Occupational Orientation Inventory (Vol. 4)
Health Belief Model (Vol. 1)
Human Subjects Review in an Online World (Vol. 1)
Intelligence Tests (Vol. 3)
Jackson Vocational Interest Inventory (Vol. 4)
Kuder Career Search (Vol. 4)
Language Difficulties, Clinical Assessment of (Vol. 2)
Memory, Assessment of (Vol. 2)
Mental Status Examination (Vol. 2)
Minnesota Importance Questionnaire (Vol. 4)
Mixed Methodology Research (Vol. 1)
Multicultural Career Assessment Models (Vol. 4)
Multicultural Career Counseling Checklist (Vol. 4)

xi

My Vocational Situation Scale (Vol. 4)
National Survey of Student Engagement (Vol. 4)
Parenting Stress Index (Vol. 1)
Performance Modeling (Vol. 4)
Personality Assessment (Vol. 2)
Personality Assessment and Careers (Vol. 4)
Person–Environment Fit (Vol. 4)
Person Matching (Vol. 4)
Prescreening, In-Depth Exploration, and Choice Model (Vol. 4)
Problem-Solving Appraisal (Vol. 2)
Process and Outcome Research (Vol. 4)
Psychometric Properties (Vol. 2)
Psychopathology, Assessment of (Vol. 2)
Qualitative Methodologies (Vol. 1)
Quantitative Methodologies (Vol. 1)
Self-Directed Search (Vol. 4)
Self-Esteem, Assessment of (Vol. 2)
Strong Interest Inventory (Vol. 4)
System of Interactive Guidance Information (Vol. 4)
Test Interpretation (Vol. 2)
Transition Behavior Scale (Vol. 4)
Translation and Adaptation of Psychological Tests (Vol. 1)
Unisex Edition of the ACT Interest Inventory (Vol. 4)
Values Scale (Vol. 4)

Biographies

Altmaier, Elizabeth M. (Vol. 1)
Arredondo, Patricia (Vol. 3)
Atkinson, Donald Ray (Vol. 3)
Bandura, Albert (Vol. 2)
Beck, Aaron T. (Vol. 2)
Bernal, Martha E. (Vol. 3)
Bingham, Rosie Phillips (Vol. 1)
Casas, Jesús Manuel (Vol. 3)
Clark, Kenneth Bancroft (Vol. 3)
Clark, Mamie Phipps (Vol. 3)
Constantine, Madonna G. (Vol. 3)
Costa, Paul T., and McCrae, Robert R. (Vol. 2)
Courtois, Christine A. (Vol. 1)
Crites, John O. (Vol. 4)
Cross, William E., Jr. (Vol. 3)
Csikszentmihalyi, Mihaly (Vol. 2)
Dawis, René Villanueva (Vol. 4)
Deci, Edward L., and Ryan, Richard M. (Vol. 2)
Delworth, Ursula (Vol. 1)
Douce, Louise (Vol. 1)
Ellis, Albert (Vol. 2)
Fretz, Bruce (Vol. 1)
Freud, Sigmund (Vol. 2)
Friedlander, Myrna L. (Vol. 1)
Gelso, Charles J. (Vol. 2)
Goldberg, Lewis R. (Vol. 2)
Goldman, Leo (Vol. 2)
Helms, Janet E. (Vol. 3)
Heppner, Puncky Paul (Vol. 2)
Hill, Clara E. (Vol. 2)
Holland, John L. (Vol. 4)
Ivey, Allen E. (Vol. 1)
Ivey, Allen E.: Counseling Theory and Skills Training (Vol. 3)
Jung, Carl (Vol. 2)
Kitchener, Karen Strohm (Vol. 1)
Krumboltz, John D. (Vol. 4)
Kuder, Frederic (Vol. 4)
LaFromboise, Teresa Davis (Vol. 3)
Leong, Frederick T. L. (Vol. 3)
Lofquist, Lloyd Henry (Vol. 4)
Marsella, Anthony J. (Vol. 3)
Meehl, Paul E. (Vol. 2)
Norcross, John C. (Vol. 1)
Osipow, Samuel H. (Vol. 4)
Parsons, Frank (Vol. 4)
Pedersen, Paul Bodholdt (Vol. 3)
Roe, Anne (Vol. 4)
Roelhke, Helen J. (Vol. 1)
Rogers, Carl R. (Vol. 2)
Ryff, Carol D. (Vol. 2)
Seligman, Martin E. P. (Vol. 2)
Skinner, B. F. (Vol. 2)
Strong, Edward Kellogg, Jr. (Vol. 4)
Strong, Stanley R. (Vol. 2)
Sue, Derald Wing (Vol. 1)
Sue, Derald Wing: Contributions to Multicultural Psychology and Counseling (Vol. 3)
Sue, Stanley (Vol. 3)
Super, Donald Edwin (Vol. 4)
Thurstone, Louis L. (Vol. 2)
Tinsley, Howard E. A. (Vol. 4)
Tracey, Terence J. G. (Vol. 2)
Trimble, Joseph E. (Vol. 3)
Tyler, Leona E. (Vol. 1)
Tyler, Leona E.: Human Multipotentiality (Vol. 2)
Vasquez, Melba J. T. (Vol. 1)
Vontress, Clemmont Eyvind (Vol. 3)
Walsh, W. Bruce (Vol. 4)
Wampold, Bruce E. (Vol. 2)

Wechsler, David (Vol. 2)
Weiss, David J. (Vol. 2)
White, Joseph L. (Vol. 3)
Williamson, Edmund Griffith (Vol. 4)

Coping

Abuse (Vol. 2)
Acculturative Stress (Vol. 3)
Adaptation (Vol. 3)
Bereavement (Vol. 1)
Cancer Management (Vol. 1)
Career Indecision (Vol. 4)
Caregiver Burden (Vol. 1)
Coping (Vol. 2)
Culture Shock (Vol. 3)
Decision Making (Vol. 4)
Disasters, Impact on Children (Vol. 1)
Forgiveness (Vol. 2)
Healthy Paranoia (Vol. 3)
Job Loss (Vol. 4)
Normative Issues (Vol. 2)
Occupational Stress (Vol. 1)
Poverty (Vol. 3)
Sexual Violence and Coercion (Vol. 1)
Social Support (Vol. 2)
Stereotype Threat (Vol. 3)
Stress (Vol. 2)
Stress Management (Vol. 2)
Work–Family Balance (Vol. 4)
Work Stress (Vol. 4)

Counseling—General

Barriers to Cross-Cultural Counseling (Vol. 3)
Career Counseling Process (Vol. 4)
Change Agent (Vol. 3)
Client Attitudes and Behaviors (Vol. 2)
Clinical Presenting Issues (Vol. 2)
Counseling Process/Outcome (Vol. 2)
Counselors and Therapists (Vol. 2)
Current Procedural Terminology (Vol. 2)
Diagnostic and Statistical Manual of Mental Disorders (DSM) (Vol. 2)
Dictionary of Occupational Titles (Vol. 4)
Empirically Based Professional Practice (Vol. 1)
Expectations About Therapy (Vol. 2)
Facilitative Conditions (Vol. 2)
Occupational Information (Vol. 4)
Occupational Information Network (Vol. 4)
Outcomes of Counseling and Psychotherapy (Vol. 2)
Relationships With Clients (Vol. 2)
Self-Disclosure (Vol. 2)
Taxonomy of Helpful Impacts (Vol. 2)
Technology and Treatment (Vol. 1)
Therapist Interpretation (Vol. 2)
Therapy Process, Individual (Vol. 2)
Treatment Compliance (Vol. 1)
Underdiagnosis/Overdiagnosis (Vol. 2)
Working Alliance (Vol. 2)

Economic/Work Issues

Affirmative Action (Vol. 3)
Americans with Disabilities Act (Vol. 1)
Career Indecision (Vol. 4)
Caregiving (Vol. 1)
Contract Work (Vol. 4)
Corrections Applications (Vol. 1)
Dictionary of Occupational Titles (Vol. 4)
Forensic Applications (Vol. 1)
Homeless Youth (Vol. 1)
Job Loss (Vol. 4)
Job Satisfaction and General Well-Being (Vol. 4)
Job Sharing (Vol. 4)
Occupational Information (Vol. 4)
Occupational Information Network (Vol. 4)
Occupational Stress (Vol. 1)
Part-Time Work (Vol. 4)
Pay Equity (Vol. 4)
Poverty (Vol. 3)
Socioeconomic Status (Vol. 3)
Stress-Related Disorders (Vol. 1)
Training in Organizations (Vol. 4)
Work-Bound Youth (Vol. 4)
Work Stress (Vol. 4)
Work Values (Vol. 4)

Human Development and Life Transitions

Adult Development (Vol. 1)
Adults in Transition (Vol. 4)
Aging (Vol. 1)
Black Racial Identity Development (Vol. 3)
Career Advancement (Vol. 4)
Career Education (Vol. 4)
Career Exploration (Vol. 4)
Career/Life (Vol. 4)
Career Maturity (Vol. 4)

Career Planning (Vol. 4)
Death and Dying (Vol. 1)
Identity Development (Vol. 3)
Leisure (Vol. 2)
Life-Role Balance (Vol. 4)
Life Transitions (Vol. 2)
Parent–Adolescent Relations (Vol. 1)
Parenting (Vol. 1)
Racial Identity (Vol. 3)
Retirement (Vol. 4)
Retirement, Implications of (Vol. 1)
School-to-Work Transition (Vol. 4)
Teenage Parents (Vol. 1)
Vocational Identity (Vol. 4)
White Racial Identity Development (Vol. 3)
Work–Family Balance (Vol. 4)

Legal and Ethical Issues

Affirmative Action (Vol. 3)
Americans with Disabilities Act (Vol. 1)
Civil Rights (Vol. 3)
Classism (Vol. 3)
Code of Ethics and Standards of Practice (Vol. 2)
Colonialism (Vol. 3)
Color-Blind Racial Ideology (Vol. 3)
Confidentiality and Legal Privilege (Vol. 2)
Credentialing Individuals (Vol. 1)
Cultural Relativism (Vol. 3)
Custody Evaluations (Vol. 1)
Duty to Warn and Protect (Vol. 2)
Ethical Codes (Vol. 1)
Ethical Decision Making (Vol. 1)
Ethical Dilemmas (Vol. 1)
Ethics in Computer-Aided Counseling (Vol. 1)
Ethics in Research (Vol. 1)
Ethnic Cleansing (Vol. 3)
Human Subjects Review in an Online World (Vol. 1)
Individuals with Disabilities Education Act (Vol. 1)
Informed Consent (Vol. 2)
Legal Issues in Parenting (Vol. 1)
Oppression (Vol. 3)
Political Correctness (Vol. 3)
Prejudice (Vol. 3)
Prescription Privileges (Vol. 1)
Racism (Vol. 3)
Reversed Racism (Vol. 3)
Sexism (Vol. 3)
Sexual Harassment (Vol. 4)
Social Class (Vol. 4)
Social Justice (Vol. 3)
Virtue Ethics (Vol. 1)

Organizations

Accreditation by the American Psychological Association (Vol. 1)
Accreditation by the Council for Accreditation of Counseling and Related Educational Programs (Vol. 1)
Alcoholics Anonymous (Vol. 1)
Asian American Psychological Association (Vol. 3)
Association of Black Psychologists (Vol. 3)
Bureau of Indian Affairs (Vol. 3)
Bureau of Labor Statistics (Vol. 4)
Department of Veterans Affairs (Vol. 1)
Indian Health Service (Vol. 3)
International Association for Educational and Vocational Guidance (Vol. 4)
International Test Commission (Vol. 1)
National Association for the Advancement of Colored People (Vol. 3)
National Career Development Association (Vol. 4)
National Latina/o Psychological Association (Vol. 3)
Society for the Psychological Study of Ethnic Minority Issues (Vol. 3)
Society for Vocational Psychology (Vol. 4)
Society of Indian Psychologists (Vol. 3)

Physical and Mental Health

Attention Deficit/Hyperactivity Disorder (Vol. 1)
Autism/Asperger's Syndrome (Vol. 1)
Bipolar Disorder (Vol. 2)
Cancer Management (Vol. 1)
Child Maltreatment (Vol. 1)
Children With Chronic Illness (Vol. 1)
Chronic Illness (Vol. 1)
Chronic Pain (Vol. 1)
Cigarette Smoking (Vol. 1)
Community-Based Health Promotion (Vol. 1)
Compulsive Sexual Behavior (Vol. 1)
Conduct Disorder (Vol. 1)
Culture-Bound Syndromes (Vol. 3)
Defenses, Psychological (Vol. 2)
Dementia (Vol. 2)
Depression (Vol. 2)
Developmental Disorders (Vol. 1)

Diagnostic and Statistical Manual of Mental Disorders (*DSM*) (Vol. 2)
Drapetomania (Vol. 3)
Eating Disorders (Vol. 2)
Externalizing Problems of Childhood (Vol. 1)
False Memories (Vol. 2)
HIV/AIDS (Vol. 1)
Hospice (Vol. 1)
Impairment (Vol. 1)
Indigenous Healing (Vol. 3)
Internalizing Problems of Childhood (Vol. 1)
Job Satisfaction and General Well-Being (Vol. 4)
Learning Disorders (Vol. 1)
Low-Incidence Disabilities (Vol. 1)
Medication Adherence (Vol. 1)
Mental Health Issues in the Schools (Vol. 1)
Mental Retardation and Developmental Disabilities (Vol. 1)
Neuropsychological Functioning (Vol. 2)
Oppositional Defiant Disorder (Vol. 1)
Panic Disorders (Vol. 2)
Personality Disorders (Vol. 2)
Persons With Disabilities (Vol. 4)
Physical Health (Vol. 2)
Posttraumatic Stress Disorder (Vol. 2)
Psychological Well-Being, Dimensions of (Vol. 2)
Psychopharmacology, Human Behavioral (Vol. 2)
Schizophrenia, Adult (Vol. 2)
Secondary Trauma (Vol. 2)
Sleep Disorders (Vol. 1)
Stress-Related Disorders (Vol. 1)
Substance Abuse and Dependence (Vol. 2)
Suicide Postvention (Vol. 1)
Suicide Potential (Vol. 2)
Traumatic Brain Injury and Rehabilitation (Vol. 1)

Professional Development and Standards

Career Development Quarterly (Vol. 4)
Code of Ethics and Standards of Practice (Vol. 2)
Conferences, Counseling Psychology (Vol. 1)
Conferences in Counseling (Vol. 1)
Confidentiality and Legal Privilege (Vol. 2)
Consultation (Vol. 2)
Continuing Education (Vol. 1)
Counseling Skills Training (Vol. 2)
Credentialing Individuals (Vol. 1)
Distance Education/Dispersed Learning (Vol. 1)
Duty to Warn and Protect (Vol. 2)
Ethical Codes (Vol. 1)
Ethical Decision Making (Vol. 1)
Ethical Dilemmas (Vol. 1)
Ethics in Computer-Aided Counseling (Vol. 1)
Ethics in Research (Vol. 1)
Informed Consent (Vol. 2)
International Developments, Counseling (Vol. 1)
International Developments, Counseling Psychology (Vol. 1)
Journal of Career Assessment (Vol. 4)
Journal of Career Development (Vol. 4)
Journal of Vocational Behavior (Vol. 4)
Mentoring (Vol. 1)
Multicultural Counseling Competence (Vol. 3)
Postdegree/Prelicensure Supervision (Vol. 1)
Postdoctoral Training (Vol. 1)
Predoctoral Internships (Vol. 1)
Prescription Privileges (Vol. 1)
Professional Associations, Counseling (Vol. 1)
Professional Degrees (Vol. 1)
Rural Practice, Challenges of (Vol. 1)
Scientist–Practitioner Model of Training (Vol. 1)
Specialization Designation (Vol. 1)
Standards and Competencies (Vol. 4)
Supervision (Vol. 1)
Virtue Ethics (Vol. 1)

Psychosocial Traits and Behavior

Bullying (Vol. 1)
Ego Strength (Vol. 2)
Empowerment (Vol. 3)
Espiritismo (Vol. 3)
Familismo (Vol. 3)
Fatalism (Vol. 3)
Gambling (Vol. 1)
Happiness/Hardiness (Vol. 2)
Help-Seeking Behavior (Vol. 3)
Hope (Vol. 2)
Identity (Vol. 3)
Intelligence (Vol. 2)
Intrinsic Motivation (Vol. 2)
Learned Helplessness (Vol. 3)
Locus of Control (Vol. 3)
Machismo (Vol. 3)
Marianismo (Vol. 3)
Meaning, Creation of (Vol. 2)
Multicultural Personality (Vol. 3)
Optimism and Pessimism (Vol. 2)
Personal Space (Vol. 3)

Power and Powerlessness (Vol. 3)
Quality of Life (Vol. 2)
Religion/Religious Belief Systems (Vol. 3)
Resilience (Vol. 2)
School Refusal Behavior (Vol. 1)
Self-Esteem (Vol. 2)
Spirituality (Vol. 3)
Spirituality and Career Development (Vol. 4)
Spirituality/Religion (Vol. 2)

Society, Race/Ethnicity, and Culture

Acculturation (Vol. 3)
Achievement Gap (Vol. 3)
Affirmative Action (Vol. 3)
African Americans (Vol. 3)
Afrocentricity/Afrocentrism (Vol. 3)
Alaska Natives (Vol. 3)
Allocentrism (Vol. 3)
American Indians (Vol. 3)
American Jews (Vol. 3)
Antisemitism (Vol. 3)
Arab Americans (Vol. 3)
Asian Americans (Vol. 3)
Assimilation (Vol. 3)
Bias (Vol. 3)
Bicultural (Vol. 3)
Bilingualism (Vol. 3)
Biracial (Vol. 3)
Black English (Vol. 3)
Black Racial Identity Development (Vol. 3)
Career Counseling, African Americans (Vol. 4)
Career Counseling, Asian Americans (Vol. 4)
Career Counseling, Gay and Lesbian (Vol. 4)
Career Counseling, Immigrants (Vol. 4)
Career Counseling, Latinos (Vol. 4)
Career Counseling, Native Americans (Vol. 4)
Certificate of Degree of Indian Blood (Vol. 3)
Civil Rights (Vol. 3)
Classism (Vol. 3)
Collectivism (Vol. 3)
Colonialism (Vol. 3)
Color-Blind Racial Ideology (Vol. 3)
Communication (Vol. 3)
Cross-Cultural Training (Vol. 3)
Cultural Accommodation and Negotiation (Vol. 3)
Cultural Encapsulation (Vol. 3)
Cultural Equivalence (Vol. 3)
Cultural Mistrust (Vol. 3)
Cultural Paranoia (Vol. 3)
Cultural Relativism (Vol. 3)

Cultural Values (Vol. 3)
Culture (Vol. 3)
Demographics, United States (Vol. 3)
Discrimination (Vol. 3)
Discrimination and Oppression (Vol. 2)
Diversity (Vol. 3)
Diversity Issues in Career Development (Vol. 4)
Enculturation (Vol. 3)
Ethnic Cleansing (Vol. 3)
Ethnic Identity (Vol. 3)
Ethnicity (Vol. 3)
Ethnic Minority (Vol. 3)
Ethnic Pride (Vol. 3)
Ethnocentrism (Vol. 3)
Eugenics (Vol. 1)
Eurocentrism (Vol. 3)
Feminization of Psychology (Vol. 1)
Filial Piety (Vol. 3)
Idiocentrism (Vol. 3)
Immigrants (Vol. 3)
Individualism (Vol. 3)
Interracial Comfort (Vol. 3)
Interracial Marriage (Vol. 3)
Kwanzaa (Vol. 3)
Latinos (Vol. 3)
Model Minority Myth (Vol. 3)
Monocultural (Vol. 3)
Multiculturalism (Vol. 3)
Multiracial Families (Vol. 3)
Nationalism (Vol. 3)
Oppression (Vol. 3)
Organizational Diversity (Vol. 3)
Pacific Islanders (Vol. 3)
Pluralism (Vol. 3)
Political Correctness (Vol. 3)
Prejudice (Vol. 3)
Race (Vol. 3)
Racial Identity (Vol. 3)
Racial Microaggressions (Vol. 3)
Racial Pride (Vol. 3)
Racism (Vol. 3)
Recruitment: History and Recent Trends in Diversity (Vol. 1)
Refugees (Vol. 3)
Reversed Racism (Vol. 3)
Santería (Vol. 3)
Second Culture Acquisition (Vol. 3)
Sexism (Vol. 3)
Sexual Harassment (Vol. 4)
Sexual Orientation (Vol. 4)
Social Class (Vol. 4)

Social Discrimination (Vol. 4)
Social Justice (Vol. 3)
Sojourner (Vol. 3)
Stereotype (Vol. 3)
Third World (Vol. 3)
Tokenism (Vol. 3)
Transracial Adoption (Vol. 3)
Universalism (Vol. 3)
Visible Racial/Ethnic Groups (Vol. 3)
White Americans (Vol. 3)
White Privilege (Vol. 3)
Worldview (Vol. 3)
Xenophobia (Vol. 3)

Subdisciplines

Bilingual Counseling (Vol. 3)
Black Psychology (Vol. 3)
Career Counseling (Vol. 4)
Career Counseling, History of (Vol. 4)
Career Counseling in Colleges and Universities (Vol. 4)
Career Counseling in Organizations (Vol. 4)
Career Counseling in Schools (Vol. 4)
Career Resource Centers (Vol. 4)
Computer-Assisted Career Counseling (Vol. 4)
Constructivist Career Counseling (Vol. 4)
Counseling, Definition of (Vol. 1)
Counseling, History of (Vol. 1)
Counseling Psychology, Definition of (Vol. 1)
Counseling Psychology, History of (Vol. 1)
Counseling the Elderly (Vol. 1)
Couple and Marital Counseling (Vol. 1)
Crisis Counseling (Vol. 2)
Cross-Cultural Psychology (Vol. 3)
E-Counseling (Vol. 1)
Exercise and Sport Psychology (Vol. 1)
Family Counseling (Vol. 1)
Genetic Counseling (Vol. 1)
Gerontology (Vol. 1)
Industrial/Organizational Psychology (Vol. 1)
Mediation (Vol. 1)
Multicultural Counseling (Vol. 3)
Multicultural Psychology (Vol. 3)
Narrative Career Counseling (Vol. 4)
Occupational Health Psychology (Vol. 4)
Personal and Career Counseling (Vol. 4)
Physical Activity Counseling (Vol. 2)
Positive Psychology (Vol. 2)
Private Practice Career Counseling (Vol. 4)
Rehabilitation Counseling (Vol. 2)
School Counseling (Vol. 1)

School Psychology (Vol. 1)
Trait-Factor Counseling (Vol. 4)
University Counseling Centers (Vol. 1)

Theories

Action Theory (Vol. 4)
Attachment Theory (Vol. 4)
Brown's Values-Based Career Theory (Vol. 4)
Career Construction Theory (Vol. 4)
Common Factors Model (Vol. 2)
Confucianism (Vol. 3)
Constructivist Theory (Vol. 2)
Counseling Theories and Therapies (Vol. 2)
Critical Race Theory (Vol. 3)
Deficit Hypothesis (Vol. 3)
Etic–Emic Distinction (Vol. 3)
High-Context Communication (Vol. 3)
Holland's Theory of Vocational Personalities and Work Environments (Vol. 4)
Krumboltz Happenstance Learning Theory (Vol. 4)
Low-Context Communication (Vol. 3)
Model Minority Myth (Vol. 3)
Orthogonal Cultural Identification Theory (Vol. 3)
Personality Theories (Vol. 2)
Personality Theories, Behavioral (Vol. 2)
Personality Theories, Cognitive (Vol. 2)
Personality Theories, Evolutionary (Vol. 2)
Personality Theories, Five-Factor Model (Vol. 2)
Personality Theories, Phenomenological (Vol. 2)
Personality Theories, Psychodynamic (Vol. 2)
Personality Theories, Social Cognitive (Vol. 2)
Personality Theories, Traits (Vol. 2)
Person–Environment Interactions (Vol. 2)
Positivist Paradigm (Vol. 2)
Roe's Theory of Personality Development and Career Choice (Vol. 4)
Self-Efficacy/Perceived Competence (Vol. 2)
Social Cognitive Career Theory (Vol. 4)
Social Identity Theory (Vol. 3)
Super's Theory (Vol. 4)
Theory of Work Adjustment (Vol. 4)
Tiedeman's Decision-Making Theory (Vol. 4)

Therapies, Techniques, and Interventions

Adlerian Therapy (Vol. 2)
Adventure Therapy (Vol. 1)
Art Therapy (Vol. 1)
Behavior Therapy (Vol. 2)

Brief Therapy (Vol. 2)
Career Interventions (Vol. 4)
Cognitive-Behavioral Therapy and Techniques (Vol. 2)
Cognitive Therapy (Vol. 2)
Conversion Therapy (Vol. 1)
Corrections Applications (Vol. 1)
Crisis Counseling (Vol. 2)
Critical Incident Stress Debriefing (Vol. 2)
Developmental Counseling and Therapy (Vol. 2)
Dialectical Behavior Therapy (Vol. 2)
Evidence-Based Treatments (Vol. 2)
Expectations About Therapy (Vol. 2)
Eye Movement Desensitization and Reprocessing (Vol. 1)
Feedback in Counseling, Immediate (Vol. 1)
Feminist Therapy (Vol. 1)
Forensic Applications (Vol. 1)
Free Association (Vol. 2)
Gay, Lesbian, and Bisexual Therapy (Vol. 2)
Group Therapy (Vol. 2)
Harmful Psychological Treatments (Vol. 2)
Homework Assignments (Vol. 2)
Humanistic Approaches (Vol. 2)
Hypnosis (Vol. 1)
Individual Therapy (Vol. 2)
Integrative/Eclectic Therapy (Vol. 2)

International Approaches (Vol. 4)
Interpersonal Learning and Interpersonal Feedback (Vol. 2)
Metaphors, Use of (Vol. 2)
Mindfulness (Vol. 1)
Music Therapy (Vol. 1)
Narrative Therapy (Vol. 2)
Outcomes of Counseling and Psychotherapy (Vol. 2)
Paradoxical Interventions (Vol. 2)
Phrenology (Vol. 1)
Play Therapy (Vol. 1)
Projective Techniques (Vol. 2)
Psychoanalysis and Psychodynamic Approaches to Therapy (Vol. 2)
Psychoeducation (Vol. 2)
Rational Emotive Behavior Therapy (Vol. 2)
Reframing (Vol. 2)
Self-Help Groups (Vol. 2)
Socratic Method (Vol. 2)
Solution-Focused Brief Therapy (Vol. 2)
Therapist Interpretation (Vol. 2)
Therapist Techniques/Behaviors (Vol. 2)
Therapy Process, Individual (Vol. 2)
Transactional Analysis (Vol. 2)
Transference and Countertransference (Vol. 2)
Translation Methods (Vol. 3)

About the Editors

Editor-in-Chief

Frederick T. L. Leong, Ph.D., is Professor of Psychology (Industrial/Organizational and Clinical Psychology Programs) and Director of the Center for Multicultural Psychology Research at Michigan State University. He has authored or co-authored more than 110 articles in various psychology journals, as well as 70 book chapters. In addition, he has edited or co-edited 10 books. Dr. Leong is a Fellow of the APA (Divisions 1, 2, 12, 17, 45, 52), Association for Psychological Science, Asian American Psychological Association, and the International Academy for Intercultural Research. His major research interests center around culture and mental health, cross-cultural psychotherapy (especially with Asians and Asian Americans), and cultural and personality factors related to career choice and work adjustment. He is past president of APA's Division 45 (Society for the Psychological Study of Ethnic Minority Issues), the Asian American Psychological Association, and the Division of Counseling Psychology in the International Association of Applied Psychologists. He is currently serving on the APA Board of Scientific Affairs, the Minority Fellowship Program Advisory Committee, and the Commission on Ethnic Minority Recruitment, Retention, and Training (CEMRRAT2) Task Force. He is the 2007 co-recipient of the APA Award for Distinguished Contributions to the International Advancement of Psychology.

Senior Editor

Madonna G. Constantine, Ph.D., is Professor of Psychology and Education in the Department of Counseling and Clinical Psychology at Teachers College, Columbia University. She received her doctorate in Counseling Psychology from the University of Memphis and completed bachelor's and master's degrees from Xavier University of New Orleans. Constantine is a highly esteemed researcher in the areas of Black psychology and multicultural counseling. The scope of her work includes exploring the psychological, educational, and vocational issues of African Americans; developing models of cross-cultural competence in counseling, training, and supervision; and examining the intersections of variables such as race and ethnicity in relation to mental health and educational processes and outcomes. Constantine is currently serving as associate editor for the *Journal of Counseling Psychology* and *Cultural Diversity & Ethnic Minority Psychology*. She also is involved in various leadership capacities in counseling and psychological associations across the country.

Associate Editor

Roger L. Worthington, Ph.D., currently serves as Interim Chief Diversity Officer at the University of Missouri–Columbia (MU), where he directs the Chancellor's Diversity Initiative. He is a member of the Board of Directors of the National Association of Diversity Officers in Higher Education (NADOHE) and serves on the editorial board of the *Journal of Diversity in Higher Education*. In the past he has also served on the editorial boards of the *Journal of Counseling Psychology* and *The Counseling Psychologist*. Worthington has an extensive record of scholarship, including theoretical and empirical articles and book chapters related to race/ethnicity, gender, sexual orientation identity, social class, and religious expression. He has been a principal investigator or co-investigator on nearly $500,000 in internal and external grants. He is the principal investigator and project director of the MU Difficult Dialogues Program, a project funded by a prestigious Ford Foundation grant. The focus of the MU Difficult Dialogues Program is to promote greater understanding of the relationships among academic freedom, academic responsibility, and intellectual pluralism in a climate characterized by divisiveness and mistrust among those holding differing cultural, religious, and political viewpoints. In addition to his role directing the Chancellor's Diversity Initiative, he is a licensed psychologist (MO) and an associate professor of Educational, School, and Counseling Psychology at MU, where he has taught courses to undergraduate and graduate students on counseling skills, ethics and law for professional psychology, research design, measurement, and human diversity.

Contributors

Volume 3

Aimee-Nicole Adams
Lehigh University

Noah E. Adrians
Marquette University

Muninder K. Ahluwalia
Montclair State University

Vanessa Alleyne
Montclair State University

Alvin N. Alvarez
San Francisco State University

Julie R. Ancis
Georgia State University

Jesus (Jesse) R. Aros
Texas A&M International University

Germine H. Awad
University of Texas at Austin

Amanda L. Baden
Montclair State University

Nick Barneclo
New Mexico State University

Fred Bemak
George Mason University

Kimberly Bena
Loyola University Chicago

Sara Bennett
Idaho Dept. of Health and Welfare

Gregory Benson
University of Wisconsin–Milwaukee

Sha'kema M. Blackmon
Loyola University Chicago

Caryn J. Block
Teachers College, Columbia University

Raymond D. Brock-Murray
Fairleigh Dickinson University

Jeff E. Brooks-Harris
University of Hawaii at Manoa

Leon D. Caldwell
University of Memphis

Taisha L. Caldwell
Southern Illinois University

Scott C. Carvajal
University of Arizona

Elif Celebi
University of Missouri

Anne Chan
Stanford University

Catherine Y. Chang
Georgia State University

Ruth Chao
University of Denver

Eric C. Chen
Fordham University

Chun-Chung Choi
University of Florida

Stephanie Clouse
University of Georgia

M. Nicole Coleman
University of Houston

Noah M. Collins
Teachers College, Columbia University

Madonna G. Constantine
Teachers College, Columbia University

Donelda A. Cook
Loyola College in Maryland

Megan Correia
Wells College

Shannon Curry
Pepperdine University

Edward A. Delgado-Romero
University of Georgia

Laura Dick
Loyola University Chicago

Matthew A. Diemer
Michigan State University

Chandra M. Donnell
Michigan State University

Peter C. Donnelly
Teachers College, Columbia University

Cristina Dorazio
Teachers College, Columbia University

Lisa M. Edwards
Marquette University

Jose Eluvathingal
University of Wisconsin–Milwaukee

Angela D. Ferguson
Howard University

Pamela F. Foley
Seton Hall University

Donna Y. Ford
Vanderbilt University

Elizabeth D. Fraga
Teachers College, Columbia University

Miguel E. Gallardo
Pepperdine University

Maritza Gallardo-Cooper
Private Practice

Edmund W. Gordon
Teachers College, Columbia University

Sheila V. Graham
Teachers College, Columbia University

Teresa Granillo
University of Michigan

Jacqueline S. Gray
University of North Dakota

India Gray-Schmiedlin
University of Milwaukee

Arpana Gupta
University of Tennessee, Knoxville

Tonisha Hamilton
Seton Hall University

Shelly P. Harrell
Pepperdine University

Jon M. Harvey
University of Georgia

Yuhong He
University of Missouri–Columbia

Ashley Heintzelman
University of Missouri–Kansas City

P. Paul Heppner
University of Missouri–Columbia

Jill S. Hill
Cornell University

Cheryl Holcomb-McCoy
University of Maryland

Farah A. Ibrahim
Oregon State University

Arpana G. Inman
Lehigh University

Margo A. Jackson
Fordham University

Morris L. Jackson
American University

Linda James-Myers
New College of California

Asma Jana-Masri
University of Wisconsin–Milwaukee

Terri L. Jashinsky
University of Wisconsin–Milwaukee

Brenda K. Johnson
Cleveland State University

Kamauru R. Johnson
Teachers College, Columbia University

Janice E. Jones
Cardinal Stritch University

Pamela Jumper Thurman
Colorado State University

Anju Kaduvettoor
Lehigh University

Bryan S. K. Kim
University of Hawai'i at Hilo

Mai M. Kindaichi
Teachers College, Columbia University

Erica King-Toler
John Jay College of Criminal Justice–City University of New York

Heather Knox
Tennessee State University

Kwong-Liem Karl Kwan
University of Missouri at Columbia

Nicholas Ladany
Lehigh University

Teresa LaFromboise
Stanford University

Richard M. Lee
University of Minnesota, Twin Cities

Szu-Hui Lee
Massachusetts General Hospital

Jennifer L. Lemkuil
University of Wisconsin–Milwaukee

Frederick T. L. Leong
Michigan State University

Ma'at E. Lewis-Coles
John Jay College of Criminal Justice

Noriel E. Lim
University of Illinois at Urbana-Champaign

Jun-chih Gisela Lin
Texas A&M University

William Ming Liu
University of Iowa

Michael I. Loewy
University of North Dakota

Ané M. Mariñez-Lora
University of Illinois at Chicago

Jaya Mathew
Fordham University

Elizabeth P. McCadden
Marquette University

Laurie D. McCubbin
Washington State University

Brenda X. Mejia
Teachers College, Columbia University

Marie L. Miville
Teachers College, Columbia University

Debra Mollen
Texas Woman's University

Ruth Montero
University of Wisconsin–Madison

Eduardo Morales
California School of Professional Psychology

Kevin L. Nadal
Teachers College, Columbia University

Sylvia C. Nassar-McMillan
North Carolina State University

Rachel L. Navarro
New Mexico State University

Hammad S. N'cho
Boston College

Helen A. Neville
University of Illinois at Urbana-Champaign

Johanna Nilsson
University of Missouri–Kansas City

Michael S. Nystul
New Mexico State University

Ezemenari M. Obasi
Southern Illinois University

Sumie Okazaki
University of Illinois at Urbana-Champaign

Yanina Paoliello
Pepperdine University

Yong S. Park
University of California, Santa Barbara

Jennie Park-Taylor
Fordham University

John J. Peregoy
Morehead State University

Ruperto M. (Toti) Perez
Georgia Institute of Technology

Ani Pezeshkian
University of California, Berkeley

Wade E. Pickren
Ryerson University

Alex L. Pieterse
George Mason University

Emily Pimpinella
Antioch University New England

Joseph G. Ponterotto
Fordham University

Paul E. Priester
Cardinal Stritch University

Stephen M. Quintana
University of Wisconsin–Madison

Kilynda V. Ray
Howard University

Rebecca M. Redington
Teachers College, Columbia University

Amy L. Reynolds
University at Buffalo

Charles R. Ridley
Texas A&M University

Luis A. Rivas
VA Caribbean Healthcare System

David P. Rivera
Teachers College, Columbia University

Rockey R. Robbins
University of Oklahoma

David Rollock
Purdue University

Andrea J. Romero
University of Arizona

LeLaina Romero
Teachers College, Columbia University

Rocio Rosales
University of Missouri

Daniel C. Rosen
Arizona State University

Gargi Roysircar
Antioch University New England

Alexandra Rutherford
York University

Lisa A. P. Sanchez-Johnsen
University of Chicago

Anne Saw
University of Illinois at Urbana-Champaign

María R. Scharrón-del Río
City University of New York–Brooklyn College

Joshua Scherer
University of Wisconsin–Milwaukee

Lewis Z. Schlosser
Seton Hall University

Sara Schwarzbaum
Northeastern Illinois University

Nicholas C. Scull
University of Wisconsin–Madison

Sheetal Shah
Southern Illinois University

Kimber L. Shelton
University of Georgia

Frances C. Shen
Southern Illinois University

Laura Smith
Teachers College, Columbia University

Melissa K. Smothers
University of Wisconsin–Milwaukee

Lisa B. Spanierman
University of Illinois at Urbana-Champaign

Jesse A. Steinfeldt
Indiana University–Bloomington

Francis L. Stevens
Tennessee State University

Robbie J. Steward
Michigan State University

Lisa A. Suzuki
New York University

Michelle A. Swagler
Independent Practice, Athens, Georgia

Vivian L. Tamkin
Southern Illinois University

Nita Tewari
University of California, Los Angeles

Chalmer E. Thompson
Indiana University–Purdue University, Indianapolis

Ivory A. Toldson
Howard University

Alisia G. T. T. Tran
University of Minnesota

Joseph E. Trimble
Western Washington University

Chia-Lin Tsai
University of Missouri–Columbia

Sherri Turner
University of Minnesota

Allison Ventura
Fordham University

Elizabeth M. Vera
Loyola University Chicago

Adam M. Voight
Michigan State University

Rebecca Wagner
Tennessee State University

Rheeda L. Walker
Southern Illinois University

Barbara C. Wallace
Teachers College, Columbia University

Bruce E. Wampold
University of Wisconsin–Madison

Yu-Wei Wang
Southern Illinois University at Carbondale

Eliza M. Wells
University of Georgia

Arthur L. Whaley
Russell Sage Foundation

Gilman W. Whiting
Vanderbilt University

Carmen B. Williams
University of Colorado

Frank C. Worrell
University of California, Berkeley

Roger L. Worthington
University of Missouri

Kuang-ming Wu
Tennessee State University

Billy Yarbrough
University of Georgia

Carlos P. Zalaquett
University of South Florida

ACCULTURATION

Acculturation can be described as cultural change associated with social group movement, be it movement within or across nations, that results in persons who have different cultures intersecting. Since the 1990s, the immigrant population in the United States has increased by more than 13 million people. More than half of this immigrant population is from Mexico, where the Spanish language is dominant, and approximately one fifth of the children of immigrant households speak a language other than English in their home. Rates of migration from other Latin American and Pacific Rim nations to the United States also are increasing, as is immigration throughout most developed nations worldwide. These trends underscore the great impetus in understanding the processes of immigrant adaptation and all its components.

As persons from multiple social groups and cultures intersect, it would be expected that their thoughts, attitudes, values, behaviors, and (in most cases) language would be influenced. Until recently, the prevailing assumption within U.S. popular culture, as well as for most Western mental health scholars, has been that when persons from different cultures interact, one culture is dominant. However, within the United States and across the world, there is increasing cultural, social, and economic diversity, as well as the formation of dominant minority communities within larger majority communities (e.g., ethnic enclaves). The development of such communities challenges more traditional acculturation models that have guided social/behavioral scientists, educators, practitioners, and even popular culture, where cultural change is believed to solely and linearly occur within minority group members.

Conceptual Origins and the Prevailing Assimilation Model

Acculturation has been defined by Robert Redfield and colleagues as the "phenomenon that occurs when two independent cultural groups come into first hand contact over an extended period of time, resulting in changes in either or both groups" (1936, p. 149). References to acculturation by social scientists in the 1940s included that of Mischa Titiev titled "Enculturation." Enculturation was described as the process of teaching a child to be a member of the society in which he or she will live, whereas acculturation was described as the process of incorporating aspects of the mainstream (host) culture into each individual's repertoire of behaviors.

Despite a clear emphasis in the original definitions on cultural exchange and mutual influence, the majority of early theory, research, and practice on acculturation focused on unidirectional cultural change. This is best represented in the assimilationist model, where the minority traditional culture is assumed to conform over time to the majority culture, and the majority culture remains static. It was thought that external acculturation, such as changing food habits and styles of clothing, as well as learning and/or adapting to the majority language, tended to take place first, followed by internal acculturation, or the adoption of cultural beliefs, values, and more complex patterns of behaviors. Assimilation models assumed that, over time, behavior patterns, attitudes, and beliefs of an immigrant population would come to resemble more closely those of the culture they entered than those of the culture they left behind. The process of acculturation then included dropping, modifying, and adopting cultural traits and was thought to occur at different rates over several generations for every person individually. From this perspective, acculturation also could be assessed in terms of the distance from the culture of origin to the majority culture, reflecting either movement toward acculturation or movement away from the majority culture. Also, it was thought that acculturation could be conceptualized primarily from consideration of factors such as place of origin, language preferences, and preferences for social contacts. The assimilation model of acculturation also was reflected in the philosophy that the United States had been founded on the notion of "the melting pot." This perspective suggested that multiple immigrant groups could be welcomed and integrated into the general U.S. society, while slowly breaking all ties to their past culture and not affecting their new society. In other words, immigrants would gradually conform into the existing society norms, values, language, and all other elements characteristic of U.S. culture, while the U.S. culture itself remained uninfluenced by their entry.

However, behavioral scientists within the past 2 decades have shown empirically more closely to what previous anthropologists and many sociologists had described. Namely, the melting pot metaphor in describing the processes of immigration for most immigrants arriving in the United States, as well as in other industrial nations, was incomplete and inaccurate. For example, one assumption underlying the assimilation model was that culture change was inherently stressful, and the quickest path to eliminate this stress was complete assimilation. In other words, the healthiest way of life was for people to put behind them all aspects of their culture of origin. Many research findings indicate that the acculturation process is not inherently stressful (although parts of it may be at times) and that assimilation may result in increased stress or worse physical health for immigrants or their descendents. Furthermore, researchers continue to provide evidence that losing functioning in individuals' original culture often is harmful to their well-being.

Another guiding assumption of assimilation-related models was that complete acceptance into the new society was thought possible for all immigrants; however, many minority ethnic groups (including immigrants and later generations) in the United States report experiencing discrimination or being treated unfairly as a result of their ethnic group membership, language, phenotype (i.e., physical features, including skin color), or other socially recognizable characteristics. In fact, contrary to assumptions underlying the assimilation model, discrimination often is felt more strongly for later generations, who are citizens and speak English fluently, as they become more knowledgeable about the customs of their new society and interact more often with societal institutions. In short, the current social and behavioral science findings suggest that the experience of many immigrants and later generations is not reflective of the melting pot metaphor, or its extension, the assimilation model of acculturation.

Progress in Theories and Methods and the Emergence of Orthogonal Models

The study of acculturation began through anthropologists' explorations of indigenous and immigrant groups immersed within a dominant culture. Researchers employed qualitative methods of inquiry that relied on their personal contact with these groups. Often anthropologists would learn about new cultures by becoming everyday members of new societies, recording their observations, and providing rich descriptions of participants' experiences. This research was insightful and critical to the philosophical and scientific advancement of the study of acculturation, though there were questions about the efficacy of this research to generalize to other participants.

In the past 25 years, there has been major advancement of quantitative approaches to the study of immigration and culture exchange, with aims to provide more objective research as well as generalizable theories and methods. This area of inquiry into acculturation includes economists, sociologists, linguists, psychologists, and other social and behavioral scientists. Researchers from these disciplines have relied heavily on quantitative methods and statistical analyses, along with increasingly precise and generalizable measures of language and, later, increasingly sophisticated assessments of cultural attitudes, knowledge, values, and behaviors. Additionally, the utilization of large federal surveys with massive sample sizes, such as the U.S. Census, has allowed sociologists and economists to investigate variations among ethnic groups on such factors as family size, income, education, and language preference. Finally, cultural psychologists have explored individual perceptions and cross-cultural interactions through the use of highly controlled laboratory experiments and small-scale surveys with measures developed to assess precisely defined cultural factors.

Within the fields of counseling and clinical psychology, acculturation began to attract substantial interest in the 1970s. During this time, acculturation theory within the behavioral sciences progressed from a single-dimension theory to a multidimensional theory. Assessment of acculturation also moved from employing ethnic categories or labels, and perhaps only a single language domain, to reflecting multiple domains including attitudes, values, identities, and social network characteristics. One of the most widely used initial measures was Israel Cuéllar and colleagues' Acculturation Rating Scale for Mexican Americans (ARSMA). This scale included items assessing preferences for language, associations, entertainment and food, ethnic identification, generation, and bilingual abilities. In reviewing current multidimensional and bilinear acculturation measures, most include language and behavior items, yet only a few instruments assess elements of cultural change that include values, knowledge, or cultural identity.

Most current acculturation models emphasize cultural exchange between cultures. Two of the most widely used scales for U.S. Latinos/as, the most widely studied group regarding acculturation, include the Bidimensional Acculturation Scale (BAS) and the ARSMA-II. A commonality of these two scales is that they emphasize the *orthogonal* nature of acculturation; that is, one does not have to lose one culture to gain another. Such models of acculturation have demonstrated that individuals can adhere to more than one culture independently and come from a theoretical tradition from the study of ethnic identity where some individuals of color were maintaining their culture of origin. It is important to note that there are significant differences between the BAS and ARSMA-II. The BAS is designed as a relatively brief measure for use with Latinos/as more generally, and it is primarily centered on language (although as it is orthogonal, it is assumed that one need not give up proficiency of, and exposure to, English or Spanish). The ARSMA-II targets immigrants of Mexican descent in particular and includes multiple identities (American/Anglo, Mexican, and Chicano/a) as well as additional domains such as cultural values and traditions. Scales for other immigrant and indigenous groups within the United States and other nations have been developed, as well as scales that can be used with multiple ethnic groups, such as Zea and colleagues' Abbreviated Multidimensional Acculturation Scale. Although more generic acculturation scales have their utility for examining general cultural change patterns across multiple cultural groups and may yield broad acculturation classifications for many individuals, it should be understood that this can occur at the cost of expressing cultural richness, cultural nuance, and cultural specificity.

Acculturation, Acculturative/Cultural Stress, and Health

Throughout the acculturation literature, there have been controversies about the effects of acculturation on health. Some researchers posit that there is a negative relationship between acculturation and mental health, where unacculturated clients experience poorer mental health due to the lack of adequate social networks and stress from exposure to unfamiliar cultural dynamics. However, others suggest that those who are more acculturated experience a greater degree of psychopathology, due mainly to the stress caused by rejection from the dominant culture within the society in the form of racism and discrimination. Also, there is some evidence that more-acculturated Asian Americans experience depression and anxiety at higher rates than less-acculturated Asians and Whites. Furthermore, higher acculturation status among native-born Mexican Americans has been associated with higher lifetime prevalence of phobia as well as alcohol/drug abuse and dependence.

Also, within many contexts, immigrants and indigenous groups who retain some traditional cultural practices are protected in mental health domains. Mexican immigrants who retain traditional cultural practices report lower divorce rates and more positive perceptions of their family. Still other data have suggested that the balance between adjusting to the host society and holding on to traditions and beliefs of the culture of origin may lead to the best mental health status.

Although the relations of acculturation to mental health are complicated and mixed, there also has been interest in examining acculturation and physical health. Typically, rapid acculturation to American values and behaviors is associated with negative health outcomes for Latinos/as. An important framework that aims to more specifically link acculturation to health is the acculturation stress perspective, which seeks to examine the *components* of acculturation that lead to distress or poor health. This framework assumes that living in an environment with more than one culture present might generate stress due to negotiating more than one set of values, norms, and identities. People of color and immigrants who experience acculturative stress tend to report greater mental health problems.

As with most acculturation measures extant before the mid-1990s, however, few acculturative stress measures are consistent with orthogonal models (that differentiate bicultural from marginalized persons, the latter most strongly associated with poor well-being). In a study from a nonmajority community using an orthogonal measure, these stressors were most strongly reported by Latino/a and Asian American youth than non-Latino/a White youth, consistent with positions that minority ethnic groups experience more pressure to assimilate because of less power and lower status. However, non-Latino/a Whites also experienced these stressors, which were significantly associated with more negative mental health markers and health risk behaviors across all groups. Likewise, bicultural conflict has also been positively associated with depressive symptoms in Chinese Americans. This bicultural stress paradigm, with its underpinnings from the cultural exchange premise of acculturation, potentially contributes to the understanding of a wide range of persons' health outcomes (immigrants and nonimmigrants, minority and majority) as they navigate through multiple cultures.

Implications for Psychotherapy and Counselors

As previously discussed, there are various conflicting theories as to the relationships among acculturation, psychological problems, and health status. However, cultural context and the acculturative process cannot and should not be left out of the therapeutic context. The question then becomes how to address acculturation and cultural beliefs in therapy. Before exploring this topic, it is important to note that acculturation issues are primarily recommended to be addressed in therapy when cultural exchanges are identified by the client as a source of incongruence and/or distress.

Clinicians and counselors should take considerable responsibility to study the available scholarship about their clients' cultures, their intersections, and clients' individual responses. Most of the literature that focuses on psychotherapy with clients from diverse ethnic backgrounds highlights the importance of cultural competency, including understanding acculturation processes. The term *cultural competency* in this case refers to the degree to which a clinician is knowledgeable about the culture of the client. However, cultural "competence" seems to suggest that providers can study a particular culture until a certain level, and once this level is achieved, they have sufficient knowledge of the culture to competently treat an individual from that culture. Just as practitioners can never know everything about a client, they also will never have a complete understanding of ever-evolving cultures. Furthermore, practitioners may have a fairly large knowledge base about a particular culture, but that does not mean cultural ascriptions of what an individual client is experiencing are accurate. Finally, because individuals may be uniquely situated among multiple cultures, their cultural experiences may be adequately understood not by focusing on any of the cultures that influence them but rather by looking at the multiple cultures as a whole, unique, cultural context for those individuals.

Thus, the best way to learn about clients' cultural context and acculturative experience is from clients themselves. This is not to say that practitioners should rely solely on clients' self-report. Rather, while it is important that clinicians obtain a sufficient knowledge base in their clients' culture(s) from credible scientific or perhaps from nonscientific sources (history, narratives, and case studies), they also must recognize their clients' unique experiences and be cautious to avoid overgeneralizations and stereotypes represented in various public literatures and media. Also, it should be understood that clients are not their culture; rather, their cultural contexts and acculturative processes influence who they are and how they view and experience the world they live in.

Understanding clients' cultural context and acculturative process requires more than attaining culture competence or cultural knowledge. It requires awareness and acknowledgment of clients' personal experiences along with cultural context in attempts to develop empathy. Most importantly, practitioners should always inquire and avoid assumptions about clients' personalized experiences based on limited information about the person or broad cultural understandings. At times, the difference between cultural interaction processes most detrimental to mental health and those most adaptive may be subtle.

Paying close attention to subtleties and individuals' cultural context within therapy has been termed by some researchers as *cultural naïveté*, which reflects humility and respectfulness in individuals' unique, culturally influenced spaces without practitioner anxiety or self-consciousness. Data suggest that immigrant clients and clients of color care more about clinicians' attitudes and reassurance that the client will be treated respectfully than they do about clinicians' skills or perceived knowledge of clients' cultures. Furthermore, clients who have experience with a culturally responsive clinician tend to experience higher levels of satisfaction, increased trust and self-disclosure, and decreased rates of attrition. Thus, it may be more beneficial for both clients and clinicians if clinicians are focused more on being culturally responsive, which includes a high degree of openness in addition to a strong foundation of culturally relevant knowledge.

Under the assumption that it would lead to cultural competence in therapy, the costs and benefits of using client–therapist acculturative or ethnic matching in considering treatment options has been examined. Findings on the effects of client–therapist matching in mental health treatment studies have been mixed. There is some evidence that ethnic matching for Latinos/as, African Americans, Asian Americans, and White Americans is related to lower rates of early termination, increased participation, and greater treatment outcomes. However, no single culture is homogenous, and a client from China can be matched with a therapist from Korea based on the fact that they are both of Asian descent as marked in a database—but they may have little else in common besides a pan-ethnic label. Furthermore, a mismatch ignoring class, gender, education, acculturation, and their intersections could lead to greater misunderstanding and poorer treatment outcomes than if no matching was attempted. A second concern about acculturative matching follows the concept of cultural naïveté. Often, it might be beneficial to avoid ethnic or acculturative matching to further facilitate inquiry and discovery. If a client and a clinician are acculturatively matched, there may be less exploration due to the assumption that they understand each other because of their similar cultural backgrounds. Furthermore, even with ethnic or acculturative matching, a client and therapist may differ greatly in the expectations and practices of therapy as most clinicians are immersed in Western cultural norms of psychotherapy, which may interfere with the therapeutic process and therapeutic alliance.

In summary, it is essential that counselors remain empathic by being culturally responsive and by paying close attention to how their own cultural context influences their actions within the therapeutic context. When working with clients who present concerns related to acculturation, it is important to remain open and respectful, and strive to understand clients' cultural context, experiences, and level of distress most strongly guided by clients' own insights.

Future Research and Practice

All research efforts and delivery of service where acculturation is relevant specify what is meant by acculturation and the ways in which acculturation might influence well-being, health, and behavior. Generally speaking, language or generational status reveals little about individuals' cultural context. More than likely, acculturation factors reflecting family relationships/dynamics, beliefs about health and disease, beliefs about personal responsibility, cultural conflict, and social networks will be more insightful in the quest to understand clients from immigrant populations. Likewise, it is vital to recognize that cultural change and cultural intersections may lead to mixed outcomes—at times leading to stressors such as family, social networks, and identity disturbances, but also to important strengths and resiliencies in terms of identity and adjustment. A growing area of research has identified positive cultural buffers, such as a positive and bicultural ethnic identity, that promote health and wellbeing. It is particularly critical for therapists and prevention program developers to recognize sources of resilience that promote well-being that many immigrants have before they transition to a new area, but that may be hard to sustain when immersed in multiple cultures or within a pervasive dominant culture.

Finally, although not widely examined in North America, researchers in other nations are examining dynamics of acculturation that are both migrant and dominant (host) culture specific. One example is the exploring of the potential match or mismatch in cultural characteristics among the interacting cultures and the associated social and health consequences. Such models may be useful if extended in the United States as well. For instance, one would expect Mien immigrants (from rural Laos) and immigrant Mexicans from Distrito Federal (an urban area including Mexico City and representing almost 20 million inhabitants) to experience different acculturation stressors depending on the urbanity and other local cultural characteristics within a particular U.S. community. Just as one should not view immigrant groups as monolithic, host communities should not be viewed that way either, because both influence the acculturative process and outcomes for the interacting groups. This gap in North American research paradigms also further reinforces the importance of counselors recognizing the complexity of cultural exchanges and the limitations of inferring clients' particular cultural contexts and experiences from an extant literature not fully developed.

Scott C. Carvajal and Teresa Granillo

See also Acculturative Stress (v3); Adaptation (v3); Assimilation (v3); Barriers to Cross-Cultural Counseling (v3); Cultural Accommodation and Negotiation (v3); Cultural Values (v3); Culture (v3); Enculturation (v3); Ethnic Identity (v3); Immigrants (v3); Multiculturalism (v3); Orthogonal Cultural Identification Theory (v3); Person–Environment Interactions (v2); Second Culture Acquisition (v3)

Further Readings

Berry, J. W. (2003). Conceptual approaches to acculturation. In K. M. Chun, P. O. Balls, & G. Marín (Eds.), *Acculturation: Advances in theory, measurement, and applied research* (pp. 17–37). Washington, DC: American Psychological Association.

Cuéllar, I., Arnold, B., & Maldonado, R. (1995). Acculturation rating scale: A revision of the original ARSMA scale. *Hispanic Journal of Behavioral Sciences, 17*, 275–304.

Gamst, G., Dana, R. H., Der-Karabetian, A., Aragon, M., Arellano, L. M., & Kramer, T. (2002). Effects of Latino acculturation and ethnic identity on mental health outcomes. *Hispanic Journal of Behavioral Sciences, 24*, 479–504.

Marin, G., & Gamba, R. J. (1996). A new measurement of acculturation for Hispanics: The Bidimensional Acculturation Scale for Hispanics (BAS). *Hispanic Journal of Behavioral Sciences, 18*, 297–316.

Redfield, R., Linton, R., & Herskovits, M. J. (1936). Memorandum for the study of acculturation. *American Anthropologist, 38*, 149–152.

Romero, A. J., Carvajal, S. C., Valle, F., & Orduno, M. (2007). Adolescent bicultural stress and its impact on mental well-being among Latinos, Asian Americans and European Americans. *Journal of Community Psychology, 35*, 519–534.

Zea, M. C., Asner-Self, K. K., Birman, D., & Buki, L. P. (2003). The Abbreviated Multidimensional Acculturation Scale: Empirical validation with two Latino/Latina samples. *Cultural Diversity & Ethnic Minority Psychology, 9*, 107–126.

Acculturative Stress

Acculturation or adaptation to a new culture involves changes in multiple areas of functioning (e.g., values, behaviors, beliefs, attitudes, etc.), and for individuals, families, and groups engaged in the acculturation process, these adjustments are often experienced as stressful. The stress that emerges from difficulties in acculturation is referred to as *acculturative stress*. Distinct from general experiences of stress, acculturative stress is understood to stem from differences in culture and language between the acculturating individual and the host culture or country. Furthermore, acculturative stress is also believed to be more closely related to symptoms of anxiety than depression and associated more with the presence of negative emotions rather than the absence of positive emotions.

Although the experience of acculturative stress is relevant for any individual living in multiple cultural worlds, which is the case for many U.S.-born ethnic and racial minority individuals, current conceptualizations of acculturative stress have emerged largely from empirical studies with immigrant groups. Within this body of literature, some of the variables that are hypothesized to be related to acculturative stress include majority language ability, assimilation pressure, acculturation style, demographic factors, distance between culture of origin and host culture, pre-immigration and migration experiences and intrafamilial acculturation levels/conflicts.

Theoretical Underpinnings of Acculturative Stress

What is currently known about acculturative stress is the result of a conceptual integration between the well-established stress and coping literature and the growing body of literature that explores the acculturation process. More specifically, the cognitive-relational model of stress and coping put forth by S. Folkman and R. S. Lazarus, which describes the processes associated with the stress experience and coping response, along with the empirical and theoretical literature that has emerged from cross-cultural psychologists, led by J. W. Berry and his colleagues, provide a strong foundation for understanding the experience of acculturative stress. A brief synopsis of both theoretical models is given next.

Stress and Coping

In the cognitive-relational model, stress is understood as a relationship between a person and his or her context that is appraised by the individual as difficult, beyond his or her current resources, or dangerous. Lazarus and Folkman note that individuals under stress evaluate what is at stake (e.g., physical safety, anticipated losses or gains) and what coping resources and options are available to them.

Coping is understood as an individual's attempt to reduce the stress and moderate the impact of the stress through either cognitive or behavioral means. Individuals under challenging circumstances will typically evaluate their experiences and behaviors and then engage in basic coping procedures. Lazarus and Folkman have identified two key coping mechanisms for managing stress: problem-focused coping and emotion-focused coping. Both coping strategies are involved in the acculturation process, but their relationship to specific acculturation strategies is still not clear.

Acculturation: Definition and Theoretical Model

R. Redfield, R. Linton, and M. Herskovits provided one of the earliest definitions of acculturation, which they described as a process that occurs when individuals of different cultures are brought together in continuous contact and which consequently leads to changes in the cultural patterns of either or both groups. Although acculturation has been conceptualized as a dynamic process, where change occurs at multiple levels and with all involved groups (dominant cultural group and minority cultural groups), the concentration of acculturation research has largely been focused on the way in which minority immigrant individuals adapt to the norms (e.g., values, beliefs, and behaviors) of the dominant cultural group. Furthermore, earlier notions of the cultural adaptation process that focused on the assimilation of new immigrants, whereby newcomers to a country would and should "shed" their original culture to the culture of the host country, have been challenged by contemporary cultural psychology scholars that emphasize an integration strategy leading to a more bicultural or multicultural identity.

Berry's acculturation model describes individual-contextual pairs of acculturation strategies, which can be adopted by either an acculturating individual or the larger society as a response to intercultural contact. At the individual level, Berry's acculturation strategies include (a) *assimilation,* when an acculturating individual does not wish to maintain his or her original cultural identity and primarily seeks social relationships with the dominant society; (b) *separation,* which is characterized by a maintenance of the original culture/identity with a wish to avoid social relationships with the dominant society; (c) *integration,* where an individual wishes to maintain relationships with his or her original culture/identity and wishes to develop social relationships with the dominant society; and (d) *marginalization,* when the acculturating individual does not maintain his or her original culture/identity and does not have a desire to develop social relationships with the dominant society.

Theoretical Integration: A New Understanding of Acculturative Stress

Resting on these two distinct, yet rich, theoretical and empirical traditions, acculturative stress has come to be understood as a complex psychocultural/psychosocial experience, where an individual, who is in the process of cultural adaptation, experiences stress related to the tasks associated with this change process. Furthermore, there are variables associated with the original culture, host culture, and individual, which may potentially exacerbate or minimize the level of acculturative stress experienced by the acculturating individual. However, the mechanisms through which these contextual and individual variables lower or heighten acculturative stress remain unclear. Using the impact of perceived discrimination as an example, it is possible that experiences of discrimination heighten an individual's level of acculturative stress because he or she appraises the tasks of acculturation as too demanding or because the noxious stimuli are negatively impacting the individual's personal resources (e.g., self-concept, coping).

Why Study Acculturative Stress?

Acculturative stress has emerged as an important specific kind of stress to investigate for a number of reasons. First, the significant and growing immigrant population calls for a better understanding of what may contribute or detract from the healthy cultural adaptation of these individuals. Second, because acculturative stress has been linked to other serious psychological outcomes, researchers and clinicians are increasingly interested in its investigation. Finally, because of increased globalization, individuals, even in less densely populated areas of the United States, are increasingly in contact with people that may identify with cultures that are different from the dominant or mainstream culture. These demographic shifts result in more intercultural contact among acculturating individuals and native-born individuals, which increase the possibility of individuals experiencing both acculturative stress and positive intercultural exchanges. Research in the area of acculturative stress may illuminate factors that are related to acculturative stress as well as factors that result in more positive intercultural experiences for all individuals.

Comorbidity With Psychological Outcomes

When individuals experience heightened levels of acculturative stress, they may exhibit a reduction not only in their mental health state but in their overall health. As is the case for stress in general, acculturative stress has been associated with negative mental health outcomes.

The relationship between acculturation and mental health has not been well established empirically. The data are equivocal, by supporting direct, inverse, and curvilinear relationships between acculturative stress and mental health outcomes. However, despite discrepancies in the literature regarding the way in which acculturative stress influences mental health outcomes for individuals, the significance of acculturative stress as a phenomenon of study is well documented. The emphasis on current research appears to be on examining the risk factors and protective factors associated with acculturative stress, some of which are briefly described next.

Risk Factors and Protective Factors Associated With Acculturative Stress

Most studies on acculturation focus only on the direct relationship between acculturation and mental health and not on possible explanatory mechanisms and processes. Recently, however, more attention has been focused on trying to understand the personal and contextual factors that either increase or decrease an individual's risk of developing acculturative stress. In the following section, some of the risk factors and protective factors that have been associated with acculturative stress are discussed. It is important to note that the factors outlined here represent not an exhaustive list of variables that potentially affect an individual's acculturation pathway, but rather an important subset of variables highlighted in recent literature.

Pre-Immigration Factors

Although individuals migrate to new countries for a variety of reasons, some of the most common reasons include political or economic turmoil in the country of origin and greater educational and financial opportunities in other countries. The reason that individuals decide to immigrate may have implications for their acculturation experience. For example, individuals who immigrate because their family or entire village has experienced severe financial ruin will move to the host country with very few monetary resources. The lack of financial resources may exacerbate the acculturative stress these individuals experience. Although not necessarily associated with the reason for immigration, another pre-immigration factor that potentially impacts individuals' acculturation is their language abilities. Immigrants who are fluent in English, for example, may experience less acculturative stress associated with the post-migration demands because they are more likely able to understand and negotiate the demands of cultural adaptation.

Migration Factors

Migration Trauma. Whereas many immigrants migrate into new countries with their families in a safe and healthy manner, others come alone or come as refugees, and still others are forced to enter new countries by traffickers or smugglers. Refugees have often experienced trauma, including witnessing the death of family members and long periods of malnutrition and inadequate health care. The trauma experienced in either their native country (e.g., war, genocide, persecution, imprisonment, torture) or en route to their new destination (e.g., rape, abuse, exploitation) can affect refugees well after their arrival. Children and women are at a higher risk for abuse and harm during the migration process than are men. For instance, women crossing borders from Central to North America without their families may have encounters with *coyotes* (i.e., illegal travel brokers) for passage and may became victims of sexual assaults and forced labor before reaching their final destinations. Consequently, the migration process, for some, becomes a major acculturative stressor.

Pattern of Arrival. The pattern of immigration can greatly impact the experience of acculturation for immigrant families. For a host of reasons, a significant number of immigrant families come to America in units. This pattern of arrival has been referred to in the literature as *step migration,* and there has been a great deal of agreement that these family separations are sources of acculturative stress. Intrafamilial separations differ in length of time, usually with the longer separations being the more challenging for the family.

Documentation Status. Undocumented immigrants are at heightened risk for experiencing acculturative stress because their acculturation is mired by the fear of deportation and, for some, the actual experience of deportation. Furthermore, their lack of documentation may cause them to avoid public institutions, such as hospitals and clinics, even if they may need these services. This, in turn, adds to their level of risk for health and mental health difficulties. Also, it is important to note that the lack of documentation also places individuals at a heightened risk for exploitation by employers who may threaten to call the authorities.

Family Factors

Intrafamilial Acculturation Conflicts. It is possible that differences in acculturation levels within families will lead to difficulties or conflicts. However, when acculturation conflicts do occur between parents and their children, they have the potential to cause significant stress for members of the entire family unit. Family conflict arising from the acculturation process is beginning to be better understood. The cultural distance between families' original culture and the host country's culture can threaten the harmony of immigrant families' intergenerational relationships. Furthermore, it is by now generally accepted that younger generations of immigrants acculturate to the Western or mainstream society at faster rates than their elders, who, oftentimes, firmly maintain their traditional customs. This discrepancy in acculturation level may result in increased familial stress and feelings of separation between family generations. It is also possible that the younger generations might experience interpersonal conflict by feeling like they must choose the host culture over their traditional, native identity.

Language/Cultural Brokering. Another outcome of differing rates of acculturation is the reliance on children as cultural and language brokers for their families. Oftentimes, because of limited social or financial resources, coupled with their limited English language abilities, parents rely on their children to help them manage and navigate the host culture. As language/cultural brokers, children essentially translate the language and culture for their parents and also serve as the liaison between their family and the larger cultural context. This role is associated with both negative and positive outcomes for children. On the one hand, it has been argued that this "parentified" role can be experienced as stressful, especially considering the important tasks and decisions child language/cultural brokers are engaged in (i.e., legal, school, financial). Furthermore, when children act as language/cultural brokers for their families, they may miss important social and opportunities and enrichment activities, which can be experienced as a loss. On the other hand, it has also been argued that it is precisely the serious nature of the tasks required of children who serve as language/cultural brokers for their family that positively impacts their self-esteem and social development.

Language Use

The linguistic world of acculturative individuals is complex. English language usage and ability have been associated with acculturative stress, whereby individuals who are less fluent in English experience higher levels of acculturative stress. Given that linguistic ability is necessary not only for simple to more complex business transactions, such as buying groceries and a home, but also for developing relationships with people, language ability may be directly related as well as indirectly related, through social relationships and connectedness, to reported levels of acculturative stress. Despite evidence that suggests the importance of English language skills for acculturating individuals, this does not necessarily mean that healthy acculturation requires surrendering one's language of origin for English. Individuals who are highly acculturated or have been in the host country for many years may experience stresses or losses associated with not being able to communicate in their language of origin with members of their cultural or ethnic enclave. Maintaining fluency in one's language of origin may be a source of pride for individuals.

Acculturation Level

The level of acculturation, that is, the level of familiarity and exposure to the new culture, which is largely associated with amount of time in the host culture, is an important variable to consider when thinking about an acculturating individual's risk for acculturative stress. Unfortunately, the empirical literature that focuses on the link between acculturation level and acculturative stress and other health and mental health outcomes is mixed. For example, it has been suggested that there is a relationship between acculturative level and acculturative stress, whereby higher levels of acculturation may lead to lower levels of acculturative stress. At the same time, there is a growing body of work that suggests that, for some individuals, greater acculturation is associated with an increase in negative physical and mental health, and, for youth, negative academic outcomes.

Nonetheless, immigrants at any level of acculturation can be at risk for detrimental psychological consequences. For example, highly acculturated individuals may realize that becoming acculturated and identified with the host culture does not always result in acceptance by mainstream society and can lead to the development of interpersonal conflict, alienation from traditional supports, frustration, demoralization, and internalization of society's prejudicial attitudes. On the other hand, low-acculturated individuals often face multiple stressors when negotiating an unpredictable majority cultural milieu, which may lead to feelings of isolation, low self-esteem, and helplessness. Research proposes that positive mental health outcomes may be achieved from balancing one's multiple cultures.

Acculturation Strategy

Research investigating Berry and others' fourfold acculturation model primarily focuses on investigating the outcomes for acculturating individuals who adopt different acculturation strategies, with many of the results pointing to the same conclusion: Integration, or a bicultural identity, is the healthiest acculturation strategy for individuals associated with the least amount of acculturative stress. The strategy associated with the highest level of acculturative stress and considered the least healthy mode of acculturation is marginalization, which describes an individual who rejects his or her original culture as well as the host culture.

Exposure to Discrimination and Racism

Despite evidence of the detrimental effects of discrimination and racism for individuals' well-being, these events are quite commonplace in society. Experiences of ethnic/racial discrimination can impact individuals' health and mental health. In the Harvard Immigration Study, C. Suarez-Orozco and M. M. Suarez-Orozco suggest that within immigrant groups, race significantly impacts the level of discrimination one experiences. Given the fact that the majority of recent immigrants are persons of color, the impact of the sociocultural context of the host country on the identity development of non-White immigrants needs to be taken into consideration. When immigrants enter the United States, they are quickly made aware of the racial stratification that characterizes the status quo system of access to opportunity.

Social Capital and Social Support

The greater sociocultural context, determined primarily by the dominant group, greatly impacts acculturating individuals. Given that an individual's successful acculturation is influenced by the flexibility, openness, and equality of the host society, it is imperative to examine the social and cultural context of the receiving community. A. Portes introduces the theory of economic sociology and, specifically, social capital, to help explain the process by which immigrants call on the monetary and nonmonetary resources of their ethnic community to assist with jobs, launch businesses, and establish a pool of suppliers and clients. It is argued that immigrants who move to an area that is richer in social capital will find the acculturation process less challenging because they have the support and resources of an ethnic enclave.

It has been hypothesized that acculturation and acculturative stress are mediated through social and personal variables. Specifically, social support has been found to be an alleviating factor and also serves as both a mediator and moderator in the acculturation–mental health link. For individuals who are in the process of acculturation, perceived social support is a primary protector against negative mental health outcomes. However, it is important to note that, regardless of how much social support individuals have, if they are continually exposed to serious acculturative stressors, they may possibly still experience heightened levels of acculturative stress.

Implications for Research and Practice

Accessing Mental Health Services

Numerous problems and potential barriers exist in the effective delivery of mental health services to the immigrant population. Individuals experiencing heightened levels of acculturative stress and/or other psychological issues (e.g., depression, anxiety) are less likely to seek psychological help. However, the underutilization of mental health services by immigrants is still not clearly understood. There are a host of reasons why immigrants may not seek psychological services, even when they may benefit from such services. Some of these reasons include, but are not limited to, miscommunication between patients and clinicians due to language or cultural barriers; low level of multicultural competence on the part of the clinician; stigmas attached to receiving counseling; the use of culturally relevant coping strategies, such as family members or indigenous healers; fear of seeking services because of lack of documentation; and intercultural mistrust with authority figures and institutions associated with the host society.

It is important that researchers examine which factors serve as barriers to the successful delivery of services for immigrants. For example, seeking help from a mental health practitioner may be a last resort for some immigrant clients, and therefore, practitioners must be sensitive to the potential severity of the problem. Finally, it is imperative for counselors to be culturally competent when working with immigrant clients, which includes an acknowledgment of the client's specific cultural values.

Acculturative Stress and Psychological Outcomes

Successful practitioners are keenly aware of the complex interplay between acculturation and psychological distress when they are providing counseling services to immigrants. For example, given the evidence that suggests that the acculturation process can be extremely stressful and can impact a client's presenting problem, a thorough client history that includes experiences before immigration, during migration, and during acculturation might be necessary.

It is also important for clinicians to understand the acculturation process and the types of stressors that may be associated with a client's acculturation strategy or level. For instance, low-acculturated clients (i.e., new immigrants) may experience homesickness, isolation, and grief over what they left behind in their native land. Contextual factors, such as lack of financial opportunities and discrimination, may exacerbate these stressors. On the other hand, for highly acculturated individuals, the acculturative stress they experience may be both quantitatively and qualitatively different from low-acculturated individuals. For example, highly acculturated individuals may not experience stress related to an inability to communicate in English, but they may experience the stress associated with attempting to maintain a bicultural identity.

Future research should concentrate on discovering within-group differences that exist during the acculturation process so that treatment can become specific and more effective. For instance, not all immigrants, even those within the same ethnic group, acculturate and appraise acculturative stressors in the same way; each may have unique resources (e.g., financial and family supports) and barriers (e.g., lack of education and language skills) that change the experience of acculturation and level of acculturative stress.

Risk and Resilience

Supportive sources within one's own ethnic community may be important in developing both culturally specific ethnic and host competencies. Counselors are encouraged to recognize and appreciate their clients' personal, family, and community resources, as they may serve to protect clients from harmful outcomes associated with acculturative stress. Although practitioners are heavily trained in the diagnosis and treatment of psychological disorders, this preparation may place an overemphasis on finding out what's wrong with individuals. Practitioners who work with immigrant individuals may be more successful if they balance the tasks of facilitating growth in areas of need with supporting and acknowledging client strengths. Similarly, researchers interested in understanding what impacts the acculturation pathway of immigrants may want to investigate both the risk factors and the protective factors associated with this process.

Moving Beyond the Traditional Counseling Role

Counseling psychologists in this new era may be required to move beyond the traditional counseling role, which is largely associated with humanistic approaches to individual and group counseling. Given the inextricable link between the person and the environment, counseling psychologists are increasingly assuming new roles as change agents at systemic levels while they also continue to develop effective interventions that focus on change at the individual level. Furthermore, counseling psychology, as a professional discipline, with its deep tradition and history in human development and multicultural theories, is poised to make a significant positive impact on the way in which immigrants adjust to the new cultural context and on the way in which the cultural context embraces and adjusts to its new citizens.

Jennie Park-Taylor and Allison Ventura

See also Acculturation (v3); Adaptation (v3); Assimilation (v3); Cultural Values (v3); Culture Shock (v3); Immigrants (v3); Multiculturalism (v3); Refugees (v3); Resilience (v2); Second Culture Acquisition (v3); Stress (v2); Stress Management (v2)

Further Readings

Berry, J. W. (1997). Immigration, acculturation, and adaptation. *Applied Psychology: An International Review, 46,* 5–34.

Constantine, M. G., Okazaki, S., & Utsey, S. O. (2004). Self-concealment, social self-efficacy, acculturative stress, and depression in African, Asian, and Latin American international college students. *American Journal of Orthopsychiatry, 74,* 230–241.

Hovey, J. D., & King, C. A. (1996). Acculturative stress, depression, and suicidal ideation among immigrant and second-generation Latino adolescents. *Journal of American Academy of Child and Adolescent Psychology, 35*(9), 1183–1192.

Portes, A., & Rumbaut, R. G. (2001). *The story of the immigrant second generation: Legacies.* Los Angeles: University of California Press.

Redfield, R., Linton, R., & Herskovits, M. (1936). Memorandum on the study of acculturation. *American Anthropologist, 38,* 149–152.

Rudmin, F. W. (2003). Critical history of the acculturation psychology of assimilation, separation, integration, and marginalization. *Review of General Psychology, 7*(1), 3–37.

Sodowsky, G. R., & Maestes, M. V. (2000). Acculturation, ethnic identity, and acculturative stress: Evidence and measurement. In R. H. Dana (Ed.), *Handbook of cross-cultural and multicultural personality assessment* (pp. 131–172). Mahwah, NJ: Lawrence Erlbaum.

Smart, J. F., & Smart, D. W. (1995). Acculturative stress of Hispanics: Loss and challenge. *Journal of Counseling & Development, 73*(4), 390–396.

ACHIEVEMENT GAP

A number of reports and studies have explored issues surrounding the education of African American, Latino/a, and other culturally and linguistically diverse (CLD) students in American school systems. Every CLD group has a different history in the United States. It is widely recognized that the educational experiences of African American students in public schools is rather unique. Specifically, African Americans as a group have been systematically and legally denied the right to an education, and past and ongoing injustices continue to affect the educational achievement of African American students. The most obvious effect is the gap between the academic performances of African American students and their White counterparts. Specifically, myriad reports indicate that Black students often graduate from high school 4 years behind White students in both reading and math. In addition to the gaps in reading and math, there are gaps between White and CLD students in grade point averages, participation in Advanced Placement (AP) classes, gifted education classes, and honors classes, as well as high school graduation rates and college enrollment and graduation rates.

The achievement gap is not a new phenomenon; it has its roots in history. One has only to recall the Supreme Court decision in the case of *Plessy v. Ferguson* to see that separate but equal was legally acceptable only 100 years ago. And it was less than 6 decades years ago that legislation was passed to desegregate education as a result of the landmark 1954 Supreme Court decision in *Brown v. Board of Education.* Although efforts to secure equity and excellence in the education of African American students have a relatively short history, there really is no excuse for ongoing inequities in the education of CLD students.

What Factors Contribute to the Gap?

There is no single achievement gap; the achievement gap has many faces. These achievement gaps individually and collectively contribute to Black and Latino/a students performing less well than White students relative to grades, test scores, graduation rates, and more. In essence, the omnibus "achievement gap" is a *symptom* of many other gaps, such as the funding gap, the resource gap, the teacher quality gap, the curriculum gap, the digital gap, the family involvement gap, and the expectations gap.

Essentially, the reasons behind the achievement gap are multifaceted and complex. The achievement gap starts at home, before children begin school, and then widens during the formal school years. For example, at the kindergarten level, there tends to be a 1-year gap between Black and White students; by the 12th grade, there is often a 4-year gap, as already noted. It is counterintuitive that the gap *widens* while students are in school.

Many factors contribute to the achievement gap(s). Borrowing from the work of Barton of the Educational Testing Service (ETS), this entry explains the primary correlates of the achievement gap and offers recommendation for change. Based on his review of several hundred studies that examined factors contributing to the achievement gap, Barton identified 14 variables that consistently and substantively contribute to the achievement gap. At least two contexts must be thoroughly examined to understand the achievement gap in a comprehensive manner. These two contexts are (1) school and (2) before school and beyond.

School Correlates

Six correlates found in school settings are thought to contribute to the math and reading achievement gaps. These school correlates must be considered in terms of their cumulative impact. For 13 years, students attend school for approximately 180 days each year. Thus, what takes place in school has a major impact on students.

Rigor of Curriculum. Research shows consistently that students' academic achievement depends extensively upon the rigor of the curriculum; yet, the curriculum tends to be less rigorous for Black and Latino/a students. Instructional rigor rests on teachers' expectations, as has been learned from research on teacher expectation and student achievement—when expectations are high, teachers challenge students. Rigor can be defined as high-level instruction and access to challenging programs, such as gifted education and AP classes. Black and Latino/a students are less likely than White students (a) to have substantial credits in academic sources at the end of high school and (b) to participate in honors, AP, and gifted education classes. Although Black students represent over 17% of the public school population, they represent only 8% of students participating in gifted education; even fewer are enrolled in AP and honors classes. Publications by the College Board, Education Trust, Educational Testing Service, and other organizations describe more extensively problems regarding lack of access to rigorous instruction, classes, and programs.

Teacher Quality and Preparation. The importance of teacher quality on student achievement cannot be ignored. Black and Latino/a students are more likely to be taught by teachers who are unqualified, including teachers who lack certification, out-of-field teachers, teachers with the fewest credentials, and teachers with the lowest test scores. In high-minority schools, 29% of teachers do not have at least a minor in the subject area in which they teach; in low-minority schools, the percentage is 21, according to Barton's report. Related to the previous issue of rigor, ill-qualified teachers will have difficulty teaching and challenging students; they are unlikely to raise students' achievement as they do not have the skills to do so.

Teacher Experience and Attendance. Inexperienced teachers, those with less than 3 years of teaching experience, for example, are more likely to teach in urban than suburban settings. In schools with high percentages of CLD students, 21% of teachers have less than 3 years of experience; in schools with low CLD enrollment, 10% of teachers have less than 3 years of teaching. Further complicating this issue, data indicate that teachers working in high-minority schools often have low attendance rates, resulting in classes being taught by substitute teachers. Again, teacher inexperience and poor attendance hinder the quality of instruction given to, and received by, CLD students, contributing to their poorer school achievement.

Class Size. In schools where there are higher percentages of CLD students, class sizes are larger. For instance, in schools where CLD students represent 75% of the population, average class size is 31. In schools where CLD students constitute less than 10% of the student population, class size averages 22. Larger classes are more difficult to manage; more time is spent on behavior than teaching, resulting in students being denied the opportunity to learn at the same rates as their White classmates in smaller classrooms.

Technology-Assisted Instruction. Schools with higher percentages of CLD students are less likely to have computers in the classrooms, Internet access, and updated, high-quality software; this situation is often referred to as the digital divide. Just as problematic is the issue of how teachers use technology in the classroom; 61% of students in low-minority schools are given assignments to conduct research on the Internet, compared to 35% for students in high-minority schools. As a result, CLD are less qualified to compete in situations where technological skills are essential.

School Safety. Classroom discipline, disruptions, and negative peer pressures (e.g., gangs and fears about being attacked at school) are reported more often by Black and Latino/a students than by other students. Students cannot learn in unsafe, threatening environments. They have difficulty concentrating and staying focused or engaged. Thus, many CLD students may have poor attendance or drop out to avoid the stresses that come with peer pressures, which adds to their poorer performance.

As just described, schools contribute to the achievement gap between CLD students and White students in significant ways. But they are not solely responsible for students' differential performance, as described next.

Before School and Beyond Correlates

Schools alone did not create the gap, nor can they close it without support from families and the larger community. Eight additional correlates of the achievement gap, based outside of school, must be addressed.

Parent Availability. The extent to which parents are available and spend quality time with their children varies by family structure and composition. A larger percentage of Black and Latino/a students, compared to White students, live in single-parent homes, and many of these are low income. For those living with mothers only, the rates are 17% for White children, compared with 49% for Black children and 25% for Latino/a children. When parental presence is low, students are left to make choices for themselves. This lack of availability results in less structure and discipline for students; they may not spend their unsupervised time studying and/or participating in school-related activities, causing them to fall further behind White students.

Parent Participation. The extent to which caregivers are involved in their children's education affects students' achievement and behavior. Reports indicate that Black and Latino/a parents tend to participate less in their children's education than other parents. Some 44% of urban parents and 20% of suburban parents report feeling unwelcome in schools. Approximately 50% of both Black and Latino/a parents and 75% of White parents attended a school event in 1999; approximately 25% of CLD parents and 50% of White parents volunteered or served on a committee. As with findings regarding lack of parent availability, student achievement suffers.

Student Mobility. There are many negative consequences to changing schools; CLD students, especially those who live in poverty, have the highest rates of changing schools (25% for Latino/a students, 27% for Black students, and 13% for White students). Data from one study indicate that 41% of students who changed schools frequently were below grade level in reading, and 33% were below grade level in math.

Reading to Young Children. Reading positively correlates with language acquisition, literacy development, test scores, and achievement. One longitudinal study spanning 1993 to 2001 found that, among 3- to 5-year-olds, 64% of White preschoolers were read to every day in the preceding week, compared with 48% for Black preschoolers and 42% of Latino/a preschoolers in 2001. The consequences of poor reading skills are serious, with students subsequently performing poorer on intelligence and achievement tests and having difficulty keeping up in other subject areas.

TV Watching. In 2000, 42% of Black, 22% of Latino/a, and 13% of White fourth graders watched 6 hours or more of TV daily. Excessive and unsupervised TV watching negatively affects students' achievement, with students doing less homework and reading, and participating in fewer after-school activities and intellectually stimulating activities.

Health and Nutrition. Of all households with school-age children, 14% have food issues and 4% report hunger. Black and Latino/a households have 2 to 3 times the food insecurity and hunger of White students. Poor health and hunger are detrimental to achievement, with such students showing less interest, less motivation, and lower concentration; their grades suffer considerably.

Birth Weight. In 2000, more Black infants (13%) were low birth weight compared with White infants (7%) and Latino/a infants (6%). Infants born with low birth weight begin life with disadvantages, many of which do not disappear. A disproportionate percentage of children born low birth weight have long-term disabilities and impaired development, as well as delayed motor and social development. These are more likely to struggle academically.

Lead Poisoning. The primary source of lead poisoning among children is living in old homes covered with lead-based paint. Whereas 6% of White children live in homes constructed before 1946, the percentage increases to 22% of Black children and 4% of Latino/a children. Excessive levels of lead cause reduction in IQ and attention span, increased reading and learning disabilities, and increased behavior problems. Compared to other students, CLD students are at the highest risk of being exposed to lead because a larger percentage lives in older homes.

Despite the data just presented, many of these variables can be improved. If these 14 variables are the most powerful in creating and maintaining the achievement gap, then it behooves counseling professionals to address them in a systemic, comprehensive, and collaborative manner. Families, educators (administrators, teachers, counselors, etc.), community leaders, health professionals, and others must collaborate to tackle this educational tragedy.

Educators must, for example, ensure that CLD students are taught by high-quality teachers and teachers with extensive experience in classrooms. School personnel and staff must receive formal preparation to work more effectively with CLD students and, thus, to raise their expectations for Black and Latino/a students, as has been proposed by advocates of multicultural and culturally responsive education (e.g., Sonia Nieto, James Banks, Linda Darling-Hammond, Geneva Gay, Gloria Ladson-Billings, and Jacqueline Irvine). Furthermore, class sizes and schools must be smaller, and teachers should receive training in culturally responsive classroom management strategies. Educators must adopt and implement programs in their schools to address safety and peer pressure. Conflict resolution programs and anger management programs would be helpful to students.

In terms of homes and communities, families will need access to learning opportunities that educate, empower, and support them in working with schools and their children. Programs addressing family involvement and literacy are two timely topics. Community leaders should collaborate with schools and families to provide students with mentors and role models. Finally, it is essential that schools, families, and businesses collaborate with the social workers and healthcare providers to address problems such as poverty, hunger, health care, and lead poisoning.

Donna Y. Ford and Gilman W. Whiting

See also Academic Achievement (v2); Civil Rights (v3); Cognition/Intelligence, Assessment of (v2); Cultural Equivalence (v3); Intelligence (v2); Intelligence Tests (v3); Socioeconomic Status (v3); Stereotype Threat (v3)

Further Readings

Barton, P. (2003). *Parsing the achievement gap. Baselines for tracking progress.* Princeton, NJ: Educational Testing Service.

Bridgeman, B., & Wendler, C. (2005). *Characteristics of minority students who excel on the SAT and in the classroom.* Princeton, NJ: Educational Testing Service, Policy Information Center.

Education Trust. (2006). *The funding gaps 2006.* Washington, DC: Author.

Ford, D.Y. (1996). *Reversing underachievement among gifted Black students: Promising practices and programs.* New York: Teachers College Press.

U.S. Department of Education. (2006). *Secretary's fifth annual report to Congress on teacher quality.* Washington, DC: Author.

Adaptation

The term *adaptation* originally derives from the biological sciences as a phenomenon of person–environment fit. In psychology, adaptation is a process by which individuals or groups make necessary or desired changes—cognitive, behavioral, and affective—in response to new environmental conditions or demands in order to meet basic needs, function, and maintain a good quality of life. Adaptation is integral to the study and practice of multicultural counseling. In a rapidly changing world with increased cross-cultural interactions, people must engage in a continuous process of overcoming internal and external obstacles in order to survive and thrive. Failure to adapt leaves individuals in a prolonged state of culture shock that can create long-term damage to mental and physical well-being.

Important Distinctions

Several distinctions are important for understanding adaptation within the context of multicultural counseling. Although cross-cultural adaptation is similar to adaptation to other major life changes (e.g., loss of a loved one), Linda Anderson speaks to what is unique to cross-cultural adaptation; that is, a person experiencing a new culture is automatically an outsider adapting to the dominant culture. The work of John Berry delineates this acculturation process as a step toward adaptation. In response to the new environment, individuals make changes to "fit" by employing an assimilation or integration strategy or "not fit" by utilizing a separation or marginalization strategy.

Colleen Ward makes an important distinction between psychological adaptation and sociocultural adaptation. Psychological adaptation arises from the stress/coping paradigm and refers to emotional changes that vary over time until equilibrium is reached (e.g., tolerance of ambiguous situations). Sociocultural adaptation comes from the social learning paradigm and refers to cognitive and behavioral changes that follow a more linear progression (e.g., accepting new cultural mores). Although these modes of adaptation are linked theoretically and statistically, they are also distinct processes with different predictor variables.

Andrew Garrison reviews adaptation as a goal of all psychotherapy. He argues that the intrinsic problem of this goal is that it comes from an individualistic point of view, a bias of Western culture. Using the individual as the unit of analysis in the study and practice of psychology neglects the notion of interdependence and adaptation goals that are good for all human beings (e.g., equitable distribution of resources). Furthermore, good mental health is often viewed as the individual adjusting to the environment, a conceptualization that ignores unhealthy aspects of cultures to which individuals are adjusting (e.g., unfair social conditions). Inherent to multicultural counseling is the empowerment of clients not only to adapt in new cultural contexts but also to impact the environment (e.g., managing global warming) such that humanity can adapt as a whole.

Future Directions

The study of cross-cultural adaptation is complex. It is a process that occurs over a long period of time and, thus, calls for longitudinal studies using both qualitative and quantitative methodologies. Furthermore, each cross-cultural interaction is unique. Thus, Berry's work calls for systematic, comparative studies. Finally, research has focused on how individuals adapt to the environment. Consideration of the impact of individuals on the environment as a process of adaptation is called for as well.

Michelle A. Swagler

See also Acculturation (v3); Acculturative Stress (v3); Assimilation (v3); Enculturation (v3); Identity Development (v3); Person–Environment Fit (v4); Person–Environment Interactions (v2)

Further Readings

Anderson, L. (1994). A new look at an old construct: Cross-cultural adaptation. *International Journal of Intercultural Relations, 18,* 293–328.

Berry, J. W., & Sam, D. (1997). Acculturation and adaptation. In J. W. Berry, M. H. Segall, & C. Kagiticibasi (Eds.), *Handbook of cross-cultural psychology: Vol. 3. Social behavior and applications* (pp. 291–326). Boston: Allyn & Bacon.

Garrison, A. (1997). Adaptationism, mental health, and therapeutic outcome. *Psychotherapy: Theory, Research, Practice, Training, 34,* 107–114.

Ward, C., Bochner, S., & Furman, A. (2001). *The psychology of culture shock* (Rev. ed.). Hove, East Sussex, UK: Routledge.

Adoption, Transracial

See Transracial Adoption

Affirmative Action

Affirmative action refers to institutional measures taken to increase the representation of women and people of color in areas of employment, government contracts, and higher education from which they have been excluded historically. The policy began as a response to the failure of businesses with government contracts to hire women, persons with disabilities, and minorities. These groups were discriminated against and denied equal access and opportunity. Hence, following the Civil Rights Act of 1964, affirmative action was initiated by Executive Order 11246 by President Lyndon Johnson in 1965. The executive order required organizations receiving government funding or contracts to adopt programs to promote the aggressive recruitment and retention of underrepresented populations.

Three major concepts form the basis for affirmative action. First, all of society is strengthened by diversity, equality, and inclusion. Second, preferences for women and minorities help to (a) neutralize unearned advantages that favor the privileged majority and (b) prevent further exclusion of women and minorities from higher education and the workplace. Finally, the federal government has the legal and social responsibility for enforcing programs to eliminate existing discriminatory practices of institutional racial preference that infringe on equal opportunity.

Over the past 3 decades, affirmative action has faced considerable opposition in the courts and public debate forums. In the late 1970s, the establishment of racial quotas under affirmative action was criticized as an antithetical practice of promoting preferential treatment. This "reverse discrimination" argument was accepted by the U.S. Supreme Court in *Regents of the University of California v. Bakke* (1978), which let existing programs remain but reduced the use of affirmative action to voluntary programs. In 1989, the Supreme Court ruled in favor of reverse discrimination claims and eliminated the use of minority set-asides where past discrimination was unproven. Still, affirmative action is often associated with being a quota system, when, in fact, affirmative action programs can only require that institutions take cognizance of the demographics of their constituents. Quotas have only been court ordered in instances after a finding of overt discriminatory practices by a company. Even in such cases, proving discriminatory practices was extremely difficult in that statistics were deemed inadmissible, as they did not prove intent. As a result of these rulings, the federal government's role in affirmative action was significantly diminished.

The Civil Rights Act of 1991 was established in effort to restore government commitment to affirmative action, but a 1995 Supreme Court decision limited the use of race as a criterion in awarding government contracts. In response to that decision, President Clinton put forward a White House memorandum that called for the elimination of any program that "(a) creates a quota; (b) creates preferences for unqualified individuals; (c) creates reverse discrimination; or (d) continues even after its equal opportunity purposes have been achieved." In 1996, Proposition 209 called for an end to the use of affirmative action in California, and the use of race- and gender-based preferences was banned in the state the following year. Affirmative action was also abolished by Initiative 200 in Washington State, further demonstrating a strong opposition to the policy on a state level.

More recently, a landmark 2003 Supreme Court decision involving the University of Michigan allowed educational institutions to consider race as one of many factors for admission as long as it was applied broadly when evaluating students and not used in a formulaic manner. As a result, more systematic affirmative action procedures—such as setting aside admissions slots for students of color or assigning weighted points for race—were eliminated. The Supreme Court ruled that affirmative action was no longer justified as a tool to redress past discrimination but was upheld as means to increase diversity at all levels of society.

These challenges to affirmative action have the potential to jeopardize minority recruitment rates and opportunities for higher education and employment. As agents of social justice, counseling psychologists must understand the issues in the controversy over affirmative action. Minimally, counselors must stay informed as to the current status of affirmative action policies and must maintain awareness of how changes to such programs affect the lives of their clients of color. Within a counseling context, clients of color may present with some of the adverse effects of being stigmatized as beneficiaries of affirmative action programs. As a result, clients may experience doubts about their own merit and self-efficacy, stereotype threat, and enhanced pressure to demonstrate competence. Counselors must be prepared to address such issues.

Peter C. Donnelly

See also Civil Rights (v3); Discrimination (v3); Organizational Diversity (v3)

Further Readings

American Psychological Association. (1996). *Affirmative action: Who benefits?* Washington, DC: Author.

Crosby, F. J. (2004). *Affirmative action is dead; Long live affirmative action.* New Haven, CT: Yale University Press.

Dovidio, J. F., & Gaertner, S. L. (2001). Affirmative action, unintentional racial biases, and intergroup relations. In M. A. Hogg & D. Abrams (Eds.), *Intergroup relations: Essential readings* (pp. 146–161). Philadelphia: Psychology Press.

Wise, T. (2005). *Affirmative action: Racial preference in Black and White.* New York: Routledge.

African Americans

According to the most recent U.S. Census Bureau report, prepared in 2000, there were 36.4 million people, or 12.9% of the total U.S. population, who identified as Black or African American. In addition, there were 1.8 million, or 0.6% of the population, who identified as Black in combination with one or more other races.

The term *African American* is an evolutionary one that gives rise to much debate regarding categorization and inclusion. *African American* is an ethnic term that includes persons who are descended from the African continent and whose families have been in the Americas for at least one generation; in contrast, the term *Black* refers to race and includes diverse ethnic backgrounds, including Caribbean and African ethnicities. However, both terms are often used interchangeably as a racial term. Conflict may often arise between native-born Blacks and Black immigrants and their children, all of whose experiences within American society help inform their decision to identify with the term *African American.* However, concerns about competing for limited resources are often cited as the reason for a wish to be less inclusive rather than more inclusive in terms of identifying group membership.

The need to categorize and group those who were not members of the dominant group in the United States began in the mid-1600s when Africans arrived to the newly established American colonies. Initial categorizations referred to racial/ethnic characteristics, including skin color, hair texture and physical phenotypes (e.g., lips, nose, and body shape), parentage, and land of origin. It is perhaps the overlap in early categorizations which have contributed to the confusion surrounding the present-day usage of *African American* to denote a racial category as well as an ethnicity. Ethnic and racial group labels for people of African descent have changed over time and political contexts. Early labels used to refer to African Americans as a group included *African, Negro, Black,* and the derogatory term *nigger.*

However, with growing cultural awareness (e.g., the Harlem Renaissance), increased political power (e.g., the American civil rights movement), and grass-roots activism (e.g., Black Panthers), social initiatives toward self-identification and labeling arose within African American communities. Community members began to take control of how they were referred to in arenas involving the written word, mass media communication, the arts, sciences, and the political lexicon. These self-chosen identifications were reflective of a shared cultural heritage, language, history, and legacy of slavery and included terms such as *Colored, Afro-American, African American,* and, of late, the lesser-used term *Neo-Nubians.*

Despite the extensive use of *African American* as a racial/ethnic label, individuals may take issue with being presumed to identify as African American. Disagreements about inclusion and identification can be linked to an individual's generation, level of acculturation, and political affiliation. Others who do not wish to be affiliated with African Americans may deny their membership because of negative associations tied to a long history that portrays African Americans as the denigrated "other," plagued by oppression. Still, others who have some part of their ethnic identity that interfaces with the African American experience (e.g., mixed race, biracial, or foreign-born individuals) may prefer to identify themselves as multiethnic or multiracial rather than identifying solely as African American, as this label may be too confining or restrictive.

People who identify or are identified as African Americans do not comprise a monolithic people. Factors such as gender, age, educational attainment, geographic location, socioeconomic status, religious and political affiliation, and occupational endeavor contribute to the variations of experiences among these people. Within-group differences relevant to cultural identity (e.g., racial identity attitudes and acculturation level) need to be considered and honored in the counseling relationship. Therefore, it is difficult to suggest a singular counseling approach that would address a variety of mental health concerns that affect individual members of this group.

Furthermore, the nature of African American experiences in America has significant implications for the use of counseling and mental health services by this community. In fact, for many years the counseling profession has had limited contact with African American clients. Racial boundaries in the United States have, in effect, created a national system of disparate access to societal resources. The counseling and mental health professions embedded in this culture are only now, in recent years, beginning to become more receptive to the needs and concerns of African Americans.

Thus, the impact of history has profoundly shaped the experiences of African Americans in the United States. The legacy of enslavement has embedded racism into the cultural milieu, which has had important psychological, physical, and socioeconomic consequences for African Americans and all racial and ethnic groups in the United States. African Americans, dehumanized and treated legally and otherwise as property, have worked to overcome the legacy of institutionalized racism that has been in place for more than 200 years. Many of the practices and laws that created slavery have since been overturned, and yet the legacy of racism continues.

Given the myriad within-group differences among African Americans, shared experiences related to the legacy of slavery and racism contextualize health and mental health, educational, and socioeconomic disparities evidenced among African Americans. Despite the tremendous strides African Americans have made in the United States, they remain overrepresented in lower socioeconomic strata. Psychosocial stressors arising from ongoing interactions with racism in the United States have led some African Americans to seek treatment. Yet, members of this group are disproportionately located among homeless and incarcerated populations, making it difficult to offer consistent, effective interventions.

Furthermore, with regard to mental health disparities, African Americans face numerous obstacles. These obstacles include overdiagnosis of schizophrenia, compared with affective disorders; less availability of, and access to, services; and overall poor quality of treatment received for mental health disorders. In comparison, disparities in the treatment of physical health issues for African Americans also remain problematic. African Americans are more likely to suffer from heart disease, stroke, obesity, breast cancer, and prostate cancer than are Whites.

To this end, gross inequities impact every aspect of this group's existence in the United States, including economics, housing, and employment. Although it is clear that exposure to trauma (e.g., neighborhood violence, genocide, racial microaggressions) influences mental health, particularly with reference to race-related stress, African Americans have also demonstrated tremendous resilience in the face of such difficulty. Resilience refers to a person's ability to recover from hardship. Counselors who encounter African American clients can use a strength-based approach that focuses on positive attributes African Americans possess rather than retraumatizing or overpathologizing this population. Strengths African Americans possess that need to be considered by counselors include the family unit, their ability to recognize the importance of education, and their use of religious/spiritual coping strategies as a way of improving their life circumstances.

Cultural Values Relevant to African Americans

There are several cultural values that African Americans embrace which help to sustain their communities. These values include familialism and connection to spirituality and religion, values that originated with Africentric cultural values. In addition, when encountering difficulty, African Americans have been described as being more likely to face the problem to find resolution and to rely upon spirituality to aid in relief from problematic situations. It is recommended that counselors and mental health professionals consider the diversity in the endorsement of these cultural values when working clinically with African American individuals and families.

Families

The family is an important social, cultural, and psychological structure within the African American community that is subject to being classified as dysfunctional by members of the dominant culture making peripheral observations. African American family units represent diverse structures, including multigenerational, single-parent, and two-parent blended or intact. The makeup of African American families can be extensive, including several generations living together and the informal adoption of fictive kin (i.e., non–blood related members of the family). The institution of slavery had required that African Americans transform the very meaning and structure of the family because slave families were fractured by slave masters who bought and sold slaves like chattel. For slave families, the Eurocentric nuclear family model did not exist; rather, broadened definitions of family, inclusive of multiple generations and fictive kin, were adaptive forms of social support. Furthermore, fictive kin and the nature of extended family networks facilitated the African American family's ability to share limited resources (e.g., child care responsibilities, housing, and economic resources).

Regardless of the structural makeup of the African American family, the unit is faced with concerns as members of the family engage and interact with components of the dominant culture. For example, the African American family as a unit is concerned with issues related to (a) sustaining economic survival; (b) achieving financial prosperity; (c) perpetuating itself despite obstacles such as child abuse, poverty, unwed mothers, and the proliferation of AIDS; (d) meeting the challenges of day-to-day survival; (e) overcoming the undereducation of its children; and (f) protecting its community from violence associated with the illegal drug trade, police shootings, or victimization in the form of random acts of violence.

Families that have a stable economic foundation, possess racial pride, provide a consistent environment for its children, use extended family networks to create a support system, are connected with a larger community, and have the skill to obtain what they need are thought to have protective factors against the development of mental illness. On the other hand, factors such as child abuse, neglect, and substance abuse are detrimental to the family unit and can influence the prevalence of mental illness within a family unit, especially when compounded by deficiencies in the aforementioned protective factors. Biological and psychological factors also influence the onset of mental illness.

Experiences within African American families vary vastly; however, commonalities of heritage, culture, and contexts inform counselors about unique considerations within African American families. For example, it is possible for the existence of various levels of acculturation and racial identities (i.e., refers to the spectrum of how one thinks about oneself as a racial being) within the context of a single African American family unit. Family members' differing racial identity statuses may contribute to discord and tension across multiple domains, such as education, employment, and relationships. Similarly, generational and regional cultural differences can influence family members' role expectations, such that intergenerational conflict and social class differences may arise. Counselors' ability to recognize the nuances that these variations create within the family and the tensions that may arise when differences exist is crucial.

Socioeconomic class has a tremendous impact on the African American family and its functioning. Within the same family, broad variations that exist within social classes can contribute to tensions related to education, status, and access. Despite these differences, African Americans are more likely than Whites to remain connected to their family unit regardless of these variations in socioeconomic status. For example, unlike their White middle-class peers, middle-class African Americans are often the first generation to reach this class status and thus are looked upon to provide economic, educational, and emotional support to family members who have not joined the ranks of the middle class. Dynamics created by shifts in social class may be stressful and overwhelming. Thus, the resources that may have been sufficient to sustain the individual when stretched to support an extensive family network may cause middle-class African Americans to experience a sense of economic paucity.

Role of the Black Church

African Americans have a long and rich tradition of involvement with the Black church. The Black church has been a sanctuary, gathering place, and social change agent in the African American community. The term *Black church* in this context serves as a collective description that includes a variety of Christian denominations (e.g., Baptist, African Methodist, Episcopalian, Catholic, Jehovah's Witness, Church of God) to which African Americans belong. African Americans also practice a variety of other religions, such as Islam, Buddhism, and African religions such as Kemet or Ifa. Given its historic role in this community,

African Americans continue to depend heavily on the Black church for support. Members of the clergy are often consulted to provide advice to members of their congregation.

At times, counselors and clergy members may need the benefit of mutual collaboration to facilitate the counseling process. Collaboration is beneficial in circumstances where members of the clergy are not equipped to address various mental health concerns or the complexities associated with psychological distress and mental illness. Counselors can receive additional insights about the individual or family that only the clergy member may be able to access. However, African Americans who identify themselves as very religious may be unwilling to attend counseling for fear that it may demonstrate a lack of faith on their behalf.

In some instances, African American adults who actively attended church as children may attend church less frequently or not at all; nevertheless, they may still identify as spiritual or religious and may depend on prayer. Prayer serves as a coping mechanism for many African Americans, particularly women. Prayer plays a vital role in the lives of African Americans, affording them the opportunity to express concerns, request intervention with various life circumstances, and seek comfort and connection to a higher power.

Therapeutic Considerations

A key component to working with a diverse group of people such as African Americans is developing multicultural counseling competence. Multicultural counseling competence refers to developing the ability to understand one's own cultural perspectives and developmental process in relation to diverse cultural perspectives and life experiences. Several aspects of multicultural competence involve being able to discuss issues of race, class, and culture without discomfort, whether the discussion is initiated by the therapist or client. With respect to African American clients, counselors can fortify their knowledge base through talking to informed colleagues, working collaboratively with members of the African American community (e.g., clergy, community leaders), reading about the cultural experiences of African Americans, and attending professional conferences to learn about issues African American face and how to effectively address these issues in clinical practice.

A primary vehicle that may be used to ascertain extensive knowledge of clients' experiences is the structured clinical interview. Through the structured clinical interview, the clinician may gather information about clients' development, family experiences, and personality in order to formulate a profile and build a holistic understanding of clients' experiences and concerns. However, some clients may experience this interview as intrusive and overly reliant on verbal expression. For example, African American clients who may not have received a formal education or do not express themselves well verbally may be at a disadvantage not only in this interview but also in traditional "talk" therapy settings. African Americans who do not trust the counseling process may be unwilling to respond openly to inquiries and may withhold pertinent information. Clinical misinterpretations of Black ways of speaking and use of language can lead to missed opportunities for understanding the nuances of African American clients.

Counselors who work with African Americans need to be prepared to work with clients traumatized by racism-related stress, which has implications for the psychological functioning of African Americans. Racism-related stress is stress generated from ongoing encounters and experiences with discrimination and prejudice. It manifests itself daily in the lives of African Americans (e.g., employment, housing, commerce, and criminal justice system) and can appear as depression, lower self-esteem, sub-par school performance, and an overall sense of dissatisfaction with one's state of well-being. Racism-related stress has been linked to increased rates of high blood pressure, stroke, diabetes, and cancer among African Americans. A holistic approach, which addresses the mind, body, and spirit to alleviate negative energy located in the psyche, may be an effective alternative to traditional medicine for treating these manifestations of stress in African Americans. Exercises that use progressive relaxation and meditation may help reduce racism-related stress.

Therapists who work with African Americans also may want to consider the influence of Africentric cultural values on clients' psychological functioning and willingness to engage in the therapeutic process. Africentric cultural values are an outgrowth of African traditionalism and the historical experiences of African Americans. These beliefs and values refer to individuals' ways of viewing the world which acknowledges the importance of one's relatedness or connectedness to others by engaging in collaborative efforts, spirituality, and presentation of one's true self to the world. Despite taking these factors into account in the counseling process, counselors may find that African

American clients who embrace Africentric cultural values may be more difficult to engage in traditional counseling and therapy; clients may have stigmas about seeking therapy or have a wish to withhold their true thoughts and feelings from the therapist.

As has been previously suggested, the counseling relationship is one built on trust, an alliance, created between therapist and client. At times, this relationship can be challenged or damaged by racial microaggressions that occur at conscious or unconscious levels during the therapeutic process. Racial microaggressions are slights that occur in the counseling relationship, when the therapist expresses a racist belief or thought. Examples of racial microaggressions that can manifest in therapy include making stereotypical assumptions about members of ethnic and racial groups, suggesting that racial-cultural differences do not exist, denying that racism occurs, and dismissing the client's concerns about issues of race. In addition, racial microaggressions are likely to give rise to further cultural mistrust in the therapeutic alliance.

Cultural mistrust occurs in therapy when African American clients become concerned that the therapist is racist or biased and that the therapist's biases will prevent both members of the counseling dyad from participating genuinely in the counseling process. On the other hand, the phenomenon of cultural paranoia is described as a healthy, adaptive response to historical racial discrimination and oppression that African Americans have experienced. Both cultural mistrust and cultural paranoia have been linked to increased rates of premature termination of the counseling process among African American clients. At times, clinicians unfamiliar with the intensity of racial dynamics may diagnose patients who appear to have paranoid ideations with paranoid schizophrenia without considering the potential influence of racial dynamics within the counseling setting or the degree to which race-related vigilance has been adaptive for the client. Because paranoid schizophrenia is overrepresented, and arguably overdiagnosed, among African Americans above other mental disorders, counselors are advised to foster an awareness of cultural paranoia.

Assisting African Americans with issues of cultural mistrust and paranoia requires a willingness to acknowledge the realities of racism in the lives of African Americans. Possessing flexibility and ability to embrace diverse worldviews can help to establish a strong therapeutic alliance with clients. Using a cognitive-behavioral approach to work with clients to help them to identify irrational thoughts and beliefs can help them to gain insight into racial dynamics as they occur and challenge fixed beliefs that all White people aim to harm African Americans. Using a cognitive-behavioral approach, counselors can assist clients with gaining control of their reactions to incidents where perceived instances of racism have occurred and can offer problem-solving techniques and strategies to address the events.

One common practice in African American family life is keeping family problems within the family. Secrets are those parts of family historical knowledge and life that distinguish family from nonfamily. Cultural values that endorse keeping family problems "within the family" may contribute to African American individuals' reluctance to enter counseling or self-disclose with their therapists. Examples of secrets that families may not want to discuss in therapy are informal adoptions, a relative with mental illness, or a family history of substance abuse. Furthermore, for many African American individuals and families, secrets related to sexual or substance abuse, marital difficulties, identity issues, or mental illness are unlikely to receive psychological attention until such concerns have escalated. Mandated individual or family therapy may engender feelings of humiliation, embarrassment, anger, and resentment, all of which need to be explored with counselors. In addition, families may view counselors as intruders into the family's business. Having an understanding of how clients become engaged in the therapeutic process can help inform counselors' strategies for overcoming personal, social, and institutional barriers toward treatment and developing a helpful working alliance. Given the tremendous influence of the family on the development of the individual member, consideration should be given to expanding the therapeutic alliance to include members of the family for assessment purposes and treatment if needed.

Referral Sources

Compared with other ethnic/racial groups, African Americans are the least likely to use counseling services. Thus, when African Americans do arrive to counseling, the situation is usually extreme and may be reflective of African Americans' cultural perspective of immediacy, dealing in the here and now. Issues of social stigma, lack of financial resources to pay for treatment, concerns about stigmas of weakness or abnormality, as well as lack of information about the counseling process are contributing factors to African Americans' underutilization of counseling to relieve psychological distress.

Frequently, African Americans who experience psychological distress do not receive adequate relief from their symptoms because they are not connected with appropriate or culturally responsive mental health professionals (e.g., psychologists, psychiatrists). African Americans are more likely to receive mental health services from hospital emergency rooms. This approach is often ineffective because although the immediate crisis is averted, follow-up is often needed to fully address or resolve systemic problems. Furthermore, overreliance on emergency room treatment can result in misdiagnosis or the overdiagnosis of serious mental disorders in this population. Outpatient services remain underutilized by this group for similar reasons.

Future Directions

Although African Americans may appear to be struggling and beleaguered by social injustice and racism, as a group they remain resilient. Their resilience is evidenced by the steady growth of the African American middle class, economic gains, and social progress. Although varied, their experiences share common links; thus, it is important for counselors to examine the cultural context of the issues African Americans bring to the consultation rooms. Greater efforts must be made to inform, educate, and encourage African Americans to use the therapeutic process to unburden themselves of the stress and trauma often associated with the overlays of social locations in the United States.

The counseling profession has made strides to improve the quality of treatment received by African American clients; however, a concerted effort must be made to help this population focus on their strengths rather than on the negative aspects of prejudice and racism. A strength-based approach can serve as a powerful tool in helping engage African Americans in the therapeutic process. Focusing on strengths can help them continue to adapt and thrive, relying on their families, religious affiliations, and communities for support, uplift, and advancement.

Erica King-Toler and Vanessa Alleyne

See also Acculturation (v3); Black English (v3); Black Psychology (v3); Black Racial Identity Development (v3); Career Counseling, African Americans (v4); Cultural Mistrust (v3); Cultural Paranoia (v3); National Association for the Advancement of Colored People (v3); Race (v3); Racial Identity (v3); Visible Racial/Ethnic Groups (v3)

Further Readings

Boyd-Franklin, N. (2003). *Black families in therapy: Understanding the African American experience* (2nd ed.). New York: Guilford Press.

Constantine, M. G. (2007). Racial microaggressions against African American clients in cross-racial counseling relationships. *Journal of Counseling Psychology, 54,* 1–16.

Constantine, M. G., Alleyne, V. L., Wallace, B. C., & Franklin-Jackson, D. C. (2006). Africentric values: Their relation to positive mental health in African American adolescent girls. *Journal of Black Psychology, 32,* 141–154.

Daniels, L. A. (Ed.). (2001). *The state of Black America 2001.* New York: National Urban League.

Grier, W., & Cobbs, P. (1968). *Black rage.* New York: Basic Books.

Jones, R. (1996). *Handbook of tests and measurements for Black populations* (2 vols.). Hampton, VA: Cobb & Henry.

Lewis-Coles, M. E. L., & Constantine, M. G. (2006). Racism-related stress, Africultural coping, and religious problem-solving among African Americans. *Cultural Diversity & Ethnic Minority Psychology, 12,* 433–443.

Neighbors, H. W., & Jackson, J. S. (Eds.). (1996). *Mental health in Black America.* Thousand Oaks, CA: Sage.

Snowden, L. R. (2001). Barriers to effective mental health services: African Americans. *Mental Health Services Research, 3,* 181–187.

U.S. Department of Health and Human Services. (2001). *Mental health: Culture, race and ethnicity. A supplement to mental health: A report of the surgeon general.* Rockville, MD: Author.

Utsey, S. O., & Ponterotto, J. G. (1996). Development and validation of the Index of Race-Related Stress. *Journal of Counseling Psychology, 43,* 490–501.

Whaley, A. L. (2001). Cultural mistrust: An important psychological construct for diagnosis and treatment of African Americans. *Professional Psychology: Research and Practice, 32,* 555–562.

AFROCENTRICITY/AFROCENTRISM

Afrocentricity/Afrocentrism is better referred to as *African-centered thought.* The term has endured several political and vernacular changes, but conceptually it has remained consistent. African-centered thought symbolizes the intellectual, psychological, and social struggle of descendants forcibly removed from Africa and placed in the Americas. It is representative of an intellectual and practical effort to reclaim a cultural legacy, consciousness, and history that positions an authentic cultural unity of the continent of Africa as the worldview lens from which human endeavors are interpreted and engaged.

Background

Afrocentricity/Afrocentrism is relatively recent nomenclature. The precursor to stake a modern literary claim recognizing a distinct cultural identity of African Americans can be found in the pioneering work of W. E. B. Du Bois in 1913, *The Souls of Black Folk*. Indirectly anchored in African-centered thought, Du Bois articulated a paradoxical condition of being an African in America. Du Bois's concept of "double consciousness" is a historical reference point for acknowledging an alternative worldview at conflict with the hegemonic Eurocentric worldview in America. Contemporary African-centered anthropologists, social scientists, and psychologists have articulated an authentic African worldview for such concepts as personality, identity, and optimal health and behavior.

African-Centered Worldview

Based on the pioneering scholarship of Cheikh Anta Diop and G. G. James in 1954, Afrocentricity/Afrocentrism postulates that an African-centered worldview places African cultural unity, history, and philosophy as the central perspective for which the world is experienced, interpreted, and engaged. Contemporary scholars such as Marimba Ani, Molefi Kete Asante, Asa Hillard, Maulana Karenga, and John Mbiti have stated that the African worldview provides a method and process of analysis that reflects the historical continuity, collective consciousness, and cultural unity of ethnocultural groups on the continent of precolonial Africa. Afrocentricity/Afrocentrism, although similar to Pan-Africanism or Black Nationalism, is not a political ideology but a cultural consciousness.

Some themes of an African worldview are ancestor veneration, social collectivity, and spiritual basis of existence. *Ancestor veneration* in Africa is the belief that ancestors are deities, much like saints and prophets in other traditions, and they are very much part of the cosmology and influence daily living. They are respected and celebrated but not worshipped. In a therapeutic setting ancestors play an important role in the healing process. *Social collectivity* by clan groupings influences the distribution of wealth and labor. Social roles are flexible to meet the needs of the collective. Research investigating African Americans must include the impact on the community or other systems that are connected to their lives. *The spiritual basis of existence* refers to the belief that all things are spiritually manifested. Spirit is the essence of existence. There is only one God, a Divine energy that flows through all things and thus creates our interdependence. Truth is revealed through signs, the rhythm of nature, symbolic imagery, the cosmos, and the human being. This value introduces the notion and acceptance of phenomena, which are critical to the analysis of human behavior from an African-centered worldview. In essence the African worldview takes a teleological orientation.

African-Centered Psychology

African-centered psychology is concerned with defining African psychological experiences from an African-centered worldview. According to Na'im Akbar, Kobi K. K. Kambon, and Wade Nobles, an African-centered worldview assumes a philosophical premise that utilizes an affective inclusive metaphysical epistemology and that employs an axiology that is based on a member-to-member values orientation, an ontology that is di-unital (the attraction of opposites or curricular thought), and a cosmology that acknowledges the interdependence of all things seen and unseen, which is the essence of the Divine Spirit. In essence African-centered psychology is conscious and unconscious.

African-centered psychological theory has emerged from roughly three general periods on the continuum of African world civilization: *Africa in antiquity, traditional,* and *re-establishment*. African-centered psychology situated in ancient Africa draws on the wisdom of the world's first known and recorded scholars of the world. During this period covering several dynasties and thousands of years, there was a particular focus on teleological orientation (attention to purpose) and maintenance of the self in a God-like fashion. Spiritual illumination through harmonious and balanced behaviors (actions and thoughts) was the criterion for a functioning African mind. During the *traditional* period African-centered conceptualizations of the self continued to focus on spiritual connectivity as the central purpose of existence. As the previous dynasties expanded and then fell, populations shifted with migrations. During this period the basic concepts for understanding the African mind remained consistent with those of the previous period, though the models and practices (i.e., rituals) were adapted for new environments. The central teleological orientation (attention to purpose) remained consistent. In fact this provided the foundation for cultural unity that preserved the various ethnic groups during hostile Arab and European invasions and colonization. During this current period of *reestablishment,* African-centered psychological theory has adopted and integrated the language and practices of its colonizers while maintaining its core theoretical tenets from the previous periods. While challenges to African cultural unity, as a result of colonial hegemony and religious missionaries, have created contention within postmodern African cities, African-centered and non–African-centered praxes coexist.

Future Directions

Afrocentricity/Afrocentrism is a representation of African thought and worldview that is placed at the central perspective of analysis. As a unit of analysis, African-centered thought is both individual and institutional. An Afrocentric/Africentric orientation can inform individual and institutional behaviors, methods, and practices. In particular, African-centered thought can provide a framework for understanding such concepts as spirituality, humanity, functioning, illness, identity development, purpose, assessment, personality, community, and civilization.

In the future, Afrocentricity/Afrocentrism, as influenced by African-centered thought, should be placed as the primary unit of analysis for the development of appropriate interventions, assessments, and theories for addressing the health of people of African descent. Non–African-centered perspectives should be seen as supplemental or alternative.

The challenge of an African-centered thought is inclusion in the traditional canon of psychological theory. Dominant Western theories have produced a condition of scientific colonialism that employs "different equals deficient" logic. Eurocentric thought, institutionally, has taken the position that alternative intellectual traditions are alternatives, deserve prolonged empirical scrutiny, and are seen as supplemental to its original position. As the issues of, for example, ethnic-specific health and educational disparities continue to exist, the claims of intellectual supremacy and universal applicability of Western thought will be difficult, if not impossible, to defend.

Worldview-oriented psychological thought offers a true depiction of humanity's cultural pluralism.

Leon D. Caldwell

See also African Americans (v3); Black English (v3); Black Psychology (v3); Black Racial Identity Development (v3); Nationalism (v3); Racial Identity (v3); Racial Pride (v3); Worldview (v3)

Further Readings

Kambon, K. K. K. (1992). *The African personality in America: An African centered framework.* Tallahassee, FL: Nubian Nation Publications.

Myers, L. J. (1988). *Understanding an Afrocentric worldview: Introduction to an optimal psychology.* Dubuque, IA: Kendall/Hunt.

Nobles, W. W. (1980). *African psychology: Towards it reclamation, reascension, and revitalization.* Oakland, CA: Black Family Institute.

Parham, T. A. (2002). *Counseling persons of African descent: Raising the bar of practitioner competence.* Thousand Oaks, CA: Sage.

Alaska Natives

Alaska Natives comprise three distinct ethnic groups: Eskimos, Aleuts, and Indians, each with their own distinct histories, cultures, customs, and traditions. American Indians/Alaska Natives constitute approximately 1% of the U.S. population. However, in Alaska, Native people comprise approximately 17% of the 625,000 people that make up the state's total population. Thus, Alaska has the 10th largest Native population and the largest Native population per capita in the United States. Alaska Native peoples live primarily in northern and western Alaska, accounting for more than 50% of the total population in those regions. Only 7% of Alaska Natives live in urban settings. The rest live in rural and bush areas, often in isolated tribal villages 40 to 60 miles apart.

Alaska Natives have a rich, proud, and varied history. Although protectors of Alaska's vast natural resources and contributors to the rich cultural heritage of the state, they also experience acculturation stresses brought on by initial and ongoing contact, first with French and Russian Europeans and then with European Americans. As a result, Alaska Natives confront social and psychological challenges that are similar to those confronted by Native Americans from other parts of the United States, including quickly changing social expectations, underemployment, high rates of incarceration, high rates of alcohol and drug abuse, and extremely high rates of suicide.

Alaska Native Cultural Groups

Eskimos

Eskimos (also known as Inuit) are the largest of the three Alaska Native ethnic groups. They comprise 52% of all Alaska Natives. Eskimo subdivisions include the Inupiat (Greenland to northern Alaska), the Yu'pik (western and southwestern Alaska), and the Siberian Yu'pik (St. Lawrence Islanders). Historically, Eskimos lived in extended and multifamily units in tents during the summer and in large underground sod houses during the winter. Although outside temperatures range from −80° F in winter to +40° F in summer, these sod houses were kept at a comfortable 70° F to 85° F by fires, sod roofs, and igloo overhouses.

Alaska Eskimos are related to, and share many of the same cultural beliefs and lifeways as, Eskimos living in Siberia, Greenland, and Canada. Historically, Eskimos practiced an animistic religion that prescribed times of social gathering, rituals, and feasts, as well as religious beliefs and practices concerning the care and respect for all living things (including people, animals, and the environment). Their religion, along with the cultural habits of summer hunting and storage, helped regulate the daily rhythm of arctic life, especially during the 3 months of total darkness and the 3 months of total light that occur in the arctic every year.

Before European contact, Eskimos practiced subsistence living by catching fish and hunting seals, walruses, whales, caribou, musk oxen, and polar bears. They used animal skins to make tents and clothes, which protected them from the extreme arctic weather. They constructed hand tools and weapons from antlers, horns, teeth, and animal bones. In summer, they hunted in boats covered with animal skin, and in winter, they traveled on sleds pulled by dog teams. When traveling in search of game, they built igloos as shelters from blocks of snow and ice.

Alaska Indians

Alaska Indians comprise 36% of the Alaska Native population. There are four major tribes of Alaska Indians: the Athabascans, the Tlingits, the Tsimshians, and the Haida. In pre-contact times, people from these four tribes inhabited the whole of Alaska, the western portions of Canada, and the northwestern portions of America. They lived in both coastal and interior regions of the Alaskan territories. They lived in highly structured societies centered on clan membership, with people in each of these clans related by genealogy, history, and possessory rights.

Alaska Indians lived in villages or in camps that followed wild game migrations. Village housing was built with local materials, such as birch bark. Migrant housing tended to be animal skin teepees or lean-to shelters. Dietary practices as a whole depended on hunting and gathering with some farming, but these practices varied somewhat among geographical regions and tribal groups. Alaska Indian religion centered primarily on respect and reverence for nature, belief in an afterlife, and, for some tribes, belief in reincarnation. After Alaska Indians' first contact with Europeans, many became Russian Orthodox or Protestant Christians. However, in recent years, some younger Alaska Indians have reconverted to their traditional tribal religions.

Aleuts

Aleuts comprise 12% of the Alaska Native population. They live on the Aleutian Islands, a chain of more than 300 small volcanic islands extending westward from the Alaskan Peninsula toward the Kamchatka Peninsula in Russia.

Alaska Eskimos and Aleuts were historically one people who migrated across the Bering Land Bridge between 8,000 and 15,000 B.C. Those who migrated south became Aleuts, and those who migrated north became Eskimos. The first reported settlement of Aleuts was in Nikolski Bay, which is suspected by some archaeologists to be the oldest continuously occupied community in the world.

Aleuts are seagoing people living on meats and processed pelts from the sea lions, otters, whales, and other animals that inhabit the north Pacific. In the relatively warmer climate of the Aleutians (with temperatures ranging from 11° F to 65° F year round), these hunting and fishing activities are carried on in all seasons. Before their initial contact with European and American cultures, there was an estimated 16,000 to 20,000 Aleuts living in the Aleutian Islands. There are approximately 12,000 Aleuts today. The dominant religion in many Aleutian communities is the Russian Orthodox faith.

Social and Psychological Challenges

Social Challenges

Before contact with European people (in the early 1700s), Alaska Natives lived free and independent lives. However, upon discovery of the rich resources of the northern Pacific and Alaskan interior by Europeans and non–Native Americans, Alaska Natives as a whole experienced both personal and economic exploitation. Early enslavements of Alaska Native peoples and population decimations from deadly European diseases (e.g., smallpox and tuberculosis) changed Alaska Natives' life ways and caused severe damage to social structures supporting psychologically healthy lives.

The traditional way of life has ended for most Alaska Natives. Most now live in wooden houses made from imported wooden planks rather than igloos, sod houses, or teepees. They wear modern clothing instead of animal skin garments. They speak English, Russian, or Danish in addition to their native languages. They now must compete in the modern economic world. The kayak and the umiak have given way to motor boats, and the snowmobile has replaced the dog team. Fishing villages are connected with a ferry system, and previously inaccessible mountain and river villages are connected by ski trails, boats, bush pilots, or snowmobiles. Telecommunication devices (e.g., televisions, telephones, and computers), needs for petroleum, and other lifestyle changes have necessitated a cash economy to supplement ancient subsistence practices. Yet, access to full participation in the modern U.S. economy has been slow among Alaska's Native people.

In 1968, the Senate Interior Committee issued a report that stated that more Alaska Natives were unemployed or seasonally employed than had permanent jobs. More than half of the Alaska Native workforce was jobless most of the year. Year-round jobs were typically few and were limited to such types of employment as school maintenance worker, postal worker, airline station agent, village store manager, or teacher's aide. Some income was gained through the sale of furs, fish, or arts and crafts. Some Natives found seasonal employment away from their villages, as firefighters, cannery workers, or construction laborers. Most provided for the bulk of their food supply by fishing, hunting, and trapping, and most relied upon a combination of means to obtain the cash needed for fuel, food staples, tools, and supplies. The wage gap was continuing to grow precipitously as immigration into Alaska by other ethnic and cultural groups continued to increase.

In 2004, a report issued by the Center for Educational Research stated that even with the increasing wage gap, Alaska Natives had gained thousands of new jobs and improved their incomes in every decade since 1960. Native women, in particular, had continued to move into the workforce. However, in the 1990s the gains were smaller, and thousands of Natives who wanted jobs could not find them. The modest income gains were not in wages but mostly in transfer payments, including the state Permanent Fund dividend.

Today Native incomes on average remain just over half those of other Alaskans, and Natives are still about a third less likely to have jobs. Native households are 3 times more likely to be poor; poverty is especially high among households headed by women. These economic problems are worse for Natives in remote rural villages. Subsistence hunting and fishing continue to be the only source of provision for many Native families, even as external pressures to maintain a contemporary economic lifestyle are increasing.

The social stress that many Alaska Natives face is even more evident as one examines the breakdown of Alaskan Native families and communities. Alaskan Native adults, who represent about one third of the state's inmate population, commit crimes that are considered to be among the most violent in nature: assault, sexual assault, sexual abuse of a minor, and murder. Alaska Natives are overrepresented in cases of child abuse by twice what would be expected given the population statistics. Among Alaska Native adolescent males, nearly one in every eight between the ages of 14 and 17 has been, or is currently, in juvenile detention.

Alaska Natives continue to be in a period of cultural, economic, and social transition. Their acculturation has not always been voluntary, and they have not had control over the extent or pace of change. As a result, many experience tremendous stress, which permeates all aspects of their lives. Whereas some Alaska Natives have successfully adjusted to a new way of life, the consequences of this constant and massive stress have put many others at risk for leading lives that are characterized by poverty, violence, and cycles of personal and social destruction. The psychological consequences of living in such circumstances can lead otherwise psychologically healthy people to overuse maladaptive coping strategies. Among Alaska Natives, the coping strategies most often used have been alcohol abuse, drug abuse, and suicide.

Alcohol and Drug Abuse/Dependence

The primary mental health challenge among Alaska Natives is alcohol and drug abuse/dependence. Alcohol was introduced to Alaska Natives only 300 years ago. Since then, alcohol and drug abuse has been a constant source of sorrow and destruction for Alaska Natives. Although exact rates of alcohol and drug abuse/dependence are not available, among Alaska Natives the alcohol-related mortality rate is 3½ times greater than the rate among non-Natives. The rate of fetal alcohol syndrome for Alaska Natives is 3 times that of the rest of the population of Alaska. The impact of alcohol and drug use has been particularly dramatic among Alaska Native youth. In 1998, of all court referrals of Native youth in the state, 55% were for the offense of possession and/or consumption of alcohol. Among Alaska Natives, alcohol contributes to high rates of motor vehicle crashes, cirrhosis, suicide, homicide, domestic abuse, and fetal alcohol syndrome.

The pattern of abuse among most Alaska Natives is drinking to pass out rather than engaging in social drinking. Moreover, alcohol abuse is chronic, and many Alaska Natives become dependent on alcohol at the same time they become users. Drug abuse, which is a newer phenomenon among Alaska Natives, has nevertheless become a serious threat to their communities. For example, in some isolated Alaskan Native villages, there is a 48% lifetime risk of inhalant abuse.

Theories about the magnitude of alcohol abuse among Alaska Natives include genetic predisposition, enculturation pressures, social prohibition, and integration theories. Genetic predisposition theories cite the lack of acetyl dehydrogenase (which breaks down the toxic substances created by alcohol metabolism in the liver) as a causal factor. This genetic variation, which is shared with some Asian races (e.g., Chinese and Japanese), causes distinctive facial reddening, accelerated heartbeat, and increased blood pressure upon the consumption of alcohol. However, this theory cannot fully account for Alaska Native alcoholism, in that Chinese and Japanese Americans have the lowest rates of alcoholism of all American ethnic groups, whereas Alaska Natives and American Indians have the highest.

Enculturation theories examine the poor fit between Native indigenous values and those of the broader American culture. These theories examine the diathesis-stress dimensions of alcohol abuse, citing desperate social and economic conditions as precursors to alcoholism. Through the self-destructive behaviors that result from internalized oppression, Alaska Natives express massive grief over the loss of their cultures and the traditional ways of life. Boredom, stoicism, intense pride, and the lack of cultural models for seeking help reinforce this proclivity to alcoholism among Alaska Natives.

Prohibition theories suggest that Alaska Natives learned binge-drinking behavior from the trappers, miners, and traders with whom they had initial contact. Alaska Natives, according to these theories, invest alcohol with tremendous power and readily accept that they cannot control its effects. In contrast, Chinese and Japanese Americans (who have the lowest rates of alcoholism in the United States) believe that alcoholism is a weakness and that people can and should control their drinking.

Finally, integration theorists combine genetic, enculturation, and social prohibition theories. They assert that alcohol abuse is fundamentally a symptom of a much more complex set of problems within the Native community, that these problems have yet to be identified, and that alcoholism, although a symptom, is also a unique contributor, in that it breeds an abundance of negative personal and community outcomes. Integration theorists remind us that regardless of the physiological, social, or psychological origins of alcoholism, the disease of alcoholism (and drug abuse as well) must be successfully treated if there is to be a livable future for Alaska's Native people.

Suicide, Depression, and Other Mental Health Issues

The Alaska Native suicide rate, which did not significantly differ from nationwide averages throughout the 1950s, began to take a dramatic turn upward in the 1960s. In the quarter-century between 1964 and 1989, the rate of Alaska Native suicides increased 500%. Today, although Alaska Natives make up just under 20% of the Alaskan population, they represent 41% of all suicides. Although rates have decreased slightly in the past 15 years, the problem continues to be widespread. In all populations, suicide rates are generally higher for adolescents. Among Alaska Natives, the number of adolescent suicide victims is even more pronounced.

Alcohol abuse is a factor in a large majority of Alaska Native suicides. Seventy-nine percent of all

Alaska Native suicide victims have detectable levels of blood alcohol. Although there is very little research on the correlates of suicide among Alaska Natives, some theorists believe that suicide in this population is associated with rapid and unpredictable social change, childhood and interpersonal losses, a limited ability to grieve, poor affective relatedness, and very high rates of depressive disorders.

Although there is less empirical research on the prevalence and treatment of other mental health issues among Alaska Natives per se, there are studies of American Indian children and adults that include samples of Alaska Natives. These studies report increasing rates of depression, low self-esteem, and anxiety, citing that Native people do not fit well into the American way of life. Learning disabilities are the second most frequent major diagnosis among American Indians and Alaska Natives. Furthermore, American Indians and Alaska Natives are slightly overrepresented among HIV/AIDS patients, suggesting greater sexual risk behaviors than are found in the U.S. population at large.

The U.S. Department of Health and Human Services Substance Abuse and Mental Health Services Administration (SAMHSA) reports that Native Americans/Alaska Natives are more likely to experience mental disorders than are other racial and ethnic groups in the United States. Of great concern is the high prevalence of depression, anxiety, substance abuse, violence, and suicide. Other common mental health problems include psychosomatic symptoms and emotional problems resulting from disturbed interpersonal and family relationships. According to SAMHSA, failure to address the "historic trauma" and culture of American Indians/Alaska Natives in health care only adds to the oppression they experience. Nevertheless, disentangling socioeconomic factors, cultural influences, civil rights issues, and the effects of race/ethnicity is difficult when seeking to understand any health condition, and even more so when seeking to understand mental health disorders.

Service Provision and Treatment Issues

Alaska Natives represent almost 30% of the public mental health clients in Alaska at an overrepresentation of almost 2 to 1 based on the general population. Nevertheless, public health officials believe that Alaska Natives are woefully underrepresented in relation to the magnitude of the mental health challenges they face. The burden of mental illness looms over Alaska Native people, extracting vitality and interrupting their futures. Worse, the stigma attached to mental illness often deters people from seeking help, thus prolonging illnesses that could be treated or even prevented.

Stigma is not the only challenge to providing mental health services to Alaska Native people. Other challenges include cultural, philosophical, and communication style differences between mental health providers and their Alaska Native clients. Moreover, some Alaska Natives believe that mental health providers use their counseling/psychology positions to extend social dominance and control over Native people's lives.

More Effective Treatments

Experts in multicultural psychology agree that effective treatments for ethnic minority clients should be based on those clients' worldview and cultural precepts. Among Alaska Natives, these cultural precepts include respect for traditional knowledge, connections with the land and all living things, use of inductive analysis (inference of a generalized conclusion from particular instances), emphasis on discovering how, and verification of individual facts derived primarily from oral forms of communication. In contrast, European American mental health providers tend to value scientifically derived knowledge, mastery and control of one's physical and social environments, deductive analysis (the conclusion about particulars follows necessarily from general premises), emphasis on discovering why, and verification of general principles derived primarily from written forms of communication. The primary challenge for European American mental health providers then is to find ways to understand and enter into the world of Alaska Natives to provide the most effective psychological treatments possible.

Within the context of providing culturally sensitive and effective treatments for Alaska Natives, several innovative programs are being introduced. Among the most promising are intertribal, business, and public service consortia, as well as tribally centered programs, that identify and treat alcohol and drug dependency as primary dysfunctions and co-occurring disorders as secondary dysfunctions. These programs typically are designed to (a) treat alcohol and substance abuse in ways that control the availability of alcohol, (b) provide educational and treatment efforts, and (c) reduce the social and environmental factors that increase the risk of harm to both the individual and the community. The treatment programs include using culturally familiar symbols, pictures, signs, and stories, addressing the impact of intergenerational trauma and chemical abuse on both families and communities, using Native languages and art forms, and employing traditional interpersonal techniques, such as talking circles and ceremonial protocols. In these programs, tribal elders often are employed both as consultants and as service providers.

A sample program, which has used this psychological treatment/community action model, has shown great success. In this program, which is operating in the Aleutian Pribilof Islands, responsibility for the mental health care of island inhabitants has been undertaken through a consortium of municipal and tribal governments and corporate management. Alcoholism and drug use decreased when island employers began to enforce sobriety policies and conduct random drug testing. Employees with substance addictions were sent off the islands for treatment, and they participated in a mentorship program when they returned. As a result, violence, felonies, suicides, and murders decreased, and psychological adjustment continued to increase as a new pride in island inhabitants' cultural heritage and self-sufficiency emerged. Social and community support was established for people who suffered with mental health issues. Moreover, there were abundant opportunities for all workers to obtain sustained year-round employment. The affluence in the communities hosting this treatment program currently matches that of many other American cities.

Finally, there has been success in helping American Indians/Alaska Natives establish more productive and fulfilling lives by providing Native-based career counseling. In programs established by the Division of Indian and Native American Programs of the Workforce Investment Act, Alaska Natives are helped to achieve economic self-sufficiency through job training, job counseling, career counseling, academic counseling, and financial aid and educational assistance. These programs provide ongoing case management in a manner that is culturally appropriate and holistic in nature. Through individual development plans, counselors and clients work together to set goals, identify needs, and find referrals to other programs and outside community agencies. Nearly 90% of the individuals served in 2000 under this program were highly satisfied with the services they received.

Future Directions for Mental Health Treatments

Although there have been some successes in providing more effective mental health treatments to Alaska Natives, through the combination of culturally relevant treatments offered within a broader social support structure, there is still a tremendous need to look at short-, medium-, and long-term solutions to alcohol and drug abuse, depression, suicide, and other mental health issues among Alaska Native peoples. There is little empirical research that investigates the correlates of treatment effectiveness, although there is some evidence that consortium and community efforts are effective. Nevertheless, Alaska Native mental health, including the mental health of future generations, will depend on both preventive and remedial efforts that (a) provide empirically validated psychological treatments; (b) address the underlying economic, sociocultural, and other factors that cause Alaska Natives to seek refuge in alcohol and other chemicals; (c) create real economic opportunities; and (d) empower Alaska Natives to participate in crafting their own solutions to potentially devastating mental health challenges.

Sherri Turner

See also Acculturative Stress (v3); Career Counseling, Native Americans (v4); Community-Based Health Promotion (v1); Depression (v2); Discrimination and Oppression (v2); Diversity Issues in Career Development (v4); Evidence-Based Treatments (v2); Multicultural Counseling (v3); Secondary Trauma (v2); Substance Abuse and Dependence (v2); Suicide Potential (v2)

Further Readings

Grandbois, D. (2005). Stigma of mental illness among American Indian and Alaska Native nations: Historical and contemporary perspectives. *Issues in Mental Health Nursing, 26*(10), 1001–1024.

Gregory, R. J. (1994). Grief and loss among Eskimos attempting suicide in western Alaska. *American Journal of Psychiatry, 151*(12), 1815–1816.

Harris, K. M., Edlund, M. J., & Larson, S. (2005). Racial and ethnic differences in the mental health problems and use of mental health care. *Medical Care, 43*(8), 775–784.

Hesselbrock, V. M., Hesselbrock, M. N., & Segal, B. (2003). Alcohol dependence among Alaska Natives and their health care utilization. *Alcoholism: Clinical and Experimental Research, 27*(8), 1353–1355.

Lee, N. (1995). Culture conflict and crime in Alaska Native villages. *Journal of Criminal Justice, 23*(2), 177–189.

Segal, B. (1997). The inhalant dilemma: A theoretical perspective. *Drugs & Society, 10*(1–2), 79–102.

ALLOCENTRISM

Allocentrism is a personality trait that characterizes the attitudinal, cognitive, affective, and behavioral patterns and preferences shared among people of a collectivist culture. Among those who are allocentric, self is defined as more interdependent than independent; ingroup goals and harmony take priority over individual goals and autonomy. People who hold allocentric beliefs tend to value social norms, self-sacrifice, cooperation, equality, and relatedness more than social recognition, self-reliance, competition, equity, and rationality. Allocentrism is usually conceptualized as an end point of a continuum, with idiocentrism as the opposite construct. The individual levels of the allocentric and idiocentric tendencies correspond to the cultural dimensions of collectivism and individualism.

Current Research

The theorization of allocentrism has sparked 2 decades of research on the relationship between allocentrism and other individual and contextual variables. Multimethod measures have been developed to assess various dimensions of allocentric tendencies, such as the INDCOL scale, individualism–collectivism scales, the Self-Construal Scale, value surveys, sentence completion exercises, and scenario stimuli.

Research has demonstrated that there are more allocentrics than idiocentrics in collectivist cultures and vice versa. Women tend to be more allocentric than men across cultures. In the United States, racial and ethnic minorities appear to be more allocentric than White Americans. Among allocentrics, high self-esteem is related to self-efficacy in forming positive interpersonal relations. Allocentric persons reported having more and better social support than did idiocentrics. Moreover, they tend to transmit values such as obedience and obligations to their children. Allocentrics, compared to idiocentrics, also are more likely to perceive their group as homogeneous (regardless of how "homogeneous" the group actually is), which in turn may affect their behavioral patterns in a group setting (e.g., workplace performance).

Allocentrism is a complex construct that is multidimensional in nature and context dependent. Allocentric tendencies can be *vertical* (i.e., defining themselves as different from others and yet subordinate to the ingroup, thus likely to sacrifice for the interests of the group) or *horizontal* (i.e., perceiving themselves to be the same as others within the group, thereby unlikely to self-sacrifice for ingroup goals). Also, individual allocentric tendencies may differ depending on the tasks, groups, and settings. For example, a person may be a vertical allocentric at home and yet a horizontal allocentric at work. Furthermore, the strength of the relationship between allocentric tendencies and other psychosocial correlates (e.g., subjective well-being) may vary depending on the level of collectivism or individualism within a given cultural context.

Future Directions

Due to the contexualized multidimensional nature of the allocentric construct, individual allocentric tendencies may shift or intersect with a plethora of other factors, such as age, ethnic values, acculturation levels, socioeconomic status, religious/spiritual affiliation, sex roles, and situated contexts. Thus, conceptualizing and measuring allocentric and idiocentric tendencies as the end points of a single, bipolar continuum is a common practice, yet may be overly simplistic. Contemporary researchers have advocated the employment of multimethod and domain-specific approaches to assess the varying dimensions of allocentrism. At the same time, the use of myriad measurements for allocentrism also makes it difficult to interpret results. More longitudinal and qualitative research may provide better information about the complexity of this construct. Finally, the construct of allocentrism has significant implications for cross-cultural counseling. In working with clients, particularly those who identify with or whose values are influenced by a collectivist culture, counselors and psychologists should pay special attention to the potential impact of allocentric tendencies on psychosocial adjustment levels, work–family issues, and intergenerational or intergroup relations. Specifically, counselors should be aware that relationships with members of the ingroups play an essential role in the self-esteem and well-being of clients who subscribe to an allocentric perspective; counselors and mental health professionals may overpathologize allocentrics as "dependent," without considering the cultural relevance and primacy of group-orientation versus self-orientation. Allocentrics may experience difficulties when pressured to compete and assert themselves in an individualist culture that values individual recognition over ingroup harmony. Also, because allocentric tendencies are multidimensional and context dependent, allocentric individuals may exhibit different behavioral patterns and value preferences when dealing with multiple ingroups in various settings (e.g., sacrifice family for work or vice versa). Younger generations who were reared by allocentric parents but grew up in an individualist society may face value conflicts and acculturation stress. Counselors should examine the cultural appropriateness of applying counseling theories and approaches that were developed in individualist contexts to working with allocentric clients. This will help counselors understand sources of conflicts and examine self-identity, as well as identify ways for clients to cope with acculturation stress.

Yu-Wei Wang and Frances C. Shen

See also Collectivism (v3); Cultural Values (v3); Identity (v3); Idiocentrism (v3); Individualism (v3)

Further Readings

Hui, C. H. (1988). Measurement of individualism-collectivism. *Journal of Research in Personality, 22*(1), 17–36.

Triandis, H. C. (1995). *Individualism and collectivism.* Boulder, CO: Westview Press.

Triandis, H. C. (2000). Allocentrism-idiocentrism. In A. E. Kazdin (Ed.), *Encyclopedia of psychology* (Vol. 1, pp. 118–119). New York: Oxford University Press.

Triandis, H. C., Leung, K., Villareal, M. J., & Clark, F. L. (1985). Allocentric versus idiocentric tendencies: Convergent and discriminant validity. *Journal of Research in Personality, 19,* 395–415.

AMERICAN INDIANS

American Indians (herein referred to as Indians, Native Americans, or Natives) have a rich and heart-rendering history and continue to contribute to the fabric of American society. The history of Native people is important for mental health professionals and researchers to understand in order to grasp the present implications of history and how they may affect psychological, familial, and social interactions. The following overview of Indian country, past and present, is divided into several sections. A brief history of Native–White relations serves as an introduction to Native peoples. This section is followed by a presentation of demographics and an introduction to the complex definitions that surround being Native. Several myths that are commonly held by non-Indian "others" regarding Native Americans are presented and clarified. This is followed by an overview of health and mental health issues affecting Natives today. The final section presents traditional Native and contemporary approaches to healing, examining the physical, spiritual, and psychological community and group approaches to mental health.

History

The history of Native peoples can be divided into two major periods: pre-contact and contact. The contact period is generally divided into several subsets, including the periods of Manifest Destiny (1492–1890), Assimilation (1890–1970), and Self-Determination (1970 to the present). Pre-contact was a period of autonomy for tribes that inhabited the Americas. Tribes adapted to the environment they lived in. Varieties of lifestyles included those of hunting and gathering, agrarian lifestyles, and a combination of both, which were determined by the environment and terrain where tribes lived. Complex social and political systems were developed by each tribe. Each group had its own set of attitudes, beliefs, social organizations, men's and women's societies, and views of creation, self, and nature. Wicki-ups, teepees (hide and bark), sod housing, and cave dwellings served as homes across the continent. Political practices included input from both men and women in clans or bands and honor societies; this latter respect for women ran contrary to European patriarchy and contributed to the cultural dissonances between colonialists and Natives.

Manifest Destiny, Assimilation, and Self-Determination

With the arrival of Christopher Columbus, a lost sailor who worked for the Spanish, in 1492, Natives were removed from ancestral homes, starved to death, and massacred as a means to secure land and resources. This westward movement was justified under the auspices of Manifest Destiny. This movement was a form of what has come to be known as *ethnic cleansing*. Native Americans suffered new sicknesses and diseases brought by colonists, illnesses that claimed more lives than combat claimed.

The assimilation era was between 1890 and 1970 and was characterized by efforts to socialize Natives through missionary activities and the practices of boarding schools. Both of these acts of forced assimilation served destructive cultural, social, and psychological influences on Native groups. With the advent of the boarding schools, children often witnessed the loss of tribal life ways. These practices represented the shift from physical genocide to cultural genocide. Common practices of corporal punishment and sexual abuse impeded healthy psychological development and, in many cases, impeded the ability to develop appropriate relationships with others.

This collective past of broken promises, discrimination, and oppressive practices has had resounding effects that have shaped the psychological well-being of many Native peoples today. These effects have been described as historical trauma, the reliving of events, oppressive and violent in nature, retold and experienced in the present through stories shared among families and in social settings. These historical traumas are intertwined with current traumas, the impacts of alcohol and other drug abuse, child abuse and maltreatment, unemployment, poor health care, and death, all of which have profound psychological and social effects.

Demographics

American Indians comprise many different groups, including over 569 federally and state recognized tribes, each with their own commitment to cultural and spiritual beliefs and practices. There are many tribal groups that are not federally or state recognized by treaties. There are tribes without signed treaties, and, through what is known as the termination period during the 1950s and 1960s, there are tribes who ceased their treaty relationships with the U.S. government. Processing treaties for federal recognition is a complex and lengthy task, as exemplified by the Little Shell Band of Montana, whose struggle has lasted more than 38 years. In deciding to terminate their quest for federal recognition, tribal groups compromise their ability to have a land base and become ineligible for health care or psychological services.

Differences within Native people are evidenced through tribal diversity and rates of intermarriage. According to recent census estimates, there are 4.5 million self-identified American Indians and Alaskan Natives, excluding Hawaiians. Specific tribal populations vary widely in their enrollment. For example, the Diné people (Navajo Tribe) maintain a membership exceeding 298,000 strong. In contrast, the Confederated Salish and Kootenai Tribes of Montana currently have a membership of 7,000, due to blood quantum enrollment criteria (i.e., the degree to which an individual can claim his or her heritage as Native). Many tribes anticipate similar declines in enrollment as a function of blood quantum criteria.

American Indians vary by level of acculturation, often paralleling the acculturation level and degree of collective forced assimilation of their tribes. Individual variations in acculturation level may be related to Native cultural identity development attitudes; length of time away from reservations, including nonparticipation in familial and cultural activities; degree of commitment to learning the culture of one's tribe(s); and generation level.

Within-group differences can be found across age, language, and social class. American Indians appear to constitute a young cultural group, as a recent estimate indicated that the median age of the population was 29, compared to 36 years for the White population. Furthermore, approximately 1.3 million Native Americans were reported to be under 18, and 336,000 were 65 years or older. However, Native elder population is growing at dramatic rates; specifically, between 1989 and 1999 the Native population aged 65 and older grew by 33%, while the non-Native population of adults over 65 increased by 9%. Additionally, there is linguistic diversity among Native people, such that 28% of all Indians/Natives 5 years of age and older speak a language other than English in their home; of that number, 18% speak English proficiently. Lastly, although there is variability in socioeconomic status among Native people, 26% were reported to live at or below the poverty level, according to recent census reports based on a 3-year average.

Many myths abound regarding Native Americans. The following section provides an overview of several of the most commonly held notions about American Indians/Alaskan Natives.

Myths

Myth 1: All Natives get a U.S. government check monthly. Natives are eligible for monies such as general assistance, housing support, and other services available to the general population, but do not receive monthly checks from the government. Some tribes do pay tribal members a "per capita" payment. These are proceeds earned by the tribe and paid out to tribal members in a fashion similar to that of dividends paid to shareholders in a corporation. Treaty-bound services not available to the general public include health and education services.

Myth 2: Natives do not pay income taxes. Native Americans pay taxes like any other group. There are some exceptions, which may include monies earned within reservation boundaries in some states.

Myth 3: All Indians look like the Plains Indian, with a dark complexion, high cheek bones, and brown eyes. Many Natives have intermarried, changing the gene pool and diversifying phenotypes among Native people. Nearly 70% of Indians/Natives are in mixed marriages, whether with Indians/Natives of other tribes and bands or with other racial and ethnic groups. Furthermore, during the Civil War, many slaves that escaped were adopted into tribes and, as a result, there are many Black Indians.

Myth 4: Natives possess knowledge of all Native American experiences across tribes. There is an expectation or myth held by the non-Native "other" for Native individuals to possess knowledge of other Native groups, contemporary, historical, or both. Combined with this false expectation is that an individual Native can speak for other groups. This can present itself as a stressor.

Myth 5: Tribes should share the wealth. This myth is grounded in the assumption that all Indian groups are one. The diversity within Native tribes can be seen in the extent to which there are alliances among groups. Tribes can be compared to corporations, in that, for example, the Ford Motor Company would not assist Chevrolet in times of financial crisis. This myth also serves as an example of how stereotypes are negotiated, building one stereotype upon another, only to develop a set of erroneous assumptions that may drive perception and behavior.

Myth 6: Native families often neglect their children. Native families had been broken historically through forced assimilation strategies. In addition, child care differences and conflicting worldviews contributed to the removal of Native children from their homes and tribes. It wasn't until the 1970s that this myth was challenged in the courts, with pleas to legislatures to change the adoption process of Indian children. This change was brought about by the lobbying of many tribes and the action of concerned individuals in the federal legislative arenas. The Indian Child Welfare Act (ICWA) became law in 1978 and subsequently was implemented in 1979. ICWA established a new set of strict requirements for child welfare cases and placed authority for Native children with tribes. This ushered in a new era for Indian/Native child welfare. This act changed adoption practices in the United States, giving preference to family and tribal members for the provision of a culturally appropriate living environment.

Health and Psychosocial Concerns

Health

The health status of Natives lags behind all other ethnic groups in the United States. The top 10 leading causes of death, in no specified order, are tuberculosis, chronic liver disease and cirrhosis, accidents, diabetes, stroke, chronic lower respiratory diseases (e.g., pneumonia), suicide, homicide, cancer, and heart disease. In addition, rates of obesity, substance abuse, sudden infant death syndrome, and mental health concerns (e.g., depression and posttraumatic stress disorder) are disproportionately higher among Native Americans. Socioeconomic conditions, including unemployment, lack of economic opportunities, and lack of availability of and access to appropriate health care, influence health status and contribute to high mortality rates. These conditions, combined with geographic isolation, limited access to medical care, high costs, and other barriers, create invisible boundaries that stand between Native peoples and appropriate health care.

Through examining rates of diagnoses, prevalence, and mortality, barriers to adequate health care and far-reaching health disparities are evidenced. For example, the Centers for Disease Control and Prevention reported that Natives are 3 times more likely than Whites to be diagnosed with diabetes, Native American adults are at greater risk than their White counterparts of developing cardiac concerns, and

Natives are less likely than Whites to be informed of having hypertension. In addition, Native Americans are reported to be twice as likely to be diagnosed with stomach or liver cancers as White men, and Native women are reported to be 20% more likely than White women to die of cervical cancer.

Although health outcomes are slowly improving for this population, Native Americans experience relatively compromised health, with one of the primary factors being substance abuse. Alcohol-related deaths are 4 to 5 times the national average among Native people, and at least one third of all visits to Indian Health Services are alcohol related. This also influences the number of deaths by accident for this group, both vehicular and nonvehicular accidents.

Crime in Indian Country

Data from the Bureau of Justice Statistics, highlighted in *A BJS Statistical Profile, 1992–2002: American Indians and Crime,* reveals a wealth of information and statistics about crime in Indian country. For example, American Indians were reported to be more likely to be arrested for aggravated assault than arrested for robbery. Native children under 17 years of age were less likely to be arrested for a violent crime than youth of all races, with the exception of murder. Native adults were twice as likely as their non-Native peers to be arrested for driving under the influence or alcohol violations, and Native youth (i.e., under 17 years) were nearly twice as likely to be arrested than non-Natives for alcohol-related offenses.

Gangs have emerged onto the reservation areas. About 23% of respondents to the *2000 National Gang Survey* indicated that they had gang problems on their reservation or Native community. Alcohol and/or drug use was a factor in 51% of the violent crimes against all races. Among victims of violence that were able to describe use by offenders, American Indians were more likely than any other racial group to report an offender under the influence of alcohol or drugs.

The combination of stress, depression, substance abuse, and psychological frustration contributes to the increases of violent and abusive behaviors throughout Indian/Native communities. The rate of violent victimization among American Indian women was more than double that among all other women. Indians/Natives were twice as likely to experience a rape/sexual assault. Violence and resultant trauma can have vast effects on the survivor or bystander. Among the manifestations include child physical and sexual abuse, child neglect, domestic violence, assault, homicide, and suicide. Suicide is 3 to 6 times greater in Indian country.

Indian Child Welfare

Before the institutionalization of the Indian Child Welfare Act (ICWA), displaced Native children had been assigned to care outside of their homes at rates between 5 and 30 times higher than their non-Native peers. Tribes responded to these alarming conditions by demanding more control over the rights to rear their own children and began to advocate for federal policy to support their position on child care. The passage of the ICWA indicated a federal initiative to address one form of institutional discrimination against Native Americans.

There are eight provisions to ICWA, two of which are noted. First, tribes were given exclusive jurisdiction over children who live on the reservations, except in cases in which federal law already has designated jurisdiction to the state. Second, agencies that place children must provide culturally appropriate services to Native families before placement occurs. The provision of ICWA becomes more complicated when the out-of-home care takes place in urban settings, where access to culturally appropriate services may be limited. Presently, American Indian children are placed in care outside of the home 4 times more often than are non-Indian children.

Considerations of Healthcare Services

Health disparities among Native Americans have been related to cultural mistrust, geographic isolation, and socioeconomic factors. For example, through the 1970s, the practice of sterilization without consent was not uncommon. Such behaviors, enacted primarily by Indian Health Service (IHS) personnel and other governmental agencies, have engendered distrust for some healthcare providers among Native Americans. In addition, urban Indians are geographically dispersed in comparison to other populations, which may compromise their access to tribe-specific health-related information and services.

There are unique considerations relevant to receiving health care services and programming on and off the reservation. On-reservation programming is provided by the IHS generally, under the Behavioral Health Program, or contracted by the tribe with IHS or other providers. Health care available off the reservations is funded at only about 2% of the IHS budget in urban areas. This leaves the majority of Indians without access to adequate health care.

Urban health and mental health services are not as clear-cut. Only about 2% of all IHS funding goes to urban Indian programs, where up to 60% of all Natives live. According to the Surgeon General's report in 1999, only 20% of Natives reported access to IHS clinics, most of these found on reservations. Medicaid is the primary insurer for about 25% of this population, and only 50% of Natives have employer-based insurance coverage, compared with 72% of Whites. Twenty-four percent of all Natives do not have health insurance, compared with 16% of Whites. When scarce resources are needed for survival, mental health becomes a luxury item.

Mental Health

Mental health needs among Native populations vary, yet there appears to be some commonalities across tribes. Similar rates of lifetime diagnosis in Native populations have been reported concerning alcohol dependence, posttraumatic stress disorder (PTSD), and major depressive episodes. For example, the Surgeon General's Report of 2000 stated that depression ranged from 10% to 30% among Native populations.

Effects of Trauma

Considerations of the profound effects of direct, vicarious, and historical trauma on Native peoples have implications for substance use, violent behaviors, and depression. The many precipitating factors of PTSD include service in combat zones; exposure to violent accidents, homicides, and suicides; sexual victimization; and poverty and homelessness. The higher rate of traumatic exposure results in a 22% rate of PTSD for Native peoples, compared with 8% in the general population. Moreover, the Vietnam Veterans Project found lifetime prevalence of PTSD to be from 45% to 57% among Native veterans, rates significantly higher than among other Vietnam veterans. Prevalence rates for current alcohol and drug abuse or dependence among Northern Plains and Southwestern Vietnam veterans have been estimated to be as high as 70% compared with 11% to 32% of their White, Black, and Japanese American counterparts.

The rate of violent victimization of Natives is more than twice the national average. Given the exposure of this population to potential stressors beyond the "norm," mental health professionals must be versed in PTSD and potential referral sources that may include traditional healing ceremonies or activities.

Values and Mental Health

Cultural values among Native people are, among themselves, very diverse. However, when considered as a collective, Native cultural values tend to contrast significantly with individualistic and dualistic orientations of Western psychology. In Indian country, traditional groups view life as a function of the interconnectedness of all things, and behavior is considered to be motivated through the interconnections with others. In these philosophies, balance among the reciprocal effects of actions and changes in the entire system leads to wellness. Furthermore, the interplay of these worldly and otherworldly (i.e., spirited) systems creates a whole. Attention to both of these systems often is desirable to effect long-lasting and effective change for clients, such that therapeutic goals include balance among individual, spiritual, and community systems.

Interventions

Effective interventions are dependent upon many factors. Counselors' attention to clients' levels of acculturation facilitates effective care. It is also critical for mental health professionals to have an understanding of the Native family and extended family systems and clients' roles in these systems. In urban and reservation settings, the therapist needs to be known and trusted in the community. This can be facilitated by attending open social gatherings and attending local school functions.

There are traditional interventions that have been found to work across settings. These include the talking circle, sweat lodge ceremonies, smudging ceremonies, and others. It is recommended that the non-Native therapist seek Native spiritual leaders with whom to develop relationships so that they may later refer clients for spiritual assistance. Non-Native therapists can work with clients on therapeutic goals while learning about clients' cultural experiences through the therapeutic process.

John J. Peregoy

See also Acculturative Stress (v3); Alaska Natives (v3); Bureau of Indian Affairs (v3); Career Counseling, Native Americans (v4); Community-Based Health Promotion (v1); Depression (v2); Diversity Issues in Career

Development (v4); Evidence-Based Treatments (v2); Indian Health Service (v3); Society of Indian Psychologists (v3); Substance Abuse and Dependence (v2); Suicide Potential (v2)

Further Readings

Beals, J., Novins, D. K., Whitesell, N. R., Spicer, P., & Manson, S. M. (2005). Prevalence of mental disorders and utilization of mental health services in two American Indian reservation populations: Mental health disparities in a national context. *American Journal of Psychiatry, 162,* 1723–1732.

Centers for Disease Control and Protection, Office of Minority Health & Health Disparities. (2005). *American Indian and Alaskan Native (AI/AN) populations.* Retrieved April 5, 2007, from http://www.cdc.gov//omhd/Populations/AIAN/AIAN.htm

Evans-Campbell, T. (2006). Indian child welfare practice within urban American Indian/Alaskan Native American communities. In T. M. Witko (Ed.), *Mental health care for urban Indians: Clinical insights from Native practitioners* (pp. 33–54). Washington, DC: American Psychological Association.

Peregoy, J. J. (1999). Revisiting transcultural counseling with American Indians and Alaskan Natives: Issues for consideration. In J. McFadden (Ed.), *Transcultural counseling* (2nd ed., pp. 137–170). Alexandria, VA: American Counseling Association.

Peregoy, J. J. (2001). Counseling with American Indian/Alaskan Native clients: Perspectives for practitioners to start with. In E. Welfel & R. E. Ingersoll (Eds.), *The mental health desk reference* (pp. 306–314). New York: Wiley.

Perry, S. W. (2004, February). *A Bureau of Justice statistical profile, 1992–2002: American Indians and crime.* Washington, DC: U.S. Government Printing Office.

U.S. Census Bureau. (2006). *We the people: American Indians and Alaskan Natives.* Washington, DC: U.S. Government Printing Office.

U.S. Department of Health and Human Services. (2001). *Mental health: Culture, race, and ethnicity, supplement to mental health: A report to the Surgeon General.* Rockville, MD: U.S. Government Printing Office.

Witko, T. M. (Ed.). (2006). *Mental health care for urban Indians: Clinical insights from Native practitioners.* Washington, DC: American Psychological Association.

AMERICAN JEWS

American Jews are a diverse group of people, with varying cultural and ethnic self-identification, degrees of religious adherence, and observances of Jewish holidays and customs. Despite the myriad ways in which one can be a Jew, however, there remains a common history, ethnocultural heritage, and, for many, a religious practice that unites this unique group. This entry introduces contemporary issues salient to understanding American Jews, including (a) the diversity of Jewish heritage and denominations, (b) Jewish identity, (c) psychological stressors for Jews, and (d) counseling issues with American Jewish clients.

Recent estimates of the number of American Jews range between 5 and 6 million, representing a substantial proportion of the estimated 12 to 17 million Jews worldwide. However, given the U.S. population has been estimated at nearly 300 million, Jews are clearly a numerical minority. Because more than one third of American Jews live in large urban centers concentrated in the Northeast and the East Coast (e.g., New York), as well as in California and Chicago, there may be a misperception concerning the actual number of American Jews. This might be especially noticeable in the three U.S. cities with the largest Jewish populations: New York, Miami, and Los Angeles.

Definitional Terms

Bicultural

The experience of American Jews might be best described as bicultural. That is, given that one's cultural self-identification is context specific, American Jews are likely to see themselves as both Jewish and American; this dual identification provides them with two different lenses from which to view the world. In addition, there are many ways to be Jewish. All at once, Judaism is a culture, a religion, an ethnicity, and a set of traditions that is embedded in Jewish people's expectations, belief systems, and family dynamics. As a result, Jews do not fit easily, if accurately at all, into the current demographic taxonomies; this may have contributed to the previous lack of attention to Jewish issues in counseling.

American Jews Versus Jewish Americans

The semantic categorization of racial and ethnic groups is often a matter of critical relevance for group members. *American Jew* has emerged within both the Jewish community and social science literature as the preferable term for individuals who identify as both Jews and citizens of the United States in that the term emphasizes the primacy of being Jewish through use of *American* as a descriptor of *Jew*. Furthermore, the term serves to acknowledge the nomadic heritage of Jews as a Diaspora people and the needs of Jews from many nations to flee those countries when oppression and antisemitism reached dangerous levels. Despite this trend, within-group differences certainly exist, and individuals whose nationality takes precedence over their Jewish heritage may be most comfortable with the use of the term *Jewish American*.

Diversity of Jewish Heritage

There is tremendous within-group variability among American Jews. For example, there are three main lineages for American Jews (i.e., Ashkenazim, Sephardim, and Mizrachim). The Ashkenazim are Jews who trace their family history to Eastern Europe, and they are the largest group (numerically) among American Jews. The Sephardim are Jews who trace their family history to the Iberian Peninsula (i.e., Spain and Portugal). Finally, the Mizrachim are Jews who trace their family history to Northern Africa and/or Western Asia. In addition to these three main lineages, there are also communities of Jews who have lived in China, India, and Ethiopia for centuries.

Diversity of Denominations

There are several active denominations among American Jews. The groups are presented in order from most to least adherent to Jewish Orthodoxy. It is important to note that most Jews omit the *o* in spelling *G-d*. This is done because Judaism prohibits erasing or destroying any Hebrew name of G-d. Finally, there are some Americans who identify as secular or cultural Jews; these people self-identify as Jewish without it having any religious connection.

Hasidic

Hasidic Jews are readily identifiable, as men wear black coats, pants, and hats, as well as peyos (i.e., side curls); women wear very modest clothing (e.g., long, conservative skirts), and some married women shave their heads and wear wigs. Yiddish is the first language, followed by Hebrew and then English. These Jews are totally immersed in Jewish life and traditions, and they strictly adhere to the three tenets of the Orthodox lifestyle: (a) keeping kosher (dietary practices), (b) observing the Sabbath (following prescribed religious traditions concerning behaviors on *Shabbat*, which occurs from sundown Friday to sundown Saturday), and (c) following family purity laws (which address sexual relations and ritual cleanliness). Secular culture is avoided; hence, Hasidic Jews live in self-contained communities. Men and women sit apart during religious services, and the Torah is believed to be the literal translation of G-d's law.

Non-Hasidic Orthodox

The dress of these Jews is similar to most Americans, except that men wear a yarmulke (head covering) and women dress more modestly. Unlike the Hasidic Jews, secular culture is an important part of the lives of the non-Hasidic Orthodox. These Jews are similar to the Hasidim in their (a) adherence to the Orthodox lifestyle, (b) belief that the Torah is the word of G-d, and (c) having men and women sit separately during religious services (which are conducted entirely in Hebrew).

Conservative

This denomination was created as a response to Reform Judaism. Men and women sit together in religious services, which are performed mostly in Hebrew. These Jews are more likely to keep kosher and observe the Sabbath than are Reform Jews, but there are many Conservative Jews who do not adhere to the Orthodox lifestyle. Like the Reform Jews, Conservative Jews have a positive attitude toward and involvement with modern, secular culture and a nonfundamentalist teaching of Judaism.

Reform

Reform Jews see Judaism as an evolving entity. This denomination was developed as a reaction to Orthodoxy to modernize Judaism during the European Enlightenment. Men and women sit together during religious services, which are conducted in both Hebrew and English. Reform Jews believe that not only the Torah but also individual conscience and informed choice guide decision making. In addition, most Reform Jews do not follow the Orthodox lifestyle. This was the first denomination to ordain women as rabbis.

Reconstructionist

Reconstructionist Jews see Judaism as an evolving tradition, with three primal elements: G-d, Torah, and the People of Israel. These Jews accept and interact with modern culture. Although the religious services and rituals are traditional, the group ideology is very progressive. For example, one's personal autonomy supersedes traditional Jewish law. Finally, this was the first denomination to hold a Bat Mitzvah ceremony for Jewish girls.

American Jewish Identity

Multidimensional Construct

American Jewish identity is a term used to designate those uniquely Jewish attributes shared among group members. Such attributes may include religious and spiritual beliefs and practices, as well as the customs, attitudes, values, and cultural practices that reflect the characteristics of Jews as an ethnic group. However, neither ethnicity nor religion alone adequately captures the complexity of what it is to be a Jew.

The term *Jewish identity* also has been used to reflect one's national heritage, language (e.g., Hebrew, Ladino, and Yiddish), culture, and, historically, race. Mordecai Kaplan's conceptualization of Judaism as a civilization included ethics and philosophies, in addition to knowledge, skills, literature, tools, arts, and laws, as critical elements that help shape the identity of American Jews. This list of shared attributes has been expanded to include those who identify with the political elements of Judaism arising from one's relationship with the State of Israel and opposition to antisemitism. Clearly, neither a single construct nor a set combination of them goes far enough to encompass Jewish identity.

Historical events and geography provide additional context for understanding American Jewish identity. The processes of immigration and acculturation have shaped the American experience for Jews, as have the unique sociopolitical, historical, and economic realities in their new country. Though many Jews have prospered in the United States, Jewish identity cannot be understood without consideration of how Jews have been affected by the forces of oppression and discrimination.

Dynamic Construct

Jewish identity may best be viewed as a dynamic construct in which Jews continually engage in a process of discovery and self-definition. Although the term *Jewish identity* may be used to capture common attributes of the Jewish people as a collective group, it is also used to express the way in which the individual, as a member of the Jewish community, reflects such attributes. That is to say, the identification of commonalities attributed to the Jewish people is not meant to imply that all Jews have the same relationship to being Jewish. Each American Jew may choose to express his or her sense of Jewish identity with behaviors or beliefs that either converge or diverge from the collective in a variety of contexts. Additionally, although it would be much simpler to understand Jewish identity as a static or fixed construct, many individuals experience significant changes related to their Jewish identity over time. As one develops personally and professionally, the importance of being Jewish may fluctuate. Moreover, the way that one expresses his or her Jewish identity may also fluctuate throughout one's life.

Core Jews

Such complexities have made the scientific study of American Jews challenging in that there is no consensus as to the specific inclusion or exclusion criteria for this group. One approach to providing such criteria is the construct of *core Jews,* a term which has been used in social science research to account for Jewish identification. These criteria, centered in one's own subjective sense of identity, include (a) all those born Jewish and who identify Judaism as their religion, (b) secular-ethnic Jews who do not report any other religion, and (c) those who have converted to Judaism. Exclusion criteria include individuals who were born Jewish and have formally adopted another religion and those who do not acknowledge being Jewish.

Empirical Research

Research that has explored Jewish identity may be divided into three levels, each aiming to explore the relationship of American Jewish individuals to perceived group attributes. The three levels are (1) cognitive, which includes one's perceptions of Jewish attributes and the salience of them in one's life; (2) affective, which is one's feelings regarding such attributes; and (3) behavioral, which is the extent to which one's actions are consistent with one's conceptualization of being Jewish. Furthermore, it is important to note that in addition to measuring the consistency of one's behavior to one's own conceptualization of being Jewish, behavioral assessments commonly measure one's actions in accordance with traditional standards (e.g., observing holidays).

Although observing and measuring the numerous ways that American Jews are capable of expressing their Jewish identity is clearly a worthwhile pursuit, it fails to provide a complete picture of the identity of American Jews. In modern society, one's identity may be defined not only in terms of religion or ethnicity but also in terms of one's gender, social class, sexual orientation, career, nationality, and numerous other collective identities. Rather than ignoring these other dimensions, research has begun to consider their relative, and sometimes competing, importance in relation to one's Jewish identity.

Psychological Stressors

The relative socioeconomic success that some Jews have attained in America, compared with other oppressed groups, may lead to the erroneous conclusion that American Jews have been fully embraced by the dominant culture. Antisemitism still operates currently, and the effects from past antisemitic atrocities, most notably the Shoah (i.e., the Jewish Holocaust), are still carried by many Jews. The psychological stress that results from being oppressed and marginalized is of central importance for understanding the reality of many American Jews.

Acts of Oppression

While the construct of Jewish identity has been defined largely by American Jews, antisemitic views propagated by those critical of group members have had a major impact on the Jewish people and beyond. Antisemitism includes the oppression, condemnation, and systematic discrimination of Jews. Throughout history, antisemitic acts of hatred against Jews have been directed at the religious, cultural, and intellectual heritage of the Jewish community. The impact of such actions include the stereotypes held both inside and outside the Jewish community that devalue Jewish people, as well as the negative ways Jews themselves have internalized such negative images. Contrary to beliefs that antisemitic activity disappeared with the Shoah, indications exist that Jews may be increasingly vulnerable to being viewed negatively and to being victims of antisemitic crimes of hate.

The Self-Hating Jew

In attempting to conceptualize the psychological impact of acts of oppression directed toward Jews, the concept of the self-hating or self-loathing Jew has emerged. Consistent with the initial stage of racial and ethnic identity development models, such terms have been used in reference to the internalization of antisemitic views held toward Jews by the dominant group and the experience of being marginalized or devalued within society. The presence or perception of antisemitism in society is therefore a precondition of developing such a negative view of oneself and entails the incompatibility of being oppressed by dominant standards while at the same time being unable to achieve them. This process reflects the acceptance of the dominant culture's belief of Jewish inferiority as one's own. Identity rejection has been observed to result most typically in feelings of anger, embarrassment, and guilt. The experience of shame has been documented as an additional response to antisemitism, reflecting feelings of inferiority, alienation, and indignity.

Antisemitism and Fear

Another observed result of antisemitism is the experience of fear. A desire to remain out of public view and, in some cases, be "invisible" are the consequences of this fear. Practically, this means avoiding the use of wearing or carrying Jewish symbols in public and keeping one's Jewish identity a secret from outsiders. Consequently, voicing concern regarding Jewish issues is not an option. Although non-Jews might conceptualize this behavior as paranoia, the historical reality of being persecuted based solely on being Jewish has conditioned this behavior within the American Jewish community. In other words, past experience has provided unfortunate empirical support for retaining this pessimistic view. Given the relative position of privilege that many Jews have attained in America, the theoretical risk of losing these privileges is simply not worth calling attention to oneself for many of Jewish descent.

The Shoah

While a history of Jewish culture is beyond the scope of this entry, it is essential to understand the contextual forces that gave rise to and sustain antisemitism both at home and abroad. The Shoah (Hebrew for *catastrophe*) refers to the genocide of approximately 6 million Jews in Nazi Germany. The Shoah is a critical incident to understand, as the majority of Jews in Europe (approximately 65%) and over one in three Jews throughout the world were killed. Although the precise psychological impact of this catastrophic event may never be known, potential consequences include beliefs that the world is dangerous for all Jews and that being Jewish is inextricably tied to suffering. These and other issues may be particularly relevant for the children and grandchildren of survivors of the Shoah. While the Shoah is, without question, the most devastating event for Jews in modernity, antisemitic acts of violence and oppression extend throughout history. It is precisely this history that has made Jews in America sensitive to any act conveying antisemitic intent. For this reason, it is the perception of antisemitism, and not any set of objectively defined acts, that becomes relevant when conceptualizing the psychological implications of oppression for the American Jew.

Numerical Minority

Another relevant contextual factor for understanding the psychological experience of the American Jew is the religious makeup of the United States. Currently, Jews comprise less than 2% of the national population. Compared to the presence of Christians (approximately 84% of the population), those identifying as non-Christian are without question a numerical minority. Furthermore, non-Christians living in the United States often experience the impact of living in the predominantly Christian society based on assumptions made as to one's practices and beliefs and the strong Christian influence in national politics. Consequently, Jewish clients may feel as though their issues and identity hold little value in the dominant culture.

Privilege and Passing

The fact that many Jews can, to some degree, make choices regarding their visibility may itself be considered a privilege. This differs from racial minorities (including many Jews) with phenotypes clearly distinguishable from the dominant group, making the option of "passing" as White not available. For many Jews of European descent, however, this may well be possible. Whereas until the 1940s Jews were considered a separate and inferior race in America, a redefinition of "Whiteness" now allows for the potential of Jews gaining equal access to becoming members of the privileged class. Many Jews in America now possess the choice of whether or not to renounce being Jewish. Despite the potential benefits of gaining access to this privileged status, the psychological toll of hiding one's identity may come with a cost. Underlying this decision may be a shame, terror, and embarrassment of one's Jewish identity and oneself.

Jews and the Origins of Counseling

In an effort to contextualize the experience of American Jews, it bears mentioning that Jews played a prominent role in the origins of counseling. Many scholars erroneously contend that the majority of counseling theories are products of White dominant culture. In fact, the origins of counseling can be traced to Freud and his colleagues in Europe, who were assimilated Ashkenazi Jews. Although these Jews had white skin, they were culturally dissimilar from the dominant group of White Christians. Since Freud's time, a multitude of Jews have had a lasting impact on the field. The continued inattention regarding Jewish contributions to the counseling profession reflects the perceived invisibility of Jews and the unfortunate persistence of antisemitism.

Counseling Issues With American Jewish Clients

Awareness, Knowledge, and Skills

It is important for all counselors, both Jewish and Gentile, to engage in a self-assessment regarding their thoughts and feelings about Jews, Judaism, and Jewish culture. This way, any negative stereotypes or beliefs regarding American Jews can be dealt with via education, supervision, and/or personal counseling. Because there are many ways to be Jewish, Jewish counselors must not assume that their American Jewish clients have the same beliefs and practices where Judaism is concerned. As such, these counselors need to understand the client's thoughts and feelings about his or her own Jewishness. The Jewish counselor must also be cognizant that internalized antisemitism could play a role in the therapeutic process, either in oneself or in the client. When a non-Jewish counselor is working with an American Jewish client, the issues are different. The main issue would be for the non-Jewish counselor to be knowledgeable about Judaism. For example, these counselors should understand that Judaism is more than a religion and that Jewish identity is quite complex.

Disclosure and Identification

Some American Jews will not openly identify as Jews unless they perceive the environment to be safe. This is because identifying oneself as Jewish can be perceived as potentially hazardous due to the long history of antisemitism. Complicating matters here is the client's level of awareness and insight. The client might think it implausible that her or his Jewish identity has relevance to the presenting problem. In this way, counselors need to tread cautiously when inquiring about religious and ethnic background. The counselor should follow the client's lead with regard to the level of disclosure about the client's Jewishness, while also creating a safe environment for the discussion of these issues. Once a client's Jewish identity has been confirmed, counselors might inquire about the client's adherence to the practice of Judaism, including identification with a particular denomination. Of course some will define themselves as secular or cultural Jews; that is, they will not practice any of the religious aspects of Judaism, yet they will self-identify as Jews.

Therapeutic Relationship

Establishing a good rapport and a positive working alliance is central to the beginning of treatment with American Jews. Some ways the counselor can succeed at this task are by knowing about the history and present experiences of Jews, including antisemitism and stereotypes. At the same time, it is important for counselors not to let assumptions guide their treatment plan. Thus, being Jewish should not be the only factor in understanding the client.

Healthy Paranoia

Another skill for counselors concerns the ability to discern clinical paranoia from healthy paranoia or cultural mistrust in American Jews. This is important because American Jews, like other oppressed cultural groups, might be appropriately mistrustful of outsiders (in this case, non-Jews). Hence, counselors should be cautious not to misinterpret the actions of American Jewish clients. Survivors of the Shoah and their descendants bring an additional dynamic with them to counseling. These American Jews may view the world as a dangerous place because of overprotective parents who were traumatized during the Shoah.

Identity Issues

Counselors working with American Jews also need to understand Jewish identity, which can be a difficult task given the complexity of the issues. As previously stated, there are both religious and secular/cultural aspects to Jewish identity, and Jewish identity is both multifaceted and context specific. Hence, to provide culturally competent care, counselors need to understand the client's perspectives on his or her own Jewish identity.

Importance of Family

For American Jews, the family is often the primary social structure, and there are emotional consequences for going against the wishes of the family. It is important to remember that because American Jews are bicultural, they may experience value conflicts between individualistic American culture and the more collectivistic nature of Jewish culture. Hence, counselors need to attend to family issues and the bicultural identity of American Jews.

Presenting Concerns

Scholars have theorized the following common presenting concerns for American Jewish clients: (a) Jewish identity issues, (b) body image and gender identity, (c) child rearing practices, (d) interfaith or interdenominational couples, (e) issues surrounding conversion to or from Judaism, (f) sexual orientation and religion, and (g) antisemitism-related experiences. Of course, American Jews may seek counseling for personal growth and development, as well as to receive treatment for any psychological disorders.

Conclusion

In conclusion, American Jews are a small yet culturally distinct group in the United States. Despite stereotypes of widespread financial success and the appearance of fitting into the dominant culture, antisemitism persists and grows. This perpetuation of antisemitism contributes to potential biases in counseling, especially when there is a lack of information and a reliance on stereotypes. By learning about Jews and Jewish culture, counselors can provide culturally competent treatment for their American Jewish clients.

Lewis Z. Schlosser and Daniel C. Rosen

See also Acculturation (v3); Acculturative Stress (v3); Antisemitism (v3); Bicultural (v3); Cultural Mistrust (v3); Cultural Paranoia (v3); Enculturation (v3); Ethnic Identity (v3); Ethnic Pride (v3); Identity (v3); Identity Development (v3); Individual Therapy (v2); Religion/Religious Belief Systems (v3); Spirituality (v3); Spirituality/Religion (v2)

Further Readings

Brodkin, K. (1998). *How Jews became White folks and what that says about race in America.* New Brunswick, NJ: Rutgers University Press.

Chesler, P. (2003). *The new anti-semitism: The current crisis and what we must do about it.* San Francisco: Jossey-Bass.

Cohen, S. M., & Eisen, A. M. (2000). *The Jew within: Self, family, and community in America.* Bloomington: Indiana University Press.

Dershowitz, A. M. (1997). *The vanishing American Jew: In search of Jewish identity for the next century.* New York: Little, Brown.

Friedman, M. L., Friedlander, M. L., & Blustein, D. L. (2005). Toward an understanding of Jewish identity: A phenomenological study. *Journal of Counseling Psychology, 52,* 77–83.

Gilman, S. L. (1990). *Jewish self-hatred: Anti-semitism and the hidden language of Jews.* Baltimore: Johns Hopkins University Press.

Herman, S. N. (1977). *Jewish identity: A social psychological perspective.* Beverly Hills, CA: Sage.

Horowitz, B. (2003). *Connections and journeys: Assessing critical opportunities for enhancing Jewish identity* [Report to the Commission on Jewish Identity and Renewal, United Jewish Association-Federation of New York]. New York: UJA-Federation.

Langman, P. F. (1999). *Jewish issues in multiculturalism: A handbook for educators and clinicians.* Northvale, NJ: Jason Aronson.

Schlosser, L. Z. (2003). Christian privilege: Breaking a sacred taboo. *Journal of Multicultural Counseling and Development, 31,* 44–51.

Antisemitism

Antisemitism is prejudice, hostility, and/or discrimination toward Jews as a racial, religious, and/or ethnic group on an individual, community, institutional, and/or societal level. Antisemitism can be categorized into three central forms: religious (anti-Judaism), racial/ethnic (classical antisemitism), and political (anti-Israeli or anti-Zionist). This definition underscores a major problem with defining and understanding antisemitism; that is, Jews cannot be adequately classified using the established taxonomies for cultural demography. This is primarily because Judaism is often viewed only as a religion and because of the erroneous assumption that all Jews are White; this inaccurate view of Judaism ignores the within-group diversity of Jews. In fact, the term *anti-Semitism* originally and erroneously referred to a Jewish racial group: Semites. There are differences in Jewish racial and ethnic origins (i.e., Ashkenazim, Sephardim, and Mizrachim) and different identities both within the diverse Jewish religious denominations (e.g., Orthodox, Hasidic, Reform, Conservative, and Reconstructionist) and within nonreligious Jews. Hence, antisemitism consists of more than religious bias.

The term *anti-Semitism* was first used by Wilhelm Marr, a German national and political conservative, in 1879 to express anti-Jewish feelings. Marr's original intent was for political purposes, which was developed more fully into a "racial" concept when applied by the Nazis and later used as an anti-Israeli referent after the creation of the State of Israel. Finally, many scholars no longer hyphenate this term as *anti-Semitism* to cease the use of this word for anything other than its original intent: Jew-hatred. This has been done because some have attempted to use the term *anti-Semitism* for other purposes. Specifically, some Arabs have claimed they cannot be anti-Semitic because they themselves are Semitic.

Others have attempted to use the term to be critical of Israel's interactions with other Semitic peoples of the Middle East. Hence, eliminating the hyphen takes the focus away from the term *Semitic*.

Prevalence of Antisemitism

Although there have been some suggestions that antisemitism is no longer a problem, a 2005 Anti-Defamation League poll found that roughly one in six

Americans (14%) hold "strongly antisemitic" views. In addition, there was a 17% increase from 2003 to 2004 with regard to the number of antisemitic incidents that were reported (i.e., 1,557 to 1,821); the 2004 figure represents the highest number of incidents in the past 9 years. Finally, of the 1,374 religiously motivated hate crimes in the United States committed during 2004, 954 (70%) were exclusively anti-Jewish, accounting for 12% of all 2004 bias crimes.

Examples of Antisemitism

Antisemitism has existed for more than 4,000 years and has manifested in a variety of ways, including negative stereotypes, oppression, discrimination, segregation, forced expulsion, pogroms, and genocide. Anti-Jewish prejudice dates back to when the ancient Hebrew people refused to accept foreign deities, particularly under Greek and Roman domination. Some examples of antisemitism from history include the (a) exile of Jews from their homeland, (b) persecution of Jews after Constantine established Christianity as the official religion of the Roman Empire, (c) centrality of Christian teachings of Jewish deicide from antiquity until Vatican II, and (d) establishment of racial antisemitism as Hitler's Third Reich came to power in Nazi Germany.

One of the most prominent examples of antisemitism is the perpetuation of the deicide myth, which is the erroneous belief that the Jews killed Jesus. Deicide, which literally means to kill a G-d or a divine being, has frequently been used to describe the death of Jesus (most Jews omit the *o* in spelling *G-d* because Judaism prohibits erasing or destroying any Hebrew name of G-d). However, it is a historical fact that the Romans, and not the Jews, were responsible for the death of Jesus. Hence, continuing to blame Jews for the death of Jesus is both antisemitic and historically inaccurate. Next is a list of other examples of antisemitism; this list is neither exhaustive nor mutually exclusive. These examples include (a) the use of anti-Jewish slurs (e.g., "heeb," "kike"); (b) the perpetuation of the blood libel myth (i.e., the belief that Jews killed Christian children for religious ceremonies); (c) violence against Jews, Jewish communities, and Jewish symbols (e.g., synagogues); (d) questioning the Jewish identity of Jews based solely on adherence to religious practices (e.g., accusing secular Jews of not being Jewish); (e) Holocaust denial; (f) accusing Jews of cosmic evil (e.g., stereotyped belief that the Jews are plotting to take over the world); and (g) asserting that Jews have no claim to Israel. Some of the more prevalent antisemitic stereotypes include (a) all Jews are simultaneously wealthy and miserly; (b) Jews control the media, the banks, and Hollywood; and (c) Jews are secretly plotting to take over the world. Antisemitism manifested itself until the end of World War II in open discrimination in jobs and housing, quotas in colleges, and myths of cowardice among Jewish soldiers. Modern antisemitism, like racism and other forms of discrimination, has become more subtle and insidious.

Internalized Antisemitism and Gender Stereotypes

Antisemitism is psychologically harmful regardless of one's ethnic or religious identification as a Jewish person. Internalized antisemitism refers to the owning of a negative self-image or identity rejection as a Jew. It may manifest in feelings of fear, anxiety, ambivalence, depression, alienation, isolation, shame, low self-esteem, identity conflict, and self-hatred related to being Jewish.

Antisemitism combined with sexism often results in gender stereotypes of Jewish men and women. Both positive and negative stereotypes have been perpetuated. For example, Jewish men are typically portrayed as intelligent and good providers who neither abuse alcohol nor hit their spouses. At the same time, they have been portrayed as neurotic, weak, boring, and unmasculine.

Caricatures of Jewish women often fall into one of two contradictory categories: the Jewish American Princess (J.A.P.) or the Jewish mother. The former is presented as pushy, aggressive, domineering, shallow, materialistic, and demanding, yet simultaneously passive, dependent, and helpless. Jewish mothers are often portrayed as overprotective, self-sacrificing, and tending to induce guilt in their children. Distorted body image and eating disorders may manifest in Jewish women who have internalized negativity related to the pervasive devaluation of "Jewish" features.

The acceptance of these negative evaluations and stereotypes may lead Jews to attempt to change or distance themselves from their Jewishness to try and escape the stereotype. Attempts to erase signs of Jewishness manifest in changing one's name, hair, accents, and physical features. Judaism, the use of the Yiddish language, or any manifestation of Jewish culture may be viewed with disdain.

Antisemitism in Counseling

Antisemitism may be related to a variety of psychological problems. For example, depression and low self-esteem may be related to internalized antisemitism. Anxiety may be related to a history of family trauma related to antisemitism, often present in Holocaust survivors and their descendants. The manifestation of antisemitism in counseling varies depending on (a) whether it lies within the counselor or the client (i.e., because of the inherent power differential), and (b) whether each of the members is Jewish or non-Jewish.

Counselors

Jewish counseling professionals should consider that Jewish clients may not view antisemitism in the same way that they do. This is especially important because of the diversity both within and between various groups of Jews. In addition, Jewish counselors must be aware of the possibility of internalized antisemitism, both in themselves and in clients. Non-Jewish counselors must consider any biases and preconceptions they might have about Jews before working with Jewish clients. Failure to do so could have serious negative implications for the Jewish client in that he or she could be harmed psychologically by the counselor who holds conscious or unconscious antisemitic views.

Clients

Jewish clients could present to counseling with problems related to internalized antisemitism. Hence, learning about one's feelings about being Jewish is important, and the skilled counselor (i.e., who is knowledgeable about antisemitism) may be able to assist the client as well. Jewish clients' discussions of antisemitic experiences need to be validated and processed. In addition, Jewish clients might encounter antisemitism from a counselor, and this could also negatively impact treatment.

Lewis Z. Schlosser and Julie R. Ancis

See also Acculturative Stress (v3); American Jews (v3); Cultural Paranoia (v3); Discrimination (v3); Ethnocentrism (v3); Oppression (v3); Racism (v3)

Further Readings

Beck, E. T. (1988). The politics of Jewish invisibility. *National Women's Studies Association Journal, 1,* 93–102.

Chesler, P. (2003). *The new Anti-Semitism: The current crisis and what we must do about it.* San Francisco: Jossey-Bass.

Feldman, S. M. (1997). *Please don't wish me a Merry Christmas: A critical history of the separation of church and state.* New York: New York University Press.

Gilman, S. L. (1990). *Jewish self-hatred: Anti-Semitism and the hidden language of Jews.* Baltimore: Johns Hopkins University Press.

Josefowitz Siegel, R., & Cole, E. (Eds.). (1997). *Celebrating the lives of Jewish women: Patterns in a feminist sampler.* New York: Haworth.

Langman, P. F. (1999). *Jewish issues in multiculturalism: A handbook for educators and clinicians.* Northvale, NJ: Jason Aronson.

Lewis, B. (2006). The new Anti-Semitism. *The American Scholar, 75*(1), 25–36.

Schlosser, L. Z. (2003). Christian privilege: Breaking a sacred taboo. *Journal of Multicultural Counseling and Development, 31,* 44–51.

Weinrach, S. (2003). I am my brother's (and sister's) keeper: Jewish values and the counseling process. *Journal of Counseling & Development, 81,* 441–444.

ARAB AMERICANS

Arab Americans are defined, in this entry, as individuals and families with ancestry from one or more of the 22 Arab League states. The Arab League includes Algeria, Bahrain, Comoros, Djibouti, Egypt, Iraq, Jordan, Kuwait, Lebanon, Libya, Mauritania, Morocco, Oman, Palestine, Qatar, Saudi Arabia, Somalia, Sudan, Syria, Tunisia, United Arab Emirates, and Yemen.

The Arab League countries span Asia and Africa. The United States and other Western countries often refer to this particular region of the world as the Middle East; however, many countries within the Middle East are non-Arab, such as Turkey, Afghanistan, and Israel; and still others, such as Iran, represent different regions (e.g., Persia) altogether. Some Arab League states are Arab speaking; others are not. Many Arab League states are predominantly Muslim, although the Arab Middle East represents only a small percentage of the world's Muslims.

Demographics

This diversity in origin, religion, language, and the like, serves to account for the respective variety of demographics within the Arab American population in the United States.

The 2000 U.S. Census was the first opportunity for selected respondents to indicate their affiliation with ethnic groups. Among all self-identified Arab Americans surveyed, 39% indicated Lebanese ancestry, 18% Arab, 12% Egyptian and Syrian ancestries, and smaller groups of Palestinians, Moroccans, Iraqis, and those signifying "other Arab."

Most metropolitan cities have sizeable Arab populations, with some identifiable community center, such as a church or mosque, community center, or even restaurant. Larger established Arab American communities, rich in Arab heritage and traditions, can be found in New York, Dearborn (Michigan), Los Angeles, Chicago, Houston, Detroit, San Diego, Jersey City, Boston, and Jacksonville (Florida). States with the largest populations of Arab Americans are California, Florida, Michigan, New Jersey, New York, Illinois, Massachusetts, Ohio, Pennsylvania, and Texas.

Although the U.S. Census numbers the Arab American community in the United States at just over 1 million, most Arab American advocacy groups consistently estimate the population to be over 3 million. These groups attribute the Census Bureau's undercount of Arab Americans, like for that of other ethnic groups, to problems in the methodological procedures of the census, particularly pertaining to the study of ethnic minority populations. Census data identify a 40% increase in Arab Americans over the decade of 1990 to 2000. The Arab American Institute (AAI), one of the leading national advocacy groups within the Arab American community, works closely with the U.S. Census Bureau, as well as conducting its own independent census and cultural research. Many of the statistics cited in this entry are taken from either U.S. Census Bureau data or AAI's Internet and written resources.

Contrary to the stereotype of Arab Americans as being Muslim, the majority are actually non-Muslim. Approximately 42% of Arab Americans are Catholic, representing Roman, Maronite, and Melkite (Greek) traditions; 23% are Orthodox, including Antiochian, Syrian, Greek, and Coptic faiths. Twenty-three percent of the Arab Americans who are Muslim represent Sunni, Shi'a, and Druze traditions.

Compared with other ethnic groups, the Arab American population comprises more younger and foreign-born individuals, as well as being somewhat more educated. According to AAI, 85% have high school diplomas, over 40% have at least a bachelor's degree (compared with the national average of 24%), and 17% have postgraduate degrees (compared with 9% of U.S. citizens).

Arab Americans represent a wide array of careers. About 64% are in the labor market, similar to the national average. The majority of working Arab Americans, at 88%, are employed within the private sector, and 73% hold managerial, professional, technical, sales, or administrative positions. AAI reports that Arab Americans are less likely to be found in governmental and service positions than their non–Arab American counterparts nationally. The mean income for Arab American households is slightly higher (i.e., 8%) than the national average.

History and Culture

According to well-known Arab American historians (e.g., Gregory Orfalea, 1988) immigration from the Arab world to the United States has taken place in waves. These waves seem to parallel various strategies of acculturation among Arab Americans.

The earliest wave, at the turn of the 20th century, paralleled that of many other ethnic groups who came to the United States in search of better educational and economic opportunity and, for some Arabs, to escape the Ottoman regime. This immigrant group was made up primarily of Christians, many of whom were uneducated merchants, from Lebanon, Palestine, Syria, and Jordan. It also included a group of scholars and writers in search of academic freedom, such as Khalil Gibran, who was among those founding the New York Pen League, or "immigrant poets," which has historically showcased some of the most important of Arab American literature of the 20th century.

The next two waves, in contrast, were primarily composed of educated Muslims. During the post–World War II, or "brain drain," wave, Palestinians, Egyptians, Syrians, Jordanians, and Iraqis, along with smaller groups of Lebanese and Yemeni left their countries, dissatisfied with political leadership in the region. Shortly thereafter, the next wave began immigrating during the 1960s, partly in response to the lessening of U.S. immigration restrictions. This group came for similar reasons and included large numbers of Palestinians who came to escape the Israeli occupation.

More recently, a fourth wave has emerged. This most recent wave has occurred as a result of the Gulf War of 1990–1991. Thousands of Iraqis have entered the United States to join their earlier counterparts. Many of these are political refugees, and many others came to flee the economic conditions caused by external sanctions imposed by other countries.

In terms of acculturation, the first wave quickly established close-knit community ties with one another in the places they settled. They also quickly became immersed, or assimilated, into the overall U.S. culture, similar to their other ethnic group counterparts at the turn of the century. The second and third waves became quickly reestablished professionally and economically, yet they maintained their own cultural traditions and values. The final wave, similar to other refugee populations, have struggled to resettle in the United States, and many suffered significant pre-immigration, immigration, and post-immigration traumas that have been difficult to overcome.

Religion and Values

Although the majority of Arab Americans are non-Muslim, Islam, the religion of the Muslim world, has had a significant influence upon Arab culture historically. Thus, there is overlap of some of the spiritual values, such as the focus on collectivism, held by both Christian and Muslim Arab Americans. Similarly, many Arab Americans, Christians and Muslims alike, value their religious faith and traditions as a symbol of their cultural heritage.

Islam is a religion that was brought to the Arabian Peninsula (known as the Saudi Arabian Peninsula of modern times) between A.D. 7 and A.D. 10 by the Prophet Muhammad. Muslims believe that he was a messenger of God, delivering God's word that was given to him by the Archangel Gabriel. These words became written as the *Qur'an*, the holy book of Islam. Islam is viewed as a religion that embodies the same messages God revealed in the previously founded world religions of Judaism and Christianity, and Muslims believe that Jesus was one of God's many prophets. The Qur'an is considered a continuation of the Bible's Old and New Testaments.

The Five Pillars, or traditions, are commonly practiced by many Muslims. *Shahadah* speaks to the belief in Allah as one God and to his Servant, the Prophet Muhammad. *Salat* requires formal worship five times daily. This ritual includes reciting a formal liturgy followed by a moment of personal meditation. *Sawm* represents the fasting period during the month of Ramadan, to demonstrate self-restraint, patience, endurance, obedience to God, and solidarity with those less fortunate. *Zakah* requires that Muslims donate 2.5% of their income toward causes of economic justice. Finally, *Hajj* prescribes journeying to the city of Mecca, Saudi Arabia. This journey is ideally undertaken during the early part of the 12th month of the Islamic (lunar) calendar.

For Muslim Arabs, the biggest holidays include Eid al-Fitr and Eid al-Adha. Eid al-Fitr is the celebration at the end of the month of Ramadan; Eid al-Adha is celebrated at the end of the pilgrimage to Mecca, usually on the 10th day of the 12th Islamic lunar month. The holy day is Friday, although in the United States, many religious institutions hold their services and other programs on weekends.

There are other important beliefs within Muslim and Arab culture, including accountability to God, self-responsibility for one's deeds, global unity, racial equality, peace, and social harmony. Beyond these spiritually oriented values, collectivism and extended family are perhaps the most significant values for Arab Americans. Despite the vast diversity in subcultures of origin across the League of Arab States, Arab American communities, or enclaves, typically have families representing multiple Arab ethnicities. Even those families choosing not to reside within such an enclave tend to value social relationships with their extended family members and other Arab Americans.

Educational and economic achievements also are highly valued. This holds true for boys and girls, men and women alike. These accomplishments are often seen as a source of family pride. Likewise, civic activities, such as leadership positions, are seen as community accomplishments and honor. Although Arab Americans are less likely to establish governmental sector careers, the sense of collectivism and altruism for the Arab American community, either locally or nationally, leads many to become involved in the political arena. Arab Americans have provided leadership to the Senate, the House of Representatives, state legislatures, and city governments, as well as having served in critical military positions in every U.S. war. High-ranking officials such as Chief of Staff John Sununu under President George Bush and Health and Human Services Secretary Donna Shalala under President Bill Clinton, along with counterparts in the U.S. military, sports, business, law, entertainment, education, fashion, arts and literature, and science and medicine, are detailed in a publication titled *Arab Americans: Making a Difference*.

Gender and Family

Male and female gender roles have been defined within Arab cultures since well before the inception of

Islam. Some early Arab societies were tribal and nomadic, and the survival of the tribe or clan relied upon each individual taking on his or her prescribed role. Males have the responsibility of economic support and therefore are more likely to engage in social relationships outside of their families and communities. Females are largely responsible for keeping kinship ties; thus, they interact more within the familial structure.

According to Islam, men and women have an equal footing before God. Compared with Western societies, Muslim women have held rights to own and inherit property, obtain educations, and seek divorce for 1,400 years. In some Arab countries, governmental restrictions may preclude these rights from being realized. In the United States, many women also have the same relative freedoms as their mainstream counterparts. On the other hand, those individuals from newer immigrant groups, as well as those who reside in close-knit Arab American enclaves, may practice more controlled gender roles, such as prohibiting dating and other coeducational activities. Some Muslim parents and families report, in fact, that they impose more restrictions on their children, specifically their daughters, than they did or would do in their countries of origin, because of perceived environmental threats to traditional values.

For example, Arab/Muslim American families and individuals interpret the Muslim practice of veiling, or wearing a *hijab* (an Arab headdress), in a wide variety of ways. Some Arab American women believe that the practice was designed by male-dominated governments to oppress women, whereas others use it as a symbol of their personal interpretation of religious or cultural values, as a political expression against Western influences in the Middle East, or because they feel safer and more valued in coeducational settings.

Although divorce is not uncommon within Arab American communities, promoting the maintenance of the nuclear family is of primary importance; thus, Arab Americans tend to have a lower divorce rate than their non–Arab American counterparts. Within traditional marriages, individuals do not place as much reliance on their partners to meet all of their needs; rather, they may rely on other family and community members. In fact, multiple generations and family members may reside within a single household, and elders are integral to the family unit. Parenting styles may tend more toward the authoritarian approach than the Western authoritative one.

Sociopolitical History and Contemporary Issues

The Arab world has historically had a troubled relationship with the United States, and this relationship extends into contemporary issues for Arab Americans.

Some scholars have attributed negative images of Arabs and Muslims within society to historical events such as the Crusades and the Ottoman Empire. In more recent times, the ongoing Palestine–Israel conflict and Iraq wars (e.g., Gulf War, Second Gulf War) have perpetuated the perception that Arabs and Arabism are a threat to U.S. interests.

Within this historical context, many Arab American advocacy groups perceive an image linking Arabs with terrorism both as faulty and inaccurate and as damaging to Arab Americans as individuals, families, and communities. Human rights organizations such as the Human Rights Watch and the Washington Report on Middle East Affairs document incidents ranging from harassment to hate crimes such as arson, vandalism, and physical assaults toward Arab Americans and others perceived to be of Muslim or Arab origins. These organizations also document the effect this backlash can have on Arab American communities locally, regionally, and nationally. Periods immediately following events and tragedies linked, either accurately or inaccurately, with individuals or groups of Arab descent appear to serve as triggers for such backlash.

Juxtaposed with some of these historical and political events over the past century are corresponding immigration and other legal issues facing the Arab American community. Over the years, according to H. H. Samhan, Arab Americans have been classified by the U.S. government as being from "Turkey in Asia," "Syrian," "Asiatic," and "Colored." These fluid yet compulsory labels have regulated immigration from the Middle East. For example, during the early 1900s, because "Syrians" were neither White nor of African descent or birth, they were deemed as ineligible for citizenship according to the immigration statutes of that time. "Asiatic" was ascribed to Arab Americans during a time period in which Asian immigration was sharply restricted. "Colored" was based on skin tone rather than country of origin.

Issues surrounding immigration and classification, in general, continue to be salient ones among Arab Americans today. Similarly to the relationship between sociopolitical and immigration histories addressed earlier in this entry, contemporary issues such as the War on Terrorism, the U.S. military engagement in Iraq, and Palestine, are intertwined with current concerns such as civil liberties and Arab American census data.

Current Issues

Advocacy groups such as the AAI and the American Arab Anti-Discrimination Committee often link contemporary issues among Arab Americans with global events involving Arab regions. Leading issues in contemporary U.S. society include those related to civil liberties, Iraq, and Palestine.

Since the World Trade Center bombings in New York City on September 11, 2001, civil rights legislation in the United States has held challenges for Americans. Though some has been associated with the profiling and targeting of Arab Americans, Muslims, and other specific groups in order to ensure homeland security, the debate about its legality affects all citizens.

Arab Americans, parallel to non–Arab American mainstream counterparts, have not been unified in their opinions about the series of Gulf Wars in Iraq. Some may have supported initial or more recent military tactics. However, many stand with other Americans in concerns about foreign policy and moral issues involved in contemporary military tactics in Iraq.

Surveys of Arabs in the Middle East as well as of Arab Americans consistently yield the perspective of impartial handling of the Palestine–Israel conflict, with the United States being perceived as operating in favor of Israel's interests, as well as its own. One Zogby International Poll indicated that, although majorities of younger-generation Arabs throughout the Middle East have favorable attitudes toward American science and technology, democracy and freedom, American entertainment (i.e., movies and television), and American-made products, the lowest attitude ratings were given for U.S. policy toward the Arab nations and Palestine. In the same poll, the "Palestinian issue" was viewed as the most critical contemporary issue of our time, with respondents overwhelmingly reporting that they would react more favorably to the United States if it were to "apply pressure to ensure the creation of an independent Palestinian state."

Counseling Issues

Taken together, the culture of origin, coupled with the sociopolitical history of Arab Americans, yields potential risks and resiliencies among this ethnic group that warrant consideration among psychologists, counselors, and other mental health service providers. Within the context of psychosocial issues for Arab American clients, effects of discrimination trauma and ethnic identity development are of primary importance.

Sylvia Nassar-McMillan has found that Arab Americans tend to somaticize their mental health concerns. For example, their anxiety may manifest in headaches or digestive problems. Thus, it is important for counselors to work in collaboration with medical and other health service providers to develop appropriate referral systems, as well as educational interventions, for their mutual clients. Arab Americans are most likely to seek medical treatment for disorders for which there are specific observable, physical symptoms; thus, they may focus more on their physical versus psychological health. They also may favor a medical model, in which the service provider is in an expert role and gives concrete advice and guidance.

Although psychological services have been provided within Arab societies for centuries, often by religious or spiritual healers, according to Alean Al-Krenawi and John Graham, there remains a stigma attached to admitting and seeking help for a psychological complaint, particularly for women. Moreover, going beyond the Arab American community to speak to an "outsider" may pose additional stigma and shame to the identity of an individual or family.

Within a counseling context, it is imperative that practitioners take into account a variety of psychosocial factors when assessing and preparing to work with an Arab American client. The first of these involves the demographic background of the client. Gender, age, religion, and sexual orientation, as well as educational level and socioeconomic status, all represent issues that may provide important historical information in understanding Arab American clients' socialization processes.

Another layer of relevant information, according to Nassar-McMillan, is the status arena—that is, the individual or family client's status in the United States. If they are permanent residents or U.S. citizens, then learning about how long the family of origin has lived in the United States is important, as is whether they reside within or outside an Arab American ethnic community. These details may shed light onto clients' level of attachment and commitment to their cultural background or heritage. Language spoken in the home also may provide a similar perspective. Country of origin also is important, because the level of Westernization of a country of origin can impact the level of acculturation of individuals or families.

Discrimination Trauma and Ethnic Identity

In light of the increasing phenomenon of hate crimes toward Arab Americans, and the fact that most Arab Americans have experienced acts of prejudice or discrimination or have witnessed fellow Arab Americans experiencing them, backlash may include mild to severe discrimination traumas. Negative stereotyping toward Arabs and Arab Americans can manifest in educational texts, in school and college settings, within employment arenas, and from news and other popular media sources; such stereotyping can further impact the trauma experience. For some individuals, this type of trauma may cause a conscious or unconscious disengagement with country of origin, especially for those who are more likely to physically "pass" as White, or European American. For others, the trauma can serve as a catalyst for becoming involved in advocacy movements to combat the perceived oppression.

In determining that individual or family clients came to the United States as refugees, counselors must be aware of the unique traumas faced by refugees in general. Levels of anxiety and depression may be higher in this group of clients. For those who served in or observed combat or other horrors of war, posttraumatic stress disorder may be pervasive. Immigrants from the Arab world, most recently from Iraq, are likely to have suffered a series of traumas spanning their pre-immigration, immigration, and post-immigration experiences. These clients may be most likely to present for counseling and other human services to meet their basic life needs, such as coping with financial, language, employment, and other barriers. In addition, they may seek medical services in response to some of their somaticized psychological issues.

Regardless of the demographic backgrounds and life experiences of Arab American clients, it is not unlikely that negotiating ethnic identity issues may become relevant within a counseling context. Individuals' level of ethnic identity as Arab Americans may vary widely depending on all of the variables described earlier. The levels to which they have internalized the oppression, both overt and subtle, over their lifetime, may also affect their ethnic pride and commitment to their Arab American ethnic identity and sense of community.

In summary, assessment strategies must be culturally relevant and appropriate. They need to focus significantly upon clients' level of acculturation and ethnic identity development. In addition, although a variety of counseling approaches may be effective when working with Arab American individual and family clients, some may be more culturally appropriate. For example, although some clients may gain valuable insight through counseling and psychotherapy, cognitive-behavioral and problem-solving strategies (e.g., solution-focused counseling) may be more effective. In addition, Arab American clients may be most familiar with a medical, authoritative model on the part of the therapist, along with relatively directive approaches. Finally, constructivist approaches may help clients explore and construct their own perceptions, as well as those involving their communities of origin.

Sylvia C. Nassar-McMillan

See also Acculturation (v3); Acculturative Stress (v3); Adaptation (v3); Antisemitism (v3); Assimilation (v3); Constructivist Theory (v2); Cultural Paranoia (v3); Discrimination (v3); Ethnic Identity (v3); Ethnocentrism (v3); Panic Disorders (v2); Racism (v3); Religion/Religious Belief Systems (v3); Spirituality (v3); Spirituality/Religion (v2)

Further Readings

Abinader, E. (2000). Children of Al-Mahjar: Arab American literature spans a century. *U.S. Society & Values: Electronic Journal of the Department of State, Vol. 5.* Retrieved June 7, 2007, from http://usinfo.state.gov/journals/itsv/0200/ijse/abinader.htm

Ajrouch, K. (1999). Family and ethnic identity in an Arab-American community. In M. Suleiman (Ed.), *Arabs in America: Building a new future* (pp. 129–139). Philadelphia: Temple University Press.

Al-Krenawi, A., & Graham, J. R. (2000). Culturally sensitive social work practice with Arab clients in mental health settings. *Health & Social Work, 25*(1), 9–22.

Barry, D., Elliott, R., & Evans, E. M. (2000). Foreigners in a strange land: Self-construal and ethnic identity in male Arabic immigrants. *Journal of Immigrant Health, 2*(3), 133–144.

Cainkar, L. (2000). Immigration to the United States. In M. Lee (Ed.), *Arab American encyclopedia.* Detroit, MI: Gale.

Council on Islamic Education. (1995). *Teaching about Islam and Muslims in the public school classroom: A handbook for educators* (3rd ed.). Fountain Valley, CA: Author.

Dwairy, M. (2006). *Culturally sensitive counseling and psychotherapy: Working with Arabic and Muslim clients.* New York: Teachers College Press.

Kasem, C. (2005). *Arab Americans: Making a difference.* Washington, DC: Arab American Institute Foundation. Retrieved from http://aai.3cdn.net/eb843914472c84a043_efm6ibdbq.pdf

Nassar-McMillan, S. C. (in press). *Counseling Arab Americans.* Boston: Houghton Mifflin/Lahaska Press.

Samhan, H. H. (2001). Arab Americans. In *Grolier multimedia encyclopedia.* Grolier Inc. Retrieved from http://gme.grolier.com

Shaheen, J. G. (1997). *Arab and Muslim stereotyping in American popular culture.* Washington, DC: Center for Muslim-Christian Understanding.

Smith, H. (1991). *The world's religions: Our great wisdom traditions* (Rev. ed.). San Francisco: HarperCollins. (Original work published 1958)

Web Sites

Arab American Institute: http://www.aaiusa.org

ARREDONDO, PATRICIA (1945–)

Patricia Arredondo, born July 17, 1945, is a nationally acclaimed Latina psychologist who has achieved prominence through her work on multicultural counseling competencies. Additionally, she is an international leader in the areas of counseling, counseling psychology, and psychology and is the founder of Empowerment Workshops, Incorporated, a consulting company that focuses on issues of diversity as they relate to the workplace. Through her research, outreach, and leadership, she has guided and inspired a generation of counselors and psychologists to examine what it means to be culturally competent to work with diverse populations. As someone who has negotiated several tensions in the field of mental health (e.g., counseling vs. counseling psychology, ethnic minority psychology vs. psychology), Arredondo serves as a visionary leader and role model for all mental health professionals.

Arredondo, a Mexican American, grew up in Loraine, Ohio, a town with a small Latino/a population at the time. Arredondo was a second-generation American on her father's side and third generation on her mother's side. Her grandmother was a Zapotec Indian from Oaxaca, Mexico, who later worked as a laborer at the steel mills in the small town near Cleveland, Ohio. The experiences of her family in the United States inspired and informed Arredondo in her work. Arredondo received her undergraduate degree in Spanish and journalism from Kent State University, received her master's in counseling from Boston College, and was the first in her extended family to receive her doctorate in counseling psychology (from Boston University). She began her career as an assistant professor in counseling psychology at Boston University, where she found her academic competence questioned; some suspected that she was hired to be a token woman and ethnic minority in her department. Arredondo left Boston University in 1985 to launch a career as the founder and president of Empowerment Workshops, Incorporated, a consulting company based in Boston.

Through her work as the founder and president of Empowerment Workshops, Arredondo took on the roles of entrepreneur, psychologist in private practice, and organizational consultant. She worked with a variety of organizations providing a range of services, including training workshops and diversity initiatives with assessments, management consultations, and management training. Arredondo's consulting company focused on assessing workplace culture, addressing barriers to workplace diversity, and offering business strategies to increase workplace diversity. Through Empowerment Workshops Arredondo reported that she gained a sense of personal and professional success.

Arredondo pioneered the use of the dimensions of personal identity model in her consulting work (see Figure 1). The model partitions identity into three dimensions: A, B, and C. The A dimensions include the following: age/generational status, culture, ethnicity, gender, language, physical/mental status, race, sexual orientation, and social class. These dimensions can have positive and negative valences, which impact self-concept, self-esteem, and empowerment, and they are the least changeable. The B dimensions are less visible and are developmental in nature: They include educational background, geographic location, hobbies/recreation, healthcare practices/beliefs, religion/spirituality, military experience, relationship status, and work experience. The C dimensions emphasize historical contexts and external forces that individuals and families must deal with. The C dimensions are personal/familial/historical, eras/events, and sociopolitical forces. Through the use of this model counselors can conceptualize clients in context and

"A" Dimensions
- Age
- Culture
- Ethnicity
- Gender
- Language
- Physical/Mental Well Being
- Race
- Sexual Orientation
- Social Class

"B" Dimensions
- Education Background
- Geographic Location
- Hobbies/Recreational
- Health Care Practices/Beliefs
- Religion/Spirituality
- Military Experience
- Relationship Status
- Work Experience

"C" Dimensions Historical Moments/Eras

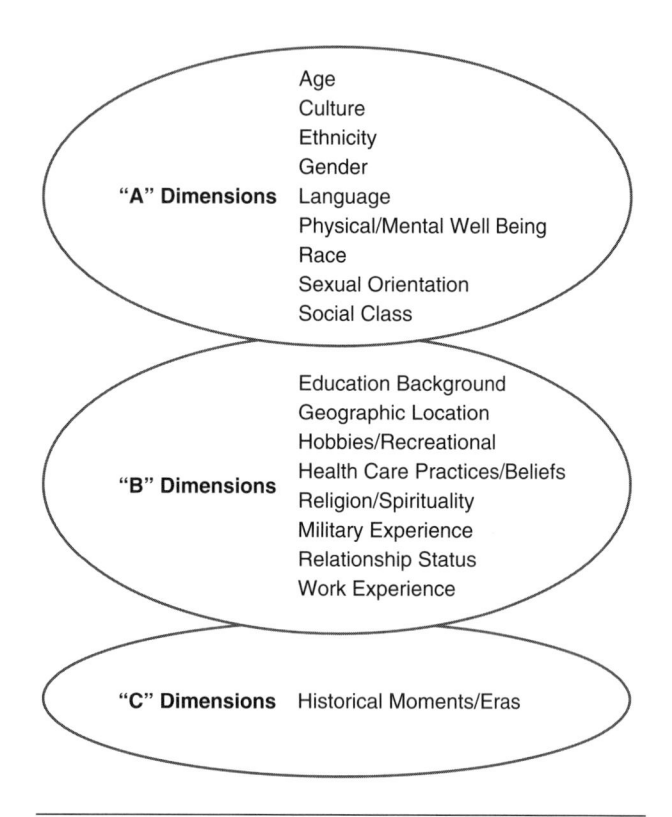

Figure 1 Dimensions of personal identity

Source: © Patricia Arredondo. Used with permission.

focus their interventions on specific dimensions. There is some emerging empirical support in the research literature for the use of the model, and the model has been adapted for use with specific populations (e.g., Latinos/as).

A highlight of her work was presenting her first book on diversity management to her parents, which Arredondo dedicated to them. In 1999, after several years with Empowerment Workshops, she returned to academia at Arizona State University (ASU) in the Department of Counseling and Counseling Psychology. At ASU she had to confront the challenge of navigating a new social network and once again having to prove her competence. Arredondo was able to continue her pattern of success and was tenured and promoted to the rank of full professor. In 2006 she became the Deputy Vice President and University Dean for Student Affairs at ASU.

Arredondo provided national professional leadership through being the first Latina president of the American Counseling Association (ACA) and the Association for Multicultural Counseling and Development, president of the Society for the Psychological Study of Ethnic Minority Issues (Division 45 of the American Psychological Association [APA]), and founding president of the National Latina/o Psychological Association. She served as chair of the Board for the Advancement of Psychology in the Public Interest of APA, cochair of the Executive Committee of the Latino Professional Network, chair of the ACA Publications committee, president of the Chicano Faculty and Staff Association of ASU, cochair of the Latino Professional Network, and member of the Board of Directors for the People of Color Network in Phoenix, Arizona.

Arredondo is best known for her work in creating, operationalizing, and advocating for the adoption of the multicultural counseling competencies. She has played a crucial role in bringing multiculturalism and culturally competent counseling to the forefront of the profession. Arredondo has promoted counselor awareness of their own cultural values and biases, counselor awareness of the client's worldview, and use of culturally appropriate intervention strategies. The multicultural counseling competencies assert that culture is core to everyone's (not just racial/ethnic minorities') life experiences. The competencies state that in human interactions there are many personal dimensions of identity to consider, including different manifestations of culture based on varying historic, ethnic, economic, and other forms of diversity. Beginning with a seminal article in 1992, Arredondo has provided leadership in the operationalization of the multicultural competencies and the adoption of the multicultural competencies and guidelines by various professional groups, including the ACA and the APA. Arredondo's work has helped to make counseling and counseling psychology relevant and responsive to an increasingly diverse and global workplace.

Arredondo has received several major recognitions, including being named a fellow of APA in Divisions 17 (the Society of Counseling Psychology) and 45 and receiving the Samuel H. Johnson Memorial Award from the Association for Multicultural Counseling and Development, the Distinguished Professional Service Award from ACA's Association for Counselor Education and Supervision, the Kitty Cole Human Rights Award from ACA, and the inaugural Distinguished Professional Career Award from the National Latina/o Psychological Association. In recognition of her lifetime contributions to the profession of counseling, Arredondo was designated a "living legend" by ACA in 2004. In addition, Arredondo was awarded an Honorary Doctorate of Humane Letters from the University of San Diego for her multicultural leadership.

Arredondo has consistently been a pioneer in terms of being an ethnic minority and woman who has broken through barriers and achieved power, prestige, and influence in the business and academic worlds. For example, in 2006 she became the highest-ranking Latina in senior administration at ASU. Although in her career she has often been the "first" woman or Latina to achieve distinctions or take on leadership roles, she has made sure that others have followed behind her; thus, her career has been consistent with her empowerment mission and an example of how culture can be the source of personal power in a career.

Edward A. Delgado-Romero and Stephanie Clouse

See also Counseling Psychology, History of (v1); Multicultural Counseling (v3); Multicultural Counseling Competence (v3); National Latina/o Psychological Association (v3); Society for the Psychological Study of Ethnic Minority Issues (v3); Tokenism (v3)

Further Readings

Arredondo, P. (1999). Multicultural counseling competencies as tools to address racism and oppression. *Journal of Counseling & Development, 77,* 102–108.

Arredondo, P. (2002). Mujeres Latinas—santas y marquesas. *Cultural Diversity & Ethnic Minority Psychology, 8,* 1–12.

Arredondo, P., Toporek, R., Brown, S. P., Jones, J., Locke, D. C., Sanchez, J., et al. (1996). Operationalization of the multicultural counseling competencies. *Journal of Multicultural Counseling and Development, 24,* 42–78.

Sue, D. W., Arredondo, P., & McDavis, R. (1992). Multicultural competencies and standards: A call to the profession. *Journal of Counseling & Development, 70,* 477–486.

Asian American Psychological Association

The Asian American Psychological Association (AAPA) is a national organization dedicated to the advancement of Asian American psychology and advocacy for Asian American communities and their psychological well-being. Its advocacy efforts include the promotion of culturally responsive mental health services for Asian and Asian American communities, the advancement and dissemination of psychological research on Asian Americans, the education and training of Asian American mental health service providers, the development of culturally appropriate mental health policies, and the establishment of professional collaborations and networks within the field of mental health. Founded in December 1972 in the San Francisco Bay Area, the AAPA has grown from a local organization with 10 regular members to a national organization of approximately 600 members in 2006. Parallel to their growth in the United States, Asian Americans constitute approximately 4% to 5% of the doctorates awarded in psychology, according to the National Science Foundation.

Despite the AAPA's contemporary origins, its formation occurred within a historical context of discrimination and toward Asian Americans within the United States. Since the arrival of Chinese immigrants in the United States in the mid-1800s, subsequent groups of Asian immigrants from a variety of ethnic groups have encountered strikingly similar patterns of individual, institutional, and cultural forms of racism. Historically, Asian Americans have been the targets of numerous anti-immigration, anti-naturalization, and anti-miscegenation laws. Currently, Asian Americans, despite their diverse ethnic origins and histories, continue to be treated as a homogeneous community and stereotyped as a "model minority" (i.e., presumably a uniformly successful racial group in terms of educational and economic achievement) and "perpetual foreigners" (i.e., a racial group of untrustworthy outsiders). Moreover, Asian Americans continue to be the targets of modern-day forms of racism ranging from homicide and physical assaults to glass ceiling barriers in the workplace to implicit quotas within higher education. Recognizing this shared history of discrimination and inspired by the larger civil rights and antiwar movements, predominantly Japanese American and Chinese American activists coined the term *Asian American* in the late 1960s to unite the various Asian ethnic groups in recognition of their shared experiences. More importantly, Asian American activists across the nation formed a range of organizations to challenge racial inequities in areas such as physical and mental health, education, and politics. Within this context, AAPA was formed in recognition of the neglect of Asian American issues within psychology and the sense of isolation among Asian American mental health professionals.

The cofounders of AAPA were two brothers, Derald Wing Sue and Stanley Sue. Both men recognized their own lack of training in working with Asian and Asian American communities and the lack of a professional network for mental health service providers. As a result, the two brothers began to organize informal gatherings to discuss Asian American issues and their roles as Asian American clinicians and scholars. D. W. Sue was chosen to be the first president of AAPA out of respect for his status as the older brother, and S. Sue was elected as secretary. In the initial days of AAPA with so few Asian American psychologists, many members of the organization were social workers, counselors, educators, and other allied health and mental health professionals. Additionally, interdisciplinary alliances with fields such as Asian American studies and with community leaders were key to the initial formation of AAPA. Indeed, one of the seminal papers in the field of Asian American psychology, S. Sue and D. W. Sue's "Chinese American Personality and Mental Health" was published in 1971 in *Amerasia Journal*, the first Asian American studies journal. At an organizational level, AAPA drew inspiration from the newly formed Association of Black Psychologists, which was founded in 1968, also in San Francisco. In particular, the activism of organizations such as the Association of Black Psychologists and academic disciplines such as ethnic studies inspired AAPA to strive for organizational and systemic transformation within the field of psychology.

AAPA has been involved at a national level in advocating for greater awareness of both Asian Americans and the issues that affect their psychological well-being. For instance, AAPA has been involved with ensuring the accurate representation of Asian Americans in the U.S. Census and in advocating against English-only language initiatives. Additionally, AAPA leaders have advocated for Asian American issues before President Carter's Commission on Mental Health, President Clinton's Race Advisory Board, President George W. Bush's New Freedom Commission on Mental Health, as well as authoring portions of the supplement to the Surgeon General's Report on Mental Health. Within psychology, AAPA and its members have been instrumental in fostering the recognition of Asian American issues within the field of psychology in general and in professional organizations such as the American Psychological Association (APA) and the National Institute of Mental Health (NIMH). Within APA, AAPA has worked toward the inclusion of Asian Americans at all levels of APA governance, the formation of the Board of Ethnic Minority Affairs and the Office of Ethnic Minority Affairs, and the inclusion of Asian Americans in editorial positions and journal review boards. As a result of this emphasis on leadership development, Asian Americans have been elected to numerous governance boards, committees, task forces, and division leadership positions within APA. Indeed, Richard Suinn, an early AAPA member, was elected as the first Asian American president of APA. Both Suinn and Alice Chang served on APA's board of directors. Moreover, Christine Iijima Hall, the first female president of AAPA, also served as the director of APA's Office of Ethnic Minority Affairs. Currently, AAPA is a member of the Council of National Psychological Associations for the Advancement of Ethnic Minority Interests, composed of all the national ethnic minority psychological organizations, and an observer on APA's Council of Representatives.

Within NIMH, AAPA has been effective in advocating for Asian American issues since its inception. In particular, the support of K. Patrick Okura, an executive assistant to the director of NIMH and an early member of AAPA's board of directors, was instrumental to AAPA's visibility. Okura organized the first Asian American mental health conference in 1972 and was vital in securing NIMH funding for the National Asian American Psychology Training Conference in 1976 under the leadership of Robert Chin and S. Sue. In 1988, the NIMH also provided funding for the National Research Center on Asian American Mental Health, with S. Sue as its first director. Additionally, Okura, along with his wife, Lily, established the Okura Mental Health Leadership Foundation with the reparations money that they received for their internment during World War II. The foundation provides leadership development opportunities to emerging Asian American mental health professionals from a variety of disciplines.

AAPA is led by an executive committee selected from its membership. The president, vice president, secretary-historian, president-elect, past president, and a four-member board of directors are all elected for 2-year terms. One member of the board is designated as a student representative. Additionally, the following officers are appointed positions: membership, communications, financial affairs, and editor of the newsletter. A central focus of AAPA's leadership is hosting a national convention on the day before the

APA convention. The convention has served as an integral event for the dissemination of the latest research and best practices within the field, mentorship across all levels of AAPA membership, and the recognition of the achievements of its members. AAPA publishes a newsletter, the *Asian American Psychologist,* three times a year to communicate with its membership about events, issues, and position announcements. AAPA also maintains an active Listserv, open to all individuals who are interested in Asian American psychology, as well as a Web site. The Web site provides information about AAPA, its activities, resources for mental health professionals, and access to online forums on a variety of research and practice-oriented topics.

Currently, AAPA also has two divisions that address issues specific to segments of the professional community: the Division on Women (DoW) and the Division of Students (DoS). The DoW was founded in 1995 under the leadership of Alice Chang. The DoW provides a forum for collaboration and mentorship among Asian American women within the field and provides a platform for the advocacy of women's issues. Similarly, the DoS was founded in 2006 by a cohort of students under the leadership of Szu-Hui Lee to give voice to, and in recognition of, the large student community within AAPA.

Alvin N. Alvarez

See also Asian Americans (v3); Civil Rights (v3); Sue, Derald Wing: Contributions to Multicultural Psychology and Counseling (v3); Sue, Stanley (v3)

Further Readings

Leong, F. T. L. (1995). *A brief history of Asian American psychology, Vol. 1.* San Francisco: Asian American Psychological Association.

Leong, F. T. L., & Gupta, A. (in press). History and evolution of Asian American psychology. In N. Tewari & A. Alvarez (Eds.), *Asian American psychology: Current perspectives.* Mahwah, NJ: Lawrence Erlbaum.

Munsey, C. (2006). A family for Asian psychologists. *American Psychologist, 37*(2), 60–62.

Web Sites

Asian American Psychological Association: http://www.aapaonline.org

ASIAN AMERICANS

Asian Americans are Americans of Asian descent. Based on the U.S. Census report, there are approximately 14.0 million U.S. residents who identified themselves as Asians. Heterogeneity is particularly important to address when it comes to a group such as Asian Americans, given that this population comprises approximately 43 different ethnic groups with more than 100 languages and dialects represented. According to the recent Census, 2.3 million individuals speak Chinese at home, the second most widely used non-English language in the United States. Immigration history and status are also diverse within this group: 8.7 million U.S. residents are born in Asia, and 25% of the nation's total foreign-born population and 52% of foreign-born Asians are naturalized U.S. citizens. The median household income for Asians in 2004 was $57,518, the highest among all race groups. Diversity of income within the Asian population was also evident. For example, median household income for Asian Indians was $68,771 and $45,980 for Vietnamese. The poverty rate for Asians was 9.8%. Asians have the highest proportion of college graduates of any race or ethnic group in the United States, with 49% of individuals ages 25 and older holding a bachelor's degree or higher level of education, 87% of individuals with high school diplomas, and 20% with an advanced degree (e.g., master's, Ph.D., M.D., or J.D.). Sixty percent of Asian households consist of a married-couple family. The projected number of U.S. residents who will identify themselves as Asian in 2050 is 33.4 million, 8% of the total projected U.S. population.

Counseling psychologists must consider the cultural context of the individuals and the cultural lens from which they view themselves and the world. Understanding the worldviews of Asian Americans from the cultural perspective is critical for an accurate understanding and assessment of how Asian Americans may respond to counseling and psychotherapy. Without accounting for the differences that exist within Asian American ethnic subgroups, it is inevitable that there will be errors of omission, that is, failures to account for culture, ethnicity, or cultural differences, as well as making false generalizations of individuals within a given culture. In this entry, key aspects of the Asian cultural perspective are highlighted. Systematic and practical barriers that impede service utilization and compromise service effectiveness as well as ways of overcoming those barriers through culturally responsive services are outlined. Recommendations for counseling Asian Americans are presented throughout this entry.

Client Variables Within the Asian Cultural Context

Cultural Values and Worldview

Asian American worldview emphasizes humility, modesty, treating oneself strictly while treating others more leniently, obligation to family, conformity, obedience, and subordination to authority. This cultural context also values familial relations, interpersonal harmony versus honesty emphasis, role hierarchy versus egalitarianism, and self-restraint versus self-disclosure.

Awareness of these values sheds light on why research and clinical findings have shown Asian Americans to exhibit greater respect for counselors, preference for a counselor who is an authority but is not authoritarian, tendency to exhibit lower levels of verbal and emotional expressiveness, preference for directive counseling styles, and crisis-oriented, brief, and solution-oriented approaches rather than insight and growth-oriented approaches. Asian Americans are likely to find difficulty with the Western model of counseling and psychotherapy, which is filled with ambiguity by design and typically conducted as an unstructured process. For Asian Americans who tend to be less tolerant of ambiguity, the mismatch with insight-oriented psychotherapy may account for the early termination and the underutilization rates that exist. Similarly, Asian cultural values of reserve, restraint of strong feelings, and subtleness in approaching problems may come into conflict with the Western model of counseling and psychotherapy, which expects clients to exhibit openness, psychological mindedness, and assertiveness.

An example of error of omission leading to false generalizations and conclusions about Asian Americans can be found in career counseling. Asian Americans report significantly high parental expectations and involvement when making career decisions and are likely to be influenced by their families. From a Western cultural worldview the inclusion of parental expectations and wishes may be interpreted as being immature and maladaptive, whereas from an Asian cultural perspective it would be aligned with the cultural norms and values. It is important to know the person being helped, understand his or her cultural context, and use his or her cultural worldview rather than other worldviews to prevent misunderstandings and inappropriate services.

Family

Family plays a central role in the mental health of Asian Americans. Families not only have the potential of facilitating mental health, but they can also serve as potential mental health stressors. Immigrant families may face difficulties with social isolation, adjustment difficulties, and cultural and language barriers, and cultural and language barriers may contribute to parent–child conflicts. Characteristics of immigrant families include a husband–wife dyad, families with dependent children, families with adult children, aging parents, split households, and reunifications, all of which render unique adjustment and relational concerns. Parenting styles also impact the life experiences of Asian Americans. Studies have found that authoritative parenting styles and the number of years lived in the United States are predictive of higher academic competence. Authoritarian and permissive parenting styles are predictive of lower self-reliance, whereas number of years lived in the United States is related to higher self-reliance. Family constancy and equilibrium, duty, obligation, and appearance of harmonious relations are important. Whereas Asian families emphasize connectedness of the family, the Western worldview prioritizes separateness and clear boundaries in relationships, individuality, and autonomy. Therefore, counselors should note that the preferred direction of change may be toward a process of integration rather than differentiation.

Acculturation

Acculturation involves a minority individual's behavioral, cultural, and social adaptations that take place as a result of contact between the individual's ethnic society and the host dominant society. Experiences of culture conflicts are inevitable during this process, resulting in mental health issues and interpersonal conflicts. Asian Americans are often caught between the Western worldviews and the traditional cultural values as they attempt to negotiate between the two. As Asian Americans became exposed to Western influence via the schools, mass media, and their peers, intergenerational conflicts often result within family units. Studies have found that Asian American women tend to acculturate faster than their male counterparts. One way that Asian Americans attempt to resolve the cultural conflicts generated by the acculturation process is by developing a sense of ethnic identity to their heritage culture.

Sue and Sue have developed a conceptual scheme for understanding how Asian Americans adjust to these conflicts. They observed that Asian Americans exhibited three distinct ways of resolving the culture conflicts experienced. First of all, there is *the traditionalist* who remains loyal to his or her own ethnic group by retaining traditional Asian values and living up to expectations of the family. Second, there is *the marginal person* who becomes over-Westernized by rejecting traditional Asian values and whose pride and self-worth are defined by the ability to acculturate into White society. The third way of resolving cultural conflict is the *Asian American,* who is also rebelling against parental authority but at the same time is attempting to integrate his or her bicultural elements into a new identity by reconciling viable aspects of his or her heritage with the present situation.

It has been suggested that an Asian American's level of acculturation may influence his or her response to both therapy process and outcome. It also is important for clinicians to be cognizant that acculturation also plays an important role in the career development of Asian Americans. For example, a high level of acculturation had been found to be positively related to job satisfaction and negatively related to occupational stress and strain. There is a wide research and clinical consensus that there is a significant relationship between levels of acculturation and attitudes toward seeking professional psychological help. More specifically, the more acculturated Asian Americans are, the more likely it is they will seek professional psychologist help. The less acculturated they are, the more likely it is they will seek help from community elders, religious leaders and communities, and student organizations. Individuals who are most acculturated are most likely to recognize the need for professional psychological help because they are most tolerant of the stigmas often associated with seeking psychological assistance.

Help-Seeking Attitudes

Asian Americans have shown patterns of underutilization of health services. Those that do make use of mental health services have shown significant dropout rate. As mentioned earlier, acculturation is found to account for ethnic differences in help-seeking behaviors of Asian American students. Those with a high acculturation level are more willing to seek help than those who are less acculturated. Levels of acculturation can also impact the attitudes held by Asian Americans toward mental health services. For example, most acculturated individuals are likely to recognize need for professional psychological help, more tolerant of stigmas, and more open to discuss problems with a psychologist than individuals who are not acculturated.

Underutilization can also be explained by the stigmas that are often attached to seeking professional psychological services by the Asian community. There are correlations found between Asian Americans' levels of acculturation and stigma tolerance and their confidence in mental health practitioners. In some cultures, there is not a cultural analogy to psychological therapy; therefore, utilization of mental health services may not be viewed as a treatment option. Stigmas and lack of understanding also account for the lower frequencies of self-referrals. In response, efforts have been placed on how to minimize premature termination among Asian American clients by accounting for cultural values, ethnocentrism and the cultural uniformity myth, cultural attitudes and beliefs, styles of interpersonal communication, and cultural determinants of the nature of interpersonal relations.

Psychological Distress and Coping Mechanisms

The prevalence of mental health problems among Asian Americans is noteworthy despite the stereotype of being the "model minority." Much literature and research attention has been paid to the unique needs and experiences of Asian Americans. The cultural context helps practitioners to understand the experiences and the expression of symptoms of distress. For Asian Americans, there may be a tendency to replace psychological symptoms with somatic ones. This tendency to somaticize may extend beyond the diagnosis stage to influence the actual therapy process itself. Failure to recognize this client characteristic among Asian Americans may result in both diagnostic and therapeutic errors. Cultural experience of Asian Americans is further contextualized by understanding their ethnic identity. Asian Americans' experience with racism and discrimination should also be taken into consideration in the therapy process. Immigration experiences and acculturative stress have been found to have predictive effects on mental health. Examining within-group differences of immigration status (e.g., international, permanent residents, and naturalized citizens) while taking into account clients' immigration history will further contextualize the life experiences of the individual Asian American client.

Asian Americans tend to endorse coping sources and practices that emphasize talking with familial and social relations rather than professionals such as counselors and doctors. In one study, among the ethnic groups examined (Chinese, Korean, Filipino, and Indian), Korean Americans were found to be more likely to cope with problems by engaging in religious activities. Indigenous coping resources such as traditional folk healers, spiritual identifications, and religious practices such as Buddhism are support resources that Asian Americans utilize. Social support is also an instrumental tool for coping among Asian Americans. Social support, including friends, family, and even international student offices, has been found to provide buffering effects on the mental health issues faced by Asian Americans. Social support variables have also shown to be predictive of academic persistence.

Barriers to Asian Americans Using Counseling Services

Cultural differences in mental health concepts, idioms of distress, stigmatization of the mentally ill and mental health service use, and preference for alternate coping strategies may contribute to the underutilization of psychological services by diverse Asian American groups. Cultural values of self-reliance and emotional self-restraint explain why Asian Americans prefer to work out issues independently. Strong stigmatization of the mentally ill and mental health service use accounts for why Asian Americans are more likely to seek support from family and friends than reaching out to professional service providers. Mainstream mental health services being inaccessible or culturally irresponsive to the needs of Asian communities continue to be barriers to Asian Americans seeking services. Structural barriers include lack of knowledge of service availability, time constraints, distance, cost of treatment and lack of financial resources, access to transportation, and English-language proficiency. Practical barriers such as cost, time, and language accessibility have been shown to pose more of a problem for less-acculturated individuals, who must learn to navigate an entirely new health care system while also adjusting to life in a new culture.

Counselor's lack of culture-specific knowledge about Asian Americans may act as a barrier to effective counseling, resulting in Asian American clients not receiving appropriate care. Misdiagnosis frequently occurs, and the existence of culture-bound syndromes points to a lack of precise correspondence between indigenous labels and established diagnostic categories. Counselors should view clients on both macro and micro levels while maintaining cultural sensitivity. Assuming homogeneity among Asian Americans and falling prey to stereotypes would compromise the therapeutic process. It is theorized that counselors' bias toward Asian Americans and other minorities comes from at least two sources: their own cultural and personal backgrounds and their professional training. When counselors' cultural background and personal characteristics are in contrast to those of Asian Americans, there is potential for cultural misunderstandings. In addition, the cultural bias of counselors toward minority groups in general can operate against Asian Americans in particular.

The professional training received by counselors can be another source of bias in working with Asian Americans. Training bias tends to operate in the form of using traditional psychotherapeutic procedures acquired from training with culturally different clients, such as Asian Americans, without first evaluating if those procedures would be culturally appropriate. Given that social and cultural variables affect Asian Americans' help-seeking behaviors, experiences of distress, manifestation of symptoms, and therapeutic process and outcome, it is important that training curriculum place emphasis on these variables as clinicians learn to implement their learning into care of Asian American clients.

Most counselors trained with Western models of psychotherapy possess certain characteristics and assumptions inherent in these models that may conflict with the cultural background of Asian Americans and thus serve as barriers to effective therapy or counseling. The major characteristics of Western models include (a) language variables, such as the use of standard English; (b) class-bound values, such as strict adherence to time schedule and an unstructured approach to problems; and (c) culture-bound values, such as emphasis on the individual (as opposed to the group or family) and verbal and emotional expressiveness. In light of some of the characteristics of Asian Americans already reviewed (e.g., intolerance of ambiguity), counselors using a Western approach with Asian American clients may run into a considerable amount of resistance. The universal applicability of Western approaches to psychotherapy and mental health services has been challenged by several investigators, and some investigators have begun developing training models that are intended to be sensitive to the Asian American cultural background and experiences.

Overcoming Barriers Through Culturally Responsive Services

Sue proposed a number of solutions to account for the barriers to receiving effective psychological services. His recommendations include (a) augmenting existing services, (b) establishing parallel or ethnic-specific services programs, and (c) creating nonparallel programs that are culturally tailored to a particular group. Many changes have taken place, including the implementation of these suggestions in ethnically dense communities.

One implementation is to provide racial/ethnic client and therapist matching within the existing public mental health system. Providing clients with a therapist of his or her same racial/ethnic background has increased some service utilization by Asian American clients. Ethnic match, language match, or both, are particularly important for Asians who did not speak English as a primary language. Ethnic and language matches are found to be associated with lower rates of premature termination and greater number of sessions. Clinical and research data show that ethnic/racial matching may have important effects in increasing the utilization of mental health services by Asian Americans. Some research shows that Asian Americans who were receiving mainstream services but were ethnically matched with their therapist returned more often than their unmatched counterparts. This approach has proven to be an effective way to augment existing services.

Ethnic-specific mental health services (ESS) is another response to Sue's call for action. The emergence of ESS involves modifications on the systemic level. Rather than just augmenting existing services, ESS is designed to improve the cultural fit of service offerings and the clients served. ESS programs are designed to address cultural barriers faced by the specific ethnic groups they treat. For example, ESS programs are frequently located within ethnic enclaves with extended service hours to accommodate transportation or work hour conflicts. ESS programs also work cooperatively with family members, indigenous healers, and community elders, which is rare within the existing public mental health system. Extensive case management services are also provided to address unique social service needs of immigrants. Mental health services may also be integrated with primary care to capitalize on the preference for integrating health and mental health treatments. Recent studies provide preliminary evidence that ESS programs are more effective than mainstream programs. Asian Americans attending ESS programs had a higher rate of return after the first session and attended a greater number of treatment sessions, even if there was no ethnic matching. Studies have found that when psychiatric inpatient units incorporate the systemic-level change of ESS, longer treatment stays and improved referral to follow-up treatment after discharge result. Inpatients are more willing to accept outpatient or residential treatment referrals. Organizational improvements to afford cultural match and/or fit are aimed to enhance service effectiveness, increase service utilization, and result in therapeutic gain to those in need.

Nonparallel programs that are culturally tailored to a particular group are also important. Such programs address the specific cultural concerns and social contexts of a particular ethnic group. Indigenous healing practices are key components to such nonparallel programs. One example of a nonparallel community program is one designed for native Hawaiians, Hale Ola Ho'opakolea. This program incorporates indigenous Native Hawaiian therapies to assist clients in overcoming their concerns. The program has reportedly led to increased mental health service use and has received high client satisfaction ratings. Although it might be difficult to obtain funding support for such innovative programs and reimbursement from insurance companies, there is some preliminary evidence that such programs play an increasingly important role in meeting the service needs of specific populations.

Overall Recommendations for Counseling Asian Americans

When working with any racial/ethnic minority individuals, it is important to consider the cultural context of that individual and the cultural lens from which the individual views himself or herself and the world. Furthermore, service providers must also acknowledge their own cultural biases and learn about the cultures, histories, and values of their Asian clients to determine the appropriateness of their therapeutic approaches and goals. To understand the cultural context and worldview of their clients, service providers should also assess the levels of adherence to Asian cultural values of their Asian American clients. Adherence to Asian cultural values would shed light on the relevance of specific cultural factors impacting therapeutic process and outcome. Service providers who are willing and able to discuss culturally specific and relevant aspects of one's life experiences would certainly highlight the counselors' levels of multicultural competency. Cultural competency on the part of the service provider would result in perceived credibility and positive impact on the therapeutic relationship. Having counselors with similar cultural backgrounds, values, and experiences may also help to foster stronger therapeutic relationships. In essence, counselors should view cultural values held by clients as an avenue for connection, mutual learning, and a window toward a more complete understanding of their clients.

Understanding the cultural context of Asian Americans would also highlight ways to work effectively with Asian American clients. Structured therapeutic interventions and directive approaches, such as cognitive-behavior therapy and problem-focused approaches, are effective, particularly for more traditional Asian American clients. Working collaboratively with clients' families, support networks, and other treatment providers is also important. Similarly, it is important for researchers and practitioners alike to note that although seeking professional help is one resource option for people of Asian descent, not choosing to utilize it does not necessarily mean there are no other, more appropriate coping methods available. Effectiveness of integrating alternative belief systems and healing approaches into service provisions certainly deems continued clinical and research attention.

Finally, it is critical that service providers be aware of the heterogeneity within Asian American groups. Within-group differences include, but are not limited to, ethnic identity, cultural background, degree of acculturation, experiences within the majority culture, circumstances of immigration, family structure, values, social class, and religious affiliation. These aspects of an individual's background and life experiences are essential to the understanding of that individual client. In essence, efforts should be made to prevent the impact of error of omission by honoring the differences that exist within Asian American ethnic subgroups and the influence of cultural context and the worldview of Asian Americans.

Frederick T. L. Leong and Szu-Hui Lee

See also Acculturation (v3); Acculturative Stress (v3); Allocentrism (v3); Barriers to Cross-Cultural Counseling (v3); Career Counseling, Asian Americans (v4); Collectivism (v3); Cultural Values (v3); Discrimination and Oppression (v2); Help-Seeking Behavior (v3); Model Minority Myth (v3); Multicultural Counseling Competence (v3)

Further Readings

Gamst, G., Dana, R. H., Der-Karabetian, A., & Kramer, T. (2001). Asian American mental health clients: Effects of ethnic match and age on global assessment and visitation. *Journal of Mental Health Counseling, 23*(1), 57–71.

Gim, R. H., Atkinson, D. R., & Whiteley, S. (1990). Asian-American acculturation, severity of concerns, and willingness to see a counselor. *Journal of Counseling Psychology, 37*(3), 281–285.

Kim, B. S. K., Atkinson, D. R., & Umemoto, D. (2001). Asian cultural values and the counseling process: Current knowledge and directions for future research. *Counseling Psychologist, 29*(4), 570–603.

Kim, J. M. (2003). Structural family therapy and its implications for the Asian American family. *Family Journal Counseling and Therapy for Couples and Families, 11*(4), 388–392.

Leong, F. T. L., Chang, D. F., & Lee, S. H. (2006). Counseling and psychotherapy with Asian Americans: Process and outcome. In F. T. L. Leong, A. G. Inman, A. Ebreo, L. Yang, L. M. Kinoshita, & M. Fu (Eds.), *Handbook of Asian American psychology* (2nd ed., pp. 429–447). Thousand Oaks, CA: Sage.

Leong, F. T. L., & Lau, A. S. L. (2001). Barriers to providing effective mental health services to Asian Americans. *Mental Health Services Research, 3*(4), 201–214.

Leong, F. T. L. & Lee, S. H. (2006). A cultural accommodation model for cross-cultural psychotherapy: Illustrated with the case of Asian Americans. *Journal of Psychotherapy: Theory, Research, Practice, Training, 43*(4), 410–423.

Sue, D. (1998). The interplay of sociocultural factors on the psychological development of Asians in America. In G. Morten & D. R. Atkinson (Eds.), *Counseling American minorities* (5th ed., pp. 205–213). New York: McGraw-Hill.

Sue, S. (1977). Psychological theory and implications for Asian Americans. *Personnel & Guidance Journal, 55*(7), 381–389.

Takeuchi, D. T., Mokuau, N., & Chun, C. A. (1992). Mental health services for Asian Americans and Pacific Islanders. *Journal of Mental Health Administration, 19*(3), 237–245.

True, R. H. (1990). Psychotherapeutic issues with Asian American women. *Sex Roles, 22*(7–8), 477–486.

Yeh, C., & Wang, Y. W. (2000). Asian American coping attitudes, sources, and practices: Implications for indigenous counseling strategies. *Journal of College Student Development, 41*(1), 94–103.

ASSIMILATION

Contemporary use of the term *assimilation* has involved two processes: (a) the process whereby an individual or a group of diverse ethnic and racial minority or immigrant individuals comes to adopt the beliefs, values, attitudes, and the behaviors of the majority or dominant culture; and (b) the process whereby an individual or group relinquishes the value system of his or her cultural heritage and becomes a member of the dominant society. The early use of the term *assimilation* refers mainly to the process by which people of diverse racial and ethnic backgrounds occupying a common territory came to achieve a cultural solidarity to sustain a national existence. Since the 19th century, the use of *assimilation* has been a political rather than a cultural concept. It has been used to justify selective state-imposed policies aimed at the eradication of minority cultures. As globalization results in ever-expanding trading and political relations, understanding the history and the process of assimilation becomes important as we support multicultural sensitivity and well-being of all cultural groups and individuals.

Historical Background

Sarah Simons in 1901 suggested that the word *assimilation* is rarely or inconsistently used in social science. The concept can be traced back to the first U.S. general treatise on immigration, published in 1848. It recorded that the United States was composed of immigrants from all over the world and that the policy of the United States was to transform everyone into British-like individuals. Scholars later called it Anglo-conformity theory. Although the practice of assimilation can be traced back thousands of years to the ancient conquerors, so well documented in the histories of Europe or Asia, this entry mainly addresses the use of the word *assimilation* in psychology, sociology, and anthropology.

Milton Gordon, in his 1964 book, noted that the early use of the word *assimilation* can be traced to the concept of the melting pot, which was first proposed by the agriculturalist J. Hector St. John Crevecoeur in 1782. In the following century, assimilation became influential in the field of American historical interpretation after Frederick Jackson Turner, in 1893, presented his paper discussing the fusion of Western frontier immigrants into a mixed English group—a new composite of American people. Politicians in the early 20th century maintained that the new types melting into one were already shaped by the American frontier in the process of nation making. The newer immigrants, mainly Southern and Eastern European at the time, were indoctrinated with the Americanism that had been established by earlier arrivals. Sociologists of that era equated assimilation with Americanization. While the concepts of Anglo-conformity and the melting pot dominated 20th-century thoughts, in the mid-1940s the sociologist Ruby Jo Reeves Kennedy studied intermarriage. She found that although intermarriage took place across national lines, there was a strong tendency for marriage to stay confined within three major religious groups, namely, Protestants, Catholics, and Jews. She posited that religion rather than nationality should determine or define assimilation and called it the "triple melting pot" theory of American assimilation.

Assimilation as a Process

Assimilation is consistently treated as a process rather than a result. It is a process that is continuous in nature and varies in degree. It is not a concept that can be dichotomized. Direct contact between an individual or a racial minority group and persons of the majority or dominant culture is required for assimilation to take place. Contacts can also be described as primary and secondary contacts. Primary contact refers to a personal network, including marriage or strong personal friendships, whereas secondary contact refers to the wider range of interactions other than with primary contacts. In general, the more numerous the points of interactions are, especially in the primary contacts, the faster the process of assimilation occurs.

Assimilation also requires both a positive orientation toward and identification with the dominant group on the part of the assimilating individual or group. In addition, assimilation is contingent upon acceptance by the dominant group because becoming a member of the dominant or host society necessitates acceptance by that society. Furthermore, assimilation comprises both internal and external change. It is more than making individuals look alike in appearance, language, or manners, that is, external change. It also involves changes in beliefs, values, and attitudes, that is, internal change. Both internal and external changes form the components of the assimilation process; changing one without the other is only partial assimilation. Other conditions, such as common language, racial and class equality, and religion, all play a significant role in the process of assimilation.

Individual Versus Group Assimilation

Whether assimilation is to be treated as a group process, individual process, or both, has been discussed among scholars. For some, assimilation occurs when one enters into social relations, absorbs meaning generated from the interactions, and passes its significance to others. To these scholars, assimilation occurs at the individual level. Other scholars, such as Sara Simons and Bernard Siegel, restrict their discussions of assimilation to the group level, thereby implying that it is a group process. An example of group assimilation would be the Indian-Anglo of India in the early 1900s. As a group, they collectively identified with British and desired to be assimilated into British. They wore European clothes and regarded England as their home, despite the fact that they had never been there.

The popular position in the literature has treated the concept of assimilation process as an individual or a group phenomenon. Some scholars suggest that for minority groups that continually receive cultural influences from a larger parent cultural group, group assimilation could be difficult or even impossible. An example of this might be the continuing influence of Mexican immigrants in the United States. In such a case, individual rather than group assimilation becomes the norm. It is important to recognize that group isolation does not necessarily dictate group assimilation. Groups may resist being assimilated as a whole or may adopt an antagonistic acculturative attitude that also will affect group assimilation.

Dominant groups have justified segregation, mass expulsion, and even genocide on the grounds that certain groups are inassimilable because of their innate inferiority. For many years, Black Americans were barred from consideration as an assimilable element of the American society, despite the fact that they made up nearly one fifth of the total population at the time of the American Revolution.

In contrast to forced segregation or expulsion, there are also programs designed for forced assimilation. This was the case in Russia where a program was designed to assimilate Jews by getting rid of their communal life at the end of 1950s. Similarly, the governments of the United States and Australia designed programs to force assimilating of their native populations in the 19th and 20th centuries.

Direction and Dominance

The assimilation process has traditionally been regarded as a unidirectional process. It implies that the assimilating individuals or groups are always being pulled toward the dominant culture. The dominant culture serves as an active element, and the assimilating individuals or groups serve as a passive element. Simon, in 1901, proposed three factors that determine the direction of the assimilation process:

1. The relative culture stage of the element involved. Simon proposed that if a culture is perceived to be superior, it is likely to be the dominant culture irrespective of the number of people in that cultural group.

2. The relative mass of the two elements. Although the number of people in a group is not as influential as the perceived superiority of a culture, the number of people in a cultural group is still a determining factor in the direction of the assimilation process.

3. The relative intensity of race-consciousness. That is, the greater the intensity of the assimilating group's racial consciousness, the more resistance is displayed by the assimilating individual or group. This consciousness may be so intense as to prevent all assimilation from taking place. For instance, the intense cultural awareness of the ancient Greeks caused the Roman conqueror to adopt the Greek culture rather than assimilate the Greeks into the Roman culture.

Some scholars also support the view of history that suggests that the majority of nationalities resulted from conquest and assimilation. This leads those thinkers to postulate that conquest changes not only the conquered, the assimilating group, but also the conquerors, the dominant group. This mutually interactive process is usually referred to as *acculturation*. Most scholars maintain that assimilation is a unidirectional process pulling the minority individuals or groups from the minority culture to the dominant culture.

Assimilation and Acculturation

It is almost impossible to study assimilation without considering the process of acculturation. These concepts are often treated as being identical or as stages of one another. The anthropologists and sociologists, who began the study of acculturation, often used these terms interchangeably. In the current literature on intercultural interactions, assimilation and acculturation are seen as separate processes that can be related to one another. Acculturation can be described as a process that involves changes in cultural practices or behaviors as well as social and institutional structural changes among individuals or groups of two or more cultural backgrounds or cultural systems as a result of contacts. It continues for as long as there are culturally different groups in contact. Both assimilation and acculturation are long-term processes that may take years or even generations to change. Sometimes this process may take centuries. They both take place most rapidly and completely in primary social contacts, which include intermarriage and other forms of intense personal relationships.

The process of assimilation differs from the process of acculturation in several important aspects. First, acculturation does not require dominant group acceptance, whereas assimilation does require such acceptance. Second, assimilation requires that the minority group have a positive orientation and identification toward the dominant group. Simply making oneself appear and act like the dominant cultural group does not constitute assimilation. Assimilation requires internal value change; that is, individuals come to be a part of an association, absorb the meaning of the association, and contribute to the correction and improvement of the association. Furthermore, assimilation requires the assimilating individual or group to relinquish the identification with the heritage group and seek identification with the dominant group that results in becoming less distinguishable from them. Acculturation does not require such a unidirectional process. It involves a two-way reciprocal relationship in which the dominant and acculturating groups make changes. Also, one may acculturate but not lose his or her personal heritage.

Whether assimilation is a phase of acculturation or vice versa has also been discussed among scholars. Robert Park, for example, is known for his notion that assimilation is the final stage of a natural progressive, inevitable, and irreversible race relations. He posits that when stabilization is achieved, race relations would assume one of three configurations: (1) a caste system, (2) complete assimilation, or (3) the unassimilated race constituting a permanent racial minority. Milton Gordon further proposed that acculturation is the first stage of assimilation and, although it does not lead to structural assimilation, inevitably produces acculturation. Among anthropologists, as documented in the Social Science Research Council 1953 Summer Seminar, acculturation is commonly treated as a necessary but insufficient condition of assimilation, which is treated as a second type of progressive adjustment. The first type of progressive adjustment is cultural fusion, which refers to a formation of a third sociocultural system through a process of intercultural contacts among two or more autonomous systems.

Other scholars, such as John Berry and his colleagues, advocate for assimilation as a phase of acculturation. They developed a bidimensional model that focuses on the process of group and individual adaptation within pluralistic societies. These two dimensions allow for a fourfold classification and four acculturation strategies. In this model, individuals or groups decide whether to maintain their cultural identity and customs or to engage in and pursue intergroup contacts. Integration occurs when one chooses to engage in intergroup contacts while maintaining one's own cultural identity. Assimilation occurs when one chooses to engage in intergroup contacts while relinquishing one's cultural identity. Separation occurs when one chooses to maintain one's cultural identity and customs while giving up intergroup contacts. When one loses cultural and psychological contacts to both cultures, the result is marginalization. In this model, assimilation is considered a phase of the process of acculturation, and integration is the preferred way to acculturate.

Chun-Chung Choi and Jun-chih Gisela Lin

See also Acculturation (v3); Adaptation (v3); Cultural Accommodation and Negotiation (v3); Cultural Values (v3); Enculturation (v3); Person–Environment Fit (v4); Person–Environment Interactions (v2)

Further Readings

Berry, J. W. (2005). Acculturation: Living successfully in two cultures. *International Journal of Intercultural Relations, 29,* 697–712.

Gordon, M. M. (1964). *Assimilation in American life: The role of race, religion and national origins.* New York: Oxford University Press.

LaFromboise, T., Coleman, H. L. K., & Gerton, J. (1993). Psychological impact of biculturalism: Evidence and theory. *Psychological Bulletin, 114,* 395–412.

Sayegh, L., & Lasry, J. (1993). Immigrants' adaptation in Canada: Assimilation, acculturation, and orthogonal cultural identification. *Canadian Psychology, 34,* 98–109.

Simons, S. E. (1901). Social assimilation. *American Journal of Sociology, 6,* 790–822.

Social Science Research Council. (1954). Acculturation: An exploratory formulation. *American Anthropologist, 56,* 973–1002.

Teske, R. H. C., & Nelson, B. H. (1974). Acculturation and assimilation: A clarification. *American Ethnologist, 1,* 351–367.

ASSOCIATION OF BLACK PSYCHOLOGISTS

The Association of Black Psychologists is a professional organization born out of the need to have issues of mental health and the psychological well-being of persons acknowledging African descent addressed more effectively. In the social context of racism and monocultural hegemony common in the United States, the profession of psychology had not escaped historic bias. The need for a cultural relevance and cultural congruence had not been acknowledged in a meaningful manner. The Association of Black Psychologists is the first organization of ethnic-minority professional psychologists to step forward and demand the American Psychological Association begin to address and better meet the mental health needs of people of color.

The foundation upon which Western psychology, and European American psychology in particular, rests with regard to its capacity to identify, address, and respond appropriately to the mental health needs of persons of African descent, more specifically those whose ancestors' forced labor built the wealth upon which the U.S. economy is built, is quite tenuous. Such a history in the evolution of psychiatry and psychology cannot be ignored because it has a great impact on the mental health and well-being of those African Americans in the society who have been and are reliant on the mental health system, its institutions, and its professionals for meeting their mental health needs.

Further, great consideration must be given to the issue of the training, policies, and practices in place, or not in place, designed to address and overcome the monocultural bias that has characterized the development and delivery of mental health services for nondominant populations. The Association of Black Psychologists would encourage practitioners and researchers to ask themselves the following series of questions: What has been and is the historical relationship between strongly held societal beliefs and professional mental health practices? When did these biased, self-serving, oppressive perspectives change? What has caused or can cause a shift toward greater recognition and appreciation of the full humanity of these people of African descent and their progeny? To what extent are the prevailing societal beliefs and attitudes reflected in current mental health perceptions, policies, and practices?

History

The Association of Black Psychologists was founded in San Francisco in 1968 by a number of Black psychologists from across the country. They united to actively address the serious problems facing Black psychologists and the larger Black community. Guided by the principle of self-determination, these psychologists set about building an institution through which they could address the long neglected needs of Black professionals. Their goal was to have a positive impact upon the mental health of the national Black community and, later, international community by means of planning, programs, services, training, and advocacy. This goal was to be met by pursuing the following objectives: (a) to organize their skills and abilities to influence necessary change, and (b) to address themselves to significant social problems affecting the Black community and other segments of the population whose needs society has not fulfilled.

The Association of Black Psychologists has grown from a handful of concerned professionals into an independent, autonomous organization of over 1,400 members. Its membership now comprises people of color from all over the world.

Mission, Purposes, and Goals

African American psychologists were the first group of ethnic minority professionals to take the courageous step of forming an organization focused on identifying and meeting the mental health needs of persons acknowledging African descent. Articulating a mission to liberate the African mind, illuminate the African spirit, and empower the African character, the Association of Black Psychologists has charted its destiny based on very high goals and ideals. In that regard, it is committed to improving health and mental health, promoting social change toward a more just and sustainable society and world, and advancing African psychology and the capacity of humanity to heal and become holistically sustainable.

The Association of Black Psychologists is committed to solving the plethora of problems confronting Black communities and the communities of other ethnic groups. To accomplish these aims, the association is governed by its board of directors and organized into local chapters. Dedicated to fulfilling its mission, the association performs several functions geared toward the establishment and maintenance of a strong core and critical mass of Black psychologists organized to support and advance research, scholarship, and practice. This agenda has included publishing the *Journal of Black Psychology* and also offering various professional and paraprofessional training programs to address the critical needs of African descent people. Among the organization's other foci are recruiting students to the field, supporting and mentoring faculty in the field, developing and promoting community mental health care programs, articulating and disseminating psychological research and knowledge grounded in the African cultural tradition and cultural frame of reference, and pursuing its mission via all available avenues.

The organizational goals of the association are many and varied, and enhancing the understanding and psychological well-being of people acknowledging African descent in the United States and throughout the world is high among them. This goal is furthered by the promotion of solid, culturally congruent and consistent research methods, strategies, and approaches to the study of Black people, their experiences, and the impact of extended oppression and multigenerational trauma. Requiring the development of theories and constructs consistent with the experience and cultural realities of Black people, the association has been a key forum for the dissemination and proliferation of such knowledge. It has also led to the establishment of guidelines and standards for researching and treating persons acknowledging African descent. A strong international component and network of support systems for Black psychologists has been developed and is being maintained for professionals and students.

The Association of Black Psychologists has also worked to develop policies on the local, state, and national levels to improve mental health outcomes, provide culturally competent services, and support effective human service delivery methods. Much of this work has come about because of the keen awareness of the pervasive racial biases and discriminatory social policies and practices common to U.S. society and evidenced throughout the world, making the association a key force in monitoring and promoting the survival and well-being of members of the racial and ethnic communities it represents. The association works with other organizations sharing its vision and mission to aid in the development and support of institutions geared toward enhancing the psychological, cultural, educational, social, and economic health of persons acknowledging African descent and their communities.

Linda James Myers

See also African Americans (v3); Afrocentricity/Afrocentrism (v3); Black Psychology (v3); Black Racial Identity Development (v3); Career Counseling, African Americans (v4); White, Joseph L. (v3)

Further Readings

Belgrave, F. Z., & Allison, K. W. (2005). *African American Psychology: From Africa to America*. Thousand Oaks, CA: Sage.

Bynum, E. B. (1998). *The African unconscious: Roots of ancient mysticism and modern psychology*. New York: Teachers College Press.

Guthrie, R. (2003). *Even the rat was white: A historical view of psychology* (2nd ed.). Boston: Allyn & Bacon.

Jones, R. L. (Ed.). (2003). *Black psychology* (4th ed.). Hampton, VA: Cobb & Henry.

Web Sites

Association of Black Psychologists: http//www.abpsi.org

ATKINSON, DONALD RAY (1940–2008)

Donald Ray Atkinson (born February 10, 1940, in Union City, Indiana) is best known for his pioneering work in the area of multicultural counseling psychology and his leadership in mentoring doctoral students of color into prominent professional positions in counseling psychology across a career spanning more than 30 years. The story of his life exemplifies the values that he promoted during his career. He grew up on the margins of poverty and served in the military before working his way through school, rearing a family on his own, and becoming one of the most frequently cited scholars in the area of multicultural or cross-cultural counseling.

Early Life

Atkinson spent his childhood in poverty in the midwestern United States, first in Indiana and then in Wisconsin. His family lived in an assortment of apartments, trailer parks, and unfinished garages while his parents worked a variety of different jobs trying to make ends meet. Atkinson was diagnosed with rheumatic fever when he was 15 years old. His only sibling died at an early age from cerebral palsy. After graduating from high school and serving in the U.S. Navy for 2 years, Atkinson moved on to college at Wisconsin State College in La Crosse where he received a B.S. in teacher education in 1964. He was able to attend college only because of a meager life insurance policy paid to his family after his brother died. For a short period of time, he worked as a teacher at a small high school in Menominee Falls, Wisconsin, while he continued his education at the University of Wisconsin–Milwaukee to earn a degree in guidance and counseling in 1966. He later became a guidance counselor at his old high school in Baraboo, Wisconsin. Eventually, Atkinson moved on to pursue his doctorate at the University of Wisconsin–Madison in 1968, where he studied under the tutelage of Marsh Sanborn.

It was during his doctoral studies that Atkinson met his first wife and started a family with the birth of two sons, Jimmy and Robert. Soon, however, Atkinson found himself raising his sons on his own as a single parent after his wife left under the stress of Jimmy Atkinson's severe developmental disability. Following a brief stint at a college counseling center at Moorhead State College, Minnesota, Atkinson moved to the University of California, Santa Barbara (UCSB), in 1972 to become an assistant professor in the counseling psychology program.

Early Career

Atkinson joined Jules Zimmer and Ray E. Hosford to become only the third faculty member in the counseling psychology program at UCSB. Over the course of Atkinson's career, the counseling psychology program at UCSB became one of the most prominent training grounds for multicultural counseling psychology. Although Atkinson was joined by numerous colleagues of considerable prominence, including such psychologists as J. Manuel Casas, Gail Hackett, Tania Israel, Chalmer Thompson, Nolan Zane, Glenn Good, Louise Fitzgerald, Elizabeth Holloway, Patricia Wolleat, Gayla Margolin, Steven Brown, Michael Mahoney, and Larry Beutler, the reputation and achievements of the program in the area of cross-cultural counseling can be substantially attributed to Atkinson's efforts and accomplishments.

During Atkinson's early years at UCSB, the counseling psychology program was not ranked among the top contributors in the field's flagship research outlet, the *Journal of Counseling Psychology* (*JCP*). Later, however, UCSB began to appear among the highest-ranked institutions in *JCP* publications, placing 10th in 1983, 6th in 1994, and 9th in 2000, largely as a consequence of Atkinson's scholarly works. Yet again, he was recently ranked 4th among scholars contributing to the literature on multicultural counseling competencies empirical research over the course of 20 years. Furthermore, Atkinson was ranked 10th in a study of contributions to the *Journal of Multicultural Counseling and Development* from 1985 to 1999, and he was identified as the top-ranked contributor of racial-ethnic minority research in *JCP* from 1988 to 1997.

Over the course of his career, Atkinson published 109 peer-reviewed journal articles, along with three books and 15 book chapters. Nevertheless, he has won only a few awards over the course of his career for his outstanding achievements, in part because he actively avoided the limelight. He achieved fellow status in the Society of Counseling Psychology (Division 17 of the American Psychological Association [APA]), the Society for the Psychological Study of Ethnic Minority Issues (Division 45 of the APA), and the American Psychological Society. In 2000, he was recognized in a Division 17 symposium at the annual APA convention as one of the "Multicultural Scholars of the Millennium." He was recognized in 2001 for his Distinguished Career Contributions to Research by Division 45, and in 2005 he was given a

Presidential Citation and Elder Recognition Medal at the National Multicultural Conference and Summit. In 2006, Atkinson was honored with the Leona Tyler Award by the Society of Counseling Psychology, the society's highest form of recognition.

Major Contributions

Although Atkinson is best known for his contributions in the area of multicultural counseling, his career did not begin on that path. In fact, Atkinson credits his doctoral students for propelling him into the field of study that became his life's commitment. Despite his active efforts to recruit women and students of color into the doctoral training program at UCSB, it was not until his sixth year as a professor there that his first publication in the area of multicultural counseling appeared (his 17th publication overall). Until that time, Atkinson's publications included a combination of topics such as behavior modification, student personnel services, and counselor training. After 1983, however, the vast majority of his scholarship began to focus on multicultural issues and many of his works became seminal to the field.

In 1983, Atkinson published one of his most frequently cited articles in *The Counseling Psychologist,* "Ethnic Similarity in Counseling." In 1993, Atkinson published (with Chalmer Thompson and Sheila Grant) "A Three-Dimensional Model for Counseling Racial/Ethnic Minorities," one of only a few major theories of multicultural counseling. Across time, Atkinson's focus within multicultural counseling began to broaden to diversity issues beyond race and ethnicity. This trend was most noticeable in the publication of his two early books: *Counseling American Minorities* (now in its sixth edition), which focused on race and ethnicity, and *Counseling Diverse Populations,* which focused on gender, sexual orientation, aging, and disability. In this way, Atkinson became one of very few scholars in the field to produce such a broad array of works that exemplify the true meaning of *multi*culturalism.

During one of the more difficult periods in his career, Atkinson often discloses that he contemplated changing the focus of his scholarship in the face of criticism that as a European American, he should not be conducting research about people of color. To this day, he credits Teresa LaFromboise with convincing him to stay the course and continue his line of research. His many graduate students, colleagues, and consumers of his scholarship are grateful that she held sway on that dilemma.

Among his numerous accomplishments during his career as an educator, Atkinson recounts tremendous fulfillment in the number of doctoral advisees he mentored who went on to pursue academic careers in counseling psychology, including but not limited to Bruce Wampold, Michael Furlong, Ruth Gim Chung, Cindy Juntunen, Jose Abreu, Linda Mathews, Susanna Lowe, Bryan Kim, Sheila Grant, and Roger Worthington, many of whom are members of racial and ethnic minority groups. There also were many others, too numerous to mention, who studied under Atkinson's mentorship and went on to make important contributions in careers outside of academic psychology. Beyond his own professional triumphs, Atkinson has been known to express his greatest pride in the accomplishments of his students. He died on January 11, 2008, from pancreatic cancer.

Roger L. Worthington and Bruce E. Wampold

See also Casas, Jesús Manuel (v3); LaFromboise, Teresa Davis (v3); Multicultural Counseling (v3); Tyler, Leona E.: Human Multipotentiality (v2)

Further Readings

Atkinson, D. R. (1983). Ethnic similarity in counseling. *The Counseling Psychologist, 11,* 79–92.

Atkinson, D. R. (2004). *Counseling American minorities* (6th ed.). Boston: McGraw-Hill.

Atkinson, D. R., & Hackett, G. (2004). *Counseling diverse populations* (3rd ed.). Boston: McGraw-Hill.

Atkinson, D. R., Maruyama, M., & Matsui, S. (1978). The effects of counselor race and counseling approach on Asian Americans' perceptions of counselor credibility and utility. *Journal of Counseling Psychology, 25,* 76–83.

Atkinson, D. R., Thompson, C. E., & Grant, S. K. (1993). A three-dimensional model for counseling racial/ethnic minorities. *The Counseling Psychologist, 21,* 257–277.

Atkinson, D. R., Wampold, B. E., & Worthington, R. L. (2007). Our identity: How multiculturalism saved counseling psychology. *The Counseling Psychologist, 35,* 476–486.

Barriers to Cross-Cultural Counseling

When counseling culturally diverse clients, counselors will often encounter many obstacles or barriers. These barriers can stem from the counselor's lack of cultural knowledge to language differences between the counselor and client. Barriers to cross-cultural counseling can negatively influence the counseling relationship as well as the outcome of counseling. The literature has even linked these cultural barriers to the underutilization and premature termination of counseling services by ethnic minorities and low-income persons. An increasing awareness of these barriers has led to changes in counselor preparation and the delivery of counseling services to culturally diverse populations. In this entry, seven barriers to cross-cultural counseling are described.

Lack of Counselor Cultural Self-Awareness

A major barrier to effective cross-cultural counseling is the counselor's lack of cultural self-awareness. Cultural self-awareness refers to the counselor's awareness and acknowledgment of his or her own cultural beliefs, attitudes, and values as well as an awareness of his or her biases and faulty assumptions about other groups. Essentially, a counselor with a heightened sense of cultural self-awareness acknowledges and recognizes when his or her culture is contradictory to a client's culture. When a counselor does not recognize that he or she has biased views and stereotypical beliefs about other groups, he or she will likely provide ineffective counseling services and experience high rates of client dropout. Also, a culturally aware counselor is able to recognize when he or she is conceptualizing a client's case based on prejudiced and/or stereotypical beliefs about a particular group of people.

Lack of Counselor Cultural Knowledge

In many cases, the counselor's lack of cultural knowledge can serve as a barrier to effective cross-cultural counseling. Cultural knowledge includes the counselor's understanding and knowledge of other cultural groups' behaviors, norms, beliefs, and attitudes. Both counselors and clients bring to counseling a set of cultural norms that have been reinforced for long periods of time. These norms then influence the way in which the counselor and client perceive their world, each other, and their approach to counseling. Counselors who are knowledgeable of their clients' cultural preferences and norms are better equipped to make appropriate clinical decisions. For example, in some cultures, passivity rather than assertiveness is revered. A counselor adhering to the Western culture may have great difficulty understanding a Chinese client's unwillingness to "demand" more from others. However, after learning more about the client's culture, the counselor introduces counseling interventions that take into account Chinese cultural norms.

When counselors lack knowledge of varying cultural groups, they will often rely on stereotypes to better understand clients from different cultural backgrounds. Stereotypes are often negative, based on faulty perceptions, and are of unspecified validity. Many argue, however, that some stereotypes or generalizations can be helpful in the process of learning to understand other cultures. African Americans are an example of an entire ethnic minority group that has been subject to historical and contemporary stereotyping. African American stereotypes have ranged from portrayals of African Americans being lazy and intellectually inferior to being violent and poor. For example, a White career counselor might assume that an African American client is not able to pay for a series of career-exploration courses. The counselor, therefore, fails to share information about the workshops with the African American client but she shares the information with a White client. Her faulty assumption is based on the stereotype that all African Americans are poor, from low-income backgrounds, or both.

Counselors are often ineffective with culturally diverse clients because they view cultural differences as deficits rather than strengths. In addition, counselors will often neglect to discuss a client's problems in the context of current social issues facing the client. Counseling professionals create barriers in counseling when they do not consider clients' problems in the context of educational, economic, social, political, legal, and cultural systems. The deficit perspective, coupled with a neglect to address social contextual issues, can hinder the cross-cultural counseling process.

Because of the vast number of cultures that clients may ascribe to, it is impossible for a counselor or therapist to know everything about every culture. Working together with a counselor, healer, or helper from an unknown culture can vastly improve a counselor's ability to be effective and the probability of success in implementing appropriate interventions.

Lack of Culturally Appropriate Counseling Skills

Distinctions can be made between general counseling skills, which may include active listening, empathy, and illustrating genuineness, and the specific skills that are central to working with a client who is culturally different. Counselors who lack multicultural counseling skills are at risk of providing culturally insensitive counseling. Examples of skill requirements specific to cultural competency are (a) determining effective ways to communicate with a client that may use a different style of thinking, information processing, and communication; (b) discussing race and racial differences early in the counseling process; (c) engaging in multiple verbal and nonverbal helping responses, recognizing responses that may be appropriate or inappropriate within a cultural context; (d) using resources outside of the field of psychology, such as traditional cultural healers; and (e) modifying conventional forms of treatment to be responsive to the cultural needs of the client. Some counseling professionals have indicated that there is no simple methodology or approach that can easily define the "how-to" in the counseling session with the culturally diverse client. One of the greatest dilemmas in the area of cultural competency is determining what counseling strategies and interventions are most effective with different cultural groups.

Language Barriers

Language may be a barrier in the cross-cultural counseling process. Language differences in counseling can lead to miscommunications, misdiagnoses, and misinterpretations. A lack of language or communication skills often emerges as a major stressor for clients who are bilingual, immigrant, or both. It is also important to consider immigrant clients' level of acculturation, which might be linked to their command of their native and English languages. Bilingual clients may have the ability to express themselves in English in a rudimentary way but may need to use their native language to discuss more emotional subjects. Because of language barriers, many immigrants will avoid counseling services for fear of being unable to communicate with counselors. Likewise, counselors may avoid immigrant clients because the language barrier frustrates them.

Because counseling is a process of interpersonal interaction, communication is paramount to the counseling process. Both parties in counseling interpret the information transmitted between them, and if interpreted inaccurately, the counseling process and outcomes can be negatively influenced. The difficulties related to communication are most prevalent when interpreting nonverbal patterns because nonverbal communication is highly influenced by culture. Types of nonverbal communication that are important in cross-cultural counseling include proxemics, kinesics, paralanguage, high–low context communication, and kinesthetic. *Proxemics* is the use of personal space and appropriate distance in social interactions. For example, Latinos/as tend to stand close, touch, and avoid eye contact, whereas White Americans ascribe to greater physical distance between individuals, avoid touching, and maintain eye contact. *Kinesics* are bodily movements such as facial expressions, gestures, posture, and eye contact. Different cultures have different meanings attached to these bodily movements and expressions. *Paralanguage* refers to vocal cues that are used to communicate, such as volume and intensity of speech and turn taking. For example, in some cultures, speaking loudly may not indicate anger, hostility, or poor self-control and speaking softly may not be a sign of weakness, lack of confidence, shyness, or depression. *High–low context communication* refers to an individual's primary communication style. For example, high-context communicators rely on nonverbal cues and behaviors, whereas low-context communicators rely on the verbal part of the interaction or the spoken word. *Kinesthetic* refers to touching. Touching in some cultures indicates a very personal and intimate gesture, whereas in other cultures extensive touching is commonplace and expected.

Client Distrust and Fears

When counseling ethnically and culturally diverse clients, counselors might encounter clients whose past experiences with oppression will hinder the development of a trusting relationship. It is not uncommon for clients of marginalized and historically oppressed groups to approach counseling with feelings associated with past experiences of discrimination and oppression. These clients might come to counseling with a great deal of "healthy suspicion" and distrust based on racial and cultural biases in the larger society. This unconscious process of bringing past conflicts into counseling is called *transference*. For example, an African American client may have difficulty trusting a White counselor because of African Americans' history of oppression in the United States. Understanding sociopolitical events and forces in the larger society is critical for counselors of culturally diverse clients.

Counselor countertransference can also create a barrier to effective cross-cultural counseling. Counselor countertransference is defined as those responses to the client that are based on the counselor's past significant relationships and experiences with persons in the client's cultural group. For example, a heterosexual male counselor may respond angrily to a homosexual male client based on the counselor's disappointment and anger with his homosexual brother. Effective cross-cultural counselors must then recognize transference and countertransference, as both are important to understanding the feelings, behaviors, and attitudes in the cross-cultural counseling relationship.

Many persons from ethnic minority and low-income backgrounds have little or no prior understanding of counseling. Therefore, when they do come to counseling, they may be distrustful of the process. Fear of being labeled "crazy," fear of deportation, and fear of disclosing "family issues and secrets" may all be experienced by culturally and ethnically different clients. Because of distrust and fears regarding the counseling process, counselors may experience clients who make an appointment but do not show for the first appointment or come to their first appointment and never return. For instance, a doctor has referred a Latina client with very little English proficiency to counseling. Without any prior information about the nature of counseling, the client is frightened by the paperwork and extensive intake procedures at the counseling agency, and she does not return for her next counseling appointment.

Racial Identity Development

Racial identity has been identified as an important concept when examining cross-cultural relationship development. Racial identity theory refers to an individual's racial self-conception as well as his or her beliefs, attitudes, and values relative to other racial groups. Racial identity development is a maturational process in which an individual uses more complex cognitive-affective ego statuses to perceive of herself or himself as a racial being. It is also assumed that the individual is also developing racial meanings about members of his or her own affiliated and reference racial groups. There is a relationship between racial identity and the quality of the client–counselor relationship. In particular, a difference in the counselor's and the client's racial identities might become a barrier to effective cross-cultural counseling. It is even possible that the psychological meaning that individuals attribute to their race and racial group affiliation can determine how a client and counselor will interact with each other. For instance, an African American counselor who harbors anger and self-hatred about her racial group may transmit her anger and frustration in counseling sessions with an African American adolescent who is immersed and exploring racial meaning. The adolescent terminates counseling after one session because she states that she "can't relate to the counselor's views on Black people." Clients and counselors of the same cultural group may experience tension or lack of rapport as a result of differing levels of racial identity development.

Lack of Multicultural Counseling Training

There is extensive literature suggesting that "traditional" and "culturally insensitive" counselor training leads to ineffective cross-cultural counseling. As such, one barrier to effective cross-cultural counseling is the lack of multicultural counseling training among counseling professionals. Despite the fact that many counselor training programs have revised their curricula to include issues pertaining to race, culture, and ethnicity, there are still counselors who have not received adequate multicultural counseling training to effectively counsel clients of culturally different backgrounds.

Cheryl Holcomb-McCoy

See also Bilingual Counseling (v3); Career Counseling (v4); Communication (v3); Counseling Skills Training (v2); Counseling Theories and Therapies (v2); Counselors and Therapists (v2); Cross-Cultural Psychology (v3); Cross-Cultural Training (v3); Multicultural Counseling Competence (v3); Racial Identity (v3); Therapist Techniques/Behaviors (v2)

Further Readings

Baruth, L., & Manning, M. L. (2006). *Multicultural counseling and psychotherapy: A lifespan perspective.* Upper Saddle River, NJ: Prentice Hall.

Ponterotto, J. G., Casas, J. M., Suzuki, L. A., & Alexander, C. M. (2001). *Handbook of multicultural counseling.* Thousand Oaks, CA: Sage.

Sue, D. W., & Sue, D. (2008). *Counseling the culturally diverse: Theory and practice* (5th ed.). New York: Wiley.

BERNAL, MARTHA E. (1931–2001)

Martha E. Bernal was the first Latina to earn a Ph.D. in psychology. She is best known for pioneering effective ways to treat children with behavioral disorders, her model of ethnic identity for Latino/a children, and providing leadership to the American Psychological Association (APA) for redressing problems with training minority students. Any one of these achievements would be sufficient for claiming a successful career; combining all three sets of accomplishments into a single career is truly meritorious. How did she accomplish so much? She did so through commitment to high standards and clarity of vision. She set high standards and goals for herself and expected much of others, including the APA, and worked tirelessly until she and others met these expectations. Moreover, her clarity of vision helped her imagine possibilities that others around did or could not. She imagined herself going to college at a time and place when women, particularly Mexican American women, were not viewed as legitimate for a college education. She imagined a new way of treating behavioral disorders despite resistance from the field. Finally, she had a vision in which the APA could promote the training of minority students who could go out and provide effective mental health treatment to underserved populations. The challenges she faced along the way to meeting her goals reveal that overcoming personal and sociocultural barriers may be as impressive as her professional accomplishments.

Childhood

Bernal's is a compelling personal story deserving of admiration and respect. Born in San Antonio, Texas, to parents who had recently immigrated from Mexico, she was raised in El Paso, Texas, in the context of significant discrimination against her and her Mexican American peers. She arrived in kindergarten to learn that speaking her native language, Spanish, would lead to punishment by teachers and administrators. Her early public schooling reflected the actual and symbolic silencing of her and her peers' voices and ambitions. This discrimination socialized them in their second-class social status relative to Anglo peers and population. Her memories of the discrimination of Mexican Americans in El Paso remained painful into adulthood. Through these early experiences, Bernal later realized she had internalized some of this racism, which required reflective and contemplative work to overcome.

She described her family as reflecting traditional Mexican values, which she considered a blessing but also a challenge to carving out a nontraditional role for her as a Mexican American woman. Despite her negative experiences in El Paso's larger community, she had warm and fond memories of growing up in a tight-knit extended family and circle of friends. She was forever thankful for the love, support, and companionship she received while growing up. One of the biggest sacrifices she made in forging a nontraditional career was the loosening of these bonds as she entered the world of academic psychology. Nonetheless, many of her childhood friendships were maintained throughout her life despite her pursuing a lifestyle that was very different from the rest of her peers.

Education

As she set her sights on a nontraditional career path, she faced many doubts from school teachers and school counselors and pressure from her Mexican American family and community not to pursue a college degree. In breaking with cultural tradition, Bernal defied her father's wishes and announced she was attending college. She worked for a year to save enough to start her long academic career. Despite his misgivings, her father provided much needed financial support to his daughter even though this posed financial hardships for him. In 1952, Bernal graduated from the Texas Western College, now the University of Texas at El Paso. She then set her sights on a graduate education, which reawakened the cultural and familial prohibitions against pursing a nontraditional career and occupational path. She somewhat naively sought an assistantship at Louisiana State University but quit after a year when she realized the assistantship was no more than a clerical position and would not provide the training in psychology for which she yearned. She earned a master's degree in special education at Syracuse University in 1959 and eventually enrolled in Indiana University's Ph.D. program in clinical psychology. While in graduate school, she and her female classmates faced sexism and sexual harassment. Despite her dissertation mentor's death prior to her finishing dissertation, Bernal received her Ph.D. in psychology in 1962, the first Latina to have ever received that degree in that field. Bernal had overcome significant personal, familial, cultural, and gender-based challenges before she could even face the significant academic challenges. Earning the Ph.D. is a testament to Bernal's intelligence and perseverance.

Research Career

Having overcome significant barriers and challenges to obtain her Ph.D. and having entered an elite status as the recipient of a Ph.D., it would be natural to assume most of the challenges related to racism and sexism were behind her. Yet, sexism and probably racism continued to influence her career. In response to applications for faculty positions, Bernal received notice that some positions did not hire women. Instead, she obtained a postdoctoral position at the University of California, Los Angeles (UCLA), before securing a faculty position at the University of Arizona in Tucson, where she stayed only 1 year, in part because of isolation, before returning to UCLA.

Pioneering Behavioral Treatment of Children

During the first half of her academic career, Bernal pioneered work on behavioral strategies for working with those with psychiatric and behavioral disorders. At the time, the field of psychology was still enamored with a psychoanalytic view of disorders in which schizophrenia, for example, was attributed to bad parenting, typically bad mothering, and for which the treatment (e.g., psychoanalysis) was costly, arguably inefficient, and not available to many. Instead, Bernal offered very humane treatment that provided cost-effective treatment to long-standing problems and symptoms. Despite receiving scorn from her psychoanalytic colleagues, Bernal persevered and received National Institute of Mental Health and other federal grants supporting her innovative work at a time when there was no affirmative action program and her minority status probably worked against her in securing these important grants. Her work, along with other colleagues, developing behavioral treatments revolutionized the field in ways that continue to be practiced in schools for children with behavioral disorders and inpatient and outpatient facilities that provide effective treatment for debilitating disabilities. Her work focused on training parents and other adults to assist in the treatment of children's psychological problems. In this way, her work was effective in reducing the psychological distress of many children. She was widely recognized as one of the nation's foremost authorities and experts in this area of research.

Latina Researcher

Bernal refocused her research in the second half of her career, beginning in the early 1980s. This re-tooling corresponded to a period of reflection and introspection as a Mexican American woman. She made the painful realization that she was not immune to the pervasive bias against the abilities of minority students and faculty. Subsequently, she sought to re-educate herself and experienced a personal transformation that led to her passion to work toward equity in psychological training for historically underrepresented groups. She was part of the early efforts for minority psychologists to organize as an influential body to provide leadership to psychology and facilitate the next generation of minority psychologists. She became active in the APA's efforts to diversify its training and make it more relevant for recruiting and training more diverse cohorts of psychologists and to help the APA provide the necessary resources to meet more of the diverse mental health needs of the nation. She called attention to the small number of minority faculty and students in clinical and counseling psychology programs and worked with the APA to develop practices that have helped to diversify the field. She quickly became the national authority on the training of minority psychologists. She had since moved from UCLA to the University of Denver. In 1986 she joined the psychology faculty at Arizona State University and joined the Hispanic Research Center. She shifted her own empirical focus to investigate Hispanic children. She proposed a groundbreaking model of Hispanic children's ethnic identity development and conducted an influential program of research with colleagues while mentoring the next generation of Hispanic scholars.

Her distinguished career was recognized with a long list of awards, including a distinguished lifetime career award from Division 45 (Society for the Psychological Study of Ethnic Minority Issues) of the APA and the Award for Distinguished Senior Career Contributions to the Public Interest by the APA. Throughout her career, Bernal could envision and realize goals for her education and psychology that others did not. Through considerable perseverance, Bernal realized these goals and, in the process, made meritorious contributions to the treatment of children's behavioral disorders, to the understanding of Hispanic children's ethnic identity, and to the training of minority students in psychology. Sadly, on September 28, 2001, Bernal succumbed to her third bout with cancer and died. Despite her passing, her work lives on, and the world and field are better because of her.

Stephen M. Quintana

See also Ethnic Identity (v3); Ethnic Minority (v3); Latinos (v3); Racial Pride (v3); Racism (v3); Sexism (v3); Social Justice (v3)

Further Readings

Bernal, M. (1988). Martha E. Bernal. In A. O'Connell & N. Russo (Eds.), *Models of achievement: Reflections of eminent women in psychology* (Vol. 2, pp. 263–276). Hillsdale, NJ: Lawrence Erlbaum.

Bernal, M. E. (1980). Hispanic issues in psychology: Curricula and training. *Hispanic Journal of Behavioral Sciences, 2,* 129–146.

Bernal, M. E. (1990). Ethnic minority mental health training: Trends and issues. In F. C. Serafica, A. I. Schwebel, R. Russell, & P. Isaac (Eds.), *Mental health of ethnic minorities* (pp. 249–274). New York: Praeger.

Bernal, M. E., Klinnert, M. D., & Schultz, L. A. (1980). Outcome evaluation of behavioral parent training and client-centered parent counseling for children with conduct problems. *Journal of Applied Behavior Analysis, 13,* 677–691.

Bernal, M. E., & Knight, G. P. (Eds.). (1991). Ethnic identity and psychological adaptation [Special issue]. *Hispanic Journal of Behavioral Sciences, 13*(2).

Bernal, M. E., & Knight, G. P. (Eds.). (1993). *Ethnic identity: Formation and transmission among Hispanics and other minorities.* Albany: State University of New York Press.

Bernal, M. E., & Knight, G. P. (1997). Ethnic identity of Latino children. In J. G. Garcia & M. C. Zea (Eds.), *Psychological interventions and research with Latino populations* (pp. 15–38). Boston: Allyn & Bacon.

Bernal, M. E., Knight, G. P., Garza, C. A., Ocampo, K. A., & Cota, M. K. (1990). The development of ethnic identity in Mexican-American children. *Hispanic Journal of Behavioral Sciences, 12*(1), 3–24.

Bernal, M. E., Sirolli, A. A., Weisser, S. K., Ruiz, J. A., Chamberlain, V. J., & Knight, G. P. (1998). Relevance of multicultural training to students' applications to clinical psychology programs. *Cultural Diversity & Ethnic Minority Psychology, 5,* 43–55.

Vasquez, M. J. T. (2002). Complexities of the Latina experience: A tribute to Martha Bernal. *American Psychologist, 57,* 880–888.

BIAS

Bias is defined as distortion of judgment or perception of a person or group based on the person's or group's race, religion, ethnicity, gender, age, sexual orientation, heritage, or ancestry, resulting in differential treatment in clinical work, diagnosis, and testing. The term *bias* has been used interchangeably with *prejudice,* specifically related to holding a distinct point of view or ideology. Stereotypes contribute to biases and negative perceptions of people who are different than oneself or perceived as an "outgroup." Concurrently, individuals may use stereotypes to form biases and predict or explain behavior of members of an outgroup, although it is possible for individuals to hold biases and believe a stereotype but not apply it to certain individuals from that group.

A recent decrease in biases may be attributed to social norms that promulgate politically correct attitudes and behaviors rooted in conformity rather than an authentic reduction of prejudice. Subsequently, outright expressions of bias have become less acceptable causing some people to appear unbiased while holding biased viewpoints and creating a close link between internalizing and expressing personal bias and social acceptability.

Individuals typically are exposed to family bias during early childhood and learn to disparage those who are different from them. During later years, children learn biases from peer groups, surrounding communities, and the mass media when they are exposed to overrepresentations of negative stereotypes and gross generalizations of groups such as ethnic and racial minorities. Bias also may occur from direct experience or conflict between one's own group and other groups that may cultivate irrational assumptions and attitudes.

Theories of bias and prejudice have historically emerged in response to circumstances and events, causing shifting theories about the origin of bias that parallel particular circumstances at a given time. A brief historical summary of racial bias provides an excellent framework for understanding current biases. During the 1920s, racial differences became a prominent social theme so theories of prejudice focused on understanding racial differences and antipathies. Race theories looked at inferiorities of outgroups and discussed the backwardness of inferior races in terms of lacking intelligence and evolutionary backwardness, which, in the 1930s, shifted dramatically away from inferiority of outgroups and the superiority of Whites to causes of bias. Social scientists began examining attitudes and beliefs held within the dominant European American group toward other racial and ethnic minority groups and the unjustness and flaws of these biases, leading to an emphasis of White prejudice rather than ethnic and racial minority inferiority.

The 1940s evolved into an era of understanding about White racism. The concepts of unconscious psychological processes and defense mechanisms were introduced as roots of prejudice, exploring psychodynamic processes and bias. The 1950s shifted away from intrapsychic processes and an individual focus presenting prejudice as a by-product of personality development and social conditioning, related to Nazi racial ideology and personality traits conducive to developing biases. The next 2 decades deemphasized individual bias, focusing on group conformity and social norms as the cause of bias. At the same time a growing civil rights movement and heightened concern with other social and political issues led to emphasizing social conditions as underlying roots to prejudice, a view that continued through the 1980s and beyond.

Bias in testing and clinical assessment, as well as treatment and service delivery, also presents issues of concern in psychology. Test disparities between racial and ethnic groups, social strata, genders, and geographic regions raise serious questions about the standardization and construction of test instruments that are culturally unbiased. Despite attempts by the *Diagnostic and Statistical Manual of Mental Disorders* to promote consistency and reduce bias, critics argue that diagnostic biases continue to result in overdiagnosis, underdiagnosis, and misdiagnosis and that testing and diagnosis perpetuate inequality, discrimination, and oppression rather than promote fair assessment and diagnosis. The result of clinical biases in testing, assessment, and treatment is culturally insensitive services and client dropout.

There are a number of theories that have been developed to explain various types of bias and prejudice. One is the justification-suppression model which explained holding back on expressing prejudice because of social norms that suppress the public expression of certain biases. When guilt or shame is absent, it is easier to justify expressing biases publicly. Another similar theory, the self-presentational theory, explains how individuals privately display prejudice while not sharing their views publicly unless the prejudicial values are acceptable as the norm. Aversive racism theory describes how racist beliefs may be repressed and denied and become unconscious, causing individuals to share their biases publicly only in situations that allow them to rationalize their unconscious values. The social dominance theory argues that there are group-based hierarchies with dominant and subordinate groups within society. Dominant groups have power over other groups and enjoy disproportionate privilege; individuals in dominant groups then support and maintain their hierarchical position. The personality model of prejudice emphasizes individual traits that are immutable across situations as the cause of prejudice. A variation of this model is the person X situation model, which asserts that situational variables, such as power or social status, interact with personality to develop prejudice. Also emphasizing the social context is the group socialization model, whereby the groups determine personal beliefs and the expression of bias, and the group normative theory, which looks at the development of prejudicial norms and social pressure for conformity in social groups.

Within these different theories, individuals are motivated to adopt certain beliefs and attitudes and frequently adopt prejudicial views to meet personal needs. Personal motivations may increase stereotyping behavior and justify the bias, generating a "blaming the victim" mentality whereby people get what they deserve.

Bias serves many purposes while negatively impacting people who are targets of discrimination and prejudice and negatively influencing counseling practice, testing, and diagnosis. Bias helps predict stereotypical behaviors from people different than oneself while solidifying negative values and inaccurate stereotypes. Bias assists in perpetuating stereotypes and heightens sensitivity to those values in ways that can be socially supported and highly destructive. Furthermore, bias explains and normalizes behavior toward members of outgroups, reaffirming one's "rightness and worthiness," and doesn't take into account differences that affect testing, service delivery, and counseling. The cultivation and perpetuation of "we" versus "they," ingroup versus outgroup mentality, and a right versus wrong way of thinking diminishes tolerance, openness, and respect toward diversity and differences and effective counseling.

Fred Bemak

See also Classism (v3); Discrimination (v3); Ethical Decision Making (v1); Ethnocentrism (v3); Oppression (v3); Prejudice (v3); Racism (v3); Sexism (v3); Stereotype (v3)

Further Readings

Dion, K. (2002). The social psychology of perceived prejudice and discrimination. *Canadian Psychology, 43*(1), 1–10.

Gaines, S. O., & Reed, E. S. (1995). Prejudice: From Allport to DuBois. *American Psychologist, 50*(2), 96–103.

BICULTURAL

The term *bicultural* describes a state of having or inheriting two or more cultures (e.g., one of an ethnic heritage and one of culture lived in) or two or more ethnic traditions. Central to the discussion of biculturalism is the construct of culture. Culture can be defined as a learned system of meaning and behavior for a group that is defined by geographic boundaries; it includes the customs, values, and traditions that people learn from the environment, family members, peers, and the community or society in which people live. Individuals within a culture have common shared values, customs, habits, and rituals; systems of labeling, explanations, and evaluations; social rules of behavior; perceptions regarding human nature, natural phenomena, interpersonal relationships, time, and activity; symbols, art, and artifacts; and historical developments.

In 1980, Raymond Buriel and Delia S. Saenz defined *biculturalism* as an integration of the competencies and sensitivities associated with two cultures within an individual. Similarly, bicultural individuals were described as having had extensive socialization and life experiences in two or more cultures and as participating actively in these cultures. These descriptions apply to a growing population of people within the United States who have affiliations with other countries and cultures (e.g., given the predominance of immigration and the increased emphasis on ethnic pride). These individuals have feelings and experiences that contribute to their becoming both a part of and separate from the dominant American culture. This duality can be seen in the number of "hyphenated" Americans among ethnic and racial minority groups such as Vietnamese Americans and Dominican Americans as well as among dominant White American groups such as Italian Americans and Irish Americans.

Biculturalism also carries with it expectations regarding cultural practice, mastery, or competence. In essence, biculturalism can manifest in the state of being comfortable with, knowledgeable of, aware of, and competent with at least two distinct cultures. However, two dichotomous perspectives on what it means to be bicultural exist, and both have empirical evidence to support them. In the first, bicultural individuals perceive their dual cultural identities as compatible and complementary, whereas in the second, bicultural individuals describe them as oppositional and contradictory. Bicultural individuals also have been seen as either individuals who have a healthy balance of two or more cultures or individuals who are confused and conflicted. Clearly, being bicultural is not as simple as being on one or another end of a cultural spectrum. Biculturalism can involve feelings of pride, being special, being unique, and having a sense of community and history. It can also include identity confusion, dual or multiple expectations, and value clashes.

Bicultural individuals differ in how they subjectively organize their dual cultural orientations (i.e., variations in orientations are associated with different patterns of contextual, personality, and performance variables). In fact, although individuals want to maintain positive ties with both cultures, certain psychosocial pressures and individual variables lead to significant variations in the process, meanings, and outcomes. The experience of navigating the world as an individual with a hyphenated identity has been described by Alan Roland as walking on a "bicultural tightrope." Bicultural individuals constantly face the challenge of integrating different cultural demands, messages, expectations, and issues of discrimination. In spite of the challenges, however, many bicultural individuals succeed at developing a bicultural identity. There are two types of bicultural individuals identified in the literature. In the first type, bicultural individuals identify with both cultures simultaneously but may do so at differing levels. They identify with being "both" (e.g., I am Haitian American). They do not perceive their ethnic minority culture and the dominant cultures as being mutually exclusive or conflicting. They integrate their cultures into their lives, are able to demonstrate competency in both cultures, and are able to switch behaviors depending on contextual demands. A second type of bicultural individual perceives the dominant and ethnic minority cultures as oppositional in orientation. Although these individuals also identify with both cultures, they are acutely aware of the discrepancies in their cultures and see these discrepancies as a source of internal conflict. Thus, these individuals keep their two cultural identities separate and often report that it is easier to be from their minority culture or from the dominant culture but hard to be both at the same time. For example, they may identify as being Korean or American as opposed to Korean American. They feel they have to choose one or the other because of the differing perspectives of their cultures.

Stereotypes

For many years, it was thought that living in two cultures has a negative impact on the development and lives of individuals. In fact, one common assumption has been that individuals who try to engage in two cultures experience identity confusion and even marginality. To help diminish this assumed confusion, parents of bicultural children were often encouraged to have their children speak only one language, most often the dominant one (e.g., in the United States, English). There are a number of colloquial expressions that highlight the negative perceptions of bicultural individuals. For example, Indians born in the United States may be called "ABCDs" which stands for American Born Confused Desi (of the Indian subcontinent). This term implies that because these individuals are U.S. born and not born in India, they do not really understand or accept their roots. It was thought that being born into or developing competence in one culture leads to the loss of identification with the other. Similarly, negative terminology has developed that is used to imply that racial and ethnic minorities may appear a certain way but have internally identified with and adopted values, norms, and behaviors of White U.S. culture. For example, African Americans may be referred to as "Oreos" (black on the outside, white on the inside), East Asian Americans may be referred to as "Bananas" (yellow on the outside, white on the inside), Latinos/as (and South Asians) may be referred to as "Coconuts" (brown on the outside, white on the inside), and Native Americans or American Indians may be referred to as "Apples" (red on the outside, white on the inside). Although the stereotypes are still deeply embedded in our cultures, it is known now that being bicultural gives individuals an opportunity to access more than one culture, and being bilingual or multilingual is often an advantage (e.g., research has found that being multilingual promotes brain development).

Ethnic Identity

There are many definitions of *ethnic identity*, some of which put it in relation to other terms such as *biculturalism* and others that define ethnic identity independently. Ethnic identity has been defined as the totality of individual's feelings about the values, symbols, and common histories that identify one as a member of a distinct ethnic group. It has also been defined as a social identity based on the culture of one's ancestral group or groups (national or tribal), as modified by the culture in which one's group currently resides. The dimensions on which ethnic identity vary are self-identification, knowledge of one's culture, and preferences toward an ethnic group. Ethnic identity can be divided into two parts—an *external* ethnic identity and an *internal* ethnic identity, whereby external ethnic identity refers to observable social and cultural behaviors and internal ethnic identity includes cognitive, affective, and moral domains. For ethnic minorities, ethnic pride, or a positive ethnic identity, can help individuals cope with the demands of the dominant culture. A number of models of ethnic identity development apply to various ethnic groups in the United States. These models typically incorporate various developmental stages or statuses that follow individuals' progression from lower levels of ethnic pride to higher levels of pride and ethnic self-appreciation.

The psychological literature has alluded to a connection between *ethnic identity, biculturalism*, and *acculturation*, and these terms are sometimes (incorrectly) used interchangeably. Whereas biculturalism and ethnic identity can be seen as states of being, acculturation is a process. Furthermore, whereas an individual with an ethnic identity is not necessarily bicultural, a bicultural individual will have at least one ethnic identity.

Ethnic Belongingness

Included in models of ethnic identity is the concept of ethnic belongingness. This construct refers to the state of feeling affiliation with or connection to those belonging to the individuals' own ethnic group. The feelings and perceptions that individuals have about their own ethnic group are also likely to impact the degree to which these individuals feel belongingness to their ethnic group. For bicultural individuals, this process is complicated by awareness of stereotypes, assumptions, and judgments that the dominant group has toward individuals' own ethnic group and that their ethnic group has toward the dominant group. Thus, the very awareness (of bias) that often accompanies biculturalism can either facilitate or hinder individuals' ethnic belongingness.

Bicultural Models

Bicultural models describe how members of racial and ethnic minority groups go through an adaptive process whereby they learn two or more behavioral repertoires. An important bicultural model is the bicultural "alteration model," which outlines the process of second culture acquisition experienced by individuals. The model suggests that it is possible for individuals to gain competence in two cultures without having to choose one culture over another or lose their original cultural identity.

In opposition to the assumption that living in two cultures is confusing or problematic for individuals, biculturalism and the ability to develop and maintain competence in both cultures is actually psychologically beneficial to individuals. Moreover, negative psychological impact from contact with both cultures can be reduced through the development of bicultural competence. In turn, bicultural competence and second culture acquisition are facilitated by the presence of a strong personal identity. It is important to note, however, that the acquisition of culture and achievement of bicultural competence tend to occur at varying rates for individuals.

To navigate two cultures effectively, individuals need to acquire competence in six dimensions:

1. Knowledge of cultural values and beliefs such as awareness of history, rituals, and everyday practices for each cultural and ethnic group with whom one has contact

2. Positive attitudes toward the goal of bicultural competence and toward both groups with whom one has sufficient contact (but not necessarily equal regard)

3. Bicultural efficacy, or the belief that one can live in an effective and satisfying way within more than one group

4. The ability to appropriately and effectively communicate verbally and nonverbally in each culture

5. Knowledge of, and competence to perform, a range of situationally appropriate behaviors and roles for each cultural group

6. Existence of a sufficient social support system in both cultures that provides a source of practical information

This model can be seen as applicable to immigrants and second-generation bicultural individuals, as well as interracial, interethnic, intercultural, and transracial individuals. It can also be seen as valuable for multicultural individuals or those affiliated with more than two cultures.

Assimilation, Acculturation, and Biculturalism

Some experts believe that the development of a bicultural identity occurs through acculturation. Research on bicultural individuals has focused predominantly on the process of acculturation. Acculturation is the process of cultural change and adaptation that occurs when different cultures come into contact within an individual. More narrowly, acculturation refers to the adaptation process of one group *to* the rules and behaviors of another group. For many years, the assimilation model was the only acculturation model. This model was built on the idea that the United States is a "melting pot."

Biculturalism is an important aspect of acculturation because the preexistence of a minority community can lead to the process in which individuals retain the culture of origin while also acculturating to the host culture. Acculturation and biculturalism can be differentiated by recognizing that acculturation refers to a cultural shift in which elements of the majority culture progressively predominate, whereas biculturalism refers to a cultural orientation in which elements of both minority and majority cultures are increasingly found in equal proportions. For example, a man from Senegal might begin to acculturate and strive to live, act, and speak as Americans do, so that in seeking to be more "Americanized," he might give less time and attention to retaining his Senegalese culture. Were this same man to be considered bicultural, he would have equal skills, knowledge, and comfort in both American and Senegalese cultures so that he would not subvert one to learn the other.

Bicultural Unidimensional Scales

Quantitative methods, primarily through use of scales, have been used to study these variables. Unidimensional and multidimensional models of biculturalism and acculturation have emerged. Unidimensional or unilinear bicultural models conceptualize acculturation along a single, linear continuum, with one end reflecting high adherence to the indigenous or ethnic minority culture and the other end reflecting high adherence to the dominant culture. There are a number of biculturalism scales used to measure biculturalism unidimensionally, including (a) the Acculturation and Biculturalism Scale (ABS) that was developed using a Latino/a sample and includes Acculturation and Bicultural subscales; and (b) the Bicultural/Multicultural Experience Inventory (B/MEI) that was developed using a Mexican American sample and measures the behavioral dimensions of acculturation and cultural identity.

Critics of these unilinear models argue that they are unable to truly represent biculturalism, which includes adherence to both indigenous and host cultures. The limitations in these models lead to more complex conceptualizations of biculturalism.

Bicultural Multidimensional Scales

Bidimensional, bilinear, or multidimensional models conceptualize acculturation along two or more dimensions, each representing higher or lower levels of identification with a culture (e.g., the culture of the indigenous/ethnic minority and the dominant culture). In these models, the bicultural identity is often seen as the optimal identity. John Berry, Joseph Trimble, and Esteban Olmedo's acculturation framework is one such model. The authors present four degrees of acculturation (i.e., bicultural, traditional, assimilated, and marginal) that take into account both identification with an ethnic group and identification with the dominant group. Individuals who strongly identify both with the dominant group and with their ethnic group are considered to be acculturated, integrated, and bicultural. These bicultural individuals are considered the ideal, and biculturalism is the goal for those who are in the process of acculturation. If individuals identify strongly with their own ethnic group and minimally with the dominant group, they are considered traditional, or ethnically embedded, separated, and dissociated. Traditionalists do not adapt in any way to their new culture. If, on the other hand, individuals identify strongly with the dominant group and weakly with their ethnic group, they are considered to be assimilated. With assimilation, there is a loss of ethnic or cultural identity. Finally, if they identify with neither group, they are considered marginal.

Similarly, bilinear or multidimensional scales were designed to measure the adaptation process on two continua—one that reflects adherence to the indigenous or ethnic minority culture and the other, adherence to the dominant culture. Two such measures include (1) the Bicultural Involvement Questionnaire, which was developed for Cuban Americans and measures the behavioral dimension of acculturation and has Hispanicism and Americanism subscales; and (2) the Bicultural Scale for Puerto Ricans.

The unilinear and bilinear scales used to assess biculturalism are not able to capture the complexity of this construct (though the latter appears to be a better measure than the former). Increasingly, researchers use qualitative measures either to complement quantitative measures or as the primary means of data collection.

Culture as Frame and Navigating Biculturalism

Individuals have culturally specific meaning systems (i.e., learned networks of ideas, values, beliefs, and knowledge) that are shared with others within the same culture. These meaning systems are interpretive frames that affect feelings, thoughts, and behaviors. Given the pervasive nature of culture as the lens or frame through which individuals filter, understand, and internalize the meaning assigned to experiences and interactions, bicultural individuals' navigation through culture can be thought of as doubly complex.

Because one's cultural identity is influenced by language, generational/immigration status, sociopolitical climate, and situational cues, bicultural individuals often have dual cultural identities that they must navigate between and which become of greater or less salience depending on the environment, situation, and goal that is of concern.

Biculturalism and Frameswitching

More recently, the idea of cultural frameswitching has emerged, or the process in which cultural meaning systems guide individuals' sociocognitive processes. Research suggests that for bicultural individuals, this frameswitching allows bicultural individuals to move between two different culturally based interpretive system lenses (i.e., in response to situational cues) that are rooted in their dual cultural backgrounds. Thus, bicultural individuals have access to multiple cultural meaning systems and switch between culturally appropriate behaviors depending on context. For example, Chinese American individuals possess both Asian and Western cultural meaning systems, and each system can be independently activated by culturally relevant icons or primes. There is much variability, however, in how bicultural individuals manage and experience these meaning systems.

Bicultural Identity Integration

Differences in bicultural identity affect how cultural knowledge is used to interpret events. Veronica Haritatos and Jana Benet-Martinez discussed a construct they call Bicultural Identity Integration (BII), which is the way bicultural individuals organize their two cultural identities. Bicultural individuals high on BII describe their two cultural identities as compatible (i.e., fluid and complementary), whereas bicultural individuals low on BII experience their two identities as oppositional (i.e., conflicting and disparate). Cultural frameswitching is moderated by BII or the perceived compatibility (vs. opposition) between the two cultural orientations. In Haritatos and Benet-Martinez's research, Chinese Americans who perceived their cultural identities as compatible (high BII) responded in culturally congruent ways to cultural cues. They made more external attributions (more Asian behavior) after being exposed to Chinese primes (e.g., picture of a Chinese dragon) and more internal attributions (more Western behavior) after being exposed to American primes (e.g., picture of an American flag). On the other hand, Chinese Americans who perceived their cultural identities as oppositional (low BII) demonstrated a reverse priming effect. That is, individuals with a low BII had more external attributions (Asian behavior) after being exposed to American primes and more internal attributions (Western behavior) after being exposed to Chinese primes.

Variations in BII, however, do not define a uniform phenomenon. Instead, the variations encompass two separate independent constructs: perceptions of distance (vs. overlap) and perceptions of conflict (vs. harmony) between an individual's two cultural identities.

Culture and Transracial Adoption

Transracial adoption, or the practice of placing (for adoption) children of one racial group with parents from another racial group, by its very nature, has long been expected to result in multiple forms of biculturalism as well as bicultural conflicts. In fact, common expectation for transracial adoptees is for them to demonstrate some degree of biculturality. However, many transracial adoptees are raised by adoptive parents who are racially different from the child, typically rearing them within the adoptive parents' own cultural traditions. These parents often do not practice, identify with, or subscribe to the values, beliefs, and traditions found in the adoptees' birth culture. Moreover, the separation (physical, environmental, and social) from the birth culture often results in little, if any, familiarity or real affiliation and identification with the birth culture. As a result, the culture with which the transracial adoptee often identifies is that of his or her adoptive parents. Furthermore, for transracial adoptees to truly become bicultural, they must become competent in, knowledgeable about, aware of, and competent within their birth culture—achievements that are even less likely to occur when the adoptions are international. Thus, for many transracial adoptees biculturalism is difficult to achieve. Because the adoptees often do not have adequate or full access to their birth culture and because they are reared by parents with cultural values, beliefs, and traditions from a culture other than their birth culture (often the dominant culture), they are most often described as assimilated rather than truly bicultural. Biculturalism, however, is sought by many adult transracial adoptees. It is achieved by visits to their birth countries and immersion into their birth culture and birth communities. Thus, the process of becoming bicultural is often one that reverses the target culture in the acculturation process; that is, the birth culture (often nondominant) becomes the target culture.

Current Issues in Biculturalism

A bicultural framework often does not take into account multiple identities, such as socioeconomic status, (dis)ability status, sexual orientation, and gender. For example, studying ethnicity and gender as separate variables would result in reductionism and denial of the full experience of ethnic women. Also, it is simplistic to assume that ethnicity is a combination of heritage and modification. Ethnicity cannot be summed up as something simply passed on from generation to generation, taught and learned. Rather, it is dynamic and has to be inclusive of many components of one's identity.

Although bicultural identities have been discussed in relation to immigrant and ethnic minority groups, it has been posited that biculturalism can be applied to globalization as well. Because of international travel and communication through media technology (e.g., television, the Internet), modern youth have developed a global identity in addition to their local identities (e.g., ethnic, cultural identities). This global identity gives them a sense of belonging to a worldwide culture that includes an awareness of global events, practices, and information. Biculturalism has also become more globally prominent. Modern conceptualizations of identity incorporate ethnic origins and heritage as parts of individuals.

Muninder K. Ahluwalia and Amanda L. Baden

See also Acculturation (v3); Acculturative Stress (v3); Adaptation (v3); Assimilation (v3); Cultural Accommodation and Negotiation (v3); Cultural Values (v3); Culture (v3); Enculturation (v3); Ethnic Identity (v3); Person–Environment Interactions (v2); Second Culture Acquisition (v3); Transracial Adoption (v3)

Further Readings

Arnett, J. J. (2002). The psychology of globalization. *American Psychologist, 57*(10), 774–783.

Benet-Martinez, V., & Haritatos, J. (2005). Bicultural Identity Integration (BII): Components and psychosocial antecedents. *Journal of Personality, 73*(4), 1015–1050.

Benet-Martinez, V., Leu, J., Lee, F., & Morris, M. W. (2002). Negotiating biculturalism: Cultural frameswitching in biculturals with oppositional versus compatible cultural identities. *Journal of Cross-Cultural Psychology, 33*(5), 492–516.

Hong, Y. Y., Morris, M., Chiu, C. Y., & Benet-Martinez, V. (2000). Multicultural minds: A dynamic constructivist approach to culture and cognition. *American Psychologist, 55,* 709–720.

LaFramboise, T., Coleman, H. L. K., & Gerton, J. (1993). Psychological impact of biculturalism: Evidence and theory. *Psychological Bulletin, 114,* 395–412.

Padilla, A. (Ed.). (1980). *Acculturation: Theory, models and some new findings.* Boulder, CO: Westview Press.

Park, R. E., & Burgess, E. W. (1921). *Introduction to the science of sociology.* Chicago: University of Chicago Press.

Phinney, J. S., & Devich-Navarro, M. (1997). Variations in bicultural identification among African American and Mexican American adolescents. *Journal of Research on Adolescence, 7,* 3–32.

Szapocznik, J., Kurtines, W. M., & Fernandez, T. (1980). Bicultural involvement and adjustment in Hispanic-American youths. *International Journal of Intercultural Relations, 4,* 353–365.

Triandis, H. C., Kashima, Y., Hui, C. H., Lisansky, J., & Marin, G. (1982). Acculturation and biculturalism indices among relatively acculturated Hispanic young adults. *Interamerican Journal of Psychology, 16,* 140–149.

BILINGUAL COUNSELING

Bilingual counseling is defined as therapeutic discourse that accommodates the client's linguistic characteristics and incorporates bilingual or multilingual factors as vital components of psychological and contextual functioning. Because language and culture are closely embedded, attention to language diversity responds to competent multicultural counseling that includes self-awareness of the counselor, knowledge of bilingual processes, and skills in bilingual interventions. The discussion that follows applies not only to bilingual individuals but also to multilingual individuals, who may exhibit a more complex language presentation in counseling.

Foundations of Bilingual Counseling

Brief Historical Perspective

In the initial stages of psychodynamic theory, Sigmund Freud documented treatment with bilinguals, but language factors per se were not addressed as instruments of therapeutic change. In the 1930s, some psychodynamic clinicians explored bilingualism, and by the late 1940s a more definite view emerged of language choice as a defense mechanism. Case studies published in the 1950s described the impact of multiple languages on psychodynamic processes such as repression, ego functions, and transference. Further investigations in the 1970s reported differential client presentation in two languages, diagnostic errors, and unique processes and interventions. The multicultural movement that followed and contributions from psycholinguistics, cognitive and clinical psychology, psychometrics, and education have widened the understanding of relevant processes evident in bilingual counseling, which are relevant regardless of the theoretical orientation of the professional.

Bilingual Processes

Bilinguals are described as having a *dual sense of self* that responds differently to distinct contextual stimuli. Language duality allows for the conceptualization of two worlds, communication of thoughts and emotions differently, bicultural dynamics, different organizational sets of knowledge, and multiple self-identities. Intact cognitions and emotions that are specific to each language help store memories in different language domains that can be retrieved by the most meaningful language at a particular period of time.

Bilingual language development may be sequential or simultaneous. Maintenance of the first language (L1) and the second language (L2) depends on ecological support, acculturation level, language use, and sociopolitical factors. Language development encompasses learning to label emotions and cognitions that are associated with early attachments. Thus, a bilingual individual may be prone to experience affective content in L1 or the language that endorses emotional meaning while affective detachment may be expected in L2. Similarly, a sense of logic and maturity may influence accessing L2 in decision making. When both languages are learned simultaneously and supported equally, the affective component may be accessible in both languages. Knowledge of the following bilingual concepts is necessary for competent practice.

Language switching, or code-switching, is a pattern where a word or phrase is replaced by another language within a sentence or a language shift for an extended period of time. The shift occurs from L1 to L2 as well as from L2 to L1, may be involuntary or voluntary, and may be predictable by context. A voluntary shift can be (a) a purposeful strategy to be better understood, (b) a result of lack of fluency, or (c) an avoidance response. Code-switching is associated with memory of emotional content, defense mechanisms, cognitive coping skills, spontaneity, creativity, diverse attributions and interpretations, taboo words, and word retrieval problems. Words that are concrete or overlap semantically are easier to translate than words having unique meanings or abstractions such as emotions. *Language mixing* integrates characteristics of two languages into one word or phrase (e.g., *Spanglish*).

Language dominance refers to the individual's most fluent language. Once a level of fluency is mastered and supported by high levels of use, L2 may shift to become the base, more accessed language.

Language proficiency involves high-order verbal cognitive abilities required in reading, writing, and oral expression. An individual may be proficient in

English but may be dominant in Spanish. In 1984, Jim Cummins indicated that non-English speakers require a period of 5 to 7 years to attain proficient English abilities, whereas interpersonal communication skills develop within 2 to 3 years of natural and informal exposure to a second language.

Best Practices

The establishment of the therapeutic alliance, language sensitivity, non-English language acceptance, multicultural competence, and the language match between counselor and client modulate successful bilingual interventions. Sound clinical practice with bilinguals targets the motives leading to choices in language use and phenomenological experiences associated with a *dual self*. Application of core counseling skills is important, particularly focusing on nonverbal messages and communicating clearly without the use of idioms or regionalisms.

The professional counselor needs to engage in self-evaluation to ascertain whether he or she has the language skills to best respond to the bilingual client. Inadvertently, the practitioner may project unintentional prejudices and power imbalances by choosing the client's L2 as the primary therapeutic language. Parallel bilingual skills between counselor and client are the ideal match to ensure understanding, maximize the applications of bilingual interventions, and provide a natural flow in therapeutic interactions as figures of speech are difficult to translate and many regional and national variations coexist within the same language. Monolingual counselors are generally not recommended but may be effective in some situations as long as the client's L2 level is highly proficient, bicultural and bilingual issues are addressed, and expression in L1 narratives is encouraged.

A bilingual practice requires availability of assessment tools and documentation in two languages. A brief telephone conversation before the face-to-face interview is valuable to assess language preference. Generally, working with two languages duplicates in-session work and case management responsibilities.

Assessment Methods

Bilingual language skills may be assessed with formal and standardized instruments as well as through interviews. Several norm-referenced tests are available to measure bilingual language dominance and language proficiency (e.g., Riverside Publishing instruments: *Woodcock Language Battery–Revised Tests* and the *Bilingual Verbal Cognitive Abilities Tests*). These instruments need to be administered by assessment specialists and may be useful for counseling goals associated with educational and vocational issues.

Comprehensive clinical interviews need to include language factors such as patterns of language use and bilingual development and history. Other areas to assess are conversational proficiency, acculturation level, language used to express emotions and cognitions, language use contexts, coping strengths associated with language use, language of prayers and dreams, general literacy skills, and ecological factors that hinder or endorse specific language usage.

Assessment also requires counselor sensitivity to the interplay of cultural, linguistic, and verbal and nonverbal communication processes. Communicating in the nondominant language may interfere with the accurate presentation of the client. Verbal and nonverbal features may be affected by limited verbal fluency, anxiety, and emotional inhibition. Affective content may be hampered by communication in a language that lacks emotional meaning. Clients may present as distant and with dissonant affect when verbalizing emotionally laden events. Frequent translations disrupt the flow of therapeutic interactions, risking client distraction and affective disengagement as well as counselor misinterpretations and excessive focus on content instead of meaning.

Bilingual Interventions

Several counseling interventions have been useful with bilingual clients. Language switching has received the most attention in research and practice. Strategically, changing languages during counseling has been used to follow the client's language and to intervene clinically. When applied in the first manner, code-switching facilitates rapport, connects with phenomenological expressions, clarifies conceptualizations, and enhances the client's construction of reality. By strategically shifting into the emotional language, the counselor may access affective catharsis, memories, and insights. In contrast, redirecting the shift to L2 will generate an inhibition response, producing a more rational and controlled stance to unrestrained or painful emotions.

In systemic interventions, bilingualism adds another dimension to family and couples therapy with shifts in languages representing systemic dynamics of conflict, resistance, ethnic identity, and acculturation. Cross-cultural couples and family members that share weak skills in a common language may require the counselor to assume the role of *language broker.*

Counselors with weak L1 fluency may encourage clients to express events and emotions to elicit affective catharsis followed by the client's translation. The client may benefit from the comparison of different affective perspectives evident in the original and translated narrative. *Language-culture–based* strategies (e.g., metaphors, proverbs, *dichos,* music, storytelling, poetry) may be powerful therapeutic tools, and combining two languages enhances spontaneity, disclosure, and problem-solving skills.

Language is also linked to ethnic identity, social justice, and environmental stressors. Addressing language issues (e.g., loss of first language, language acquisition problems) may reveal pertinent clinical data (e.g., pressure to communicate in L2 to avoid discrimination, loss of cultural membership, ethnic identity confusion, educational problems, family conflicts).

Open communication with the client about the counselor's bilingual language skills may address the client's comfort level with the counselor's linguistic abilities as well as any foreign accent evident, which may reflect biases and communication issues.

To prevent process interference, the professional literature unfavorably supports counseling with *language facilitators.* Special circumstances such as low-incidence languages, emergencies, and assessment needs justify the use of a trained language facilitator. David Bradford and Abilio Muñoz (1993) and Freddy Paniagua (2004) provide useful guidelines.

Future Directions

Bilingual counseling requires adequate supervision and training as well as clear delineation of the competency level of the bilingual practitioner. This emerging specialty will require substantially more empirical exploration, new training models, and innovative practice methods.

Maritza Gallardo-Cooper

See also Barriers to Cross-Cultural Counseling (v3); Career Counseling (v4); Career Counseling, Asian Americans (v4); Career Counseling, Immigrants (v4); Career Counseling, Latinos (v4); Communication (v3); Counseling Skills Training (v2); Multicultural Counseling (v3); Multicultural Counseling Competence (v3); Translation Methods (v3)

Further Readings

Ali, R. K. (2004). Bilingualism and systemic psychotherapy: Some formulations and explorations. *Journal of Family Therapy, 26,* 340–357.

Altarriba, J., & Santiago-Rivera, A. L. (1994). Current perspectives on using linguistic and cultural factors in counseling the Hispanic client. *Professional Psychology: Research and Practice, 25,* 388–397.

Bradford, D. T., & Muñoz, A. (1993). Translation in bilingual psychotherapy. *Professional Psychology: Research and Practice, 24,* 52–61.

Burck, C. (2004). Living in several languages: Implications for therapy. *Journal of Family Therapy, 26,* 314–339.

Clauss, C. S. (1998). Language: The unspoken variable in psychotherapy practice. *Psychotherapy: Theory, Research, Practice, and Training, 35,* 188–196.

Cummins, J. (1984). *Bilingualism and special education: Issues in assessment and pedagogy.* Clevedon, UK: Multilingual Matters.

Fabbro, F. (1999). *The neurolinguistics of bilingualism.* East Sussex, UK: Psychology Press.

Javier, R. A. (1989). Linguistic considerations in the treatment of bilinguals. *Psychoanalytic Psychology, 6,* 87–96.

Marcos, L. R. (1976). Bilinguals in psychotherapy: Language as an emotional barrier. *American Journal of Psychotherapy, 30,* 552–560.

Marcos, L. R., & Urcuyo, L. (1979). Dynamic psychotherapy with the bilingual patient. *American Journal of Psychotherapy, 33,* 331–338.

Paniagua, F. (2004). *Assessing and treating culturally diverse clients: A practical guide* (3rd ed.). Thousand Oaks, CA: Sage.

Perez-Foster, R. P. (1998). *The power of language in the clinical process: Assessing and treating the bilingual person.* Northvale, NJ: Jason Aronson.

Santiago-Rivera, A. L., & Altarriba, J. (2002). The role of language in therapy with the Spanish-English bilingual client. *Professional Psychology: Research & Practice, 33,* 30–38.

BILINGUALISM

Bilingualism is defined as the ability to communicate or be fluent in two languages. *Multilingualism* (a related term) refers to the ability to communicate or be fluent in three or more languages. Early definitions dating back to the 1930s refer to bilingualism as having "native-like" control of two languages. Nevertheless, research in the fields of linguistics, psychology, sociology, education, neurology, and politics has expanded the concept of bilingualism far beyond the simplistic view of communicating in two languages. Current definitions are as complex as each of the languages a bilingual individual chooses to communicate in.

An important distinction necessary to begin to understand the concept of bilingualism is the difference between *ability* (or degree of bilingualism) and *use* (or function of bilingualism). To communicate proficiently in a given language, an individual must possess four basic skills: listening, speaking, reading, and writing. Some have argued for the inclusion of thinking as a fifth language ability. To use the abilities properly, a bilingual individual must exist in what is known as a *language community,* for these abilities do not develop in a vacuum. Moreover, contact between different language communities provides the bilingual individual with the context to know when to listen, speak, read, write, and think in which language.

Language Ability

Human beings are uniquely equipped for language production. The brain performs all the executive functions (such as information processing and controlling the physical aspects of speech). The diaphragm muscle, lungs, nose, mouth, lips, tongue, and vocal cords are all involved in speech production and regulation. The ear, ear bones, cochlea, brain stem, and auditory cortex are involved in hearing. Facial expressions and hand gestures also play a role in spoken language as well as sign language.

These actions of *language performance* represent the outward evidence that an individual has language competence. *Language competence* is the general term that lets us know an individual is proficient in a given language (e.g., that an individual has a mental system established for that particular language and can analyze and produce it). *Language abilities* are the more specific, direct, and quantifiable evidence that an individual can communicate in a given language.

Language abilities are multidimensional in nature. They include active skills (e.g., speaking and writing) and passive skills (e.g., listening and reading). A person may speak a language but not be able to read in that language or understand the spoken language. An individual may understand others who speak in a given language but not be able to speak it themselves. These abilities can be developed formally (e.g., school, continuing education classes), informally (e.g., contact with another language community such as friends or the media), or through a mixture of both formal and informal methods (e.g., language immersion programs, living abroad).

An individual who can only communicate in one language is referred to as a *monolingual* (or *monoglot*). An individual who has developed an approximately equal level of proficiency in her or his language abilities across a variety of situations in both languages is commonly referred to as a *balanced bilingual.* This is what most people typically think of when referring to bilingual individuals: a person who is equally fluent and has the same knowledge base in two languages. It is important to note that being monolingual may not necessarily be a good reference point to compare with or understand bilinguals.

Dominant bilingualism is another type of bilingualism used to describe a person who can communicate in two languages but is partial to one of them because she or he is more proficient in it. Although not always the case, this more proficient language is usually the one the person learned first (e.g., their *first language, native language*, or *mother tongue*). Another type of bilingualism is called *semilingualism* (or distractive bilingualism). This controversial term describes an individual who has some deficiencies in both languages when compared with monolinguals in each of those languages. These deficiencies typically include a smaller vocabulary, incorrect grammar, lack of creativity and spontaneity with both languages, and a difficulty with thinking and expressing emotions in either language. The term has been wrought with controversy because of its negative connotations and its emphasis on expectations of failure and underachievement.

Language Use

The experience of a bilingual individual is not independent of her or his context. Contact between different language communities helps languages grow, helps individuals learn their language(s) better, and helps communities relate better with each other. Studying functional bilingualism facilitates the understanding of a bilingual individual's language use in the context of her or his language community.

Understanding language use in bilingualism entails exploring the following questions: (a) Who is the speaker? (b) Who is the listener(s)? (c) What is the situation or context? (d) What is the specific topic of conversation? and (e) What is the purpose of language use? For example, why does speaker A change from Spanish to English when talking to listener B at location C about topic D? How is it that speaker E can talk in English to speaker F when the topic is G but not when the topic is H? Understanding bilingual communication thus moves beyond the concept of language proficiency and language skills.

The term *diglossia* refers to the notion of a community having more than one language available for use. The situation typically involves a majority (or high language variety) and a minority (or low variety) language. Language communities often perceive a majority language as more prestigious and as the key to upward mobility. They thus tend to use it in formal or official contexts (e.g., school, business, correspondence with the government). Minority languages are more often used in informal or personal situations (e.g., home, family, correspondence with friends). For example, a television reporter in Hawai'i may talk about a football game during a broadcast in standard English but discuss it with her friends at home in pigeon English (a form of English that retains its basic grammatical rules while integrating those of other languages such as Hawaiian, Japanese, Chinese, and Portuguese).

This phenomenon of language shift is often visible in immigrant populations. First-generation immigrants maintain their own language while attempting to learn the host language. Second-generation immigrants intent on assimilating to the majority culture embrace the host language and begin using it in contexts once reserved for their native language. By the time third-generation immigrants choose a language in which to communicate, the majority language may be the only choice available to them.

Code-switching is a common phenomenon that occurs when a bilingual individual alternates between languages. It can happen in complete sentences, within one sentence, or at the single word level. "Voy a print*ear* el homework" (I'm going to print the homework) is an example of code-switching. Code-switching is what some members of the Spanish-English bilingual community have termed *spanglish*.

Bilingualism Myths and Cognitive Advantages

The predominant belief during the "period of detrimental effects" (early 1800s to 1960s) was that bilingualism had a negative impact on individuals. It was thought that learning more than one language could confuse a child in the learning of their first language, could cause a decrease in intelligence (e.g., lower IQ), could decrease spiritual growth, and could cause cultural identity or split personality problems in children. Some also argued that two languages were learned independently of each other and that the knowledge of learning one did not transfer into the other. Others believed that as more was learned in one language, less could be learned in the other.

The "period of additive effects" (1960s–present) represented a shift in the understanding of bilingualism and its effects in cognitive development. Recent research has demonstrated that being mindful that there is more than one way to communicate enhances a number of cognitive skills. Flexibility, creativity, concept formation, memory, analogical reasoning, classification skills, divergent thinking, and inhibitory control are some of the advantages of bilingualism. Research has also shown that bilinguals develop increased *metalinguistic skills* (e.g., the ability to talk about language, analyze it, think about it, separate it from context, and judge it). This analysis of one's own knowledge of language and control over this internal language process has been shown to facilitate earlier reading acquisition, which can lead to higher levels of academic achievement. Independent of academics, being able to communicate in two or more languages increases career opportunities and options for places to live, as well as a range of options for interpersonal interactions (which in turn enhances interpersonal skills). Finally, recent research has also shown that the increased cognitive activities inherent in bilingualism delay the onset of Alzheimer's disease and other cognitive disorders.

Luis A. Rivas

See also Acculturation (v3); Barriers to Cross-Cultural Counseling (v3); Bicultural (v3); Bilingual Counseling (v3); Career Counseling, Immigrants (v4); Communication (v3); Counseling Skills Training (v2); Immigrants (v3); Multicultural Counseling (v3); Multicultural Counseling Competence (v3); Second Culture Acquisition (v3); Translation Methods (v3)

Further Readings

Baker, C. (2006). *Foundations of bilingual education and bilingualism* (4th ed.). Philadelphia: Multilingual Matters.

Baker, C., & Jones, S. P. (1998). *Encyclopedia of bilingualism and bilingual education.* Clevedon, UK: Multilingual Matters.

Bhatia, T. K., & Ritchie, W. C. (2004). *The handbook of bilingualism.* Oxford, UK: Blackwell.

Bialystock, E. (2001). *Bilingualism in development: Language, literacy, and cognition.* Cambridge, MA: Cambridge University Press.

Hakuta, K. (1990, Spring). Bilingualism and bilingual education: A research perspective. *FOCUS: Occasional Papers in Bilingual Education* (No. 1). Washington, DC: National Clearinghouse for Bilingual Education.

Wei, L. (2000). *The bilingualism reader.* Oxford, UK: Routledge.

BIRACIAL

The term *biracial* refers to individuals who are born to parents who are each of a different racial background. For example, the child of an African American mother and an Asian American father would be considered biracial. Similarly, a person with one White parent and one Native American parent would also be considered biracial. The term *multiracial,* which is used to describe individuals of two or more races, is inclusive of the term *biracial.* An example of a multiracial individual would be someone with White, Native American, and African American parentage.

It is important to note that distinctions between race and ethnicity are complex and, at times, controversial within U.S. society. Currently the U.S. Census considers *Hispanic* an ethnicity rather than a racial category. Therefore, an individual with one Latino/a parent and one White parent, for example, would not be considered biracial, though he or she may feel as though he or she is of a mixed cultural background. This is complicated by the fact that many social scientists believe that race is a social construct, with racial groupings being based on historical classifications rather than true genetic differences among people. The term *multiethnic,* which refers to individuals of multiple ethnic backgrounds, is sometimes preferred to describe individuals of mixed heritage because ethnicity is a broader term that denotes a shared identity and ancestry among members of a particular cultural group. However, the term *multiethnic* would also describe someone of Japanese and Chinese descent, and this experience would be seen as different from a more traditional multiracial (e.g., Japanese and White) experience.

It is also important to recognize that many individuals who fit the definition of *biracial* may not choose to use this term to describe themselves. They might elect to identify with only one side of their racial background (opting for a monoracial identity) or use other terminology such as *mixed.* Indeed, individuals of mixed racial background have various options of self-identification that are based on demographic background, familial influences, skin color, and other cultural experiences.

Historical Perspectives

The number of biracial individuals has increased over the years, particularly with increasing rates of interracial relationships and the repeal of antimiscegenation (racial mixing) laws in the late 1960s. Dating back to the early 18th century, antimiscegenation laws sought to maintain the purity of White European bloodlines in U.S. society by limiting the birth of biracial children. Such norms held to the rule of *hypodescence,* or "one-drop rule," a rule that even the slightest degree of racial mixing eliminated the possibility for an individual to legally identify as White. Although the offspring of interracial relationships have been noted in American history for centuries, it was not until the civil rights movement and the repeal of antimiscegenation laws that the U.S. government was pushed to formally acknowledge and give equal liberties to the many adults involved in interracial relationships as well as those who were of mixed racial background.

In addition to the legal and cultural norms that implied that biracial offspring and mixed race relationships were taboo, the government also traditionally classified individuals in a way that limited how people of mixed racial heritage could identify themselves. For the 210-year span between the first national census in 1790 and the recent decennial census in 2000, individuals had to identify themselves as belonging to only one racial group. At times, however, efforts were made to track individuals of mixed African/White heritage. On the 1890 national census a *mulatto* was defined as someone three- to five-eighths Black; a *quadroon* was one-quarter Black, and an *octoroon* was one-eighth Black. These definitions applied only to Black/White biracial combinations and were eliminated by the next census in 1900, as they had very little rational justification or public support. Between 1900 and 2000, no effort was made to distinguish people of mixed racial heritage, and the classification trend fell back to using the "one-drop rule" to determine who could and could not identify as White. Any individual with "one drop" of non-White blood had to identify legally with the non-White portion of her or his racial background, thus emphasizing the importance of purity in White ancestry.

The 2000 U.S. Census marked the first time in history in which respondents were allowed to indicate more than one race for their self-classification. This landmark change allowed biracial and multiracial individuals to acknowledge their mixed background. An estimated 6.8 million, or 2.4% of the U.S. population, selected more than one race. This modification of the traditional census format was not met without controversy, however, as many civil rights groups viewed the counting of individuals belonging to more than one race as a potential threat to their political strength. Nevertheless, the change seemed to mark a cultural shift that has allowed for individuals of biracial or multiracial backgrounds to express the full range of their heritage and not be artificially placed into specific minority groups. This new option for classification, along with the legalization of interracial marriages over the past 30 years, has led to what researchers have called a *biracial baby boom*. Indeed, there is increased visibility and awareness about individuals of mixed racial background in the media as well as in academic arenas. It is expected that the biracial population will continue to grow, and in turn, counselors and psychologists will come in contact with more youth and adults of mixed heritage.

Biracial Identity Development Models

Researchers and clinicians across many areas of psychology have worked to understand the process by which individuals of mixed racial heritage develop conceptualizations of themselves and their racial identity. The primary effort in this area has been the development of models to identify and examine how biracial individuals create personal and racial identity. These models have changed over time, paralleling changes in historical and sociopolitical perspectives regarding biracial individuals in the United States, as well as increased research about biracial development.

The earliest description of biracial development was Everett Stonequist's marginal person model. In 1937 Stonequist wrote about biracial individuals as individuals who were linked to two different worlds but never truly belonged in either. Stonequist believed that mixed racial heritage would complicate normal identity development by creating confusion with a person's ability to identify with a specific social, racial, or ethnic group. This negative description of identity stood as the primary source of understanding for biracial individuals for many years, until models were introduced that described biracial development as somewhat less pathological and, proceeding through a series of distinct stages, could explain various identity outcomes.

The first of the stage models of racial identity was a 1971 model by William E. Cross, Jr., which focused on Black racial identity. Although not specific to individuals of mixed heritage, Cross's model was highly influential to subsequent models of biracial identity development. In his model, Cross saw racial identity development occurring across a series of distinct stages. Soon, many authors were producing models of biracial development that portrayed biracial individuals as going through a series of distinct, linear, developmental stages throughout their life span. James Jacobs, another contributor to the body of literature about stage models, saw biracial individuals as first noticing racial and ethnic differences between people, then understanding what personal meaning these differences held, and finally synthesizing these meanings to become an individual of combined heritage. Similarly, George Kich saw biracial individuals first becoming aware of statuses of differentness, then personally struggling for acceptance, and finally accepting a biracial identity.

Many stage models, although significantly different from Stonequist's first description of biracial identity, still held onto the basic premise that biracial development would be inherently more difficult or less healthy than monoracial development. This assumption began to shift with W. S. Carlos Poston's five-stage model of biracial identity development. Poston's model suggested that biracial individuals progress through five stages: (1) awareness of personal identity; (2) choice of a specific group categorization; (3) enmeshment or denial from having to select one identity that may not perfectly fit the biracial individual; (4) appreciation for having broader, multiple, ethnic identities; and (5) integration of all different identities into one unified self. This model was one of the first that provided a positive outcome for biracial individuals by incorporating the idea that biracial individuals could create a healthy, integrated sense of racial identity.

Stage models dominated the literature about biracial identity development until recently, when limitations of these models became evident. One concern with stage models was that newer research suggested that biracial identity development may not proceed in a linear fashion or be uniform for all individuals. In addition, many stage models fail to recognize the significance that environmental influences, such as early life experiences, family settings, culture, and other salient aspects of life, could influence the identity development of biracial individuals. These limitations have led many researchers to advocate for more complex, fluid, and multifaceted models of development that highlight biracial identity within specific cultural and environmental contexts.

Maria Root's ecological identity model is a recent model designed to incorporate contextual influences on biracial identity. This model highlights the myriad influences that can affect an individual's racial identity, including history, geographic location, family, physical appearance, gender, socioeconomic status, and sexual orientation, among others. Root's model also suggests that there are several outcomes of identity development for biracial individuals, without claiming that these outcomes will either occur in a specific order or even necessarily occur for all biracial individuals. The five identity outcomes in Root's model are (1) acceptance of ascribed identity as labeled by others, (2) identification with dual racial or ethnic groups, (3) personal identification with a single racial group, (4) identification with a new group, such as biracial, or (5) adoption of a symbolic race or ethnicity by taking more pride with or placing more emphasis on one side of the individual's race. According to Root's model, biracial individuals may elect any of these outcomes at various points in their lives, depending on personal experiences and contextual influences.

Changes in basic understanding and conceptualization of biracial individuals across both the scientific community and the culture of the United States are largely reflected by changes in models of biracial identity development. Understanding of biracial identity started by society initially viewing biracial existence as inherently problematic and maladaptive out of the belief that biracial individuals could never wholly identify with, or fit into, a larger racial group. This perception has changed over time to eventually conclude that biracial individuals may form a cohesive identity, but to do so these individuals would have to go through universal and concrete steps before forming a positive identity. Finally, modern perspectives are reflected in current identity models, which identify the roles that external ecological forces play in the lives of biracial individuals and the fluid process of identity.

Psychological Functioning in Biracial Individuals

Researchers have studied biracial children, adolescents, and adults to better understand their psychological functioning. Psychologists have been interested in whether early descriptions of biracial individuals as confused and marginalized were accurate and how biracial identity develops in different situations. These studies have highlighted the influence of historical and societal perspectives on race and how these can affect the well-being of biracial individuals. One of the most common findings relates to the experience of discrimination, based on being biracial, and the negative effects of stereotypes. Biracial individuals often describe experiences of discrimination, particularly those involving physical appearance, that took place during their childhood and even as adults. Furthermore, stereotypes about biracial individuals as confused and unhealthy contribute to widespread assumptions that being of mixed race is problematic. Other stereotypes, particularly of biracial women, include perceptions of exotic and sexualized behavior. Like stereotypes of any other groups, these generalizations can be internalized and negatively affect biracial individuals and can also contribute to discrimination targeted toward them.

Research also suggests that biracial youth may experience additional challenges and benefits as a result of their mixed racial heritage. One example is developing a personal identity. Whereas all adolescents grow and struggle with their sense of identity, multiracial adolescents also must integrate aspects of a racial identity that is unique because of its complexity and because of the fact that it does not fit into rigid, monoracial categories. Although being multiracial does not necessarily predict negative consequences for youth and adolescents, research suggests common challenges faced by multiracial youth, such as pressure (from family or others in society) to identify with one ethnicity over the other. For example, an African American/White female may be persuaded to identify with her African American background from her parents although she identifies more with her White peers, who may also reject her. Rejection from either family or peers can contribute to identity confusion and internalized negative stereotypes.

Whereas early research and theory focused on the negative aspects of mixed heritage individuals, recent research has highlighted strengths and positive aspects of biracial identity. Researchers have recognized that biracial individuals have the opportunity to be exposed to more cultural traditions and languages and may develop increased respect and appreciation of their parents' cultures. In addition, some studies have noted that biracial individuals have more positive attitudes toward other groups of different races than do those of monoracial backgrounds, highlighting the utility of being exposed to multiple cultures.

Qualitative studies also have shed light on the positive aspects of being biracial. In some studies, biracial adults noted there were challenges in various contexts of their lives, especially when they were growing up, but that overall they appreciated and took pride in being of mixed race. Furthermore, many of these individuals exhibited resilience and positive coping strategies as they faced various challenges, such as discrimination and prejudice. Taken together, there are many strengths that contribute to positive and healthy psychological functioning in biracial individuals, and it is expected that researchers will continue to elucidate these assets and resources as they work to understand the complexity of the biracial experience.

Counseling Biracial Individuals

Clinicians who work with biracial clients should be aware of challenges and strengths possessed by individuals of mixed race, as well as current research about identity development and psychological functioning. It is important to remember that biracial individuals may not present to counseling with racial identity as their primary concern; however, their identity will likely influence various other presenting concerns they may bring to therapy. Thus, it is important for clinicians to explore the meaning of race and ethnicity in the lives of clients to better understand their importance and role.

Clinicians working with biracial individuals are also encouraged to remember that identity development may not be linear and that each person may not pass through the same set of stages or changes. Although it is expected and likely that an individual will grapple with identity factors during adolescence, for example, it also is possible for individuals to revisit various identity issues throughout life, depending on personal and contextual factors. For example, a biracial college student who grew up in a diverse community may find herself moving to a less diverse city where her university is located. At this new setting she may find that she is confronted with challenges regarding how others perceive her identity and understand ethnicity. She may find that she revisits issues related to her racial background and may work to redefine herself in this new context.

Though there is some research to suggest that having an integrated identity may be helpful and adaptive for individuals of mixed race, it is not necessarily the only healthy or functional identity outcome for everyone. Indeed, many individuals may choose to identify as monoracial and still experience well-being and healthy psychological functioning. Clinicians should be aware of the multiple options for identification that exist for an individual and should not assume that choosing a biracial label is the only marker of positive psychological functioning.

Finally, because biracial identity can be influenced by numerous contextual factors, it is important for clinicians to understand a client's environment and the ways it influences a client's identity. Root's ecological model of identity serves as a useful framework for identifying the various aspects of a client's context that may play a role in his or her choice of identity, such as geographic location or physical appearance. Clinicians are also encouraged to explore the difference between how others see the client (the public or ascribed identity) and how the client sees himself or herself (the personal or private identity). Understanding the degree of convergence or divergence of these identities, as well as its influence on a client's well-being, can help provide a deeper understanding of a client's identity.

Multiracial Families

Interracial relationships are those relationships formed between two individuals whose racial backgrounds differ from one another. Two individuals with different racial heritages in a romantic relationship are often identified as an *interracial couple*. A U.S. Census 2000 brief reported an estimate of 246,000 Black–White unions that exist out of the 50 million marriages within the United States. Although

Black–White unions dominate the percentage of interracial marriages within the United States, interracial relationships are not limited to these two racial backgrounds. Other examples include an Asian female and an African American male, a Latino male and a White female, and a Native American male and an African American female. Although interracial relationships are still met with opposition, historical and societal changes have led to greater acceptance of younger generations who choose to become romantically involved with individuals of a different race.

Despite this growing acceptance, interracial couples may face additional issues that are not encountered by couples of the same race. Interracial couples sometimes experience hostility from society as well as from their own families and, in extreme cases, may be excluded from the family if relatives are not accepting of the relationship. Negative stereotypes and myths about biracial offspring may also contribute to negative attitudes toward adults who choose partners who are of a different race from themselves. Furthermore, the challenges of an interracial relationship can be exacerbated by the potential differences in the couples' cultural values. These cultural values will influence various aspects of the relationship such as gender roles and expectations of partners, communication styles, and parenting styles, among many others.

Researchers have discussed various counseling interventions to use with parents and children of multiracial families. It is important for counselors to examine their personal views and biases on interracial marriages and biracial or multiracial individuals so as not to bring those biases into the therapeutic relationship. Adolescents especially may be in great need of support from someone with a nonjudgmental stance who does not ascribe judgments based on stereotypes. For these youth, bibliotherapy, for example, reading about experiences that are similar to their biracial experiences, may be a useful intervention. Also, helping clients communicate their questions or concerns to other family members about being biracial is important for clients' acceptance of themselves. Children of mixed racial heritage may question why their physical appearance is different than that of their parents. Parents can communicate with their children an appropriate label to consider for their family so that children know what to say when confronted with the question, "What are you?" Clinicians can also provide psychoeducation to parents and families as they attempt to learn about the experience of having a mixed family and the unique issues they may be facing.

Future Research

Psychologists have noted that research about biracial individuals is still in the early stages of development but is definitely growing. With the increasing numbers of biracial individuals and clients in the United States, it is expected that researchers will continue to explore issues of identity, psychological functioning, and counseling interventions with these populations over the next years. There are several areas for future research that will further the field and expand our understanding of biracial individuals. One area includes conducting studies that explore more diverse samples. Past research has focused primarily on biracial individuals of Black and White heritage, but little research exists with combinations of other races. To understand the common experiences faced by all biracial individuals, as well as the unique issues related to those of specific racial combinations (e.g., Native American–Black), more research is needed.

Another area for further research relates to the methodology that is employed to study biracial issues. The majority of past research has relied on qualitative studies, and although this has provided useful models and frameworks, the field is poised to begin studying the biracial experience with larger populations to identify findings that can be generalizable. Indeed, many identity development models that were developed through qualitative studies can be tested with larger, diverse samples of biracial individuals. In addition, researchers may consider utilizing mixed method studies that combine qualitative and quantitative approaches to explicate processes of identity development that change over time.

Another area for further research is the exploration of issues related to multiple identities. It is clear that being biracial is only one aspect of any individual's identity, as every person also represents diversity with respect to gender, age, sexual orientation, disability, and other aspects of culture. To have a comprehensive understanding of the experiences and background of any individual, it is critical to understand the complexity of identity and how various aspects of culture interact. Some researchers have begun to explore biracial lesbians, for example, in an effort to understand the experience of being of mixed race, female, and attracted to the same sex. Continued research about multiple identities will further the field in understanding the complexity of biracial identity and psychological functioning.

Lisa M. Edwards, Noah E. Adrians, and Elizabeth P. McCadden

See also Bicultural (v3); Cultural Relativism (v3); Ethnic Identity (v3); Ethnicity (v3); Identity Development (v3); Multiracial Families (v3); Race (v3); Racial Identity (v3); Social Identity Theory (v3); Transracial Adoption (v3)

Further Readings

Gillem, A. R., & Thompson, C. A. (2004). *Biracial women in therapy: Between the rock of gender and the hard place of race.* Binghamton, NY: Haworth Press.

Miville, M. L. (2005). Psychological functioning and identity development of biracial people: A review of current theory and research. In R. T. Carter (Ed.), *Handbook of racial-cultural psychology and counseling* (pp. 295–319). Hoboken, NJ: Wiley.

Poston, W. S. C. (1990). The biracial identity development model: A needed addition. *Journal of Counseling & Development, 69,* 152–155.

Root, M. P. P. (1992). *Racially mixed people in America.* Thousand Oaks, CA: Sage.

Root, M. P. P. (1996). *The multiracial experience.* Thousand Oaks, CA: Sage.

U.S. Census Bureau. (2001, November). *The two or more races population: 2000.* Retrieved from http://www.census.gov/population/www/cen2000/briefs.html

Wehrly, B. (2003). Breaking barriers for multiracial individuals and families. In F. D. Harper & J. McFadden (Eds.), *Culture and counseling: New approaches* (pp. 313–323). Boston: Pearson Education.

Web Sites

Association of MultiEthnic Americans: http://www.ameasite.org
MAVIN Foundation: http://www.mavin.net

BLACK ENGLISH

Black English, also referred to as Black English Vernacular (BEV), African American Vernacular English (AAVE), or Ebonics, is a dialectal adaptation of Standard American English found primarily within the African American community. The term refers primarily to patterns of speech that some scholars believe developed during the slavery period in America, as Africans learned English by adapting it to the linguistic patterns of their native dialect. Other scholars argue that Black English developed out of pidgin English, an amalgamation of Standard American English and several African dialects, which facilitated communication within a culturally heterogeneous slave population. It is largely held that this method of communication, while varying regionally, gained a level of permanence throughout the African American community because of the segregation it frequently experienced. Although Black English has traditionally been depicted negatively within American society, contemporary pop culture has adopted many Black English colloquialisms and added them to the American English lexicon.

Syntax of Black English

Studies of the syntax of Black English have frequently attributed its deviations from Standard English to West African language rules. For example, the lack of consonant pairs in many West African languages is seen as responsible for the elimination of consonants in Black English; thus, for example, the word *just* becomes *jus.* Similarly, the lack of *r* and *th* sounds in West African languages leads to substitutions such as *souf* for *south* and *dis* for *this.* Frequent absence of the verb *be* in present-tense Black English (e.g., "They so noisy!") can be attributed to the lack of such an equivalent in many West African languages.

Controversy Involving Black English

In 1996, the Oakland Unified School District of Oakland, California, sought to increase academic performance among African American students by recognizing Black English, or Ebonics, as a distinct language and its speakers as bilingual. The school district intended to enhance English proficiency among poorly performing African American students by, among other things, linking their experience to that of English as a second language learners. It was the school district's contention that Black English was the primary language of the home for many African American students, and their limited English proficiency was, as with other ethnic groups, related to interference from their most commonly spoken tongue.

This proposed curricular conceptualization met significant resistance within the field of education as well as within segments of the African American community itself. Many saw Black English as simply incorrectly spoken English or as broken English and not a language deserving of recognition or curricular considerations. Others misinterpreted the intentions of the Oakland Unified School District as seeking to instruct students in Black English as opposed to Standard English. Although the Oakland School District's initial attempt to incorporate vernacular speech patterns into English instruction was met with opposition, this topic continues to surface among educators of African American students.

Hammad S. N'cho

See also African Americans (v3); Afrocentricity/Afrocentrism (v3); Communication (v3); Ethnic Identity (v3); Racial Identity (v3)

Further Readings

Mufwene, S. S., Rickford, J. R., Bailey, G., & Baugh, J. (1998). *African-American English: Structure, history and use.* New York: Routledge.

Rickford, J. R., & Rickford, R. J. (2002). *Spoken soul: The story of Black English.* New York: Wiley.

Smith, E. (1995). Bilingualism and the African American child. In M. Ice & M. Saunders-Luca (Eds.), *Reading: The blending of theory and practice* (pp. 90–91, 93). Bakersfield: California State University.

Smitherman, G. (1977). *Talkin and testifyin: The language of Black America.* Boston: Houghton Mifflin.

Van Keulen, J. E., Weddington, G. T., & Debose, C. E. (1998). *Speech, language, learning and the African American child.* Boston: Allyn & Bacon.

BLACK PSYCHOLOGY

Black psychology is an emerging discipline broadly defined as an evolving system of knowledge concerning elements of human nature, specifically study of the experience and behavior of people of African descent (Black populations). Historically, Black psychology stems from African philosophy, yet early perspectives in the United States focused on reacting to Western psychology's characterization of Blacks as psychologically inferior. Contemporary perspectives proactively create racially sensitive models and establish African-centered models of human behavior for understanding the Black experience. Drawing upon emerging Black and African-centered psychological perspectives will contribute to the future of cross-cultural counseling with people of African descent.

The Emerging Discipline of Black Psychology

Historical Foundations

The historical foundations of Black psychology extend back to the educational systems of Ancient Egypt (Kemet, 3200 B.C.). During that time, African scholars developed complex philosophies, or systems of knowledge, which predated Greek philosophy. The African philosophical belief systems, contemporarily known as worldviews, informed members of society about how to understand reality and the structure of all things in the universe, including human relations and values. Duadi Azibo, Kobi K. Kambon, Linda James Myers, and Wade W. Nobles are a few of the notable Black psychologists who discuss the philosophical foundations of Black psychology based on four major components of African worldview: (1) Cosmology, the structure of the universe or reality, reflects interdependence, collectivism, and unity with nature; (2) ontology, the essential nature of reality, including the self, is a spiritual divine energy manifesting in the physical or material realm; (3) epistemology, the nature of knowledge, regards knowing reality through affective and cognitive self-knowledge using symbolic imagery and rhythm; and (4) axiology, the basic value system, focuses on positive human relations. Prior to the emergence of these African worldview concepts in Western academia, early Black psychologists were establishing their legitimacy and researching the inferior status of Blacks in traditional psychology.

Early Black Psychologists

In 1920, Francis Summer became the first Black person in America to earn a Ph.D. in psychology. In 1938, Herman Canady convened the first group of Black educators in psychology as a caucus within the American Teachers Association (ATA) at its annual convention in Tuskegee, Alabama (the ATA was the primary professional organization for Black educators at the time). The group's main goal was to promote the teaching and the application of psychology, particularly at Black schools and among Black scholars.

Subsequently, numerous Black psychologists in the early 20th century published theories and research critiquing racist social policies. The research of Kenneth and Mamie Clark on racial preferences among Black preschool children helped to determine the 1954 landmark case *Brown v. Board of Education,* which affirmed the unconstitutionality of separate but equal schools. Ironically, early theory and research also fostered a perspective of Blacks as deficient, claiming that the effects of discrimination and oppression left Blacks with few strengths, self-hatred, and low self-esteem. In the late 1960s, the emergence of the Black Power movement and Black Nationalism inspired some African American psychologists to combat the deficit view and eventually form the first independent Black psychological association.

Association of Black Psychologists

The Association of Black Psychologists was founded in 1968 following a formative group of African American psychologists voicing frustration and outrage with the policies and practices of the American Psychological Association (APA). The Black psychologists attending the APA San Francisco conference in 1968 made several proposals requesting that APA address concerns regarding the effects of racism in multiple settings, such as the Black community, educational settings, psychological research, testing, and graduate training programs. Dissatisfied with the response, the formative group decided to establish an organization that would advance a Black psychology, separate and distinct from Western psychology.

In 1972, numerous Black scholars under the editorship of Reginald L. Jones published the inaugural text *Black Psychology.* Here, Wade W. Nobles introduced the African philosophical foundations of Black psychology and Joseph White formally advocated for a theory of Black psychology out of the authentic perspective of Black people in the United States. By 1974, under the inaugural editor William David Smith, the Association of Black Psychologists launched the *Journal of Black Psychology* to provide a peer review platform for publishing empirical research, original theoretical analysis of data, and discussions of current literature in the domain of Black populations. In 1984 the journal published a 10-year content analysis indicating a small increase in empirical articles using the traditional deficit view to explain Black behavior and a need for explanatory models based upon African descent values and the diverse cultural experiences among Blacks. During the journal's second period of self-evaluation (1985–1999), the results of which were published in 2001, the trend of articles focused on Black personality development addressing racial/cultural identity and racial/cultural consciousness. In recent years the journal has focused on a number of health psychology special issues addressing substance abuse prevention, HIV/AIDS, gender, sexuality, and suicidal behavior and articles examining the psychological impact of racism and discrimination among Blacks. Today both the Black and African-centered perspectives contribute to the diversity of publications in this emerging discipline.

Black and African-Centered Psychology Perspectives

The Black (also called African American) psychology perspective is the study of the experience of Black populations, particularly in the United States, using principles adapted from traditional psychology to create racially and culturally sensitive models. The perspective uses traditional empirical methods to dismantle the prevailing view of the 1960s through 1980s that African Americans are culturally deficient against the normative standard of European American beliefs, values, and lifestyles. Unlike the deficit view, Black psychology's racial and cultural models emphasize cultural strengths and limitations in the context of social and environmental factors.

Alternatively, the African-centered psychology perspective concerns understanding human nature, using African philosophical values, thus going beyond oppressive social contexts. The perspective defines experience from an African-centered psychological orientation, emphasizing worldview dimensions of spirituality, collectivism, oral tradition, affective senses, and harmony in relationships. Equivalent to using traditional empirical methods of observing behavior is understanding human nature through feelings or emotional and cognitive processes of self-knowledge or self-realization. Although systematic research is limited, African-centered psychology models for understanding people of African descent—for example, the Azibo nosology diagnostic system of psychopathology and Na'im Akbar's classification of mental disorders—are emerging. Models of positive

Black identity, Black families, and education are but a few examples of both Black and African-centered psychology perspectives.

Black Identity

First theorized by Charles Thomas (cofounding chair of the Association of Black Psychologists), William E. Cross, Jr.'s 1971 linear stage–based racial identity theory, labeled the Nigrescence model, gave rise to extensive research on how Blacks identify with and psychologically interpret the meaning of their racial group in the context of racism and social oppression. Most notably Janet E. Helms and other scholars went on to revise and expand racial identity theory, which now includes status-based, life-span development perspectives, multidimensional models, and measures of racial identity such as the Cross Racial Identity Scale and the Black Racial Identity Scales. A decade of empirical inquiry using the scales examines within-group differences of racial identity and its association with demographic variables, academic achievement, problem behaviors, acculturation, socialization, racism-related variables, and counselor preference of Blacks in cross-cultural counseling.

Concurrently, Wade Nobles's 1972 theory of African self-concept or African self-consciousness laid the foundation for decades of African-centered psychology research. Using African philosophical assumptions about human nature, the African self-consciousness view stresses awareness of one's past history, one's collective spiritual consciousness, and one's individual and group self-concept. Subsequent models of African-self consciousness focus on a spiritual and collective identity as the core of the Black personality. Various scholars conducted assessment and research of the African personality with such scales as the African Self-Consciousness Scale and the Black Personality Questionnaire. Psychometric scales such as the Afrocentrism Measure, the African Value for Children Scale, and the Spirituality Scale continue in use to advance understanding of the Black experience via the African-centered perspective.

Black Families

Black families are defined as extended family networks that involve immediate family, friends, neighbors, church members, and fictive kin or members not biologically related. African American perspectives examine both structural and functional aspects of family, emphasizing acculturation, socialization, and coping factors. Black perspectives also take care not to pathologize or highlight deficit views of Black families, but to promote the strengths and consideration of socioeconomic, historical, and political factors that affect families. African-centered perspectives additionally emphasize the family values of spirit, interconnection, children, cooperation, responsibility, and respect for elders.

Education

Black psychology perspectives on education are defined by emphasis on the educational experiences, needs, and career development of African Americans. Perspectives of the 1960s and 1970s addressing elementary school age children included combating culturally deficient paradigms about intelligence, language, dialect, and learning styles. In the past 2 decades researchers have turned to emphasizing the role of culture and advocating for culturally congruent education acknowledging racial/ethnic identity, socialization, home, spirituality, and community practices among youth and college-age students. Emerging African-centered initiatives teach youth about unique cultural concepts such as the *Nguzo Saba* principles (*Umoja*—unity, *Kujichagulia*—self-determination, *Ujima*—collective work and responsibility, *Ujamaa*—cooperative economics, *Nia*—purpose, *Kuumba*—creativity, and *Imani*—faith) of the African American holiday Kwanzaa and the *Ntu* (meaning "energy") system of health and healing. The concept of *Maat*, referring to the principles of truth, justice, righteousness, reciprocity, harmony, balance, and order, is another cultural value system emerging in educational and Black psychological initiatives.

Future Directions

Black psychology is an emerging discipline transformed from reacting to Western psychology to constructing models that explain the Black experience from perspectives that are racially sensitive and emphasize the strength of African cultural values. Future theory and research will likely employ overlapping Black and African-centered approaches to generate practice models supportive of adaptive functioning and the diverse counseling needs of African Americans. Counseling paradigms that articulate the Black experience in both the context of racial oppression and the African worldview will increase

Black psychology as a resource for cross-cultural counseling with people of African descent.

Ma'at E. Lewis-Coles

See also Acculturation (v3); African Americans (v3); Afrocentricity/Afrocentrism (v3); Association of Black Psychologists (v3); Black Racial Identity Development (v3); Clark, Kenneth Bancroft (v3); Clark, Mamie Phipps (v3); Cross, William E., Jr. (v3); Discrimination (v3); Helms, Janet E. (v3); Kwanzaa (v3); Racism (v3); Spirituality (v3); Worldview (v3)

Further Readings

Belgrave, F. A., & Allison, K. W. (2006). *African American psychology: From Africa to America.* Thousand Oaks, CA: Sage.

Cokley, K., Caldwell, L., Miller, K., & Muhammad, G. (2001). Content analysis of the *Journal of Black Psychology* (1985–1999). *Journal of Black Psychology, 27*(4), 401–438.

Guthrie, R. V. (1976). *Even the rat was white: A historical view of psychology.* New York: Harper & Row.

Jones, R. (Ed.). (2004). *Black psychology* (4th ed.). Hampton, VA: Cobb & Henry.

Kambon, K. K. (1998). *African/Black psychology in the American context: An African-centered approach.* Tallahassee, FL: Nubian Nation.

Nobles, W. (1986). *African psychology: Towards its reclamation, reascension & revitalization.* Oakland, CA: Black Family Institute.

Parham, T. A. (2002). *Counseling persons of African descent: Raising the bar of practitioner excellence.* Thousand Oaks, CA: Sage.

Parham, T. A., White, J. L., & Ajamu, A. (1990). *The psychology of Blacks: An African-centered perspective.* Upper Saddle River, NJ: Prentice Hall.

Web Sites

Association of Black Psychologists: http//www.abpsi.org

BLACK RACIAL IDENTITY DEVELOPMENT

Black racial identity development (BRID) theory explains the processes by which Black people (the term *Black* is used here, rather than *African American*, to reflect the terminology in models of identity development) develop a healthy sense of themselves as racial beings and of their Blackness in a toxic sociopolitical environment. BRID is generally viewed as a derivation of more general racial/cultural development theory, in that it describes the importance of race in an individual's self-concept. However, BRID is distinctive in its attention to the unique experience of Black people in dealing with racial discrimination and oppression.

The concept of race has played a historically important role in the lives of Black people in the United States, as reflected in the early writings of W. E. B. Du Bois. In the most recent literature, Black identity development has been associated with factors such as psychological health, academic achievement, acculturation, psychosocial competence, self-actualization, self-esteem, and student involvement.

Models of Black Racial Identity Development

Black racial identity development has often been conceptualized in models that describe linear stages through which Black individuals move from a negative to a positive self-identity in the context of their racial group membership. One of the earliest and most influential models of BRID was developed by William E. Cross, Jr., as part of his Nigrescence (the process of becoming Black) theory. Cross used a five-stage model to describe a Black person's feelings, thoughts, and behaviors as he or she moves from a White frame of reference to a positive Black frame of reference: pre-encounter, encounter, immersion/emersion, internalization, and internalization/commitment.

In the *pre-encounter* stage, Black people consciously or unconsciously manifest an anti-Black worldview while seeking to assimilate and acculturate into dominant White society. Low self-esteem and poor psychological health are characteristic of individuals at this stage. The *encounter* stage is marked by two processes: (1) an experience that challenges the pre-encounter individual's pro-White/anti-Black worldview, and (2) a reinterpretation of one's racial identity as a result of this experience. At this stage, a Black person finds support in the search for a Black identity and makes the conscious decision to identify with being Black. A strong pro-Black attitude and withdrawal from, and hostility toward, dominant White culture typifies the *immersion/emersion* stage, signifying a switch from the "old" anti-Black/pro-White worldview. The individual has an acute sense of Black pride, but a positive Black identity has not yet been internalized.

Feelings of guilt and anger at having been conditioned by White culture are common. At the *internalization* stage, Black people succeed in reconciling the antagonism of their pre-encounter and immersion/emersion worldviews. The individual's resentment of White culture subsides and a nonracist, multicultural orientation prevails. Social action demarcates the ultimate stage, *internalization/commitment,* from the previous stage. Here, Black people not only incorporate a positive Black racial identity into their self-concepts, but they also make a commitment to activities that promote social justice and civil rights.

The Nigrescence model has received the most attention in the psychological literature of all the BRID models, particularly for its association with a measurement instrument developed by Janet Helms—the Racial Identity Attitude Scale–Black—which has been used to operationalize BRID in a number of studies. Cross and his colleagues have since revised the Nigrescence model, collapsing the internalization and internalization/commitment stages into one stage (internalization) and expanding each stage into multiple "identity clusters" to address the criticism that numerous identities may be manifested at each stage.

Another model of BRID, proposed by Bailey Jackson, explains a slightly different version of racial identity development. Whereas Cross suggested that dominant culture worldviews could be internalized on a subconscious level, characteristic of his pre-encounter stage, Jackson's four-stage model describes an initial *passive acceptance* stage in which Black people accept and conform to White cultural norms. The second stage, *active resistance,* is characterized by the rejection of, and feelings of anger toward, White culture. The *redirection* stage is associated with pride of one's Black culture and a mollified anger toward White culture. Thus, although Cross combined elements of these two identities into one stage, immersion/emersion, Jackson conceptualizes them as two distinct processes. Finally, the *internalization* stage is marked by both an acceptance of the healthy aspects of the dominant White culture and a commitment to taking action to redress the deleterious aspects.

Mainstream Versus Underground Theories

The BRID theories previously described focus on the universal processes of group identity development that Black people undergo to arrive at a psychologically healthy racial self-concept. These models have been referred to as *mainstream* theories of Black racial identity. Another set of theories—called *underground* theories for their relative noninclusion in the broader psychological community—generally take a more Africentric perspective and do not hold the assumption that all Black individuals begin the process of identity development with anti-Black attitudes. Historically, W. E. B. Du Bois argued that Black sociocultural influences can aid in racial identity development and that one's self-concept is not necessarily a reaction to racial oppression. According to underground theories, the reconciliation between one's "African self" and one's "American self" is the essential task in developing a healthy BRID. However, there is disagreement among underground theorists over how to reconcile these two "selves": Some theorists claim that African Americans benefit from attending to both their "Blackness" and the broader White society, whereas others argue that an integrated identity comes only when one strongly identifies with all things Black.

Applications for Training and Counseling

BRID theories have important practical implications in their capacity to help counselors recognize the differences in racial identity development among Black clients. An individual's level of racial identity development has an important bearing on his or her attitudinal and behavioral predispositions in the counseling relationship. Helms used the updated four-stage Nigrescence model to project the nature of counseling relationships with a Black counselor and client across the stages of identity development.

For example, a pre-encounter client would likely be disappointed about being assigned a Black counselor and would exhibit hostility or embarrassment toward the counselor. A pre-encounter counselor may treat Black clients in a punitive, condescending fashion. Black clients in the encounter stage may be hypersensitive to the approval of a Black counselor and may, accordingly, be apologetic and avoid issues they deem non-Black. A counselor in this stage can show fear over whether or not the Black client will approve of him or her and also anticipation for the opportunity to connect with a member of his or her racial group. Clients in the immersion/emersion stage will feel positively toward a Black counselor only after determining that the counselor has a high enough level of "Blackness." There may, therefore, be an early combative, testing element to the relationship.

The internalizing client may prefer a Black counselor, but race no longer has primacy in the selection process. Counselors in the internalizing stage aim to help the client achieve self-actualization, and they focus on the issue of race insomuch as it is an important part of actualization.

Helms states that for a counselor to help a client progress through stages of racial identity development, he or she must be at least one stage ahead of the client in his or her own development. If the counselor and client are at the same stage, or if the client is at a more advanced stage than the counselor, then a counseling impasse may occur.

Another important application of BRID to counseling is its role in helping counselors understand the role that oppression plays in Black clients' development. This awareness serves as a clarion call for many to explore systemic interventions and take action outside the confines of their offices to combat sociopolitical factors, such as racism and poverty, that impact clients' psychological health.

Future Directions

Early formulations of BRID, such as Cross's Nigrescence model, have been criticized for conceptualizing BRID as a linear process and focusing upon BRID in late adolescence/early adulthood. However, Thomas Parham and Janet Helms have reconceptualized BRID to reflect a more fluid notion of identity development in which individuals can move both forward and backward through the different statuses across the life span.

Eleanor Seaton and colleagues recently found that Black individuals may both progress and regress across BRID stages over time, supporting this more fluid conceptualization of racial identity development. Tabbye Chavous and colleagues have further illuminated the complexity of BRID via cluster analyses, suggesting BRID may also involve the salience of race in one's identity, feelings regarding one's racial group, and attitudes regarding how Blacks are perceived by others in the United States. The complexity of BRID in recent research provides promising future directions for theory and research.

Although theories of BRID have done much to explain an individual's racial identity, there has been less exploration of the intersections of BRID with other aspects of identity, such as gender, class, and sexual orientation. The interactions of these factors with Black identity may have important implications. Likewise, there may also be important yet unexplored geographic considerations in BRID. Most BRID theories were conceived in the climate of Western cultures; the development of Black people's racial identities in non-Western cultures is much less understood. Similarly, theories of BRID, and underground theories in particular, emphasize the importance of reconnecting with aspects of one's African heritage, yet the processes for doing so are still unclear.

Adam M. Voight and Matthew A. Diemer

See also African Americans (v3); Afrocentrism/Afrocentricity (v3); Ethnic Identity (v3); Identity (v3); Identity Development (v3); Multicultural Counseling (v3); Oppression (v3); Racial Identity (v3)

Further Readings

Chavous, T. M., Bernat, D. H., Schmeelk-Cone, K., Caldwell, C. H., Kohn-Wood, L., & Zimmerman, M. A. (2003). Racial identity and educational attainment among African American adolescents. *Child Development, 74,* 1076–1090.

Constantine, M. G., Richardson, T. Q., Benjamin, E. M., & Wilson, J. W. (1998). An overview of Black racial identity theories: Limitations and considerations for future theoretical conceptualizations. *Applied & Preventive Psychology, 7,* 95–99.

Cross, W. E. (1971). The Negro to Black conversion experience: Toward a psychology of Black liberation. *Black World, 20,* 13–27.

Helms, J. E. (1984). Towards a theoretical explanation of effects of race on counseling: A Black and White model. *Counseling Psychologist, 12,* 153–165.

Sellers, R. M., Shelton, J. N., Cooke, D. Y., Chavous, T. M., Rowley, F. A. J., & Smith, M. A. (1997). Multidimensional model of racial identity: A reconceptualization of African American racial identity. *Personality and Social Psychology Review, 2,* 18–39.

Vandiver, B. J., Cross, W. E., Worrell, F. C., & Fhagen-Smith, P. E. (2002). Validating the Cross Racial Identity Scale. *Journal of Counseling Psychology, 49,* 71–85.

BUREAU OF INDIAN AFFAIRS

As one of the oldest agencies within the U.S. government, the Bureau of Indian Affairs (BIA) shares a complex and traumatic history with Native Nations. Originally part of the War Department, the BIA was transferred to the Department of the Interior in 1849 by an act of Congress. Since its establishment as a federal agency, the BIA as well as its precursors have been tasked with managing and overseeing most matters relating to Indian affairs and relations between Indian Nations and the U.S. government; examples include educational services, land and other asset management, health care, and economic development.

As the relations between Native Nations and the United States have changed dramatically since colonization, the roles of the BIA have also transformed. The agency's responsibilities have changed to reflect evolution of the U.S. government's policies toward Native Nations that have been shaped by treaties, laws, and court rulings. These responsibilities have ranged from enforcing policies of removal, "civilization," assimilation, and termination of American Indian tribes to implementing policies that support tribal sovereignty, self-determination, and self-government. However, the relationship between the BIA and Native Nations remains complex.

Historical Context

Removal and Reservations

From 1824 to 1849, the BIA was housed within the War Department; the agency was then known as the Office of Indian Affairs. The placement of the agency was reflective of the mostly constant hostile and conflictual nature of U.S. and Native relations. Through warfare, other uses of military force, and the creation of treaties (many of which were fraudulent) with Native Nations, the United States gained control of more than 90% of Indian lands. As part of the removal policy and also the treaty-making process, the government created the reservation system, lands where tribes were permanently removed to or relocated and forced to remain under military sanction. In exchange for ceding their ancestral lands, Native Nations were promised in treaties they would be provided food, education, other goods, and annuities, thereby creating a state of dependency on the U.S. government. However, treaties were chronically violated through official corruption within the government, specifically, the Office of Indian Affairs, and continued hostile acts of European American settlers against Native peoples.

Following the Indian Removal Act of 1830, the Office of Indian Affairs oversaw the removal of southeastern tribes (primarily Cherokee, Muscogee Creek, Seminole, Choctaw, and Chickasaw) to what was then called Indian Territory, today known as the state of Oklahoma. Whereas some citizens of these tribes had relocated to lands west of the Mississippi prior to the removal act, the U.S. military, under the auspices of the Office of Indian Affairs, forcibly removed others to Indian Territory. For example, in 1838, the Cherokees, most of whom had not migrated to Indian Territory, were forcibly removed from their ancestral lands on a thousand-mile march that became known as the Trail of Tears. More than 4,000 people died on the journey. The primary objective of the removal was to open up more than 25 million acres of eastern land to European American settlement.

Assimilation

In 1847, the Office of Indian Affairs was renamed the Bureau of Indian Affairs, and 2 years later the agency was transferred to the Department of the Interior, which had been newly established by Congress. Following the era of removal, relocation, and creation of the reservation system, the official U.S. policy toward American Indians changed to one of assimilation. This policy aimed to extinguish Native culture and "civilize" or "Americanize" Indians; it was enforced mostly through the boarding school system formally administered by the BIA, and it continued governmental control of land also under the auspices of the BIA.

The General Allotment Act, or Dawes Act of 1887, abolished communal title of reservation lands and forced families onto individual allotments typically of 80 to 160 acres to be held in trust by the government. Whatever reservation land was left after allotment was sold. In less than 4 years, more than 12 million acres had been designated as "surplus," and just 10 years later, nearly 29 million acres had been designated as surplus. One result of the Dawes Act was the fragmentation of reservation land, further disrupting tribes' communal relationship with the land and placing physical distance between tribes' citizens and families. For the U.S. government, the primary aim of the act was twofold: to obtain more land, opening it up for European American settlement, and to "civilize" Native Nations into European American society and culture.

In 1879, the Carlisle Indian Industrial School was founded by Captain Richard Pratt in Carlisle,

Pennsylvania, and operated until 1918. Pratt is infamous for saying, "Kill the Indian and save the man." The Carlisle School was the model upon which all other governmental boarding schools were based and operated, most under regimented military-style rules. Indian children were forced to attend boarding schools that were generally located very far away from their tribes and families; separations from family members would often last for years. Everything from clothing, haircuts, language use, food, and lifestyle in the schools were "American" and were meant to "civilize" the children mandated to attend those schools. In addition to the subjects of arithmetic and U.S. history, children were taught to read, write, and speak English. Speaking their Native languages or practicing any cultural activities or traditions was prohibited and typically met with severe physical punishment. Less than 10 years after the founding of the Carlisle School, 41 boarding schools operated under the BIA's management, most of which were administered through Christian religious organizations.

When tribes and parents refused to allow their children to be taken away to boarding schools, BIA agents would incarcerate parents and withhold rations of food, clothing, blankets, and other necessities from the tribe, forcing them to submit to the government's will. Indian boarding schools, rather than being institutions that fostered healthy child and adolescent development, were institutions that allowed perpetration and perpetuation of emotional, physical, and sexual abuse of the children who attended them. The boarding school system operated in much the same way into the 1960s. The abuse that occurred in the schools, as well as the resulting disastrous and traumatic effects on Native Nations and cultures, are felt in nearly every aspect of life and have been well documented. Loss of language, religious and spiritual practices, cultural knowledge, traditional parenting practices, and cultural identity and heritage have profoundly damaged Native Nations, communities, families, and individuals. This damage is evident in the high incidence of suicide, alcoholism and other substance abuse/dependence, child abuse and neglect, domestic violence, and other social and behavioral problems within many Native communities.

Termination

Beginning in the early 1950s, in an effort to permanently cut federal funding of Native Nations and further assimilate American Indians into American society, federal Indian policy was that of termination. This referred to the U.S. government terminating federal relations with Native Nations. The government withdrew federal recognition of many tribes during this time, which effectively disallowed federal benefits and services to such Nations. For affected Nations, this policy was economically and politically crippling.

Another aspect of federal termination policy included relocation programs. These programs, administered via the BIA, relocated American Indian families to urban areas for perceived job training and economic opportunities, again perpetuating the belief that assimilation was a means to a better life. One major effect of relocation programs was further dilution in Native community strength, as relocated members were seldom able to travel back home because of economic reasons. The descendants of this relocated generation experienced even further disconnection from their cultures and communities.

Contemporary Policies

Self-Determination and Self-Governance

The late 1960s and into the 1970s saw passage of several congressional acts that seemed to support Native self-determination, for example, the 1968 Indian Civil Rights Act, the 1975 Indian Self-Determination Act, the 1978 Indian Child Welfare Act, and the 1978 Indian Religious Freedom Act. Each act reaffirmed tribal sovereignty and the special trust relationship between Native Nations and the United States. Additionally, they provided Native Nations greater jurisdiction over their affairs in each of these important areas.

This policy has transformed today to one of self-governance in which the United States recognizes Native Nations' governments; Nations are able to directly address and negotiate with the U.S. government for their own interests. In terms of the BIA, the policy of self-governance provides Native Nations much more autonomy over administration of federal monies and economic and social programs. However, conflicts of interest still arise, for example, protection of water and land rights. Oftentimes the BIA, whose task is to protect such rights on behalf of Native Nations, is confronted with competing interests from other Department of Interior agencies (e.g., Bureau of Land Management). Such conflicts of interest may result in poor outcomes for Native interests, thereby maintaining tension in an already complex relationship.

Jill S. Hill, Rockey R. Robbins, and Megan Correia

See also Alaska Natives (v3); American Indians (v3); Career Counseling, Native Americans (v4); Indian Health Service (v3); Society of Indian Psychologists (v3)

Future Readings

Henson, C. L. (1995). From war to self-determination: A history of the Bureau of Indian Affairs. *American Studies Today Online.* Retrieved from http://www.americansc.org.uk/Online/indians.htm

Reyhner, J., & Eder, J. (1989). *A history of Indian education.* Billings: Eastern Montana College, Bilingual Education Program.

Smith, A. (2005). *Conquest: Sexual violence and American Indian genocide.* Cambridge, MA: South End Press.

Wilkins, D. E. (2007). *American Indian politics and the American political system* (2nd ed.). Lanham, MD: Rowman & Littlefield.

Wilson, J. (1998). *The earth shall weep: A history of Native America.* New York: Grove Press.

Witko, T. M. (2006). *Mental health care for urban Indians: Clinical insights from Native practitioners.* Washington, DC: American Psychological Association.

Casas, Jesús Manuel (1941–)

Jesús Manuel (Manny) Casas was born in the small town of Avalos, Chihuahua, Mexico. His rich racial/ethnic heritage includes roots in Spain and indigenous Mexico. His paternal great-grandmother was Apache, having been saved by Mexican wagon masters from U.S. cavalry raids on her village and subsequently taken to Mexico where she was raised by his great-grandfather's family. Something that ties him historically to California, the state in which he has lived most of his life, is the fact that in the 1800s his paternal great-grandfather spent a major portion of his life driving a wagon train from the north central part of Mexico to Sacramento, California, and back again.

Casas immigrated to the United States at a young age and was educated in the racially hostile environs of the U.S. educational system during the late 1940s and 1950s. Part of this historical period is best captured in Casas's own words from his 2001 published life story:

> On the first day of school, my mother, along with a limited-English speaking friend, walked me and a friend to school, got me to the classroom and left. As I entered the classroom, I experienced the kind of aloneness, fear, and alienation that, if it were in my power, no other child would ever have to experience. No one looked like me. No one spoke my language. I couldn't communicate with anyone, including the teacher. To solve this communication problem, the teacher came up with a unique and intellectually challenged strategy. I would be seated in the back of the room—not the bus—the room, where I could listen and with time eventually pick up the English language. (Casas et al., 2001, p. 84)

And so began Casas's lifelong devotion to advocating for immigrant families—particularly poor Latino/a families and children.

Despite the discrimination he experienced during his primary and secondary schooling, he graduated at the top of his high school class and went on to college at the University of California, Berkeley. After graduating, he taught in the public schools for 5 years before going on to graduate school. He earned his Ph.D. at Stanford University in 1975. After 2 years as a counseling psychologist at the University of California, Los Angeles, he began his career at the University of California, Santa Barbara. Over the course of his more than 30 years as a psychologist, Casas has become widely recognized as a distinguished scholar of Chicano/a psychology. He is now the senior Chicano faculty member in the University of California system.

Though Casas is best known for his work in developing the field of Chicano/a psychology, he has also done considerable work in general multicultural counseling. He is a Fellow of the American Psychological Association (APA) Division 17 (Society of Counseling Psychology) and Division 45 (Society for the Psychological Study of Ethnic Minority Issues). He is also the recipient of many awards, most recently the National Latina/o Psychological Association Psychologist's Distinguished Contributions to Latino(a) Psychology Award in 2006, and he was honored as an elder at the 2007 APA National Multicultural Summit and Conference.

He has been a reviewer or editorial board member for 19 journals, including *The Counseling Psychologist, Journal of Counseling Psychology, Journal of Multicultural Counseling and Development, Cultural Diversity & Ethnic Minority Psychology,* and *American Psychologist.* He has authored or coauthored 140 articles and has presented 129 papers at professional conferences internationally. He has published in the flagship journals of his field and has either written, edited, or contributed to most of the seminal works in multicultural counseling. Casas's works are among the most frequently cited in the field of multicultural counseling, and his works have literally contributed to defining the field and pushing it to use more rigorous research methods.

With all of these accomplishments, one of Casas's greatest strengths is as a teacher and mentor. To produce scholars who are also caring teachers, he combines his immense knowledge of the literature and Socratic teaching style with the care and interest of a parent. Among his many protégés who have gone on to establish their own records of excellence in multicultural counseling psychology are some of the field's most dedicated and eminent counseling psychologists. Casas has collaborated with dozens of prominent multicultural counseling psychologists—far too many to name here.

Casas's role as a practitioner has been primarily in the area of advocacy and consultation. He has consulted with over 50 governmental and nongovernmental organizations, mostly as a multicultural or diversity consultant. To this point, Casas was one of the only Latino psychologists to work toward increasing the sensitivity, knowledge, and practices of selective Fortune 500 companies who, early on, acknowledged their need to reach and access the growing Latino/a population. Through this work, he developed training models and manuals that are still in use today. More importantly, Casas has been an advocate for the Chicano/a communities and other oppressed groups during his career. Very few people know the amount of time, energy, and resources that he has poured into the local Chicano/a community in Santa Barbara. For instance, he has served on numerous boards of nonprofit organizations that work toward increasing the educational and social well-being of Latino/a children and families (e.g., Head Start). He continues to be a member of the Santa Barbara Mental Health Commission. In this position he serves as an advocate for those populations that are inappropriately served or underserved by the mental health system. More to the point, when asked why he wanted to be on the Commission, Casas said, "Someone needs to watch how they are spending the money and to make sure it gets to the families that need it."

Casas has secured millions of dollars worth of grants from public and private foundations. He has been responsible for channeling more than $10 million of grant money to the County of Santa Barbara for use in the development of interventions for high-risk children. In addition, he has served as the cochair of the University of California Chancellor's Outreach Advisory Board, overseeing the distribution of millions of dollars earmarked for increasing the pipeline of students of color eligible for admission to the University of California.

Casas continues his work as an advocate, consultant, educator, and researcher, As an advocate, he is directing much of his energy to work with the local community to identify and implement the best practices and interventions that can be used to combat the growing menace of gang violence. As a consultant, Casas is volunteering his time to work with the Universidad del Valle de Guatemala to help the university to develop the first Ph.D.-level counseling psychology training program in Guatemala. He welcomes this venture because it gives him a chance to test the generalizability of many existing multicultural theories and practices with the very diverse and indigenous population of Guatemala. With respect to research, he is "examining old wine in new bottles." More specifically, to increase the understanding of ethnic identity, he is examining, comparing, and contrasting this construct with other psychological constructs that together are the essence of the "self."

Casas's lifelong devotion to bettering the conditions of his people through his work has taken a more personal turn in recent years. It is common to see him out in the community with his two young, recently emigrated godsons, Joel and Manuelito, in whom he is already instilling the love of learning and commitment to the community. These boys are now benefiting from the care, nurturing, and structure that so many students and clients have received from Casas. In their eyes are reflected Dr. Casas's dream . . . and the love they have for their *abuelito.*

Michael I. Loewy and Roger L. Worthington

See also Career Counseling, Latinos (v4); Cross-Cultural Training (v3); Diversity (v3); Ethnic Minority (v3); Immigrants (v3); Latinos (v3); Machismo (v3);

Multicultural Counseling (v3); National Latina/o Psychological Association (v3); Organizational Diversity (v3); Racism (v3); Society for the Psychological Study of Ethnic Minority Issues (v3)

Further Readings

Brady, S., Casas, J. M., & Ponterotto, J. G. (1983). Sexual preference biases in counseling: An information processing approach. *Journal of Counseling Psychology, 30,* 139–145.

Casas, J. M., & Keefe, S. E. (Eds.). (1978). *Family and mental health in the Mexican-American community.* Los Angeles: University of California, Los Angeles, Spanish-Speaking Mental Health Research Center.

Casas, J. M., Ponterotto, J. G., & Gutierrez, J. M. (1986). An ethical indictment of counseling research and training: The cross-cultural perspective. *Journal of Counseling & Development, 64,* 347–349.

Casas, J. M., Turner, J. A., & Ruiz de Esparza, C. (2001). Machismo revisited in a time of crisis: Implications for understanding and counseling Hispanic men. In G. R. Brooks & G. E. Good (Eds.), *The new handbook of psychotherapy and counseling with men: A comprehensive guide to settings, problems, and treatment approaches* (Vol. 2, pp. 754–779). San Francisco: Jossey-Bass.

Ponterotto, J. G., & Casas, J. M. (1987). In search of multicultural competence within counselor education programs. *Journal of Counseling & Development, 65,* 430–434.

Ponterotto, J., & Casas, J. M. (1991). *Handbook of racial/ethnic minority counseling research.* Springfield, IL: Charles C Thomas.

Ponterotto, J. G., Casas, J. M., Suzuki, L. A., & Alexander, C. M. (Eds.). (1995). *Handbook of multicultural counseling.* Thousand Oaks, CA: Sage.

Ruiz, R., & Casas, J. M. (1981). A model of culturally relevant and behavioristic counseling for Chicano college students. In P. Pedersen, J. C. Draguns, W. J. Lonner, & J. Trimble (Eds.), *Counseling across cultures.* Honolulu: University of Hawaii Press.

CERTIFICATE OF DEGREE OF INDIAN BLOOD

A Certificate of Degree of Indian Blood (CDIB) or Alaska Native Blood is a federal document that certifies that an individual possesses a specific degree of blood of a federally recognized tribe, band, nation, pueblo, village, or community. Generally, the tribal rolls of federally recognized tribal nations are used to determine parental lineage and, therefore, blood quantum for Bureau of Indian Affairs–issued CDIBs. A CDIB is established through genealogical documents that verify ancestral bloodlines through one or both Native parents. Though possession of a CDIB does not establish membership in a tribe, some tribes do require a minimum degree of blood for both membership and/or access to benefits such as health care, education, and others. Membership rules vary from tribe to tribe. For example, in 1985, Congress passed the Quarter Blood Amendment Act that declared that Indian students must be at least one-quarter blood to receive financial support for higher education. A CDIB was the document used to establish eligibility.

The Ute tribe has the highest blood quantum requirement for membership (five eighths) whereas other tribes, such as the Western Cherokee, require only a traceable roll number. The most common blood quantum requirement by many tribes is one fourth.

CDIBs are not without controversy. There is evidence that colonization initiated blood quantum in an effort to deny civil rights to "inferior persons" identified as "Negroes and Indians." According to J. D. Forbes, many colonies used blood quantum to determine who should be afforded the "privileges of Whiteness." Those with greater amounts of White ancestry were thought to be more competent than those with lesser amounts. A greater degree of White blood entitled an Indian citizen to greater privileges, such as the ability to buy and sell property and the right to vote. This literature suggests that it was believed by early colonists that Indian people would not sustain their culture, and the CDIB was one way to monitor how quickly the bloodline was assimilated into the majority culture. Controversy exists for other reasons as well:

1. Census rolls of the 1800s and early 1900s are not always correct. If ancestors were not included in the original rolls, for whatever reason, it is impossible to accurately trace lineage.

2. Because of the politics and privilege of the times, not all tribal people claimed Indian blood.

3. Not all tribes are federally recognized and therefore not entitled to CDIBs or to the benefits that the CDIB may afford them even though they are indigenous people.

4. Many Freedmen, or descendants of Black slaves "owned" by tribes, consider CDIBs to be racist and believe that the CDIB promotes discrimination. These Freedmen were often given tribal membership when freed but were not entitled to CDIBs because they did not possess an Indian bloodline. This situation resulted in Freedmen who were tribal members being excluded from any tribal rights.

5. Finally, and the reason stated often, many people believe that no government agency has the right to determine who is and who is not Indian.

Pamela Jumper Thurman

See also Alaska Natives (v3); American Indians (v3); Bureau of Indian Affairs (v3); Ethnicity (v3); Indian Health Service (v3); Race (v3); Visible Racial/Ethnic Groups (v3)

Further Readings

Department of the Interior, Bureau of Indian Affairs (BIA), 25 CFR Part 70; RIN 1076-AD98. Certificate of Degree of Indian or Alaska Native Blood. *Federal Register*, April 18, 2000 (Vol. 65, No. 75).

Forbes, J. D. (2000, November 27). Blood quantum: A relic of racism and termination [Native Voice column]. *People's Voice*. Retrieved from http://www.thepeoplespaths.net/Articles2000/JDForbes001126Blood.htm

CHANGE AGENT

The term *change agent* has been used generally to denote any person, activity, or experience that facilitates change. An alteration in both psychological and behavioral functioning is the expected result of the interplay between individual and organizational competencies, such as knowledge, skills, and awareness. The basis for measuring this change relates to movement along a continuum of Self-System awareness.

Originally, *change agent* was used to refer to leaders or facilitators of change induction groups, or T-groups (basic skills training groups). Early change induction groups in the early 1900s were utilized by only a few, isolated individuals. The focus of the early T-groups was varied and unstandardized, based on the specific focus of the facilitator's goal for the population. In the first quarter of the century, no true effort was made to combine the philosophies of groups or group leaders.

World War II proved to be the catalyst for research on change agents. With the need to quickly modify the everyday living practices of people to meet the requirements of military systems, much emphasis was placed on the potential effects of group dynamics. The inefficiency and limited availability of psychiatric and psychological personnel precluded individual efforts of classification and remediation. Consequently, group therapy and the role of change agents became a noteworthy topic, and the notion of efficient psychological and behavioral change still drives most of the individual and group therapy today.

Self-System awareness in psychotherapy may be conceptualized best by Julian B. Rotter's notion of internal versus external locus of control and how it produces change or motivates individuals to change. As noted earlier, the term *change agent* may refer to any persons, activities, or experiences. Change produced at the Self (internal locus of control) end of the continuum concerns attitudes, beliefs, and thoughts—all of which are unobservable but often produce the most permanent and stable change. Change seen at the System (external locus of control) end is often quantifiable, or, at least, observable—however, not necessarily linked to authentic or lasting change. Change agents must focus on both behavioral and cognitive aspects when addressing individuals' intrapersonal/interpersonal functioning.

Mental health clinicians serving as change agents look to enhance individuals' self-regulation. Rather than place external pressures, forces, or consequences on behavior and affective expression, clinicians seek to assist individuals in satisfying, productive intrapersonal and interpersonal functioning. However, change agents must take precautions to avoid invalidation of the cultural experience of others or assessing the affect, behavior, and cognitions of others without consideration of sociocultural context.

Both the American Psychological Association and the American Counseling Association have addressed the need for facilitating change while considering the sociocultural contexts in their ethics codes. American Psychological Association Ethics Code Principle A concerning Beneficence and Nonmaleficence presumes that, because clinicians' "scientific and professional judgments and actions may affect the lives of others, they are alert to and guard against personal, financial, social, organizational, or political factors that might lead to misuse of their influence." Principle E speaks of Respect for People's Rights and Dignity and expects that clinicians "are aware of and respect cultural, individual, and role differences, including those based on age, gender, gender identity, race, ethnicity, culture, national origin, religion, sexual orientation, disability, language, and socioeconomic status and consider these factors when working with members of such groups." The American Counseling Association mentions its encouragement of clinicians to "actively attempt to understand the diverse cultural backgrounds of the clients they serve" in the Introduction to Section A: The Counseling Relationship.

Social scientists and clinicians are expected to take the lead in advocating for change in relation to the consideration of these factors in theory, research, and practice. The degree to which multicultural issues receive attention in the future will depend on the willingness and effectiveness of social scientists in modeling the change that is yet to come to fruition in larger society.

Edward A. Delgado-Romero and Jon M. Harvey

See also Cross-Cultural Training (v3); Cultural Encapsulation (v3); Ethical Codes (v1); Locus of Control (v3); Multicultural Counseling (v3); Multicultural Counseling Competence (v3); Multiculturalism (v3)

Further Readings

American Counseling Association. (2005). *ACA code of ethics.* Alexandria, VA: Author.
American Psychological Association. (2002). Ethical principles of psychologists and code of conduct. *American Psychologist, 57,* 1060–1073.

CIVIL RIGHTS

Civil rights have been generally defined as affirmative legal promises governments make to protect the privileges and power of a specified group of people or citizens of a nation. Civil rights movements have been the way by which many marginalized groups have gained legal protection against discriminatory actions. The laws protecting the civil rights of citizens may be written or implied. Examples of such written laws in the United States are constitutional amendments such as the 13th Amendment outlawing the enslavement of peoples and the 19th Amendment protecting the right for women to vote. In a self-proclaimed democracy such as the United States, these rights have been revered as essential components of a just society. The right to "life, freedom and the pursuit of happiness," for example, is a phrase well known to many Americans. The United States' own history, however, reveals the violation of these civil rights for multiple communities defined by racial, ethnic, gender, sexual orientation, social class, and religious group memberships among others.

To understand the needs and become advocates in the struggles of marginalized groups, mental health providers must first have a foundation and knowledge of the histories of these groups. The following is an outline of historical civil rights violations of marginalized groups in the United States and subsequent movements fighting for the protection of those rights.

History of Marginalized Groups

African Americans

African Americans, more than any other group, have been at the center of civil struggles throughout U.S. history. Their struggle for liberty began with the first law passed by the Virginia Assembly in 1661 making persons of African descent slaves for the duration of their lives. The U.S. Constitution implicitly recognized the right of White landowners to hold slaves; it was not until the implementation of the 13th Amendment of 1865 that slavery and involuntary servitude were outlawed. Jim Crow laws helped circumvent these rights by allowing the virtual enslavement of poor Blacks through sharecropping and legalized segregation of schools, transportation, and public accommodations well into the 20th century. The 14th Amendment of 1868, intending to protect emancipated slaves from the physical and legal retaliation of their former masters, also failed to do so as African Americans were persecuted by organized terrorist groups such as the Ku Klux Klan. Following the Supreme Court decision of *Plessy v. Ferguson* in 1896, legal segregation and the principle of "separate but equal" were sanctioned by the law. By far the most influential civil rights organization in the African American movement, the National Association for the Advancement of Colored People (NAACP) pressed the issue of equality all the way back to the Supreme Court. Today the legacy of the *Brown v. Board of Education of Topeka* decision in 1954 demanding the desegregation of public schools helps protect the rights of people of color; women; lesbian, gay, bisexual, transgender (LGBT) persons; and persons with disabilities. The leaders of the civil rights movement of the 1950s and 1960s, including Martin Luther King, Jr.,

Malcolm X, and Rosa Parks, were the inspiration for tactics and concepts that sparked and empowered subsequent movements for women, Latinos/as, Asian Americans, Native Americans, the LGBT community, and the poor.

Asian Americans

Asian Americans have not only been subject to violations of civil right liberties, but they systemically have been the direct target of such injustice. The Chinese Exclusion Act of 1882, for example, was enacted to ensure that Asians did not become naturalized citizens and could not vote. The Immigration Act of 1924 further barred all Asians ineligible for American citizenship from entering the United States. The creation of "Chinatowns" in many coastal cities is largely a result of the denial of full participation in society for early Asian immigrants. The forced relocation and internment of more than 120,000 Japanese Americans during World War II is one of the most atrocious violations of the civil rights of Asian Americans in U.S. history. Following the bombing of Pearl Harbor by the Japanese government in December 1941, Japanese Americans were forced to sacrifice their livelihoods and were imprisoned in internment camps, where living conditions risked their health and family unity. Although the Civil Liberties Act of 1988 provided an official government apology and monetary reparations for internee survivors, the wound of this violation remains open in the hearts of many Asian Americans today.

In the 1960s Asian American activists joined other groups of color in the fight for racial equality and social justice, demanding the United States take notice of what became known as the Yellow Power movement. The Asian American movement of the 1960s was led primarily by college-age students of Chinese and Japanese descent seeking to be recognized by the largely White anti–Vietnam War movement of the time. One of the most important legacies of the movement has been the implementation of Asian American studies across institutions of education. Today Asian American activists continue to struggle for political, economic, and cultural inclusion and equality.

Native Americans/American Indians

The lives of Native Americans, also referred to as American Indians, and their struggle for civil rights began with the arrival of the first Europeans on the Western Hemisphere. Stripped of the land on which they lived, Native Americans were driven by gunpoint on harsh and arduous journeys to Indian Territories. From 1838 to 1839, more than 16,000 Cherokees were driven from their homeland; more than one fourth of these people died in the march that has become known as the *Trail of Tears*. Cruel measures of forced assimilation, often led by missionaries, endorsed the removal of young Natives from their families into boarding schools, where tribal customs and use of language were subject to severe punishment. It was not until the enactment of the Indian Reorganization Act of 1934 that Native Americans were given the right to a system by which tribes could autonomously adopt representative, democratic institutions in their traditional forms of government. Although a setback of these rights occurred with the communist scare after World War II, the civil rights movement also provided opportunities for the improvement of civil rights for Native Americans. Pan-Indian organizations such as the American Indian Movement embraced the confrontation tactics practiced successfully by African Americans during the 1960s. The American Indian Civil Rights Act of 1968 further guaranteed American Indians living under tribal governments many rights and liberties of other Americans. The struggle of American Indians continues, however, as socioeconomic disparities continue to maintain poverty, poor health, and poor education among this population.

Latino/a Americans

Latino/as have been the targets of violent attacks based on their race/ethnicity leading to a struggle for civil rights similar to those of other marginalized groups. The heterogeneity of this population, however, has resulted in a history often separated by struggles by nationalities. For example, Mexican Americans (also known as Chicanos/as) have a long-standing history on U.S. soil and have helped fight for the labor rights of people across racial lines. César Chávez organized and led migrant farm laborers with the United Farm Workers union movement by creating community service programs, emphasizing nonviolence, and articulating the needs and rights of farm workers. The young Brown Berets of the 1960s aimed to protect Chicano/a youth from police harassment. Although Puerto Rico was included as a U.S. territory in 1917, Puerto Ricans continue to be denied voting rights, which is a concern for some Puerto Rican Americans. The most prominent struggle that the Latino/a community continues to face is the recognition of the rights of large numbers of Latino/a immigrants living in the United States. Basic rights such as provision of health care, fair wages, and legal protection continue to be denied this growing population.

Women

The women's movements in the United States were heavily influenced by the abolitionist movement and the civil rights movements of the 1960s. The political rights of women were virtually nonexistent prior to the 19th century to the extent that wives were denied ownership of property, prohibited from leaving their husbands, and barred from custodial rights to their children. The movement for women's rights has been active since the 1700s and continues today with historical works from Mary Wollstonecraft, Susan B. Anthony, Harriet Taylor, Betty Friedan, Sara Evans, Alice Walker, Audre Lorde, and bell hooks, among others. Advocates for woman's rights have successfully demanded a wide variety of civil liberties, such as the right to vote, legalization of abortion, the right to initiate divorce, and the entrance of women to the political and labor workforce, which have had a lasting impact on issues of education, religion, sexuality, and gender identity. Feminists today continue to advocate for economic, political, and social equality and an end to oppressive conditions for women of all races.

Other Marginalized Groups

The LGBT community continues to fight for equality for all regardless of sexual orientation or gender identity. Groups such as Henry Gerber's Society for Human Rights of 1924 have been fighting for "gay rights" for nearly a century. The federal and some state governments continue to resist support of LGBT civil rights legislation. In 2007, sexual and gender identity are not covered by federal civil rights codes or protected under the laws against hate crimes. Although some individual states have civil union clauses, the struggle for the legal recognition of same-sex marriages and unions continues, as does discrimination against the LGBT community legally and socially across most of the country.

In an effort to raise awareness of poverty in the United States, Martin Luther King, Jr. and colleagues launched the Poor People's Campaign. The movement mobilized African Americans, Native Americans, Whites, and Mexican Americans to lobby Congress for social and economic equality. Large numbers of Americans continue to live below the poverty level today. The most visible members of this community are the homeless, a population disproportionately stricken with mental illness. Despite the dire needs of this marginalized group, the civil rights of the poor are often ignored by a nation still hostage to the myth of the American dream and equally blind upward mobility.

Mental Health Civil Rights

Historical traumas have left members of these marginalized groups weary of the institutionalized systems that have not only failed them but have often been the perpetrators of their plights. Mental health providers are faced with the responsibility of healing remnants of these historical wounds, and they are encouraged to serve as social advocates in continuing to demand equal rights for those peoples to whom they are still denied. The call for the multicultural competence of all counselors working with marginalized groups is, in itself, a civil rights movement. It is the right of every individual living in the United States to be met with culturally competent mental health providers when seeking treatment. As researchers, practitioners, and educators, counselors at large are part of a movement whose goal is to recognize and eradicate the ways in which racism, sexism, heterosexism, classism, and other forms of discrimination continue to affect members of marginalized groups today.

Sheila V. Graham

See also Affirmative Action (v3); African Americans (v3); American Indians (v3); Asian Americans (v3); Classism (v3); Discrimination (v3); Diversity Issues in Career Development (v4); Latinos (v3); Multicultural Counseling Competence (v3); Organizational Diversity (v3); Prejudice (v3); Racism (v3); Sexism (v3); Social Discrimination (v4); Social Justice (v3)

Further Readings

Bradley, D., & Fishkin, S. F. (1998). *The encyclopedia of civil rights in America.* Armonk, NY: Sharpe Reference.

Martin, W. E., & Sullivan, P. (Eds.). (2000). *Civil rights in the United States.* New York: Macmillan Reference USA.

Zinn, H. (2005). *A people's history of the United States: 1492 to present* (2nd ed.). New York: Harper Perennial Modern Classics.

CLARK, KENNETH BANCROFT (1914–2005)

Kenneth Bancroft Clark was one of the most influential psychologists and social activists of his generation. Born in the Panama Canal Zone in 1914, Clark moved with his family to Harlem, New York, when he was 4 years old. After graduating from Washington High School in New York City, he enrolled in Howard University, a prominent historically Black university in Washington, D.C. It was at Howard that Clark would work with African American scholars like E. Franklin Frazier and Francis Cecil Sumner, whose ideas about racism and integration would influence his thoughts throughout his career. From Howard, he returned to New York to attend Columbia University. He would become the first African American to earn a Ph.D. in psychology in the school's history. In 1938, he married Mamie Phipps (Clark), an influential psychologist in her own right. The two had met at Howard and continued their relationship when Mamie came to New York to study psychology at Columbia. Clark would live and work in Harlem for much of the remainder of his life.

Clark was perhaps best known for his contribution to the 1954 decision of the U.S. Supreme Court in the matter of *Brown v. Board of Education of Topeka*. His research was an integral part of the case challenging the legality of segregated schools. He worked closely with his wife, Mamie, to use their research to change the way that race and prejudice are viewed in America. Over the course of his career, he would help found a community health center, chair several educational research projects, and hold several key positions within the fields of psychology and education (including the presidency of the American Psychology Association) and a seat on the New York State Board of Regents. Clark passed away in Hastings-on-Hudson, New York, in 2005.

Clark's early work focused on racial identity development in African American children. In a set of experiments known as the doll studies, African American children were presented with dolls that were identical in every way except for skin color. Some of the dolls were brown to represent African American children, and some were pinkish to represent White children. Clark and the research team asked participants a series of questions about the dolls, such as "Which one is you?" and "Give me the doll that you like the best." The results from this series of experiments indicated that even as young as age 3, a majority of African American children were aware of the classifications of White and African American. The results also revealed that although many children identified themselves with the African American doll, a large proportion expressed a preference for the white dolls and a rejection of the brown dolls. In the eyes of many African American children, white dolls were associated with goodness and intelligence, whereas brown dolls were associated with ignorance and other negative characteristics.

Clark found these results particularly disturbing. The views of the children in the study highlighted the profound psychological conflict facing African American children in the United States at that time. Clark argued that as African American children grew, the already difficult process of identity development was further complicated for them by the cultural definitions of race. The children knew that they were African American and were also aware of the insulting value that culture had placed on this group.

Clark became preoccupied with understanding what factors created the perception of African Americans as bad and Whites as good. He theorized that these ideas were the result of pervasive cultural prejudice. The way that African Americans were treated in virtually every sphere of American life taught children that African Americans were inferior to Whites. The effect of this universal devaluing of the African American race was to confuse and discourage African American children. It has been observed that although this line of research and thinking was relevant to the state of social science knowledge and the political climate of the time, this focus on the deleterious effects of racism and racial segregation contributed to a "deficits approach" to the study of ethnic identity that it would take another generation of social scientists to offset.

Clark felt strongly that the education system had a responsibility to protect children from the dangers of prejudice. He believed that it was a school's legal and moral obligation to provide a safe learning environment in which all children could learn and develop. He criticized segregated schools because they failed to do this. In his research, he pointed out that almost universally, segregated schools for African Americans were aesthetically inferior and lacked the resources afforded to schools for Whites. Within the schools, the biased attitude of teachers and administrators also affected students. Clark cautioned that these repeated associations of African Americans with inferior status would lead to irreversible damage to children's identity, self-esteem, and ability to function as productive members of society. He also asserted that the lessons of democracy and equality taught in schools could not be credibly proposed within a system that promoted the humiliation of a portion of its people. For African American children to have a fair educational opportunity, school segregation would have to be eliminated.

Clark continued to promote these ideas through research and activism. However, the culture of racism and prejudice in America at that time made it difficult for many to see his point of view. Despite this, he continued pressing the ideas of integration and fair educational opportunities for all students.

Perhaps no single effort illustrates Clark's desire to see change in his community more than the founding of the Northside Center for Child Development in 1946. Recognizing the need for affordable psychological care for the children of Harlem, Clark and his wife, Mamie, used their own money to fund a community center offering these services in their neighborhood. Today, Northside is still functioning in Harlem. Though it has grown beyond its humble beginnings, it still operates under the Clarks' original principles of community service and activist research.

Shortly after the founding of the Northside Center, Clark became involved in the National Association for the Advancement of Colored People (NAACP) legal battle against segregation. As a result of the papers that he and Mamie published establishing the negative effects of prejudice, Clark had gained some notoriety as one of the leading psychologists in this area. The research provided a new kind of evidence that could be used to challenge the legality of segregation. Beginning in 1951 and for several years thereafter, Clark served as a social science consultant to the NAACP. He would eventually testify as an expert witness in the 1954 *Brown v. Board of Education of Topeka* case, which called for an end to school segregation. He explained the dangers of segregation and emphasized that thorough integration was the only way to offer African American children a fair education. His testimony was cited as crucial in the Supreme Court's decision to overturn previous cases that had supported "separate but equal" educational facilities.

Though Kenneth was pleased that his and Mamie's research had been used to effect legal change, he was troubled by the fact that schools remained illegally segregated even after the *Brown* verdict. While he and Mamie continued their research and their work at Northside, Kenneth pressed education officials at the local and national levels to make the changes that had been mandated by the court's ruling. For the remainder of his career, he worked on various advisory boards and research councils pushing for this change. In 1962, Clark served as chair of Harlem Youth Opportunities Unlimited. The organization's overall goal was to explore the reasons for the high rates of juvenile delinquency in Harlem and to devise a plan of action to reduce the problems. A few years later, Kenneth and a group of colleagues formed the Metropolitan Applied Research Center. The group of individuals, which represented a variety of professions, met with the common goal "to serve as a catalyst for change and as an advocate for the poor and powerless in American cities." Although Clark worked hard on these and many other projects, political opposition and feasibility concerns prevented many of the suggestions that he proposed from taking place as quickly as he would have liked.

Despite some setbacks, Clark remained active throughout his career. The same year that he began working with Harlem Youth Opportunities Unlimited, he began his 20-year term with the New York Board of Regents. He continued to hold several professorships, publish scores of articles and books, serve as president of the American Psychological Association, and establish several research and advisory corporations in the areas of psychology, education, and economics. For him, social justice began with an educational experience for all children that allowed them to feel respectful of themselves and their status as human beings. He worked tirelessly in his community, in the schools, and in the courts and government halls to ensure this environment of equality and respect for all children, always from his command of the knowledge and his commitment to social action.

Kamauru R. Johnson and Edmund W. Gordon

See also African Americans (v3); Black Psychology (v3); Black Racial Identity Development (v3); Civil Rights (v3); Clark, Mamie Phipps (v3); Community-Based Action Research (v1); Discrimination (v3); National Association for the Advancement of Colored People (v3); Prejudice (v3); Racial Identity (v3); Racism (v3); Social Discrimination (v4); Social Justice (v3)

Further Readings

Cherry, F. (2004). Kenneth Clark and social psychology's other history. In G. Philogene (Ed.), *Racial identity in context: The legacy of Kenneth B. Clark* (pp. 13–33). Washington, DC: American Psychological Association.

Clark, K. (1955). *Prejudice and your child.* Boston: Beacon Press.

Clark, K., & Clark, M. (1939). The development of consciousness of self and the emergence of racial identification in Negro preschool children. *Journal of Social Psychology, 10,* 591–599.

Clark, K., & Clark, M. (1940). Skin color as a factor in racial identification of Negro preschool children. *Journal of Social Psychology, 11,* 159–169.

Clark, K., & MARC Staff. (1972). *A possible reality: A design for the attainment of high academic achievement for inner-city students.* New York: Emerson Hall.

Markowitz, G., & Rosner, D. (2000). *Children, race and power: Kenneth and Mamie Clark's Northside Center.* New York: Routledge.

CLARK, MAMIE PHIPPS (1917–1983)

Mamie Phipps Clark, one of the first Black women to earn a Ph.D. in psychology, was the cofounder and director of the innovative Northside Center for Child Development in New York City. Founded in 1946, Northside is a multidisciplinary, multiracial service for children, adolescents, and parents with psychological and educational needs in the Harlem community. Clark's vision for Northside and her implementation of this vision for more than 30 years attest to her enormous contribution to strengthening and improving the lives of ethnic minority children and their families.

In addition to her professional contributions, Clark is also well known for her pioneering study of racial self-identification in African American children, conducted for her master's thesis at Howard University. Her subsequent studies on racial identification in both Black and White children, published with her husband, psychologist Kenneth B. Clark, were used to prepare the famous "Social Science Statement" supporting the racial desegregation of American schools in the 1954 United States Supreme Court case, *Brown v. Board of Education of Topeka.*

Early Life

Clark was born in 1917 in Hot Springs, Arkansas, and, like all Black children, attended a segregated school. Her father, Harold H. Phipps, was a physician; her mother, Katie Florence Phipps, was a homemaker. Clark described her childhood as comfortable, secure, and happy despite an omnipresent awareness of racism and the personal experience of legalized discrimination. Coping with these facts of everyday life in the Jim Crow South required resilience and determination. Phipps drew on both of these qualities in her decision to pursue postsecondary education.

Upon graduating from high school, Phipps chose to attend prestigious Howard University in Washington, D.C., with a desire to major in mathematics. She enrolled in 1934 at the age of 16. At Howard she quickly discovered that the segregated public school system had ill-prepared her to meet the intellectual demands of her new environment. She realized that there were huge gaps in her education, but she acted quickly to compensate: "Well, I had to study harder. I really did. I went to summer school. I went to summer school the first two summers when I was in college, to make up the deficiencies. . . . But I was taking five courses in summer school, and that's a lot of courses" (Clark, 1976, p. 12).

Training in Psychology

Clark's desire to pursue mathematics at Howard gave way to an interest in child development and psychology, partly because of the lack of encouragement given female students in mathematics and partly because of the influence of her future husband, Kenneth Clark. She transferred into the field with the support of Francis Cecil Sumner, the head of Howard's psychology department and the first African American to receive a doctorate in psychology. There were no Black women on the staff of the department. Clark reported retrospectively that the absence of Black women with advanced degrees in psychology itself represented a silent challenge.

Mamie Phipps married Kenneth Clark in 1937. She graduated with her bachelor's degree from Howard in 1938 and spent the summer working in the law offices of Charles Hamilton Houston, a pioneering Black civil rights attorney. She also discovered the work of psychologists Ruth and Eugene Horowitz (later Hartley) on self-identification in nursery school children. She decided to merge her interests in race and child development in her master's research, resulting in her thesis, "The Development of Consciousness of Self in Negro Pre-school Children." In this work, she explored the development of racial identity in 300 Black children in segregated nursery schools in the Washington, D.C., area. Over the course of the next year, she published three more articles with Kenneth, looking at the effects of skin color and segregation on the racial self-identification of Black children.

In 1939, Mamie Clark was granted her M.A. degree and received a fellowship to begin doctoral work at Columbia. She chose to work with White psychologist and known racist Henry Garrett rather than with Kenneth's mentors Gardner Murphy and Otto Klineberg because, as her husband Kenneth later reported, she felt that working with Murphy or Klineberg would be too easy. In 1944 Clark received her Ph.D. Her dissertation was titled "The Development of Primary Mental Abilities with Age." During her doctoral studies she also gave birth to two children, Kate (1940) and Hilton (1943).

The Birth of Northside

After graduation, Clark looked for work outside academia. Despite her husband's recent academic appointment at the City College of New York, it was very clear to Clark that full-time university appointments for doctoral-level Black psychologists were rare and those for doctoral-level Black women psychologists nonexistent. After a series of adverse experiences working in various agencies, she became convinced that there was a distinct need for more services for neglected and abandoned minority children in New York City.

With the realization that a satisfying career would ensue only if she created one for herself, Clark envisioned a psychological testing and service center for minority children. With Kenneth, she approached a number of agencies for support. None was forthcoming. Thus, with a loan from Harold Phipps, the Clarks opened a basement office in the Paul Dunbar Apartments on the north side of Harlem in February of 1946. They named it the Northside Testing and Consultation Center but, in 1947, changed the name to the Northside Center for Child Development. For the next 30 years, Mamie Clark's vision would drive Northside.

Treatment Philosophy

Northside's primary and overarching objective was (and is) to provide psychological and educational services to minority children and their parents to help them cope with and overcome the pervasive impact of racism and discrimination. The Clarks' philosophy of treatment and their vision for Northside at times collided with prevailing psychiatric thought, which tended to focus exclusively on intrapsychic deficiencies. By contrast, the Clarks consistently promoted the understanding and treatment of children's emotional and behavioral difficulties holistically from a strengths-based, psychosocial, and environmental perspective. This meant that the services offered at Northside were eclectic and underwent constant revision to meet the needs of the community. For example, when it became clear early in the Center's history that minority children were overrepresented in classes for the mentally deficient, the staff at Northside retested children and showed that they did *not* meet the criteria for this designation but *were* subjected to social and educational neglect. They then developed remedial reading classes that became a core component of client services. The success of these efforts provided acceptance of the Center in the larger Harlem community.

Another critical aspect of Northside's service philosophy was that all children, regardless of race, should be served by a multiracial and multidisciplinary team of professionals and paraprofessionals. This reflected not only the Center's eclecticism but also the Clarks' unwavering belief in the pernicious effects of racial segregation on all children. Despite differences in race, class, and professional status among the staff, Mamie Clark strove to maintain a nonhierarchical atmosphere. She also believed in providing a pleasing physical environment for the children and their families. The offices at Northside, whether in the original basement or in the later multi-floor facility in Schomburg Towers, were safe, attractive, and stimulating for the children and parents served within their walls.

Activism in the Community

Along with her work at Northside, Clark was active in the larger Harlem community and the greater New York City area. She worked with Kenneth on the Harlem Youth Opportunities Unlimited project, as well as serving on its advisory board. She was active in the initiation of the national Head Start program. Beyond psychology and child development, she served on the board of directors of numerous educational and philanthropic institutions. In brief, Clark was deeply involved in her community.

Clark was the executive director of Northside until her retirement in 1979. Her death from cancer followed shortly thereafter, in 1983. As one of her staff members characterized her directorship of the Center: "When an unusual and unique person pursues a dream and realizes that dream and directs that dream, people are drawn not only to the idea of the dream, but to the uniqueness of the person themselves. I think this is what Dr. Mamie was like . . . Northside, including today's school, really revolved on her ingenuity, her dream. . . ." (Johnson, 1993, as cited in Markowitz & Rosner, 2000, p. 246).

Alexandra Rutherford and Wade E. Pickren

See also Black Psychology (v3); Black Racial Identity Development (v3); Civil Rights (v3); Clark, Kenneth Bancroft (v3); Community-Based Action Research (v1); Discrimination (v3); Ethnic Minority (v3); Prejudice (v3); Racial Identity (v3); Racism (v3); Social Discrimination (v4); Social Justice (v3)

Further Readings

Clark, M. P. (1976). [Interview with Ed Edwin]. Columbia University Libraries Oral History Research Office. Retrieved from http://www.columbia.edu/cu/lweb/digital/collections/nny/clarkm/index.html

Clark, M. P. (1983). Mamie Phipps Clark. In A. N. O'Connell & N. F. Russo (Eds.), *Models of achievement: Reflections of eminent women in psychology* (pp. 267–277). New York: Columbia University Press.

Lal, S. (2002). Giving children security: Mamie Phipps Clark and the racialization of child psychology. *American Psychologist, 57,* 20–28.

Markowitz, G., & Rosner, D. (2000). *Children, race, and power: Kenneth and Mamie Clark's Northside Center.* New York: Routledge.

CLASSISM

According to the nonprofit resource center Class Action, *classism* can be defined as the systematic assignment of characteristics of worth and ability based on social class and the systematic oppression of subordinated groups (people without endowed or acquired economic power, social influence, and privilege) by the dominant groups (those who have access to control of the necessary resources by which other people make their living). It includes individual attitudes and behaviors, systems of policies and practices that benefit the upper classes at the expense of the lower classes, the rationale that supports these systems and this unequal valuing, and the culture that perpetuates them.

Before going on to develop this definition of *classism,* it is necessary to also define which classes are subordinate to which others. Many scholars, whether they are sociologists, economists, or psychologists, begin their attempts to define class structure by acknowledging that there is no conclusive definition. The language used to describe groups of interest varies widely, including such terminology as *poor, low income, disadvantaged, working class, blue collar, white collar, wealthy,* and *upper class;* class indicators (the criteria used to differentiate class membership) include such considerations as income, attitudes and beliefs, educational level, job prestige, power in the workplace, and differences between manual and physical labor. Each of these formulations captures some, but not all, of the truth about the lived experience of social class, but the most useful definition for a discussion of classism as a form of oppression will be one that incorporates considerations of social power and powerlessness. Along these lines, authors Betsy Leondar-Wright and Michael Zweig have offered similar formulations that include the following elements:

- *Poverty class:* Predominantly working-class people who, because of unemployment, low-wage jobs, health problems, or other crises, are without enough income to support their basic needs.
- *Working class:* People who have little power or authority in the workplace, little control over the availability or content of jobs, and little say in the decisions that affect their access to health care, education, and housing. They tend to have lower levels of income, net worth, and formal education than more powerful classes.
- *Middle class:* Professionals, managers, small business owners, often college-educated and salaried. Middle-class people have more autonomy and control in the workplace than working-class people, and more economic security; however, they rely upon earnings from work to support themselves.

- *Owning class:* People who own enough wealth that they do not need to work to support themselves; people who own and control the resources by which other people earn a living. The owning class includes people who, as a result of their economic power, also have significant social, cultural, and political power relative to other classes.

Conceptual Framework

To better understand classism, it is necessary to locate it within a conceptual framework that helps further clarify it. First, classism is a form of oppression and, as such, does not refer simply to prejudiced attitudes that people of one social class group might have regarding members of another class. Rather, classism, like racism, sexism, and heterosexism, is an interlocking system that involves domination and control of social ideology, institutions, and resources, resulting in a condition of privilege for one group relative to the disadvantage of another. Of course, members of both dominant and subordinated groups are capable of harboring prejudiced attitudes, but only dominant groups have the institutional and cultural power to enforce their prejudices via oppression. Making this distinction between prejudice and oppression is significant in that, in a world where the status quo is characterized by social inequities, all prejudices are not created equal; some are the expressions of real sociocultural power hierarchies.

Second, classism, like other forms of oppression, often exists within individuals at an unconscious level, so it can be perpetuated by well-intentioned people who are genuinely unaware that they are acting on learned cultural assumptions about the differences between poor people and wealthier people. Becoming aware of classism, then, does not imply that one was previously deliberately scornful of poor people or overtly lacking in concern for them. Even people who participate in charitable activities benefiting the poor, and poor people themselves, are exposed to cultural attitudes regarding the poor and incorporate them into their worldviews and self-concepts.

Finally, although isolating one form of oppression is useful for the purposes of summary and definition, the lived experience of social class is complex, and class and classism exist at intersections with other aspects of identity such as race and gender. Different forms of oppression have an interlocking nature, and their function often serves to perpetuate each other.

For example, sexism operates so that most people living in poverty are women, and racism and classism inform each other in critical ways. In the minds of many Americans, the typical poor individual is represented by a person of color, yet most welfare recipients are, in fact, White. At the same time, people of color are much more likely to live in poverty, with the 2004 poverty rates for racial groups being 25% for Blacks, 22% for Latinos/as, 10% for Asians, and 9% for Whites, according to the University of Michigan's National Poverty Center. Considering both race and gender together with regard to class reveals the very high poverty rates of about 40% for Black and Latina female-headed households.

Examples of Classism in Everyday Life

In a nation that has long defined itself in opposition to the old-world class structures and explicit caste systems found in other societies, it is not surprising that classism would be one of the least recognized of the "-isms." Although some are easily identifiable, many forms of classism escape the notice of the most well-intentioned people. Examples of classism include the general cultural and institutional invisibility of poor and working-class people, negative attitudes and beliefs regarding poor and working-class people, educational inequities, healthcare inequities, disparities in the judicial system, environmental injustice, social acceptance of unlivable minimum wages, and the deprecation of organizations of working people.

Cultural and Institutional Invisibility of Poor and Working-Class People

Perhaps the best example of the unexamined invisibility of poor people in the mainstream U.S. cultural experience is the widespread astonishment at the depth of American poverty revealed in the aftermath of Hurricane Katrina, which struck the Gulf Coast in 2005; journalists and television reports of the time chronicled both the disaster itself and the nation's startled response to it. In her 2002 article on classism in the United States, called "Cognitive and Behavioral Distancing From the Poor," psychologist Bernice Lott described the primary characteristic of classism as "cognitive and behavioral distancing from the poor," a response that renders the poor invisible in many interpersonal and institutional contexts. The field of psychology is no exception; as Lott explained, a lack of attention to issues related to poverty and classism is evident even in the consideration of multicultural issues. The result is that psychological theory, research, and practice are not particularly accessible or relevant for poor people, and middle-class psychologists who attempt to offer services in poor communities may find that their work is compromised by previously unexamined classist attitudes. Similarly, the experiences of poor and working-class people are largely without representation in art, literature, or popular culture; there are few working-class voices in the national discourse on public policy issues; and intellectualism and critical thinking are largely assumed to be the province of wealthier Americans.

Negative Attitudes and Beliefs

Writing about the time that she spent working in low-wage jobs, author Barbara Ehrenreich described her encounters with the contemptuous attitudes that are often directed toward poor and working-class people. Although most middle- and owning-class people would not consider themselves to view others unfavorably simply on the basis of their financial status, there is a considerable amount of evidence to suggest that poor people are often seen in a negative light. Television sitcoms often present poor and working-class people as narrow-minded and ignorant, even if comically so; classist attitudes are referenced in jokes about people with southern accents and people who live in trailers. Owning-class people, by contrast, can become national celebrities on the basis of the wealth they own, with the media chronicling their everyday activities. Lott's 2002 article (mentioned in the previous section) is a review of research that provides evidence of this widespread, if often unconscious, aversion. For example, study participants endorsed traits such as *crude, lazy, stupid, dirty,* and *immoral* more often for poor people than for middle-class people, and they listed stereotypes for poor people that included *uneducated, lazy, dirty, drug/alcohol user,* and *criminal*. Descriptors like these point to a tendency to locate the factors contributing to poverty within poor people themselves, effectively deflecting attention from larger societal forces that obstruct pathways out of poverty for poor families.

Educational Inequities

American cultural lore includes a belief in education as a social equalizer within a meritocratic society, yet the reality is that the gap between the educational experiences of children from poor families and their wealthier peers continues to widen. This trend has been documented by scholars such as Jonathan Kozol, the author of several books examining the interface of class, race, and schooling in America, including *The Shame of the Nation* (2005). Students who attend public schools in poor communities are more likely to be taught by poorly paid, uncertified teachers, and their schools are more likely to have fewer computers, fewer library books, fewer classes, fewer extracurricular opportunities, and fewer teachers than schools attended by wealthier students. Correspondingly, less money overall is spent per student on behalf of children in poor neighborhoods, a gap that spans from $8,000 per student on the low end to $18,000 per student in wealthier neighborhoods, according to Kozol. Those poor students who do receive adequate preparation for college-level work will face financial obstacles that few can surmount. In a report called "Losing Ground," the National Center for Public Policy and Higher Education documented that the costs of a college education are escalating at a rate higher than both inflation and family income, lowering the rates of attendance by low-income students while those from middle- and owning-class families continue to attend college in record numbers. The educational equity gap, then, becomes one of the ways that "the rich get richer and the poor get poorer," as college degrees are themselves associated with increases in earning potential; the College Board estimates that over a lifetime, the gap in earnings between those with a high school diploma and a B.A. or higher exceeds $1,000,000.

Healthcare Inequities

The annual United Nations Human Development Report usually addresses health and well-being in third-world countries, yet in 2005 it documented the widening healthcare gap in the United States, the wealthiest country on Earth. The United Nations found that, although the United States spends more money on health care than any other country, only certain groups of Americans enjoy the benefits. Among poor people and people of color, health indicators are worse in the United States than in some developing countries. Infant mortality, for example, has increased for the past 5 years and is now equal to that of Malaysia. The Kaiser Commission, which studies healthcare and insurance trends, reported that by 2004, the number of Americans without health insurance grew to 45.5 million, with 80% of the uninsured coming from working families. Not surprisingly, people without insurance are more likely to have problems getting medical care, less able to purchase prescribed medications, more likely to let preventable conditions escalate into serious ones, and more likely to let serious problems go untreated. As more and more poor and working-class families are permitted to go without access to health care, they are increasingly vulnerable to the multiple health risks of poverty, which include elevated rates of nearly every sort of threat to survival, including heart disease, diabetes, exposure to toxins, cognitive and physical functional decline, and homicide, among many others.

Disparities in the Judicial System

Under this heading can be found one of the clearest forms of classism: bail. This overt form of discrimination hides in plain sight as the poor remain in prison cells while wealthier people accused of the same crimes go free. More generally, millions of Americans are financially without access to civil legal process, and funding for legal aid services is sufficient only to provide counsel to a small proportion of those who need it. Laura Abel at New York University's Brennan Center for Justice has explained that a scenario familiar to viewers of law-and-order television programs—that legal aid services are provided to Americans who cannot afford an attorney—never comes to pass for most poor people. For example, the Brennan Center showed in 2007 that fewer than one out of four tenants facing eviction in New York City Housing Court had legal representation; in particular, 5,000 low-income senior citizens come before New York City housing court each year with no legal representation. Overall, 67% of all potential evictees had incomes under $25,000, making clear the linkages between poverty, lack of access to legal counsel, and homelessness.

Environmental Injustice

Classism and racism intertwine to affect the way that waste and "dirty industries" are managed in American communities. In urban areas, this means that waste dumps and pollution-producing operations are predominantly located where poor people and people of color live. In economically depressed rural areas like the Central Appalachian mountain region, poor families contend with the effects of strip-mining and its most extreme form, mountain-top removal. Through the use of mountain-top removal, coal companies access underlying coal deposits by blasting off the tops of the Appalachian Mountains, a cost-cutting, profit-enhancing method that has already resulted in the decapitation of some 300,000 acres of mountain area in West Virginia alone; estimates are that at current rates of demolition, an area the size of Rhode Island will have been decapitated by 2012. Nearby valleys and streams are filled in with everything from the blast that is not coal—the so-called overburden—while the coal-washing process leaves behind vast slurry ponds of coal sludge, a thick mixture of soil, water, and the toxic chemicals used in coal processing. On October 11, 2000, a 72-acre, 2.3-billion-gallon impoundment near Inez, Kentucky, failed. A torrent of slurry was released into the surrounding countryside, resulting in what the U.S. Environmental Protection Agency called one of the South's worst environmental disasters. This catastrophe received little national media attention, although it ruined property, destroyed drinking water systems, and killed local animal and aquatic life in one of the poorest counties within one of the poorest regions of the United States. This dangerous situation continues to threaten the people of the Central Appalachian region, which is the location of at least 700 more slurry impoundments.

Classism and the Minimum Wage

The continuing low level of the minimum wage gives rise to inherent ethical contradictions, suggesting that attitudes toward poor and working-class people may influence public debate (or lack thereof) regarding this issue. Without people working in minimum-wage jobs to carry it along, everyday life in America would come to a standstill. Our society relies upon the labor of people who work in child care, take care of the elderly, clean offices, and serve food, yet the citizens who perform these necessary jobs cannot earn enough money to support themselves and their children. The federal minimum wage was not increased at all for a 10-year period beginning in 1996, and in terms of real purchasing power, it was allowed to fall during that time to its lowest level in 50 years, eventually representing only 64% of the poverty line. In May 2007, the U.S. Congress passed a measure to raise the minimum wage to $7.25 per hour—yet this amount is still not sufficient to lift a family of four above the poverty threshold. The consequences for working people who try to survive in these jobs are clear; the National Coalition for the Homeless reported in 2005 that as many as 25% of people in U.S. homeless shelters have jobs. Less obvious are the advantages that middle- and owning-class people enjoy as a result, in that they can afford to buy more products and services more cheaply when employers do not pay employees enough to live on.

An alternative perspective on the minimum wage is the living wage. As explained by the Economic Policy Institute, the living wage is a pay rate that would bring a full-time worker within 100% to 130% of the poverty line (130% being the maximum amount that a family can earn and still be eligible for food stamps). Although 58 local governments have passed living wage ordinances for their own cities or counties (beginning with Baltimore, Maryland, in 1994), this debate has yet to receive sustained attention on a national level. Different constituencies could be expected to bring different perspectives to this debate, but an attempt to understand classist attitudes must include the notion that unconscious devaluing of poor and working-class people may be at work to discourage such an examination.

Deprecation of Organizations of Working-Class People

Classist attitudes can also be seen in the way that groups of poor and working-class people are regarded if they come together to advocate for themselves. Organizations such as unions comprise the sole opportunity for working-class people to have a voice in workplaces where they do not own or control resources, have no authority in the content or availability of jobs, and do not occupy roles in the corporate power structure. They have used that voice to achieve such innovations as the end of child labor and the establishment of the 8-hour (as opposed to the unlimited hour) workday. These organizations also help bring low-wage earners out of poverty; in 2005, the AFL-CIO reported that union workers earn an average of 28% more in weekly wages than their nonunion counterparts. Yet, in August 2005, a Harris Poll found that a majority of U.S. adults surveyed (68%) rated labor organizations negatively—hardly a surprising finding given the increasingly unfavorable portrayal of unions in American culture. Whereas entertainment vehicles or news reports may offer sympathetic accounts of individual poor people or families, organizations of poor and working-class people are typically portrayed unfavorably, for example, as greedy, troublesome, or corrupt. Past labor officials have indeed been found guilty of corruption—as have high-ranking members of financial, pharmaceutical, agribusiness, medical, and defense-contracting corporations, among many others. Yet, there is not an across-the-board dismissal of these organizations, nor do we begrudge their right to meet collectively to protect their interests—professional organizations, chambers of commerce, and lobbying groups are all examples of such organizing.

Classism in View

An understanding of classism, then, begins with a clearer vision of poor and working-class people among us and their conspicuous absence from important cultural and institutional representations of American life. It requires a new awareness of personal attitudes and assumptions regarding the poor. Finally, it means not only recognizing the circumstances under which poor people live but also the aspects of our social system that hinder poor families in their efforts to surmount poverty.

Laura Smith

See also Deficit Hypothesis (v3); Discrimination (v3); Discrimination and Oppression (v2); Oppression (v3); Poverty (v3); Prejudice (v3); Racism (v3); Sexism (v3); Social Class (v4); Social Discrimination (v4); Social Justice; (v3) Socioeconomic Status (v3)

Further Readings

Carr, S. C., & Sloan, T. S. (Eds.). (2003). *Poverty and psychology.* New York: Kluwer Academic/Plenum.

Correspondents of the *New York Times*. (2005). *Class matters.* New York: Henry Holt.

Ehrenreich, B. (2001). *Nickel and dimed: On (not) getting by in America.* New York: Henry Holt.

Hill, M., & Rothblum, E. D. (Eds.). (1996). *Classism and feminist therapy: Counting costs.* New York: Harrington Park.

hooks, b. (2000). *Where we stand: Class matters.* New York: Routledge.

Kozol, J. (2005). *The shame of the nation.* New York: Crown.

Leondar-Wright, B. (2005). *Class matters.* Gabriola Island, BC: New Society.

Lott, B. (2002). Cognitive and behavioral distancing from the poor. *American Psychologist, 57,* 100–110.

Smith, L. (2005). Psychotherapy, classism, and the poor: Conspicuous by their absence. *American Psychologist, 60,* 687–696.

Zweig, M. (2000). *The working class majority.* Ithaca, NY: Cornell University Press.

COLLECTIVISM

Collectivism is defined as an orientation that reflects the values, attitudes, and behaviors of a person–group relationship in which family and group life is emphasized and the concept of the self is less essential. Collectivism emphasizes an interdependence among individuals in their ingroups (e.g., family, tribe, nation), with the expectation that members give priority to the goals of the group, and shapes the norms of group behavior. For example, children in collectivistic cultures are not encouraged to individuate from their parents; instead, children tend to obtain psychological well-being and a sense of security through obedience to, and dependence on, their parents. In essence, in collectivistic cultures, groups bind and mutually obligate individuals.

Ingroup and Outgroup

An important defining feature of collectivistic cultures pertains to the dynamics of ingroups and outgroups. In collectivistic cultures, individuals usually belong to a few ingroups (e.g., family, coworkers, and friendship circles). The welfare of their ingroups is viewed as a priority, and individuals are expected to make efforts for the groups' well-being. Specifically, they are encouraged to retain connectedness among individuals, promote ingroups' goals and interests through cooperation, and avoid open conflicts. Because of the emphasis on group harmony, cooperation, and collective goals, individuals in the ingroups are perceived as interdependent and selfless. For example, individuals tend to be concerned about the impact of their behavior on members of their ingroups and tend to shape their behavior based on the norms of the groups. Moreover, individuals from a collectivistic culture tend to share resources with ingroup members and feel cared for and a sense of belongingness by being involved in the lives of other ingroup members.

Although relatedness is a defining element of collectivism among individuals in the ingroups, it does not apply to everyone else in outgroups. In collectivistic cultures, individuals' attitudes tend to be sharply different toward others in outgroups. For example, a cooperative relationship is highly unlikely with others who belong to outgroups. Individuals tend to treat those in outgroups with distance and clear boundaries.

Collectivism and Psychological Functioning

Scholars who have examined relations between collectivism and psychological functioning have found that collectivism contributes significantly to social, collective, and related aspects of the self-concept. For example, researchers found that collectivism was associated with decentrality of self-concept and perception of the self as part of larger social groups and endeavors; consequently, the personal needs and goals of members of collectivistic cultures should be deferred for the unity of the collective group. Moreover, personal traits that are facilitative to the maintenance of group connectedness are especially favorable in collectivistic cultures, such as being willing to sacrifice for collective benefits, being skillful in maintaining close relationships with ingroup members, and being mindful of preserving group harmony. Not surprisingly, when in conflictual situations, individuals attend to preserving relationships rather than achieving justice. Direct confrontation is usually tension provoking and undesirable in solving a conflictual situation. Studies on relationality and groups also suggest that collectivism is associated with equality. People from collectivistic cultures who showed more willingness to remain in relationships indicated ingroup preference, even in personally costly ones, and presented different forms of face-saving. Additionally, collectivism was found to have a correlation with a flexible and more ambiguous personality in that people from collectivistic cultures tend to place more focus on contexts, have less concern for consistency, and be less interested in self-enhancement as they tended to adjust themselves to their ingroups. Moreover, in organization research, collectivism was found to be associated with lower preference to work alone, lower performance in solo tasks, and more focus on work conditions and human relations. Thus, collectivism does appear to be related to psychological processes.

Collectivism Versus Individualism

Individualism and collectivism are often conceptualized as two opposite constructs and represent very different norms of behavior. In general, cultures of Africa, Asia, and Latin America are categorized as collectivistic, whereas cultures of Western Europe and North America are noted as individualistic. In examining the dimensional structure of collectivism, research suggested that the simple approach of viewing collectivism as the opposite of individualism does not sufficiently represent the complexities within these two constructs. Most of the recent conceptual models and empirical research support collectivism/individualism as a separate domain-specific, independent dimension depending on contextual and social cues. Moreover, it seems appropriate to view societies as simultaneously dealing with both collectivistic- and individualistic-oriented values. Consistent with the notion of separate dimensions, another model has divided collectivism into kin- and non–kin-related collectivism, as well as kin- and non–kin-related individualism. This model implies that the meaning of collectivism varies across ingroups and cultures. In other words, collectivism is associated with certain groups but not others, and it takes different forms across different cultures.

Collectivism Across Cultures

Studies on individualism and collectivism have been using samples from countries across the world. A recent meta-analysis of the comparative research literature of individualism and collectivism found that 50 out of 83 studies examined international comparisons, and 35 examined within-U.S. comparisons. In the studies of international comparisons, 50 countries were represented, with countries in South Asia and East Asia being most represented. The findings suggest that Americans are less collectivistic oriented than other regions of the world, except for some English-speaking countries. Within-U.S. comparisons examined differences among European Americans, African Americans, Asian Americans, and Latino/a Americans. The results from these studies indicate that European Americans are significantly lower on collectivism than Asian Americans and Latinos/as, although the effects were small, but do not differ from African Americans on collectivism. However, different collectivistic cultures emphasize different elements of collectivism. For example, Asian collectivistic cultures value group harmony and modesty in one's presentation. Conversely, collectivistic cultures of the Mediterranean and Latin America construe respect/dignity as the central value; that is, individuals are expected to preserve their honor and act dependably.

Measurement

The measurement of collectivism, as reflected in more than 2 dozen inventories, has been based primarily on Likert ratings of values and attitudes. Some of the existing scales measure individualism and collectivism as a single bipolar construct. The majority, however, measure individualism and collectivism as separate orthogonal constructs. Measuring collectivism (and individualism) has been very difficult, in part because of the many varieties of collectivism and collectivistic cultures. For example, some collectivistic cultures emphasize equality (e.g., Sweden), whereas others emphasize hierarchy (e.g., India). Nonetheless, common content components of collectivism scales are useful to depict key elements of collectivism, such as relatedness to others, a sense of belongingness to groups, a sense of duty to groups, harmony, seeking others' advice, contextual self, valuing hierarchy, and working in groups. Most of the current research literature on collectivism can be categorized into three areas: (a) the dimensional structure of collectivism and its model development, (b) the relationship between collectivism and psychological functioning domains (e.g., self-concept, self-efficacy, well-being, attribution, and relationality), and (c) international comparisons and within-U.S. comparisons.

Counseling Implications to Collectivism

Collectivism can have a profound impact on all aspects of the counseling process. For example, individuals from collectivistic cultures are more likely to attribute the cause of an event to situational factors (e.g., environmental stressors) and less to personal characteristics. Such attributions can affect a client's perceptions of his or her presenting problems and thus are relevant for the counselor to carefully assess. Also, a counselor's choice of appropriate intervention strategies should be in line with a client's worldview (e.g., collectivism). For example, intervention strategies that promote a sense of autonomy and self-worth would be inappropriate to a client who endorses collectivism with an emphasis on interdependence. Instead, it may be more appropriate to help a client from collectivistic cultures to find ways to meet both personal needs and group expectations. In addition, traditional emphasis on direct and open communication in a counseling relationship may create uncomfortable feelings in a collectivistic-oriented client who prefers indirect and high-context communication.

In sum, collectivism represents an important culture-based psychological construct related to how the self is conceptualized relative to important ingroups and outgroups across different cultures. It is also a worldview that is related to a host of psychological processes, which underscores the utility of the construct in understanding human adjustment. A competent counselor is one who understands how collectivism and individualism influence the counseling process and takes an active approach to develop culturally appropriate intervention strategies to help his or her clients.

P. Paul Heppner, Chia-Lin Tsai, and Yuhong He

See also Allocentrism (v3); Barriers to Cross-Cultural Counseling (v3); Confucianism (v3); Cross-Cultural Psychology (v3); Cross-Cultural Training (v3); Cultural Values (v3); Filial Piety (v3); Individualism (v3); International Approaches (v4); Multicultural Career Assessment Models (v4); Multicultural Counseling (v3); Work–Family Balance (v4)

Further Readings

Oyserman, D., Coon, H. M., & Kemmelmeier, M. (2002). Rethinking individualism and collectivism: Evaluation of theoretical assumptions and meta-analyses. *Psychological Bulletin, 128,* 3–72.

Rhee, E., Uleman, J. S., & Lee, H. K. (1996). Variations in collectivism and individualism by ingroup and culture: Confirmatory factor analyses. *Journal of Personality and Social Psychology, 71,* 1037–1054.

Triandis, H. C., Bontempo, R., & Villareal, M. J. (1988). Individualism and collectivism: Cross-cultural perspectives on self-ingroup relationships. *Journal of Personality and Social Psychology, 54,* 323–338.

Williams, B. (2003). The worldview dimensions of individualism and collectivism: Implications for counseling. *Journal of Counseling & Development, 81,* 370–374.

COLONIALISM

Colonialism refers to a nation extending its sovereignty over territory beyond its homeland by establishing colonial settlements, dependencies, trading posts, or plantation colonies, in which native inhabitants are ruled, displaced, or extirpated. The goal of colonialism is to strengthen the homeland by controlling the natural resources, labor, and market of the colonial territory. Usually, colonizers will impose their sociocultural mores, religion, and language on the indigenous population. The term *colonialism* also refers to a set of values, including racism, ethnocentrism, and imperialism, which aim to justify the means by which colonial settlements are established on foreign land.

Types of Colonialism

Settlements, dependencies, trading posts, and plantation colonies are distinct ways in which colonialism has been achieved. Settlements involved people emigrating from a mother country, such as England, Spain, or France, and permanently displacing or killing indigenous populations. Dependencies occurred when colonizers did not arrive as a mass settlement but as rulers over existing native populations. Trading posts occurred primarily to engage in trade rather than to rule or settle in the larger territory. Finally, plantation colonies, used primarily in the Caribbean, involved importing slaves into colonial settlements, who eventually outnumbered the primary settlers and ruled the hinterland.

History of Colonialism
Pre-European Colonialism

Although most world history texts cite the European Age of Exploration as the origins of colonialism, substantial evidence suggests that African and Asian colonial settlements predate European settlements by centuries. The Olmec heads found along the Mexican Gulf Coast provide the most striking evidence of African colonies in the Americas more than 3,000 years ago. North African rule over European territory is also well documented through the legacy of the Moorish societies in Spain and France and Hannibal's reign over Rome and Italy. Genghis Khan led the most notable Asian colonial establishment by conquering nations and installing the Mongol Empire across Asia, Western Europe, and North Africa. The Mongol Empire was the largest contiguous empire in world history.

The First Wave of European Colonization

European colonization, which has its roots in Portuguese and Spanish exploration of the 15th century, in many ways shaped present-day debates over colonialism. Portuguese explorers successfully established trading posts on the Atlantic islands and along the West African coast and eventually rounded the Cape of Good Hope to reach India in 1498. In 1492, Spain financed Christopher Columbus's voyage to discover an alternate route to India by sailing west. Columbus reached the Bahamas Islands, thinking he was in Asia. He returned to Spain to obtain more resources to conquer the so-called New Land. On his second voyage, he reached Haiti, thinking he was in India, and led his army to exploit the native population. Columbus's exploits included mass murder, enslavement, torture, and rape. His human rights abuses led to some of the first debates on colonialism, which included mostly religious leaders who either condemned or justified Columbus-style atrocities against Neolithic populations.

After observing Portugal and Spain's economic boosts, Northern European nations, particularly the Netherlands, England, and France, began to stake claim to the Americas as well. Religion influenced all European colonial establishments. Spanish nations used colonialism to seek fabled Christian kingdoms, establish theocracies, and finance religious wars. Conversely, some of the largest colonial settlements from England spawn from people fleeing religious intolerance in their homeland. However, monetary gains were the cornerstone of most human rights violations. Colonizers found that harvesting crops on the hinterland reaped great profits, so they enslaved native populations and sub-Saharan Africans. Historians estimate that Western settlers enslaved more than 10 million Africans to provide the labor necessary to harvest the colonies.

Independence in the Americas

In 1776 the 13 British colonies declared their independence and became the precursor to the modern-day United States of America. Subsequently, Haiti became the second independent nation and the first Black republic in the Western Hemisphere, when Toussaint L'Ouverture led the Haitian revolution against France. The Haitian revolution also led to the first organized slavery abolition movement in a metropole, or mother country. Spanish occupation in the Americas ended with the Latin American wars.

Western Expansion, New Imperialism, and the Scramble for Africa

In the 19th and 20th centuries, new nations in the Americas formed by European colonizers focused on conquering the western frontier. In North America, settlers subjected the Native American population to preemptive war, detention centers, and population transfers, such as in the Trail of Tears. However, the White settlers' diseases crippled the Native American population more than their prowess.

In the Eastern Hemisphere, European nations set out a new colonial agenda with *New Imperialism,* after losing most of their stake in the Americas. New Imperialism, starting with the *Scramble for Africa,* formally established a competition between the United Kingdom, the French Third Republic, and the German Empire to conquer as much territory through armed force as possible. In the Scramble for Africa, which commenced in 1880 and boiled over into World War I, European powers established dependencies in and claimed as colonial territory all of Africa except Ethiopia and Liberia (Liberia was colonized by the United States with former slaves).

Racist pseudoscientific theories and religion were used as propaganda to justify the African expansion and subsequent atrocities committed against Africans. However, major corporations, such as the De Beers Mining Company, provided the most solid platform for European exploits of Africa. During the European conquest of Africa, wars between Westerners and native Africans proliferated (e.g., the Anglo–Zulu War), and eventually European superpowers began to war with each other as they competed for territory.

The Scramble for Africa ended after World War I; however, most of Africa was still under European control. From the period immediately after World War I (1914–1918) to the mid-20th century, anticolonialism and anti-imperialism movements became powerful, spurred by communism, colonized war veterans (e.g., Senegalese sharpshooters who fought with France), and colonized elites (e.g., Algerian Franz Fanon). The French colonial empire suffered a devastating blow in the Algerian Revolution. Worldwide, sympathy increased for colonized populations, and the institution of colonialism lost popularity.

Decolonialism, Neocolonialism, and Postcolonialism

Decolonialism was most prevalent after World War II; however, cold war tensions between the two new world superpowers, the United States and the Soviet Union (USSR), spawned neocolonialism. The USSR aligned itself primarily with anti-imperial movements, by providing training and weapons to militias planning a coup (e.g., the African National Congress and Castro's Cuban Revolution). The United States, afraid that the USSR was building dependencies, began to compete with Soviet interest by spreading democracy. U.S. and USSR competition for allies led to civil war in many third-world nations (e.g., Angola and Vietnam) and wrongful CIA- and KGB-implicated assassinations of key leaders, such as Patrice Lumumba of the Democratic Republic of the Congo and Sylvanus Olympio of Togo.

In the postcolonial era, there have been many critiques of the impact of colonialism and whether colonialism exists today. Colonialism permanently changed the social-cultural, geographical, political, and economic landscape of the world. Indigenous populations of Africa, the Americas, and Australia continue to live as second-class citizens on their native lands, whereas generations-old businesses and banks that financed acts of genocide and other atrocities reap residual benefits from the legacy of colonialism. The debate on colonialism is omnipresent and still very active to this day. Recently, the February 23, 2005, *French Law on Colonialism* contained an article that mandated high-school teachers to teach the "positive values" of colonialism to their students. French Prime Minister Jacques Chirac repealed the law in 2006.

The United States, a product of both colonialism and an independence movement, is the primary focus of the postcolonial era. Critiques allege the existence of an *American Empire,* which imposes its values on other countries to build a new style of dependency. Defenders argue that the American Empire does not exist, or they propose that the United States is a *Benevolent Empire,* which builds relationships with other nations by helping them overcome struggles, as in the Spanish-American Wars. Internally, the United States continues to grapple with its own colonial legacy. To the dismay of social advocates, history texts in the United States are replete with colonialism-related omissions (e.g., Columbus's second voyage and atrocities against Native Americans).

Implications for Counseling

The legacy of colonialism has implications for counseling practice and research. First, the psychological impact of colonialism and survival of indigenous values among previously colonized people influences the counseling relationship. Second, cultural imperialism is a natural by-product of colonialism, leading many counselors to make assumptions about a client's traditions and values that are shaped by the majority culture. In addition to cultural imperialism, theories of ethnocentrism, racism, White supremacy, and pseudoscience used to justify colonialism have lingered well past decolonialism and influence counseling research and practice.

Ivory A. Toldson

See also Acculturation (v3); Adaptation (v3); Assimilation (v3); Discrimination and Oppression (v2); Enculturation (v3); Ethnocentrism (v3); Identity (v3); Indigenous Healing (v3); Multiculturalism (v3); Oppression (v3); Racism (v3); Second Culture Acquisition (v3)

Further Readings

Biel, R. (2000). *The new imperialism: Crisis and contradictions in North–South relations.* London, New York: Zed Books.

Duara, P. (2004). *Decolonization: Perspectives from now and then.* New York: Routledge.

Fanon, F. (1980). *A dying colonialism.* London: Writers and Readers.

Sartre, J.-P. (2001). *Colonialism and neocolonialism.* London: Routledge.

COLOR-BLIND RACIAL IDEOLOGY

Over the past 2 decades scholars and popular authors have written about racial color-blindness as a way to characterize racial beliefs in the post–civil rights era. At its core, *racial color-blindness* refers to the belief that racism is a thing of the past and that race no longer plays a role in understanding people's lived experience. Conceptually, racial color-blindness has its roots in the law field and traditionally has been applied mainly to the Constitution. More recently, scholars have redefined the term to better capture the new social relations within the current racial climate. As early as 1997, the field of psychology questioned the underlying assumption that ignoring race and color was a desirous and appropriate approach to interracial interactions. In a pamphlet on color-blind racial attitudes, the American Psychological Association (APA) concluded that "research conducted for more than two decades strongly supports the view that we cannot be, nor should we become, color-blind" (p. 3). The APA further provided a critique of the color-blind perspective, arguing that a color-blind approach "ignores research showing that, even among well-intentioned people, skin color . . . figures prominently in everyday attitudes and behavior" (p. 2). The APA thus argued that to get beyond racism it is essential to take into account differences between the lived experiences of people.

Defining Racial Color-Blind Ideology

There are a number of complementary but competing definitions of *racial color-blindness*. Couching racial color-blindness as an expression of modern-day racism, sociologist Eduardo Bonilla-Silva identified four frames or types: *abstract liberalism* (i.e., emphasizing political liberalism and the availability of equal opportunities to everyone, regardless of race, and the belief that political/economic interventions only serve to create a schism between racial groups); *naturalism* (i.e., interpreting racial clustering as a natural and preferred occurrence); *cultural* (i.e., using essentialist arguments to explain racial disparities, thus rooting racial differences in cultural practices); and *minimization* of racism in today's society. Ruth Frankenberg, also a sociologist, viewed racial color-blindness as a perspective consisting of two types: *color-evasion* (i.e., placing an emphasis on racial sameness to the detriment of seeing or acknowledging differences in experiences and political realities) and *power-evasion* (i.e., the belief that resources are fairly distributed to everyone and success is attributed to individual effort).

In the *Guidelines on Multicultural Education, Training, Research, Practice, and Organizational Change for Psychologists,* authored by the APA, the interpersonal aspects of racial color-blindness are emphasized. Based on this perspective potential racial differences are minimized in favor of universal or human experiences. There is a great deal of commonality across cultures; however, the color-blind perspective dismisses potential differences based on racial group membership and downplays how these differences may shape human experiences. This limited awareness of the manifestation of race and racism in society is the foundation for most conceptualizations of racial color-blindness. Regardless of the definition, racial color-blindness is also thought to help justify existing racial practices or policies that ultimately create and support existing racial inequalities.

Consistent with these articulations, researchers argue that racial color-blindness reflects a broader ideological stance. Racial ideology is complex, but essentially it can be conceptualized as a global term referring to the dominant views about race within a hierarchical society. Ideology in this regard consists of a shared worldview about race that helps to justify and legitimize the current racial status quo; it accounts for individual beliefs and dominant societal racial beliefs or ideas that are commonly understood and transmitted through a variety of civil society and structural mechanisms. From this perspective racial color-blind ideology is a set of commonly held beliefs that minimize and distort the existence of institutional racism. This perspective is most consistent with the minimization type of color-blind racism identified by Bonilla-Silva and the power-evasion type proffered by Frankenberg.

Recently, scholars have challenged the assumption of the emergence of a new racism. Based on the review of the interdisciplinary literature in the United States and in other English-speaking countries, Colin Wayne Leach concluded that old-fashioned racism or the endorsement of racial inferiority/superiority ideology and actions have not been supplanted by more covert forms of racial expressions. Although he did not name racial color-blindness in his critique, Leach raised questions about whether or not a shift has occurred in the manifestation of racism since the passage of civil rights laws.

In sum, racial color-blindness is premised on the persistence of racism as manifested in contemporary racial disparities across a range of indexes, including housing, health, and employment. The complex set of beliefs used to restrict awareness of the persistence of racism is part of a larger ideological stance that serves to legitimize and further perpetuate racial inequalities. There is some debate about whether racial color-blindness is a new phenomenon or whether it reflects a dimension of racism that, until relatively recently, has received attention in the social science literature.

Measuring Racial Color-Blindness

Leslie Carr, one of the first social scientists to quantitatively examine racial color-blindness, assessed the concept with one item: "Are you color-blind when it comes to race?" He identified two types of racial color-blindness among White college students: (1) liberal (i.e., those who identified themselves as color-blind but supported affirmative action policies) and

(2) conservative (i.e., those who identified themselves as color-blind and opposed affirmative action policies), both of which were significantly related to increased racial prejudice. Later studies, however, refute the utility of using one item to capture the complexities of color-blind racial ideology.

Some researchers have created a set of survey questions to assess concepts consistent with racial color-blindness but have not explicitly adopted a color-blind racial ideology framework. For example, Samuel Sommers and Michael Norton collected statements reflective of lay theories of racism. Factor analysis of endorsement of these statements suggested a three-factor solution; one factor represented denial of the problem of racism. In their study, participants who held greater modern racism beliefs were less likely to view denial of the problem statements (e.g., "Believes that prejudice against Blacks is no longer a problem) as an expression of racism.

The Color-Blind Racial Attitudes Scale (CoBRAS), developed by Helen Neville and her colleagues, is among the first scales to assess the minimization and distortion of institutional racism most consistent with the ideological view. Sample items on the scale include "Everyone who works hard, no matter what race they are, has an equal chance to become rich" and "Racism may have been a problem in the past, but it is not an important problem today." Emerging data on the CoBRAS have suggested an association between color-blind racial ideology and theoretically relevant constructs, including increased racial and gender intolerance, anti–affirmative action beliefs, and belief in a just world among Whites and internalized racism among racial and ethnic minorities.

Racial Color-Blind Ideology in Counseling

When counselors ignore the influence of race and racism, they may minimize the potential influence of race and ethnocultural factors on the therapeutic process inadvertently. This, in turn, may serve to isolate racial minorities in seeking or remaining in counseling services. Several studies have assessed the association between racial color-blindness and the therapeutic process, although not always explicitly using this terminology. Findings suggest that among White psychologists and trainees, minimization of institutional racism is related to decreased multicultural competencies, including the ability to contextualize clients' presenting concerns and express client empathy. In fact, racial color-blindness has been found to be related to both observed and self-reported multicultural counseling competencies over and beyond that accounted for by multicultural coursework and racial group membership.

Helen A. Neville

See also Affirmative Action (v3); Assimilation (v3); Diversity (v3); Multicultural Counseling Competence (v3); Political Correctness (v3); Prejudice (v3); Racial Identity (v3); Racism (v3); Reversed Racism (v3); Worldview (v3)

Further Readings

American Psychological Association. (1997). *Can—or should—America be color-blind? Psychological research reveals fallacies in a color-blind response to racism* [Pamphlet]. Washington, DC: Author.

American Psychological Association. (2003). Guidelines on multicultural education, training, research, practice, and organizational change for psychologists. *American Psychologists, 58,* 377–402.

Bonilla-Silva, E. (2001). *White supremacy and racism in the post civil rights era.* Boulder, CO: Lynne Rienner.

Carr, L. (1997). *Color-blind racism.* Thousand Oaks, CA: Sage.

Frankenberg, R. (1993). *White women, race matters: The social construction of Whiteness.* Minneapolis: University of Minnesota Press.

Neville, H. A., Lilly, R. L., Duran, G., Lee, R., & Browne, L. (2000). Construction and initial validation of the Color-Blind Racial Attitudes Scale (CoBRAS). *Journal of Counseling Psychology, 47,* 59–70.

COMMUNICATION

Communication is difficult to define as it can be understood from a variety of perspectives. Dominic Infante, Andrew Rancer, and Deanna Womack suggest that communication occurs between humans when the meaning of symbols is manipulated to stimulate meaning. From this perspective, communication is important for promoting cooperation. Humans are social in nature and require cooperation if they are to get along and thrive. Communication also involves acquiring and sharing information through various venues such as the 24-hour news services, newspapers, and the World Wide Web.

Models of Communication

Ronald Adler and Neil Towne and Infante, Rancer, and Womack described several models of communication. The linear model describes communication in simple unidirectional terms—how information from a sender is communicated to a receiver. In this process, a sender encodes a message (by preparing an existing ideal for transmission) and sends the message through a channel (e.g., letter) to a receiver, who decodes (interprets) the message. The linear model proposes that noise and environment are important variables that can influence communication. Noise involves factors that can undermine the process of communication (e.g., psychological stress), and environment relates to factors such as personal experiences and physical setting that can influence communication.

The transactional model suggests that communication is not simply unidirectional (a sender transmitting a message to a receiver) but also is influenced by feedback that can include the responses of the people involved. From this perspective, individuals are referred to as communicators and not senders or receivers, as they are alternately senders and receivers throughout the communication process.

Communication and Counseling

Communication can impact counseling in a variety of ways, such as through listening skills and multicultural issues.

Listening Skills

Adler and Towne noted that more people spend time listening than any other form of communication. Effective communication skills are emphasized in counseling. This is especially true in marriage and family counseling where communication problems are a central focus. In this process, family members are often taught to use listening skills to obtain a phenomenological perspective (seeing others' point of view). Listening skills that promote the phenomenological perspective include open-ended statements, paraphrasing, minimal encouragers, clarifying, and reflection of feeling.

Communication of empathy is a particularly important listening skill. According to Carl Rogers, empathy is considered a core condition in counseling and can be defined as communicating a sense of caring and understanding. According to this definition, empathy involves not just caring but being perceived as caring. In other words, a person could care about a person but not get credit for caring, unless the caring is effectively communicated to the other person.

Multicultural Issues

In terms of multicultural communication in counseling, *multiculturalism* will be defined in an all-inclusive manner, including race, ethnicity, gender, sexual orientation, class, disability, and more. Miscommunication can occur in multicultural counseling as a result of not considering cultural issues associated with language differences and nonverbal behavior. Language differences can include counselors using standard English with bilingual clients, resulting in inaccurate assessment of clients. Nonverbal behavior can also create challenges in multicultural counseling. For example, it might be problematic for a European American counselor to misinterpret the direct eye contact of an African American client as anger.

Derald Wing Sue and David Sue examined the subtleties of nonverbal communication through various dimensions. A counselor may benefit from noting similarities and differences with comfort and emotional reactions to personal and interpersonal space (e.g., how close the counselor and client sit), physical movement (e.g., eye contact, hand gestures), and vocal cues (e.g., loudness, silence, rate). Sue and Sue emphasize the importance of recognizing these and other contextual and process modes of communicating during counseling.

Marvin Westwood and F. Ishu Ishiyama provided guidelines that could be used to address communication issues in multicultural counseling.

- Counselors should check with clients regarding the accuracy of their impressions associated with nonverbal communication.
- Counselors can help clients experience catharsis by encouraging them to use their own language to express a feeling when another language cannot adequately describe how they are feeling.
- Counselors should attempt to learn culturally appropriate responses to accurately describe clients' experiences.
- Counselors can use creative arts modalities, such as music and art, to overcome communication barriers.

Multicultural Model for Communication in Counseling

Westwood and Ishiyama summarized a culturally embedded model for understanding communication. Unlike previous models of communication in the counseling relationship, this model assumes that cross-cultural clients enter the session with a unique language and way to relate socially. As such, it is assumed that the primary effort of initial counseling sessions is for clients to begin to understand their unique way of seeing themselves in their world (intrapersonal communication). As clients feel they are both beginning to understand themselves and are being understood by their counselors, there will be simultaneous development in being understood verbally and nonverbally (interpersonal communication), which is the unique focus of traditional models. There are three primary assumptions included in this model:

- Communication involves culturally constructed verbal and nonverbal behavior, which is often not conscious and varies between cultures.
- Individuals' perceptions of communication are at least partially determined by one's own culture, which influences both counselors and clients.
- Communicative processes are directly influenced by the situation and feelings of clients and counselors.

The multicultural model suggests that counselors are most effective when both counselor and client attempt to promote client self-understanding. In this process, the counselor can facilitate cross-cultural client communication by demonstrating an understanding of clients' unique experiences and perspectives, understanding how clients uniquely express their perspective both verbally and nonverbally, and developing multicultural competencies.

Future Directions

When counselors emphasize multicultural communication in counseling, they increase the likelihood of validating the client, enhancing the counselor–client relationship, and improving the likelihood of reaching the counseling goals. Both beginning and veteran counselors demonstrate respect and better assist their clients by understanding their own communication style, understanding the communication style of the dominant cultures, and understanding the communication style of each client. Future research can explore these unique dynamics.

Michael S. Nystul and Nick Barneclo

See also Barriers to Cross-Cultural Counseling (v3); Bilingual Counseling (v3); Bilingualism (v3); Language Difficulties, Clinical Assessment of (v2); Multicultural Counseling Competence (v3)

Further Readings

Adler, R. B., & Towne, N. (2002). *Looking out/Looking in.* Orlando, FL: Harcourt.

Evans, D. R., Hearn, M. T., Uhlemann, M. R., & Ivey, A. E. (2004). *Essential interviewing: A programmed approach to effective communication* (6th ed.). Belmont, CA: Thomson-Brooks/Cole.

Infante, D. A., Rancer, A. S., & Womack, D. F. (1990). *Building communication theory.* Prospect Heights, IL: Waveland Press.

Rogers, C. (1951). *Client-centered therapy.* Boston: Houghton Mifflin.

Sue, D. W., & Sue, D. (2008). *Counseling the culturally diverse* (5th ed.). New York: Wiley.

Westwood, M. J., & Ishiyama, F. L. (1990). The communication process as a critical intervention for client change in cross-cultural counseling. *Journal of Multicultural Counseling and Development, 18*(4), 163–171.

CONFUCIANISM

Confucianism is an omnibus term for a set of thoughts that compose an ethos, a sentiment, that has been shaping China for many millennia. Confucianism is a group of proposals for proper socioethical ways of life, providing a foundation to the individual's commitment to sincerity, honesty, and interpersonal harmony. Its impacts are multidimensional in politics, family, interpersonal relations, and education, with deep moral and religious implications. It originated in the *Analects,* supposedly of Confucius, and its ancient commentaries began at Mencius. Elements of Confucianism are popular in Taiwan, Hong Kong, and China and in the United States, where Confucianism is popular among Asian Americans and traditional Chinese. Asian parents emphasize education, a time-honored Confucian ideal. In Confucian ethos, Asian Americans value family; a member's decision (e.g., on house-buying) involves other members' consultation, approval, and even financial support.

Confucianism has had to contend with other trends, such as Taoism and Buddhism. In the Sung Dynasty (960–1279), Neo-Confucianism made Confucianism the dominant philosophy among the educated, who drew from Taoism and Buddhism to formulate a new metaphysics of a sociopolitical hierarchy nonexistent in older Confucianism. This Neo-Confucian synthesis was established as dominant orthodoxy by Chu Hsi (1130–1200).

Confucianism envisions harmonious social relations in proper respectful comportment, the gentleman's way of life in polished manners, with rites and ceremonies to fulfill responsibilities of one's societal positions to promote the Five Relations: ruler–subject, father–son, elder–younger brothers, husband–wife, and friend-to-friend.

Reforming the society begins at reforming the individuals, through whom we establish loving respectful order in families and develop into orderly state and world concord. Rulers must initiate and exemplify the reform in person and in performance.

Personal desire for goodness nurtures family structural concord, to support individuals and spread to society at large. Social solidarity in various aspects is formed by people's loyalties, respect, and proper conduct.

Fulfilling the codes of conduct is a form of socialization. The codes are accepted with individual expressions. Ideally, psychological issues are considered within this goal-context of virtues as fulfillment of the ideal Five Relations.

Stressing individuals as part and parcel of families and interpersonal relationships, Confucianism is a constitutive ingredient in the Chinese value system and relevant to cross-cultural counseling. China assumes family and Five Relations (parent–child, husband–wife, etc.) as a context of living. Individual well-being depends on the harmony of family relationships. Exclusive consideration of private needs is perceived as selfish, not "independent" as in the West. Confucianism is where a good personal trait (virtue) is gentle modesty, to allow others to express their needs and help fulfill them. Seen from the West's independence, many Chinese may appear withdrawn, indecisive, and shy in self-expression.

Unwittingly, however, Western individualistic ethos does include respecting others' individual rights and laws that are communal (e.g., traffic laws, election laws). Counselors working with clients who value Confucianism should stress community as a resource for coping, because, Confucianism would say, community *composes* individual integrity, giving birth to it, raising it. Exclusively stressing unique individuality, taking community as its auxiliary, is one major cause of mental stresses. Confucianism calls for a shift in counseling paradigm from individual-centeredness to individual–community interdependence.

Ruth Chao and Kuang-ming Wu

See also Asian Americans (v3); Career Counseling, Asian Americans (v4); Collectivism (v3); Cross-Cultural Psychology (v3); Cultural Values (v3); Filial Piety (v3); Multicultural Counseling Competence (v3); Multiculturalism (v3); Worldview (v3)

Further Readings

Chan, W. T. (1963). *A sourcebook in Chinese philosophy.* Princeton, NJ: Princeton University Press.

Mair, V. (Ed.). (1994). *The Columbia anthropology of traditional Chinese literature.* New York: Columbia University Press.

CONSTANTINE, MADONNA G. (1963–)

Madonna G. Constantine is an African American female counseling psychologist who has been described by many as an inspired researcher, prolific author, respected mentor, and leader in the exploration of multicultural and social justice issues in psychology. Her extensive record of research has blazed new trails in the exploration of multicultural counseling competence and the impact of racism on psychological practice. Moreover, as a collaborator and mentor, Constantine embodies the best of the scientist-practitioner model, conveying her dedication to research and its relevance for practice to the hundreds of students and colleagues from all over the United States that she has mentored both formally and informally.

Career Path

Constantine was born and raised in Lafayette, Louisiana, the third of five children in her family.

With a lifelong natural curiosity about people, she realized at an early age that she wanted to become a psychologist. Constantine completed her undergraduate studies at Xavier University in New Orleans, Louisiana, where she graduated *cum laude* in 1984 with a major in psychology and a minor in English. She received an M.A. in business, industry, and social agencies counseling from Xavier in 1986 and a Ph.D. in counseling psychology from Memphis University in 1991, where she matriculated as the first student of color in the program's history.

Upon completing her predoctoral internship at the University of Notre Dame's Counseling Center, Constantine began her professional career as a practitioner, accepting a staff position at the University of Texas's Counseling and Mental Health Center in Austin. After 5 years there, Constantine sought a new career direction that would allow her to develop her research interests more fully, and in 1995 she joined the counseling psychology faculty at Temple University in Philadelphia. Three years later, in 1998, she was recruited by Teachers College, Columbia University, to their Counseling Psychology Program, where she works as a full professor as of this writing.

National Leadership and Service

Throughout her career, Constantine has served her field as both participant and leader in a number of professional organizations and national service activities. She is a member of Divisions 17 (Society of Counseling Psychology), 35 (Psychology of Women), and 45 (Society for the Psychological Study of Ethnic Minority Issues) of the American Psychological Association (APA), and is a lifetime member of the Association of Black Psychologists. She is also a member of the American Counseling Association (ACA), the Association of Multicultural Counseling and Development, the National Career Development Association, and the Association for Counselor Education and Supervision. In particular, she has been a leader within Division 17 since the early 1990s, when she became the chair of the division's Ethnic and Racial Diversity Committee (which subsequently became the division's Section on Ethnic and Racial Diversity); she served as past chair from 1997 to 1999. On behalf of Division 17, Constantine also has served as Program Committee chair (1999–2000), Awards Committee cochair (2001–2002) and chair (2002–2003), Fellowship Committee chair (2005–present), and liaison to the APA's Ethnic Minority Affairs Committee (1996–2003). She was the Program Committee cochair for the 2001 National Counseling Psychology Conference in Houston, Texas, and also has served as member-at-large for Division 45. In addition, Constantine has served as a grants review panel member for both the U.S. Department of Health and Human Services (2000) and the National Institute of Mental Health (2001), and she has served as a member of the Committee for the Examination for the Professional Practice of Psychology Licensing Exam (since 2002) and a member of numerous committees and task groups within APA.

Constantine's editorial experience is extensive and comprises service to some of the most important journals in the field of psychology. She is currently a consulting editor of the *Journal of the Professoriate* (since 2005) and associate editor of *Cultural Diversity & Ethnic Minority Psychology* (since 2004) and the *Journal of Counseling Psychology* (since 2007). She also served previously as associate editor of the *Journal of Black Psychology* (2002–2006) and senior and associate editor of the *Journal of Multicultural Counseling and Development* (1999–2003). Constantine has received appointments to the editorial boards of the *Journal of Counseling Psychology* (2000–2006), *Career Development Quarterly* (2005–2008), *Cultural Diversity & Ethnic Minority Psychology* (2000–2003), the *Journal of Career Assessment* (2001–2003), *Professional Psychology: Research and Practice* (2000–2003), *The Counseling Psychologist* (1999–2002), the *Journal of Psychotherapy in Independent Practice* (1997–2001), and the *Journal of Counseling & Development* (1996–1999).

Awards and Honors

Constantine's professional accomplishments have garnered numerous national accolades, beginning with two awards that recognized the promise of her early scholarship. In 1999, she was honored by Division 45 of the APA with the Early Career Contributions to Ethnic Minority Psychology Award, and the following year she received the Fritz and Linn Kuder Early Career Scientist-Practitioner Award from Division 17 of the APA. Constantine also has been honored with Fellow status in each of these divisions, having been named a Fellow of Division 17 in 2002 and of Division 45 in 2003. She also is the recipient of five Outstanding Teaching Awards from Teachers College, Columbia University. In 2001, Constantine received the ACA Award for Outstanding Research, and in 2005 she received the Samuel H. Johnson Award for Exemplary Service and Scholarship from the Association of Multicultural Counseling and Development as well as the Exemplary Scholarship Award from the Association of Black Psychologists. More recently, Constantine was honored with the Distinguished Scholar Award from the American Educational Research Association's Committee on Scholars of Color in Education (2006) and the Distinguished Research Award from its Division of Counseling and Human Development (2006).

Scholarship

The proof of Constantine's commitment to psychological research lies in her astonishing productivity and the scholarly significance of her contributions. In mid-career at the time of this writing, she has authored or coauthored at least 110 journal articles and more than 40 book chapters, and she has edited or coedited four books—all in the 13 years since her first journal article in 1995. Her scholarship coheres around four interrelated themes: (1) the education, training, and supervision of counselors and psychologists; (2) vocational and psychological issues of underserved populations; (3) multicultural counseling competence; and (4) racism in psychology and education.

With regard to the education and training of psychologists, Constantine's work has illuminated everything from the internship selection process to the complexities of the clinical supervisory relationship, especially where multicultural issues are concerned. Her studies of underserved populations and corresponding vocational and psychological issues have included explorations of racial identity, Africentric cultural values and coping styles, contextual and cultural factors in vocational development and career decisions, and the cultural adjustment experiences of international students. Constantine's body of work on multicultural counseling competence is among the strongest to be found within the field of psychology. It comprises studies that systematically examine the components and effects of multicultural competence from the vantage points of clients, counselors, and supervisors, considering both self-reported and observed ratings of multicultural competence; it also includes a significant focus on the multicultural competence of school counselors.

Finally, Constantine's research on racism in psychology and education represents a major contribution to our understanding of the dynamics of oppression within these fields as well as in society as a whole. This important social justice theme bookends Constantine's work to date: Her first publication in 1995 documented the racist attitudes and behavior encountered by psychologists of color in Division 17, and her recent (2007) work on racial microaggressions has further developed this theme along several dimensions. As defined by Constantine and her colleague and collaborator Derald Wing Sue, *racial microaggressions* are the commonplace indignities and demeaning messages that are conveyed to people of color on a daily basis, often by perpetrators who are unaware of the racist connotations of their speech or behavior. Constantine's research has identified the various types of racial microaggressions experienced by Black clients, graduate students, and faculty members as perpetrated by their White counselors, supervisors, and colleagues. Utilizing primarily qualitative methodologies that allowed participants' own voices to emerge, Constantine's contributions are momentous for psychologists interested in multicultural competence and social justice. In revealing the extent to which unaware racism still pervades the field of psychology, undermines psychological practice, and produces damaging results for people of color, this research should serve to spur the field to deepen its examination of all oppression-related biases and its commitment to multicultural competence.

Achievement in a Relational Context

In her 1994 book *Teaching to Transgress,* bell hooks described a liberatory, feminist, multicultural context for teaching and learning as "a radical space of possibility." The ability to create such spaces epitomizes Madonna Constantine as a professional and as a person. Her collaborative and feminist spirit, her reticence to showcase herself as an individual, and her avid support and mentorship of students and colleagues alike are legendary.

Laura Smith

See also Afrocentricity/Afrocentrism (v3); Association of Black Psychologists (v3); Counseling Skills Training (v2); Cultural Values (v3); Multicultural Counseling (v3); Multicultural Counseling Competence (v3); Oppression (v3); Racial Identity (v3); Racial Microaggressions (v3);

Critical Race Theory

Critical race theory (CRT), initially created as a body of legal theory, is an organizing framework useful in understanding human behavior and social processes relevant to racial group categorizations and racial stratification. Critical race theory examines the oppressive dynamics of society to inform individual, group, and social transformation. Rather than embracing a color-blind perspective, CRT places race at the center of the analysis and provides a critical perspective on how racial stratification continues to influence the lives of racial/ethnic minorities in the United States. In this context, color-blindness refers to the minimization or denial of a substantive role for race in the understanding of life outcomes for different racial groups. Critical race theory provides a framework consistent with multicultural psychology and is useful in the conceptualization and practice of counseling and psychotherapy in cross-cultural contexts. Mental health professionals working in cross-cultural contexts can use CRT to facilitate a deeper understanding of how racial stratification is manifested in everyday experience and the enduring role that race plays in the lives of individuals, families, and groups, as well as in the therapeutic process.

Basic Tenets and Dominant Themes

Scholars across disciplines have identified several dominant and unifying themes that describe the basic tenets of CRT. Based on the core CRT literature, 10 basic tenets/dominant themes can be articulated that describe CRT's conceptual foundation.

1. Race is a social construct, not a biological phenomenon.

2. Racism is endemic to American life and should not be regarded as an aberration.

3. Racism benefits those who are privileged and serves the interests of the powerful to maintain the status quo with respect to racial stratification.

4. CRT represents a challenge to the dominant social ideology of color-blindness and meritocracy.

5. Racial identity and racial identification are influenced by the racial stratification that permeates American society.

6. Assimilation and racial integration are not always in the best interests of the subordinated group.

Racism (v3); Scientist–Practitioner Model of Training (v1); Social Justice (v3); Society for the Psychological Study of Ethnic Minority Issues (v3)

Further Readings

Constantine, M. G. (2001). Predictors of observer ratings of multicultural counseling competence in Black, Latino, and White American trainees. *Journal of Counseling Psychology, 48,* 456–462.

Constantine, M. G. (2002). Predictors of satisfaction with counseling: Racial and ethnic minority clients' attitudes toward counseling and ratings of their counselors' general and multicultural counseling competence. *Journal of Counseling Psychology, 49,* 255–263.

Constantine, M. G. (2007). Racial microaggressions against African American clients in cross-racial counseling relationships. *Journal of Counseling Psychology, 54,* 1–16.

Constantine, M. G., Anderson, G. M., Berkel, L. A., Caldwell, L. D., & Utsey, S. O. (2005). Examining the cultural adjustment experiences of African international college students: A qualitative analysis. *Journal of Counseling Psychology, 52,* 57–66.

Constantine, M. G., & Sue, D. W. (Eds.). (2005). *Strategies for building multicultural competence in mental health and educational settings.* Hoboken, NJ: Wiley.

Constantine, M. G., & Sue, D. W. (Eds.). (2006). *Addressing racism: Facilitating cultural competence in mental health and educational settings.* Hoboken, NJ: Wiley.

Constantine, M. G., & Sue, D. W. (2007). Perceptions of racial microaggressions among Black supervisees in cross-racial dyads. *Journal of Counseling Psychology, 54,* 142–153.

Constantine, M. G., Warren, A. K., & Miville, M. L. (2005). White racial identity dyadic interactions in supervision: Implications for supervisees' multicultural counseling competence. *Journal of Counseling Psychology, 52,* 490–496.

Miville, M. L., Constantine, M. G., Baysden, M. F., & So-Lloyd, G. (2005). Chameleon changes: An exploration of racial identity themes of multiracial people. *Journal of Counseling Psychology, 52,* 507–516.

Perez, R. M., Constantine, M. G., & Gerard, P. A. (2000). Individual and institutional productivity or racial and ethnic minority research in the *Journal of Counseling Psychology. Journal of Counseling Psychology, 47,* 223–228.

Smith, T. B., Constantine, M. G., Dunn, T. W., Dinehart, J. M., & Montoya, J. A. (2006). Multicultural education in the mental health professions: A meta-analytic review. *Journal of Counseling Psychology, 53,* 132–145.

7. CRT considers the significance of within-group heterogeneity and the existence of simultaneous, multiple, intersecting identities.

8. CRT argues for the centrality, legitimacy, and appropriateness of the lived experience of racial/ethnic minorities in any analysis of racial stratification.

9. CRT insists on a contextual analysis by placing race and racism in a cultural and historical context, as well as a contemporary sociopolitical context.

10. Informing social justice efforts and the elimination of racial oppression are the ultimate goals of critical race theory.

The first basic tenet of CRT is that *race is a social construct, not a biological phenomenon.* It is not rooted in biology or genetics but rather is a product of social contexts and social organization. Based on the social construction thesis, CRT holds that races are categories that society creates, revises, and retires as needed. This tenet is based on scientific research demonstrating that the human phenotypic expressions used to indicate racial categorization (i.e., those physical characteristics shared by many people of a common heritage) constitute only a minute segment of people's genetic makeup and account for approximately .1% of genetic variability between races. Genetically, people are more similar than different. Furthermore, science has found no reliable link between physical traits and higher-order characteristics such as personality, intelligence, and morality. A central question that emerges from CRT is why and how pervasive social ideology continually overlooks scientific fact and attributes semipermanent characteristics to different races. CRT challenges the idea that race should be disregarded because it is not valid scientifically. Assigned racial group categorizations continue to have a strong impact on differential life outcomes, as well as on how people perceive and interact with each other. Race continues to influence the structure and functioning of a broad range of societal institutions, including education, health care, employment, media, and the legal system.

Second, *racism is endemic to American life and should not be regarded as an aberration.* Socially constructed racial categorization is currently and has historically been a fundamental organizing principle of society. Individual, cultural, and institutional expressions of racism reflect the racial stratification that is part of the fabric of the United States of America. In a CRT analysis, racism is ordinary practice and part of the dominant cultural ideology that manifests in multiple contexts. Race and racism are central and defining factors to consider in understanding individual and group experience. Racism can express itself in very mundane, as well as quite extraordinary, ways. It affects the course and quality of life through access to valued societal resources, opportunities, and information. Thus, CRT critiques the position that racism is primarily an attitudinal or psychological problem and argues that conceptualizing it in this way hides its pervasiveness, insidiousness, and enduring nature.

A third basic tenet of CRT is that *racism benefits those who are privileged and serves the interests of the powerful to maintain the status quo with respect to racial stratification.* Those with power and influence in society have little incentive to eliminate racism. This feature is known as "interest convergence" or material determinism. Efforts to eliminate racism occur only when the change will benefit the privileged group in some way. This tenet encourages exploration of the role of societal need and power interests in the way that specific qualities are associated with particular racial groups. This idea of differential racialization examines how characteristics ascribed to a particular race change depending on the needs and interests of the majority group. Historically, these have included economic power, safety from a perceived threat, and a quest for racial or ethnic purity, among others. In addition, sentiments and stereotypes associated with a particular group change with societal conditions. For example, during World War II, Japanese Americans were in extreme disfavor, moved to internment camps, and assigned stereotypes such as "cruel" and "evil." As another example, people of Black African descent were depicted as simple-minded and childlike during slavery when justification for servitude was needed. However, more recently, African Americans are depicted as aggressive, threatening, and criminal, which serves to justify the practice of racial profiling and disproportionate rates of imprisonment, among other phenomena.

Fourth, CRT represents *a challenge to the dominant social ideology of color-blindness and meritocracy.* Race neutrality and the myth of equal opportunity ignore the reality of the deeply embedded racial stratification in the United States and the impact it has on quality of life. These dominant ideological assumptions result in a deficit analysis of differences between Whites and people of color. The traditional paradigm of equal opportunity camouflages the realities of power asymmetry and unearned privilege afforded to dominant groups. Within this predominant paradigm of color-blindness and meritocracy, a Latina worker's failure to be promoted would be attributed exclusively to individual deficiencies with factors such as an "old boys club" ignored or discounted. A CRT analysis would illuminate the dynamics of race and differential access to opportunities for advancement that create disparities in life outcomes.

A fifth important theme relevant to CRT is that *racial identity and racial identification are influenced by the racial stratification that permeates American society.* The perceived salience of race, the significance of racial/ethnic group membership to self-concept, the degree to which racial/ethnic heritage and practices are embraced or rejected, and the affiliations and identifications that are made within and outside of one's own racial/ethnic group are all impacted by the dominant cultural narrative of White superiority. Trustworthiness, intelligence, leadership, credibility, and standards of attractiveness are among the characteristics more quickly attributed to Whites when in comparison with people of color. When there is an idealization of Whiteness by persons of color, behavior may be influenced by the need to meet the approval of Whites, and there may be collusion with attitudes of color-blindness and race neutrality to be "acceptable" to Whites. This idealization of Whiteness can be associated with the internalization of negative stereotypes and result in distancing and disidentification with respect to one's own racial/ethnic group. However, dissonance can be created when a preference for Whiteness comes face-to-face with the inescapable reality of the permanence of living as the racial/ethnic group within which one was born. Biracial and multiracial individuals and families frequently must negotiate identity and identification within a society where part of their heritage is valued as superior and is more privileged than other parts. This is most striking when one parent is White. However, this dynamic can also be present in situations where parents are members of different racial/ethnic groups of color (e.g., Japanese and African American). From a CRT perspective, positive and healthy racial identification, which does not collude with the perpetuation of racial stratification, requires exposure, familiarity, and affirming contexts that provide alternative and empowering meanings associated with one's racial/ethnic group or groups.

Sixth, within a CRT framework, *assimilation and racial integration may not always be in the best interests of the subordinated group.* In practice, racially integrated settings occur in mainstream institutions that are majority White in composition and/or in the distribution of power. Due to the dominant ideology of White supremacy, messages of inferiority and deviance are easily available and internalized by people of color in predominantly White settings. In addition, fairness may be perceived differently by those with diverse racial experiences. For example, integration that separates children of color into different classrooms in the name of integration actually benefits White children in providing them with exposure to a "diversity" experience. Dominant cultural values and practices, sense of identity, belonging, security, and esteem are not at risk for the White children. However, the children of color face greater risk of conformity demands, encouragement to keep differences relatively invisible, alienation, disconnectedness, withdrawal, and internalized racism. This is particularly true when the institutional culture insists on a "we are all the same" value structure and silences or marginalizes voices that threaten this ideology that renders people blind to the dynamics and expressions of racism. When affirmation, validation, within-group support, and opportunities for racial and cultural socialization are missing or weak, racial integration (as it is currently practiced) can have negative effects on members of racial/ethnic minority groups.

A seventh dominant theme in CRT is *the significance of within-group heterogeneity and the existence of simultaneous, multiple, intersecting identities.* This is often referred to as anti-essentialism or intersectionality. All people have overlapping identities, and multiple lenses through which the world is experienced. CRT challenges the idea that any person has a unidimensional identity within a single category (e.g., race/ethnicity) or that racial groups are monolithic entities. There is tremendous diversity within broad racial/ethnic group categories. For example, a person of Middle Eastern descent might be a fifth-generation Lebanese man or a recently immigrated Iranian Jewish woman. Many critical race scholars recognize that poverty and race intersect in complex ways, so that the predicament of very poor racial/ethnic minority families differs in degree from that of their White counterparts. Gender, immigration status, language, and sexual orientation are among the many dimensions of diversity that exist within broad racial/ethnic group categories. It is necessary to understand the dynamics of subordination within these dimensions of diversity and the ways that these forms of oppression (e.g., classism, sexism, heterosexism) intersect with racism.

Eighth, CRT argues for *the centrality, legitimacy, and appropriateness of the lived experience of racial/ethnic minorities in any analysis of racial stratification*. People of color have different stories to tell regarding the way that race affects their life experiences. These stories have not had as significant an influence on policies, practices, and opinions as have the dominant cultural narratives about race that permeate the media and minds of most Americans. People of color have unique perspectives on racial matters, and their voices speak of experiences involving marginalization, devaluation, and stigmatization of which their White counterparts have very little knowledge. Racial minority status grants particular expertise and competence in speaking about race and racial matters. According to CRT, this experiential knowledge is a strength and critical to analyzing the dynamics and results of racial stratification in an authentic and meaningful way. Given that storytelling is a significant aspect of human communication, CRT has advocated for marginalized people to tell their often unheard and unacknowledged stories and for these perspectives to be applied to the existing dominant narratives that influence the law. The CRT process of counter-storytelling refers to the illumination of the cultural and personal narratives, family histories, and metaphorical stories that present a contrast to dominant societal narratives about race. These stories are viewed as central sources of information necessary for an authentic and comprehensive understanding of racial stratification and subordination.

Ninth, CRT insists on a *contextual analysis by placing race and racism in a cultural and historical as well as a contemporary sociopolitical context*. CRT challenges ahistoricism and locates current manifestations of racial stratification within a broader historical landscape that has shaped the present forms and expressions of racism. Interdisciplinary perspectives and methods emerge from this contextualized approach.

Finally, a tenth dominant theme within CRT involves the recognition that *social justice and the elimination of racial oppression are the ultimate goals* of a CRT analysis and orientation. CRT provides a liberatory and transformative response to racial stratification and oppression. Research from a CRT framework should contribute to efforts that (a) facilitate the empowerment of marginalized and disenfranchised groups, and (b) inform strategies for eliminating racism and other forms of oppression.

Origins and Interdisciplinary Applications

The early roots of CRT lie in a variety of fields and movements including anthropology, sociology, history, philosophy, law, and politics. W. E. B. Du Bois, César Chávez, Frederick Douglass, and the Black Power and Chicano movements of the 1960s and 1970s helped inspire the development of its core ideas. CRT, as a formal idea, was first conceived in the 1970s, when a team of activists, lawyers, and legal scholars became wary that the strides made in civil rights activism and policy during the 1960s were eroding. There was clear consensus among these individuals that a different theoretical framework was needed to fight the newer, subtler forms of racism that had pervaded society. The earliest authors of CRT included civil rights lawyer Derrick Bell, legal scholar Alan Freeman, and Latino scholar Richard Delgado. Bell is arguably the most prominent source of thinking critical of traditional civil rights discourse and is considered by many as CRT's "intellectual father figure." He employed three major arguments in his analyses of racial patterns in American law: constitutional contradiction, the interest convergence principles, and the price of racial remedies. The late Alan Freeman was also instrumental in the development of CRT and wrote a number of foundational articles that critiqued racism in the U.S. Supreme Court's jurisprudence. Through scholarly dialogue and over the course of many meetings and conferences, CRT was actualized. Delgado, Kimberle Crenshaw, and Mari Matsuda have been significant contributors to CRT discourse from the 1980s to the present. During the capitalist boom of the 1980s and 1990s, critical race theorists focused primarily on the task of combating the country's racial indifference. A current focus of CRT scholars and activists is on the issue of "unmasking color-blindness."

It is noteworthy that culturally specific subdivisions have developed under the umbrella of CRT. These include Latino/a critical race studies (LatCrit), Asian American critical race studies (AsiaCrit), American Indian critical race studies (TribalCrit), critical race feminism, and a queer critical (Queer-Crit) interest group. The LatCrit contingent, as well as the AsiaCrit division, focuses its work on immigration policy and theory, language rights, assimilation, and discrimination based on nationality, accent, or both. Scholars associated with the TribalCrit subdivision study indigenous people's rights, sovereignty, and land claims. QueerCrit theorists focus primarily on the relationship between race and societal norms regarding sexual orientation. Some scholars have explored the interplay between feminism, sexual orientation, and CRT in their study of critical race feminism. This subgroup also examines issues such as relations between men and women of color; sterilization of Black, Latina, and Indian women; and the impact of changes in welfare, family policies, and child support laws.

The field of critical White studies has also emerged from CRT. A variety of questions have been generated that explore issues related to "Whiteness" and challenge its legitimacy as a normative standard. These questions include examining the meaning of being White, how Whiteness became established legally, how certain groups changed status in terms of their category of Whiteness, White power and White supremacy, and the unearned privileges that come with being a part of the majority culture or race.

During the first decade of the 21st century, work related to CRT is flourishing in many disciplines, and it is being applied by numerous scholars, students, and activists. Although CRT began as a movement in law, it has spread rapidly to other disciplines and has been utilized to understand the ways racial stratification operates on implicit, explicit, institutional, and individual levels to impact how those in a racialized society live and die. CRT has been continually increasing in educational scholarship, especially with regard to understanding school discipline and hierarchy, tracking, controversies over curriculum and history, and IQ and standardized testing. Within political science, CRT has been used to examine voting strategies, increasing voting power and representation and guaranteeing that the opinions and perspectives of minority groups are taken into account in the political process and major policy decisions. Critical race theorists in the legal system incorporate the ideas into their arguments to combat inequality and bias. The distribution of environmental dangers and biohazards has been analyzed from a CRT perspective, citing that sewage treatment plants are disproportionately placed in minority communities or on Indian reservations. Other issues receiving attention from "race crits" across disciplines include resolving the racism prevalent in the U.S. criminal justice system, examining racism in globalization and immigration, developing new immigration policies, protecting language rights, combating hate speech, fighting discrimination in higher-paying jobs, rectifying disparities in the delivery of health and well-being services, demystifying the concept of race as a biological phenomenon, protecting the rights of minorities to retain their heritage and free them from the need to assimilate to advance in U.S. society, and making necessary reforms appealing to the majority group so that legislation and other appropriate measures will be approved and stand the test of time.

Critical Race Theory, Psychology, and Multicultural Counseling

Although the core assumptions of CRT can be found throughout the multicultural psychology literature and underlie many of the approaches to counseling in cross-cultural contexts, there has not been a large body of work within the field of psychology that explicitly refers to CRT. However, since the end of the 20th century, there has been increased attention to the application of CRT within psychology. The primary contribution has been the work of James Jones and his 1998 proposed psychological critical race theory, in which he articulates five psychological explanations for the continuing racial disparities in the United States. These explanations, rooted in the dominant themes of CRT yet applicable to psychological research, are (1) the spontaneous and persistent influence of race, (2) the idea that fairness is derived from divergent racial experiences, (3) the asymmetrical consequences of racial policies, (4) the paradoxes of racial diversity, and (5) the salience of racial identity. Jones contends that race is both socially constructed and psychologically constructed such that racial categorizations exaggerate group differences and lead to divergent experiences for different racial groups. General CRT argues that the early civil rights era view of a disregard for race under the law will not lead to equality because of the permanence of race and racism. Similarly, utilizing psychological research, psychological CRT holds that social justice efforts must incorporate attention to race as a central dynamic in social disparities. The push and pull between commonalities and differences, belongingness and distinctiveness continues to be a tension experienced on individual, interpersonal, group, and macro-systemic levels. Jones proposes the diversity hypothesis, which holds that maintaining, valuing, and validating strong and positive group identity (e.g., racial identity) as well as a simultaneous superordinate identity (i.e., our humanness) is necessary for both psychological well-being and movement toward social justice.

Other approaches to the application of CRT within psychology examine the ways that racial stratification (a) creates social conditions (e.g., crime, joblessness, poverty) that may be risk factors for mental health problems, and (b) generates and increases exposure to specific race-related stressful circumstances (e.g., hate crime, racial profiling). This approach also explores how a system of racial oppression has the potential to express itself through unique mental health problems that are not explicitly recognized in traditional conceptualizations of psychopathology. The focus is on understanding psychological problems that are generated by the dilemmas, dissonance, and challenges to the construction of a positive, coherent, sense of self that emerges in the societal context of a dominant ideology of White supremacy. These include concerns such as nihilistic tendencies, anti-self issues, and suppressed anger. In mainstream contexts, persons of color exhibiting behavior associated with these concerns may be positively reinforced to the extent that the behavior colludes with notions of White superiority and construes race or racism as irrelevant. Examples include being reinforced for stating that race is currently not a determinant of success in America, making disparaging remarks about members of one's own racial/ethnic group, or shedding any signs of cultural distinctiveness related to race/ethnicity so as to be indistinguishable from Whites in all ways except phenotype. However, within a CRT framework, these behaviors indicate internal conflicts that threaten self-esteem and are likely to influence interpersonal interaction and quality of life.

With respect to counseling and psychotherapy applications, CRT has been used to explore the racial experiences of marriage and family therapists in training, as well as to analyze the content of the *Journal of Marriage and Family Therapy*. These efforts reinforce the need to (a) listen to racially marginalized voices of clients, students, and supervisees about their race-related experiences, and (b) be willing to explore the meanings of race and racism with them. The ways that racial stratification has impacted status and opportunities, intersections with other social locations and multiple identities, and potential strategies for building a healthy sense of self can all be informed by CRT. Questioning dominant social ideology and exploring social justice implications are also facilitated through a CRT analytic frame. CRT provides an interdisciplinary theoretical base that is compatible with multicultural counseling and can facilitate the development of multicultural competence among counselors and therapists.

Table 1 presents 10 basic tenets/dominant themes of CRT and an example of the application of each theme to multicultural counseling and psychotherapy. CRT can be applied to diagnosis and assessment, case conceptualization, and treatment planning, as well as the client–therapist relationship. Counselors and therapists can utilize the 10 themes to process the role of racial stratification in a client's life and the expression of CRT themes in a client's behavior and relationships. The application of CRT in counseling and psychotherapy also provides clients with resources that may be helpful in shaping their own lives in the realistic context of racism and White privilege.

Conclusion

The future applications of CRT rely on the racial landscape of the United States in the coming decades. Although there has been some suggestion that the country will experience a transition into a more inclusive and diverse society, there is also concern that racial divisions will deepen and the gap between our language of equality and our practice of racial stratification will continue to widen. CRT provides a useful framework for generating insights into the dynamics of socially constructed racial categorizations, the racialized nature of social dynamics, and the impact of the system of racial oppression on human behavior and psychological functioning. The theory represents a paradigm shift from a traditional "we are all the same" posture, which masks power asymmetries and protects the interests of the dominant group, to an analysis that insists on the explicit identification of racial dynamics and the influence of racial stratification on life experiences and life outcomes.

Cross-cultural counseling can be further strengthened through the systematic application of CRT to facilitate more comprehensive and inclusive case conceptualizations, treatment planning, and the delivery of appropriate and responsive services to marginalized racial/ethnic populations. Furthermore, adopting a CRT perspective in counseling will require participation in social justice efforts that can have a positive impact on the psychological well-being of clients. Ultimately, a CRT perspective encourages action to eliminate the influence of the societal values of racial

Table 1 Basic tenets of critical race theory (CRT) and applications to counseling and psychotherapy

Basic CRT Tenet	Example of a Counseling Application
1. Race is a social construct, not a biological phenomenon.	Include consideration of the subjective meaning of racial group categories to client and therapist.
2. Racism is endemic to American life and should not be regarded as an aberration.	Be aware that racism is embedded in the social structure such that how it impacts the lives and thinking of clients and therapists may not be easily articulated and can remain unquestioned, simply experienced as "normal."
3. Racism benefits those who are privileged and serves the interests of the powerful to maintain the status quo with respect to exploring the role of racial stratification.	Assess both therapist and client resistance to naming racism as a contextual factor in the client's life experience and to racial dynamics in the therapeutic process.
4. CRT represents a challenge to the dominant social ideology of color-blindness and meritocracy.	Ignoring race and assuming neutrality risks rendering core aspects of a client's life experience and identity invisible communicates support of conformity to an idealized White norm and thus limits the effectiveness of psychotherapy, as important issues may be minimized or missed.
5. Racial identity and identification are influenced by the racial stratification that permeates American society.	Analysis of racial identity issues must be understood in the context of the existence of racial hierarchies such that some groups are devalued and others are idealized.
6. Assimilation and integration are not always in the best interests of the subordinated group.	Assess racial socialization and exposure to racially affirming and devaluing contexts and messages. Consider strengthening within-group social support as indicated.
7. CRT considers the significance of within-group heterogeneity and the existence of simultaneous, multiple, intersecting identities.	Socioeconomic class, gender, phenotypic expression, birthplace, sexual orientation, age, religion, and other characteristics interact with racial group to impact the nature of race-related experience. It is important to avoid assumptions of within-group homogeneity in case conceptualization and treatment planning.
8. CRT argues for the centrality, legitimacy, and appropriateness of the lived experience of racial/ethnic minorities in any analysis of social stratification.	Encourage narratives that reflect the client's race-related experience, observations, and understandings. Engage in explicit counter-storytelling strategies when indicated. Facilitate the empowerment of clients to express, create, and reauthor both personal and cultural narratives to reflect increased understanding of racial stratification and critical consciousness.
9. CRT insists on a contextual context, as well as a sociopolitical context.	Comprehensive case conceptualization and treatment planning requires locating the client within his or her cultural, historical, developmental, and sociopolitical context.
10. Informing social justice efforts and the elimination of racial oppression are the ultimate goals of CRT.	Identify and challenge policies and practices of educational and treatment settings that reflect and perpetuate racial stratification.

superiority and racial stratification in the practice of counseling and psychotherapy.

Shelly P. Harrell and Ani Pezeshkian

See also Color-Blind Racial Ideology (v3); Cross-Cultural Psychology (v3); Discrimination and Oppression (v2); Ethnic Identity (v3); Ethnicity (v3); Multicultural Psychology (v3); Oppression (v3); Race (v3); Racial Identity (v3); Racism (v3); Social Class (v4); Social Identity Theory (v3); Worldview (v3)

Further Readings

Brown, T. (2003). Critical race theory speaks to the sociology of mental health: Mental health problems produced by racial stratification. *Journal of Health and Social Behavior, 44,* 292–301.

Crenshaw, K., Gotanda, N., Peller, G., & Thomas, K. (Eds.). (1995). *Critical race theory: The key writings that formed the movement.* New York: New Press.

Delgado, R., & Stefancic, J. (Eds.). (2000). *Critical race theory: The cutting edge* (2nd ed.). Philadelphia: Temple University Press.

Jones, J. M. (1998). Psychological knowledge and the new American dilemma of race. *Journal of Social Issues, 54,* 641–662.

CROSS, WILLIAM E., JR. (1940–)

William E. Cross, Jr., is an African American social psychologist who is best known for his Nigrescence model of Black racial identity. The power of Cross's original Nigrescence model, which was first articulated in 1971, is evident by its adoption in the theorizing about other cultural identities, including minority, racial, ethnic, feminist, womanist, and gay/lesbian identities. The later versions of the model (i.e., the revised and expanded models in 1991 and 2001, respectively) have not only advanced the theorizing about Black racial identity, but the 2001 revision also resulted in a psychometrically supported measurement model, the Cross Racial Identity Scale. Cross is one of the most frequently cited names in the Black racial identity literature.

Background

Cross's interest in the identity of African Americans came, in part, out of the segregated social context of the times in which he grew up. He was the fourth child and first son of William and Margaret Cross; his father was a Pullman porter, a job that was steady and resulted in economic security, and his mother worked at different times as a maid and a factory worker. Although both of his parents had about 2 years of college—advanced education for their time—the social context did not allow them to translate their education into related employment. Thus, although Cross's parents valued education, they did not see it as a guaranteed avenue leading to advancement.

Cross's parents encouraged their children to read broadly and to value learning, but they also communicated messages to their children that are now well documented in the research literature. Cross's father encouraged him to go to college but also pressured him to pursue a skilled trade that would enable him to support himself as an adult. He did not want his son to be educated but unemployable. Cross chose not to pursue a skilled trade, initially a source of tension between him and his father, and was the only one of his siblings (Dolores, Shirley, Charlene, Charles, and Judith) to attend college. Cross's mother communicated a different message. She insisted that Cross could do anything he wanted to do, but she also pointed out that to be successful, he needed to be much better at it than others, if he expected to succeed and be taken seriously. She also indicated that even if he were better than others, he might not be rewarded at the level that he should. Thus, there was this unstated notion of a racialized world, present in the household but never made explicit. However, until he was about 10 years old, Cross's mother actively protected him and his siblings from some of the negative events that were happening in society as they were growing up. Cross describes the notion of becoming aware of race at about age 10 as a sledgehammer that initially took all of the fun out of life.

Origins of Cross's Nigrescence Model

Although there were many things that contributed to the development of the original Nigrescence model, three of these stand out: pursuing clinical psychology for his master's degree, the Black Power movement in the mid- to late 1960s, and the death of Martin Luther King, Jr., in 1968. After completing his bachelor's degree in psychology, Cross enrolled in a master's program in clinical psychology in 1963. In this program, with its emphasis on process, Cross developed a keen interest in identity change and became fascinated with experiencing changes in the self without conscious awareness of the process.

Although Cross had encountered Black professionals before he had attended college, he describes these individuals as too different from his experiences to identify with as role models. However, the Black movement's emphasis on African Americans having the power to be anything they chose to be—an idea initially inculcated by his mother—led him to embrace this idea in a way that he had not done earlier. Reading books like *From Superman to Man,* with its documentation of the consanguinity of many Blacks and Whites, supported this notion. Cross concluded that what the Black movement and specific subgroups like the Black Panthers were doing was putting African Americans through a *conversion* experience that resulted in a change in African Americans' conceptualization of being Black. In keeping with his training as a psychologist and the preeminence of stage theories in the psychological literature (e.g., Freud, Piaget, Kohlberg, Erikson), Cross conceptualized this identity change in terms of five stages: pre-encounter, encounter, immersion/emersion, internalization, and internalization/commitment.

The assassination of Martin Luther King, Jr., in 1968 served to further the development of Cross's thinking. This event became his *encounter,* as described in the original Nigrescence model, leading him to immerse himself in Blackness, something that he had not yet fully done. The assassination reminded Black people in the United States of (a) the hatred and segregationist beliefs grounded in *miseducation,* (b) their existential connections to being Black, and (c) the importance of responding as a community. Going to Princeton in 1969 put Cross in a forum where he could discuss his ideas with other intellectuals; this environment supported the seminal publication of his original Nigrescence model in the journal *Black World* in 1971.

From the Original to the Expanded Nigrescence Model

In 1991, Cross revised his model to account for greater identity variability at the pre-encounter and internalization stages. In the original formulation, everything linked to pre-encounter was thought to be negative and potentially pathological. Cross realized that the pre-encounter stage also needed to account for African Americans who do not base their identity on an attachment to Black people and Black culture (i.e., people with low racial salience). To capture the negative dimensions of pre-encounter, themes of racial self-hatred and miseducation were advanced. Thus, the *revised* model separates negative (miseducation and racial self-hatred) and low-salience (assimilation and other low racial salience exemplars) dimensions in the explication of pre-encounter.

This multidimensionality was also extended to internalization. All internalization identities accorded moderate to high salience to Blackness, but some were monocultural perspectives (e.g., Black Nationalist or Afrocentric perspectives), others had a dual-cultural frame (Black bicultural and biracial perspective), and others seemed to combine their sense of Blackness with two or three additional identities (multicultural perspectives). In the revised model, Cross also argued that the content of the identity stage was unrelated to individual well-being. In other words, assimilation, Afrocentricity, and multiculturalism identities may be divergent but equally efficacious pathways toward mental health.

The revised model explicates that at some point in life, a person may experience Nigrescence or Black identity change as a corrective to negative identity dynamics (miseducation or racial self-hatred). Change may also occur in a person who starts out in life with an assimilated worldview but, due to some encounter, may gravitate toward an identity that accords moderate to high salience to race. Thus, the revised model allowed researchers and therapists to better predict and explain the wide range of identity types and levels of well-being found in any large sample of African Americans.

The development of the *expanded* Nigrescence model in 2001 was due, in large part, to the development of the Cross Racial Identity Scale (CRIS), a scale that was originally conceived of as an operationalization of the revised model. In developing the CRIS, Cross and his colleagues began to describe racial identity in terms of attitudes rather than stages. The expanded model consists of four sets of attitudes (with the same names as the original four stages), each incorporating several worldviews that are relatively independent. Thus, an individual's racial identity is best described in terms of his or her racial identity attitude *profile* and not the stage that the individual is in.

Cross's Legacy

Cross's contributions to counseling and psychology have been tremendous. First, he has made a tremendous contribution in the theoretical realm. His initial conceptualization of Black racial identity as a stage model with movement from poor mental functioning to mental health stimulated several decades of research and theorizing on Black identity and other cultural identities and continues to have an impact on these fields to this day. The changes in the Nigrescence model over the past 3 decades (1971, 1991, 2001) have also demonstrated the important and oft-neglected relationship between theory and empirical research, and the most recent conceptualization is likely to stimulate another generation of researchers.

Second, although Cross's place as a theorist is well established, he has also had a tremendous impact on the empirical literature. There have been numerous empirical studies on the stages that he proposed in 1971 and the relationship of those stages to psychological functioning. The Racial Identity Attitude Scale, developed by Thomas Parham and Janet Helms in 1981, was based on a Q-sort that Cross had developed to examine Black racial identity stages, and was the preeminent measure of Black racial identity attitudes for more than 2 decades. Scores on the CRIS, which is the operationalization of the expanded model, have been validated for use in adolescent, emerging adult, and adult populations (a feat that has not been accomplished with any other measure of this type) and provides a context for the study of Black racial identity attitudes from a life-span perspective. Additionally, generalizable profiles of Black racial identity attitudes based on the expanded Nigrescence model have been reported for the first time in the empirical literature.

Cross's work has demonstrated that Black identity is a complex construct that is worthy of serious research scrutiny. He and his colleagues have shown that it is possible to develop a sound measure of Black racial identity attitudes that holds up under rigorous psychometric scrutiny. Finally, although Cross's focus has been on Black identity, his ideas are applicable to other cultural groups and are likely to have a continuing and profound impact on research examining cultural identity attitudes.

Frank C. Worrell

See also African Americans (v3); Afrocentricity/Afrocentrism (v3); Bicultural (v3); Black Psychology (v3); Black Racial Identity Development (v3); Monocultural (v3); Multiculturalism (v3); Racial Identity (v3)

Further Readings

Cross, W. E., Jr. (1971). The Negro-to-Black conversion experience. *Black World, 20*(9), 13–27.

Cross, W. E., Jr. (1991). *Shades of Black: Diversity in African American identity.* Philadelphia: Temple University Press.

Cross, W. E., Jr. (2001). Encountering Nigrescence. In J. G. Ponterotto, J. M. Casas, L. A. Suzuki, & C. M. Alexander (Eds.), *Handbook of multicultural counseling* (2nd ed., pp. 30–44). Thousand Oaks, CA: Sage.

Cross, W. E., Jr., & Fhagen-Smith, P. E. (2001). Patterns of African American identity development: A life span perspective. In C. L. Wijeyesinghe & B. W. Jackson (Eds.), *New perspectives on racial identity development: A theoretical and practical anthology* (pp. 243–270). New York: New York University Press.

Cross, W. E., Jr., & Vandiver, B. J. (2001). Nigrescence theory and measurement: Introducing the Cross Racial Identity Scale (CRIS). In J. G. Ponterotto, J. M. Casas, L. A. Suzuki, & C. M. Alexander (Eds.), *Handbook of multicultural counseling* (2nd ed., pp. 371–393). Thousand Oaks, CA: Sage.

Gardner-Kitt, D. L., & Worrell, F. C. (2007). Measuring Nigrescence attitudes in school-aged adolescents. *Journal of Adolescence, 30,* 187–202.

Vandiver, B. J., Cross, W. E., Jr., Fhagen-Smith, P. E., Worrell, F. C., Swim, J. K., & Caldwell, L. D. (2000). *The Cross Racial Identity Scale.* Unpublished scale.

Vandiver, B. J., Cross, W. E., Jr., Worrell, F. C., & Fhagen-Smith, P. E. (2002). Validating the Cross Racial Identity Scale. *Journal of Counseling Psychology, 49,* 71–85.

Worrell, F. C., Vandiver, B. J., Cross, W. E., Jr., & Fhagen-Smith, P. E. (2004). The reliability and validity of Cross Racial Identity Scale (CRIS) scores in a sample of African American adults. *Journal of Black Psychology, 30,* 489–505.

Worrell, F. C., Vandiver, B. J., Schaefer, B. A., Cross, W. E., Jr., & Fhagen-Smith, P. E. (2006). Generalizing Nigrescence profiles: A cluster analysis of Cross Racial Identity Scale (CRIS) scores in three independent samples. *The Counseling Psychologist, 34,* 519–547.

CROSS-CULTURAL PSYCHOLOGY

Cross-cultural psychology is the study of similarities and differences in individual psychological functioning in various cultural and ethnic groups, as well as the relationships between psychological variables and sociocultural, ecological, and biological variables. Cross-cultural psychology regards culture as essential to psychological functioning, as an integral context for psychological development and behavior.

Cross-cultural psychology consists mainly of diverse forms of comparative research so as to discern various distinct cultural factors—many of which are related to ethnicity—that are relevant to forms of development and behavior. Cross-cultural research typically seeks evidence of how culture can be taken as a set of variables, independent or contextual, that affect various aspects of individual behavior.

Cross-Cultural Psychology Versus Ethnic Minority Psychology

Differences in interpretation of "culture" account for the differences between cross-cultural psychology and ethnic-minority psychology. They differ in two ways, although they sometimes overlap and are taken as synonymous by some psychologists.

Ethnic minority psychology focuses on various ethnic groups such as African Americans. Cross-cultural psychology, in contrast, emphasizes differences between two or more cultures. Besides, ethnic minority psychology rooted in the United States has a briefer history than cross-cultural psychology does. Only after the civil rights movement of the 1960s was the Association of Black Psychologists founded, in 1968. The *Journal of Black Psychology* was first published in 1974 and the *Hispanic Journal of Behavioral Sciences* in 1979.

Historical Background

Traditional research in psychology has understandably been carried out mostly by thinkers of Western (ultimately Hellenic) cultures. The concepts and tools of psychological research came into being in an era of industrial systems of ideas, while consideration of culture has been relegated to a secondary role in psychology, appearing, at most, as moderating or qualifying footnotes to the major theoretical propositions assumed to be universally applicable.

In the meantime, however, there slowly emerged an awareness that such psychological theories in the traditional thinking mode, being Anglo-European, may well be of quite limited relevance to non-Western communities. It was thought that consideration of cultural aspects in psychological research would render psychology more widely relevant.

The era of cross-cultural psychology commenced soon after World War II ended. Its rapid expansion can be attributed to a shared motivation to understand the attendant horrors of war and to expand the intellectual horizons of psychology beyond parochial, nationalistic boundaries. With an emerging international perspective accompanying the cold war, the study of human behavior in cultural context evolved quite rapidly. The half decade of 1966 to 1970 saw the start of the quarterly *Cross-Cultural Psychology Bulletin* (originally called *Cross-Cultural Social Psychology Newsletter,* published periodically) and the *International Journal of Psychology,* as well as an initial *Directory of Cross-Cultural Psychological Research.*

Those years were marked also by the publication of a multisocietal study of cultural influences on cognitive conflict, a paperback volume titled *Cross-Cultural Studies,* and the flagship publication in cross-cultural psychology, *Journal of Cross-Cultural Psychology,* launched in 1970. By the late 1970 and early 1980s, enough research had been done to justify several major handbooks in cross-cultural psychology in general and in human development in particular. From the 1990s until the beginning of the 21st century, there appeared several new and updated handbooks on cross-cultural psychology. In 1998, Marshall H. Segall, Walter J. Lonner, and John W. Berry published an article, "Cross-Cultural Psychology as a Scholarly Discipline," on the critical role of culture in psychology. Several books through the 1990s into the 21st century (e.g., *Cross-Cultural Psychology: Research and Applications*) highlight many emerging themes in cross-cultural psychology.

In addition to the literature that emerged, scholarly and professional organizations on cross-cultural psychology were founded and have continued to flourish. Since its inauguration in Hong Kong in 1972, the International Association for Cross-Cultural Psychology has been holding biennial international congresses, and it continues to play a central role in the further development of cross-cultural psychology. Other important organizations include the International Union of Psychological Sciences and the International Association of Applied Psychology, among many others. By attracting diverse participants to their conventions and disseminating the most recent research and programs, these organizations facilitate dialogues on cross-cultural psychology across the world.

In the meantime, Berry and Pierre R. Dasen proposed three goals in cross-cultural psychology: to transport and test the current psychological knowledge and perspectives by examining them in other cultures, to explore and discover new aspects of the phenomena being studied in local cultural terms, and to integrate what has been learned from the first two points in order to generate psychology capable of addressing human basic processes and cultural variations worldwide.

Perspectives of Cross-Cultural Psychology

Various approaches in cross-cultural psychology can be classified in four ways: (1) etic versus emic; (2) dichotomous versus integrative; (3) absolutistic versus relativistic versus universalistic; and (4) individualistic versus collectivistic.

Etic Versus Emic

Following linguist Kenneth L. Pike, many cross-cultural psychologists used the contrasting terms *etic* and *emic,* to refer to etic comparative studies across cultures and emic intensive internal exploration of psychological phenomena in local cultural terms.

On the etic approach in early days, some Western psychologists used psychological notions and instruments that are designed, produced, and validated in the European American setting alone, to research psychological phenomena in other settings, cultural and national. This approach was recently criticized by Paul B. Pedersen because of its limited interpretation of the relationship between culture and psychological functioning. Emic research, on its part, focuses on culture-specific psychological phenomena and is expected to provide indigenous culture-based meanings probably missed in an overall etic approach.

After extensive use of emic approaches in cultures has produced instruments that satisfy etic criteria, comparative examination, with these instruments, of behaviors in various cultures would produce valuable information on cultural differences or similarities in psychological functioning. If superficial differences in behavior thus obtained reflect underlying shared psychological functioning, then they would support the notions of psychological universals. This possibility leads psychologists to consider another way of envisioning cross-cultural psychology today, namely, the integrative approach.

Dichotomous Versus Integrative

An alternative to the dichotomous approach, such as emic versus etic, is integration of psychological research. The integrative approach aids in revising and refining a theoretical understanding of human behavior, especially when theories are needed to apply to the widest audience possible. For example, cross-cultural research has helped refine understanding of child-rearing practices and attachment, and has helped modify what was considered as optimal attachment in child-rearing (based on research solely in the United States) to accommodate important child-rearing differences around the world.

Furthermore, uncovering cross-cultural differences helps render counseling more effective. Appreciation of similarities and differences in the relations between clients and mental health professionals depends much on information about people's cultural backgrounds. Cross-cultural research has helped in the development of culturally sensitive psychological assessments and treatments that have critically rendered psychotherapy effective.

Finally, cross-cultural research provides important connections among people and psychologists around the world, helping produce new modes of international intercultural cooperation among scholars, practitioners, and clients. New organizations that cut across many sorts of borders—social, economic, racial, national, as well as cultural—involve psychologists and health professionals from around the world, creating unions that would have been impossible otherwise.

Absolutism Versus Relativism Versus Universalism

The absolutist approach assumes that human phenomena are basically and qualitatively identical throughout all cultures. Sincerity is sincere, sadness is sad, no matter how or where one observes them, and so culture has practically no meaning or displays no specific characteristics.

Assessments of such ubiquitous characteristics are likely to be made through the use of standard instruments (perhaps via linguistic translation) and simplistic interpretations, taking into account no alternative, culturally based views. This orientation resembles the imposed etic perspective that was characteristic of some early cross-cultural research.

Cultural relativism, a term coined by anthropologist F. Boas and expanded and disseminated by Melville J. Herskovits, was initially a warning against invalid cross-cultural comparisons with an ethnocentric perspective. Later, Berry and his colleagues took up the term *relativism* to mean the opposite of absolutism. Thus, the relativists have no interest in intergroup similarities, in stark contrast to the absolutists, who assume and explore broad species-wide similarities.

The absolutists are prone to attempt context-free measurements with standardized psychological instruments, frequently making universal evaluative comparisons. As a result, they open themselves to errors of imposing "etics" when working in societies other than their own. In contrast, the relativists tend to lean toward emic research, considering context-free concepts and measurements as impossible, and so would try to avoid all cross-cultural comparisons; if they ever made the comparison, it would be as nonevaluative as at all feasible.

Psychologists with a universalistic perspective search for features of psychological functioning that appear common across all peoples. Berry proposed a rule of two steps: Culture comes first, comparison second. The framework begins with research in one cultural group A, firmly rooted in an indigenous tradition. Such research commences in examinations, both anthropological and psychological, of various cultural and individual behaviors and their plausible links and then draws cross-indigenous or cross-cultural research out of cultural groups B, C, D, and so forth. Thus emerges a universal psychology, rooted in both cultural-indigenous research and comparative cross-cultural analysis, achieved by gathering all indigenous psychologies and comparing them.

Individualism Versus Collectivism

Individualistic versus collectivistic approaches have been variously characterized. The approaches were said to be idiocentric-allocentric at the individual level versus idiocentric-sociocentric at the collective-cultural level; or individual and group loyalties versus culture of relatedness and separateness. In any case, the subjects in individualistic cultures have individualistic values and behaviors, and those in collectivistic cultures have collective values.

Such value dichotomy is reflected in other psychological processes and behaviors as well. Harry C. Triandis reported that even the meaning of *culture* differs in the kinds of information sampled from the culturally different environment. Such complex features in individualism versus collectivism can be conceptualized as "polythetic constructs" with the following aspects of self, goals, and the conflict between norms and attitudes.

The collectivists view the self as interdependent with others, sharing resources in a family manner. The individualists view the self as autonomously independent of groups, and whether or not to share resources is decided by individuals separately. Individuals are the units of analysis of social behavior. In contrast, the collectivists use groups. Individualists are concerned with individuals' own successes; collectivists are concerned with group success.

Goals are envisioned differently as perspectives differ. For collectivists, individual goals are ingroup compatible; for individualists individual goals are irrelevant to the group's goals. When individual goals and group goals collide, collectivists give priority to group goals, and individualists give priority to individual goals.

The conflict of norms versus attitudes is stressed differently. The collectivist determinants of social behavior are equally (a) norms, duties, and obligations, and (b) attitudes and personal needs. In contrast, individualist determinants are primarily attitudes, personal needs, perceived rights, and contracts. Whereas collectivists emphasize unconditional relatedness, individualists emphasize rationality in decision.

Areas of Research

Cross-cultural psychology involves many areas in psychology, including cognition, values, and mental health. The major research harvested by cross-cultural psychology can be categorized into six areas: (1) values, (2) personality, (3) gender issues, (4) development, (5) mental illness and well-being, and (6) counseling.

Values

Implicit in cross-cultural studies of values are guidelines on improvements in group relations, international negotiation, and globalization. Many different worldviews, conceptualizations of the world, affect what people in which society think is fair or what matters. These differences are their different views of the world to result in different manners of relating one to another.

Naturally, then, any two groups with different values (say, American students and international students) can form a community cross-culturally related, where interactions are prone to erroneous interpretations and judgments. Therefore, training in intercultural understanding is incumbent on all those in the counseling field, deserving close attention by scholars and professionals alike.

Personality

Cultural and cross-cultural analyses have thrown doubt over the existence of monolithic meanings of the key notions in psychology (e.g., personality, the self, etc.). Personality, as any other concept, is socially constructed, particularly based on Western assumptions. A high level of correspondence between higher-order personality models and everyday conceptions of personality has been found, indicating that personality is a cultural product. Some researchers (e.g., Kenneth J. Gergen) question any meaning in "personality" that exists identically in *all* contexts, seeing that some personality traits are meaningful solely in their respective specific contexts.

Despite such reports, many personality assessments (e.g., the Minnesota Multiphasic Personality Inventory or the Millon Clinical Multiaxial Inventory) were developed in Western psychology and then applied to culturally diverse populations to obtain cross-cultural validity. High degrees of cross-cultural validity, reported by some researchers such as James N. Butcher, who conducted the MMPI-2, may have prompted a proposal of the universality of personality.

Gender Issues

Cross-cultural research on gender has also yielded crucial findings. The core finding is that gender-related phenomena are embedded in cultures, whether the phenomena are sex-related differences in behavior or relations between sexes. Sex-role socialization has been studied in children and adolescents. On the role gender plays in later stages of life, women in traditional societies may well gain status with age advancement, which is a situation different from that in Western societies. Such variations call for renewed explanations based on different cultural definitions of women.

A related issue is sex-role differences and their underlying dimensions as cross-cultural. The expressive-instrumental dimension assumed to underlie differential sex-role socialization has been questioned. Some scholars reported greater expressiveness of males and more androgyny in general, in traditional cultures, than in Western cultures. Thus, some societies may routinely socialize children into androgynous patterns. Socialization of both females and males for great relatedness, sensitivity to others, and expressiveness may exist in highly collective societies, more so than in less collective communities.

Attitudes and stereotypes about gender roles have been continually popular among researchers. John E. Williams and Deborah L. Best reported that the ideals of both men and women in 14 countries were more masculine than self-ideals; in most countries, men traditionally carry an ideal image, not women. It appears universally valid to claim that breaking the stranglehold of outmoded stereotypes on sexual differences would facilitate equality between the sexes.

Development

Cultural attributes seem to remain important and serve as crucial contexts for psychological development. Cross-cultural research on human development has presented a challenging corrective to knowledge and theory based on Western experience. In fact, despite increasing cross-cultural research on development, developmental psychology has remained parochial. Gustav Jahoda noticed that researchers in development commonly accept a convergence of Piagetian and Vygotskian approaches. Following Charles M. Super and Sara Harkness's developmental niche (by analogy of "ecological niche" in biology), Dasen proposed a new diagram in studying human development, to show how, in Africa, parental psychology affects social and cognitive development. Barbara Rogoff proposed a similar orientation to cognitive development to show that such development has two features: (1) Culture and behavior (or thought) are not separate variables but are mutually embedded, so culture is not an independent variable; and (2) child socialization is jointly managed by children and adults.

Fred Rothbaum and his colleagues, with an interaction model, compared Japanese and American infant–mother interactions to test whether maternal behaviors shape infant behavior or whether they mutually shape each other. The interaction model was deemed valid by significant differences between newborns in motor activity level and later changes in infant and mother behavior. Such work has brought conceptual and methodological refinements in cross-cultural research on infant–mother attachment and early stages of development.

Interest in cross-cultural studies of life-span development is emerging. Studies have been made on life satisfaction in later years and on attitudes to the elderly. Research findings on life-span development focused on later life experiences show cross-cultural variations. For example, students in Turkey, but not in India, showed favorable attitudes to the elderly.

Mental Illness and Well-Being

Applications of cross-cultural psychology to problems of daily life are particularly evident in counseling psychology. At the same time, academic studies continue in such topics as the relationship between culture and psychopathology and between culture and diagnosis. Most psychologists now agree that the sociocultural context is a critical origin of psychological problems and that it is important to understand this cultural context. Among the issues to be researched are relationships between health and various cultural factors such as socialization, education, disability, and organizational structures of health institutions.

Depression is an example among many to this claim of culture as relevant to psychological problems. The *Diagnostic and Statistical Manual of Mental Disorders* indicates that culture can influence symptoms and experiences of depression. To reduce misdiagnosis, ethnic and cultural specificity need to be considered in diagnosis.

This raises a fundamental question, however, on how universal the notion of "depression" is. Sushrut Jadhav claims that it is questionable to indiscriminately apply *depression* or other such terms to non-Western clients, for there is insufficient evidence to detect depression as an objective entity transportable from one cultural setting to another.

From the perspective of relativist cross-cultural psychology, it is questionable that diagnostic systems and structured interviews developed in the West can ever serve as a universal framework for all cultures. These critics say the same syndromes hardly exist in the same form in other cultures, nor do individual symptoms necessarily exist in the same way across diverse cultures. For example, "fear" manifests quite differently from culture to culture; for example, among Hispanics, *ataques de nervios* are characterized by, among others, a feeling of rising heat. Counselors without such awareness will have difficulty understanding the Hispanic client's fear, particularly if the psychologist relies on a standard interview without questions related to such a way of experiencing fear.

Counseling

It is becoming increasingly common, all over the world, for counselors to come from cultures that differ from those of their clients, thus rendering cross-cultural counseling a challenging task. When other cultures and worldviews enter the picture, the situation can turn dauntingly complex.

Two aspects of cross-cultural research that are highly relevant to counseling are cross-cultural emphasis and intercultural focus. Pedersen specifies that cross-cultural counseling pays attention to qualitative differences across cultures and interculturally focused counseling work with ethnic and racial groups within a culture-pluralistic society. Despite different emphases, however, both aspects share many similar principles, including the necessity of cultural knowledge and sensitivity and understanding the crucial role culture plays in an individual's life.

In cross-cultural counseling, culturally sensitive diagnosis and treatment in counseling are essential, as based on the following factors. The counselor must be aware both of what is usually done in the clients' culture to resolve their presenting problems and of usual treatment in the counselor's own culture. In addition, the counselor must also be aware of how well the clients are acculturated to their host culture. If the clients are fairly well acculturated, counselors can feel more comfortable in designing a treatment plan similar to their usual design for native clients. If the clients have recently arrived from other cultures, counselors may want to consider how to temper the treatment plan with supplements familiar to the clients. The clients must be willing to accommodate the proposed supplements.

Ruth Chao

See also Barriers to Cross-Cultural Counseling (v3); Career Counseling (v4); Collectivism (v3); Counseling Skills Training (v2); Cross-Cultural Training (v3); Cultural Relativism (v3); Cultural Values (v3); Ethnicity (v3); Etic–Emic Distinction (v3); Immigrants (v3); Individualism (v3); Multiculturalism (v3); Multicultural Psychology (v3); Nationalism (v3); Personality Theories (v2); Universalism (v3)

Further Readings

Berry, J. W., Poortinga, Y. H., & Pandey, J. (Eds.). (1997). *Handbook of cross-cultural psychology.* Boston: Allyn & Bacon.

Boesch, E. E. (1996). The seven flaws of cross-cultural psychology: The story of a conversion. *Mind, Culture, and Activity, 3,* 2–10.

Greenfield, P. M. (1997). You can't take it with you: Testing across cultures. *American Psychologist, 52,* 1115–1124.

Herskovits, M. J. (1948). *Man and his works: The science of cultural anthropology.* New York: Knopf.

Jahoda, G. (1986). A cross-cultural perspective on developmental psychology. *International Journal of Behavior and Development, 9,* 417–437.

Matsumoto, D. (Ed.). (2001). *Handbook of culture and psychology.* New York: Oxford University Press.

Pedersen, P. B. (2000). *A handbook for developing multicultural awareness.* Alexandria, VA: American Counseling Association.

Pike, K. L. (1967). *Language in relation to a united theory of the structure of human behavior.* The Hague, the Netherlands: Mutton.

Ratner, C. (2002). *Cultural psychology: Theory and method.* New York: Plenum.

Rothbaum, F., Weisz, J., Pott, M., Miyake, K., & Morelli, G. (2000). Attachment and culture: Security in the United States and Japan. *American Psychologist, 55,* 1093–1104.

Segall, M. H., Lonner, W. J., & Berry, J. W. (1998). Cross-cultural psychology as a scholarly discipline. *American Psychologist, 53,* 1101–1110.

Shiraev, E., & Levy, D. (2004). *Cross-cultural psychology: Critical thinking and contemporary applications* (2nd ed.). Boston: Pearson.

CROSS-CULTURAL TRAINING

Cross-cultural training, also referred to as multicultural counseling competence training, denotes the process of instructing psychologists-in-training to work effectively across cultures in their practice and research activities. The term *cross-cultural* (or *multicultural*) has been defined in the counseling psychology literature in two distinct ways. One definition of *cross-cultural* is broad and inclusive of a wide variety of reference group identities (e.g., race, ethnicity, sexual orientation, social class). More traditional uses of the term, which emerged in the 1960s, were specific to different ethnicities, within and beyond the borders of the United States. On the basis of salience of race as a marker in the United States, many scholars during the 1980s and 1990s argued for a more specific definition of *cross-cultural* (*multicultural*) that focuses on domestic racial, ethnic, and linguistic minority groups. Because there has been increased attention to international issues in the field of counseling psychology during recent years (for instance, three of the five presidents of the Society for Counseling Psychology between 2003 and 2007 positioned counseling psychology in a global sphere), *cross-cultural,* for the purposes of this entry, refers to race and ethnicity within both domestic and international contexts.

The rapidly changing demographics of the U.S. domestic population and the transnational reach of counseling psychology make cross-cultural training increasingly critical in the overall education of applied psychologists. However, despite the importance the American Psychological Association (APA) has placed on cross-cultural training and the growing percentages of people of color in the United States served by applied psychologists, clients from diverse racial and ethnic backgrounds nonetheless continue to average fewer sessions, terminate more quickly, and utilize services less often than their non-Hispanic White counterparts. Racial and ethnic minority individuals oftentimes do not view counseling as addressing their needs, or perhaps untrained, culturally insensitive therapists leave too many minority clients feeling misunderstood. If clients are not considered within their sociocultural contexts as they understand and experience them, a host of potential negative implications might ensue with regard to case conceptualization (e.g., minimizing the importance of contextual factors), diagnosis (e.g., overpathologizing clients from different cultures on the basis of their different worldviews), and treatment (e.g., difficulty establishing the therapeutic alliance, inappropriate interventions). Therapeutic services designed from a universalist framework—a theoretical approach based on White middle-class male values that assumes a set of universal laws of human functioning—may not be appropriate in contexts where diverse worldviews and cultural values prevail. On the other hand, counselors (of various ethnicities) who have received cross-cultural training and demonstrate adequate levels of multicultural competence and sensitivity generally will minimize mistakes made in cross-cultural counseling and thus provide better, more appropriate services to clients of various racial and ethnic backgrounds.

Changing demographics in the academy also call attention to the importance of cross-cultural sensitivity in university classrooms and other training settings (e.g., practica). Traditional forms of pedagogy that rely on the universalist approach are not relevant for many students of diverse racial and ethnic backgrounds. To recruit and retain graduate students from a variety of racial and ethnic backgrounds, training programs must make the curriculum relevant for these students. Although demographic trends reveal increasing numbers of domestic students of color in undergraduate psychology programs (25% in 2000), many do not enroll in graduate study, or they withdraw before obtaining their doctorates. The teaching and training of psychology must become culturally relevant and appropriate for students from diverse racial and ethnic backgrounds so that they can (a) feel respected and validated in academic environments, thus leading to greater rates of completion; (b) bring relevant knowledge, grounded in empirical research, back to their communities; and (c) transform the ways in which psychological services are provided to a wide range of people. Based on data collected by the APA Research Office in 2000, the immediate reality remains that the majority of psychologists in the workforce (91%) and psychologists-in-training (78%) are White, and many are apathetic or resistant to cross-cultural training. With regard to internationalization, increasing numbers of international students are enrolling in applied psychology graduate programs and are being hired in academic positions in the United States or abroad in their countries of origin.

Counseling psychologists of all ethnicities, races, and nationalities are well-positioned to be leaders in the area of cross-cultural training because the variety of skills that they possess are essential in this realm. Certainly, creating environments conducive to effective cross-cultural training is challenging. Educators not only need mastery of content knowledge but also must possess excellent group facilitation skills, demonstrate appropriate self-disclosure, employ theoretical models and empirical research to guide training, and skillfully manage intense emotions that might emerge during discussions of such affectively loaded topics as racism, ethnocentrism, and White privilege.

Historical Context

A long-standing history exists that deals with the constructs of culture and race in psychology. Initial conceptual and empirical work regarding cross-cultural psychology sought to identify equivalent individual variables across cultural groups; that is, the focus was to detect universal laws of human functioning, which perhaps only varied by context. Early attention to the notion of race in psychology often was based on models of biological inferiority and cultural deprivation paradigms, blatantly reflecting and reinforcing White supremacy. In a society as diverse as U.S. society, with a wide variety of worldviews and healing practices among different cultures, it would seem obvious that a universalist approach would be ineffective with clients from various racial and ethnic backgrounds. However, the field of psychology was unable to transcend the universalist approach and is still struggling to do so, perhaps due to institutional racism and White privilege.

The concept of cross-cultural training in psychology gained momentum alongside grassroots activism, such as the civil rights and other liberal movements for social change. It was not until *Brown v. Board of Education of Topeka,* when psychological research was accepted as evidence in federal courts, that the stage was set for improved attention to race in therapy. The advent of minority-focused psychological associations, such as the Association of Black Psychologists (1968), Asociación Por La Raza (1970), Asian American Psychological Association (1972), and Society of Indian Psychologists (1975), provided further impetus for attention to cross-cultural training that transcended deficit paradigms. Concomitantly, the APA's evolution with regard to racial issues has facilitated the development of cross-cultural training initiatives. For example, during the National Conference on Levels and Patterns of Professional Training in Psychology (widely known as the Vail Conference of 1973), leaders decided that diversity training would be included in all APA-accredited doctoral programs; however, this was not immediately enforced. Subsequently, structural changes in the APA, such as the development of the APA Office of Ethnic Minority Affairs in 1979, the Board of Ethnic Minority Affairs in 1980, and Division 45 (Society for the Psychological Study of Ethnic Minority Issues) in 1986, compelled greater attention to culturally relevant training issues.

Since early forms of the multicultural guidelines in the 1980s and the *Guidelines for Providers of Psychological Services to Ethnic, Linguistic, and Culturally Diverse Populations* in 1993, almost 20 years had passed before the APA Council of Representatives approved as APA policy the *Guidelines on Multicultural Education, Training, Research, Practice, and Organizational Change for Psychologists* in 2002. Guideline 3 specifically encourages psychologists "to employ the constructs of multiculturalism and diversity in psychological education" and emphasizes the importance of incorporating culturally relevant practice into undergraduate and graduate instruction, including research advisement and clinical supervision.

Key Components

During the early 1980s, Derald Wing Sue and his colleagues pioneered the development of a tripartite model of cross-cultural, or multicultural, training. Sue's model included three distinct yet interrelated areas multiculturally competent counselors should possess: (1) knowledge of the cultural values and worldviews of diverse populations, (2) awareness of one's own cultural socialization and biases, and (3) skills for interventions with diverse client populations. The domains of knowledge, awareness, and skills have become widely accepted as the components of multicultural counseling competence and continue to be the prevailing training model today. Beginning in the 1990s Patricia Arredondo and her colleagues extended the tripartite model by delineating practical and specific training strategies, objectives, and techniques in each domain.

Since Sue's early work, a growing body of research has documented the ways in which cross-cultural training is most effective. In a meta-analysis examining the findings of 30 years of published studies on multicultural training effectiveness (1973–2003), Timothy Smith and colleagues found that theoretically grounded training is twice as beneficial as training that is not based on theory. Several other key variables also were consistently predictive of higher levels of cross-cultural competence, such as advanced racial identity statuses, lower levels of racism, and greater levels of emotional empathy. These findings underscore the importance of trainee racial self-awareness as a critical aspect of cross-cultural training. Apparently, the one course method is not sufficient, and the most beneficial approach, according to Charles Ridley and colleagues, is one that integrates multicultural issues into every aspect of a training program.

P. Paul Heppner, in his 2005 Society for Counseling Psychology Presidential Address, emphasized that in an era of increasing globalization, the boundaries of counseling psychology will cross an even wider variety of countries and cultures, which further necessitates incorporating cross-cultural competence in training. He suggested a number of activities that could promote such competence: immersion experiences abroad, formal coursework, proficiency in languages other than English, cross-cultural textbooks and curricula, and learning opportunities with international students within U.S.-based training programs.

Final Note

Greater specificity in the APA code of ethics and continued development of the *Guidelines* to explicitly outline the ways in which psychologists can effectively work with people from a variety of backgrounds is critical. Continued research is one way to accomplish this; empirically documenting what factors make cross-cultural training work best and for whom is crucial. Although training models are needed for trainees of all racial and ethnic backgrounds (those whose socialization and education are primarily U.S. based and those from other countries who complete graduate studies in U.S. colleges and universities), specific models are needed to help White graduate students overcome apathy, resistance, and ideologies grounded in White supremacist values (e.g., the perception of the superiority or universality of their worldviews). Minimum standards must be established to ensure that graduates possess the necessary knowledge, awareness, and skills to be effective in increasingly diverse domestic and global contexts. A challenge for the field of counseling psychology is to maintain its momentum on U.S.-based social justice initiatives while also attending to transnational issues.

Lisa B. Spanierman

See also Barriers to Cross-Cultural Counseling (v3); Constantine, Madonna G. (v3); Counseling Skills Training (v2); Cross-Cultural Psychology (v3); International Developments, Counseling (v1); International Developments, Counseling Psychology (v1); Multicultural Counseling (v3); Multicultural Counseling Competence (v3); Sue, Derald Wing: Contributions to Multicultural Psychology and Counseling (v3); Therapist Techniques/Behaviors (v2)

Further Readings

Abreu, J. M., Chung, R. H. G., & Atkinson, D. R. (2000). Multicultural counseling training: Past, present, and future directions. *The Counseling Psychologist, 28,* 641–656.

American Psychological Association. (2002). *Guidelines on multicultural education, training, research, practice, and organizational change for psychologists.* Washington, DC: Author.

American Psychological Association Research Office. (2003). *Demographic shifts in psychology.* Retrieved from http:/research.apa.org/gen1.html

Arredondo, P., & Arciniega, G. M. (2001). Strategies and techniques for counselor training based on the multicultural counseling competencies. *Journal of Multicultural Counseling and Development, 29,* 263–273.

Arredondo, P., Toporek, R., Brown, S. P., Jones, J., Locke, D. C., Sanchez, J., et al. (1996). Operationalization of the multicultural counseling competencies. *Journal of Multicultural Counseling and Development, 24,* 42–78.

Heppner, P. P. (2006). The benefits and challenges of becoming cross-culturally competent counseling psychologists: Presidential address. *The Counseling Psychologist, 34,* 147–172.

Leong, F. T. L., & Ponterotto, J. G. (2003). A proposal for internationalizing counseling psychology in the United States: Rationale, recommendations, and challenges. *The Counseling Psychologist, 31,* 381–395.

Marsella, A. J., & Pedersen, P. (2004). Internationalizing the counseling psychology curriculum: Toward new values, competencies, and directions. *Counselling Psychology Quarterly, 17,* 413–423.

Ponterotto, J. G., Casas, J. M., Suzuki, L. A., & Alexander, C. M. (Eds.). (2001). *Handbook of multicultural counseling* (2nd ed.). Thousand Oaks, CA: Sage.

Pope-Davis, D. B., & Coleman, H. L. K. (1997). *Multicultural counseling competencies: Assessment, education and training, and supervision.* Thousand Oaks, CA: Sage.

Ridley, C. R., Mendoza, D. W., & Kanitz, B. E. (1994). Multicultural training: Reexamination, operationalization, and integration. *The Counseling Psychologist, 22,* 227–289.

Smith, T. B., Constantine, M. G., Dunn, T. W., Dinehart, J. M., & Montoya, J. A. (2006). Multicultural education in the mental health professions: A meta-analytic review. *Journal of Counseling Psychology, 53,* 132–145.

Sue, D. W., & Sue, D. (2008). *Counseling the culturally diverse: Theory and practice* (5th ed.). New York: Wiley.

Cultural Accommodation and Negotiation

Cultural accommodation refers to the process by which individuals may take on values and beliefs of the host culture and accommodate them in the public sphere, while maintaining the parent culture in the private sphere. *Cultural negotiation* refers to the process whereby individuals must navigate two or more cultures that have values, beliefs, and behaviors that can be perceived as conflictual or incompatible.

Cultural Accommodation

Accommodating to culture suggests an adjustment or adaptation to a culture or a set of cultural beliefs, practices, or traditions—a construct that mirrors acculturation. When bilingual individuals speak a language (e.g., English), they may take on cultural values (e.g., individualism) and beliefs that are embedded in the language and that are not part of their own language or culture.

Frederick T. L. Leong identified three steps to the cultural accommodation approach: (1) The client's acculturation level and the cultural biases in an extant theory or model that hinder the cultural validity of the theory are identified. (2) Culture-specific constructs, values, and concepts from the clients' cultures that accommodate the theory or model to the clients are chosen. (3) The accommodated theory is examined for its incremental validity in comparison with the unaccommodated theory to determine the efficacy of the accommodated theory with respect to relevance, utility, sensitivity, and appropriateness. For example, the acculturation level of a Chinese American female seeking counseling for career indecision should first be assessed. As a second-generation, youngest daughter with no brothers, she may have a traditional Chinese perspective on her place in the family and community but also feel bicultural (acculturated to both American and Chinese cultures) and struggle with differences in expectations (e.g., good daughter) and stressors (e.g., pressure to marry). In step 2, Chinese interdependent values of filial piety, duty, honor with attention to hierarchy, and gender roles must be considered. Finally, efficacy comparisons between the unaccommodated (e.g., independence vs. interdependence) and the accommodated theories must be made.

Cultural Negotiation

Cultural negotiation is an adjustment process that takes place at individual, interpersonal, and systemic levels and occurs across cultural contexts. It occurs when individuals (e.g., immigrants adjusting to a new country or bicultural individuals having two cultural backgrounds) navigate diverse settings (e.g., school, home, work) and shift their identities and values depending on the norms of each environment. This allows individuals to fulfill differing expectations, obligations, and roles and to maintain relationships inside and outside their own cultural communities.

Cultural negotiation is needed to balance differing value systems, familial and community expectations, peer relationships, and identities. If conflict arises for bicultural individuals, they must negotiate between two, possibly dissimilar contexts: the culture of their family and the culture in which they live, work, and experience the world. For example, an Indian American female may weigh individualistic values with interdependent values when making a career decision. These negotiations also manifest in behavioral differences in multiple settings, including language usage (i.e., what language to speak at home and what language to speak at school), physical manifestations (e.g., body language, manner of dress), and activities (e.g., playing soccer, ethnic folk dancing).

Amanda L. Baden and Muninder K. Ahluwalia

See also Acculturation (v3); Assimilation (v3); Cultural Values (v3); Culture (v3); Enculturation (v3); Identity Development (v3); Multiculturalism (v3); Orthogonal Cultural Identification Theory (v3); Person–Environment Fit (v4); Person–Environment Interactions (v2); Second Culture Acquisition (v3)

Further Readings

Leong, F. T. L. (2002). Challenges for career counseling in Asia: Variations in cultural accommodation. *Career Development Quarterly, 50,* 277–284.

Leong, F. T. L., & Tang, M. (2002). A cultural accommodation approach to career assessment with Asian Americans (pp. 265–279). In K. S. Kurasaki, S. Okazaki, & S. Stanley (Eds.), *Asian American mental health: Assessment theories and methods.* New York: Kluwer Academic/Plenum.

Markus, H. R., Mullally, P. R., & Kitayama, S. (1997). In U. Neisser & D. A. Jopling (Eds.), *The conceptual self in context: Culture, experience, self-understanding* (pp. 13–61). Cambridge, UK: Cambridge University Press.

Oyserman, D., Sakamoto, I., & Lauffer, A. (1998). Cultural accommodation: Hybridity and the framing of social obligation. *Journal of Personality and Social Psychology, 74,* 1606–1618.

Padilla, A. (Ed.). (1980). *Acculturation: Theory, models and some new findings.* Boulder, CO: Westview Press.

CULTURAL ENCAPSULATION

Cultural encapsulation is the lack of understanding, or ignorance, of another's cultural background and the influence this background has on one's current view of the world. The purpose of this encapsulation, or "cocoon," is to allow people to protect themselves from the rapid global changes occurring in technology, families, economy, education, and social health. Cultural encapsulation can lead to a counselor applying his or her own experiences to the client's experiences despite the reality that both developed in different worlds, cultures, and values. To define one's experience as the truth or reality may result in potentially harming the client, given the possible differences between the counselor and client.

Christopher G. Wrenn revisited the conceptualization of cultural encapsulation and classified people's reactions to global change in two ways: as either a sense of hopelessness or a denial of the reality of the change or situation. This denial of the reality of change may lead counselors to make assumptions and generalizations about people and the world based on their limited group of clients; for example, clients who choose to see a counselor have money to do so and have a situation that compels them to see a mental health professional. For example, erroneous assumptions could be made about the etiology of depression based on a limited sample of clients who verbally express their depressive symptoms, are willing to seek help through counseling, and have economic means to see a counselor for a specific amount of time. Depression may have a different developmental pathway because of one's group norms about symptom expression and help seeking (e.g., seeing a family friend, elder, or religious leader that is less expensive and more appropriate for one's age, gender, religion, or culture).

The development of a counselor's cultural encapsulation can stem from one's culturally biased assumptions about counseling and psychology. Paul Pedersen identified eight assumptions:

1. American psychology is superior to other national psychologies.

2. Theories and measurements are validated for their use in other cultures.

3. The "self-reference criterion" of evaluating one's ideas and behaviors in terms of one's own viewpoint is useful.

4. Other disciplines doing similar activities can be excluded.

5. The Western cultural bias within the literature is unintentional.

6. Engagement in international issues where advocating for victims is critical is unnecessary.

7. Indigenous psychology can be included in the universal view of psychology.

8. Empirical research supports one's cultural bias.

According to Wrenn, to avoid cultural encapsulation and these assumptions, counselors need to examine their beliefs, assumptions, and stereotypes daily and eliminate them if they are no longer present in society. Counselors must anticipate changes in the information that they hold as current truths and encourage those who think differently. Finally, counselors must avoid the tendency to be self-righteous in their beliefs about themselves and others.

Laurie D. McCubbin and Sara Bennett

See also Allocentrism (v3); Barriers to Cross-Cultural Counseling (v3); Bias (v3); Cultural Mistrust (v3); Cultural Relativism (v3); Cultural Values (v3); Culture (v3); Ethnocentrism (v3); Eurocentrism (v3); Multiculturalism (v3); Person–Environment Interactions (v2); Pluralism (v3); Worldview (v3)

Further Readings

Pedersen, P. (1994). *A handbook for developing multicultural awareness* (2nd ed.). Alexandria, VA: American Counseling Association.

Wrenn, C. G. (1962). The culturally encapsulated counselor. *Harvard Educational Review, 32,* 444–449.

Wrenn, C. G. (1985). Afterword: The culturally encapsulated counselor revisited. In P. Pedersen (Ed.), *Handbook of cross-cultural counseling and therapy* (pp. 323–329). Westport, CT: Greenwood Press.

Cultural Equivalence

It is not uncommon for assessment tools to obtain unintended and unwanted sources of variance—or cultural bias—that lead to test results that are not easy to accurately interpret across cultures. Cultural equivalencies reflect a body of research methods that can be used to minimize cultural bias and measurement error in the development and/or adaptation of assessment tools. More specifically, conceptual, content, linguistic, technical, and normative equivalencies are five established dimensions of cultural equivalence that are used to minimize measurement error in cross-cultural applications.

1. *Conceptual Equivalency.* Conceptual equivalency examines the extent to which a construct has a similar nature and meaning when applied in a different cultural context. For example, does the notion of "self" mean the same thing in British culture as it does in Ghanaian culture? Ethnosemantic procedures can be used to evaluate conceptual equivalency. This is accomplished by eliciting words that span a specific domain (i.e., self), ordering such words according to predefined dimensions (e.g., good-bad, individual-collective), utilizing word associations to understanding the meaning of such words, and employing direct observations to attach associated behaviors to these words.

2. *Content Equivalency.* Content equivalency investigates if the operationalization of the construct is relevant to the population under study. For example, are the best elements used to describe and examine the notion of "personality" the same in Chinese culture as it might be in Native American culture?

3. *Linguistic Equivalency.* Linguistic equivalency is mainly concerned with translation accuracy from language A (e.g., English) to language B (e.g., Hindi). Back translation is a commonly used method to establish linguistic equivalency. This involves having a person fluent in both languages translate the original instrument from language A to language B. Next, a second person would take the recently translated instrument in language B and translate it back into language A. A research team would then test to see if the instrument that has undergone back translation is identical to the original instrument.

4. *Technical Equivalency.* Technical equivalency is concerned about the cultural appropriateness of the measuring techniques being used with a specific population. This equivalency is concerned with the appropriateness of response formats (True vs. False, Likert Scale, etc.), reading level, cognitive complexity, and any other variables that might lead to significant over- or underreporting. Use of informants, audio/visual aids, and ethnographic methods are some ways that barriers associated with technical equivalency can be minimized.

5. *Normative Equivalency.* Norms are important in having a standard so that observations of similarities and deviations can be made for a specific sample

population in question. Thus, normative equivalency requires norms to be available for the population being studied. Indices of normative equivalency might include variables like ethnicity, gender, age, educational obtainment, and socioeconomic status to name a few.

Social scientists must be aware of the importance that cultural variables can have in the acquisition of data. While much more work is needed to empirically demonstrate the nature of the aforementioned dimensions of cultural equivalence and/or the identification of new dimensions, the interpretation of results are only as good as the instruments and methodology used to obtain the raw data.

Ezemenari M. Obasi and Sheetal Shah

See also Assessment (v4); Bias (v3); Cross-Cultural Psychology (v3); Culture-Free Testing (v3); Etic–Emic Distinction (v3); Psychometric Properties (v2); Qualitative Methodologies (v1); Quantitative Methodologies (v1); Translation Methods (v3)

Further Readings

Canino, G., & Bravo, M. (1994). The adaptation and testing of diagnostic and outcome measures for cross-cultural research. *International Review of Psychiatry, 6*(4), 281–286.

Marsella, A. J., & Leong, F. T. L. (1995). Cross-cultural issues in personality and career assessment. *Journal of Career Assessment, 3*(2), 202–218.

CULTURAL MISTRUST

Cultural mistrust is an adaptive attitudinal stance in which a person of color is suspicious and guarded toward European Americans, particularly European American authority figures. It is adaptive in that if one accepts the contention that the current social paradigm is inherently racist, then a person of color cannot assume that a European American person has his or her best interests at heart. This attitudinal stance was first described in William Grier and Price Cobbs's classic book, *Black Rage*. Grier and Cobbs called this survivalistic stance *cultural paranoia*. Many writers later changed the term to *cultural mistrust* in an effort to emphasize that it is an adaptive strategy rather than a form of psychopathology.

Cultural Mistrust Research

A review and meta-analysis by Arthur Whaley indicates that there is a significant correlation between cultural mistrust in African Americans and their attitudes and behaviors related to mental health services use. However, the effect size for cultural mistrust was not significantly different for counseling and psychotherapy studies as compared with other types of studies, suggesting that the mental health context was neither more nor less threatening than other social situations. Younger African Americans tended to exhibit more cultural mistrust attitudes than did older African Americans.

Whaley argues that cultural mistrust is an important psychological construct for the diagnosis and treatment of African Americans. This construct, therefore, must be acknowledged by clinicians as a legitimate method of coping with racism and discrimination. In this context, discussing racism with clients, even those with severe mental illness, would be a relevant part of treatment.

Cultural Mistrust and Counseling

A European American counselor confronting the racial and ethnic differences between the counselor and an African American client in the initial session does not, in and of itself, offset the cultural mistrust that some Black individuals have of Whites in general. Conceptualization of the client problem consistent with the client's belief system, methods of resolution compatible with the client's culture, and counseling goals consistent with that of the client are necessary to build credibility with culturally diverse clients. When an African American client who has high cultural mistrust is assigned to a European American counselor, the client may expect the counselor to be less accepting, trustworthy, and less of an expert. Clients who do not belong to the same racial or ethnic group as their counselor and who have cultural mistrust toward their counselor may terminate counseling at a high rate. Cultural paranoia also may prevent some African American clients from self-disclosing to European American therapists.

According to Whaley, African Americans with severe mental illness who report high levels of cultural mistrust are more likely to have more negative attitudes toward White clinicians. They favor clinicians from their own racial group, although they may believe that European American clinicians receive better training. Reginald Alston and Tyronn Bell suggested that cultural mistrust may influence the way in which African Americans with disabilities approach rehabilitation counseling. Existence of cultural mistrust in a mild form could be healthy and adaptive for African Americans to sharpen their social wits and enhance their survival. However, a study by Bell and Terence Tracey indicated that among African American students, mistrust of European Americans is not always psychologically healthy. A moderate amount of trust of Whites is related to perceptions of personal well-being. It also is important to note that aspects of cultural mistrust can be mistaken for unhealthy paranoia.

Paul E. Priester and Jose Eluvathingal

See also Adaptation (v3); Barriers to Cross-Cultural Counseling (v3); Black Psychology (v3); Black Racial Identity Development (v3); Career Counseling, African Americans (v4); Coping (v2); Cultural Paranoia (v3); Defenses, Psychological (v2); Eurocentrism (v3); Healthy Paranoia (v3); Idiocentrism (v3); Relationships With Clients (v2); White Privilege (v3); Worldview (v3)

Further Readings

Terrell, F., & Terrell, S. L. (1981). An inventory to measure cultural mistrust among Blacks. *Western Journal of Black Studies, 5,* 180–184.

Whaley, A. L. (2001). Cultural mistrust and mental health services for African Americans: A review and meta-analysis. *The Counseling Psychologist, 29,* 513–531.

Cultural Paranoia

The concept of "cultural paranoia" was first introduced by William H. Grier and Price M. Cobbs in their 1968 book *Black Rage.* These two Black psychiatrists explained that this condition is not a form of psychopathology, but instead is a healthy and adaptive response by African Americans to their historical and contemporary experiences of racial oppression and discrimination in the United States. Charles R. Ridley, an African American psychologist, reintroduced the concept of cultural paranoia more than a decade later to explain why Black clients do not disclose to White psychotherapists. Ridley stated that because the encounter in counseling and psychotherapy is a microcosm of the larger American society, Black clients may not disclose personal information to White therapists for fear that they may be vulnerable to racial discrimination. Thus Black mental health professionals make a distinction between *cultural paranoia,* a form of adaptive coping, and *clinical paranoia,* a symptom of mental illness.

There have been some psychologists who questioned the use of the term *paranoia* to describe a situation that does not involve psychopathology or mental illness. Homer Ashby and Phyllis Bronstein criticized Ridley for using the term *cultural paranoia* during an exchange in the February 1986 issue of the *American Psychologist.* Arthur Whaley tried to resolve the debate by arguing that paranoia is not a simple "present–absent" symptom, falling along a continuum from mild to moderate to severe. According to Whaley, cultural aspects of paranoia in terms of lack of trust, especially among African Americans, fall on the mild, nonclinical end of the paranoia continuum. Whaley also pointed out that the term *cultural mistrust,* for which there is consensus among those on both sides of the debate, is one that is appropriate to describe African Americans' ways of coping with racism and oppression.

The Cultural Mistrust Inventory (CMI) was developed by Francis and Sandra Terrell to assess this response style in African Americans. Using the CMI, Whaley demonstrated that what was originally labeled "healthy cultural paranoia" is indeed not a form of psychopathology. In addition, Ekta Ahluwalia used the CMI in her doctoral dissertation to study African Americans, Native Americans, Latinos/as, and Asian Americans. Ahluwalia found that Native Americans and African Americans had the highest CMI scores among the ethnic groups. Because both Native Americans and African Americans had unique histories with regard to racism and oppression in the United States, her findings provide support for the notion that the CMI is tapping these cultural experiences.

Whaley conducted qualitative and quantitative reviews of the literature on the CMI and found it to correlate positively and negatively with different measures of psychosocial functioning. The positive associations tend to involve indicators of emotional functioning, whereas the negative correlates include measures of social behavior in interracial situations. This pattern of findings may reflect the fact that the protective qualities for ethnic/racial minority mental health emanate from lack of investment in tasks that increase the risk of exposure to racial prejudice and discrimination. A major element in addressing cultural paranoia or cultural mistrust in counseling and psychotherapy is to acknowledge racism as a reality for people of color and explore the reasons for mistrust. It is also important to recognize that the behavioral manifestations of cultural mistrust are not indicative of psychopathology. Recently, Dennis Combs and his colleagues showed the CMI to be positively associated with a measure of perceived racism and unrelated to measures of depression and clinical paranoia in African Americans. This empirical research is a direct test of the assumption, and supports it, that cultural paranoia is a healthy coping behavior in response to racial oppression and discrimination.

Arthur L. Whaley

See also Adaptation (v3); Barriers to Cross-Cultural Counseling (v3); Black Psychology (v3); Black Racial Identity Development (v3); Career Counseling, African Americans (v4); Coping (v2); Cultural Mistrust (v3); Defenses, Psychological (v2); Eurocentrism (v3); Healthy Paranoia (v3); Idiocentrism (v3); Relationships With Clients (v2); White Privilege (v3); Worldview (v3)

Further Readings

Ahluwalia, E. (1991). Parental cultural mistrust, background variables, and attitudes toward seeking mental health services for children (Doctoral dissertation, University of North Texas, 1990). *Dissertation Abstracts International, 51*(9-B), 4271.

Ashby, H. U. (1986). Mislabeling the Black client: A reply to Ridley. *American Psychologist, 41,* 224–225.

Bronstein, P. (1986). Self-disclosure, paranoia, and unaware racism: Another look at the Black client and the White therapist. *American Psychologist, 41,* 225–226.

Combs, D. R., Penn, D. L., Cassisi, J., Michael, C., Wood, T., Wanner, J., et al. (2006). Perceived racism as a predictor of paranoia in African Americans. *Journal of Black Psychology, 32,* 87–104.

Grier, W. H., & Cobbs, P. M. (1968). *Black rage.* New York: Basic Books.

Ridley, C. R. (1984). Clinical treatment of the nondisclosing Black client: A therapeutic paradox. *American Psychologist, 39,* 1234–1244.

Ridley, C. R. (1986). Optimum service delivery to the Black client. *American Psychologist, 41,* 226.

Terrell, F., & Terrell, S. L. (1981). An inventory to measure cultural mistrust among Blacks. *Western Journal of Black Studies, 5,* 180–184.

Whaley, A. L. (2001). Cultural mistrust: An important psychological construct for diagnosis and treatment of African Americans. *Professional Psychology: Research and Practice, 32,* 555–562.

Whaley, A. L. (2001). Cultural mistrust and mental health services for African Americans: A review and meta-analysis. *Counseling Psychologist, 29,* 513–531.

Cultural Relativism

Cultural relativism maintains the view that all cultures are equal in value and therefore should not be judged on the basis of another cultural perspective. The cultural values and beliefs connected to religious, ethical, normative behaviors, customs, and political tenets are specific to the individuals within a given human society.

Culture is considered to be the collective knowledge and experiences of any given human society that is passed on from generation to generation. This collective knowledge often helps organize language, emotional expression, and norms of behavior within the group and thus provides members with a sense of group cohesion. Cultural relativism maintains the view that the values and beliefs of one culture have specific meaning and importance from the particular worldview of the individuals within that cultural group, community, or both. Hence, people who live outside of a particular culture may or may not perceive another cultural group's worldview acceptable and consistent with their own.

The emergence of multiculturalism within the field of psychology has raised several questions and challenges regarding the universality of the human experience. The history of psychology is rooted in Western European ideology and doctrines. Historically, theoretical constructs and concepts have developed from a Eurocentric perspective, which has permeated all aspects of psychology: diagnosis, treatment, and research of human functioning and psychological disorders. Scientific literature is replete with comparative studies using a "normative" group with a minority group. The "normative" group is often composed of cultural beliefs, customs, and values consistent with a majority-group worldview, thus leading researchers and clinicians to conclude that one group is more deficient or pathological than another group. This perspective, by definition, perpetuates a deficiency model of behavior and ignores the role and importance of cultural contexts in the ways that people think, behave, and define their experiences.

Psychological research that employs a multicultural context has given voice to the importance of understanding human functioning and behavior from both etic (culturally universal) and emic (culturally specific) contexts. This form of research provides an awareness of the importance of internal and external validity, that is, how behavior is consistent within *and* across cultures and societies.

According to cultural relativism, patterns of behavior are not universally normal or deviant but must be understood relative to a specified cultural context. Individuals define their experiences and behave in ways that are consistent within their own cultural community. Cultural relativism supports the belief that mental health should be understood through the context of normative behavior within a specific culture. Therefore, when counselors are working with individuals from a specific culture, they should examine the worldviews of that cultural perspective, so that behaviors, attitudes, and perceptions can be viewed from within the context of that culture. For example, for many individuals within Asian cultures, filial piety defines patterns of behaviors that denote respect and devotion for one's parents. Therefore, behaviors and attitudes that fall within the confines of filial piety should be considered "normal" within that cultural frame. Counseling interventions and treatment modalities need to embrace cultural patterns that are consistent with the worldview of filial piety so that they can be more effective with the members of that cultural group. In this way, therapeutic strategies that are consistent with cultural worldviews will provide individuals within that group with sensitivity and empathy that are congruent with their cognitive, emotional, and psychological experience.

Angela D. Ferguson

See also Cross-Cultural Psychology (v3); Cultural Values (v3); Culture (v3); Ethnocentrism (v3); Filial Piety (v3); Multicultural Counseling Competence (v3); Multiculturalism (v3); Pluralism (v3); Worldview (v3)

Further Readings

Headland, T. N., Pike, K. L., & Harris, M. (Eds.). (1990). *Emics and etics: The insider/outsider debate.* Newbury Park, CA: Sage.

Sue, D. W., & Sue, D. (2008). *Counseling the culturally diverse: Theory and practice* (5th ed.). New York: Wiley.

Cultural Values

Culture is a pattern of responding to basic needs for food, shelter, clothing, family organization, religion, government, and social structures. Culture can be further described as discrete behaviors, traditions, habits, or customs that are shared and can be observed, as well as the sum total of ideas, beliefs, customs, knowledge, material artifacts, and values that are handed down from one generation to the next in a society. Cultural artifacts are the objects or products designed and used by people to meet reoccurring needs or to solve problems. Institutions are structures and mechanisms of social order and cooperation governing the behavior of two or more individuals. Cultural norms are rules that are socially enforced. Social sanctioning is what distinguishes norms from values.

Values are core beliefs and practices from which people operate. Each culture possesses its own particular values, traditions, and ideals. Integrity in the application of a "value" over time ensures its continuity, and this continuity separates a value from simple beliefs, opinions, and ideals. Cultural groups may endorse shared values. However, a given individual within that culture may vary in agreement with the group cultural values.

Role of Cultural Values

Cultural universalism asserts that all human beings create culture in response to survival needs. Only humans rely on culture rather than instinct to ensure survival of their kind. What seems unique to humanity is the capacity to create culture. Cultural relativism informs us that each culture possesses its own particular traditions, values, and ideals. Judgments of what is right or wrong, good or bad, acceptable or taboo are based on particular cultural values. Values underlie preferences, guide choices, and indicate what is worthwhile in life. Values help define the character of a culture, but they usually do not provide a specific course of action. Values generally prescribe what one "should" do but not how to do it. Because values offer viewpoints about ideals, goals, and behaviors, they serve as standards for social life. All groups, regardless of size, have their own values, norms, and sanctions.

Although it may seem obvious that values are rooted in the culture from which they originate, this has not always been the way values have been operationalized.

For many years in the United States, the fundamental values of White European American males were often accepted as universal rather than culturally specific. Deviations from mainstream values were labeled as abnormal and inferior rather than merely different. Psychologist Gilbert Wrenn challenged the notion that White European American culture was universal by writing about the "culturally encapsulated counselor," and the multicultural counseling movement has expanded the notion of culturally bound values.

Formation of Cultural Values

Cultural values are formed through environmental adaptations, historical factors, social and economic evolution, and contact with other groups. Individuals develop cultural perceptual patterns that determine which stimuli reach their awareness. These cultural perceptual patterns also determine judgments of people, objects, and events. When the individual or society prioritizes a set of values (usually of the ethical or doctrinal categories), a value system is formed.

Values dictate what is important. They serve as a guide for the ideals and behavior of members of a culture. As guided by its values, culture can be seen as a dynamic system of symbols and meanings that involves an ongoing, dialectic process where past experience influences meanings, which in turn affects future experience, which in turn affects subsequent meaning. Cultural values provide patterns of living and prescribe rules and models for attitude and conduct.

For example, several culture-specific values have been identified for specific groups. It should be noted, however, that there is considerable within-group variability in what is valued. In traditional Hispanic and Latino/a cultures, the following have been identified as shared cultural values among many of its members: an emphasis on family unity, welfare and honor (*familismo*), a preference for close personal relationships (*personalismo*), and respect (*respeto*) for elders and authority figures.

Traditional African American values have been identified as including the following: an emphasis on collectivism, kinship, the importance of extended families, the centrality of spirituality, and holistic thinking. Commonly among African Americans, both the nuclear family (parents and children) and the extended family (relatives, friends) are important. The concept of *familismo* among African Americans generally includes both biological and nonbiological members.

Another shared cultural value of African American families is that of *role flexibility*. The head of the household may not necessarily be the father, as many African American homes are headed by the mother or grandparents.

Traditional "American" values (derived from a White European male perspective) include individualism, competition, accumulation of material possessions, nuclear families, the separation of religion from other aspects of culture, and mastery over nature. It is important to recognize that these values may not be internalized equally among all European Americans; thus, a great deal of variability exists in the adoption and expression of traditional "American" values.

Cultural values guide interactions, and these values can come into conflict with the values of a dominant cultural group and can lead to acculturative stress. Cultures are not confined to racial or ethnic groups. Cultural values can be found in diverse groups by gender, sexual identity, class, country of origin, disability, or a variety of variables. Therefore, an individual can belong to a host of cultures simultaneously, and the issue of navigating cultures with incompatible value systems (e.g., religion and sexual identity) may lead to a fragmented sense of identity or self-hatred.

Categories of Cultural Values

Some researchers suggest that cultural values can be divided into six main categories: (1) ethics (notions of right and wrong, good and evil, and responsibility); (2) aesthetics (notions of beauty and attractiveness); (3) doctrinal (political, ideological, religious, or social beliefs and values); (4) innate/inborn (values such as reproduction and survival; this is a controversial category); (5) non-use/passive (includes the value based on something never used or seen, or something left for the next generation); and (6) potential (the value of something that is known to be only potentially valuable, such as a plant that might be found to have medicinal value in the future).

In multicultural societies, cultures may come into conflict. *Parochialism* occurs when members of a given culture believe their way is the "only" way. They do not recognize other ways of living, working, or doing things as being valid. *Equifinality* has been suggested as a more appropriate assumption to make in a multicultural world. This assumption asserts that the way of any given culture is not the only way.

Instead, there are many culturally distinct ways of reaching the same goal or living one's life. Another conflict may involve *ethnocentrism*. This occurs when members of a culture recognize the existence of other cultures and yet believe their way is the "best" way and all other cultural valuations are inferior. The notion of *cultural contingency* may be a more appropriate response in a multicultural world; that is, cultural values are seen as choices that are equally valid for the individuals involved.

Role of Psychologists

Psychologists are charged with dealing with cultural values in several ways. First, they are compelled to understand their own cultural values and how these values affect their work and worldview. Therefore, psychologists should be aware of their own cultural values, and in cases where their cultural values may lead to harm with culturally different clients, psychologists must refer these clients to culturally competent practitioners. In addition, psychologists should actively learn about the cultural values of their clients and, where possible, work with these cultural values as strengths rather than as liabilities or pathological beliefs. For example, psychologists might involve cultural spiritual leaders in the treatment of culturally different clients. The notion of cultural competence extends to all other professional arenas of psychologists, including education, teaching, research, and consultation.

Edward A. Delgado-Romero and Billy Yarbrough

See also Barriers to Cross-Cultural Counseling (v3); Cross-Cultural Psychology (v3); Culture (v3); Ethnic Identity (v3); Ethnicity (v3); Multicultural Counseling Competence (v3); Multiculturalism (v3); Pluralism (v3); Race (v3); Racial Identity (v3); Worldview (v3)

Further Readings

American Psychological Association. (2003). Guidelines on multicultural education, training, research, practice and organizational change for psychologists. *American Psychologist, 58,* 377–402.

Paniagua, F. A. (2005). *Assessing and treating culturally diverse clients: A practical guide.* Thousand Oaks, CA: Sage.

Pedersen, P. B., Draguns, J. G., Lonner, W. J., & Trimble, J. E. (Eds.). (2002). *Counseling across cultures* (5th ed.). Thousand Oaks, CA: Sage.

CULTURE

Culture consists of implicit and explicit patterns of behavior acquired and transmitted by symbols and their embodiments in artifacts. The essential core of culture consists of traditional (i.e., historically derived and selected) ideas and their attached values. Culture systems may be considered as products of action and conditioning elements of further action. A. L. Kroeber and Clyde Kluckhohn collected and analyzed several hundred definitions of culture and arrived at this definition, which the authors believed would be acceptable by most social scientists: *Culture* is one of the most important concepts in 20th-century social sciences. A reflective look at the way the concept of culture is used would be enlightening because different disciplines and schools of thoughts have their own definitions and there is no common understanding. In addition, understanding the issues of cultural unity and diversity has increasingly become relevant in our daily lives.

Historical Perspective

Kroeber and Kluckhohn's definition represents a summary of what American anthropologists and social scientists would call culture in the 1940s and 1950s. In contrast with this definition, in the 1920s and 1930s, culture was simply defined as "the learned behavior." However, Kroeber and Kluckhohn argued that although the concept of culture is based on the study of behavior and behavioral products, culture cannot be conceptualized as only the behavior or the investigation of behavior. Instead, part of culture consists of norms for or standards of behavior, and another part consists of ideologies justifying or rationalizing certain ways of behavior. Finally, every culture includes broad general principles of selectivity and ordering ("highest common factors") about behavior.

Definitions of Culture

The word *culture* originates in Middle English ("a cultivated piece of land") from the French word *culture* and from the Latin verb *culturare* ("to cultivate"). All versions of the word ultimately come from the early Latin *colere* ("to till or cultivate the ground"). A review of overarching themes and patterns in definitions of culture in various disciplines might be beneficial to our understanding of culture. Each theme has its own strengths and weaknesses, and there are inevitable overlapping and interpenetrating relationships between and among themes.

Seven types or themes of definitions of culture can be listed:

1. *Structure/pattern:* Definitions that look at culture in terms of a system or framework of elements (e.g., ideas, behavior, symbols, or any combination of these or other elements)

2. *Function:* Definitions that see culture as a tool for achieving some end

3. *Process:* Definitions that focus on the ongoing social construction of culture

4. *Product:* Definitions of culture in terms of artifacts (with or without deliberate symbolic intent)

5. *Refinement:* Definitions that frame culture as a sense of individual or group cultivation to higher intellect or morality

6. *Power or ideology:* Definitions that focus on group-based power (including postmodern and postcolonial definitions)

7. *Group membership:* Definitions that speak of culture in terms of a place or group of people, or that focus on belonging to such a place or group

Culture and Psychological Processes

Theories explaining culture from a perspective of psychological processes contribute to the understanding of the processes through which specific individuals' actions and behaviors influence the actions and behaviors of others and become norms, customs, and rituals. They help to explain how the specific clusters of thoughts and action can become commonly shared among some populations but not others. Biological foundations, motivational systems, affective/emotional systems, cognitive/communication systems, and linguistic perspective will be presented as five of the examples of psychological theories.

According to the *biological foundations approach,* biological foundations of the cognitive mechanisms give rise to the aspects of culture. There are two perspectives that could be reviewed under the biological foundations approach: evolutionary and neurological. The evolutionary perspective suggests that human beings may be especially likely to communicate information that has affective content relevant to survival and reproduction. Consequently, knowledge structures that are suggestive of these affective states may be likely to become culturally shared.

The neurological foundation tradition emphasizes the coevolution of psychological and cultural phenomena. The main idea of coevolution is that human beings evolved to be cultural. Human beings are evolutionarily shaped and genetically predisposed to seize and make use of cultural resources available in their local environments. Another neurological foundation of culture is "plasticity." Completely preprogrammed development is neither adaptive nor efficient. Instead, human ontogeny entails a built-in reliance on environmental patterns for species-typical development. This plasticity, or reliance on environmental patterns, provides a window for the cultural shaping of the human development. Another neurological foundation of culture, the notion of sensitive period, is defined as the ability to experience certain cultural patterns (e.g., tendencies of phoneme discrimination, visual perception, and culture-specific emotions) during a sensitive period of development. In other words, human beings are exposed to certain cultural patterns during a sensitive period of their development, and this early shaping of experience may make later shaping by other cultures more difficult.

According to the *motivational systems* approach, there is an existential need to make sense of big questions such as the meaning of life. Another motivational foundation is an epistemic need to make sense of day-to-day reality. Reality is often multiple and ambiguous, and people require culture, social influence with a historical and material dimension, to help define reality. A specific case of this need is observed in interpersonal communication, where people are motivated to engage in a micro-level form of cultural process, the production of common ground.

Terror management theory, an example of the motivational systems approach, proposes that culture emerged to serve as a psychological buffer against the existential anxiety that results from the awareness of our own mortality. Culture minimizes existential anxiety by providing a conception of the universe (cultural worldview) that fills the world with order, meaning, and permanence. Culture also provides a set of standards of valued behavior that, if satisfied, provides self-esteem to individuals. Culture acts as a buffer because many cultural beliefs and behaviors offer symbolic immortality (e.g., life after death, naming children after grandparents). In addition, culture provides a set of rules, standards, and principles according to which a person can be judged to be a socially acceptable or good person. One of the broad hypotheses that the terror management theory makes is that awareness of one's own mortality leads to enhanced attempts to defend one's own cultural worldview. For example, one study indicated that mortality salience increases derogation of alternative cultural worldviews and punishment of individuals who violate cultural rules.

The *affective/emotional systems* approach uses the affect/emotions as the foundation of culture. An affective foundation of culture is the concept of affective primacy, which is defined as direct, automatic shaping of moods, feelings, and preferences by everyday worlds. People are often likely to acquire affective charge of practices or artifacts unwittingly, in the process of engaging cultural worlds. For example, immersed in cultures where it is taboo to eat pork, people are likely to feel disgusted at the thought or scent of cooking pork products.

The *cognitive/communication systems* approach can be represented by Bibb Latané's dynamic social impact theory (DSIT). This theory adopts a theory of social influence to explain how cultures develop and change over time. It assumes that people influence and are influenced by others through the process of communication, which is defined as any type of social exchange of information. DSIT posits that influence will occur whenever groups of people interact on social attributes. Three factors—strength, immediacy, and number—are the basis of social influence. Strength is defined as individual differences in supportiveness or persuasiveness. Some people are more attractive, richer, or more educated than others; consequently, these characteristics may lead them to have a stronger influence on others around them. Immediacy includes proximity in physical or social space. Finally, social impact depends on the number of other individuals who share a particular attitude. The more people who agree with our opinions, the less likely we will be able to change them. In short, people are more influenced by persuasive, close, and numerous others.

To explain the creation and continuation of culture, DSIT uses concepts of clustering and correlation to explain how cultures are formed and consolidation and continuing diversity to address temporal change in cultures. Clustering represents the fact that as people are influenced by those in their local area, pockets of shared opinions will form, leading to regional differences. DSIT posits that communication will lead to spatial clustering of attributes. In other words, over time, people will be increasingly likely to share similar attitudes with those living close to them. A second prediction of DSIT is that attitudes that are originally unrelated across individuals within a group will become increasingly correlated over time. Finally, DSIT predicts that attributes will consolidate or decrease in diversity, as people influence each other over time. Although consolidation leads to majority influence and majority sizes will tend to increase, the diversity will continue to exist.

Finally, *linguistic perspective* links culture to static features of languages. Language determines each culture by representing reality in a particular manner. Thus, every language is a vast pattern system with culturally ordained forms and categories. Through language, human beings communicate, analyze nature, notice or neglect types of relationships and things, channel their reasoning, and build consciousness. This theory posits that use of language in human interaction may play an important role in the evolution and maintenance of cultural representations. The theory has four main assumptions:

1. Language is a carrier of cultural meanings.

2. Cultural meanings are evoked when language is used in interpersonal communication.

3. The use of language in communication will increase the accessibility of existing shared representations in the culture. In addition, through communication, private idiosyncratic representations will be transformed into publicly shared representations, which in turn form the cognitive foundations of culture.

4. Evolved and shared representations will then be encoded into the language and the cycle continues.

In sum, biological, motivational, affective/emotional, cognitive, and linguistic theories contribute to the understanding of culture and help explain how specific clusters of thoughts and action can become commonly shared among some populations but not others. Next, concepts of cultural worldview and cultural values of several groups are discussed.

Cultural Values

Cultural values are characterized by dimensions considered important to members of a cultural group and which may subsequently guide their norms and behavior. Researchers have stated that the cultural values of a given cultural group guide the members of that group to find solutions to common human problems. Accordingly, it has been argued that an analysis of cultural values is necessary if the uniqueness of any cultural group is to be fully understood.

Differences in Cultural Values Among Cultural Groups

Overall, many studies examining racial/ethnic groups compared with White culture in the United States report differences. In general, it has been found that racial/ethnic and immigrant groups are characterized by activity that places an emphasis on spontaneous self-expression of emotions, desires, and impulses; collateral social relationships or relationships whose individual goals are subordinate to group goals; and subjugation to nature and present time. In contrast, research demonstrates that White cultural groups are characterized by social relationships that are individualistic, view action and spontaneity as more important than self-control, strive for mastery over nature, and have a time orientation that is focused on the future.

Although racial/ethnic and immigrant groups may endorse similar value orientations, they attach different meanings to the same value orientations and may differ in why these value orientations are important to their particular cultural group. Researchers have begun to investigate the specific cultural values of racial/ethnic groups to gain a clearer understanding of the meanings of these values for different groups.

Asians

Among Asians there exist significant differences due to ethnicity, migration or generational status, assimilation, acculturation, religion, socioeconomic status, educational level, and political climate in their country of origin. Nonetheless, values common to many Asian cultural groups include an emphasis on harmony in relationships, emotional restraint, precedence of group interests over individual interests, importance of extended family, deference to authority, obedience to and respect for parents, emphasis on hard work, importance of fulfilling obligations, and a high value placed on education. In addition, families are often patriarchal, relationships among family members may be well defined, elders are often respected and cared for, and an individual's behavior may reflect upon the entire family.

Researchers have identified six Asian cultural values: collectivism, conformity to norms, emotional self-control, family recognition through achievement, filial piety, and humility. Saving face is another cultural value, which is reflected in indirect communication styles being more desirable.

African Americans

African Americans' sense of self and cultural traditions have been derived from various cultural and philosophical principles shared with West African tribes. Researchers also state that people of African ancestry continue to maintain cultural connections to these traditions. In addition, an African-centered worldview provides important information around which African Americans build their beliefs. These include the beliefs that there is a spiritual essence that permeates everything, everything in the world is interconnected with the principle of consubstantiation or the sense that everything within the universe is connected as a part of a whole, and that the collective is the most important element of existence. In addition, Afrocentricity also includes the beliefs that self-knowledge is assumed to be the foundation of all knowledge.

Moreover, African Americans value family, which includes not only blood relatives but also extended family and fictive kin. Other values include a spirit of coexistence, maintaining a strong connection to the church, education as a means of self-help, a present time orientation with less emphasis on particulars, harmony with nature, collateral relations with others, and communication patterns that include body movement, postures, gestures, and facial expressions in addition to verbal communication. Despite having experienced hardship, African Americans also demonstrate persistence, forgiveness, and resilience.

European Americans

European Americans consist of various cultural groups that descend from European countries. Among the cultural values that have been identified for European Americans is individualism, which stresses independence and autonomy. Additionally, researchers have identified an importance on productivity, rigid time orientation, and a focus on the nuclear family. For the most part, these cultural values differentiate this cultural group from others in that importance is placed on the individual rather than the group.

Latinos/as

Diversity among Latino/a groups exists across geography, country of origin, race, class, traditions, acculturation, and historical and sociopolitical circumstances. However, some shared cultural values have been identified for Latinos/as; these include *familismo, personalismo, simpatia, respeto,* and the expression *si Dios quiere* (if it is God's will). *Familismo* refers to strong family orientation in that Latinos/as value close relationships, cohesiveness and interdependence, and cooperation among family members.

The value of *personalismo* refers to valuing and building interpersonal relationships and the importance of warm, friendly, and personal relationships. This describes the orientation that Latinos/as have toward people rather than toward impersonal relationships. *Simpatia* also demonstrates this orientation that emphasizes harmonious interpersonal interactions. *Respeto* demonstrates the importance of interpersonal harmony, which governs all positive interpersonal relationships and dictates the appropriate deferential behavior toward others on the basis of age, socioeconomic position, sex, and authority status.

The expression *si Dios quiere* (if it is God's will) describes the value of fatalism, which is an indication or form of acceptance that Latinos/as have no control over what God has willed. This value makes sense given that Latinos/as often make reference to their belief in higher powers as a way of making meaning.

Further, among Latinos/as cooperation is important, cultural pride is significant, family structure is hierarchical with deference to elders and males, and adherence to family roles is important. Latinos/as also believe in a holistic connection between the mind and body that permeates their health and illness beliefs. In addition, the church and faith play a significant role and shape Latino/a core beliefs such as the importance of sacrifice, service to others, and long suffering even in the face of adversity.

Native Americans

Despite the vast diversity among Native Americans, researchers have identified specific values among this cultural group. Among these values, a collectivist cultural value has been identified. Specifically, personal accomplishments are honored and supported if these accomplishments benefit the group. Similarly, it is believed that all things are connected and have purpose. In addition, the importance of spirituality is among the cultural values of Native Americans. In particular, Native Americans believe in a creator that is considered male and female and is in command of all the elements. Additionally, Native American cultural values come from a spirituality that emphasizes coexisting in harmony with nature. From this comes the cultural value of sharing, as all things belong to the Earth.

Native Americans also value elders because of the wisdom they have acquired. In addition, there is a respect for the past and the contributions of the ancestral spirits. Other cultural values include a focus on nonverbal communication, reciprocal relationships that emphasize cooperation, a preference for a fluid time orientation, and respect for tribal rituals.

Given that these cultural values are central for a particular cultural group, it offers many implications for their worldviews, how they interpret and perceive environments and situations, and how they make decisions. With the understanding of cultural values, the understanding of culture may become more advanced. Thus, in clarifying and defining cultural values we may have a better understanding of what culture means to specific groups.

Elif Celebi and Rocio Rosales

See also Acculturation (v3); Barriers to Cross-Cultural Counseling (v3); Collectivism (v3); Communication (v3); Cross-Cultural Psychology (v3); Cross-Cultural Training (v3); Cultural Values (v3); Enculturation (v3); Ethnic Identity (v3); Ethnicity (v3); Individualism (v3); Multicultural Counseling Competence (v3); Multiculturalism (v3); Person–Environment Interactions (v2); Race (v3); Racial Identity (v3); Worldview (v3)

Further Readings

Carroll, J. B. (Ed.). (1956). *Language, thought and reality: Selected writings of Benjamin Lee Whorf.* Cambridge: MIT Press.

Carter, R. T. (1991). Cultural values: A review of empirical research and implications for counseling. *Journal of College & Development, 70,* 164–173.

Faulkner, S. L., Baldwin, J. R., Lindsley, S. L., & Hecht, M. L. (2006). Layers of meaning: An analysis of definitions of culture. In J. R. Baldwin, S. L. Faulkner, M. L. Hecht, & S. L. Lindsley (Eds.), *Redefining culture: Perspectives across the disciplines* (pp. 27–52). Mahwah, NJ: Lawrence Erlbaum.

Greenberg, J., Simon, L., Pyszczynski, T., Solomon, S., & Chatel, D. (1992). Terror management and tolerance: Does mortality salience always intensify negative reactions to others who threaten one's worldview? *Journal of Personality and Social Psychology, 63,* 212–220.

Herring, R. D. (1992). Understanding Native American values: Process and content concerns for counselors. *Counseling and Values, 34,* 134–137.

Kenrick, D. T., Maner, J. K., Butner, J., Li, N. P., Becker, D. V., & Schaller, M. (2002). Dynamic evolutionary psychology: Mapping the domains of the new interactionist paradigm. *Personality and Social Psychology Review, 6,* 347–356.

Krebs, D., & Janicki, M. (2004). Biological foundations of moral norms. In M. Schaller & C. S. Crandall (Eds.), *The psychological foundations of culture.* Mahwah, NJ: Lawrence Erlbaum.

Kroeber, A. L., & Kluckhohn, F. R. (1952). *Culture: A critical review of concepts and definitions.* New York: Random House.

Latané, B. (1996). Dynamic social impact: The creation of culture by communication. *Journal of Communication, 46,* 13–25.

Paniagua, F. (1998). *Assessing and treating culturally diverse clients.* Thousand Oaks, CA: Sage.

Parham, T. A. (2002). *Counseling persons of African descent.* Thousand Oaks, CA: Sage.

Peregory, J. J. (1993). Transcultural counseling with American Indians and Alaskan Natives: Contemporary issues for consideration. In J. McFadden (Ed.), *Transcultural counseling: Bilateral and international perspectives* (pp. 163–191). Alexandria, VA: American Counseling Association.

Sandhu, D. S. (1997). Psychocultural profiles of Asian and Pacific Islander Americans: Implications for counseling and psychotherapy. *Journal of Multicultural Counseling & Development, 25,* 7–22.

Santiago-Rivera, A. L., Arredondo, P., & Gallardo-Cooper, M. (2002). *Counseling Latinos and* la familia*: A practical guide.* Thousand Oaks, CA: Sage.

Sue, D. W. (1978). World views and counseling. *The Personnel and Guidance Journal, 56,* 458–462.

Sue, D. W., & Sue, D. (2008). *Counseling the culturally diverse: Theory and practice* (5th ed.). New York: Wiley.

CULTURE-BOUND SYNDROMES

The term *culture-bound syndromes* was first coined in 1951 to describe mental disorders unique to certain societies or culture areas. The syndromes may include dissociative, psychotic, anxiety, depressive, and somatic symptoms and do not necessarily fit into contemporary diagnostic and classification systems of Western nosology.

Although there is no consensus among mental health professionals about the extent and ways in which cultural factors influence the manifestation and diagnosis of mental disorders, the American Psychiatric Association's inclusion of a *Glossary of Culture-Bound Syndromes* within the most recent *Diagnostic and Statistical Manual of Mental Disorders* (*DSM*) constitutes a significant step toward addressing the difficulties encountered in the application of *DSM* criteria across cultural boundaries and suggests a concerted effort to increase universal utility of diagnostic and classification systems of Western nosology by integrating a group of mental disorders long marginalized as culture-specific. The inclusion of these categories also reflects an increasing recognition of the important role of culture in assessment and treatment as well as a growing acceptance of cultural differences in the diagnostic process. It should be noted that these syndromes were compiled on the basis of decades of interdisciplinary research (i.e., anthropology, psychiatry, and psychology).

According to the *DSM*, culture-bound syndromes refer to "recurrent, locality-specific patterns of aberrant behavior and troubling experience that may not be linked to a particular DSM diagnostic category. Many of these patterns are indigenously considered to be 'illness,' or at least afflictions, and most have local names" (p. 898). The glossary included in the *DSM* lists more than 20 culture-specific diagnoses along with descriptive features.

These syndromes can be categorized into the following major definitional iterations:

1. A mental illness that is not attributable to an identifiable organic cause, is often recognized locally as an illness, and does not correspond to a recognized Western medical category

2. An illness that is not attributable to an identifiable organic cause, is recognized within local culture as an illness, and resembles a Western disease category but may lack some symptoms considered as salient in Western culture

3. A discrete disease entity not yet recognized in Western culture

4. A nondescript illness that may or may not have an organic cause and may correspond to a subset of a Western disease category

5. Illnesses in the idiomatic rhetoric category that represent culturally accepted explanatory mechanisms but may not correspond with Western idioms and, in Western culture, may suggest culturally inappropriate thinking and perhaps delusions or hallucinations

6. Illnesses in the category of generalized culture-bound syndromes that are characterized by behaviors such as trance, hearing, seeing, or communicating with the dead or spirits, which may or may not be seen as pathological within local culture but could indicate psychosis, delusions, or hallucinations in Western culture

7. Unreal syndromes that allegedly occur in a given cultural setting, which, in fact, does not exist

As an example, *shenjing shaijo* ("weakened nerves" or "neurasthenia") is on the list of culture-specific diagnoses in the *DSM* and also is included in the *Chinese Classification of Mental Disorders, Second Edition*. It is characterized by a set of symptoms, including fatigue, headaches, concentration difficulties, sleep disturbance, and memory loss, and, in many cases, the symptoms would meet the criteria for *DSM* Mood or Anxiety Disorder. An apparent psychiatric illness with no identifiable organic cause, shenjing shaijo is recognized in the Chinese culture but has locally salient features different from Western diseases and does not typically have symptoms considered critical in Western psychiatry.

Another example is *rootwork*. In the southern United States and in Caribbean societies, rootwork is a set of cultural interpretations that explain illnesses such as generalized anxiety, fear, and dizziness, in terms of hexing, witchcraft, voodoo, or the influence of an evil person. It is not so much an actual illness as a locally accepted explanatory mechanism of "illnesses."

Points of Tension

Defined as a network of domain-specific knowledge structures shaped by members of a given cultural group, culture is internalized into each individual's self-concept and functions as a template to guide one's expectations, perceptions, and interpretations. Culture exerts its influence over individuals through regulating notions of self, reality, social behaviors, and patterns of emotional expression. As such, culture shapes the experience, expression, and meaning of illness by offering specific contents to thoughts and feelings, which, in turn, manifest as psychological discomfort.

Developing a universally applicable set of descriptive criteria of mental disorders thus remains a daunting task, resulting in much dispute about the utility of the concept.

The focus on the debate over the term *culture-bound syndromes* often centers on confusions or conflations among the various culture-bound syndrome categories. Given the heterogeneity of these syndromes in the *DSM*, they are loosely connected at best. Questions remain about the elusive nature of the concept and, in particular, about the lack of clarity regarding the inclusion and exclusion criteria. More specifically, for example, to what extent are the defining features based on peculiarities of the diagnostic process used? Some argue that because the criteria for culture-bound syndromes are socially constructed, every diagnosis, however appropriate, occurs in a broad sociocultural context. The principles of diagnostic systems, therefore, need to be flexibly structured so that the inclusion and exclusion criteria can be applied more directly in the context of the local culture. Questions are raised about how essential characteristics of culture-bound syndromes should be understood within the cultural context. Moreover, given that how individuals perceive, interpret, and respond to mental illness is different from the actual symptoms of the disorder, how much emphasis should be placed on subjective complaint as opposed to symptom manifestation?

Another issue concerns the relationship of culture-bound syndromes to standard diagnostic systems, such as the *DSM*. It has been argued that many mental disorders do not necessarily conform to the categories in the *DSM*, and significant differences are noted across cultures, in part, because of differing beliefs about self and reality as well as different ways of conceptualizing and displaying mental experiences. In this view, mental disorders are believed to be socially and culturally construed. Although the *DSM* has some utility across differing cultural boundaries, the reliability and validity of these classificatory systems are inevitably reduced as a result of the nonuniversality of cultural experiences in relation to mental illnesses.

Counseling Implications

With the influx of immigrants from various cultural groups, U.S. society has become more diverse, and greater demands are being placed on counselors in all types of agencies to provide services that are culturally responsive and effective. Because culture is such a rich vein of information, counseling practice is inevitably embedded in multiple sociocultural realities and contexts. As such, the concept of culture-bound syndromes is important for counselors because minority clients, particularly those who are recent immigrants, may bring with them their own indigenous patterns and conceptions of mental illness into the counseling process and relationship. That is, counseling in general, and mental illness in particular, are likely perceived, experienced, and interpreted differently by the client than by counselors. Counselors thus face the challenge of negotiating with their client a diagnosis in the assessment process, which may occur in a number of ways. Some may, for example, share with the client's view of the illness as a culture-bound syndrome and offer interventions that are consistent with the folk medicine treatment. Others may empathize with the client's subjective complaint but decide to educate the client about the causes and nature of the illness as they perceive it. Still others may discount the client's experience of illness as merely exotic, given the imprecise nature of the concept of culture-bound syndrome. The assessment process, the final diagnosis, as well as the interventions are thus dependent, to a considerable extent, upon the multicultural awareness, knowledge, and skills of counselors.

In relation to culture-bound syndromes, multiculturally competent counselors endeavor to become aware of, and knowledgeable about, the location of culture-bound syndromes in their sociocultural context by raising questions such as the following: Who are those who experience the culture-bound syndromes? What contextual factors may affect the manifestation of these syndromes? To what extent do members of some cultural groups complain of somatic discomforts that are, in fact, psychological in origin because their discomfort is locally recognized as an illness? What is the role of culture in the healthcare system? How has Eurocentrism been reflected in the history of the psychiatric diagnostic system most commonly used today?

In an effort to further improve their skills in the assessment of cultural influences on experiences, counselors may need to use the *DSM* guidelines for assessing cultural context by considering (a) the client's cultural identity; (b) cultural expressions and explanations of the illness; (c) cultural factors in relation to psychosocial environment and levels of functioning, such as cultural perceptions of social and situational stressors, social support, level of functioning, and disability; (d) cultural similarities and differences (e.g., social status, language preference) between the client and counselors that may affect the development of a collaborative working alliance; and (e) a summary statement that describes how cultural factors and issues influence comprehensive diagnosis and care.

Counselors may also benefit from a holistic approach when formulating and classifying the culture-bound syndromes, particularly in making distinctions between subjective complaints and symptom manifestation. In doing so, counselors will likely reduce diagnostic and interpretational biases during the assessment process.

Eric C. Chen

See also Cross-Cultural Psychology (v3); Cultural Values (v3); Culture (v3); *Diagnostic and Statistical Manual of Mental Disorders* (*DSM*) (v2); Ethnicity (v3); Help-Seeking Behavior (v3); Multicultural Psychology (v3); Psychopathology, Assessment of (v2); Spirituality/Religion (v2)

Further Readings

American Psychiatric Association. (2000). *Diagnostic and statistical manual of mental disorders* (4th ed., Text rev.). Arlington, VA: Author.

Guarnaccia, P. J., & Rogler, L. H. (1999). Research on culture-bound syndromes: New directions. *American Journal of Psychiatry, 156,* 1322–1326.

Hughes, C. C. (1996). The culture-bound syndrome and psychiatric diagnosis. In J. E. Mezzich, A. Klienman, H. Fabgrega, & D. L. Parron (Eds.), *Culture and psychiatric diagnosis: A DSM–IV perspective* (pp. 289–305). Washington, DC: American Psychiatric Press.

Tseng, W. (2001). *Handbook of cultural psychiatry.* San Diego, CA: Academic Press.

CULTURE-FREE TESTING

Culture-free testing is far more hypothetical than real. It assumes, if not requires, there are no cultural influences in any measurement and assessment of an individual or group on some trait. This further suggests that measurement and assessment can be designed to only tap into true individual or group traits and not draw on any culture-related error variances that may and do occur. Historically, culture-free measurement was seen as merely error-reduced measurement. Error here means unintended and undefined variance thought of as being unavoidable yet reducible through solid methodology.

Culture-Free Testing in Two Test Paradigms or Models

However, the artifact of culture-free testing is easily recognizable in current research paradigms that presume with big enough samples that researchers can control and even eliminate cultural influences or patterns in the data through either matrix algebra or calculus-based statistical methods: classic test theory (Observed Score = True Score + Error) and modern test theory with its Raschian, function-based calculus, respectively.

As such, culture-free testing may be the psychometric equivalent of a myth, or perhaps better stated as a cipher, at present. Namely, in the absence of any quantity or example of a bona fide culture-free test, scientific opinion cannot confirm culture-free testing as a reality, at present. Thus, it may be tempting to summarily dismiss culture-free testing without fully knowing why.

However, its guiding principles have been useful in discouraging, let alone discontinuing, the use and creation of "separate yet equal" versions of tests for men, women, and various ethno-cultural groups.

Historical Backdrop

Seminal works in the 1950s on the role of values in constructing a valid theory of human action and the need to improve the accuracy of what psychological tests measured have influenced the field to consider that culture serves as a context for understanding an individual. The subsequent waning of an inclusive theory of action and the booming growth of trait-factor testing and measurement meant that "culture as context" became supplanted by the notion of "culture as barrier." Therefore, a standardized test was presumed to be largely culture free through the 1950s and into the 1960s. By the 1970s, culture-free testing was made an explicit assessment goal from both positivist and civil rights perspectives. As culture-free testing could not be validated by its own data, it did not last long, giving way to the notion of culture-fair testing in the late 1970s and into the early 1980s. Not surprisingly, culture-fair testing, in turn, was not supported by its data, despite the rigors of classic test theory test validation.

It should be noted, however, that the culture-free testing movement still affected testing significantly. For example, a single Strong Interest Inventory with overall, male, female, and other group norms exists instead of separately developed Strong Campbell instruments for each, as was the case in the not too distant past. Thus, the now nonremarkable modern testing practice of using the same instrument yet with different norms was a direct result of this notable psychometric evolution before it dead-ended in classic test theory.

Implications in Modern Test Theory

Culture-free testing may seem a noble, if not odd, idea that cannot be realized in classic test theory and its matrix algebra assumptions, but what about modern test theory with its calculus-based functions? These equations allow for group differences to be "smoothed out" by an algorithm made up of hundreds, if not thousands, of responses. Thus, modern test theory statistics are not presumably influenced by culture because they are "non-norm norms" or "not group yet group-based comparisons." Hence, though methodologically debatable, key assumptions of culture-free testing can and do "live on" because of their modern test theory mathematics.

In practice, as might also be expected, cultural and other group effects can and do affect some item characteristic curves or other modern test theory–based data indices. Indeed, cultural data nonuniformly impact an item or a test's accuracy and consistency. Thus, item/test function shape "morphs" or changes when "true," nonuniform group differences occur, of which culture is one. In short, modern test theory's inferred assumptions about being culture free or culture fair do not prevail, despite some mathematical support that it should.

True to postmodern and constructivist assumptions, tests generally work best with those resembling the norming, or even non-norm, group. This too may extend to test developers and test users. Similar to the ciphered culture-free test, confirming data supporting culture-free testing appears to be wanting, and though theoretically plausible in places, it does not now appear to be forthcoming in practice any time soon.

Jesus (Jesse) R. Aros

See also Bias (v3); Career Counseling, Immigrants (v4); Cross-Cultural Psychology (v3); Cultural Equivalence

Further Readings

Anastasi, A. (1982). *Psychological testing* (5th ed.). New York: Macmillan.

Biggs, D., & Porter, G. (1994). *Dictionary of counseling*. Westport, CT: Greenwood Press.

Braun, H., Jackson, D., & Wiley, D. (2002). *The role of constructs in psychological and educational measurement*. Mahwah, NJ: Lawrence Erlbaum.

Cronbach, L., & Meehl, P. (1955). Construct validity in psychological tests. *Psychological Bulletin, 52,* 281–302.

Hansen, J. I. C. (1992). Does enough evidence exist to modify Holland's theory to accommodate for individual differences of diverse populations? *Journal of Vocational Behavior, 40,* 188–193.

Hansen, J. I. C. (1992). A note of thanks to the women's movement. *Journal of Counseling & Development, 70,* 520–521.

Kluckhohn, C. (1951). Values and values orientation in the theory of action. In T. Parsons & E. A. Shils (Eds.), *Toward a general theory of action* (pp. 288–443). Cambridge, MA: Harvard University Press.

McArthur, C. (1992). Rumblings of a distant drum. *Journal of Counseling & Development, 70,* 517–519.

Murphy, G. (1955). The cultural context of guidance. *Personnel and Guidance Journal, 34,* 4–9.

Culture Shock

Culture shock is a complex set of symptoms associated with the experience of migration to or contact with a new environment and the process of adjusting to this new environment. Historically, culture shock was conceptualized as a consequence of stress caused by contact with a new culture, resulting in feelings of anxiety, sadness, and confusion related to the loss of social rules and accustomed cultural cues. Contemporary definitions tend to characterize culture shock as a state of emotional and physical discomfort one experiences when coming into contact with a new culture and the opportunity for adaptation, acculturation, and integration into the host culture. As the population of the United States continues to become more diverse and multicultural, it is important that mental health professionals identify the physical and emotional elements of culture shock and how to develop appropriate interventions when working with clients experiencing such issues.

Historical Perspective

The term *culture shock* first came into existence in the mid-1950s when K. Oberg conceptualized culture shock as an experience of strain and anxiety resulting from living in a new culture accompanied by feelings of sadness and loss. In the late 1970s, the concept of culture shock evolved into a more cognitive reaction, which was manifested as feelings of impotence or inability to deal with an environment because of unfamiliarity with the dominant culture. In the 1980s, a more comprehensive definition of *culture shock* was put forth by S. Rhinesmith, who asserted that culture shock occurs when an individual experiences concurrently the challenges associated with living in a new environment and the loss of a familiar cultural environment.

Contemporary Views

Existing research and literature today focus on diverse aspects of culture shock, such as its symptoms and manifestations. Culture shock typically includes symptoms or feelings of anxiety, isolation, frustration, disorientation, sadness, helplessness, powerlessness, vulnerability, and extreme homesickness. When individuals migrate to a foreign country, their separation from a familiar environment, which includes friends and family members, could result in a sense of personal loss and, thus, a loss of intimacy that was once accessible to them. All of these feelings affect the mental health of individuals experiencing culture shock. As a result, they can isolate themselves from contact with others in the new culture, thus precipitating symptoms such as changes in sleep patterns and appetite and extreme feelings of sadness and worthlessness. Such symptoms, coupled with feeling overwhelmed by new cultural norms, may cause some immigrants to become depressed or to engage in obsessive and/or compulsive behaviors in an attempt to gain control of the foreign situation. All of these symptoms can have a detrimental effect on individuals' sense of self-efficacy, as they may find it difficult to complete the tasks that were once routine for them.

Somatic reactions to culture shock also can be manifested in the lives of individuals who have migrated to a new culture. Because individuals are constantly (both consciously and unconsciously) processing new information (i.e., language, cultural values, and daily customs) about the host culture, they can experience cognitive fatigue, which can contribute to headaches or migraines. Furthermore, internalized feelings of anxiety about residing in a new country and adapting to a new culture can precipitate panic attacks, extreme sweating, irregular heart beats, high blood pressure, and gastrointestinal disturbances. In addition, marked feelings of homesickness can result in other somatic reactions, such as severe back pain and muscle pain.

Implications for Counseling

With the changing demographics of the United States and the influx of immigrants to nations around the world, it is important that mental health professionals acquire the knowledge and skills to work effectively with people experiencing culture shock. Ways that mental health counselors can be cognizant of potential culture shock symptoms include assessing immigration status and generational status of individuals, assessing their length of stay in the country, and evaluating their experiences of adjustment to the new culture. Finally, physical manifestations of culture shock must be taken into account when counseling individuals who have recently immigrated. Mental health interventions that work with clients' adjustment to and sense of efficacy living in a culture different from their own will be beneficial to their physical and mental well-being.

Cristina Dorazio and Madonna G. Constantine

See also Acculturation (v3); Acculturative Stress (v3); Adaptation (v3); Assimilation (v3); Enculturation (v3); Cultural Values (v3); Culture (v3); International Developments, Counseling (v1); Person–Environment Fit (v4); Person–Environment Interactions (v2); Psychological Well-Being, Dimensions of (v2); Stress (v2)

Further Readings

Constantine, M. G., Anderson, G. M., Berkel, L. A., Caldwell, L. D., & Utsey, S. O. (2005). Examining the cultural adjustment experiences of African international college students: A qualitative analysis. *Journal of Counseling Psychology, 52,* 57–66.

Merta, R. J., Stringham, E. M., & Ponterotto, J. G. (1988). Simulating culture shock in counselor trainees: An experiential exercise for cross-cultural training. *Journal of Counseling & Development, 66,* 242–245.

Misra, R., & Castillo, L. G. (2004). Academic stress among college students: Comparison of American and international students. *International Journal of Stress Management, 11*(2), 132–148.

Oberg, K. (1960). Culture shock: Adjustments to new cultural environments. *Practical Anthropology, 4,* 177–182.

Winkelman, M. (1994). Culture shock and adaptation. *Journal of Counseling & Development, 73,* 121–126.

Deficit Hypothesis

Social science and medical literature, including research on mental health and counseling, has frequently been based on presuppositions that all individuals who differ from members of the sociopolitically dominant cultural group in the United States (i.e., male, heterosexual, Caucasian, Western European Americans of middle-class socioeconomic status and Christian religious affiliation) are deficient by comparison. This *deficit hypothesis* is particularly apparent in scientific literature presumptions that attribute psychological differences from Caucasians to deviance and pathology.

Inferiority Premise

Regarding members of U.S. racial and ethnic minority groups (or people of color)—African American, Hispanic/Latino/a American, Asian American, and American Indian people—the inferiority model is one example of a deficit hypothesis. The inferiority model assumes that the dominant Caucasian group represents the standard for normal or ideal behavior and that cultural groups who differ from these norms are biologically limited and genetically inferior by comparison. In contrast, psychology literature includes critiques that cite how data have been distorted or fabricated to support the inferiority model.

For example, based on the belief that smaller skull size and underdeveloped brains were biologically determined measures of the inferior intelligence of people of color, Samuel George Morton, in the 19th century, published research findings that supported the prevailing inferiority view. Subsequent scholars (e.g., Stephen Jay Gould) disputed these findings by examining Morton's data and reporting errors of calculation and omission. Nevertheless, the inferiority deficit hypothesis persisted in the mental health and social science literature and practices of the 20th century. Eminent leaders in early American and British psychology perpetuated the inferiority belief of their times.

In 1904 G. Stanley Hall, the first president of the American Psychological Association, published his belief that Africans, American Indians, and Chinese people were in an adolescent or immature stage of biological evolution compared with the more advanced and civilized development of Caucasian people. Cyril Burt, an influential British psychologist whom many consider the father of educational psychology, published fabricated data to support his contention that Negros inherit inferior brains and lower intelligence compared with Caucasians. In 1976, Robert Guthrie presented a critique of the flawed scientific evidence offered by several researchers who had claimed to verify the inferior intelligence of American Indians and Mexican Americans. In part due to the conclusions drawn from an inferiority deficit hypothesis, people of color who exhibited symptoms of psychological distress were considered unworthy or incapable of benefiting from most psychological or educational interventions. Thus, they were ignored, jailed, or confined to segregated mental hospitals.

The inferiority premise has resurfaced in current times, for example, in the 1994 publication of Richard Herrnstein and Charles Murray's *The Bell Curve: Intelligence and Class Structure in American Life*.

Similar to previous investigations based on an inferiority hypothesis, the research of these authors concluded that intelligence is largely inherited and correlated with race; that those who have inferior intelligence (i.e., people of color) should serve those who have superior intelligence (i.e., Caucasians); and that programs purported to promote the intellectual functioning of people of color (e.g., Head Start) are useless, and thus their resources and funding should be reallocated to serve people who are capable of benefiting (i.e., Caucasians of superior intelligence). Subsequently, scholars (e.g., Ronald Samuda, Franz Samelson, Alan Reifman) have refuted these findings and presented empirical evidence that challenges and rejects these conclusions.

Cultural Deprivation Premise

In the context of the social activism of the 1950s and 1960s in the United States, the genetic inferiority premise of the deficit hypothesis shifted to a cultural deprivation premise. Similar to the inferiority model, the cultural deprivation model assumes that the dominant Caucasian group represents the standard for normal or ideal behavior. However, this model attributes psychological differences from Caucasians to the various ways in which people of color are socially oppressed, deprived, underprivileged, or deficient in comparison.

The term *cultural deprivation* emerged from scholars' writing about poverty in the United States during the 1950s and 1960s (e.g., Frank Riessman's 1962 book, *The Culturally Deprived Child*). The deficit hypothesis of cultural deprivation posits that poverty-stricken racial/ethnic minority groups perform poorly in psychological and educational testing and exhibit psychologically unhealthy characteristics because they lack the advantages of Caucasian middle-class culture (e.g., in presumably superior education, books, toys, and formal language). Not only does this premise mistakenly imply that people of color have no valuable cultures of their own, but it also infers that the destructive influences of poverty and racial/ethnic discrimination cause irreparable negative psychosocial differences in their personality characteristics, behavior, and achievement compared with more favorable middle-class Caucasian standards.

In rebuttal, scholars have criticized the scientific merit of the research design and interpretations of findings from studies claiming to support the cultural deprivation model. For example, Abram Kardiner and Lionel Ovesey published a book in 1951, titled *The Mark of Oppression*, in which they concluded that the basic Negro personality, compared with the general Caucasian personality, is a manifestation of permanent damage, in response to the stigma and obstacles of the social conditions faced by Negroes in U.S. society, which prevents them from developing healthy self-esteem and promotes self-hatred. Scholarly critiques have noted that the authors made these generalizations on the basis of 25 psychoanalytic interviews with African American participants, all of whom but one had identified psychological disturbances, in comparison to a so-called control group of one Caucasian man. Furthermore, Kardiner and Ovesey's conclusions were disputed for failing to recognize that individuals may respond in a variety of ways (including healthy and unhealthy responses) to stress, hardships, and oppression.

One useful purpose served by studies based on the cultural deprivation premise was the attention paid to the psychosocial and environmental barriers facing people of color and their families. On the other hand, most studies focused only on abnormal and negative aspects in the lives of people of color (e.g., crime and juvenile delinquency). One detrimental implication for cross-cultural counseling is that counselors may similarly attend to and focus on only negative aspects in their assessment and interventions with clients of color. Thus (as noted by scholars such as Elaine Pinderhughes), counselors may misattribute as pathological these clients' responses to oppression instead of recognizing aspects that may be positive, healthy, and resilient.

Applications to Other Nondominant Groups

In addition to applications with people of color, the deficit hypothesis may form the basis for some counseling research and practice with other nondominant groups (e.g., by gender, sexual orientation, or religious affiliation). In other words, the deficit hypothesis may be apparent in presumptions that attribute psychological differences from the dominant group in U.S. society (e.g., male, heterosexual, or Christian) to deficiency or pathology. For example, Carol Gilligan's research findings have disputed an underlying deficit hypothesis regarding gender differences in moral development (i.e., that female participants are deficient in moral reasoning compared with males).

Her research has demonstrated that the moral reasoning of girls and women is different from, instead of inferior to, that of boys and men.

Alternative Premises

Two alternative premises to those that use only one standard of comparison (e.g., Caucasians) are models of counseling and psychotherapy based on cultural differences or diversity. Another alternative perspective to the deficit hypothesis is that of optimal human functioning. In contrast to presuming mental health deficiency in cultural group members who differ from the dominant group, the basic premise of optimal human functioning is that there are many ways to be human and promote healthy development in response to different cultural contexts and human conditions. One implication for cross-cultural counseling research and practice is that this model for conceptualizing healthy development includes both emic (culturally specific) and etic (universal) considerations. These alternative models of personality and human development offer propositions to explore beyond the ethnocentric limitations of the deficit hypothesis.

Margo A. Jackson and Jaya Mathew

See also Barriers to Cross-Cultural Counseling (v3); Bias (v3); Discrimination (v3); Ethnocentrism (v3); Eurocentrism (v3); Monocultural (v3); Oppression (v3); Prejudice (v3); Racism (v3); Sexism (v3); Social Discrimination (v4); Universalism (v3); Visible Racial/Ethnic Groups (v3); White Privilege (v3)

Further Readings

Gilligan, C. (1982). *In a different voice: Psychological theory and women's development.* Cambridge, MA: Harvard University Press.

Guthrie, R. V. (2004). *Even the rat was White: A historical view of psychology* (2nd ed.). Upper Saddle River, NJ: Pearson.

Walsh, W. B. (Ed.). (2003). *Counseling psychology and optimal human functioning.* Mahwah, NJ: Lawrence Erlbaum.

DEMOGRAPHICS, UNITED STATES

Considerable changes in the population characteristics of the United States, both in numerical and in percentage terms, reflect an unprecedented demographic complexity in the history of the nation. Thirty-one percent of the total U.S. population is composed of ethnic and racial minorities. In addition, 11% of the total U.S. population is foreign born; of these, 51.7% are from Latin America and 26.4% are from Asia. For the first time in history, the United States is experiencing a large proportion of children and young adults who are not of European ancestry and do not speak either a Germanic language (including English) or a Slavic language as their first language.

Demographic Changes

Changes in the information collected in the most recent U.S. Census, such as mixed-race status, same-sex couples, and grandparental caregiving, have provided a rich, albeit complex, demographic landscape. Some of the demographic changes influencing the research, teaching, and practice of counseling psychology are summarized in this section.

Race and Ethnicity

The ratio of persons of color to Whites increased from 1 out of every 8 persons in 1900 to approximately 1 out of every 3 in 2000. Most of the increase in racial and ethnic diversity occurred in the latter part of the 20th century, with an increase of 88% from 1980 to 2000 in the combined non-White and Latino/a population. The Asian and Pacific Islander population tripled while the White population dropped 12 percentage points between 1970 and 2000. In addition, the option to select more than one racial group in the 2000 census identified 6.8 million (2.4%) multiracial individuals. The increase in racial and ethnic diversity in the United States has been attributed mainly to unprecedented international migration rates from Latin America and Asia/Pacific Islands and higher birth rates for these groups. Latinos/as, an ethnic category that includes any race, is the fastest-growing segment of the population with an increase from 6.4% in 1980 to 12.5% of the total population in 2000.

Age

The proportion of older people is increasing and that of younger people is decreasing, particularly for White groups. The number of people age 65 years and older increased 10 times since 1900, with a total of

35 million, or 12.4% of the population, in 2000. This number is expected to increase again substantially in the 2010s when baby boomers begin approaching conventional retirement age. The proportion of the population of children under 15 years of age has declined since 1900, dropping from 1 out of every 3 (35.5%) individuals to 1 out of every 5 (21.4%) in 2000. The increase in racial diversity in immigration has also influenced the age composition of the United States, with younger age cohorts having a greater percentage of individuals of color than older age cohorts. Latinos/as have the youngest median age and have the highest percentage of children under 15 (32%), while non-Latino Whites have the oldest median age and lowest percentage of children under 15 years of age.

Households and Family Structure

The U.S. Census 2000 reflected a growing complexity in household composition. Fifty-two percent of all households were composed of married couples while 9% of coupled households were composed of unmarried couples, a figure that increased 63% from 1990 to 2000. The number of unmarried couples is likely larger because the census restricted responses to only heads of households and their partners. African Americans and Native Americans/Alaskan Indians had the largest percentages of unmarried couples with 16.9% and 17.4%, respectively, while Asians had the lowest reported rates with 4.7%. The one-person household experienced the greatest growth and was 26% of all households in 2000. In addition, 1 out of every 9 households described as composed of unmarried partner couples were same-sex unions in the 2000 census. Approximately 1 out of 4 same-sex couples are parenting children under 18 years old.

About 5.8 million grandparents were identified as living with their grandchildren in the U.S. Census 2000, and 2.4 million were identified as the primary caregivers of these children. Grandparents residing with their grandchildren and serving as caregivers were more common with non-Whites and Latinos/as. However, Latino (35%) and Asian (20%) grandparents living in mutigenerational households are less likely to be caregivers than African Americans (52%) and Native Americans/Alaskan Natives (56%).

Mental Health Care Need and Use

Findings from different studies converge to highlight high prevalence of unmet mental health care needs. Forty-six percent of adults in the United States are predicted to meet diagnostic criteria for a mental health disorder in their lifetime, according to findings from the National Comorbidity Survey Replication. The Survey also found that only 41% of adults in need of mental health services received treatment with rates of unmet need greater for ethnic and racial minority groups, the elderly, and the poor. Data on mental health service use for children and adolescents are even more disheartening, with 79% of those with mental health needs going unmet. Similar to the adult population, ethnic/racial minority children and adolescents have higher rates of unmet mental health needs (African Americans 76.5%, Latinos/as 88.4%, Other 89.7%) than Whites (76%).

Ethnic/racial minority status, low educational level, and low income have been found to be associated with premature termination of mental health services. For example, once services are initiated, African American families have been found to have attrition rates greater than 50%. African Americans have also been found more likely to receive low-quality psychiatric care, which may partially explain the high attrition rates. Being Latino/a, particularly of Mexican descent, has been associated with low use of mental health services. Only 15% of Mexican immigrants and 37% of U.S.-born Mexican Americans with psychiatric disorders have been found to receive care from a general practitioner, mental health professional, other professionals, or informal helpers to address their mental health needs.

In addition, findings from the McArthur Foundation National Survey of Midlife Development in the U.S. suggest that individuals with minority sexual orientation (e.g., lesbian, gay, bisexual) have higher prevalence rates of major depression, panic attacks, psychological distress, and generalized anxiety disorder than do heterosexual men and women. Lesbians, gay men, and bisexual individuals have been found to use mental health services more than their heterosexual counterparts and account for 7% of adults between the ages of 25 and 74 receiving mental health services.

Implications for Counseling Psychology

The demographic characteristics of counseling psychologists in the United States, as reflected in the membership to American Psychological Association's Society of Counseling Psychology, suggest that approximately 11% of counseling psychologists at the doctoral level self-identify as non-White or Latino/a, falling short of reflecting Census 2000 data by two thirds. The average age of counseling psychologists (57 years) reflects the fact that 78% of members are White, which is the oldest racial group in the United States. This high number of older members also suggests that the number of younger people entering the field is relatively low and that fewer counseling psychologists will be available to address the needs of Latinos/as, Asians, and Blacks, who are the youngest groups, and of individuals with minority sexual orientations in the near future.

Recent research suggests that ethnic match between therapist/counselor and client is not a strong predictor of mental health service use or premature termination of treatment, suggesting that culturally competent and responsive care may be more predictive of use and continuation of services than the ethnic or racial status of the counselor. This emphasis on cultural competence and culturally responsive care has two major implications for both practicing and counseling psychologists in training. First, it suggests a focus on ethnic-specific or minority group–specific (e.g., individuals with minority sexual orientations) mental health needs and program development. Second, it emphasizes the increasing importance that counseling psychology training programs include in their curricula ethnic-specific engagement and treatment retention strategies and minority group–specific concerns. Moreover, the increasing ethnic and racial diversity of the United States and the greater visibility of lesbians, gay men, and bisexual individuals point to the need to recruit more young individuals to join the profession.

Ané M. Maríñez-Lora and Stephen M. Quintana

See also African Americans (v3); Alaska Natives (v3); Asian Americans (v3); Cross-Cultural Training (v3); Diversity (v3); Diversity Issues in Career Development (v4); Ethnic Minority (v3); Immigrants (v3); Latinos (v3); Multicultural Counseling Competence (v3); Pacific Islanders (v3); Socioeconomic Status (v3); Visible Racial/Ethnic Groups (v3); White Americans (v3)

Further Readings

Cochran, S. D., Sullivan, J. G., & Mays, V. M. (2003). Prevalence of mental disorders, psychological distress, and mental services use among lesbian, gay, and bisexual adults in the United States. *Journal of Consulting and Clinical Psychology, 71,* 53–61.

Gates, G. J., & Ost, J. (2004). *The gay and lesbian atlas.* Washington, DC: Urban Institute Press.

Hobbs, F., & Stoops, N. (2002, November). *Demographic trends in the 20th century* [U.S. Census Bureau, Census 2000 Special Reports, Series CENSR-4]. Washington, DC: Government Printing Office.

Kataoka, S. H., Zhang, L., & Wells, K. B. (2002). Unmet need for mental health care among U.S. children: Variation by ethnicity and insurance status. *American Journal of Psychiatry, 159,* 1548–1555.

Kazdin, A. (1996). Dropping out of child psychotherapy: Issues for research and implications for practice. *Clinical Child Psychology and Psychiatry, 1,* 133–156.

Kessler, R. C., Berglund, P. A., Demler, O., Jin, R., Merikangas, K. R., & Walters, E. E. (2005). Lifetime prevalence and age-of-onset distributions of *DSM-IV* disorders in the National Comorbidity Survey Replication (NCS-R). *Archives of General Psychiatry, 62*(6), 593–602.

Maramba, G. G., & Hall, G. C. N. (2002). Meta-analyses of ethnic match as a predictor of dropout, utilization and level of functioning. *Cultural Diversity & Ethnic Minority Psychology, 8,* 290–297.

Vega, W. A., Kolody, B., Aguilar-Gaxiola, S., & Catalano, R. (1999). Gaps in services utilization by Mexican Americans with mental health problems. *American Journal of Psychiatry, 156,* 928–934.

Wang, P. S., Lane, M., Kessler, R. C., Olfson, M., Pincus, H. A., & Wells, K. B. (2005). Twelve-month use of mental health services in the U.S.: Results from the National Comorbidity Survey Replication (NCS-R). *Archives of General Psychiatry, 62*(6), 629–640.

Wierzbicki, M., & Pekarik, G. (1993). A meta-analysis of psychotherapy dropout. *Professional Psychology: Research and Practice, 24,* 190–195.

Discrimination

To discriminate is to make distinctions or to acknowledge that differences exist. Therefore, discrimination is an act or practice of making distinctions based on perceived or actual differences. Although the word *discriminate* has neither a negative nor a positive connotation, the term *discrimination* often carries a negative undertone. Because these two terminologies do not carry the same meaning, Carl Friedrich Graumann and Margaret Wintermantel termed the latter *social discrimination.* This entry is concerned with social discrimination, which is defined as any behavior made by a person toward another that is based exclusively on the other's innate characteristics or group membership. Social discrimination involves denying people fair treatment because of their group membership or personal attributes without considering their individual merit or ability.

Discrimination is not the same as stereotypes or prejudice. Unlike these two constructs, which involve primarily cognitive elements, discrimination involves *actions* that are often dependent on people's motivation level and ability to discriminate. It may manifest itself in more than one form (i.e., subtle and direct) and on two different levels (i.e., individual and institutional). Discrimination may be further classified into numerous types, the most common ones being race, ethnicity, gender, age, religion, class, sexual orientation, ability, and mental illness. Existing theories on discrimination suggest that it may be caused by both individual (e.g., personality) and structural factors (e.g., intergroup conflict).

Discrimination Versus Stereotypes and Prejudice

While the construct of discrimination is conceptually related to prejudice and stereotypes, several important distinctions merit consideration. Stereotyping involves placing things or people into categories in an oversimplified manner. Hence, stereotypes are overgeneralized mental representations that may carry a positive or a negative meaning. Because stereotypes are frequently acquired through hearsay, it is difficult to know if they are true or false. A number of social cognitive theorists, including Gordon Allport, believe that humans naturally place things and people in categories to create a sense of coherence in our world and to increase personal comfort. For Henri Tajfel, the exaggerations of group attributes often associated with stereotypes stem from the inability of humans to process excess information. Whereas stereotypes involve a person's positive or negative belief or opinion about the characteristics of a certain group and its members, prejudice is an individual's negative attitude toward, or tendency to make negative attributions of, a particular group. For instance, if a person perceives Asians as competitive and frugal (stereotypes), and if these attributes are viewed negatively, then this person will likely have negative attitudes (prejudice) toward Asians.

Unlike prejudice and stereotypes, which involve cognitive and affective components, discrimination entails observable behaviors, which can be blatant or subtle. Although it may be logical to assume that negative attitudes can lead to discriminatory actions, the relationship between discrimination and prejudice is not straightforward. In fact, studies that document inconsistencies between attitudes and behaviors have been in existence since the 1930s. Nonetheless, some scholars argue that these observed discrepancies may be due to measurement error rather than to actual inconsistencies between the two constructs: Whereas attitudes are usually assessed using global scales, behaviors are often measured specifically.

Ability and Motivation to Discriminate

Two factors have been proposed to help explain the lack of consistency between attitudes and behaviors: ability and motivation to discriminate. Because discrimination involves actions that are intended to disadvantage certain people, it would require the person discriminating to have the ability to do so. Jennifer L. Eberhardt and Susan T. Fiske relate one's ability to discriminate to the concept of power. They assert that discrimination occurs when people in power make important choices that ultimately restrict the opportunities of individuals from certain groups. For instance, an individual may hold negative beliefs about a certain group yet may be unable to cause harm. Thus, according to this definition, if the consequences of the person's actions do not lead to disparities in the way groups are treated, discrimination may not occur.

One's motivation to discriminate is another important factor when considering the connection between attitudes and behaviors. In general, strong, negative attitudes and feelings (e.g., anger and hatred) toward certain groups increase people's level of motivation to discriminate against members of such groups. Some believe that tension between groups and perceived threat, which intensifies existing negative attitudes, further stimulate people's tendency to act on their beliefs and desires. Attitudes with less intensity, on the other hand, are less likely to be transformed into action. Although there has been much scholarly interest in examining how prejudice leads to discrimination, researchers are becoming increasingly interested in examining the factors that allow people to resist acting on their negative attitudes.

Forms and Levels of Discrimination

Discrimination takes on several forms. According to David Schneider, *straight-line discrimination* (i.e., direct) involves deliberate and conscious negative behaviors that target individuals from certain groups. On the other hand, *subtle discrimination* (i.e., indirect) is characterized by a range of different behaviors, which may involve a decision not to help and other nonverbal actions.

Discrimination occurs on two levels. On the individual level, discrimination is described as the unequal treatment of an individual based on group membership. Unfair hiring practices that base eligibility on an applicant's group affiliation (i.e., racial, religious, etc.) is one of the most common examples of discrimination. Individual-level discrimination can be deliberate or subtle in form. On the societal level, *institutional discrimination* is characterized by a pattern of unequal treatment of individuals based on their group membership. Such patterns are sewn into the fabric of the society or institutions and are often perpetuated unconsciously by prejudice. Institutional discrimination occurs when prejudice permeates the public domain and becomes part of public policy, thus limiting opportunities for certain groups. Like individual-level discrimination, institutional discrimination can be either deliberate (e.g., the decision of lawmakers not to allow certain groups to vote) or subtle (e.g., requiring both male and female police recruits to pass a strength test normed on men before becoming an officer).

Theoretical Background

Social Identity

Humans naturally organize their lives into structures and develop habits to feel comfortable and secure. Identity facilitates the creation of meaning and structure in people's lives. Theorists believe that having the security of knowing one's self according to one's own history and one's social group membership is vital to people's mental health. Furthermore, individuals frequently derive meaning from their lives by comparing themselves to those who belong to other groups. For instance, masculinity is meaningful only when a person contrasts it with femininity. Although the process of making comparisons extends beyond just physical characteristics, external attributes are what people often use to differentiate themselves from others.

Two theories are widely recognized with regard to social identity. In social identity theory, social groups are seen as an important source of identity. The theory posits that, in general, people like to view themselves positively and they want to feel positive about themselves. To achieve this, people join groups that will either improve their positive identity or enhance the worthiness of the group to which they already belong. To achieve positive self-regard, people often feel motivated to make distinctions between their own group and other groups. Not surprisingly, they are more likely to favor their own group. Some scholars assert that although hostility toward members of the other group is not central to social identity theory, it is a natural corollary. Social identity theory maintains that conflict develops not only from limited physical resources, which is a realistic threat, but also from scarce social resources, which form a symbolic threat. Social resources include norms, moral principles, and beliefs that people hold. When a minority group advances norms that are different from those of the majority, members of the majority group may feel threatened by the new value system.

Self-categorization theory, which was derived from social identity theory, underscores the relevance of the cognitive aspect of group identity. This theory purports that group identity is not always salient to an individual's identity and that it may become relevant only when certain environmental cues trigger the individual's identification with certain groups. For instance, being the only White man in a room full of Asian women may trigger certain feelings that one has about being male and being White.

Ingroup–Outgroup Bias

William G. Sumner coined the terms *ingroup* (relating to members of one's own group) and *outgroup* (relating to members of other groups) in 1907. Sumner argued that it is natural for humans to derogate members of the outgroup because it promotes devotion to the ingroup and its accepted norms. Two codes that govern group behavior according to Herbert Spencer are the codes of "amity" and "enmity." The code of amity is characterized by positive feelings toward members of the ingroup, while the code of enmity involves negative feelings and behaviors toward those of the outgoup. Sumner later termed this phenomenon of favoring the ingroup and derogating the outgroup *ethnocentrism*. For Sumner, devotion to one's group is necessary for the survival of its members; this notion is rooted in the evolutionary theory and in social Darwinism.

Ingroup bias occurs when people give preferential treatment to members of their group or when individuals evaluate a member of their group more favorably than they do nonmembers. For instance, students in one university are likely to evaluate their sports team, regardless of their performance, more favorably than teams from other universities. In fact, findings from a number of studies suggest that individuals are more likely to show positive behaviors toward members of their own ingroup than members of the outgroup even if there are no direct benefits to showing favoritism to members of one's own group. Accordingly, this also means that people are likely to discriminate against members of the outgroup even if doing so presents no perceived value to them or their group.

Social Dominance

Another influential theory that has been proposed recently to explain the basis of social discrimination and inequality is social dominance theory. Social dominance theory states that human societies naturally organize themselves into groups. These groups reflect social hierarchies wherein groups in power enjoy substantial privilege and social value while subordinate groups suffer negative consequences and stigma. There are three distinct group systems within this theory: the age system (which privileges adults and middle-age people over the young), the patriarchal system (favoring males over females), and the arbitrary set system (which is made up of socially constructed group distinctions based on situational and historical factors, including race, social class, religion, etc.).

Social dominance theorists believe that the systematic nature of group discrimination results from people's shared knowledge and beliefs that serve to legitimize and uphold discriminatory practices. These scholars suggest that these shared ideologies influence how resources are allocated, which in turn serve to perpetuate existing prejudice and discriminatory behaviors. According to James Sidanius, the acceptance of principles that legitimize discrimination is due, in part, to people's desire to be in power, a psychological orientation known as the *social dominance orientation.* This orientation is viewed to be influenced not only by individual factors (e.g., personality), but also by contextual factors (e.g., power differential).

Sidanius and his colleagues also assert that focusing solely on the individual's psychological motivation and social construals (as in the case of social identity theory) to explain the nature of discrimination ignores the important social consequences of the actions (i.e., systematic oppression or structural inequality) or the structural causes of the behaviors. On the other hand, they maintain that focusing mainly on structural theories fails to explain individual differences in behaviors. Several theorists argue that social dominance theory addresses the limitations of the two approaches by focusing on both structural and psychological aspects of discrimination, its universal and subtle forms, and the interaction between different systems (e.g., individual predispositions, social contexts, and cultural ideologies).

Common Types of Social Discrimination

Race and Ethnicity

Racial discrimination refers to the unequal treatment of people on the basis of race. Although the definition of race is often disputed, racial discrimination usually references unequal treatment of people based on widely shared notions of race that are based largely but not exclusively on physical attributes (including the color of their skin, the shape of their eyes, etc.) and cultural heritage. Rich accounts of racial discrimination and oppression exist in the histories of the United States and other countries.

Although the United States has made improvements to reduce discriminatory behaviors through public policy, several historical factors continue to perpetuate racism, which has been present since the time of slavery. Inequalities in job opportunities and educational access with regard to racial differences are still prevalent, and minority groups continue to have lower income and higher unemployment rates compared with their White counterparts. Though overt racial discrimination decreased over the years, modern institutional discrimination has taken its place. Racial discrimination emphasizes the inferiority of the minority groups, which can invoke different emotions for members of the subjugated group, such as feelings of humiliation, shame, frustration, anger, and even hatred toward members of other groups. Hence, discrimination has important psychological implications for its victims. The development of various psychological symptoms, such as depression and anxiety, has been linked with the stressful experiences of those who have been the targets of discrimination.

The continued arrival of immigrants, including refugees, in the United States, reinforces the concept of ethnic and racial difference (the idea of "us vs. them"). Xenophobia (the irrational fear of strangers) brings about feelings of distrust of and discomfort around immigrants. These feelings may activate people's prejudice, which in turn increases their motivation to discriminate. Discrimination toward immigrant groups is well documented throughout history and has been associated with competition over limited employment opportunities. For instance, one of the underlying causes of the 1992 Los Angeles riots was the high rate of unemployment and the changing ethnic makeup of the city. As Hispanic immigrants began to populate historically African American neighborhoods, Koreans took over businesses that were formerly owned by Blacks. As a result, a number of riot victims experienced substantial distress and trauma characteristic of post-traumatic stress disorder. Although there are larger institutional issues linked with the L.A. riots, this incident also serves as an example that prejudice and discrimination may occur even between members of various minority groups.

Access to education is another issue relevant to discrimination that continues to stimulate public debate. Affirmative action is a policy that began as a measure to correct institutional discrimination against traditionally underrepresented groups. Whereas some people believe that affirmative action can promote the advancement of historically disadvantaged groups, others argue that it is an act of reverse discrimination that discriminates against poor Whites and Asians. Certain psychological outcomes have been associated with affirmative action. It has been found that affirmative action sometimes decreases the recipients' level of motivation and self-efficacy, and that individuals who believe that they were hired because of their minority status suffer the stigma of incompetence. Furthermore, they may be subjected to prejudice and further discrimination, especially by those who feel that they are undeserving. The pressure of performing to expectations adds to the stress that these individuals face.

Gender

Gender discrimination refers to behaviors that deny individuals opportunities and privileges on the basis of their gender. Unlike the category of sex, which classifies people according to their biological or phenotypic differences (i.e., male or female), gender encompasses both biological and social components. When people talk about gender, they are usually referring to the social or cultural attributes of being male or female (i.e., masculinity and femininity).

The treatment of men and women has varied significantly by country throughout history. Nonetheless, some scholars claim that the existing body of evidence suggests that women in most societies are perceived as subordinate to men. In the United States, women were not afforded the same employment opportunities as men, who were more likely to receive better educational opportunities. Women have historically accepted roles ascribed to them by their male-dominated society. It was not until after the Seneca Falls Convention of 1848 that more women began to play a more active role in advocating for their rights. Moreover, Title VII and Title IX of the Civil Rights Act (which removed employment and educational barriers for women, respectively) were designed to help improve the opportunities of women in the educational and occupational arenas. However, the current state of inequality between men and women suggests that these policies, which are intended to protect women, are not implemented effectively. Women continue to work in low-status jobs and are paid less than men who hold the same position.

Some theorists argue that benevolent prejudice, not hostile sexism, is the main cause of ongoing gender discrimination. Paternalism, which allows men to assert their privilege as the dominant gender, can be used to argue that men use their position of power to women's benefit, an idea that seems favorable to women. Men in male-dominated societies reason that they carry a great deal of responsibility to protect and provide for women. This paternalistic idea, however, has hurt women more than it helped them because it supports patriarchy. Research on affirmative action, which also promotes the preferential hiring of women, suggests that women who believe that they get hired because of their gender are less likely to be motivated, interested, and committed to their occupations. They are also more likely to negatively evaluate their ability and performance on a task.

Finally, women have frequently been viewed as sex objects throughout history. Research found that women are more likely than men to be the target of sexually derogatory comments and to be perceived as sexual objects. These sexist incidents were found to be associated with depression, anger, and decrease in self-esteem.

Sexual Orientation, Ability, and Mental Illness

People who are discriminated against because of their sexual orientation, ability, or mental illness share one thing in common: They possess characteristics that many people would consider to lie outside a socially constructed idea of normality. Hence, they can be easily seen as members of the outgroup. Discrimination based on sexual orientation refers to behaviors that deny people opportunities and rights because of their sexual orientation (e.g., homosexuality and bisexuality). Because it is often perceived that attraction to a person from the opposite sex is normal and natural, anything that deviates from this biological norm is seen as "abnormal." A large majority of gays, lesbians, and bisexuals report experiencing discrimination because of their sexual orientation, and their rate of victimization (due to hate crimes) is higher than that of the national population, especially for gay males. Furthermore, many gays and lesbians also report being denied employment because of their sexual identity, while those employed but treated unfairly in their work environment are more likely to have negative attitudes about work. Population-based studies also indicate that lesbian and gay youth have higher rates of major depression, generalized anxiety disorder, and substance abuse and dependence compared with the general population. Epidemiologists associate these observed rates to perceived discrimination (stigma) felt by gay men and lesbians. Gay men also face the stigma of being perceived as having AIDS or HIV. The fear of the AIDS epidemic may further motivate heterosexual people with homophobia to discriminate against gay men.

Like homosexuality, a person's disability has been seen as a deviation from what is considered normal. Discrimination due to one's disability occurs when a competent person with a disability (i.e., physical or mental impairment that limits the execution of certain activities) is denied the same opportunities as those who do not have disabilities. Historically, individuals with disabilities were institutionalized and separated from people who were considered "normal." Ability-based discrimination can be traced back to the eugenics movement and to the idea of natural selection. Supporters of the movement feared that human civilization would be bound to failure if the "inferior" classes multiplied to produce more "defective" children. People with visible disabilities, in particular, face the stigma of being seen as different. They have also experienced hate crimes, which have been associated with post-traumatic stress, depression, anxiety, and anger. People with disabilities make up the largest minority group in the United States. They have a very high unemployment rate, which many argue is the result of the failure of the larger society to accommodate people of different abilities. For instance, many establishments do not offer Braille for individuals with visual impairment or an interpreter for those who are deaf or hard of hearing.

Since the United Nations broadened the definition of disability to include mental illness, many have referred to mental illness as a form of disability. Supporters of the eugenics movement were not only concerned with people with physical disabilities; they were also worried about people with mental illness, regarding the mentally ill as "feebleminded." Today, many people with mental illness are still stigmatized and seen as abnormal. Despite efforts to educate people about the etiology of mental illness, many still attribute mental illness to physical or moral weakness, resulting in a number of individuals with mental illness suffering humiliation for their conditions. In some cultures (e.g., South Asians) that value close-knit relationships with community members, mental illness brings shame to the family because it carries a stigma. Accordingly, they may delay seeking treatment because they fear degradation and the stigma that comes with the illness.

Other Types of Discrimination

Discrimination has many types. Certain types may be more controversial than others, depending on the current state of affairs. Moreover, some people may be more likely than others to fall victim to discrimination because they belong to more than one discriminated group. Gay Black men, for example, may be more likely to suffer from hate crimes than heterosexual Black men or gay White men. Understanding how the interactions between the different types of discrimination affect both the risk for becoming a victim of discrimination and the possibility of subsequent mental health problems is an important issue to consider.

Noriel E. Lim and Sumie Okazaki

See also Affirmative Action (v3); Antisemitism (v3); Bias (v3); Classism (v3); Deficit Hypothesis (v3); Discrimination and Oppression (v2); Diversity Issues in Career Development (v4); Ethnocentrism (v3); Prejudice (v3); Racism (v3); Sexism (v3); Social Class (v4); Social Discrimination (v4); Social Identity Theory (v3); Stereotype (v3); Tokenism (v3)

Further Readings

Allport, G. (1954). *The nature of prejudice.* Garden City, NY: Addison-Wesley.

Crosby, F., Bromley, S., & Saxe, L. (1980). Recent unobtrusive studies of Black and White discrimination and prejudice: A literature review. *Psychological Bulletin, 87,* 546–563.

Eberhardt, J. L., & Fiske, S. T. (1996). Motivating individuals to change: What is a target to do? In C. N. Macrae, C. Stangor, & M. Hewstone (Eds.), *Stereotypes and stereotyping* (pp. 369–415). New York: Guilford Press.

Graumann, C. F., & Wintermantel, M. (1989). Discriminatory speech acts: A functional approach. In D. Bar-Tal, C. F. Graumann, A. W. Kruglasnski, & W. Stroebe (Eds.), *Stereotyping and prejudice: Changing conceptions* (pp. 183–204). New York: Springer.

Healey, J. F. (2004). *Diversity and society: Race, ethnicity, and gender.* Thousand Oaks, CA: Pine Forge Press.

Hogg, M. A., & Abrams, D. (1990). Social motivation, self-esteem, and social identity. In D. Abrams & M. A. Hogg (Eds.), *Social identity and social cognition* (pp. 28–47). Oxford, UK: Blackwell.

Marshall, S. (2004). *Difference and discrimination in psychotherapy and counselling.* London: Sage.

Monteith, M. J., Ashburn-Nardo, L., Voils, C. I., & Czopp, A. M. (2002). Putting the brakes on prejudice: On the development and operation of cues for control. *Journal of Personality and Social Psychology, 83,* 1029–1050.

Mullen, B., Brown, R., & Smith, C. (1992). Ingroup bias as a function of salience, relevance, and status: An integration. *European Journal of Social Psychology, 22,* 103–122.

Operario, D., & Fiske, S. T. (1998). Racism equals power plus prejudice: A social psychological equation for racial oppression. In J. L. Eberhardt & S. T. Fiske (Eds.), *Confronting racism: The problem and the response* (pp. 33–53). Thousand Oaks, CA: Sage.

Schneider, D. (2004). *The psychology of stereotyping.* New York: Guilford Press.

Sidanius, J., Pratto, F., van Laar, C., & Levin, S. (2004). Social dominance theory: Its agenda and methods. *Political Psychology, 25,* 845–880.

Sidanius, J., & Veniegas, R. C. (2000). Gender and race discrimination: The interactive nature of disadvantage. In S. Oskamp (Ed.), *Reducing prejudice and discrimination: The Claremont symposium on applied social psychology* (pp. 47–69). Mahwah, NJ: Lawrence Erlbaum.

Tajfel, H., & Turner, J. C. (1979). An integrative theory of intergroup conflict. In W. Austin & S. Worchel (Eds.), *The social psychology of intergroup conflict* (pp. 33–47). Pacific Grove, CA: Brooks/Cole.

Turner, J. C., Oakes, P. J., Haslam, S. A., & McGarty, C. (1994). Self and collective: Cognition and social context. *Personality and Social Psychology Bulletin, 20,* 454–463.

DIVERSITY

As a response to the shifting population demographics in the United States, issues related to diversity have received increased attention in recent years. The word *diversity* simply means difference, but the term is most commonly used to refer to differences among people. The ways in which individuals may differ from one another are considerable. Some perspectives argue for a narrow diversity focus, whereas others believe that diversity should encompass the myriad ways that people may differ from one another.

Defining Diversity

Some scholars adopt definitions of *diversity* that focus on particular demographic differences among individuals. Specifically, differences in ethnicity, race, and gender have been the most emphasized dimensions of diversity. The focus on these particular identity elements stems from the sociopolitical history of prejudice and discrimination toward women and minorities. Furthermore, focusing on differences based in ethnicity, race, and gender draws attention to the differential distribution of power in the United States. Traditionally, women and individuals of color have not had the power allotted to men and Whites. Therefore, some scholars argue that certain elements of diversity, such as ethnicity, race, and gender, have more serious social ramifications than other elements and, as a result, should receive primary focus. Proponents of this view believe that treating all elements of diversity equivalently would mask and invalidate the history of discrimination and marginalization suffered by groups that are not near the top of the power hierarchy. More recently, others have argued that additional demographic characteristics, such as sexual orientation, age, and religion, should also be included in definitions of diversity given the emerging evidence of discrimination based on these social categories. Those who focus on power differentials and resulting discrimination tend to concentrate on demographic elements of diversity.

Other scholars contend that focusing on demographic aspects of diversity is limiting, and therefore they adopt broader definitions where other differences between people may be recognized. In addition to less-accentuated aspects of demographic diversity, such as age, sexual orientation, and religion, others contend that differences in personality, ability, work styles, and ideology are also important dimensions of diversity that have been underemphasized. Advocates of broader definitions of diversity argue that no one group benefits from diversity over others. They contend that by expanding the definition, one may be more likely to gain the support of White men and others who may feel marginalized by more narrow conceptualizations of diversity. It is argued that the emphasis should be on improving the educational and working environment for everyone, not just individuals from traditionally marginalized groups. Therefore, it is argued that a more inclusive definition of diversity benefits everyone.

The approach to diversity that one adopts has implications for counseling practice and research. For example, a therapist who adopts a narrow approach to diversity while working with an older Latina lesbian may overlook critical issues related to age, gender, or sexual orientation by focusing only on ethnic aspects of the client's experience. On the other hand, a therapist who adheres to a broad diversity perspective may fail to attend to pertinent issues in the therapeutic relationship by downplaying the importance of ethnicity or race in an African American client's experience. Sometimes the adoption of a broad perspective of diversity is symptomatic of an unacknowledged discomfort with more provocative aspects of diversity (e.g., race or sexual orientation) on the part of the therapist. For example, a White therapist who is uncomfortable with people of color may always avoid issues of race by emphasizing other broader aspects of diversity, allowing the therapist to avoid acknowledging or working through his or her prejudices. Both broad and narrow definitions of diversity offer their own sets of strengths and weaknesses. In the end, individuals should weigh the costs, benefits, and implications of adhering to either approach.

Ideological Perspectives of Diversity

The two most prominent ideological perspectives that influence how individuals conceptualize and view diversity are the melting pot and multiculturalism.

Melting Pot

The *melting pot* refers to the idea that individuals of different cultural backgrounds in the United States assimilate to share one common national identity. This conceptualization of diversity presumes that differences among individuals can be harmoniously blended into one cohesive social product. In this view, differences among people are thought to help facilitate the achievement of a common goal. One criticism of the melting pot perspective is the implicit expectation that ethnic minorities and others should shed their native cultural norms and values and assimilate to dominant U.S. culture (e.g., White, middle-class culture). Furthermore, there is an assumption that individuals who attempt to shed their cultural traits and assimilate to dominant U.S. culture will be accepted as one of the majority. As many have noted, groups that exhibit physical differences from those of the majority often have great difficulty being accepted into the majority culture. For example, it is a common experience for Asian Americans to be asked what country they are from when, in fact, they were born in the United States. Furthermore, individuals who have a strong cultural and ethnic identity may see assimilation as something to avoid at all costs. The idea of losing or shedding cultural norms, behaviors, and identity is highly undesirable to individuals who value their cultural background and heritage.

Multiculturalism

Multiculturalism refers to the idea that social differences should be acknowledged, celebrated, encouraged, and preserved. Within the context of multiculturalism, diversity is affirmed and considered a valuable asset. One of the myths surrounding multiculturalism is that it is inherently divisive given the emphasis on cultural difference. Contrary to the melting pot ideal, the goal of multiculturalism is not to blend cultural differences but to maintain and take advantage of social differences. Research has found that multiculturalism can help achieve unifying superordinate goals, such as democracy, freedom, and justice, by fostering an open dialogue and facilitating contact for individuals from different backgrounds.

Counseling psychologists were among the first to address multicultural issues within psychology. The changing demographics of the United States served as a clarion call to counseling psychologists to develop culturally relevant skills for working with diverse populations. As a result of the multicultural movement within counseling psychology, practitioners and educators began to emphasize the importance of building cultural expertise and increasing multicultural competence. Some counseling psychologists contend that awareness or acknowledgment of cultural differences is not a desirable end goal because it does not lead to effective outcomes in therapy or society. Instead, they argue that mutual enrichment for all parties is necessary to achieve the true goals of multiculturalism. One component necessary for achieving mutual enrichment is the acknowledgment of power differences through open and honest dialogue about equity and opportunity in society.

Some counseling psychologists argue that several components are necessary if a therapist wishes to increase his or her level of cultural competence. First, therapists need to acknowledge their own privilege as well as the biases that may be present in a given social situation. Second, therapists who aim for cultural competence value others' feedback, listen carefully, and diligently work to reduce their own prejudiced attitudes. Finally, a multiculturally competent therapist aims to increase awareness of his or her own biases and assumptions, gain knowledge about the cultural context in which clients are embedded, and become adept in advancing positive change.

Similar to the controversy surrounding the conceptualization of diversity, there has also been debate within the field of counseling psychology about adopted definitions of multiculturalism. Some argue that multiculturalism should be defined broadly and include differences based on race, ethnicity, gender, sexual orientation, disability, and socioeconomic status, among other elements of social difference, whereas others contend that conceptualizations should be more limited and focused. Proponents of the more focused view contend that the adoption of broad definitions of multiculturalism allows individuals to treat all differences equally, therefore obfuscating the deeper level issues related to race, ethnicity, and gender. By adopting a broad conceptualization of multiculturalism, individuals from dominant groups (e.g., Whites) may treat all human difference equally, thereby avoiding issues related to their role in the oppression of women and minorities. The espousal of a more focused multicultural definition allows individuals to delve deeper and explore the values, beliefs, and norms of different cultural groups as well as their role in prejudice and discrimination.

Diversity in the Workplace

Several scholars have noted the benefits of increasing diversity in organizations. In addition to the social justice–oriented goals of increasing equality and reducing discrimination in organizations for individuals of diverse backgrounds, organizations also increase overall organizational effectiveness when they successfully include and manage diverse employees. One benefit of diversity for organizations is that they increase overall profits when they can successfully retain and acquire employees from diverse backgrounds. Not only does successful retention of diverse employees reduce turnover costs, but it also aids in the acquisition of highly talented minorities and women to the organization. Individuals from underrepresented backgrounds have a tendency to seek employment in organizations that have successfully retained other individuals from diverse backgrounds. The inclusion of individuals from diverse backgrounds in an organization aids in creating a work environment that fosters creativity, which results in broader market perspective. For example, people of different cultural groups tend to want to buy a product that is supported or created by a person from their group. The presence of a multiculturally diverse staff also may help clients from diverse backgrounds feel more comfortable when seeking services from a counseling center or practice. If they perceive the environment to be open to their interests and experience, they may be more likely to seek and remain in therapy. It may be quite overwhelming for a person of color, for example, to walk into a counseling center where there are no people of color and discuss issues related to their experiences as a minority. When organizations take into account viewpoints of women and men of different cultural, ethnic, and social backgrounds, they increase their client base.

Another aspect of an organization that is improved with diversity is problem solving. Diverse groups bring a broader range of experiences that can help in problem solving because heterogeneous groups produce solutions of better quality than those produced by homogenous groups. The mere presence of people with diverse opinions improves the quality of the decision processes regardless of whether or not the minority view was used. Overall, diverse groups provide an organization with a competitive advantage because efficiency in problem solving increases and results in better decisions.

As diversity increases in an organization, the organization members become more flexible and able to adapt to problems and issues that arise. Organizational flexibility is increased if diversity and its successful management result in broadened procedures and less-standardized management methods. The organization becomes more fluid and adaptable because it must adjust to the increase of women and men of different cultural and social backgrounds. Successfully managing diversity within an organization leads to system flexibility that results in a better and more efficient working environment.

Although the benefits of diversity in the workplace have been documented, arguments against increasing diversity in the workplace persist. Opponents of diversity in organizations argue that the increase of minorities and women in the workplace weakens organizational effectiveness by increasing conflict among employees and, in turn, reducing their productivity. Therefore, some organizations aim to keep their organizations as homogeneous as possible to avoid the perceived conflict that would be produced if they increased the level of diversity in their organizations.

Furthermore, detractors of diversity argue that increasing diversity in the workplace also results in a greater number of ill-equipped and unqualified employees. This view stems from negative stereotypes about beneficiaries of affirmative action who are usually perceived to be minorities and women. Unfortunately, one of the prevailing myths surrounding affirmative action is that unqualified persons obtain positions over more-qualified individuals. Affirmative action programs that utilize quotas to increase the number of minorities and women in the workplace have been deemed illegal and very rarely exist in organizations. When they are detected, they are usually quickly dismantled. Furthermore, studies have shown that beneficiaries and nonbeneficiaries of affirmative action in organizations yield similar productivity levels and outcomes.

Scholars argue that the consequences of increased diversity in an organization are related to the perceived commitment to diversity from the upper echelons of an organization. Organizations that lack strong vision and leadership in terms of how to address diversity issues have the most conflict in their organizations. The organizations that are most successful in managing diversity are the ones that encourage fairness at all levels and attempt to utilize all the skills and benefits that diverse employees bring to an organization.

Diversity in Higher Education

In recent years, greater attention has been given to the role of diversity in higher education. The widely publicized affirmative action cases at the University of Michigan (i.e., *Grutter v. Bollinger, Gratz v. Bollinger*) reinvigorated the debate surrounding the role of diversity and affirmative action in institutions of higher education across the United States. Proponents of diversity in higher education cited the benefits to students and society, while opponents referred to the perceived cost associated with diversifying an institution.

Colleges and universities are charged with the task of preparing students for their future as citizens. Students receive not only education that is pertinent to their career goals but also informal training on how to function in a democratic and diverse society. Their daily interactions in college help prepare them for the adult world outside the college context. Arguably, the time spent in the college environment is among the only chances in life where people may acquire skills designed to aid them in becoming competent workers and citizens in a culturally diverse society.

Scholars have argued that diverse environments help facilitate psychological and intellectual growth needed for college students to lead fulfilling lives after college. First and foremost, diverse environments help students become more active learners. Most people engage in automatic thought processes that require little effort. The goal of most professors in the classroom is to help stimulate critical and effortful thinking. Students must engage in controlled or effortful thinking when they learn something new because they have no prior experience with the content and therefore must think carefully about how to accommodate the new information.

Novel situations also promote effortful thinking. Students on a college campus who grew up in racially homogenous environments may experience a set of novel situations when they set foot on a diverse college campus. In addition to formal situations such as the classroom, informal interactions that may occur in residence halls, public dining areas, and other places provide students with opportunities to interact with individuals from backgrounds different from their own. Other elements that promote critical thinking include instability, discontinuity, and discrepancy.

These elements stem from cognitive-developmental theories that suggest that there needs to be some level of discomfort and uncertainty to promote critical and effortful thinking. Novelty, instability, discontinuity, and discrepancy all help aid the effortful processing of new information. Diverse college campuses provide an environment for these processes to work so that students can grow intellectually.

Social science research has documented the ways in which students are enriched in a learning environment. A student's quality of thinking depends, in part, on his or her social environment. One mechanism that further enriches the learning environment, by fostering critical thinking, is disequilibrium. Disequilibrium is achieved when an idea is presented that causes students to rethink notions they may have regarding a given idea. This may occur when a student from a different background asks a question from a different perspective and, as a result, challenges others to rethink their notions regarding the subject.

Affirmative Action

Affirmative action has had a long and controversial history since it was first mentioned in President John Kennedy's Executive Order 10925 of 1961. The order required federal contractors to take "affirmative action" to end discrimination against minorities. In 1964, Title VII of the Civil Right Act prohibited discrimination in employment. Title VII allowed individuals who were discriminated against to sue their employers. In 1967 President Lyndon Johnson extended the policy to include women into the protected category. Employers were required to submit reports about their recruitment and hiring efforts and to explain how they would counteract inequality in their organization. Employers at some institutions of higher education started to keep careful records of the demographic characteristics of their applicant pools.

The topic of affirmative action often incites strong emotional responses either in favor of or against the policy. Individuals launch into heated debates without actually defining what they mean by *affirmative action*. Some social science scholars define affirmative action as any effort undertaken by organizations and institutions that are designed to ensure equality of opportunity and outcome for everyone. Federal employers are required by law to implement affirmative action programs in their organizations and institutions. Private institutions, although not required by law, also often put into practice affirmative action programs as a means to increase diversity in their institutions.

The mechanism by which diversity in the workplace and higher education is increased is through affirmative action. Affirmative action programs in the workplace may vary in their goals. Some emphasize recruitment of qualified minorities and women, whereas others implement additional programs designed to ensure retention of their diverse employees. Other programs may focus on the promotion of minorities and women within the workplace. Most often, affirmative action programs are designed to recruit and hire individuals in the organization, and diversity management programs manage the diversity within the organization after the employees have been hired.

In higher education, affirmative action programs are implemented to increase racial and ethnic diversity on college campuses. The goal of most higher education institutions that value diversity is to admit enough individuals to develop a critical mass of minority students. These policies aim not only to increase the numbers of diverse students but also to admit those who are capable of withstanding the demands of college work. Furthermore, some social scientists argue that affirmative action policies are necessary to guarantee fairness in institutions of higher education because affirmative action programs emphasize outcomes. It is not enough to increase opportunity for underrepresented groups; one must implement procedures to ensure that opportunity translates into results.

The importance of effectively managing diversity will become more vital as the United States becomes more diverse. Individuals of European descent who can be categorized as Caucasian are projected to be less than 50% of the population by the year 2050, thereby making people of color the majority. Attention to issues of diversity is especially crucial in the workplace and in higher education given the role these institutions have in helping individuals lead successful and fulfilling lives. Multiculturally competent counseling professionals who are trained in areas of diversity may be called upon to provide training services to organizations and institutions of higher learning. The training that counseling psychologists receive may help organizations and institutions communicate effectively by encouraging open dialogue and aiding in the deconstruction of biases and prejudices. The shifting population demographics in the United States necessitates further investigation of all aspects of diversity to ensure that individuals have a chance to live in an equitable, just, and democratic society.

Germine H. Awad

See also Affirmative Action (v3); Assimilation (v3); Career Counseling (v4); Culture (v3); Demographics, United States (v3); Diversity Issues in Career Development (v4); Identity (v3); Interracial Comfort (v3); Multiculturalism (v3); Organizational Diversity (v3); Political Correctness (v3); Racial Identity (v3); School Counseling (v1)

Further Readings

Blaine, B. E. (2000). *The psychology of diversity: Perceiving and experiencing social difference.* Mountain View, CA: Mayfield.

Cox, T. H., & Blake, S. (1991). Managing cultural diversity: Implications for organizational competitiveness. *Academy of Management Executive, 5,* 45–58.

Crosby, F. J. (2004). *Affirmative action is dead: Long live affirmative action.* New Haven, CT: Yale University Press.

Gurin, P., Lehman, J. S., & Lewis, E. (2004). *Defending diversity: Affirmative action at the University of Michigan.* Ann Arbor: University of Michigan Press.

Locke, D. C. (1990). A not so provincial view of multicultural counseling. *Counselor Education & Supervision, 30,* 18–25.

Smith, T. B. (2004). *Practicing multiculturalism: Affirming diversity in counseling and psychology.* Boston: Allyn & Bacon.

Stockdale, M. S., & Crosby, F. J. (2004). *The psychology and management of workplace diversity.* Malden, MA: Blackwell.

DRAPETOMANIA

Drapetomania was an alleged disease afflicting enslaved Africans in the antebellum southern United States, causing them to attempt to escape their servile societal station. The term combined the Greek words *drapetes* ("a runaway slave") and *mania* ("madness"). Most contemporary references to this "disease" treat it as a prototypical historical example of racism masquerading as psychological science in clinical practice. Some, however, have cited drapetomania in broader indictments of the entire mental health field.

Resisting Enslavement as Symptomatic of Mental Disease

In an 1851 report commissioned by the Louisiana State Medical Association, physician Samuel Adolphus Cartwright summarized putative physical characteristics and health conditions of those of African descent in the state. He identified drapetomania as a unique, though vaguely defined, condition, with the key symptom of fleeing from enslavement.

Citing supposed physiological differences and the Christian Old Testament as evidence that people of African descent were destined to obey and serve, Cartwright concluded that drapetomania was a risk whenever masters either treated the enslaved as equals or treated them with cruelty.

Drapetomania could be prevented by beatings, administered if enslaved Africans showed sulkiness or dissatisfaction without obvious cause. Forbidding alcohol, eliminating visits to neighbors at night, and withholding adequate food, shelter, and clothing also were measures taken to prevent drapetomania. According to Cartwright, treating people of African descent like children, using this combination of controls, would reaffirm and support Africans' basically docile and submissive nature and thus effectively cure them from running away. Failure to treat drapetomania adequately might yield another novel disorder identified by Cartwright—*dysaesthesia aethiopis*—characterized by intellectual dullness, refusal to work, proneness to mischief, and unresponsiveness to punishment from overseers.

Although many rationalized African enslavement with similar arguments, there is no evidence that this proposed diagnosis particularly affected mental health theory or practice of the time. In fact, W. A. Sawyer reports that Cartwright's report generated published skepticism from medical colleagues, who rejected his arguments as being informed more by his politics than by science.

Contemporary Views

Twentieth-century social scientists typically cite drapetomania as a classic example of racist pseudoscience. Alexander Thomas and Samuel Sillen notably discussed drapetomania as an early point in a long line of medical justifications of dehumanizing treatment of African Americans through genetic deficiency theories and faulty, self-serving epidemiology.

Thomas Szasz, often credited with drawing modern professional attention to drapetomania, argued that Cartwright's racist nosology highlights the general inappropriateness of applying medical analyses to so-called mental problems. Szasz saw psychiatric labels as simply stigmatizing objectionable behavior of socially marginalized people and justifying societal interventions disguised as medical care. While drapetomania is not a widespread view, some recently have used its example to question the validity of diagnoses like oppositional defiant disorder and attention deficit/hyperactivity disorder.

David Rollock

See also African Americans (v3); Attention Deficit/ Hyperactivity Disorder (v1); Deficit Hypothesis (v3); Discrimination (v3); Discrimination and Oppression (v2); Oppositional Defiant Disorder (v1); Oppression (v3); Prejudice (v3); Racism (v3)

Further Readings

Cartwright, S. A. (1851, May). Report on the diseases and physical peculiarities of the Negro race. *New Orleans Medical and Surgical Journal*, pp. 691–715.

Sawyer, W. A. (1988). Brickell vs. Cartwright: Confrontations in the antebellum medical literature. *Southern Medical Journal, 81*(6), 774–780.

Szasz, T. S. (1971). The sane slave. *American Journal of Psychotherapy, 25*, 228–239.

Thomas, A., & Sillen, S. (1972). *Racism and psychiatry*. New York: Brunner/Mazel.

Empowerment

The term *empowerment* was first used in the mid-17th century. Historically, it has been described as the process of giving power to, or empowering, others. In other words, empowerment may be understood as a way of assisting others to help themselves. In contemporary descriptions of empowerment, the term has become mainstream and well-known, and it is a frequently used term in society. Modern definitions are similar to historical definitions, but modern definitions are broader and include the process of enabling others to gain control and power. Empowerment involves the practice of increasing power—from individuals to large communities—so that individuals and collective groups can take action to improve their situations. This description explains empowerment as a way of enabling people to possess or to delegate power. Empowerment may derive from outside influences, but it is also something that can be generated within a person, which is called *self-empowerment*.

Explanation

History

There are various settings in which empowerment may take place, including in vocational settings. In vocational settings, empowerment may be defined as the process of encouraging and allowing employees to take the initiative to improve the quality and conditions within their work environment. Empowerment also allows workers to improve the operation or the service of the organization with which they are employed. Several forms of empowerment exist, such as individual empowerment, social empowerment, and political empowerment. The commonly referenced examples of empowerment include the civil rights movement in the 1950s and 1960s and the women's movement, which began in the mid-1800s, both of which sought after political empowerment for supporters. Some of the well-known leaders in political empowerment include César Chávez, Mahatma Gandhi, Malcolm X, Nelson Mandela, and Martin Luther King, Jr.

Multicultural Issues

Issues of empowerment are important with regard to multiculturalism, and in particular to oppressed groups and marginalized populations. Empowerment is related to cultural competence as both focus on how groups have experienced issues such as racism and discrimination. Empowerment contributes to change and improvement in the quality of people's lives and also to the improvement of societies. From a social justice perspective, empowerment involves giving people the right to make their own decisions and choices and allowing people to act on those decisions and choices. Empowerment can be generated within individuals to address inequalities in their lives, or it can be generated across communities to help larger groups gain control over their life situations. Empowerment may bring about more choice and freedom for individuals and groups and may lead them to be more involved in organizations and advocacy efforts. Furthermore, empowerment can facilitate gained respect, strong relationships with others, and the sense of connection to a larger community.

Conceptualization of Empowerment

The process of becoming empowered involves more than just gaining access to power. Becoming empowered also involves a change in the way that people think, such that awareness and critical thought occur. Additionally, empowerment is not something that can be forced upon others. If an individual or group attempts to generate empowerment within others, the conditions should be created that facilitate its development; it should not be forced. Empowerment theory explains that empowerment involves the process of changing beliefs and attitudes within the self or among others, which subsequently leads to social change. Empowerment has been described as ecologically embedded and operating within intricate connections among individuals, groups, and community settings. Thus, empowerment is a concept that changes over time and takes on different forms depending on the individual.

Critical Consciousness

An underlying aspect of empowerment theory discusses the development of critical consciousness within those who are attempting to create change in their thinking. Critical consciousness is the process of recognizing oppression and taking action against this recognized oppression. Theories of empowerment explain the development of critical consciousness as involving three psychological processes: group identification, group consciousness, and efficacy. These psychological processes usually occur one after the other, either independently or in conjunction with each other. The first process involves group identification procedures. Group identification is described as the identification of common experiences and concerns, a preference for one's own group, and culture and norms. The second psychological process of critical consciousness involves what is called group consciousness. Group consciousness is the understanding of the discrepancy in status and power among different groups. The third process of critical consciousness is self-efficacy and/or collective efficacy, which refers to the belief in the ability to perform a given task or responsibility. For example, empowerment with regard to efficacy refers to people's perceptions of their capability to generate social change. Critical consciousness is a significant contributor to the development of empowerment because groups and individuals believe in their abilities to create change and will be more likely to be empowered.

Counseling

In counseling, empowerment is viewed as a way in which to concentrate on issues of lack of power, which is also referred to as powerlessness, and to mediate the role that lack of power plays in the formation and maintenance of social problems. Issues of empowerment are often present in counseling, with an emphasis on the clients' beliefs about themselves. This emphasis can generate clients to contribute to change—both the change they want for themselves and the change they want to see in others. This contribution to change is often referred to as community and social change. The role of empowerment in counseling suggests a new way of viewing counseling, as empowerment may also lead to the development of programs and policies that create empowered environments.

In counseling, empowerment is most often conceptualized at the individual level. Individual empowerment may also be known and described as psychological empowerment. Empowerment in counseling settings involves working with clients to make changes that they want to make in their lives. Zimmerman describes three aspects of individual, or psychological, empowerment: intrapersonal, interactional, and behavioral. Intrapersonal is described as how people think about themselves and includes concepts such as self-efficacy and motivation. The interactional component refers to social environments and how people think about and relate to their social environment. The final component, behavioral, relates to the actions that people take to put into effect their influence on the social and political environment. This is accomplished through participation in community organizations and activities. Understanding of these three components is important in counseling relationships because strength in all three components is necessary for people to become empowered.

Terri L. Jashinsky

See also Adventure Therapy (v1); Civil Rights (v3); Counseling Skills Training (v2); Cultural Accommodation and Negotiation (v3); Discrimination (v3); Ethnic Pride (v3); Learned Helplessness (v3); Multicultural Counseling (v3); Multiculturalism (v3); National Association for the Advancement of Colored People (v3); Oppression (v3); Power and Powerlessness (v3); Racial Pride (v3); Social Justice (v3)

Further Readings

Bemak, F., Chi-Ying, R., & Siroskey-Sabdo, L. A. (2005). Empowerment groups for academic success: An innovative approach to prevent high school failure for at-risk, urban African American girls. *Professional School Counseling, 8*(5), 377–389.

Gutierrez, L. M. (1995). Understanding the empowerment process: Does consciousness make a difference? *Social Work Research, 19*(4), 229–237.

Peterson, N. A., Lowe, J. B., Aquilino, M. L., & Schneider, J. E. (2005). Linking social cohesion and gender to intrapersonal and interactional empowerment: Support and new implications for theory. *Journal of Community Psychology, 33*(2), 233–244.

ENCULTURATION

Given the ongoing dramatic racial/ethnic diversification of the United States, the need for counselors to understand the unique cultural backgrounds of their clients presents an important challenge. A useful construct in this effort is enculturation.

Construct Definition and Clarification

In 1948 Melville J. Herskovits first described enculturation as the process of socialization into, and maintenance of, the norms of one's indigenous culture, such as the salient values, ideas, and concepts. It includes learning the cultural characteristics, such as language and traditions and customs, which distinguish the members of one group of people from another.

A term that often is confounded with enculturation is acculturation. The term *acculturation* has been used to describe the process of contact between members of two cultural groups, particularly when groups of people migrate from their countries of origin to other countries. John W. Berry and his colleagues described acculturation as consisting of (a) contact and participation and (b) cultural maintenance. The process of contact and participation is reflected in the extent to which people become involved in other cultural groups or remain primarily among themselves. On the other hand, the process of cultural maintenance is represented in the extent to which cultural identity and characteristics are considered important and maintained.

However, the latter part of the acculturation definition is problematic because it largely overlaps with the definition of *enculturation*. Although the characterization of acculturation in terms of cultural maintenance may work well for migrants who have been socialized into their indigenous cultural norms before arriving in a new country, it may not accurately describe the experiences of all racial/ethnic minority individuals, particularly those who were born in the new country. These persons, particularly individuals who are several generations removed from migration, may never have been fully enculturated into their ethnic group's cultural norms by their parents and family, who also may have been born in the new country. For these persons, the application of cultural maintenance process may be inappropriate because they might never have been completely socialized into their indigenous cultural norms in the first place. In addition, these persons may be socialized to their indigenous cultural heritage more fully later in life and, hence, engage in the process of enculturation during this time. For these reasons, the term *enculturation* better captures the diversity of racial/ethnic minority persons in the United States in terms of their generations since migration and the resultant variability in levels of adherence to the norms of their ancestral cultures, in comparison to the cultural maintenance concept within the acculturation construct.

Hence, *enculturation* is now used to describe the process of (re)socializing into and maintaining the norms of the indigenous culture, whereas *acculturation* is used to describe the process of adapting to the norms of the dominant culture. Within the field of counseling, enculturation (and acculturation) has been used to study clients' help-seeking attitudes and behaviors and their participation in the counseling process.

Construct Dimensions

In describing enculturation, it is also important to consider the dimensions on which the construct can be observed and assessed. Originally, enculturation (and acculturation) had been characterized as involving changes in two personal dimensions: behaviors and values. The behavioral dimension of enculturation includes language use and participation in various cultural activities (e.g., food consumption), whereas the values dimension reflects relational style, person–nature relationships, beliefs about human nature, and time orientation. Definitions of enculturation (and acculturation) have continued to grow progressively more comprehensive and integrative. Currently, enculturation is described in terms of changes at three levels of functioning: behavioral, affective, and cognitive.

In 2001 Bryan S. K. Kim and Jose M. Abreu reviewed the item contents of 33 instruments designed to measure enculturation (and acculturation) and proposed a set of dimensions along the conceptual framework described earlier. Kim and Abreu proposed that enculturation (and acculturation) consists of the following four dimensions: behavior, values, knowledge, and identity. Behavior refers to friendship choice, preferences for television programs and reading, participation in cultural activities, contact with ancestral culture, language use, food choice, and music preference. Along the cognitive level of functioning, Kim and Abreu proposed two dimensions: values and knowledge. The value dimension refers to attitudes and beliefs about social relations, cultural customs, and cultural traditions. The knowledge dimension refers to culturally specific information, such as names of historical leaders in the culture of origin and significance of culturally specific activities. Along the affective level of functioning, Kim and Abreu proposed the inclusion of identity, which refers to attitudes toward one's cultural identification, attitudes toward ancestral groups, and level of comfort toward people of ancestral groups.

Psychological Implications

To understand the psychological experiences of racial/ethnic minority individuals as they engage in the process of enculturation within the context of acculturation to the dominant U.S. cultural norms, it is helpful to consider a model proposed by Berry and his colleagues. These scholars theorized the following four acculturation "attitudes" based on combining either high or low levels of enculturation and acculturation: integration, assimilation, separation, and marginalization. Integration occurs when individuals are proficient in the cultures of both their indigenous group and the dominant group. Hence, people in this status are both highly enculturated and strongly acculturated. Separation occurs when an individual maintains and perpetuates the culture of origin (high enculturation) and does not absorb the culture of the dominant group (low acculturation). Assimilation occurs when an individual absorbs the culture of the dominant group (high acculturation) while rejecting the indigenous culture (low enculturation). Finally, marginalization represents the attitude of an individual with no interest in maintaining or acquiring proficiency in any culture, dominant or indigenous (low acculturation and low enculturation). Marginalization is perhaps the most problematic of the four statuses because marginalized individuals will lack sense of belongingness in either culture.

On the other hand, the integration (or biculturalism) status may be the healthiest status for individuals. The literature on biculturalism suggests that people who can effectively function in both indigenous and dominant cultures may exhibit increased cognitive functioning and better mental health. Described as having bicultural competence, these individuals tend to have high degrees of (a) knowledge of cultural beliefs and values of both cultures, (b) positive attitudes toward both groups, (c) bicultural efficacy, or belief that one can live in a satisfying manner within both cultures without sacrificing one's cultural identity, (d) communication ability in both cultures, (e) role repertoire, or the range of culturally appropriate behaviors, and (f) a sense of being grounded in both cultures.

Future Directions

In the late 1980s a Delphi study was conducted to examine the future prospects for enculturation (and acculturation) as a construct of interest among scholars in counseling. The results revealed a consensus among these experts in predicting that the construct of enculturation (and acculturation) would play an increasingly important role in counseling theory, research, and practice during the 1990s, as the numbers of racial/ethnic minorities in the United States continue to rise rapidly. At the time of this writing, a search of the PsycINFO database using "enculturation" as the keyword yielded 290 citations, with 236 references having the publication date of 1990 or later. Hence, it appears that there is a trend toward an increased focus on enculturation. However, more research work in counseling seems needed for this prediction to be fully realized.

Bryan S. K. Kim and Yong S. Park

See also Acculturation (v3); Assimilation (v3); Barriers to Cross-Cultural Counseling (v3); Bicultural (v3); Cultural

Accommodation and Negotiation (v3); Cultural Values (v3); Culture (v3); Ethnic Identity (v3); Multiculturalism (v3); Orthogonal Cultural Identification Theory (v3); Person–Environment Interactions (v2); Pluralism (v3); Racial Identity (v3); Second Culture Acquisition (v3)

Further Readings

Chun, K. M., Organista, P. B., & Marin, G. (Eds.). (2003). *Acculturation: Advances in theory, measurement, and applied research.* Washington, DC: American Psychological Association.

Hofstede, G. (2001). *Culture's consequences: Comparing values, behaviors, institutions, and organizations across nations* (2nd ed.). Thousand Oaks, CA: Sage.

Kim, B. S. K., & Abreu, J. M. (2001). Acculturation measurement: Theory, current instruments, and future directions. In J. G. Ponterotto, J. M. Casas, L. A. Suzuki, & C. M. Alexander (Eds.), *Handbook of multicultural counseling* (2nd ed., pp. 394–424). Thousand Oaks, CA: Sage.

LaFromboise, T., Coleman, H. L. K., & Gerton, J. (1993). Psychological impact of biculturalism: Evidence and theory. *Psychological Bulletin, 114,* 395–412.

Segall, M. H., Dasen, P. R., Berry, J. W., & Poortinga, Y. H. (1999). *Human behavior in global perspective: An introduction to cross-cultural psychology* (2nd ed.). Boston: Allyn & Bacon.

ESPIRITISMO

Espiritismo is the belief that problems, conceptualized by Western psychologists as being related to mental health issues, are caused by spirits. These spirits can be forced away from the person through interventions offered by a folk healer, the *espiritista*. After the spirits leave, the person returns to mental health.

The core beliefs of espiritismo were developed by Frenchman Allan Kardec. He wrote a book of orations, *Le Livre des Esprits* (The Spirits' Book) that attracted European and Latin American intellectuals. His work was available in Cuba and Puerto Rico by the 1860s. By the 1870s it had had a marked effect on religious practices in the Spanish- and French-speaking Caribbean and Latin America. In Cuba, espiritismo was used as a foundation for the African-derived religious system known as Santería. According to Kardec, espiritismo consists of an invisible world populated by spirits that surround the visible world. The spirits can enter the visible world and attach themselves to human beings. Some of these spirits are presently incarnated as human beings and others are not. In other words, it is the belief that the soul is immortal and that the spirits of dead persons can communicate with incarnated persons or that they may intervene directly in the lives of people.

Spirit mediums, or espiritistas, serve the purpose of communicating between the incarnated spirits and the spirits of the dead. Healing by the espiritistas consists primarily of removing harmful spiritual influences from the person and strengthening positive ones. This is done through a number of interventions: lighting special blessed candles, saying specific prayers, or donating a specified amount of money to a charity.

Similar beliefs and practices are seen in other cultures. An example of a related phenomenon is Arab culture's belief in the *jinn*. Jinn are creatures who are similar to angels but are under the dominion of Satan. Problems described as mental health issues in Western psychology are seen as being caused by jinn. An individual is placed under possession of the jinn either through the black magic incantations of another or by visiting locations where the jinn dwell and failing to ask for God's protection while there.

The diagnostic process for jinn possession is to visit a *sheik,* the cultural equivalent of an espiritista. The sheik reads passages from the Qur'an and closely observes the individual to differentiate between wholesale possession and temporary jinn visitation. Possession is marked by seizure activity during the Qur'an reading and requires a formal exorcism. On the other hand, a temporary visitation by the jinn, marked by twitching fingers during the Holy reading, requires the incantation-specific prayers or drinking a glass of water into which a Qur'anic verse has been placed.

While espiritismo and jinn possession are similar, there are distinct differences. In espiritismo, it is the souls of the departed who are vexing the victim, whereas jinn are supernatural creatures separate from humans. The main similarity lies in conceptualizing mental health concerns on a metaphysical plane and requiring treatment that includes forms of exorcism, prayer, or theistic ritual activity. It is useful for counselors to be familiar with these concepts when engaging in cross-cultural counseling, as these beliefs may impact the clients' expectations toward the counseling process. It is not recommended that counselors naively attempt to include such practices within their counseling practice.

Paul E. Priester, Gregory Benson, and Asma Jana-Masri

See also Barriers to Cross-Cultural Counseling (v3); Cross-Cultural Training (v3); Indigenous Healing (v3); Religion/Religious Belief Systems (v3); Santería (v3); Spirituality (v3); Spirituality and Career Development (v4); Spirituality/Religion (v2)

Further Readings

Al-Ashqar, U. S., & Zarabozo, J. A. (1998). *The world of jinn and devils.* Boulder, CO: Al-Basheer.

Comas-Diaz, L. (1981). Puerto Rican espiritismo and psychotherapy. *American Journal of Orthopsychiatry, 51,* 636–645.

Kardec, A. (2005). *The spirits' book.* New York: Cosimo.

ETHNIC CLEANSING

Ethnic cleansing refers to the implementation of a well-defined policy that aims to establish an ethnically homogenous group in a specific territory or society through the expulsion of an unwanted minority group in a systematic manner. Such a policy may be carried out directly through deportation, forced emigration, or violence, or it may involve the use of more passive forms of coercive action such as harassment or discriminatory legislation. A broader definition of *ethnic cleansing* includes the discrimination of one group against another civilian group, delineated by a demographic variable that extends beyond ethnicity to include other sociocultural divides such as race, religion, national origin, or ideological considerations. Ethnic cleansing of minorities is often motivated by a desire of a particular group to consolidate its power by eliminating the conditions for potential and actual opposition in order to create a political stronghold throughout a region. That is, although causes of ethnic cleansing are mainly rooted in political gain for a particular group, ethnic cleansing is embellished by, and inseparable from, prejudiced attitudes and discriminatory practices on the basis of ethnicity, race, or religion. Each of these forms of discrimination reflects the general tendency for human beings to fear dissimilarity.

Concerted efforts also may be made to remove all physical traces of the expelled group in the territory (e.g., the destruction of civilian infrastructure and cultural sites), thereby effecting radical demographic changes. Because ethnic cleansing is such a brutal tactic intended specifically to create a hostile, if not life-threatening, environment for members of the target group, it is characterized by widespread and flagrant human rights violations.

Included in the broad definition of ethnic cleansing is genocide. Among the most active and aggressive forms of ethnic cleansing, genocide is used to eradicate entire segments of a population, with the implicit or explicit aim of creating cultural, racial, and ethnic homogeneity. In an effort to prevent atrocities similar to the Holocaust of Nazi Germany during World War II, when an estimated 6 million European Jews were tortured and executed, the United Nations passed a resolution in 1948 that recognized genocide as a crime against humanity. This resolution, *The Convention on the Prevention and Punishment of the Crime of Genocide,* defined genocide as any criminal act committed by an individual, group, or government, in time of peace or in time of war, with intent to destroy a national, racial, ethnic, or religious group. These punishable acts include killing members of the target group, causing them serious bodily or mental harm, deliberately inflicting conditions that will bring about the group's physical destruction in whole or in part, imposing measures to prevent births within the group, and forcefully transferring children of the group to other groups.

Examples of ethnic cleansing include the forced displacement of Native Americans by White settlers in North America in the 18th and 19th centuries, the Armenian massacres by the Turks in 1915–1916, the Nazi Holocaust, and the Soviet Union's deportation of certain ethnic minorities from the Caucasus and Crimea during the 1940s. Precipitating events among the recent cases of ethnic cleansing in the late 20th century often include complex regional struggles between different political constituencies that have pushed minorities to the edge of extinction. When ethnic clashes among factions occur, mass rape, sexual torture, and psychological trauma are common. Women and children are particularly vulnerable because many men leave their families and communities to join resistance groups. During the armed conflicts in the former Yugoslavia in the 1990s, for example, the vicious treatment and massacre of ethnic groups was the consequence of belligerent mobs targeting civilians to expel ethnic minorities in the population and hasten military surrender.

Another recent example of ethnic cleansing is the Rwandan genocide in 1994. This example is of particular importance because of the scale of fighting and the rapid speed of the massacre. Within a few months of the start of political and ethnic fighting in Rwanda, waves of violence claimed between 500,000 and 1 million lives, most of them ethnic Tutsis. Another 2 million civilians were forced to abandon their homes.

The violence associated with ethnic hatred in Rwanda has threatened the stability of the region in Africa, with the potential to ignite a wide conflagration throughout the continent. This ripple effect destabilizing the region is most recently evident in the Darfur crisis of ethnic cleansing in western Sudan at the start of the 21st century. Some 200,000 innocent civilians of Darfur have died, and 2.5 million have been displaced since fighting among rebels, the Sudanese army, and a militia of Arab nomads began in early 2003. Many civilians died in refugee camps because they were subject to further attacks. Lack of food, water, and medicine has also led to mass starvation and disease epidemics. Although the Darfur atrocities have drawn widespread condemnation, the international community remains slow or ineffective in stopping the violence that continues at the time of this writing. As in the past, the degree and pace of responses to ethnic cleansing in Darfur at the international level hinge largely on the calculation of perceived interest and the actual costs of intervention and enforcement within the diversity of the international society. Although the long-term effects of such destructive atrocities are not known, it is evident that practices of ethnic cleansing are comprehensively toxic.

Experiences and Needs of Ethnic Cleansing Survivors

Survivors of ethnic cleansing may be at heightened risk for developing physical and mental health problems. They may experience psychological traumatization subsequent to the violence committed against them through the development of symptom patterns that are subsumed under the diagnosis of post-traumatic stress disorder (PTSD) in the American Psychiatric Association's *Diagnostic and Statistical Manual of Mental Disorders*. Symptoms of PTSD are common among refugees when they have been the victims of, or have witnessed, torture, rape, and other horrific events.

The severity of these symptoms, however, differs widely from individual to individual and also depends on the type, duration, and nature of the trauma experienced. Although the concept of PTSD may serve as a useful tool for understanding victims of psychological traumatization, PTSD is not necessarily a universal response to traumatic stress. That is, trauma as experienced by refugee youth and families may be moderated by personal, contextual, and cultural factors.

When ethnic cleansing occurs, the prolonged armed conflict displaces many civilians, and many of them seek refuge outside their countries to escape political turmoil as well as religious, racial, or political persecution. During the internal political upheavals in their countries in the 1970s and 1980s, for example, large scales of refugees from Latin America slipped across the international border into the United States.

When ethnic cleansing survivors are forced to abandon their homelands, the horror they endured may end when they successfully take shelter outside their country, but the stress they experience may not subside; rather, it may manifest in a different form. As war refugees, they have been uprooted from their familiar social and cultural milieu, which, combined with their exposure to violence, can have severe negative impacts on their health and well-being. Similar to other groups of immigrants, war refugees in a foreign country also face obstacles, such as linguistic constraints and cultural differences, in their adjustment process. The process is further complicated by the cumulative effects of resettlement, familial separation, and previous exposure to the violent, abusive, and dehumanizing world of war. These myriad potential counseling issues, combined with clinical manifestations characteristic of PTSD, create a unique challenge for counseling professionals working with survivors of ethnic cleansing. War refugees may suffer the psychological impact of separation from family and friends. The psychosocial impact of relocation and the disruption of a social support system may lead to loss of self-identification, social isolation, and loss of the sense of security. Such family disintegration disrupts the protective function of a social network that can mitigate the psychological effects of trauma and distress among individuals—children in particular. When children experience the violent death of, or separation from, parents during a war, severe grief, sleep disorders, depression, intense fears, feelings of vulnerability, and other emotional problems are common. Such difficulties faced by refugee children may be exacerbated by the inability of their surviving family members, who may suffer psychological distress themselves as well, to respond to the emotional and psychological needs of the children.

For refugee youth, their ability to cope with traumatic life events is further complicated by stress in relation to relocation, educational pursuits, and their identity development. In the United States, for example, it is the age, rather than academic background, of refugee children that determines their grade placement in schools. Young refugee children may thus be apt to quickly learn the new language and adjust to the new culture, whereas refugee adolescents may find resettlement a more daunting task due, in part, to inadequate education, lack of family support and community resources, and significant linguistic and cultural differences. Some may eventually develop behavior problems (e.g., aggression, vandalism), drop out of school, or run away from home.

Counseling Implications

Counseling professionals working with ethnic cleansing survivors need to design interventions that achieve a high level of social and cultural specificity. Effective interventions assist refugee youth and families as they negotiate profound social, cultural, economic, familial, and psychological transitions. These considerations underscore the importance of a systemic approach that examines the interplay between trauma and distress as related to political violence and forced migration, as well as the transitions associated with life in a foreign country. This perspective also necessitates the need to locate the refugee's experiences within multiple social spaces, including that of life before war, wartime, and within multiple systems, including families, neighborhoods, schools, villages, and service institutions.

Specifically, in designing intervention strategies, counseling professionals must keep in mind a number of overarching principles. First, attention needs to be given to the importance of cultural variables, as well as individual resilience, that moderate the effects of traumatic experiences. Because the severity of symptoms of ethnic cleansing survivors differs widely from individual to individual and from time to time, many survivors experience mild or occasional symptoms that do not interfere with their daily functioning. Second, consistent with the hierarchy of human needs, any intervention should address basic human needs (e.g., food, water, shelter, and security) first, followed by psychological needs (e.g., belongingness and personal identity). Creation of a stable structure, physical and psychological, proves advantageous for survivors because of the lack-of-control and general disruption characteristics of experiencing such comprehensive physical and psychological displacement. Third, survivors of ethnic cleansing may experience survivor's guilt, that is, the guilt of being one of the few who successfully escape from dangerous situations. They may have no information about the whereabouts of their family, relatives, and friends left behind. As they struggle to rebuild their life, the feeling of survivor's guilt may interfere with a survivor's process of recovery from psychological trauma. Counseling professionals must strike a balance between helping their clients reconstruct their traumatic story and supporting them to go through the grieving process at their own pace. Group counseling as a treatment modality may be particularly effective in providing the therapeutic power of universality and instillation of hope necessary for ethnic cleansing survivors to restore their social bonds with others and their connections with ordinary life.

Eric C. Chen

See also American Indians (v3); Antisemitism (v3); Bias (v3); Cross-Cultural Psychology (v2); Cultural Encapsulation (v3); Cultural Mistrust (v3); Discrimination (v3); Discrimination and Oppression (v2); Ethnicity (v3); Ethnocentrism (v3); Nationalism (v3); Oppression (v3); Posttraumatic Stress Disorder (v2); Prejudice (v3); Racism (v3); Refugees (v3); Secondary Trauma (v2); Stereotype (v3); Xenophobia (v3)

Further Readings

American Psychiatric Association. (2000). *Diagnostic and statistical manual of mental disorders* (4th ed., Text rev.). Washington, DC: Author.

Chen, E. C., & Park-Taylor, J. (2006). Intersection of racism and immigration: Implications for educational and counseling practice. In M. G. Constantine & D. W. Sue (Eds.), *Addressing racism: Facilitating cultural competence in mental health and educational settings* (pp. 43–64). New York: Wiley.

Ehrenreich, J. H. (2003). Understanding PTSD: Forgetting "trauma." *Journal of Social Issues, 3,* 15–28.

Herman, J. L. (1992). *Trauma and recovery.* New York: Basic Books.

Nicholl, C., & Thompson, A. (2004). The psychological treatment of post-traumatic stress disorder (PTSD) in adult refugees: A review of the current state of psychological therapies. *Journal of Mental Health, 13,* 351–362.

Shannon, V. P. (2005). Judge and executioner: The politics of responding to ethnic cleansing in the Balkans. *Journal of Genocide Research, 7,* 47–66.

United Nations. (1999, September). *Reports of the Secretary-General to the security council on the protection of civilians in armed conflict.* New York: Author.

United Nations. (2001, March). *Reports of the Secretary-General to the security council on the protection of civilians in armed conflict.* New York: Author.

Weine, S. M., Becker, D. F., Vojvoda, D., Hodzic, E., Sawyer, M., Hyman, L., et al. (1998). Individual change after genocide in Bosnian survivors of "ethnic cleansing": Assessing personality dysfunction. *Journal of Traumatic Stress, 11,* 147–152.

Ethnic Identity

Ethnic identity, broadly defined, is a dynamic and multidimensional construct that represents the part of one's self-concept that is derived from a sense of belonging and commitment to a particular ethnic group. Other key components of ethnic identity include self-identification, the importance of ethnicity in one's life, ethnic group affiliation, positive feelings and attitudes toward one's ethnic group, and the belief that others view one's ethnic group favorably. Ethnic identity also is manifest in a shared sense of identity, values, attitudes, heritage, and lineage with other members of the ethnic group, as well as in individual and collective engagement in the language, customs, and traditions of the ethnic group.

Historical Perspectives

The conceptualization and operationalization of ethnic identity have undergone numerous changes over the years. Historically, ethnic identity was defined according to membership in a given ethnic group, whether ascribed by the individual or by others. Early definitions also focused heavily on ethnic group preferences and attitudes. For example, the famous doll studies by Kenneth B. Clark and Mamie P. Clark in the late 1940s revealed that African American girls were more likely to assign positive attributes to white dolls, not black dolls. However, early methods of studying ethnic identity often conflated notions of ethnicity and ethnic identity, privileged the opinion of others over the individual, and conceptualized ethnic identity as a relatively static construct. The dynamic process of ethnic identity development and its multidimensional nature were largely overlooked.

Ethnic identity is now conceptualized within the framework of Henri Tajfel's social identity theory, which postulates that people have an innate need to belong, and identification with a group contributes to a positive overall self-concept and sense of well-being. But, as the Clark and Clark doll studies revealed, membership in a devalued ethnic group can lead people to distance themselves from their ethnic group or to report a greater preference for the dominant group. An alternative strategy when excluded or threatened by another group is for people to identify more strongly with their ethnic group, develop a sense of ethnic pride, and emphasize the distinctiveness of their own group. This perspective of ethnic identity places a greater emphasis on personal agency and a subjective sense of self, as well as psychological and emotional affiliation with an ethnic group.

There remains an ongoing debate over the similarities and differences between ethnic identity and racial identity. Although the two constructs share much in common (e.g., both ethnic identity and racial identity are types of social identities), racial identity is believed to emerge based on experiences with racism and oppression due to phenotypic differences, such as skin color or facial features. Ethnic identity, by contrast, is believed to develop from a more basic need to belong and identify with similar others. Although prejudices and cultural pressures are significant in understanding ethnic identity, the primary emphasis is not on oppression and sociopolitical stratification as it is in the case of racial identity.

Various developmental models have emerged to explain the formation of ethnic identity. In general, these models propose that one's ethnic identity initially starts as an unexamined aspect of one's self that eventually becomes examined. The individual subsequently goes through a period of exploration of and immersion into the group's beliefs, traditions, and behaviors until the process concludes with ethnic identity achievement and clarity. One problem with these stage models, however, is that they imply that individuals go through a fairly predictable trajectory of ethnic identity development. It is more likely the case that people cycle through these different aspects of identity negotiation depending on personal circumstances and the social context.

More recently, a multidimensional perspective of ethnic identity has emerged, which challenges the idea of ethnic identity as a single, unitary construct. Most scholars agree that ethnic identity includes cognitive, affective, and behavioral components, including self-identification, salience and centrality of ethnicity in one's life, a sense of belonging and affiliation, private regard (e.g., positive affect toward one's group), public regard (e.g., perceived favorability of one's group), and interest and participation in ethnic-specific activities. It is thought that these different aspects of ethnic identity are accessible, salient, or central to the individual based on the moment or situation. Thus, the nature and manifestation of ethnic identity can be viewed as context dependent. For example, a person may suddenly develop strong ethnic group pride with the public success of another ethnic group member. Furthermore, specific aspects of ethnic identity may have unique or differential effects on the psychological functioning of individuals, depending on the circumstances. Pride in one's ethnic group, for instance, tends to be related to self-esteem, but it may be associated with lower self-esteem when a person experiences greater discrimination because of individual sensitivity to rejection.

Influences on Ethnic Identity

Prominent variables influencing ethnic identity include ethnic socialization, acculturation, and discrimination. Parents play a particularly important role in children's ethnic identity development through engaging in ethnic socialization—a process of teaching children about their ethnicity and the experiences they may have with the broader society because of their ethnic group membership. For example, immigrant parents may speak to children in their native language, eat ethnic-specific foods, celebrate cultural holidays and traditions, and socialize with other ethnic group members. Moreover, parents may make an earnest effort to teach the history and to instill the values of their culture to their children. These direct and indirect ethnic socialization experiences gradually become internalized by children and help to shape their ethnic identities.

For those individuals who belong to an ethnic group within a larger, ethnically diverse society, acculturation processes also impact ethnic identity. Acculturation refers to a process of change in one's cultural attitudes, values, and behaviors that result from contact with another culture or society. Level of acculturation, in turn, is believed to affect how individuals relate to their own group as a subgroup of the larger society, thereby influencing quality and degree of ethnic identification. A unidimensional model of acculturation proposes that ethnic group identification is inversely related to adaptation to the mainstream culture. To illustrate, a Mexican immigrant to the United States who retains a strong sense of ethnic identity as a Mexican would have weak ties to American culture in this model; on the other hand, high levels of acculturation to American culture would be associated with a weakened ethnic identity as a Mexican. By contrast, a bidimensional model of acculturation proposes that identification with one's traditional or ethnic culture is independent of one's identification with the other culture, allowing for biculturalism—identification and awareness of oneself as a member of multiple ethnic or cultural groups. Both models have received empirical support, although there is increasing evidence in support of the bidimensional model. The implication of each model is that the development of ethnic identity does not necessarily occur in cultural isolation.

The association between ethnic identity and discrimination or bias against one's ethnic group is a complex one. On the one hand, when confronted with discrimination, people may increase or decrease their level of ethnic identification to maintain a positive self-concept and well-being. On the other hand, ethnic identity affects perceptions of discrimination or victimization as well. Some scholars have found that a stronger ethnic identity heightens sensitivity to personal discrimination, whereas others have found that individuals are motivated to minimize perceptions of bias against one's ethnic group, possibly to preserve a positive self-concept and well-being. This bidirectional association between ethnic identity and discrimination highlights the dynamic social processes that underlie issues of ethnicity and race.

Future Directions

The concept of ethnic identity has been of increasing interest to counseling research and theory, particularly for how it relates to psychological functioning and interpersonal relationships. The different perspectives of ethnic identity (e.g., ethnic identity as a unitary vs. multidimensional construct, or as a static state vs. a multistage developmental process) lend to the challenge of understanding how ethnic identity relates to such issues of psychological functioning as self-esteem, well-being, or mental illness. Future efforts to uncover the exact mechanisms through which ethnic identity affects psychological adjustment will allow for the better integration and utilization of ethnic identity in clinical interventions and in prevention strategies promoting optimal development.

Alisia G. T. T. Tran and Richard M. Lee

See also Acculturation (v3); Bias (v3); Black Racial Identity Development (v3); Clark, Kenneth Bancroft (v3); Discrimination (v3); Enculturation (v3); Ethnicity (v3); Ethnic Pride (v3); Identity (v3); Identity Development (v3); Racial Identity (v3); Self-Esteem (v2); Social Identity Theory (v3); White Racial Identity Development (v3)

Further Readings

Ashmore, R. D., Deaux, K., & McLaughlin-Volpe, T. (2004). An organizing framework for collective identity: Articulation and significance of multidimensionality. *Psychological Bulletin, 30*(1), 80–114.

Clark, K. P., & Clark, M. P. (1947). Racial identification and preference in Negro children. In T. M. Newcomb & E. L. Hartley (Eds.), *Readings in social psychology* (pp. 169–178). New York: Henry Holt.

Helms, J. E. (1995). An update of Helms' White and people of color racial identity models. In J. G. Ponterotto, J. M. Casas, & L. A. Suzuki (Eds.), *Handbook of multicultural counseling* (pp. 181–191). Thousand Oaks, CA: Sage.

Phinney, J. S. (1990). Ethnic identity in adolescents and adults: Review of research. *Psychological Bulletin, 108*(3), 499–514.

Tajfel, H. (1978). *Social identity and intergroup relations.* Cambridge, UK: Cambridge University Press.

ETHNICITY

Ethnicity refers to a social group category defined by the shared historical, national, social, political, and cultural heritage of a people. Ethnicity includes a reference to shared ancestry, language, customs, traditions, and similar physical characteristics among a group of people. In addition, ethnicity tends to be informed by the social group's particular geographic area. For example, in the United States, an individual may be racially classified as Black because he or she is associated with the social, political, and economic experiences, in addition to similar physical characteristics, of that social group, but be ethnically classified as Jamaican because he or she shares the historical, national, social, political, and cultural heritage with others from the Caribbean country of Jamaica. Ethnicity is assumed to have broad implications for how individuals understand themselves and experience the world around them. Therefore, ethnicity is thought to shape individuals' experiences of psychological well-being.

Given the connection between ethnicity, culture, and psychological well-being, ethnicity is a significant variable to explore in cross-cultural counseling situations. Social group categories provide reservoirs for meaning and context for individual and shared group experiences. Therefore, knowing an individual's ethnicity can provide a counselor with a framework for understanding the individual from a particular cultural perspective.

Race Versus Ethnicity

Race and ethnicity are often, erroneously, used interchangeably in public discourse and in scholarly and research literature. Oftentimes in the United States, ethnicity is used as a euphemism for race because the former tends to connote a more positive conception than race, which tends to be a politically charged construct. However, to be precise, race and ethnicity, though interrelated, are distinct constructs. Ethnicity is informed by an individual's race but represents a specific aspect of his or her cultural experience. Whereas race represents a limited number of social groups (e.g., Black, White, or Asian) based upon the varying social, political, and economic needs of society, ethnicity represents a larger number of specific and unique social groups (e.g., Haitian, Irish, or Japanese) based upon the historical culture of a people.

When considering culture, one must take into account the values, customs, traditions, attitudes, social norms, and patterns of interaction of a people. Given the complexity and array of the components of culture, considering broad racial categories only restricts the nuanced experiences of said culture. Therefore, ethnicity allows for greater distinction within broad racial categories such that significant but subtle differences between various subgroups are recognized. Consider the racial group Asian, which encompasses individuals representing more than 25 different ethnic groups with distinct social, political, and economic histories. With this vast array of ethnicities, knowing that someone is Asian provides very little information when compared with knowing that someone is Vietnamese, Cambodian, Chinese, or Pakistani.

Identity

Even though ethnicity allows for greater distinction among groups of people, counselors must also remain aware of within-group differences among members of ethnicities. Counselors consider how the individual understands his or her own ethnicity in relation to his or her sense of self. Ethnic identity is one way to think about those within-group differences. Whereas *ethnicity* refers to the social group category, *ethnic identity* refers to an individual's sense of belongingness or connection to his or her ethnic group. In this sense, ethnic identity includes the degree to which an individual adheres to the attitudes and values, upholds the customs and traditions, and perceives the world from a perspective that is consistent with his or her ethnicity. This means that a Jamaican person who espouses attitudes and values, participates in cultural activities, and experiences the world in a manner that is consistent with other Jamaicans is said to have a positive ethnic identity as Jamaican. This may be contrasted against a Jamaican individual who does not participate in Jamaican cultural activities, perhaps espouses attitudes and values that differ from those of other Jamaicans, and experiences the world in a manner that is inconsistent with other Jamaicans—this individual can be described as having a less positive ethnic identity.

Furthermore, it is assumed that ethnic identity has implications for self-esteem in that an individual's affiliation with a particular group influences the degree to which he or she may incorporate aspects of that group identity into his or her self-concept. Consequently, if an individual has a strong sense of connection with a social group he or she is more likely to incorporate the positive and negative characteristics associated with that group into his or her personal identity. Using the Jamaican example, if the individual has a strong Jamaican identity, then it is highly likely that the group concept and esteem of that ethnicity will have an influence on his or her personal concept and esteem.

In the context of the United States, considering an individual's specific ethnicity, the social and political history and current status of that group, and the individual's immigration status has implications for the relevance of ethnicity for a person. It also has influence on the sense of esteem associated with an ethnicity. For example, the social status of an individual's ethnicity may be different in the United States than in his or her home culture, which may have implications for the individual's ethnic identity. Therefore, in addition to being aware of a client's ethnicity, counselors should also consider the individual's level of ethnic identity. The processes of enculturation and acculturation are useful concepts to explore when considering ethnicity in the counseling relationship.

Enculturation and Acculturation

No culture exists in isolation from others. This is most evident in the United States for racial and ethnic groups where multiple groups live parallel in a broader societal context. The constructs of enculturation and acculturation describe the processes that allow cultures to remain distinct while simultaneously existing in the context of other cultures.

Enculturation and acculturation are processes that explain the degree to which ethnicities retain, or relinquish, aspects of their culture when they are located in the context of a broader culture. Specifically, *enculturation* refers to the process through which members of an ethnicity learn about, and come to appreciate, the various aspects of their culture, including values, customs, traditions, attitudes, social norms, and patterns of interaction. *Acculturation* refers to the process through which members of an ethnicity learn about the differences between, and boundaries around, aspects of their culture and those of the broader, host culture.

Enculturation and acculturation are dynamic, adaptive processes that have a profound influence on ethnic groups and their individual members. This is to say that the degree of enculturation and acculturation for different ethnicities may be different depending on several factors, including (a) immigration status (i.e., personal choice or refugee status), (b) intensity of cultural exposure (i.e., degree/type of ethnic socialization to home or host culture), (c) experiences with prejudice and discrimination, and (d) the numerical balance between the home culture and the host culture. Counselors are encouraged to consider each of these factors as an influence on an individual's ethnic identity. This is to say that there are likely many within-group differences for individual members of an ethnicity based upon these factors that may be masked if one were to only look at the ethnic group broadly.

Implications for Counseling

There is an extensive literature in the counseling field examining ethnicity and (a) individual psychological health, (b) its influence on the counseling relationship, (c) processes affecting identity development, (d) an individual's experience with discrimination, (e) relevant counseling issues for specific ethnicities, and (f) relevant counseling interventions for specific ethnicities. Generally speaking, researchers and counselors agree that knowledge of a client's ethnicity, among other aspects of his or her cultural background, is critical in providing effective and ethical counseling services. Competent and effective counselors should always consider these aspects of their own and their clients' backgrounds. Ethnicity and, subsequently, ethnic identity are integral aspects of individuals' life experiences and their psychological well-being. In providing counseling services, counselors must strive to find a balance between knowledge of a client's ethnicity, understanding the relevance of his or her ethnicity, and considering other important individual aspects of the client.

M. Nicole Coleman

See also Acculturation (v3); Bicultural (v3); Cross-Cultural Psychology (v3); Cultural Values (v3); Culture (v3); Demographics, United States (v3); Ethnic Identity (v3); Ethnic Pride (v3); Identity (v3); Orthogonal Cultural Identification Theory (v3); Race (v3); Racial Identity (v3); Racial Pride (v3)

Further Readings

Berry, J. W. (1993). Ethnic identity in plural societies. In M. E. Bernal & G. P. Knight (Eds.), *Ethnic identity: Formation and transmission among Hispanics and other minorities* (pp. 271–296). Albany: State University of New York Press.

Helms, J. E., & Talleyrand, R. (1997). Race is not ethnicity. *American Psychologist, 52*, 1246–1247.

McGoldrick, M., Giordano, J., & Garcia-Preto, N. (2005). *Ethnicity and family therapy* (3rd ed.). New York: Guilford Press.

Phinney, J. S. (1996). When we talk about American ethnic groups, what do we mean? *American Psychologist, 51*, 918–927.

Ponterotto, J. G., Casas, J. M., Suzuki, L. A., & Alexander, C. M. (Eds.). (1999). *Handbook of multicultural counseling.* Thousand Oaks, CA: Sage.

Sue, D. W., & Sue, D. (2002). *Counseling the culturally diverse* (4th ed.). New York: Wiley.

Tajfel, H., & Turner, J. C. (1986). The social identity theory of intergroup behavior. In S. Worchel & W. Austin (Eds.), *Psychology of intergroup relations* (pp. 7–24). Chicago: Nelson-Hall.

ETHNIC MINORITY

The term *ethnic minority* is used to describe an individual who belongs to an ethnic group that is marginalized by society because of social and cultural characteristics that are different from, or devalued by, the dominant ethnic or cultural group. In the United States in 2007, Americans of European descent are considered the dominant ethnic group, or ethnic majority, and all others are considered ethnic minority groups. Examples of the major ethnic minority groups in the United States include African Americans, Hispanic/Latino/a Americans, Asian Americans, Pacific Islanders, American Indians, Alaska Natives, and Arab Americans. Ethnic minority groups in the United States can be further defined by country of origin, with individuals identifying solely as a member of their country of origin (e.g., someone who identifies as "Mexican" or "Chinese") or individuals identifying with both the country of origin and the United States (i.e., someone who identifies as "Filipino American" or "Jamaican American"). Members of immigrant countries may also identify solely as "American" and dissociate with their country of origin altogether.

To fully understand who is an ethnic minority, it is necessary to elaborate on the terms *ethnic* and *minority*. An ethnic group includes people who share common characteristics, which may include race, country of origin, language, religion, customs, beliefs, and values. These common characteristics are typically transferred through successive generations, and ethnic characteristics take on different meanings through and within each generation. Although ethnic categorizations exist, it is virtually impossible to correctly label every ethnic group present in the United States. This is due primarily to the great heterogeneity within and among ethnic groups, such as differences in regions, customs, generations, and languages/dialects. For example, although Korean American persons may identify as part of the same group, they may differ based on regions (e.g., those whose heritage is from North Korea may differ from those from South Korea), customs (e.g., subgroups may participate in different traditions or practices), generations (e.g., immigrants may hold different values than second-generation Korean Americans), and language (e.g., some members may speak Korean only, others may speak English only, and others may speak both).

The meaning of ethnicity has evolved since the founding of the United States. In line with the voluntary and involuntary immigration of people to the United States, the term *ethnic* was used primarily as a descriptor to identify people who were of non–Anglo-Saxon Protestant descent. In this regard, ethnic was used to describe racial, religious, country-of-origin, and language differences. At different points in the history of the United States, the term *ethnic minority* was attributed to religious minorities (e.g., Catholics and Jews), as well as non–Anglo-Saxon Americans (e.g., Irish and Italians). Throughout time, these European American immigrant groups, which previously may have been considered "ethnic minorities," assimilated to the dominant culture's way of life. These groups may have assimilated primarily because they recognized that belonging to the White racial group afforded them power and privileges. Additionally, with the immigration of Hispanic/Latinos/as and Asians, as well as with civil rights for African Americans, it became evident that Americans of European descent held the power and privilege, and all others were less valued and oppressed.

The word *minority* is taken from the Latin term *minor,* meaning "smaller." When used literally, within the context of a societal or social setting, the term *minority* means "the smaller group as compared to a larger group." In its current usage, the term *minority* is commonly understood as a descriptor of social status assigned to the subordinate groups in a given society or culture, without necessarily connoting smaller population sizes. Majority groups are those that hold the power and have privileges in a given society, and minority groups are those that are negatively affected by an unequal power distribution. Minority groups can be based on race, gender, sexual orientation, ability, religion, and ethnicity, among other group membership characteristics. For example, women would be considered the gender minority group, gays/lesbians/bisexuals would be considered sexual minority groups, and non-Christians (e.g., Jews, Muslims, and atheists) would be considered religious minority groups.

In the present-day United States, *ethnic minority* is used primarily as a label for people who self-identify or are identified as belonging to an ethnic group of non-European descent. Although not necessarily a numerical minority in many areas of the country, a defining characteristic of an ethnic minority is the prejudice, discrimination, and ethnic injustices to which these groups are subject. These ethnic injustices are pervasive and include historical, institutional, and individual discrimination that is based on one's ethnicity (e.g., Japanese American internment during World War II, poor working conditions and wages for Mexican and Filipino farmworkers in California, discriminatory treatment toward Caribbean domestic workers). Ethnic injustices should not be confused with racial injustices, which include historical, institutional, and individual discrimination that is based on race (e.g., slavery, racial segregation, racial microaggressions or hate crimes against Asians or Blacks). Although laws have been enacted to protect American citizens against discrimination based on ethnicity, ethnic minorities are presently not proportionately represented in most spheres of American society. The power structure of the United States favors ethnic groups of European descent, as exemplified through media, education, government, politics, and economics.

The term *ethnic minority* may have both positive and negative implications. Some scholars have rejected the term because the word *minority* may have a connotation of being "minor," less than, or objectified, whereas *majority* has the connotation of being "major," superior, or most important. By identifying in this way, ethnic minority individuals may indicate that they subconsciously or unconsciously view themselves as inferior or subordinate to the European American majority group, while European American majority individuals may confer that they are of the superior, dominant group.

Some scholars prefer the term *ethnic minority* because it is inclusive of all racial and cultural minorities. For example, in the U.S. Census, Hispanic/Latinos/as are not considered a racial group. Instead, they are identified as an ethnic group and are divided racially into two groups: White Hispanics and non-White Hispanics. However, because Latinos/as (both White and Black) have experienced histories of oppression and discrimination, their experiences would parallel other ethnic minority groups. So although not all

Latinos/as would be considered racial minorities, all may be defined as ethnic minorities. Accordingly, the term *ethnic minority* is an inclusive term to accept people of all marginalized ethnicities, regardless of their racial group.

Because of these implications, there are substitute terms that might be used alternatively with *ethnic minority*. *People of color* is a term that was used to differentiate from the subordinate implications of *minority*. Individuals may also use this term as an empowering way to take back the racially charged term *colored people* that was used to segregate African Americans before the civil rights movement. Because *people of color* was a term that was coined by individuals of ethnic minority groups, it is a term that ethnic minority individuals may feel more connected to, in comparison with most racial and ethnic identifiers (e.g., American Indian, Hispanic, Filipino) that were given by the groups' oppressors or colonizers. Using *people of color* would be similar to how some groups empower themselves by using identifiers that were created by members of their own groups (e.g., Native, Latino/a, or Pilipino).

Some negative implications of the term *people of color* include that it pits these people of color against Whites, acknowledging implicitly that Whites are the standard and that people of color are the "other." Additionally, individuals of ethnic minority groups with light skin color (e.g., some Hispanic/Latinos/as and some Asians) may not feel comfortable or connected with identifying as a person of color, because of physical skin color differences. *Racial minority* is a term that is used in the same manner as *ethnic minority*, to signify those racial groups that have been oppressed by the dominant group. However, the term may still hold an undertone of subjugation or inferiority and may not be inclusive to all ethnic groups. Finally, sometimes the term *racial/ethnic minority* is used to be inclusive of oppressed racial and ethnic groups.

Identity and terminology may have several implications in counseling. First, a counselor should be aware of the various ways that a client may identify both racially and ethnically. A person's racial identity includes the ways that a person identifies with his or her racial group (e.g., Black, Asian), and a person's ethnic identity includes the way that a person identifies with his or her ethnic group (e.g., Haitian American, Vietnamese American). An ethnic minority client may identify as both a racial and ethnic minority or may not identify as either. Accordingly, a counselor must take into consideration that a client's racial and ethnic identities may affect her or his worldview, which may influence a counseling relationship.

Counselors should also be knowledgeable of both visible and invisible ethnic minority groups. Some ethnic minority groups are "visible," or identifiable, in that upon first look a counselor may be able to identify their racial group; these groups may include African Americans, Asian Americans, and darker-skinned Hispanic/Latino/a groups. Yet there may be other ethnic minority groups that may not be easily visible or identifiable; these groups include light-skinned Hispanic/Latino/a groups, multiracial persons, and Native Americans. Individuals from these invisible minority groups may identify strongly as an ethnic minority, but their ethnic identity may be ignored because of their physical appearances.

Kevin L. Nadal and David P. Rivera

See also Affirmative Action (v3); African Americans (v3); Alaska Natives (v3); American Indians (v3); Arab Americans (v3); Asian Americans (v3); Classism (v3); Diversity Issues in Career Development (v4); Ethnic Identity (v3); Eurocentrism (v3); Identity (v3); Latinos (v3); Multiracial Families (v3); Pacific Islanders (v3); Racial Identity (v3); Social Class (v4); Society for the Psychological Study of Ethnic Minority Issues (v3); Visible Racial/Ethnic Groups (v3)

Further Readings

Franklin, J. H. (1971). Ethnicity in American life: The historical perspective. In J. H. Franklin, T. F. Pettigrew, & R. W. Mack (Eds.), *Ethnicity in American life* (pp. 9–21). New York: Anti-Defamation League of B'nai B'rith.

Phinney, J. S. (1996). When we talk about American ethnic groups, what do we mean? *American Psychologist, 51*(9), 918–927.

Sue, S. (1991). Ethnicity and culture in psychological research and practice. In J. Goodchilds (Ed.), *Psychological perspectives on human diversity in America* (pp. 51–85). Washington, DC: American Psychological Association.

ETHNIC PRIDE

Ethnic pride is a positive feeling of being a member of one or more ethnic groups. As a component of ethnic identity, ethnic pride includes an appreciation and understanding of one's culture and history. Ethnic pride does not involve being arrogant, racist, or ethnocentric. Instead, ethnic pride, or pride in general, can be considered a source of self-respect and dignity. Ethnocentrism and racism, on the other hand, refer to discriminating against people because of their ethnicity and believing in the superiority of one ethnic group over another ethnic group.

For some individuals and cultures, having a high degree of ethnic pride is discouraged, and acculturation and assimilation are instead emphasized. However, ethnic pride and acculturation (or assimilation) are not mutually exclusive concepts. For example, it is possible for someone to have a high (or low) level of ethnic pride and also be more (or less) acculturated to mainstream American society. In some cultures, such as the Latino/a, African American, and Native Hawaiian cultures, there is a growing movement to embrace and be proud of one's ethnicity and culture.

Ethnic pride can be increased through activities that promote empowerment and a positive feeling toward one's ethnic group. This may be accomplished through exposure to ethnic role models, reading books, watching movies, traveling, eating ethnic foods, listening to music, and dancing.

Ethnic pride has been examined in relation to various health and academic outcomes. In general, however, there is a relative dearth of information in this area, and additional research is needed. Overall, these studies have found that high levels of ethnic pride are associated with a greater knowledge of health risks and less favorable attitudes toward smoking; among African American fourth graders, high levels of ethnic pride are associated with high academic achievement scores in school and standardized tests. Other research has found that high levels of ethnic pride are associated with less drug use and exposure among African American, Mexican American, and mixed ethnicity students, while high levels of ethnic pride are associated with more drug use among White students. In sum, these studies point to the important role of ethnic pride in physical, psychological, and academic outcomes.

Lisa A. P. Sanchez-Johnsen

See also Acculturation (v3); Afrocentricity/Afrocentrism (v3); Assimilation (v3); Enculturation (v3); Ethnic Identity (v3); Ethnocentrism (v3); Identity (v3); Psychological Well-Being, Dimensions of (v2); Racial Identity (v3); Racial Pride (v3); Racism (v3)

Further Readings

Ma, G. X., Shive, S. E., Tan, Y., Toubbeh, J. I., Fang, C. Y., & Edwards, R. L. (2005). Tobacco use, secondhand smoke exposure and their related knowledge, attitudes and behaviors among Asian Americans. *Addictive Behaviors, 30*(4), 725–740.

Marsiglia, F. F., Kulis, S., & Hecht, M. L. (2001). Ethnic label and ethnic identity as predictors of drug use among middle school students in the southwest. *Journal of Research on Adolescence, 11*(1), 21–48.

Phinney, J. (1992). The Multi-Group Ethnic Identity Measure: A new scale for use with adolescents and young adults from diverse groups. *Journal of Adolescent Research, 7,* 156–176.

Smith, E. P., Atkins, J., & Connell, C. M. (2003). Family, school and community factors and relationships to racial-ethnic attitudes and academic achievement. *American Journal of Community Psychology, 32*(1/2), 159–173.

Vazquez, C. I. (2004). *Parenting with pride—Latino style.* New York: Rayo.

ETHNOCENTRISM

The revolutionary climate of the 1960s within U.S. society challenged the existing boundaries of civil rights to include racial/ethnic minorities. Concurrently, an emergence of leading racial/ethnic minority scholars in counseling and psychology set the stage for the extensive examination of the influence of individuals' cultural backgrounds (i.e., values, attitudes, shared history, customs, race, habits, social rules of behavior, social status, perceptions of locus of control and responsibility) on psychological development and treatment process and outcomes in counseling relationships.

Culture was perceived as the lens through which individuals viewed and interpreted the world, and a growing number of professionals explained differential patterns in diagnoses, treatment, and counseling outcomes by highlighting practitioners' inattentiveness to differences between clients' cultural backgrounds and the primarily Eurocentric norms promoted by many practitioners. In addition, the predominance of White Americans within the profession seemed to perpetuate the legacy of racist attitudes, which assumed superiority based on differences in phenotype and culture. The term that describes this characteristic of seeing one's own community norms and group identity as the models against which all others should be judged as aberrant, strange, and inferior is *ethnocentrism*. Although, much of the literature highlights attention to White majority group members' ethnocentrism, it is important that readers note that all individuals who have strong cultural group identity or who have little awareness of a group identity have the capacity to assume an ethnocentric stance in day-to-day activities.

Positive Versus Negative Effects

The ethnocentric perspective can have both affirming and detrimental implications for self-concept and interactions with others. Social identity theory purports that as individuals understand themselves, the following personality qualities are enhanced: personal identity, affiliation with others within group, confidence, understanding of self, psychological well-being, and self-esteem. However, the sole or primary culture-specific focus can negatively affect individuals' ability to accept the relativism of their and others' cultural identity.

However, in spite of this mix of both positive and negative characteristics associated with a strong positive group identity (one aspect of being ethnocentric), many individuals assume that such is automatically equated with only negative implications. Empirical evidence supports the notion that one can simultaneously have a strong positive group identity and accept the legitimacy of the culturally different. Nevertheless, the most effective strategy to balance the effective expression of respect for both self and other, when the two value systems collide, remains somewhat unclear.

Because empirical evidence supports the notion that individuals can simultaneously have a strong positive group identity and respect those of other groups, it is imperative that practitioners are sufficiently multiculturally competent to effectively bridge any differences existing between themselves and all clients. However, in spite of the mandate for multicultural counseling training in all accredited programs, this competence varies significantly among practitioners.

Counselors' Ethnocentrism in Counseling

Practitioners' ethnocentric responses to clients are spontaneous and, too often, sources of unconscious, psychological harm to clients who persist in the relationship. Clients with strong positive self-concepts will prematurely terminate the counseling relationship. The following are examples of common errors made in counseling relationships, when ethnocentrism is not monitored: use of negative judgment words to describe the clients' experience, behavior, or primary support network; pathologizing differences and using assessments without considering population-demographic characteristics on which the measures are normed; engaging clients based solely on perceptions of phenotype or stated group identity; responses that indicate unawareness of one's own identity; unwillingness to examine transference or countertransference (i.e., consistently defining clients' responses in counseling as resistant to intervention); expressed insensitivity or lack of respect for clients' perception of experience associated with their unique group membership; premature problem-solving and advice-giving based on what the counselor believes the client ought to be or do; generating alternatives without considering the negative implications for ingroup and outgroup membership or preparing the client for potential shifts related to proposed changes; distancing oneself from the client by expressing no understanding of the client's experience; not specifically addressing stark differences between self and client that might influence the client's perception of the relationship and of the counselor as a person (i.e., sex, race, ethnicity, age); disaffiliating from one's group or client's perceptions of one's group when client expresses concern about counselor's group membership (i.e., I'm not racist; I'm not sexist; I'm not like all of the others like me, I'm different); not inviting the client to share perceptions whenever there is any indication of counselor's insensitivity. As a result, the client's culture is not respected, and the counselor's culture is not used in a manner that enhances the therapeutic working alliance. The increased probability of inaccurate assessment results, unstable rapport, insufficient collection of important information, inappropriate diagnoses, and negative outcomes are results from such interactions. Sensitivity is warranted particularly with clients who are ethnocentric in their own identity.

Presenting Concerns of the Ethnocentric Client

Ethnocentric clients might exhibit various presenting concerns: difficulty with interactions across groups, including difficulty finding and maintaining bonds, understanding commonalities, and accepting differences; higher levels of insecure self-identity, which could have a direct impact on individual self-esteem and self-concept; issues regarding acculturation; and issues associated with limited awareness of their own ethnocentrism. These concerns require counselors' intervention to enhance ethnorelativism versus ethnocentrism so as to not deculturate clients. For optimal outcomes in counseling to occur, it is imperative that practitioners effectively monitor their own ethnocentrism.

Effects of Ethnocentrism in the Counseling Relationship

The counseling profession has attempted to monitor the phenomenon of ethnocentrism within the counseling relationship through multicultural counseling, which refers to a process in which a trained professional from one cultural/racial/ethnic background interacts with a client of a different cultural/racial/ethnic background for the purpose of promoting the client's cognitive, emotional, psychological, and/or spiritual development. The acquisition of culture-specific knowledge has become the norm as diversity increases within the general populace. Some scholars have developed counseling models that provide a guide for practitioners to self-monitor ethnocentrism within sessions. All are efforts to minimize harm to clients because of unmonitored ethnocentrism. However, key questions remain unanswered: Is cultural relativism a real or ideal training objective? Can practitioners who maintain ethnocentric attitudes and beliefs effectively counsel culturally different clients? Can practitioners effectively and strategically self-monitor ethnocentrism during the counseling session in a manner that benefits the client? With increasing diversity within both the general populace and graduate student cohorts in counseling programs, what are ways in which training programs could strategically maximize the degrees of multicultural competence among all graduates? Finding answers to these questions will facilitate a clearer understanding of how ethnocentrism might be addressed more effectively in both training and service delivery.

Robbie J. Steward and Chandra M. Donnell

See also Acculturation (v3); Barriers to Cross-Cultural Counseling (v3); Civil Rights (v3); Classism (v3); Cross-Cultural Training (v3); Cultural Encapsulation (v3); Cultural Relativism (v3); Discrimination (v3); Diversity Issues in Career Development (v4); Enculturation (v3); Eurocentrism (v3); Identity (v3); Multicultural Counseling (v3); Multiculturalism (v3); Prejudice (v3); Racism (v3); Social Discrimination (v4); White Privilege (v3); Worldview (v3)

Further Readings

DeCremer, D. (2001). Relations of self-esteem concerns, group identification, and self-stereotyping to in-group favoritism. *Journal of Social Psychology, 141*(3), 389–400.

Fish, J. M. (2000). What anthropology can do for psychology: Facing physics envy, ethnocentrism, and a belief in "race." *American Anthropologist, 102*(3), 552–563.

Gaertner, L., Iuzzini, J., Witt, M. G., & Orina, M. M. (2006). Us without them: Evidence for an intragroup origin of positive in-group regard. *Journal of Personality and Social Psychology, 90,* 426–439.

Phinney, J. S., Lochner, B., & Murphy, R. (1990). Ethnic identity development and psychological adjustment in adolescence. In A. Stiffman & L. Davis (Eds.), *Ethnic issues in adolescent mental health* (pp. 53–72). Newbury Park, CA: Sage.

Roysircar, G. (2004). Cultural self-awareness assessment practice examples from psychology training. *Professional Psychology: Research and Practice, 38,* 658–666.

Steward, R. J. (1998, March–April). *PAR—A theoretic model for self-assessment and practice toward multicultural counseling competence.* Paper presented at the American Counseling Association World Conference, Indianapolis, IN. (ERIC Document Reproduction Service No. ED419185)

Sue, D. W. (2004). Whiteness and ethnocentric monoculturalism. Making the "invisible" visible. *American Psychologist, 59,* 761–769.

Verkuyten, M. (2005). Ethnic group identification and group evaluation among minority and majority groups: Testing the multiculturalism hypothesis. *Journal of Personality and Social Psychology, 88,* 121–138.

ETIC–EMIC DISTINCTION

For centuries, the field of psychology has been interested in understanding behavior and cultures. In effect, social and behavioral scientists have identified two critical approaches in understanding human behavior and cultures: an *etic perspective* and an *emic perspective.* Based on universal comparisons of behaviors that can be generalized across cultures, the *etic* approach is consistent with the use of quantitative hypothetical-deductive methods wherein researchers or outsiders are the primary judges of the validity of an experience. Conversely, based in a belief that unique values and norms of a given culture are key to understanding behaviors meaningful to indigenous members of a given society, the *emic* approach is consistent with qualitative research methodologies wherein members of the society or insiders become the primary sources of validity of a particular experience. With the increasing knowledge that behavior or phenomena can be universal and yet be culturally bound, the etic–emic distinction and how these two perspectives are negotiated in theory, research, assessment, and practice have become germane to the field of counseling psychology.

Originally coined in 1954 by the linguist Kenneth L. Pike, the etic–emic distinction was first referenced in psychology by David French in 1963 when he examined the relationship between anthropology and studies of perception and cognition. In 1969, John W. Berry adapted its use to cross-cultural psychology. Since this period, scholars engaged in multicultural psychological research have employed these two epistemologies to conceptualize and operationalize both comparative and indigenous research.

Interestingly, although well established and widely used in different fields—linguistics, anthropology, education, medicine, philosophy, psychiatry, social work, sociology, public health, psychology, folklore, semiotics, and management—these terms have been viewed in opposition to each other, resulting in a long-standing controversy over the efficacy of the two perspectives. In fact, there have been several shifts in the debate on its dichotomous versus symbiotic nature. In essence, the controversy over the definitions and applications of the approaches has continued to fuel the etic–emic debate.

Etics and Emics: A Dichotomous Perspective

The tension over whether etic–emic approaches are contrasting or complementary seems to come from researchers who have different assumptions about concepts, behaviors to be assessed, and methods of analysis. For instance, etic researchers examine more than one culture or language at a single moment in time. Because of this brief intervention, etic approaches are an effective means of providing a broader perspective on behavior while meeting practical demands (e.g., financial constraints, time pressures). Within this approach, concepts or classifications are known in advance (as based on prior research) rather than determined during analysis. Etic concepts are judged against criteria that are external to the system, absolute, and directly measurable. Furthermore, the etic view does not perceive all aspects of a situation to be part of a larger setting. Instead, etic data can be obtained through analysis of partial information.

Conversely, the emic approach tends to be culture-specific and applied to one culture or language at a time or over a sustained period of time. Within this approach, concepts are discovered rather than predicted and viewed against criteria that are relevant to the internal functioning of the system. The emic view thus perceives each component as interconnected and functioning within a larger structural setting. This allows for the understanding of the culture as a whole rather than a series of disconnected parts.

These dichotomous polarities inherent in the defining characteristics have led scholars to equate etic and emic with descriptors such as scientific versus subjective, cross-comparative versus ethnographic, and formal versus informal methodologies. In effect, it has led etic researchers to question emic perspectives and emic researchers to question etic perspectives for conceptual and methodological weaknesses. Etic perspectives have been dismissed for their assumption of cultural universality wherein all behaviors are perceived as equally present in all cultures with minimal modifications required when examining issues. Within this focus, cultural or contextual factors are minimized. On the other hand, emic perspectives are criticized for being overly culturally specific with limited generalizability to a larger population. These criticisms have tended to keep the two approaches somewhat separate.

Etics and Emics: An Integrated-Symbiotic Perspective

However, not all researchers ascribe to this separation, and many have argued for examining the complementary nature of the two approaches. For instance, Pike perceived the relationship to be symbiotic with the two perspectives being equally valuable because they examine the same data from two different standpoints. Similarly, Patricia Greenfield argued that the two approaches are complementary in that emic approaches serve well within an exploratory context while etic approaches work well when testing hypotheses. Other scholars, such as French, have ascribed to Pike's view of etics as an entry point to emics. Within this context, one approaches the phenomena across cultures from a common ground perspective, leading up to studying specific aspects of the phenomena within a culture.

In attempting to address the forced dichotomization between etic and emic approaches, Berry expanded on Pike's ideas about the symbiotic nature of the two perspectives. Berry noted that researchers' choice of orientation (etic/emic) has consequences in the way (method) research may be conducted. In attempting to compare behaviors across cultures (etic) while at the same time understanding behavior that is meaningful to a particular culture (emic), Berry proposed a framework that highlights the essential and interconnected nature of the two perspectives.

In initiating cross-comparative research, Berry cautioned against what he termed *imposed etics* or what Harry C. Triandis later called *pseudoetics*, or false etics. Both authors believed that although the intentionality is that of an etic orientation, researchers typically begin with a concept or instruments based in their own culture, in essence, coming from their own emics. Because the "emics" of researchers might be categorically different from those of participants, false assumptions can be made about the validity of concepts or instruments within or across cultures. Furthermore, entering a system with what "appears" to be an etic concept can provide only a preliminary approximation of the phenomena.

Thus, both advocate for a convergence of the two approaches through engaging in what Berry refers to as *parallel emics,* wherein modifications are made to the external criteria or categories (imposed etics) to develop instruments within each culture independently. Once indigenous assessments are created for each culture, cross-cultural comparisons can be made. Concepts that appear as universal across cultures are then referred to as *derived etics,* whereas concepts that vary across cultures are considered to be culture-specific and hence truly *"emic."*

Contemporary Perspectives

Understanding etic and emic distinctions is critical to understanding behaviors within and across cultures. Although the concept of etics is commonly associated with an outsider standpoint and emics with an insider viewpoint, scholars in the field of multicultural and cross-cultural psychology argue that concepts can have both a universal and a culture-specific base. In light of this, contemporary views highlight the importance of an integrated etic–emic perspective that can help examine phenomena through a functional, conceptual, and contextual equivalence.

Arpana G. Inman

See also Cross-Cultural Psychology (v3); Cross-Cultural Training (v3); Cultural Encapsulation (v3); Multicultural Psychology (v3): Pedersen, Paul Bodholdt (v3); Qualitative Methodologies (v1); Quantitative Methodologies (v1); Sue, Derald Wing: Contributions to Multicultural Psychology and Counseling (v3); Worldview (v3)

Further Readings

Berry, J. W. (1969). On cross-cultural comparability. *International Journal of Psychology, 4,* 119–128.

Berry, J. W. (1989). Imposed etics-emics-derived etics: The operationalization of a compelling idea. *International Journal of Psychology, 24,* 721–735.

Berry, J. W. (1999). Emics and etics: A symbiotic conception. *Culture and Psychology, 52,* 165–171.

Berry, J. W., & Kim, U. (1993). The way ahead: From indigenous psychologies to a universal psychology. In U. Kim & J. W. Berry (Eds.), *Indigenous psychologies: Research and experience in cultural context* (pp. 277–280). Newbury Park, CA: Sage.

Feleppa, R. (1986). Emics, etics, and social objectivity. *Current Anthropology, 27,* 243–255.

Fischer, A. R., LaRae, M. J., & Atkinson, D. R. (1998). Reconceptualizing multicultural counseling: Universal healing conditions in a culturally specific context. *The Counseling Psychologist, 26,* 525–588.

French, D. (1963). The relationship of anthropology to studies in perception and cognition. In S. Koch (Ed.), *Psychology: A study of a science: Vol. 6. Investigations of man as socius: Their place in psychology and the social sciences* (pp. 388–428). New York: McGraw-Hill.

Greenfield, P. M. (1997). Culture as process. Empirical methodology for cultural psychology. In J. W. Berry, Y. H. Poortinga, & J. Pandey (Eds.), *Handbook of cross-cultural psychology: Vol. 1. Theory and method* (2nd ed., pp. 301–346). Needham Heights, MA: Allyn & Bacon.

Harris, M. (1976). History and significance of the emic/etic distinction. *Annual Review Anthropology, 3,* 329–350.

Headland, T. N., Pike, K. L., & Harris, M. (Eds.). (1990). *Emics and etics: The insider/outsider debate.* Newbury Park: Sage.

Mead Niblo, D., & Jackson, M. S. (2004). Model for combining the qualitative emic approach with the quantitative derived etic approach. *Australian Psychologist, 39,* 127–133.

Pike, K. L. (1967). *Language in relation to a unified theory of the structure of human behavior.* The Hague: Mouton.

Triandis, H. C. (1972). *Culture and social behavior.* New York: McGraw-Hill.

Triandis, H. C. (2000). Dialectics between cultural and cross-cultural psychology. *Asian Journal of Social Psychology, 3,* 185–195.

EUROCENTRISM

Eurocentrism is defined as judging the experiences of non–European-descended individuals (i.e., African Americans, Latinos/as) against a European American standard. Eurocentrism often leads to negative attitudes and beliefs about groups of people and can confirm mainstream stereotypes about non-European group members. In essence, a Eurocentric belief system assumes that European American culture (i.e., Western culture) is the norm and should be viewed as the standard against which other cultures are judged. Both implicit and explicit Eurocentrism serve as a basis for prejudice. Though Eurocentrism has significant implications for mental health and psychology, little research exists on the subject.

The Eurocentric worldview is based on Western values and characteristics such as individualism, competitiveness, dualistic thinking, a belief in control over nature, hierarchical decision-making processes, standard English, a rigid time orientation, Judeo-Christian beliefs, patriarchy, the Protestant work ethic, future orientation, "objective/rational" thought, property ownership, and nuclear family structure. When one expects others, regardless of their cultural background, to behave in ways that reflect these values, deviations are pathologized and often serve as the basis of some form of group-based oppression. Eurocentrism, in the context of U.S. society, as well as other multicultural societies, is harmful in that non-Western cultural values (e.g., collectivism, living within an extended family system) are viewed, at best, as novel and, at worst, "deficient" in relation to European American cultural values. Viewing the experiences of others from a Eurocentric perspective may lead to exclusion, marginalization, and discrimination when individuals do not possess and display traits valued within European American culture. Eurocentrism can occur at individual, cultural, and institutional levels and can be manifested in overt and covert ways.

Everyday Eurocentrism

When immigrants come to the United States, there is often an underlying expectation that they will ultimately assimilate into mainstream American (i.e., Eurocentric) cultural lifestyles. For example, in many work and educational settings, employees or students might be expected to wear Western-style clothing or speak standard English despite the fact that many individuals may prefer non-Western, traditional, indigenous dress, or prefer to communicate in their native languages, even if they are capable of speaking English. The pressure to "fit in" and become Americanized may challenge non-Western individuals to assimilate and abandon their own personal and cultural preferences. This expectation may be tacit as well as explicit. Students who come to school dressed in non-Western, traditional clothing may be ostracized from peers or, in extreme cases, may be told that they must modify their dress (e.g., banning the practice of wearing head coverings or religious artifacts).

Eurocentrism can also result in life-changing consequences for those who do not fit the standard. Employment research has found that employers are much less likely to call back job applicants with African- versus European-sounding names and to make actual job offers. This type of preference may suggest a Eurocentric bias as well as a pattern of discrimination with regard to interview selection practices. This type of biased behavior and assumptions about what type of behavior is preferred are also relevant to the field of psychology.

Eurocentrism in Psychology

Manifestations of Eurocentrism can also be found within the practice of psychology. For example, although the *Diagnostic and Statistical Manual of Mental Disorders* (*DSM*) has been used to diagnose various forms of mental illness for decades, many of the *DSM* diagnostic categories are vulnerable to racial disparities. For example, there is an overrepresentation of African American boys who have diagnoses of conduct disorder, attention deficit/hyperactivity disorder, and other behavioral disorders than what one would expect given their statistical representation in the population. It has been argued that African American boys are given these diagnoses in greater proportions than their White counterparts because teachers, physicians, and mental health professionals use Eurocentric standards of conduct to judge these children and are faster to diagnose them with "disorders." Furthermore, mental health professionals have also been accused of minimizing the impact of racism and other forms of discrimination on the mental health of non-White individuals. The lack of inclusion of such factors in the assessment process may contribute to inaccurate diagnoses and a tendency to conceptualize pathology in the individual rather than interpreting the situation as being rooted in social problems. For instance, recent longitudinal research has found that African American youth who perceive discrimination are more likely to manifest symptoms of depression and conduct problems than their counterparts who do not perceive such discrimination. Other research with Asian American youth has found that experiences of cultural marginalization contribute to depression. Thus, in addition to the problems that Eurocentrism can influence in educational or workplace settings, Eurocentrism and its potential consequences (e.g., racism, discrimination) can affect non-Western individuals' mental health and the way that mental health professionals perceive them.

It is also important to recognize that the process of counseling has been accused of being Eurocentric. Historically, counseling theories and techniques were developed by White counselors and therapists of European American descent, who worked exclusively with White clients. Scholars have noted that although many therapeutic techniques have been developed and empirically validated as being effective, limited research has been conducted with respect to the effectiveness of such interventions with people of color and clients who are not of European descent. The lack of available research on evidence-based treatment for people of color could be seen as an outcome of Eurocentrism within the field of psychology. As a result, the field of psychology has a less-developed knowledge base about the most effective ways to intervene with non-Western clients.

Within psychology and other mental health professions, Eurocentrism can have adverse effects on individuals and institutions because of the societal power and authority scientific professions like psychology have in the United States.

On the other hand, psychology has also played an important role in efforts to change social policy that has facilitated discrimination. For instance, Mamie P. Clark and Kenneth B. Clark conducted psychological research that helped convince the U.S. Supreme Court that educational segregation resulted in prejudice and discrimination that harmed African American youth. It is important that psychologists remain vigilant against the historical and contemporary effects of Eurocentrism in relation to research, policy development, organizational behavior, and clinical practice.

Sha'kema M. Blackmon and Elizabeth M. Vera

See also Allocentrism (v3); Barriers to Cross-Cultural Counseling (v3); Bias (v3); Cross-Cultural Psychology (v3); Cultural Encapsulation (v3); Cultural Relativism (v3); Cultural Values (v3); Discrimination (v3); Discrimination and Oppression (v2); Ethnic Pride (v3); Ethnocentrism (v3); Idiocentrism (v3); Monocultural (v3); Racial Pride (v3); Social Discrimination (v4); Universalism (v3); White Americans (v3); White Privilege (v3); Worldview (v3)

Further Readings

Bertrand, M., & Mullainathan, S. (2003). *Are Emily and Greg more employable than Lakisha and Jamal? A field experiment on labor market discrimination.* Retrieved March 15, 2006, from http://povertyactionlab.org/papers/bertrand_mullainathan.pdf

Brody, G. F., Chen, Y. F., Murry, V. M., Ge, X., Simmons, R. L., Gibbons, F. X., et al. (2006). Perceived discrimination and the adjustment of African American youths: A five-year longitudinal analysis with contextual moderation effects. *Child Development, 77*(5), 1170–1189.

Cunningham, W. A., Nezlek, J. B., & Bananji, M. (2004). Implicit and explicit ethnocentrism: Revisiting the ideologies of prejudice. *Personality and Social Psychology Bulletin, 30*(10), 1332–1346.

Hwang, W. C. (2006). The psychotherapy adaptation and modification framework: Application to Asian Americans. *American Psychologist, 61*(7), 702–715.

Katz, J. H. (1985). The sociopolitical nature of counseling. *The Counseling Psychologist, 13*(4), 615–624.

Kim, S. Y., Gonzales, N. A., Stroh, K., & Wang, J. L. (2006). Parent-child cultural marginalization and depressive symptoms in Asian American family members. *Journal of Community Psychology, 34*(2), 167–182.

Kress, V. V. W., Eriksen, K. P., Rayle, A. D., & Ford, S. J. W. (2005). The *DSM-IV-TR* and culture: Consideration for counselors. *Journal of Counseling & Development, 83,* 97–104.

Stewart, E. C., & Bennett, M. J. (1991). *American cultural patterns: A cross-cultural perspective.* Yarmouth, MN: Intercultural Press.

Familismo

Familismo refers to a strong sense of identification with, and loyalty to, nuclear and extended family. It also includes a sense of protection of familial honor, respect, and cooperation among family members. Through these values, individuals place their family's needs over their own personal desires and choices. Researchers indicate that familismo-related values foster the creation or facilitation of the whole, rather than that of the individual. Scholars further define familismo as the most important cultural aspect defining the beliefs and attitudes of Latinos/as. Thus, it becomes fundamental that therapists working with Latino/a populations understand the concept of familismo and its impact on the well-being of Latinos/as.

Familismo is best understood from a multidimensional perspective, which includes three dimensions: structural, behavioral, and attitudinal. The structural dimension defines the spatial and social boundaries in which behaviors and attitudes within the family acquire meaning. The inclusion or exclusion of nuclear and extended family members defines these boundaries. The behavioral dimension refers to the support shared among family members. Visiting and calling family members reflect this dimension. The attitudinal component of familismo refers to the commitment to family relationships, including individual's identification with the nuclear and extended family. Like most constructs, familismo should be examined from a dialectical perspective where both positive and negative aspects are highlighted.

Traditional views on family dynamics have facilitated the misinterpretation of familismo. Some therapists may perceive strong family bonds among Latinos/as as signs of codependency, enmeshment, or pathology, leaving many Latinos/as feeling misunderstood and inaccurately diagnosed. Because strong family relationships among Latinos/as can cause confusion in the interpretation of symptoms, familismo should first be interpreted as a cultural variable that may also serve as a therapeutic and individual strength.

Research indicates that factors underlying the concept of familismo may positively influence Latinos/as' treatment adherence and their psychological well-being. Encouraging and strengthening family cooperation and support could be a way through which mental health providers use familismo to promote treatment adherence. They may encourage family members to set goals and make decisions that may benefit the clients' well-being. In turn, this may reinforce the clients' self-esteem and positively affect their decision-making process.

Further studies show that a strong sense of familismo may decrease cultural and intergenerational problems within the family. These studies hypothesize that the concept of familismo would lower adolescents' feelings of depression, anxiety, alcohol use, and conduct problems and increase involvement with school activities. Thus, reinforcing familismo may serve as a useful tool for therapists fostering the well-being of Latino/a adolescents.

Given that familismo is a key cultural dynamic present in Latino/a communities, it becomes crucial to understand how its function may affect the well-being of Latinos/as. Therapists are encouraged to examine their personal and professional values of family structure and interdependence as they work with Latino/a clients.

Miguel E. Gallardo and Yanina Paoliello

See also Barriers to Cross-Cultural Counseling (v3); Career Counseling, Latinos (v4); Cross-Cultural Psychology (v3); Cultural Values (v3); Culture (v3); Diversity (v3); Ethnic Identity (v3); Ethnic Pride (v3); Latinos (v3); Multicultural Counseling (v3); Multiculturalism (v3); Multicultural Psychology (v3); National Latina/o Psychological Association (v3); Work–Family Balance (v4)

Further Readings

Antshel, K. M. (2002). Integrating culture as a means of improving treatment adherence in the Latino population. *Psychology, Health & Medicine, 7*(4), 435–449.

Bacallao, M. L., & Smokowski, P. R. (2005). "Entre dos mundos": Bicultural skills training with Latino immigrant families. *The Journal of Primary Prevention, 26*(6), 485–509.

Santiago-Rivera, A. L., Arredondo, P., & Gallardo-Cooper, M. (2002). *Counseling Latinos and* la familia. Thousand Oaks, CA: Sage.

Fatalism

Mental health scholars have long been interested in fatalism. In 1959 Bruce P. Dohrenwend, in an extension of the sociologist Émile Durkheim's late-19th-century writings, posited that fatalism was a common cause of mental disorder and suicide. Fatalism was thought of as a societal response to excessive regulation and oppressive discipline, in the extreme like that experienced by prisoners. In psychological paradigms, fatalism has most frequently been grounded in the generalized expectancies framework, for example, internal–external locus of control. In this perspective fatalistic persons believe they have little or no influence on events that will happen to them. Other common prominent characterizations of fatalistic beliefs include a stable future orientation and malleable attributions of the causes of previous events.

Many scholars have thought individuals' overall fatalism would lead to poor adaptation, lack of behavioral control, and, in turn, poor health and well-being; results have been mixed, however. One approach to derive more consistent findings has been to define situation-specific fatalistic beliefs that may inhibit specific protective actions, such as those related to coping with disease, unemployment, or natural disasters. The way global fatalism has typically been constructed also has limitations when applied to more collectivist groups. One major challenge has been to discriminate what reflects spirituality or faith, which may be adaptive in many circumstances, from that of a negative expectation about outcomes where persons do have agency. An example of this problem appears in the literature of fatalismo in Latinos/as, the extent to which a person believes his or her destiny is not under his or her control. Although fatalism was thought to be parallel to fatalismo, fatalismo, when described by Latinos/as, includes components of spirituality as well as external locus of control, but neither fully encompasses it. It would be inappropriate to assume fatalismo is broadly associated with poor mental health, maladaptive behaviors, or passivity toward one's life. When extended to populations of Asian descent, fatalism may include beliefs of a higher order, a characteristic not inherent in typical Western conceptualizations.

Given multiple definitions of fatalism and questions about its comparability and meanings across cultural groups, scholars and practitioners should not assume all fatalistic-type beliefs are maladaptive. Promising approaches for intervention and therapy may focus on negative expectations toward future outcomes for which the respondent does have substantial agency and incorrect negative attributions for past events.

Scott C. Carvajal

See also Barriers to Cross-Cultural Counseling (v3); Collectivism (v3); Cross-Cultural Psychology (v3); Cultural Values (v3); Discrimination and Oppression (v2); Learned Helplessness (v3); Locus of Control (v3); Meaning, Creation of (v2); Multicultural Psychology (v3); Optimism and Pessimism (v2); Positive Psychology (v2); Power and Powerlessness (v3); Worldview (v3)

Further Readings

Guzmán, M., Santiago-Rivera, A., & Hasse, R. (2005). Understanding academic attitudes and achievement in Mexican-origin youths: Ethnic identity, other-group orientation, and fatalism. *Cultural Diversity & Ethnic Minority Psychology, 11*(1), 3–15.

Neff, J., & Hoppe, S. (1993). Race/ethnicity, acculturation, and psychological distress: Fatalism and religiosity as cultural resources. *Journal of Community Psychology, 21*(1), 3–20.

Yeh, C., Inman, A., Kim, A., & Okubo, Y. (2006). Asian American families' collectivistic coping strategies in response to 9/11. *Cultural Diversity & Ethnic Minority Psychology, 12*(1), 134–148.

Filial Piety

Filial piety is the cultural value and responsibility to treat one's parents with the highest respect. *Filial* refers to anything related to a son or daughter, and *piety* refers to the virtue of being reverent and compliant. The value includes the notion of taking care of one's parents, while showing love, respect, courtesy, and support. It includes the importance of avoiding rebellion, disgrace, or loss of face of one's family and ancestors. It is a collectivist value, in that an individual respects the worth, beliefs, and standards of a collective (i.e., one's family, tribe, ethnic group, or community) rather than of the individual. An individual is often expected to put her or his parents' needs before her or his own. This may include making decisions that best benefit one's parents and family, while making self-sacrifices for one's parents.

The term derives from Chinese and Confucian traditions, which have been passed down to subsequent generations through storytelling. The most notable written work is *The Twenty-Four Examples of Filial Piety*, a collection of stories chosen and compiled by Guo Jujing during the Yuan Dynasty (1280–1368 C.E.) while he was mourning his father's death. In this collection are stories of exemplary actions of filial children from the times of primordial Emperor Shun down to the 12th century. For example, in "Wu Meng Attracts Mosquitoes to Drink His Blood," the title character takes off his shirt at night to allow mosquitoes to bite him instead of his ailing parents. In these stories, the child's actions are praised by the community, and she or he is revered for being an ideal respectful child.

Although *filial piety* was first coined as a Chinese term, it is a value that takes similar forms in other Asian and Latino/a cultures. Other East Asian cultures (namely, Japanese and Korean) subscribe to the aforementioned values of filial piety, whereas other Asian groups may have similar values with slight differences. Asian Indians may uphold *dharma*, which includes individual ethics, duties, and obligations to one's family, while Filipinos may maintain *utang ng loob* (debt of gratitude), which embraces selfless obligations to one's parents, with an expectation of reciprocity from other family members. In Latino/a culture, filial piety is most similar to *familismo*, which is a strong identification and attachment of individuals with their nuclear and extended families.

Because many Asian cultures tend to maintain specific gender roles (i.e., men as authority figures, women as caretakers), acts of filial piety may differ for men and women. Examples of filial piety for men may include holding provider roles (i.e., paying for parents' expenses, making family decisions), whereas examples of filial piety for women may include more homemaking roles (i.e., cleaning and cooking for the parents/family). Examples of filial piety for both genders include individuals choosing colleges that would be most convenient for their parents (both geographically and financially) or an individual living at home as an adult to take care of her or his aging parents.

Kevin L. Nadal

See also Asian Americans (v3); Career Counseling, Asian Americans (v4); Career Counseling, Latinos (v4); Collectivism (v3); Confucianism (v3); Cross-Cultural Psychology (v3); Cultural Values (v3); Familismo (v3); Family Counseling (v1); Identity Development (v3); Latinos (v3); Loss of Face (v3); Parent–Adolescent Relations (v1); Parenting (v1); Worldview (v3)

Further Readings

Ikels, C. (Ed.). (2004). *Filial piety: Practice and discourse in contemporary East Asia.* Stanford, CA: Stanford University Press.

Yeh, K.-H. (2003). The beneficial and harmful effects of filial piety: An integrative analysis. In K. Yang, K. Hwang, P. B. Pedersen, & I. Daibo (Eds.), *Progress in Asian social psychology: Conceptual and empirical contributions.* Westport, CT: Praeger/Greenwood.

Healthy Paranoia

Healthy paranoia is a healthy, normative, and adaptive response to racism perceived by Black Americans. The term was first used by Grier and Cobbs to describe the inclination they observed among Blacks to mistrust Caucasians in the areas of education, business, law, work, interpersonal relations, politics, and counseling. They suggested that cultural mistrust, in a mild form, was healthy and adaptive and fostered the development of healthy paranoia. This cultural response style, based on experiences of racism or oppression, helped Blacks to function effectively in a predominantly European American society. For example, concerns about being unfairly treated or judged may lead some Black Americans to exercise caution or engage carefully in tasks evaluated by Caucasians. Many mental health professionals assert that cultural aspects of paranoia, associated with a history of racism and discrimination in American society, must be distinguished from psychopathology. Healthy paranoia is a defense against an oppressive environment that has been hostile to the interests of Blacks. This protection limits trust, facilitates understanding of social situations, and enhances survival. Misinterpretation of healthy paranoia as pathological delusion is one cause of the misdiagnosis of Black clients.

Healthy paranoia research has focused on the effects on diagnosis (e.g., overdiagnosis of paranoid schizophrenia in Black patients), counseling process (e.g., help-seeking attitudes of Black students), counseling outcomes (e.g., premature termination), and educational and occupational expectations. Healthy paranoia can have significant effects on the personal lives of Black individuals because it inhibits personal expression, an experience that is often undesirable and painful. It also can affect a wide range of situations, such as preference for counselors and other helping professsionals.

Implications for Counseling

Counselors in today's society need to develop race-specific expertise in addition to general counseling skills. Awareness of their own cultural identity and personal biases, along with knowledge and skills specific to the experiences of culturally diverse clients, is essential to conducting effective psychotherapy with populations of color. In particular, understanding and attending to issues of healthy paranoia can facilitate the provision of culturally sensitive and effective counseling services to Black clients. Knowing the history of a Black client who has experienced prejudice and discrimination can help therapists evaluate whether mistrust of a particular therapist is attributable to healthy paranoia or pathological paranoia. Counselors' recognition of healthy paranoia as an adaptive coping response to an oppressive situation or context can prevent overdiagnosis or misdiagnosis of clients of color and can enhance the delivery of culturally competent services to clients of color.

Carlos P. Zalaquett

See also African Americans (v3); Barriers to Cross-Cultural Counseling (v3); Black Racial Identity Development (v3); Career Counseling, African Americans (v4); Cross-Cultural

Psychology (v3); Cultural Mistrust (v3); Cultural Paranoia (v3); Discrimination and Oppression (v2); Eurocentrism (v3); Multicultural Counseling Competence (v3); Racial Identity (v3); Underdiagnosis/Overdiagnosis (v2); White Privilege (v3)

Further Readings

Grier, W. H., & Cobbs, P. M. (1968). *Black rage.* New York: Basic Books.

Sue, S. (2006). Cultural competency: From philosophy to research and practice. *Journal of Community Psychology, 34,* 237–245.

Whaley, A. L. (1998). Cross-cultural perspective on paranoia: A focus on the Black American experience. *Psychiatric Quarterly, 69,* 325–343.

Whaley, A. L. (2001). Cultural mistrust and the clinical diagnosis of paranoid schizophrenia in African American patients. *Journal of Psychopathology and Behavioral Assessment, 23,* 93–100.

HELMS, JANET E. (1947–)

Janet E. Helms, born in Kansas City, Missouri, is a scholar and educator best known for her work on the theory and measurement of racial identity development and her active involvement in psychological organizations. Over a period of approximately 25 years, Helms's theory of racial identity development has emerged as a set of highly interrelated conceptualizations that describes a process through which people of varying races cope and, invariably, *fail* to cope with societal racism. Helms's more recent scholarship has focused on test bias. In this body of work, she and her collaborators strive to address the questions of *why* racial disparities exist in cognitive abilities tests and *how* test constructors, practitioners, and policymakers can diminish this bias. As theoretician, researcher, mentor, educator, and advocate, Helms represents a positive force in the field of psychology. Her contributions have been applied not only to counseling and psychotherapy training and practice but also to education, law, organizational studies and practice, research methodology and ethics, and public policy. The reach of her work extends outside of the United States to countries such as Brazil, South Africa, Ghana, and Uganda.

Racial Identity Theory

With regard to her theory on racial identity development, Helms contends that a study of race and racism needs to take into account the manner in which people are cognitively, affectively, and conatively affected by the appraisals that people make about them and, recursively, by the appraisals they make about themselves and others. *Racial* appraisals are but one aspect of this process that becomes internalized and highly integrated with other aspects of identity. In the early statuses of racial identity development and in the absence of deliberate efforts to illuminate and correct distortions about people based on race, many people adopt information processing strategies that accept a status quo perspective about racism. In other words, people may fail to question the negative or negligible treatment of non-Whites, the heralding of White people and White culture, or the seeming inevitability of Blacks and Latinos/as, as examples, to occupy positions of low prominence in education relative to Whites. Crucial to the status quo perspective are mechanisms that exist at all levels in the sociopolitical ecology that upholds a tolerance for *not* questioning or that encourages the deflection of these aspects of reality. People adopt information processing strategies of obliviousness, selective attention to reality, and denial to cope with these racial stimuli. However, even though these strategies can help release some of the discomfort or pain associated with the stimuli, they may not be effective. With increased exposure to history, accuracy about people from all backgrounds, and so forth, comes the opportunity for growth in racial identity development. Moreover, as people transcend the different statuses of racial identity, they can gradually replace inchoate information processing strategies (obliviousness, denial, selective attention) with strategies that are more consistent with mental health qualities, like complexity in thinking, flexibility, a willingness to approach rather than avoid situations, and so forth.

Built upon the formulations of W. E. Cross, Jr., Helms's research and theoretical writings on racial identity development began in the early 1980s. With T. A. Parham, Helms created a scale to assess Blacks' racial identity attitudes, one aspect of racial identity. This scale was used in subsequent studies to explore the relationship of racial identity attitudes of Blacks to an array of psychological variables, such as Black college students' preference for counselors based on counselor race. The scale also spawned a proliferation of measures and theories by others, setting a precedent in identity development model and assessment development. Significantly, in addition to reformulating Cross's identity development model for Blacks, Helms developed three other models that completed her overarching theory of racial identity, the White identity model, the people of color model, and the racial interaction model.

In her racial interaction model, Helms demonstrated how counselors can effect meaningful change in counseling when racial stimuli are presented. Helms proposed that when counselors developed advanced status racial identity schemata, they were in better positions to help their clients in counseling. By contrast, in parallel relationships, in which the counselor and client share similar racial identity schemata, and in regressive relationships, where the counselor's schemata are less sophisticated than the client's, little or no change is likely. These formulations were later elaborated to apply to other situations that involved an influential or expert person who is expected to teach, guide, or lead others (e.g., teachers with students, organizational leaders with employees, group leaders with subordinate or nonexpert members).

Impact of Race and Racism

What is apparent throughout Helms's research and theoretical writings is her strong insistence that race and racism need to be understood as phenomena that have an ostensible impact on socialization. Indeed, she urges researchers to strive to achieve a full understanding of these phenomena in order to know when and how to attend to these influences on personality development, interpersonal and group dynamics, and mental health functioning. In Helms's lectures, writings, and life stories are lessons about the vicissitudes of racism. When listening or reading carefully, one can learn that racism is not merely an act of negative bias or maltreatment (discrimination), nor is it something that evenly maligns one group against another (bigotry) with little regard for a history that entitles one group, Whites, and subordinates others (e.g., African Americans and Asian Americans). Her contributions are often woven tales of what life is like from someone who resides in two "warring" worlds, as drawing from the words of W. E. B. Du Bois: a dominant or "received view" perspective and the nondominant group perspective.

Importantly, as a consummate educator, Helms repeatedly makes a case for studying racism's impact on psychological functioning and development by encouraging researchers and practitioners alike to break from convention. To learn about race and racism, one must use direct assessments, not the skillful avoidance or codified wording that characterizes social norms. *Direct* assessments involve querying participants about their perceptions of themselves and others as racial beings and of the relevance of race, as they see it, within their sociopolitical contexts. Direct assessments are challenging. Racial discourse can provoke anxiety and suspicions, even create alarm about how one will be judged. But in its place, what can be seen as the norm in conventional research are studies in which participants are asked merely to report a racial designation. When conducting these indirect assessments, researchers restrict themselves in gleaning meaningful information about the potential relevance of race to their focus of study. Instead, they rely on speculations on how the participants' reported designations configure into their findings, leaving the scientific world with little knowledge about race or the possible relevance of race to their findings. Helms's work *and* words can be used as exemplars for how we can learn a great deal about the psychology of race and racism.

Education, Career, and Awards

Helms received her B.A. and M.A. degrees in psychology at the University of Missouri in Kansas City. She earned her doctorate in psychology, with a specialization in counseling psychology, in 1975 from Iowa State University of Science and Technology. Her first job was as an assistant professor at Washington State University in Pullman, Washington in 1975, and she followed this with an academic position at Southern Illinois University from 1977 to 1981. From 1981 to 1999, she worked at the University of Maryland, College Park, beginning as an assistant professor and later promoted to full professor. While at the University of Maryland, she served for a short period as codirector of the Counseling Psychology Program and as an affiliate of the Women's Studies Program. She maintained a private practice for many years while working in the suburban Maryland/Washington, D.C., area.

In 2000, Helms began her academic post at Boston College and was eventually named Augustus Long Professor of Counseling Psychology a short time later. Helms is the founding director of the Institute for the Study and Promotion of Race and Culture at Boston College. She has published more than 60 articles and four groundbreaking books, including *Black and White Racial Identity: Theory, Research, and Practice; A Race Is a Nice Thing to Have: A Guide to Being a White Person or Understanding the White Persons in Your Life;* and (with Donelda Cook) *Using Race and Culture in Counseling and Psychotherapy: Theory and Practice.* She is associate editor of the *Assessment Journal* and is on the editorial board of the *Journal of Multicultural Counseling and Development.* She is Fellow of the American Psychological Association (APA) in Division 17 (Counseling Psychology) and Division 45 (Study of Ethnic Minority Issues). She is a Division 17 representative on the APA Council of Representatives and the APA's representative on the Joint Committee on Testing. She also is a member of the Association of Black Psychologists. She is the recipient of numerous awards, including the first Janet E. Helms Award for Mentoring and Scholarship in Professional Psychology at Columbia University, Teachers College. She also won the APA Division 17 Leona Tyler Award. In 2006 she was the recipient of the APA Distinguished Award for Education and Training in Psychology.

Chalmer E. Thompson

See also Black Racial Identity Development (v3); Cross, William E., Jr. (v3); Deficit Hypothesis (v3); Identity (v3); Identity Development (v3); Race (v3); Racial Identity (v3); Racism (v3); White Racial Identity Development (v3)

Further Readings

Helms, J. E. (1984). Toward a theoretical explanation of the effects of race on counseling: A Black and White model. *The Counseling Psychologist, 12*(4), 153–165.

Helms, J. E. (Ed.). (1990). *Black and White racial identity: Theory, research, and practice.* New York: Greenwood Press.

Helms, J. E. (1992). *A race is a nice thing to have: A guide to being a White person or understanding the White persons in your life.* Topeka, KS: Content Communications.

Helms, J. E. (1995). An update of Helms's White and people of color racial identity models. In J. G. Ponterotto, J. M. Casas, L. A. Suzuki, & C. M. Alexander (Eds.), *Handbook of multicultural counseling* (pp. 181–198). Thousand Oaks, CA: Sage.

Helms, J. E., & Cook, D. A. (1999). *Using race and culture in counseling and psychotherapy: Theory and process.* Needham Heights, MA: Allyn & Bacon.

HELP-SEEKING BEHAVIOR

Help-seeking behavior can be understood as the steps an individual, a couple, or a family takes to enter into a relationship with a counseling professional. There seems to be a gap between those who need counseling services and those who utilize them, which can be attributed to multiple factors across several dimensions. The understanding of help-seeking behavior needs to include an exploration of clients' race, ethnicity, social class, gender, and geographic origin, among other variables. Additionally, it is important to examine the availability, cost, and access to services, previous utilization experience in counseling, clients' level of belief in the helpfulness of the counseling process, and whether counseling is sought voluntarily or is imposed. Help seeking by the client cannot be viewed apart from the relationship between the clients and the counselors offering the help, or apart from the organization with which the provider is affiliated. In the process of examining the variables that affect help-seeking behavior, it is important to consider that no variable can be understood alone, independent from other variables, or isolated from contextual dimensions. Understanding the complexity and variety of help-seeking behavior of clients has implications for the successful or unsuccessful outcome of the counseling process.

Historical Background

Healing practices across cultures to relieve emotional or relational distress are not new. The act of engaging in a relationship, however, whereby one person, a couple, or a family relate to another person in a professional setting for behavioral or cognitive change and emotional or relational relief, is a relatively new, 20th-century, Western phenomenon. This development is due, in part, to sociopolitical changes the century brought to individuals and families in the West as a result of the Industrial Revolution, including the decline of extended family proximity in urban centers, the decline of authority over the life of the family, and the adjustments needed as a result of shifts in gender roles. In the first five decades of the 20th century, clients sought relief from emotional or psychological distress with the only professionals available at the time, that is, psychoanalysts or psychiatrists. Mentally ill patients were often hospitalized, sometimes for the rest of their lives, without their consent. Outpatient treatments existed but were limited to individuals who could afford the private practice fees of psychoanalysts and psychiatrists.

Increases in client demand for counseling professionals started to occur in the United States in the 1960s and 1970s as a result of important legislative initiatives. The Community Mental Health Act of 1963, for example, funded the establishment of mental health centers across the country. This law and others that followed, including the deinstitutionalization of state mental hospital patients that took place in 1975, initiated an increase in demand for outpatient services, substance abuse services, family counseling, and other clinical services.

In the latter half of the 20th century, three historical shifts affected help-seeking behavior. The feminist movement spearheaded feminist counseling in the 1970s and resulted in women's demand for counseling that would help them to challenge assumptions related to the nature of their mental health, their suffering, and their position in the family. Systemic ideas influenced the development of couple and family counseling, in responding to couples or families seeking help on a variety of clinical issues. Changing immigration patterns in the last three decades of the 20th century resulted in an increased demand for counseling on the part of immigrant communities.

Race and Ethnicity

The expansion of the traditional provision of counseling services to low-income ethnic minorities and immigrants has not been met without challenges. Dropout rates are high for ethnic and racial minorities and immigrants, particularly if they are in lower socioeconomic strata.

There is an important relationship between an individual's racial or ethnic background and his or her social class, level of education, minority or majority status, level of identity development, exposure to racism and discrimination, or religious affiliation in terms of how they affect help-seeking behavior. African Americans, Latinos/as, Asian Americans, and other ethnic minority groups tend to underutilize counseling services and are less likely than Caucasians to access outpatient mental health services. African Americans drop out after the first counseling encounter at much higher rates than do other minority and nonminority groups. Exposure to racism and discrimination may make a prospective African American client distrustful of providers of a different race or ethnicity. Asian Americans may underutilize counseling services because they may lack knowledge regarding services, either because of continued stigma associated with formal help seeking or because of cultural prescriptions against self-focus. Latinos/as' help-seeking behavior may reflect cultural prescriptions that include an unwillingness to seek help for psychological, nonmedical reasons and a degree of fatalism that precludes perceptions of self-agency. Once racial and ethnic minority clients seek the help of a counseling professional, the encounter is likely to involve a provider rooted in the cultural middle-class values of individuality, self-disclosure, self-awareness, self-improvement, rationalism, and future planning. A growing body of literature suggests that conventional services do not seem to respond adequately to the values, needs, and cultural characteristics and preferences of racial and ethnic minorities.

The religious affiliation of racial and ethnic minorities may impact the help-seeking behavior. Individuals, couples, or families who rely on clergy and a religious community for their spiritual needs may find it difficult to seek the help of secular social services, that is, services not affiliated with a religious group.

Low-income racial and ethnic minority clients can often be other-referred (as opposed to self-referred) to receive counseling by legal, medical, or school systems. Frequently, counseling is mandated as a means of social control of racial and ethnic minority clients of low socioeconomic status as an alternative to jail or termination of parental rights. Other-referred and mandated clients drop out of services at higher rates than self-referred or voluntary clients because of lack of knowledge about, lack of preparation for, or distrust regarding the counseling process.

Immigration Status

Help-seeking behavior also varies according to immigrant status (i.e., first or second generation) and acculturative processes. For immigrant groups who belong to racial, ethnic, or language minorities, lower levels of acculturation are associated with lower levels of utilization of counseling services, higher dropout rates, and higher rates of mandated referrals or referrals from other sources. For example, cultural or language incongruence is strongly related to utilization of services, as when the collectivistic orientation of certain groups clashes with the individualistic worldview of the service providers or when linguistic barriers between providers and clients affect utilization rates and outcomes.

Social Class

Help-seeking behavior varies across social class in terms of access to resources, continuity with services, and whether or not individuals with emotional, psychological, or relational distress choose the help of a counselor for their problems. Social class cannot be understood in isolation but in context with other variables, for example, immigration status and race or ethnicity. As counseling is an activity that involves the belief that speaking to a stranger about intimate matters is helpful, the outcome of counseling needs to be understood in terms of the relationship to a client of any social class background who seeks help within a middle-class, Western counseling cultural system.

Gender

There are gender differences in help-seeking behavior. As with social class, race, and ethnicity, gender cannot be viewed in isolation from other variables. Research data show that a large percentage of counseling relationships are initiated at the request of women, and women constitute by far the largest percentage of clients in counseling. This is due to a variety of reasons, including different cultural patterns of expression of psychological distress in men and women, roles traditionally held by women as family caretakers, and women's tendency to view themselves as needing to take more responsibility for the relational needs of the family, among others. From this point of view, counseling can be considered a female cultural behavior, in addition to a middle-class cultural value, because it involves the acceptance of the free expression of emotional content and openness to vulnerability. Some men, particularly in patriarchal or hierarchical family structures, might consider talking to a stranger about intimate family matters a sign of weakness, incompetence, or lack of control.

Implications

Once clients seek help, it appears that a major factor that contributes to positive outcomes is a perceived congruence between the values of the provider of counseling services and of the client seeking help. How providers of counseling services react to the different variables involved in help-seeking behaviors, attitudes, and expectations can greatly affect the outcome of the counseling relationship. Providers who accept the differences rather than fight against them, who prepare their clients for the services they are about to engage in, and who provide culturally and linguistically relevant services have a better chance of retaining the clients who seek their help.

Sara Schwarzbaum

See also Acculturation (v3); Barriers to Cross-Cultural Counseling (v3); Collectivism (v3); Cultural Mistrust (v3); Ethnic Minority (v3); Immigrants (v3); Outcomes of Counseling and Psychotherapy (v2); Self-Disclosure (v2); Social Class (v4); Race (v3); Worldview (v3)

Further Readings

Evans, K. M., Kincade, E. A., Marbley, A. F., & Seem, S. R. (2005). Feminism and feminist therapy: Lessons from the past and hopes for the future. *Journal of Counseling & Development, 83*(3), 269–277.

Falicov, C. J. (1998). *Latinos and family therapy.* New York: W. W. Norton.

Hays, P. (2001). *Addressing cultural complexities in practice.* Washington, DC: American Psychological Association.

Kliman, J. (1998). Social class as a relationship: Implications for family therapy. In M. McGoldrick (Ed.), *Re-visioning family therapy: Race, culture, and gender in clinical practice* (pp. 50–61). New York: Guilford Press.

McCarthy, J., & Holliday, E. I. (2004). Help seeking and counseling within a traditional male gender role: An examination from a multicultural perspective. *Journal of Counseling & Development, 82*(1), 25–30.

Sanchez-Hucles, J. (2000). *The first session with African Americans: A step-by-step guide.* San Francisco: Jossey-Bass.

HIGH-CONTEXT COMMUNICATION

Anthropologist Edward T. Hall introduced the construct of high-context (HC) communication to describe the degree to which people rely on contextual factors rather than the explicit and transmitted part of the message to derive meaning in communication. In HC communication, people derive meaning from mutually shared information of the context that is associated with a communication event. HC communicators pay less attention to the explicit, communicated speech to gather information. HC communication involves indirect messages, less emphasis on verbal content, and heightened sensitivity to others. HC communicators gather meaning by inferring meaning from the person's circumstances.

Hall proposed that the nervous system has developed an information-processing mechanism that can effectively cope with information overload through a culturally determined process called *contexting*. This process posits that individuals need to select only a portion of the total information available in an event to create meaning. The information that is not selected for processing but needed to create meaning is filled in by context. According to Hall, as contexting increases in a communication event, less information is needed from the explicit code to create meaning. While contexting requires time to develop, when it is accomplished, HC communication tends to be predictable, stable, and efficient.

Culture shapes the contexting process by socializing individuals to organize their past experiences according to a prescribed system of symbolic representations. This pattern of symbolic representations determines the cultural norms, rules, and expectations that guide how people communicate with one another. HC predominance is found in Japanese, Korean, Chinese, Latin American, African, Arabic, and Mediterranean cultures. Individuals within these cultures tend to be well-informed about others in their ingroup.

When a client says to the counselor, "You've been really helpful, but I don't think I will need any more counseling," a HC communicator would not interpret the statement at face value. The counselor may have observed that the client did not make eye contact while verbalizing his or her intent to end counseling and that the client identifies with a culture that discourages interpersonal confrontations. Based on HC communication, the counselor may hypothesize that the client is not satisfied with counseling and may ask the client questions about how therapy can be more helpful.

Yong S. Park and Bryan S. K. Kim

See also Allocentrism (v3); Collectivism (v3); Communication (v3); Counseling Skills Training (v2); Cultural Values (v3); Culture (v3); Low-Context Communication (v3); Relationships With Clients (v2); Self-Disclosure (v2)

Further Readings

Gudykunst, W. B., & Ting-Toomey, S. (1988). *Culture and interpersonal communication.* Newbury Park, CA: Sage.

Hall, E. T. (1976). *Beyond culture.* Garden City, NY: Anchor Press.

Hall, E. T., & Hall, M. R. (1990). *Understanding cultural differences.* Yarmouth, ME: Intercultural Press.

HISPANICS, HISPANIC AMERICANS

See LATINOS

IDENTITY

The concept of identity has been defined as an internalized psychic system that integrates an individual's inner self and the outer social world into a congruent whole. The integration of a personal self and social outer world has been viewed as a developmental process and one that, according to Erik Erikson, requires the individual to synthesize fragments of childhood identifications into a single structure during late adolescence and early adulthood. Identity formation has long been viewed in this way; however, the notion that individuals synthesize fragments of childhood identifications into a single structure during adolescence may no longer be an adequate model in which to fully understand the development of identity. Many researchers and theorists now contend that traditional theories of identity development do not fully explain the development of an individual's group or social identity such as gender, ethnicity, class, and sexual orientation. A prominent criticism of foundational theories of identity development is that they were constructed based on traditional Eurocentric individualistic culture. Consequently, traditional theories may not aptly apply to women, non-White European racial/ethnic groups, and collectivistic cultures whose family systems, cultural norms, and developmental milestones may be different from traditional Eurocentric cultural patterns. It is at this point that psychologists began looking at elements of personal identity and the sociopolitical and cultural forces that affect identity.

Much of the research examining identity has focused on traits or dynamics that are considered universal for all human beings (e.g., self-esteem, introversion–extraversion, and levels of anxiety) regardless of race, culture, gender, sexual orientation, or class. At this level, researchers and clinicians treat human experiences as being similar, for example, the experiences of aging, coping with life stress, and interpersonal relationships. However, the extent to which any one of these traits and dynamics may be high or low, prominent, amplified, or muted differs as a result of sociodemographic categories such as culture, class, gender, ethnicity, or sexual orientation.

All individuals must merge cognitive, emotional, and social factors to construct one's sense of self. Although the process of integration is similar for many people, Erikson's theory does not account for differences people may experience while integrating multiple identities based on demographic categories (e.g., gender, race, sexual orientation, physical ability). An individual's unique traits and characteristics, family dynamics, cultural and ethnic norms, beliefs and attitudes, and experiences of oppression significantly contribute to the development of one's inner self and social outer world. These factors may either inhibit or facilitate the developmental process of exploration, resolution, and commitment needed for the expression and saliency of one's identity. As the field of psychology has incorporated a broader understanding of identity, many researchers and theorists have come to recognize that individuals are cultural beings and are affected differently by various dimensions of personal identity and contextual factors. The relationship between psychological and sociocultural forces in individuals' lives has expanded conceptualizations of the manner in which individuals develop awareness and acceptance of themselves in relation to self, others, their place and definition in society, and membership(s) in social groups.

Social and Group Identity

Henri Tajfel's social identity theory is an integration of social psychological theories that describe the process by which individuals identify with respective social groups. People categorize themselves and are categorized by others in terms of social reference groups, which often serve to maintain shared attitudes, beliefs, and values common to insider members. A feeling of "belonging" is an important aspect of every person's sense of self. Social groups help create a frame of reference that contributes to an individual's place and definition in society. Personal identity development addresses the question "Who am I?" whereas social identity addresses the question "Who am I, relative to others?" The latter question is rather poignant for nondominant group members, who often experience issues of societal oppression, discrimination, and marginalization that are connected with their group identity. When taking these factors into account, exploration of identity may include the need to be aware of, evaluate, and self-identify with respective social groups (e.g., gender, race/ethnicity, sexual orientation, class, religion), while experiencing oppression and marginalization associated with membership in those respective groups. Identification with a social group that is viewed negatively by society is filled with cognitive and affective challenges that must be negotiated and integrated with the self. Consequently, integrating inner and outer perceptions of oneself becomes a complex process, potentially involving positive perceptions of oneself on a personal level, but also having to negotiate negative perceptions of oneself as a member of a respective social group. Commitment and resolution toward an integrated "self," as proposed by traditional identity theorists, can therefore become more challenging and difficult.

Identity Development Models

During the past 20 years, identity development models have emerged primarily because of the interest in multicultural counseling. Several models have been developed to describe racial identity, feminist and womanist identity, gay and lesbian identity, biracial identity, and social class worldview. Identity models provide a conceptual framework to describe the psychological and sociocultural affiliation and connectedness to respective social groups. Typically each model describes a progression through a series of stages or ego statuses of nonacceptance/unawareness to self-acceptance/awareness of a specific social group. Each ego status involves distinct developmental tasks, which must be resolved for successful progression to the next status. Some models focus on the impact of "isms" (e.g., racism, sexism, heterosexism) as contributing factors to acceptance or nonacceptance of a respective social identity. For example, Janet Helms's models of racial identity describe the process of development by which members in respective social groups must overcome internalized racism in order to achieve a self-affirming racial group identity. The general assumption of Helms's and other social identity development theories is that if an individual can embrace the attitudes, behaviors, and beliefs relative to his or her social identity, his or her psychological well-being will be positive.

This description regarding the process of identity development is a very general theme found in many identity development models and should not be interpreted as a uniform process for all members within a respective social group or across social groups. Experiences of "isms" are internalized differently from person to person and from group to group and should be explored from both an etic and an emic perspective. Identity development involves the process of integrating an individual's cognitive, emotional, and social experiences with aspects of his or her inner self (e.g., personality traits, anxiety, self-esteem, introversion–extroversion).

Until the recent past, models of identity have focused on single social identities. Researchers and theorists have argued that single-identity models are inadequate to describe and understand individuals' multiple social identities from this perspective. Many people are members of more than one social group. For example, women of color identify as women and as racial group members. Additionally, both memberships place these individuals in marginalized, nondominant groups. Given that most identity models and identity theories focus on one identity, they often omit experiences related to the convergence of multiple identities within one individual. Membership in overlapping social identities may also extend to experiencing and internalizing multiple forms and layers of oppression. Psychological and sociocultural factors influence the development of one's social identities and thus affect the way in which an individual integrates those identities to construct a congruent whole.

Individuals are cultural beings, and all aspects of an individual's identity are interconnected (including race, gender, class, sexual orientation). The development of an individual's identity involves integrating the cognitive, emotional, and social experiences related to his or her social identity with aspects of his or her inner self (e.g., personality traits, anxiety, self-esteem, introversion–extroversion). An individual's sociocultural context serves as a filter through which the cognitive, emotional, and social experiences of his or her social outer world are integrated with aspects of his or her personal self to construct a congruent whole. This complex process of integration is particularly salient for individuals who are members of nondominant groups. They often have the challenging task of integrating multiple, sometimes conflicting, aspects of themselves to form a single structure of identity. Counseling strategies need to embrace the idea that identity development for nonmajority members includes sociocultural factors, as well as personal aspects of the self. In this way, the individual is better able to integrate all facets of his or her multiple selves and develop a more congruent, whole sense of self.

Angela D. Ferguson

See also Adult Development (v1); Black Racial Identity Development (v3); Ethnic Identity (v3); Identity Development (v3); Orthogonal Cultural Identification Theory (v3); Racial Identity (v3); Social Identity Theory (v3); White Racial Identity Development (v3)

Further Readings

Erikson, E. H. (1968). *Identity, youth, and crisis.* New York: W. W. Norton.

Helms, J. E. (1994). *Black and White racial identity: Theory, research, and practice.* Westport, CT: Greenwood Press.

Triandis, H. C. (1989). The self and social behavior in differing cultural contexts. *Psychological Review, 96,* 506–620.

IDENTITY DEVELOPMENT

Identity development is the complex process by which people come to develop a sense and understanding of themselves within the context of cultural demands and social norms. Identity development has been seen historically as a primary developmental task of adolescence—the transition from dependency in childhood to increasing responsibility for one's own needs, interests, drives, aspirations, and desires in adulthood. This transition involves a cognitive reorganization in how youth think about themselves in relation to others as they gain physical, social, and psychological maturity. However, societal and historical shifts have complicated the developmental markers for adolescence, causing the demarcation of adolescence to become difficult to define. Additionally, despite being associated with adolescence, identity development is an ongoing process that continues throughout adulthood where one forms an identity within a larger and transitional cultural context. For example, changes in the body due to puberty, shifts in sociocultural context due to war or the civil rights movement, changes in individual role responsibility due to parenthood or divorce, and changes in cognitive processing due to aging support a life-span view of identity formation. Moreover, cultural factors such as race, ethnicity, gender, class, and sexual orientation also affect the identity formation that take place on the way to and through adulthood.

Historically, psychological theories of identity development date back to Sigmund Freud's psychosexual stages of development, which describe underlying motivations and impulses that shape the sense of self. However, Erich Fromm suggests that identity is more fluid than characterized by Freud and involves an awareness of oneself as a separate individual, in addition to a sense of agency and self-efficacy in one's own actions in the context of social group norms. Fromm's view also supports a view where identity formation begins prior to adolescence, when the development of a sense of self that is separate from parental figures begins and extends into adulthood, when agency and a sense of self-efficacy may be challenged with new life roles. These differences between Freud's and Fromm's seminal theories have led to two divergent views of identity formation in contemporary theories: the structural stage models of identity development and the more fluid and nonlinear sociocultural models of identity development.

Stage Models of Identity Development

Erik H. Erikson is the seminal figure in the area of identity development, having formulated a compelling conceptualization of development across the life span. Extending Freud's psychosexual model, Erikson introduced a psychosocial model of identity development drawing from disciplines such as anthropology and social ecology. He was one of the first theorists to consider the development of personality as a lifelong process and identified eight developmental stages beginning at birth and extending throughout the life span. Each of the stages presents new "tasks," or conflicts, that influence the ongoing process of identity development. The ability to negotiate conflicts successfully during each of the stages results in the development of psychological resources, which serve as the foundation for a fully integrated sense of self.

Although identity developmental tasks are encountered across the life span, identity development has been considered the primary psychosocial task of adolescence or, as characterized by Erikson, identity versus identity confusion. Adolescence is a time when, according to Erikson, individuals begin to integrate their childhood experiences, inner drives, opportunities, abilities, and social values into a sense of who they are as individuals. Within this framework, the central task of this stage is to develop a stable and authentic personal identity. Identity formation is stimulated by adolescents accelerating their psychological, physical, and social individuation from the family. Through investment in peer groups and observations of role models, adolescents learn to develop a sense of self that can be valued and shared with others.

The process of establishing an identity is not, however, easy. Adolescents, faced with many important adult and life-changing responsibilities, can become confused about their role both personally and professionally and may become unable to resolve their identity conflicts. Consequently, doubt may begin to develop about the adolescent's ability to find a valued place in society. If pervasive, these doubts may lead to some form of identity confusion. According to Erikson, a phenomenon that reduces identity confusion is called identity commitment.

Commitment is a form of allegiance to values and ideologies. Adolescents explore alternative viewpoints and select principles that best fit their moral standards, values, and ideals. The adolescent's fidelity to his or her ideals helps forge important bonds that help create a sense of security and stability to navigate through the doubts associated with identity confusion and progress toward identity achievement. Research has shown that being high on commitment makes for greater sense of stability, or adjustment. For example, research in vocational development confirms that commitment to career goals is associated with identity development.

One criticism of this stage and most other stage models is that the terms are vague and difficult to operationalize, making the models difficult to measure empirically. However, researchers such as Anne Constantinople and Allen Waterman, among others, have extensively examined identity development and have found some empirical evidence supporting the validity of Erikson's model. Another criticism is that the stage model does not account for individual or cross-cultural differences; thus, it may not be applicable across different sociocultural contexts. Additionally, the model does not account for the sometimes nonlinear or cyclical movement among the various stages, which has been found to occur.

James E. Marcia, in 1966, expanded Erikson's conceptualization by including the concept of status regression, which allowed for the movement of identity to shift from a higher-order status to a lower-order status. Status regression is supported in the developmental research as being part of the normative and continuous process of identity development. Marcia also extended Erikson's model by delineating an ego identity status paradigm, which suggests that individuals experience identity crises involving a process of questioning, reflecting, and working through individual stages of conflict. Resolving these identity crises facilitates higher-order development, whereas not resolving them may lead to regression or becoming stuck in a particular status. The four components of Marcia's status model are identity diffusion, moratorium, foreclosure, and identity achievement.

Identity Diffusion

This status classifies people who are not committed to a set of values, ideals, and so forth, and are not actively searching for an identity, which leads to an identity that is poorly defined and rather diffuse, as the name suggests. These individuals may seem to drift aimlessly. Research has demonstrated that people who have fulfilled the exploration-commitment process tend to be more interpersonally competent and mature than those who are diffused. Diffusion is considered to be the least advanced of the statuses followed by foreclosure, moratorium, and identity achievement. It is also generally considered that individuals will develop greater identity achievement with age and that relatively few in later adolescence will be diffused.

Moratorium

This status is marked by individuals who are actively searching identity alternatives and have not yet committed to an identity. These individuals tend to be ambivalent about achieving an identity and may oscillate between rebellion and conformity. Furthermore, these individuals struggle to find answers and explore various roles. Consequently, they may try different roles in a temporary and uncommitted fashion and have difficulty firmly deciding on a given set of beliefs, values, or aspirations. Because these individuals are actively exploring new ways of being, they are on the path to identity achievement. However, because moratorium involves much ambiguity—particularly in cultures and societies that value decisiveness, commitment, and goal-directed behavior—these individuals tend to score high on measures of anxiety.

Foreclosure

This is the status most commonly endorsed during early adolescence and typically declines with age. Foreclosed individuals have committed to an identity without having explored other options. These individuals tend not to be anxious and appear goal directed, yet tend to be inflexible and defensive. They are strongly committed, though their commitments are not intrinsic. Rather, their sense of self is often based on the desires or values of family, peers, teachers, religious figures, or media personalities. Consequently, their identity commitment does not reflect an authentic expression of self but of conformity to others' values. Consequently, they may not progress to the identity-achieved status.

Identity Achievement

Individuals in this status have explored various alternative identities and have committed to an identity. These individuals are thought to have successfully negotiated the psychosocial task of adolescence, negotiated the challenges of moratorium, and coped with identity crises. As a result, they have made a firm commitment to a given identity and are able to articulate how and why they have decided upon their particular choices. Individuals develop a comfort with themselves and their life direction. Furthermore, individuals are able to accept their limitations and appreciate their individual strengths. Identity-achieved individuals tend to score high on measures of moral development, autonomy, and creativity and perform well under stress.

Marcia identified another factor essential for the development of a mature identity in addition to commitment: exploration. Exploration refers to an individual's active questioning of various alternatives for their identity. Exploration also involves the concept of self-efficacy, which suggests, according to Nancy Betz and Gail Hackett, that individuals who approach specific tasks with a sense of competence and confidence tend to be more engaged in the task and have more positive outcomes.

Nonlinear Identity Development Models

Departing from the clearly delineated stage models, nonlinear models are more integrative in nature and may more accurately reflect cross-cultural identity shifts. Michael D. Berzonsky's social cognitive model of identity emphasized the differences in the sociocultural processes used by individuals to construct, conserve, and accommodate their identities. Berzonsky described three identity orientations: informational, normative, and diffuse/avoidant. Information-oriented individuals actively seek out and process information that is relevant to their identity transition. The normative identity orientation describes those who conform to the expectations and desires of authority figures. These individuals tend to disregard information that conflicts with their beliefs or values and thus appear unreceptive to differing views. Finally, diffuse/avoidant individuals tend to display an unwillingness to confront the problems and challenges associated with identity development.

Berzonsky also described the context of the attributes one uses to define one's own identity development. As a result, he identified three identity orientations: (1) social identity, which is rooted in public self-image and includes factors such as reputation, popularity, and the impressions one manages for others; (2) personal identity, which includes private self-attributes such as values, goals, and psychological makeup; and (3) collective identity, which is grounded in extended social groups such as family, community, nation, and racial and ethnic groups. Berzonsky's view of social, personal, and collective group identification as three layers of one's identity that are negotiated in the process of identity formation highlights the importance of models that take into account diverse cross-cultural experiences. Particularly important are the racial identity and ethnic identity development models, in addition to emerging models of social identity and social class.

William Cross's 1991 theory of Nigrescence, Janet Helms's 1990 theory of racial identity development, and Jean S. Phinney's 1996 theory of ethnic identity development have all expanded and redefined the meaning of identity development within the context of a cross-cultural society. These models of sociocultural identity development all can be integrated into Berzonsky's three identity orientations of social, personal, and collective identity. The social layer involves the racial and ethnic perceptions and behaviors of others, the personal layer involves the racial perception of self, and the collective layer involves the larger societal view of one's own racial and ethnic group. The racial identity and ethnic identity models also allow for fluid progression and regression within the delineated stages and are shaped by exposure to, and internalization of, various cross-cultural interactions. These interactions may include oppressive experiences and positive cross-cultural experiences during the life span.

Additionally, Henri Tajfel and John Turner proposed the social identity theory perspective, which suggests that cross-cultural identity is affected by the psychological processes that take place when one identifies with a group. Social identity theory posits that when someone identifies with a group, the person develops bias in favor of the ingroup and bias against other groups that may be seen as in competition with the ingroup. Identification with a group has been linked with an increased level of self-esteem and sense of positive ingroup racial attitudes. Social identity theory has been successfully applied to the study of racial identity and has been empirically supported for separate groups, including Latinos/as, Asians, and African Americans.

Another layer of identity that is often salient within an individual is social class status, which may also affect one's identity development in a cross-cultural society. Social class identity development as described by Lee Nelson and colleagues occurs as one has experiences within the context of the particular social class in which the individual begins to identify. Over time these experiences become internalized and lead to identity shifts throughout adulthood that occur so that new experiences confirm the internalized beliefs the individual has developed about himself or herself. Ultimately, an individual learns to conform to the behavioral, attitudinal, and value-based expectations of his or her internalized class. Nelson and colleagues found that nearly all of the participants in their study described experiences of social isolation and deprivation when trying to move up in social class through higher education, which may have a large impact on the identity that is developed.

New Advances in Identity Development

A criticism of the models of identity development that articulate linear forms of development is that they reflect a conflict-based model where an individual (particularly an adolescent or an individual not exposed to other groups) navigates between stages of either identifying or not identifying with others' views to arrive at a stage in which there is no longer this internal conflict and one has actualized his or her own identity. The new models of identity development conceptualize identity development as multidimensional and transitional given the context. These new models depart from conflict-based models and involve acceptance of the transitional and fluid nature of identity at any given moment.

In 1998 Robert M. Sellers and colleagues introduced the multidimensional model of racial identity, which is a multidimensional and integrated model of identity development and includes the fluid concept of saliency in identity development. More specifically, the extent to which one's own racial or ethnic group becomes an integral part of one's identity depends on the saliency of the attribute to the individual. The multidimensional model of racial identity takes into consideration the multitude of salient groups that an individual may identify with (e.g., gender, age, race, occupation). This integrative theory is an important departure from the stage models of identity development. It allows for flexibility across different particular cultural contexts for the individual to choose which aspect of identity becomes salient.

In 2001 Daniel P. McAdams added an important component to the area through his narrative view of identity development. McAdams's life story model of identity states that individuals create stories about themselves and weave their own stories as they selectively remember and recount episodes that are salient to them. McAdams posited that people tell and retell their own life stories in social contexts, and these stories can be seen as a way of negotiating how they have thought of themselves throughout time.

Specifically, according to McAdams, the *I* is the narrator that creates the story and the *me* is the self-concept that is created as a result. This narrative approach model, steeped in cross-cultural and societal processes, facilitates an integrative view using the individual as the source and context for his or her own identity development given the various stages and happenings that have been most salient to them. In McAdams's model, identity is formed not through resolving conflicts, as suggested by Erikson, or choices, as suggested by Marcia, but through creating authentic narratives about the self. Overall, McAdams's and Erikson's approaches suggest that identity development is fluid and influenced by both intrapersonal psychological processes and interpersonal societal experiences throughout the life span.

Implications for Counseling

With the multiple theoretical approaches to identity development and the multiplicity of cultural factors that impact identity development, shifts inherent throughout the process of identity formation have important implications for counselors. Counselors can facilitate clients' identity searching and committing to identity alternatives as well as recognize the normative stress involved in identity exploration. By encouraging identity development, clients can develop an authentic sense of self that is able to accommodate the different experiences clients have had and will have throughout their lives. Thus, by gaining an understanding of clients' identity development, counselors learn how the clients' cultural worldview and view of self impacts the framework through which the client understands his or her presenting concerns, which may serve to facilitate the therapeutic alliance and the growth and healing of the client.

Future Directions

The view of identity development as being multidimensional has been supported in the racial and ethnic identity development research, yet identity development differences between those in an individualistic society and those in a collectivistic society have not been sufficiently investigated. It has been suggested that the psychosocial process of individuation occurs differently for men and women and perhaps differently across different cultural contexts. For example, those from individualistic societies are typically taught to value autonomy and independence from an early age. Yet those from collectivistic cultures learn to value relationships and connectedness, indicating potential variances within the identity development processes of those with both cultures. Future identity research could explore the vicissitudes of identity development across contexts as well as the consistencies across contexts.

Additionally, the process of sexual identity development warrants more study. There have been extensive studies on sexual body development in adolescence; however, the psychological processes that take place as relationships with same- and opposite-sex friends and partners are forged have not been fully studied. Furthermore, the stigmatization and negotiation within a social network where one's sexual orientation may not be readily distinguishable, and the effect this may have on an individual's identity, warrant further study.

Ruth Montero, Nicholas C. Scull, and Stephen M. Quintana

See also Adult Development (v1); Black Racial Identity Development (v3); Cross, William E., Jr. (v3); Ethnic Identity (v3); Helms, Janet E. (v3); Identity (v3); Orthogonal Cultural Identification Theory (v3); Racial Identity (v3); Social Identity Theory (v3); White Racial Identity Development (v3)

Further Readings

Berzonsky, M. D. (2004). Identity processing style, self-construction, and personal epistemic assumptions: A social-cognitive perspective. *European Journal of Developmental Psychology, 1*(4), 303–315.

Berzonsky, M. D., & Neimyer, G. J. (1994). Ego identity status and identity processing orientation: The moderating role of commitment. *Journal of Research in Personality, 28,* 425–435.

Betz, N. E., & Hackett, G. (1986). Applications of self-efficacy theory to understanding career choice behavior. *Journal of Social & Clinical Psychology, 4*(3), 279–289.

Blustein, D. L., Devenis, L. E., & Kidney, B. A. (1989). Relationship between the identity formation process and career development. *Journal of Counseling Psychology, 36*(2), 196–202.

Constantinople, A. (1969). An Eriksonian measure of personality development in college students. *Developmental Psychology, 1*(4), 357–372.

Cross, W. (1991). *Shades of Black: Diversity in African American identity*. Philadelphia: Temple University Press.

Erikson, E. H. (1963). *Childhood and society*. New York: W. W. Norton.

Erikson, E. H. (1968). *Identity: Youth and crisis*. New York: W. W. Norton.

Fromm, E. (1941). *Escape from freedom*. New York: Farrar & Rinehart.

Helms, J. (1990). *Black and White racial identity theory, research, and practice*. Westport, CT: Praeger.

Marcia, J. E. (1966). Development and validation of ego identity status. *Journal of Personality and Social Psychology, 3,* 551–558.

Marcia, J. E. (1967). Ego identity status: Relationship to change in self-esteem, "general maladjustment," and authoritarianism. *Journal of Personality, 35,* 118–133.

McAdams, D. P. (2001). The psychology of life stories. *Review of General Psychology, 5*(2), 100–122.

Nelson, M. L., Englar-Carlson, M., & Tierney, S. C. (2006). Class jumping into academia: Multiple identities for counseling academics. *Journal of Counseling Psychology, 53*(1), 1–14.

Phinney, J. (1996). When we talk about American ethnic groups, what do we mean? *American Psychologist, 51,* 918–927.

Phinney, J. S., & Kohatsu, E. L. (1997). Ethnic and racial identity development and mental health. In J. Schulenberg, J. L. Maggs, & K. Hurrelmann (Eds.), *Health risks and developmental transitions during adolescence* (pp. 420–443). New York: Cambridge University Press.

Sellers, R. M., Smith, M. A., & Shelton, J. N. (1998). Multidimensional model of racial identity: A reconceptualization of African American racial identity. *Personality and Social Psychology Review, 2*(1), 18–39.

Tajfel, H., & Turner, J. (2001). An integrative theory of intergroup conflict. In M. A. Hogg & D. Abrams (Eds.), *Intergroup relations: Essential readings* (pp. 94–109). New York: Psychology Press.

Waterman, A. S. (1982). Identity development from adolescence to adulthood: An extension of theory and a review of research. *Developmental Psychology, 18*(3), 341–358.

IDIOCENTRISM

The word *idio* means own, personal, private, peculiar, and distinct. The word *centrism* refers to adopting the middle position between two extreme viewpoints. The combination of these words, *idiocentrism,* should be used when measuring individual-level orientations reflecting individualistic cultures. Individualistic cultures are common in countries in North America and Western and Northern Europe, and the term *individualism* represents general attributes of such cultures. Individualistic cultures often are described in contrast to collectivistic cultures, which are more common in Asia and Africa. The term *allocentrism* should be used when measuring individual-level orientation in collectivistic cultures. Separating the terms *idiocentrism* from *individualism,* and *allocentrism* from *collectivism,* helps eliminate confusion concerning across- versus within-culture analyses. However, the term *individualism* continues to be used as a substitute for *idiocentrism* in the literature.

Idiocentrism is reflected in attitudes, beliefs, norms, roles, and values. Several personality characteristics, such as competition, emotional distance from ingroups, self-reliance, and hedonism, are associated with idiocentrism. Further, idiocentrism is a situation-specific disposition that can be measured along a normal distribution and, as such, allows for examination of idiocentric dispositions in both individualistic and collectivistic cultures. Thus, individuals vary in the degree they value individualism, and a person can be more or less idiocentric within either an individualistic or a collectivistic culture. Idiocentrics in a collectivistic culture will tend to strive for their individual goals and may feel repressed by the culture and desire to break away from it. Allocentrics in individualistic cultures will seek for something communal to belong to, such as organizations, gangs, and other types of groups.

Characteristics of Idiocentrism

Harry C. Triandis proposed that there are four main elements of difference between individualism and collectivism: (1) the self (independent vs. interdependent), (2) goals (goal priority based on self vs. group), (3) relationships (rationality vs. relatedness); and (4) social behaviors (determined by attitudes vs. norms). In individualistic cultures, the self is viewed as stable and internally located, and the surrounding environment is changeable. For allocentrics, the environment is stable and the self is changeable, adjusting to the environment.

Idiocentrics focus on individual ability, unique characteristics, personal freedom, expression, independence, self-enhancement, and actualization; the self is the vehicle for such enhancement and actualization. Being achievement oriented, idiocentrics tend to have higher levels of academic motivation and place more importance on social competition and recognition than do allocentrics. Further, idiocentrics' personal likes and dislikes determine their behavior, and they are likely to attribute events or behaviors to internal dispositional factors. Their communication style is associated with content rather than context, focusing on what is said rather than how it is said.

Similarly to allocentrics, idiocentrics have ingroups (e.g., family, tribe, and nation), but their ingroups are often small, for example, consisting of first-degree relatives or a few friends. In addition, idiocentrics do not behave differently toward their ingroups compared with other groups (outgroups), which is a pattern of allocentrics. Idiocentrics also tend to be emotionally disconnected from larger ingroups and value their own personal goals over the goals of their ingroups. For example, when there is a conflict between idiocentrics and their ingroups, the goal or need of the individual is given priority over that of the group. Basically, idiocentrics' social experiences are structured and arranged in relation to the self. Allocentrics, on the other hand, have internalized the values of their ingroups, and following these values and expectations becomes a normal and expected activity.

Because idiocentrics tend to be focused more on themselves than others, there is a tendency for them to be lonelier and have less of a social support system compared with allocentrics. They also tend to be more emotionally unstable, experience higher rates of depression and suicide, and be less adjusted in intimate, romantic relationships. They also show less preference for seeking professional help for their problems.

Empirical Findings

Since the 1980s, individualism and collectivism have been of growing interest to scholars and researchers. Empirical data have shown consistently that there is substantial variation among cultures regarding behavior and psychological processes. The first empirical study that identified the factors of individualism and collectivism was published in 1980 by Geerte Hofstede. In 2002, the first meta-analytic study on individualism and collectivism was published by Daphna Oyserman, Heather M. Coon, and Markus Kemmelmeier. These authors identified over 170 articles on the topic. In terms of personal constructs and individualism, Oyserman and colleagues found support for relationships between higher scores on individualism and optimism, inflated sense of self, dispositional attribution style, goal orientation, and direct communication. In addition, for individuals who scored high on individualism, self-esteem was associated with more personal success than family life, and more personal control was associated with less depression. In counseling, individualism has been associated with a lesser ability to conceptualize clients from a multicultural perspective, and many scholars have pointed out the importance for mental health professionals to be aware of possible cultural (individualistic) bias when working with clients from other cultures.

Future research on idiocentrism should examine the conflict that children from collectivistic cultures may experience when living and growing up in Westernized, individualistic cultures. However, concerns have been raised regarding the low number of adequate and reliable measures of idiocentrism and how difficult it is to measure this construct as well as the related constructs of idiocentrism, collectivism, and allocentrism. Thus, additional scale development studies are needed as well as studies that would help clarify within- and between-group differences in terms of idiocentrism.

Johanna Nilsson and Ashley Heintzelman

See also Acculturation (v3); Acculturative Stress (v3); Allocentrism (v3); Collectivism (v3); Cross-Cultural Psychology (v3); Cross-Cultural Training (v3); Cultural Encapsulation (v3); Cultural Values (v3); Culture (v3); Enculturation (v3); Familismo (v3); Individualism (v3); Locus of Control (v3); Worldview (v3)

Further Readings

Constantine, M. G. (2001). Predictors of observer ratings of multicultural counseling competence in Black, Latino, and White American trainees. *Journal of Counseling Psychology, 48,* 456–462.

Hofstede, G. (1980). *Culture's consequences: International differences in work-related values.* Beverly Hills, CA: Sage.

Kim, U., Triandis, H. C., Kagitcibasi, C., Choi, S., & Yoon, G. (1994). *Individualism and collectivism: Theory, method, and applications.* Thousand Oaks, CA: Sage.

Oyserman, D., Coon, H. M., & Kemmelmeier, M. (2002). Rethinking individualism and collectivism: Evaluation of theoretical assumptions and meta-analyses. *Psychological Bulletin, 128,* 3–72.

Triandis, H. C. (1995). *Individualism and collectivism.* Boulder, CO: Westview Press.

Triandis, H. C. (2001). Individualism-collectivism and personality. *Journal of Personality, 69,* 907–924.

Triandis, H. C., & Gelfand, M. J. (1998). Converging measurement of horizontal and vertical individualism and collectivism. *Journal of Personality and Social Psychology, 74,* 118–128.

IMMIGRANTS

Immigrants are people who leave their country of birth to live in a different country, most often on a permanent basis. Currently, people are immigrating to the United States by the thousands, hoping to find work and a better or safer life. The Office of Immigration Statistics reports that, in the United States, in 2005 alone, 1,122,373 people became legal permanent residents, which was a significant increase from 957,883 in 2004. Countries that are frequent contributors of immigrants are Mexico, India, and China. In light of this information, mental health professionals must be prepared to work with the increasing immigrant population of color in the United States.

Brief History of Immigration

Up until 1875, the United States did not restrict immigration. However, later the exclusionary sections of the Immigration Acts of 1875, 1882, and 1891 barred people from entering the United States who were deemed unsavory, including convicts, prostitutes, the mentally insane, those who could not provide for themselves, polygamists, and those who suffered from contagious diseases. The Chinese Exclusion Act of 1882 singled out people from China, preventing their immigration. To enforce these acts, stations, as on Ellis Island, were set up for the purpose of checking, rejecting, or accepting immigrants and processing their papers.

There was a lag in immigration during World War I, but after the war was over, immigration increased to the point where a national origins quota system was developed to limit the number of people from each country who were eligible to immigrate, as instituted by the Johnson–Reed Act of 1924. Passports, which were used in World War I for security reasons, became the norm and were necessary to enter the country. During this time, eugenicists, who believed that intelligence and morality are determined by race, were influential and were asked to speak at congressional hearings. Eugenicists advocated that the races should not be mixed because they felt that other races were less intelligent, inferior, and degenerate. This line of thinking in the social sciences bled into the immigration policies, and people who were considered "White" had an easier time of getting into the country.

In 1924, Mexico was exempt from the quotas, and states like California and Texas welcomed Mexican immigrants into the labor force. Another factor that increased Mexican immigration was that Mexicans were considered "White" because of their ancestry and not because of their actual skin color. In 1929, the State Department made the decision to restrict Mexican immigration, but illegal immigration at the U.S.–Mexico border was not strictly monitored, and immigrants continued to cross the border at unofficial points. To enforce the quota system, Congress implemented the U.S. Border Patrol to apprehend illegal immigrants, and the Immigration and Naturalization service was born in 1933 to deal with immigration processing demands and sanctions.

As time went on, Congress became more lenient in its immigration policy. For example, in 1943, Congress repealed the Chinese Exclusion Act. Also, due to the Displaced Persons Act of 1948 and the Refugee Relief Act of 1953, many refugees displaced by World War II, who would otherwise be unable to immigrate under the national origins quota system, were able to enter the United States. During the 1950s and 1960s, Presidents Dwight Eisenhower, John Kennedy, and Lyndon Johnson used their executive powers to relax existing U.S. immigration laws. Consequently, political refugees such as Hungarians and Yugoslavians (Hungarian Refugee Act of 1956), Hong Kong Chinese (the Refugee-Escapee Act of 1957), and Cubans (the Cuban Adjustment Program of the 1960s) were also granted political asylum and, later, immigrant status.

With the aid of the U.S. Congress, President Johnson enacted President Kennedy's proposal to abolish the national origins quota system, which appeared to be based on ethnic discrimination. Congress instituted a preference system in the Immigration Act of 1965, which admitted immigrants on a first-come, first-served basis. Unification of families was the goal of the major preferences, which covered 74% of the preference slots. For example, the largest single preference (24%) was for brothers and sisters of naturalized citizens. Encompassed in the third preference (10%) were professionals or persons of exceptional ability in the arts and sciences. The sixth preference consisted of skilled or unskilled labor for which a shortage of employable and willing persons exists in the United States. Although the national origins quota system was removed, in 1978 a worldwide ceiling of legal immigrants annually allowed was implemented.

While Congress encouraged immigration by instituting programs to help refugees, illegal immigration was vigorously deterred. The Immigration Reform and Control Act of 1986 instituted sanctions against employers who hired undocumented workers, and individuals found to be working illegally were deported. To further discourage illegal immigration, under a 1996 welfare bill, illegal immigrants became ineligible for most federal and state benefits, such as food stamps and Supplemental Social Security Income, with the exception of emergency medical care, immunizations, and help with disaster relief. On the other hand, refugees and asylum seekers are able to become legal residents after 1 year of living in the United States. Legal immigrants, who are permanent residents and green card holders, are eligible to apply for citizenship after they have lived in the United States for 5 years and have completed English language and civic tests.

The dramatic rise in immigration to the United States in the past 30 years has resulted in about 3 million non–native-born children and 10.8 million children who were born in the United States and have non–native-born parents. These new immigrant families are more ethnically, linguistically, and socioeconomically diverse than previous immigrant populations, who were mainly from Western Europe. These immigrant populations have resulted in schools in many cities across the United States serving a growing number of immigrant students of color. To fail to address the counseling needs of immigrant students is to ignore the social, psychological, linguistic, and academic difficulties these students encounter in their acculturation process.

Therapists must be aware of the history of immigration in the United States and the current immigration policy when working with immigrant clients. For example, an immigrant who is living here illegally will have a different set of concerns than a legal immigrant with a green card. The acculturation adaptation process of immigrants holding green cards differs from that of political refugees who enter because of circumstances such as fleeing war, ethnic cleansing, political oppression, or religious persecution in their countries of origin.

Challenges Immigrants Face

Financial Stress

Rubén G. Rumbaut reported that immigrants may be more likely than natives to be poor and to work in low-status jobs. This finding is not necessarily indicative of immigrants' lack of skills; rather, it illustrates the societal factors that bar immigrants from obtaining ideal employment. Francisco L. Rivera-Batiz talked about how many immigrants (86.8%) were employed in blue-collar occupations, and few (25.45%) had schooling beyond 10 years, which makes it difficult for illegal immigrants to succeed economically. It can be difficult, even for educated immigrants, to obtain desired jobs, as the training they received in their native country might not be accepted in the United States and they may not seek respecialization to obtain U.S. licenses and certifications. Immigrants who enter the United States illegally are vulnerable to exploitation by employers who pay lower wages because illegal immigrants are not protected by the government and if they complain, they risk revealing their illegal status and deportation. To illustrate the payment gap, men who are legal immigrants are reported to receive 41.8% more for pay than illegal immigrants. Illegal immigrants also do not receive many of the benefits that legal immigrants do, and they may experience stress from being unable to access services for themselves and their families.

Prejudice

Upon entering the United States, many immigrants face prejudice and discrimination based on both their immigrant status and ethnicity. U.S. citizens have expressed a fear that immigrants will take jobs away from citizens because they are willing to work for less money, and there are pervasive negative stereotypes about immigrants being lazy and criminal in their conduct. In an effort to curb illegal immigration, certain states have passed propositions that severely limit illegal immigrants' access to services such as health care, welfare, and education (i.e., Proposition 187 in California, which was directed mostly toward illegal

Mexican immigrants). There is evidence that people who were in favor of these legislations exhibited more prejudice toward immigrants and were concerned about the economic implications of immigration. Prejudicial attitudes like these create an uncomfortable and unwelcoming environment for immigrants, both legal and illegal, and add to their acculturation adaptation difficulties and psychological distress.

Psychological Distress

Many immigrants experience psychological distress, but are less likely to seek treatment, due to cultural attitudes as well as a lack of health insurance. Even if immigrants are in treatment, there is a chance that they will be incorrectly diagnosed. Somatization as a symptom of psychological distress is relatively common and unlikely to be detected by Western mental health professionals, which may result in underdiagnosis of disorders in immigrants. Somatization is particularly prevalent in collectivistic, context-dependent cultures in which the expression of emotional distress is inhibited or when individuals from these societies have an acute sense of the mind–body connection at times of stress. Thus, identifying individuals as suffering from somatization may be difficult, particularly because immigrants often seek medical help from doctors as opposed to mental health professionals, and they frequently reject psychiatric consultation.

Family Difficulties and Conflicts Due to Immigration

Parent–Child Acculturation Differences

Immigration is a stressful process for the family partially because the members may each adapt differently to the host or new society. For example, young elementary school children adapt more easily than adults as they are not yet set in their cultural customs and are more easily influenced by new customs and values learned in school. As a result, conflict may arise when children's American values clash with their parents' more traditional ones. However, it is not always the parents who adhere to traditional values. Immigrant families sometimes do not immigrate together; sometimes, one or both of the parents go to the United States first to secure jobs, leaving the children with relatives in their native country. It may be years before the parents are able to bring the children over to live with them. As a result, some children may be more traditional than their parents and may be offended by their parents' behavior. They also may be reluctant to obey their parents when they have lived apart from them for so long. All these dynamics of age and time of entry can threaten the family structure and cause stress for immigrant families. Thus, the therapist needs to be aware of the many different immigrant family dynamics.

Difficulties of Immigrant Children

Gargi Roysircar delineated difficulties that many immigrant students face, including lack of family and social supports, trauma from war or refugee camp experiences, poverty, and health concerns. One major stress experienced by immigrant students is the language barrier. However, children may gain more English skills than their parents, thus making the students responsible for interpretation and helping their parents understand the American educational system. Not only does language "brokering" by children present awkward role reversals within families, it also makes immigrant students solely responsible for their own learning within the education system, a heavy burden for any student to bear, not to mention one who is transitioning across cultures. These difficulties can cause many different conduct problems and confusion in immigrant children, such as acting out or being silent, having somatic complaints, showing poor attendance at school, and experiencing difficulty making friends. The immigrant students' native-born counterparts and teachers are most often completely unknowing and unsuspecting of these difficulties and their effects on the immigrant students. The consequent sense of isolation, loneliness, and harassment from other students becomes a common barrier that impedes immigrant students' successful transition to a new school environment.

Increasing Help-Seeking Behaviors in Immigrants

Help-seeking behavior is a major barrier to immigrants receiving support. Often, the cultures from which many immigrants originated do not have the same formal help structures (such as counselors and social workers) and rely mostly on informal structures (such as family, friends, and spiritual leaders). More than simply teaching immigrants how to utilize the resources available in school and the community, counselors (especially those in the school system) can help students and teachers appreciate the cultural differences in help-seeking preferences and potential stigmas and taboos about seeking help. Teachers, who are in frequent contact with immigrant students, become allies in helping direct students to appropriate resources in the school. Along with teachers, school counselors can serve immigrant students through small group work on transitioning and bicultural issues or through a buddy or mentor system. The purpose is to provide information and ease the inhibition of seeking help. Surrounding immigrants with a support network builds a protective system that enables them to develop and broaden their cultural, linguistic, and emotional hardiness so that they can be successful in school and in their personal lives.

Counseling Immigrants

When counseling immigrants, there are many factors to consider. Family structure, experience of prejudice, legal status, and reasons for immigrating are only a few of the facets of the immigrant experience. It is helpful for counselors to be familiar with these factors when counseling a client, as they will affect how the client adapts to the new culture and how he or she responds to counseling and other available help resources. Because of the rapidly changing face of U.S. communities and schools, counselors must consider seriously the societal dynamics created when new immigrants enter educational, employment, and neighborhood environments. The introduction of greater plurality in U.S. communities and schools can be seen as an opportunity to broaden the educational experience of all members of a community rather than forcing the re-education and assimilation of immigrants.

Gargi Roysircar and Emily Pimpinella

See also Acculturation (v3); Acculturative Stress (v3); Adaptation (v3); Assimilation (v3); Bicultural (v3); Bilingual Counseling (v3); Career Counseling, Immigrants (v4); Cultural Accommodation and Negotiation (v3); Demographics, United States (v3); Multicultural Counseling (v3); Multiculturalism (v3); Refugees (v3); Second Culture Acquisition (v3)

Further Readings

Bemak, F., & Chung, R. C. (2003). Multicultural counseling with immigrant students in schools. In P. B. Pedersen & J. C. Carey (Eds.), *Multicultural counseling in schools: A practical handbook* (pp. 190–210). Boston: Pearson Education.

Marsella, A. J., Friedman, M. J., Gerrity, E. T., & Scurfield, R. M. (1996). *Ethnocultural aspects of posttraumatic stress disorder: Issues, research, and clinical applications.* Washington, DC: American Psychological Association.

Ngai, M. M. (2004). *Impossible subjects: Illegal aliens and the making of modern America.* Princeton, NJ: Princeton University Press.

Office of Immigration Statistics. (2006). *Yearbook of immigration statistics: U.S. legal permanent residents: 2005.* Retrieved May 13, 2006, from http://www.uscis.gov/graphics/shared/statistics/yearbook/index.htm

Portes, A., & Rumbaut, R. G. (1996). *Immigrant America: A portrait* (2nd ed.). Berkeley: University of California Press.

Rivera-Batiz, F. L. (1999). Undocumented workers in the labor market: An analysis of the earnings of legal and illegal Mexican immigrants in the United States. *Journal of Population Economics, 12,* 91–116.

Roysircar, G. (2004). Child survivor of war: A case study. *Journal of Multicultural Counseling and Development, 32*(3), 168–180.

Roysircar, G. (2006). A theoretical and practice framework for universal school-based prevention. In R. Toporek, L. H. Gerstein, N. A. Fouad, G. Roysircar, & T. Israel (Eds.), *Handbook for social justice in counseling psychology* (pp. 130–145). Thousand Oaks, CA: Sage.

Roysircar-Sodowsky, G., & Frey, L. L. (2003). Children of immigrants: Their worldviews value conflicts. In P. B. Pedersen & J. C. Carey (Eds.), *Multicultural counseling in schools: A practical handbook* (pp. 190–210). Boston: Pearson Education.

Rumbaut, R. G. (1997). Ties that bind: Immigration and immigrant families in the United States. In A. Booth, A. C. Crouter, & N. Landale (Eds.), *Immigration and the family: Research and policy on U.S. immigrants* (pp. 3–46). Mahwah, NJ: Lawrence Erlbaum.

Sodowsky, G. R., Lai, E. W. M., & Plake, B. (1991). Moderating effects of sociocultural variables on acculturation attitudes of Hispanics and Asian Americans. *Journal of Counseling & Development, 70,* 194–204.

Smith, M. L. (1998). *Overview of INS history.* Retrieved May 13, 2006, from http://www.uscis.gov/graphics/aboutus/history/articles/oview.htm

Waters, M. C. (1997). Immigrant families at risk: Factors that undermine chances for success. In A. Booth, A. C. Crouter, & N. Landale (Eds.), *Immigration and the family: Research and policy on U.S. immigrants* (pp. 79–87). Mahwah, NJ: Lawrence Erlbaum.

Indian Health Service

The Indian Health Service (IHS) is the agency within the U.S. Department of Health and Human Services responsible, since 1955, for providing federal health services to American Indian and Alaska Native (AI/AN) people. Its charge as the principal healthcare provider and health advocate for AI/ANs is to collaborate with federal entitlement programs, state or local healthcare programs, and private insurance providers to mobilize the necessary funding and adequate healthcare provision for the AI/AN population. This includes approximately 1.8 million of the nation's estimated 3.3 million AI/ANs who belong to more than 562 federally recognized tribes. Most IHS services are designated for AI/ANs who live on or near reservations/villages located in 35 states, primarily in the western United States. However, some AI/ANs who live in urban areas are served by this agency.

The provision of health services to members of federally recognized tribes grew out of a special government-to-government relationship between the federal government and Indian tribes established in 1787. This unique relationship is based on Article I, Section 8 of the U.S. Constitution and has been given substance through numerous Supreme Court decisions, treaties, legislation, and executive orders that acknowledge the federal government's obligation to provide free health care to AI/AN people in exchange for their cessation of over 400 million acres of tribal land.

In 1975, the U.S. Congress passed the Indian Self-Determination and Education Assistance Act (Public Law 93-638) to provide tribes the option of either assuming from the IHS the administration and operation of health services and programs in their communities or remaining within the IHS direct healthcare system. Congress consequently passed the Indian Health Care Improvement Act (IHCIA; Public Law 94-437) in 1976. The IHCIA is a health-specific law that provides appropriate authority for the delivery of health services to AI/ANs and supports the options of P.L. 93-638. The goal of this legislation is to provide comprehensive directives to the federal government regarding the delivery of services to AI/ANs and to encourage the maximum participation of tribes in the planning and management of those services.

The stated mission of the IHS, in partnership with AI/AN people, is to raise their physical, mental, social, and spiritual health through comprehensive and culturally acceptable personal and public health services. To that end, it assists tribes in developing their health programs through activities such as health management training, technical assistance, and human resource development. It provides hospital and ambulatory medical care and preventive and rehabilitative services. The agency also helps develop community sanitation facilities for Indian homes that have neither a safe water supply nor an adequate sewage system. Preventive measures involving environmental, educational, and outreach activities are combined with therapeutic measures. Within these broad categories are special initiatives in areas such as injury control, alcoholism, diabetes, and mental health.

The operation of IHS programs is overseen by 12 regional administrative units called area offices. Each area office provides administrative support in the forms of distributing funds, monitoring programs, evaluating activities, and providing technical support to the hospitals, clinics, and other facilities within its region. IHS-funded services are delivered through three mechanisms: direct IHS services, tribal services, and Urban Indian Health Programs. These services are provided to those qualified AN/ANs who meet IHS eligibility criteria. For those qualifying, health services are delivered directly at IHS facilities, through tribally contracted and operated health programs or at IHS contract health service facilities. The federal system consists of 49 hospitals in 12 states, 180 health centers in 12 states, 273 health stations in 18 states, and 8 school health centers. In addition, 34 Urban Indian Health Programs provide limited health and referral services to approximately 150,000 AI/ANs living in cities throughout the country.

As of 2003, the IHS staff was 64% non-Indian and 36% Indian. The IHS clinical staff consists of approximately 840 physicians, 380 dentists, 100 physician assistants, and 2,580 nurses. The mental health government employees with the IHS include 71 psychologists, 33 psychiatrists, and 127 social workers, not including tribal psychologists and social workers. The agency also employs allied health professionals, such as nutritionists, health administrators, engineers, and medical records administrators. There is approximately a 10% vacancy rate for health professional positions in the IHS.

AI/ANs are at higher risk for mental health disorders than any other racial or ethnic group in the United States. Their overrepresentation might be due to the high rates of homelessness, incarceration, alcohol and drug abuse, and stress and trauma. More than one third of the demands made on health facilities in Indian country are related to mental health, alcoholism, and substance abuse concerns. The IHS is limited to basic psychiatric emergency care and does not provide ongoing, quality mental health care. Instead, the approach adopted by the IHS is one of responding to immediate mental health crises and stabilizing patients until the next episode (J. Perez, personal communication, July 21, 2003). Select examples of other AI/AN health disparities include the following: Their life expectancy is 6 years less than that of other U.S. citizens; their tuberculosis rate is 4 times the national average; complications due to diabetes are almost 3 times the national average; and their infant mortality rate is 1.7 times greater than the rate for European American infants.

In 2004 the U.S. Commission on Civil Rights censured the federal government for not living up to its treaty obligations through proper funding and effective administration of the IHS in a report based upon their fact-finding mission in New Mexico in 2003. The report, titled *Broken Promises: Evaluating the Native American Health Care System,* noted great disparities in the health and medical care of AI/ANs in general and even greater disparities for urban AI/ANs. The major contributor to health disparities in Indian country has been the chronic underfunding of the IHS. It is currently operating at an estimated 57% of the budget it requires. It received an appropriation of approximately $3.1 billion for fiscal year 2006. This amount rendered a per capita IHS personal healthcare expenditure of $2,133 as compared with $5,518 for the total U.S. population (the federal government spends $3,803 on average for prison inmates). Funding for urban programs, which serve 25% of the AI/AN population, is only 1% of the total IHS appropriation. In fiscal year 2005, the budget for the IHS mental health program was $55 million; for the Alcohol and Substance Abuse Program it was $139.1 million. In addition to this fiscal barrier, the U.S. Commission on Civil Rights report cited cultural, social, and structural barriers within the IHS that limit access to health care. For example, many AI/ANs are persistently dissatisfied with the IHS because of the constant turnover of care providers, remote and inadequate facilities, extensive wait time for services, lack of continuity of care, and misdiagnosis or late diagnosis of diseases. Furthermore, the IHS does not provide formal language assistance to its patients and relies on staff or family members to act as translators.

Nevertheless, despite having inadequate funds, the IHS has helped to reduce some health disparities. For example, the life expectancy for AI/ANs is now 71 years of age, up from 65 years in 1976. In many cases the agency has identified solutions to the health problems common in AI/AN communities, yet Congress has failed to provide the necessary resources to implement those solutions. The AI/AN professional staff within the IHS has increased 125% since the inception of the agency scholarship and loan repayment programs, established in 1981 to help reduce the shortage of health professionals within the IHS. Many of the recipients of these scholarships and loans are AI/ANs. The IHS is currently applying technology to distance education and service delivery to bring primary care and specialty medicine to remote areas through telemedicine programs and partnerships.

It appears as if the *de jure* response of the federal government to overcome the shortcomings of the IHS is to encourage increased local community control through tribal P.L. 93-638 self-determination contracts and compacting. The government also appears to rely *de facto* upon supplemental funding from tribes with gaming revenues from casinos for health care, human resource development, and health disparity research. Certain tribes have demonstrated the efficacy of economic development and community collaboration for the enhancement of the emotional, physical, spiritual, and social health of AI/AN people. However, many rail against these measures on the grounds that they facilitate the government's continued neglect of its treaty obligations and rely on a means of economic development that may not be robust.

Teresa LaFromboise

See also Alaska Natives (v3); American Indians (v3); Bureau of Indian Affairs (v3); Career Counseling, Native Americans (v4); Community-Based Health Promotion (v1); Depression (v2); Indigenous Healing (v3); Society of Indian Psychologists (v3); Substance Abuse and Dependence (v2); Suicide Potential (v2)

Further Readings

Indian Health Service. (2002). *Facts on Indian health disparities.* Washington, DC: Author.

Roubideaux, Y. (2002). Perspectives on American Indian health. *American Journal of Public Health, 92,* 1401–1403.

Snyder, A. (2005). Reforming American Indian/Alaska Native health care functioning: The role of Medicaid. *American Journal of Public Health, 95,* 766–768.

U.S. Commission on Civil Rights. (2004). *Broken promises: Evaluating the Native American health care system.* Washington, DC: Author.

Zuckerman, S., Haley, J. M., Roubideaux, Y., & Lillie-Blanton, M. (2004). Access, use, and insurance coverage among American Indians/Alaska Natives and Whites: What role does the Indian Health Service play? *American Journal of Public Health, 94,* 53–59.

INDIGENOUS HEALING

The term *indigenous* has been used primarily in anthropology and social sciences to refer to customs or people who are native to a specific region. In this context, *indigenous* implies a cultural referent that is non-native; this perspective has been characterized traditionally as Western European to the extent that most early anthropologists were European. Thus, people and ways of life that were characterized as indigenous were markedly different from those of the Western European orientation. Furthermore, in the context of anthropology, designation as "native" or "indigenous" implied deficiency, a premise that served to reinforce colonialism and oppression.

Recently, mental health researchers have applied *indigenous* to various forms of emotional, spiritual, and physical healing practices. *Indigenous healing* can be defined as beliefs and practices that originate within a culture and are designed specifically for the needs of cultural ingroup members. The notion of healing may imply specific roles and expectations of the helper, including the use of intuition, inspiration, or both; being chosen, gifted, or called to be a healer; manipulating higher energies through applying specific knowledge; and being a conduit between tangible and spiritual worlds.

Characteristics of indigenous healing and healers have been offered in the literature. Some theorists have described the "universal shamanic tradition" to outline intrinsic qualities of indigenous healing: reliance on use of community, group, and family networks to protect and reconnect individuals and/or problem solve to address pressing concerns; community participation in spiritual and religious traditions intended for healing; and a consideration of healers as keepers of spiritual wisdom, empowered with transcendent skills. Other characteristics of indigenous healing include metaphysical etiology of illness (e.g., influence of deities, figures, or energies), harmony between universal contrasts (e.g., male–female or good–evil), energy and motion (e.g., laying on of hands), and the involvement of the collective (e.g., families, tribe, or community). Lastly, indigenous healing practices tend to define wellness as the homeostasis of physical, social, personal, and spiritual dimensions of the human experience and the holism of mind, body, and spirit. Thus, unlike counseling and psychotherapy, healing methods that have been steeped in the cultural worldviews of Western Europe and reflect consonant values (e.g., individualism, linear thinking, internal locus of responsibility, and separation of mind and body), indigenous healing methods are thought to originate outside of Western frameworks and operate from contrasting values (e.g., collectivism, circular thinking, external locus of responsibility, and the essential interconnection of mind, body, spirit, and the universe).

Examples of indigenous healing practices salient for specific cultural groups have been presented in the mental health literature; within-group differences, such as acculturation level, ethnicity, and adoption of diverse worldviews, are to be addressed with clients when mental health practitioners consider integrating indigenous practices in the context of counseling and therapy. For example, indigenous Native American healing practices include the Vision Quest, which is a rite of passage that serves to elevate the individual to a different plane of consciousness through the concentration of life energy in the sweat lodge and herbal treatment from a medicine man. Healing practices that can be considered indigenous for people of African descent can include practices endemic to the Black church, such as prayer, collective readings, and unique relationships between a higher power, the community, and the self.

Among Latino/a populations, the practices of *yerberos* (i.e., herbalism) and *Santería* (i.e., a religion in which Christian deities have been ascribed unique powers and which is characteristic of native African and Caribbean belief systems) may be applied to restore balance through the application or ingestion of liniments and/or herbs, lighting candles or burning herbs, or prayer. Indigenous healing practices of East Asian and Indian cultures (e.g., *kampyo* or Chinese herbal medicine in Japan, or *ayurveda* in India) similarly apply herbs and dietary considerations to restore balance between the energy counterparts.

Manipulation of energies through acupuncture, physical movement (e.g., yoga, tai-chi, qi-gong, and reiki), or diet are other methods of restoring balance and regularity to the flow of universal energies in the body.

Counseling professionals are encouraged to build their familiarity with indigenous healing practices relevant to diverse cultural groups in an effort to promote their multicultural counseling competence. Donald R. Atkinson and his colleagues presented a three-dimensional model, in which counselors are advised to consider liaising with indigenous healers when clients indicate that such methods of healing are salient to them. Furthermore, counselors can familiarize themselves with diverse indigenous healing methods through building connections with local healers.

Mai M. Kindaichi

See also Barriers to Cross-Cultural Counseling (v3); Cross-Cultural Psychology (v3); Cultural Values (v3); Espiritismo (v3); Etic–Emic Distinction (v3); Health Belief Model (v1); Multicultural Counseling Competence (v3); Religion/Religious Belief Systems (v3); Santería (v3)

Further Readings

Atkinson, D. R., Thompson, C. E., & Grant, S. K. (1993). A three-dimensional model for counseling racial/ethnic minorities. *The Counseling Psychologist, 21,* 257–277.

Frame, M. W., Williams, C. B., & Green, E. L. (1999). Balm in Gilead: Spiritual dimensions in counseling African American women. *Journal of Multicultural Counseling and Development, 27,* 182–192.

Garrett, M. T., & Wilbur, M. P. (1999). Does the worm live in the ground? Reflections on Native American spirituality. *Journal of Multicultural Counseling and Development, 27,* 193–206.

Lee, C. C., Oh, M. Y., & Mountcastle, A. R. (1992). Indigenous models of helping in non-Western countries: Implications for multicultural counseling. *Journal of Multicultural Counseling and Development, 20,* 1–10.

INDIVIDUALISM

Individualism is a common term in the counseling and psychological literature used to describe certain cultures and specific individual attributes valued in these cultures. The term *individualism* is often used in contrast to *collectivism.* Both terms describe a cultural syndrome that reflects shared attitudes, beliefs, norms, and values that are found among individuals who live in specific geographical regions and speak a particular language during a specific historical period. Individualistic cultures, such as the mainstream European and North American cultures, place a high value on individuals being independent and self-sufficient. In contrast, collectivistic cultures, more often found in Asia and South America, focus on relational harmony and collective values. Of all the variations that exist among cultures, the individualistic–collectivistic cultural syndrome appears to be the underlying structure of such difference and thus may be the most important. These differences do not only impact the individual but also have a broader impact on, for example, economic, historical, and political systems and structures.

Historical Foundations

European political philosophers of the 18th and 19th centuries, including John Locke, Jean-Jacques Rousseau, and Alexis Tocqueville, provided some of the foundation for the contemporary conceptions of individualism and collectivism by debating ideas about individual freedom versus the collective right within the state. Significant historical events such as the 1775 American and 1789 French Revolutions, both emphasizing equality and liberty, brought attention to the idea of individual freedom. Additionally, many of the early U.S. citizens who had fled Europe because of religious and political oppression were influenced by ideals expressed in the French Revolution. These ideals also came to shape the U.S. Constitution and its focus on protecting individual rights and also the U.S. culture at large.

In many parts of the world, there appears to be a movement toward individualism from collectivism, with prosperity playing a key role. As individuals become more financially well off, they become increasingly independent from their ingroup (e.g., family, tribe, nation), which is a sign of individualism. It is further argued that the more complex a culture is, the more likely it is to be individualistic. Indices of complexity include product per capita, personal computers per capita, the size of cities, and percentage of the population that is urban. Additionally, increased social and geographic mobility, exposure to mass media from individualistic countries, small families (small families tend to raise their children with a more individualistic mind-set) are all believed to contribute to individualism. Raising children to be self-reliant and independent, in turn, supports individualism at a cultural level.

Variations and Types

Whereas some suggest that individualism and collectivism are dichotomous variables representing opposites on a bipolar continuum, others argue that they can coexist and that individuals can present with aspects of both individualism and collectivism. Harry C. Triandis suggested that there may be different dimensions of individualism and collectivism, such as that American individualism differs from Swedish individualism, and the collectivism of Israeli kibbutzim is different from that of Korean collectivism.

Trying to uncover variations among the individualism–collectivism construct, Triandis and Michele Gelfand identified four types of individualist-collectivist patterns (horizontal individualism, vertical individualism, horizontal collectivism, and vertical collectivism). Horizontal patterns entail the self being different from others, emphasizing hierarchy, whereas vertical patterns assume that the self is similar to others, emphasizing equality. Countries such as Australia value equality, and others, such as the United States and India, value hierarchy. More specifically, horizontal individualists are characterized by self-reliance with a desire to be unique but not distinguished. Vertical individualists are also self-reliant but with a desire to be distinguished, and they do this through individual competition with others. On the other hand, vertical collectivists are willing to sacrifice their own goals for those of the group, and they only value competition when it is between their ingroup and other groups.

Characteristics

Whereas the term *individualism* is proposed to represent the general attributes of a given culture, the term *idiocentrism* is to be used when describing or measuring individual-level orientations of individualism. Such use of terminology helps clarify the differences between the individual and the cultural level of analysis and allows for examination of idiocentric individuals in a collectivist culture (and for allocentric individuals in an individualistic culture). At this point, however, the literature has not been consistent in its use of the terms *individualism* and *idiocentrism*.

According to Triandis, individualism and collectivism vary in four main areas: (1) self (independent vs. interdependent), (2) goals (goal priority based on self vs. group), (3) relationships (rationality vs. relatedness), and (4) social behaviors (determined by attitudes vs. norms). Specifically, in cultures that emphasize individualism, people tend to be independent and autonomous from their ingroups. In these cultures, there is value placed on the development of the self and on individuals' abilities and skills. Internal attributes, including thoughts and emotions, help organize persons' behaviors and meaning making. In these cultures, individuals' goals are prioritized over those of the group, and their behavior is guided based on individual attitudes rather than on the norms of the ingroup. Generally, the more individualistic the culture is, the stronger the emphasis on the independent self.

Empirical Research

Since the 1980s, individualism and collectivism have been of interest to scholars and researchers. Empirical data have consistently shown that there is substantial variation within cultures regarding behavior and psychological processes, and most of this research has focused on identifying the attributes of individualism and collectivism. The first empirical study that identified the factors of individualism versus collectivism was published in 1980 by Geert Hofstede, who examined IBM employees in 53 countries. In this study, the United States was identified as the most individualistic country.

In 2002, Daphna Oyserman, Heather M. Coon, and Markus Kemmelmeier published the first meta-analytic study of individualism and collectivism. The results showed that European Americans scored higher on individualism than individuals from countries such as Japan, Korea, Hong King, India, Taiwan, and Poland. The study also showed some unexpected results, such that there was no difference in individualism between European Americans and Indonesians, and that European Americans scored lower on individualism than individuals in Puerto Rico but higher in collectivism than people in Japan. Comparison of racial and ethnic groups within the United States showed that European Americans reported higher scores on individualism than Asian Americans but lower than African Americans. These results suggest that individualism, as well as collectivism, does not fully follow the expected patterns and that additional studies are needed to further understand cultural differences among cultures, countries, and continents. Specifically, more data are needed from certain continents such as Africa, in which only a few populations have been examined in terms of individualism–collectivism.

Mental Health, Illness, and Treatment

In individualistic cultures, individual maturity and mental health are associated with competence, ego strength, responsibility, and autonomy. Success is viewed as an individual accomplishment gained through ability and effort. Similarly, mental illness and failures are also seen as due to ability and effort and located within the individual. Compared with collectivistic cultures, higher rates of loneliness, depression, suicide, and marital dissatisfaction are found in individualistic countries. The role of counselors such as psychodynamic and person-centered counselors (whose theories were developed in Europe and North America) is to help clients to act on their own behalf via the use of insight and self-exploration. Clients are viewed as responsible for their own actions and decisions, and interventions are focused on fixing clients' internal deficiencies.

In the past decades, many scholars have pointed out biases and limitations of Westernized, traditional, and individualistic approaches to mental health and treatment. One common criticism is that the European American White male has been used as the norm for assessing behavior, resulting in a focus on individuation and separation as developmental processes and the view of autonomous behavior as healthy and desirable. Consequently, such views of development and counseling may be limited and biased for women and individuals of other cultural backgrounds.

Johanna Nilsson and Ashley Heintzelman

See also Acculturation (v3); Acculturative Stress (v3); Allocentrism (v3); Collectivism (v3); Cross-Cultural Psychology (v3); Cross-Cultural Training (v3); Cultural Encapsulation (v3); Cultural Values (v3); Culture (v3); Enculturation (v3); Familismo (v3); Idiocentrism (v3); Locus of Control (v3); Worldview (v3)

Further Readings

Hofstede, G. (1980). *Culture's consequences: International differences in work-related values.* Beverly Hills, CA: Sage.

Oyserman, D., Coon, H. M., & Kemmelmeier, M. (2002). Rethinking individualism and collectivism: Evaluation of theoretical assumptions and meta-analyses. *Psychological Bulletin, 128,* 3–72.

Triandis, H. C. (1993). Collectivism and individualism as cultural syndromes. *Cross-Cultural Research: The Journal of Comparative Social Science, 27,* 155–180.

Triandis, H. C. (1995). *Individualism and collectivism.* Boulder, CO: Westview Press.

Triandis, H. C. (2001). Individualism–collectivism and personality. *Journal of Personality, 69,* 907–924.

Triandis, H. C., & Gelfand, M. J. (1998). Converging measurement of horizontal and vertical individualism and collectivism. *Journal of Personality and Social Psychology, 74,* 118–128.

INTELLIGENCE TESTS

Intelligence is a general mental capability that involves reasoning, planning, solving problems, thinking abstractly, comprehending complex ideas, and learning quickly from experience. The need to operationalize and make useful the construct of intelligence in educational, clinical, and employment settings led to a proliferation of standardized intelligence tests. *Standardization* refers to the development of consistent administration and scoring practices and predetermined guidelines regarding the interpretation of test scores.

Intelligence tests measure various abilities that may include auditory and visual memory, quantitative reasoning, verbal reasoning, conceptual and abstract reasoning, perceptual and motor processing, spatial reasoning, sequential reasoning, and attention and focus. Most measures assess multiple ability areas and often include both verbal and nonverbal reasoning tasks, although purely nonverbal measures also exist. The most frequently used individually administered intelligence tests are the Wechsler series of scales and the Stanford-Binet.

Intelligence and its relationship to educational achievement and future success is complex and may be influenced by cultural factors. Understanding the potential impact of socioeconomic status, stereotype threat, and other variables related to one's racial or ethnic group may be vital in obtaining an accurate estimate of an individual's intelligence. This entry discusses the potential impact of culture in intelligence testing, specifically (a) intelligence tests and their use with diverse racial and ethnic groups, (b) culture and alternative forms of intelligence, (c) contextual and cultural considerations in measuring intelligence, and (d) culture and applied assessment.

Intelligence Tests and Their Use With Diverse Racial and Ethnic Groups

Persistent discrepancies between racial and ethnic groups on standardized intelligence tests have been interpreted based upon a deficit model (i.e., lower scores are due to deficiencies). The degree to which an individual does well on an intelligence test is determined, in part, by what he or she has learned in his or her cultural context. Cultural context determines, in part, what constitutes intelligent behavior. The impact of these considerations becomes salient as these measures are used to classify and track students for special programs (e.g., gifted, special education).

All intelligence tests yield racial and ethnic group differences, particularly on verbal scales. Nonverbal tests of intelligence (e.g., Universal Nonverbal Intelligence Test) provide an alternative to verbally based tests. These nonverbal measures yield smaller racial and ethnic group differences when compared with verbal measures. Nonverbal measures include tasks tapping symbolic and spatial memory, analogical reasoning, and spatial reasoning. These measures are considered to be culturally reduced but not culture-free tests.

Many intelligence measures are standardized to yield an overall mean of 100 with a standard deviation of 15. Scores for particular racial and ethnic groups include Whites/Caucasians, 100; Blacks/African Americans, 85; Hispanics, midway between Blacks and Whites; Native Americans, approximately 90; and Asians and members of the Jewish community, above 100. These numbers reflect only averages, and the differences within each racial and ethnic group clearly exceed between-group differences.

In addition to overall intelligence score differences, variations in ability profiles are also noted. Ability profiles refer to the pattern of scores obtained across various subtests or areas. For example, Native Americans and Hispanics score relatively higher in nonverbal reasoning in comparison to verbal reasoning. Asians possess relative strengths in numerical reasoning and nonverbal reasoning in comparison to verbal abilities. The profile for Blacks/African Americans has been less consistent, but some studies have revealed higher verbal reasoning abilities in comparison to visual. Cultural explanations have been posed to justify these profile differences as cultures reinforce particular forms of ability. On some intelligence tests (e.g., Wechsler series), extra points are awarded for quick performance on particular tasks. Not all cultures, however, emphasize speed. Indeed some would prioritize perseverance and meticulousness. A number of cross-cultural studies have found group differences in defining "intelligence."

Culture and Alternative Forms of Intelligence

Intelligence can be expressed in a number of ways; therefore, different forms of intelligence have been identified in the literature. Howard Gardner's work identified the existence of multiple intelligences, including the following: interpersonal, intrapersonal, linguistic, logical-mathematical, bodily-kinesthetic, musical, and spatial. His theory specifically acknowledges the importance of culture in determining which abilities will be valued in various contextual settings.

Social intelligence encompasses social awareness and social facility. Social awareness refers to having empathy, attunement, empathic accuracy, and social cognition. Social facility includes synchrony, self-presentation, influence, and concern. Each of these domains requires cultural understanding and sensitivity to operate effectively in the social environment.

Emotional intelligence is defined as the abilities to (a) perceive accurately, appraise, and express emotion; (b) understand emotion and emotional knowledge; and (c) regulate emotions to enhance emotional and intellectual growth. The literature indicates that given that emotional responses are learned within a cultural context, understanding the complex nature of emotional intelligence requires understanding of cultural background.

Measures have been developed to assess these different domains of intelligence. The formats of these tests range from self-report paper-and-pencil instruments to behavioral indicators, including responses to scenarios.

Contextual and Cultural Considerations in Measuring Intelligence

A number of contextual and culturally linked variables have been identified that impact performance on intelligence tests. These include variables related to the individual being assessed (e.g., socioeconomic status, home environment, stereotype threat) and variables that pertain to the measures themselves (e.g., test bias, cultural loading, cultural equivalence, differential item functioning).

Researchers have debated the influence of socioeconomic status (SES) in predicting intelligence. Variables addressing SES have included parental occupation, school attainment (i.e., years of schooling completed), family income, and home atmosphere (e.g., cultural activities, reading materials). In general, results indicate that when SES is controlled (i.e., equated), the differences in intellectual performance between Whites and people of color are reduced. There is evidence that the correlations between SES indicators and intelligence may vary for different racial and ethnic groups.

Studies addressing the relationship between intelligence and home environment indicate that stimulating and nurturing home environments yield intellectually bright children. *Home environment* refers to the learning experiences provided within the family context, including reading to the child, providing play materials, academic/intellectual aspirations for children, language development models (e.g., emphasis on use of language, opportunities to enlarge vocabulary), and provisions for general learning (e.g., opportunities to learn inside and outside the home).

Stereotype threat (i.e., anxiety regarding one's performance on an ability test based upon stereotypes of his or her racial or ethnic group membership) has been applied to intelligence testing. This anxiety is salient when a negative stereotype (e.g., "Blacks are not intelligent") may be confirmed by one's performance and not by one's ability. Stereotype threat has been shown to lower the standardized test performance for groups whose stereotypes are linked to inferior abilities.

Test bias refers to the existence of systematic error in the estimation of some true value of test scores related to group membership. Bias is addressed empirically through studies of validity (i.e., construct, content, predictive). Validity refers to whether a particular test measures what it purports to measure. If a test is valid for some groups and not for others, then it is biased. Test bias with respect to racial and ethnic group membership is cultural bias. Most well-standardized intelligence tests have withstood challenges of cultural bias. To prevent cultural bias, test developers may invite expert panels to review item content during the test development process, recruit standardization samples that reflect proportional sampling of various racial and ethnic groups based upon the national census, and identify specific reliability and validity procedures pertaining to particular racial and ethnic groups.

Cultural loading refers to the fact that all tests are developed within a cultural context. Therefore, they are inherently "loaded" to reflect the knowledge, values, and conceptions of intelligence for the cultural group upon which the test is based. A test can be culturally loaded but not culturally biased.

Cultural equivalence refers to a number of critical considerations in ability testing. For example, the content of the test items should be familiar to all racial and ethnic group members. The language and content of the test should have similar meaning for different racial and ethnic groups. The ability being examined should have equal relevance for different cultural groups.

Differential item functioning has been used to formulate alternative methods of scoring to address racial and ethnic group differences on aptitude measures. One such scoring method is based upon the cultural unfamiliarity hypothesis. Items on tests such as the Scholastic Assessment Test (SAT) include "hard" or "rare" as well as "easy" vocabulary words. Easy verbal items touch upon more culture-specific content and may be perceived differently depending upon one's cultural group. Harder items, on the other hand, are less ambiguous and therefore will be perceived similarly by members of all culture groups.

Application of Cultural Considerations to Intelligence Testing

The problems that arise when culture is not considered in the process of intelligence testing are well documented. In the 1960s and 1970s disproportionate numbers of Black and Spanish-surnamed students were identified as retarded based upon standardized intelligence measures. Many were identified as "six hour retardates" given their limited academic skills during the school day, with higher-level survival and adaptation skills demonstrated in their communities. Court cases have challenged the use of intelligence tests with students of color.

Professionals must provide services to immigrants and refugees using translated versions of tests and interpreters. Intelligence tests have been exported to other countries and renormed and revalidated. To ensure appropriate assessment practices, clinicians must consider the examinee's cultural background and experiences and understand the limitations of intelligence tests. An examiner must always strive to be better than the tests used.

Lisa A. Suzuki

See also Academic Achievement, Nature and Use of (v4); Achievement, Aptitude, and Ability Tests (v4); Achievement Gap (v3); Bias (v3); Cognition/Intelligence, Assessment of (v2); Cultural Equivalence (v3); Intelligence (v2); Quantitative Methodologies (v1); School Counseling (v1); Socioeconomic Status (v3); Stereotype Threat (v3)

Further Readings

Freedle, R. O. (2003). Correcting the SAT's ethnic and social-class bias: A method for reestimating SAT scores. *Harvard Educational Review, 73,* 1–42.

Gardner, H. (2006). *Multiple intelligences: New horizons.* New York: Basic Books.

Goleman, D. (2006). *Social intelligence: The new science of social relationships.* New York: Bantam Books.

Helms, J. E. (1992). Why is there no study of cultural equivalence in standardized cognitive ability testing? *American Psychologist, 47,* 1083–1101.

Steele, C. M., & Aronson, J. (1995). Stereotype threat and the intellectual performance of African Americans. *Journal of Personality and Social Psychology, 69,* 797–811.

Valencia, R. R., & Suzuki, L. A. (2001). *Intelligence testing and minority students: Foundations, performance factors, and assessment issues.* Thousand Oaks, CA: Sage.

Interracial Comfort

Interracial comfort is described as the comfort level that a person feels around members of a race different from his or her own. Interracial comfort can be measured as awareness of the person, the presence or absence of anxiety about the other person, and the ability to go about the task at hand without being so cognizant of the other person's race. Interracial comfort can be applied to friendships, work, dating, relationships and marriage, or meeting complete strangers on the street. Oftentimes people have different ideas about their own interracial comfort based on the role that the person from a different race is playing; for example, a person may experience a different comfort level working with a person from a race different from his or her own versus his or her ideas about dating or marrying a person from a race different from his or her own.

Our ideas about interracial friendships undoubtedly begin at home and can be reinforced or challenged when we enter school. School environment is clearly a factor in developing interracial friendships. Students who attend small, diverse schools will probably have more opportunities to form friendships with students of various races than will students who attend very large schools, because the larger the school is, the more opportunities there are to socialize with people who are of similar background. Another aspect of school-related interracial comfort is participating in teams, either academic or athletic, which allows for group success, cooperative learning, and an increase in multicultural sensitivity.

Interracial comfort in the area of dating and romance has been increasingly accepted throughout the United States and has increased as attitudes about members of diverse racial groups have changed. As people move from interracial dating into interracial marriage, ideas seem to shift. Until the mid-1960s, interracial marriage was a felony. The perceptions held by society seem to have shifted to allow interracial unions to exist; however, prejudice and stereotypes contribute to negative perceptions of couples who have married interracially. Some people believe that interracial marriages destroy traditions normally held by the family. Some argue that interracial marriages will not last because of incompatibility caused by racial differences. U.S. Census data from 2000 indicate that citizens reported 1,432,908 Latino/a–Caucasian marriages, 504,119 Asian American–Caucasian marriages, 287,576 African American–Caucasian marriages; 97,822 Latino/a–African American marriages, 40,317 Asian American–Latino/a marriages, and 31,271 Asian American–African American marriages.

It is clear that social norms provide the backdrop for interracial comfort for many people. It is also clear that early experiences can alter perceptions that people hold about members of racial groups other than their own. Interracial comfort appears to be something that needs to be explored throughout the life span, starting with positive school experiences and progressing through work and social experiences held by the individual.

Janice E. Jones

See also Acculturation (v3); Biracial (v3); Color-Blind Racial Ideology (v3); Diversity (v3); Enculturation (v3); Interracial Marriage (v3); Personal Space (v3); Race (v3); Racial Identity (v3); Racial Microaggressions (v3); Racism (v3); Tokenism (v3)

Further Readings

U.S. Census Bureau. (2000). [Census data]. Retrieved from http://www.census.gov/main/www/cen2000.html

INTERRACIAL MARRIAGE

Interracial marriage is defined as a matrimonial union between members of two different races. It can be seen as a form of miscegenation (i.e., mixing of different races) or exogamy (i.e., a union outside of one's social group), depending on whether race or culture is applied to the definition.

Race is a term intended to designate the main subdivisions of the human species. Its core intention is to distinguish groups based on physical characteristics, such as skin pigmentation and hair texture. *Culture*, on the other hand, defines the way people play out their personal belief system, and thus, culture presents a more dynamic orientation to this issue. Because all humankind embody both race and culture, it is important to understand the roles they play in the lives of individuals who marry outside of their identified race, culture, or both.

Nature of Racial Designation

Contemporary researchers suggest that race is largely a social construction that has little biological significance, despite the societal emphasis placed on race. Seemingly arbitrary and inconsistent boundaries have been established for determining racial heritage in the United States. For example, there are more than 560 federally recognized American Indian tribes in the United States. While the qualifications for membership into these tribes differ, some people of American Indian descent do not qualify for this racial designation unless they have a minimum blood quantum of one fourth. Accordingly, possessing less than 25% Indian heritage is a racial disqualification for group membership, regardless of cultural practices and beliefs.

On the other hand, African Americans have been subjected to a one-drop rule. That is, persons with any degree of African ancestry—no matter how far back the lineage—are considered to be African American, regardless of an absence of cultural beliefs and practices. Amazingly enough, no other racial group in the world is subjected to this one-drop designation, and these differing policies of racial designation illustrate the social influence on defining race.

As these examples illustrate, inconsistent designations of race highlight the arbitrary nature of the definition, even though society subscribes to a strong biological rationale for utilizing racial designations.

Legislative Influences on Interracial Marriages

This adherence to a strictly biological racial designation contributed to U.S. legislation supporting race-based segregation such as the Jim Crow laws, which were enacted in the late 1800s. This legislation was upheld in many southern states into the 1960s when the civil rights movement was initiated. Jim Crow laws stated that it was unlawful not only for White people to marry persons of Negro, Mongolian, Malay, or Hindu descent but also for Negro men and women to cohabit (i.e., share the same sleeping quarters) with White persons. Anyone found to be in violation of these laws was subjected to either imprisonment for up to 12 months or monetary fines. In 1967 *Loving v. Virginia,* the Supreme Court ruled against the remaining 13 states that upheld the antimiscegenation laws. This ruling initially spurred an uprising of Blacks protesting against White supremacy. Only after the settlement of this uprising did the phenomenon of interracial marriage begin to rise in occurrence.

As recently as 1983, the Texas Civil Liberties Union called for the removal of three justices of the peace who had refused to perform interracial marriages. Although there are currently no states that explicitly ban miscegenation, the practice continues to be a social taboo in many communities.

Current Trends

In spite of the obstacles interracial couples face, interracial marriages are on the rise in the United States.

Census data indicate that interracial marriages have increased steadily over time, from 310,000 in 1970, to 651,000 in 1980, to 1.16 million in 1992, and to 2.7 million in 2000. American demographic changes are leading to increased contact among young people across racial and cultural lines in schools, in the workforce, and in better-integrated communities. By 2050, it is estimated that the percentage of U.S. population claiming mixed racial heritage will triple, climbing to 21%.

The incidence of interracial sex experienced an incline after the Supreme Court ruling of *Loving v. Virginia* in 1967. This increase led to a surge in the population of people who identify as biracial. As the population of these individuals increased, the basis for comparison became more difficult as larger numbers identified not with a single minority group but as a more ambiguous categorical group, biracial.

Interracial marriages today are more likely to occur between White females and Black males than in the past. However, Hispanics, American Indians, and Asians lead the trend of intermarriage with White partners. These statistics are likely to differ depending upon the U.S. region within which the couple resides. People living in the northern region show higher rates of interracial marriage than those living in the southern region. This trend, in part, is attributed to the historically significant migration of Black people to the northern regions coupled with the slow reaction of the southern states in responding to the civil rights movement.

Counseling Issues Facing Interracial Couples

Given this rise in racial and cultural integration, counselors must be prepared to address multiple levels of issues unique to interracial marriages, including being able to distinguish between cultural issues and common issues. When seeking counseling, interracial couples do so for reasons such as finances, fidelity, and child rearing; however, the societal landscape of racial intolerance and the sometimes unintentional push for assimilation adds an extra dimension of difficulty for interracial couples, giving a multiplicative effect to contextual factors.

Family of Origin and Social Support

Interracial couples may face a chaotic change from previously harmonious relationships with their respective extended families. Driven by implicit racist beliefs, otherwise loving fathers or mothers may disapprove of their daughter or son marrying outside of their race. This disapproval may cause couples to disconnect from families of origin, thus causing relational strain and psychological distress.

This disconnection also may cause interracial couples to turn to sources of support outside the family, even though these sources (i.e., friends, colleagues, and community members) can potentially present greater societal oppression, stereotypical assumptions, and acceptance challenges. In an attempt to remove themselves from situations of racism and intolerance, interracial couples may intentionally isolate themselves or develop new communities that support their relationship.

Racial Identity

Parents of biracial children often feel a sense of inadequacy in assisting their children's identification with biculturalism. Society often identifies children of dual racial parentage with whichever race their physical features most resemble. However, the child may not be *Black* enough to fit in with African American peers; conversely, the child may not be *White* enough to fit in with Caucasian peers. Subsequently, the child is placed in a tenuous situation wherein he or she cannot find acceptance anywhere. Integrating a healthy self-concept is a complex task for any adolescent, and social marginality magnifies this process for biracial youth.

Since the child may not strongly resemble either parent, biracial children may also have a difficult time identifying with either of their parents in attempting to resolve this duality. It is also possible that the child will arbitrarily identify with his or her most influential parental figure, which can ultimately result in peer conflict if the child's physical appearance does not support his or her choice of racial identification. As children become more aware of their own biracial heritage, societal racism becomes more salient and can disrupt the process of healthy identity formation.

While it is difficult to watch their children navigate through their racial identity formation, interracial couples also must resolve their own racial identity issues. While transitioning through life stages, marital intimacy may be disrupted if one spouse perceives that his or her partner, who may not hold similar cultural beliefs and practices, is subsequently unable to appreciate these unique and often difficult experiences.

Counseling Implications

There exists a double-edged sword in working with interracial couples. Issues related to ethnic, racial, and cultural differences may be underlying presenting concerns (e.g., money, fidelity, child care) that bring a couple to therapy. However, counselors must be cautious in their zeal to attribute a racial explanation to these relational issues. It is inappropriate to define interracial couples simply by their interracial bond. To be competent, counselors need to become aware of the layered contexts in which the relationship exists.

In addition to their own awareness, counselors need to assist their clients in cultivating an appreciation for their own doubly rich cultural family systems. It is helpful to encourage couples to share their life stories, relate to each other's worldview, expect and respect culturally complex differences, and express the wide range of values, expectations, and cultural components found in their individual life stories that have now been merged together.

Because there exists a multitude of potential racial matches (e.g., Black–White, Latino/a–American Indian, Korean–Vietnamese), interracial couples do not form a homogenous group. There are between-group racial differences to consider, just as there are within-group racial differences. Thus, there is not a "one size fits all" counseling approach to working with the issues facing interracial couples. Instead, a multiculturally competent counselor must be aware of the internal and systemic contexts surrounding the relationship and must individually tailor treatment programs to the unique needs of this vastly diverse population.

India Gray-Schmiedlin and Jesse A. Steinfeldt

See also Bicultural (v3); Biracial (v3); Color-Blind Racial Ideology (v3); Cultural Values (v3); Culture (v3); Diversity (v3); Interracial Comfort (v3); Multicultural Counseling (v3); Multicultural Counseling Competence (v3); Multiracial Families (v3); Race (v3); Racial Identity (v3); Tokenism (v3); Transracial Adoption (v3)

Further Readings

Gullickson, A. (2006). Black/White interracial marriage trends, 1850–2000. *Journal of Family History, 31*(3), 289.

Ho, M. K. (1990). *Intermarried couples in therapy.* Springfield, IL: Charles C Thomas.

"Jim Crow" laws. Retrieved March 19, 2007, from http://www.nps.gov/malu/documents/jim_crow_laws.htm

McFadden, J. (2001). Intercultural marriage and family: Beyond the racial divide. *The Family Journal: Counseling and Therapy for Couples and Families, 9,* 39–42.

Qian, Z., & Lichter, D. (2007). Social boundaries and marital assimilation: Interpreting trends in racial and ethnic intermarriage. *American Sociological Review, 72,* 68–94.

Reber, A. S., & Reber, E. S. (2005). *The Penguin dictionary of psychology* (3rd ed.). New York: Penguin.

Volker, T., Karis, T. A., & Wetchler, J. L. (2003). *Clinical issues with interracial couples: Theories and research.* New York: Haworth Press.

IVEY, ALLEN E. (1933–): COUNSELING THEORY AND SKILLS TRAINING

Allen E. Ivey graduated from Stanford University in 1955 and received his Ed.D. from Harvard University in 1959. Early in his career, he served as Director of Counseling at Bucknell University and Colorado State University. Ivey began teaching at the University of Massachusetts, Amherst, in 1968, where he served as a professor for more than 30 years. He is the author of more than 35 books and more than 200 articles, chapters, and monographs. His work has been translated into 18 languages. In addition to his work as a scholar, Ivey founded Microtraining Associates, an independent publishing company that has led the way in producing videos and books related to skills training and multicultural development. Ivey's prolific work has had a significant impact on four major areas: multicultural counseling, skills training, developmental counseling, and counseling theory.

To understand Ivey's contribution to multicultural counseling, it is important to understand how three other lines of scholarship have influenced his ideas about cultural diversity. First, he developed the microskills training method that has become the most popular way to teach new counselors to use introductory helping skills. Second, Ivey was the originator of developmental counseling and therapy, a therapeutic approach based on Jean Piaget's theory of development. Third, Ivey has led the way in articulating the relationship between multiculturalism and traditional counseling theories.

Skills Training

In the 1970s, Ivey published two groundbreaking books describing microcounseling, a structured approach to training counselors in discrete helping skills (microskills) such as attending behavior, open invitation to talk, reflection and summarization, paraphrasing, and interpretation. Although the first edition of this book did not focus on culture, the second edition described the cultural-environmental-contextual implications of microtraining. Rather than focusing solely on internal variables, like self-actualization, counselors can help clients focus on external variables that may impact development. This early recognition of the need to explore the cultural environment led to the realization that appropriate attending and helping skills differ from one cultural context to another.

Part of Ivey's motivation for combining his interests in skills training and cultural diversity was inspired by feedback from cross-cultural counselors who observed that the same skills did not have the same impact on clients from different cultural backgrounds. Based on this feedback, Ivey realized that some attending behaviors, like direct eye contact, were helpful in one cultural context but may damage rapport with clients from another background. This led to the development of the concept of culture-centered skills. In 1993, Paul Pedersen and Ivey directly applied the microskills training method to the topic of culture-centered counseling and concluded that developing culture-centered skills involves increasing the counselor's ability to interact with different cultures. These authors stressed the now familiar idea that the effective use of *skills* should be based on both *awareness* and *knowledge*. The key to the development of culture-centered skills is to examine a specific culture, identify concrete skills that may be useful with this particular group, and develop a helping theory that can be tested in practice.

In the same way that microskills training has been applied to culture-centered counseling, Ivey has infused the idea of culture into skills training. The development of cultural skills has been an increasingly consistent theme in each subsequent edition of the classic text *Intentional Interviewing and Counseling*. In the most recent (2007) edition, Ivey and coauthor Mary Bradford Ivey suggest that the purpose of counseling is to facilitate client development in a multicultural society. Ivey and Ivey summarize the fundamental relationship between skills and culture by concluding that the same skills may have different effects on people from varying cultural backgrounds. Therefore, effective cross-cultural counseling requires awareness that racial and ethnic groups may have different patterns of communication.

Developmental Counseling

The theme of development has also had a significant impact on Ivey's ideas about culture. Ivey described his developmental counseling and therapy approach as a way to apply developmental concepts—drawn from Piaget, Erik Erickson, and Sigmund Freud—directly to the arena of counseling. In 1986, Ivey suggested that development always occurs within a cultural context and that counseling is influenced by both the therapist's and the client's cultural and historical backgrounds. In 1991, Ivey expanded the cultural emphasis in developmental counseling to highlight the idea of multicultural development. He suggested that counselors should facilitate clients' movement through different stages of cultural identity development. By focusing on culture in counseling, therapists can help clients move through stages related to conformity, dissonance, resistance and immersion, introspection, and synergistic awareness. The most recent (2005) description of this developmental approach expanded the definition of culture to include race and ethnicity as well as gender, religion, economic status, nationality, physical capacity, and sexual orientation. *Evolution of consciousness* and *liberation of consciousness* were described as goals related to facilitating cultural identity development in counseling. Clients are encouraged to tell their stories in ways that foster movement through different types of development and may result in both expanded awareness and congruent social action. Ivey's synthesis of culture and development has contributed to the recognition of cultural identity development as a central theme in the multicultural counseling literature.

Counseling Theory

Ivey has been very influential in defining the relationship between multiculturalism and traditional theories of counseling and psychotherapy. In the first edition of his popular textbook surveying theories of counseling and psychotherapy, Ivey concluded that most counseling theories were based on White, middle-class culture and questioned whether it was appropriate to generalize these theories to other cultural contexts. Long before culture became a popular theme in the counseling literature, Ivey's book was the first survey-of-theories text to directly address multicultural issues. A multicultural perspective has become a more overt theme in each subsequent edition of this book. In the most recent edition, Ivey described multiculturalism as a metatheory creating a framework that describes how different theories of counseling and psychotherapy represent different worldviews. Each theory was developed within a particular cultural context and will represent the biases of that culture in trying to understand clients and foster change. In this way, multicultural counseling encourages therapists to view the individual-in-context as well as understanding psychological theories within their own cultural context. In response to Ivey's groundbreaking work, the centrality of culture has been widely accepted in the counseling literature.

Legacy

Three key strengths can be seen throughout Ivey's long and illustrious career. First, he has been at the forefront of exploring new ideas that may benefit the field of counseling and psychotherapy. Second, Ivey has been able to bring together pluralistic ideas from diverse sources and synthesize them in new ways. Third, he has always been deeply invested in translating theoretical ideas into pragmatic actions and teaching them to others in practical ways. Throughout his career, he has weaved together his interests in skills training, development, counseling theory, and multicultural diversity. Because of his dedication to pluralistic synthesis as well as practical application, Ivey's legacy will continue to have a significant impact on the way counselors think and act for decades to come.

Jeff E. Brooks-Harris

See also Counseling Skills Training (v2); Cross-Cultural Training (v3); Cultural Values (v3); Culture (v3); Developmental Counseling and Therapy (v2); Multicultural Counseling (v3); Multicultural Counseling Competence (v3); Pluralism (v3); Relationships With Clients (v2)

Further Readings

Ivey, A. E. (1971). *Microcounseling: Innovations in interviewing training.* Springfield, IL: Charles C Thomas.

Ivey, A. E. (1986). *Developmental therapy: Theory into practice.* San Francisco: Jossey-Bass.

Ivey, A. E. (1991). *Developmental strategies for helpers: Individual, family, and network interventions.* North Amherst, MA: Microtraining Associates.

Ivey, A. E. (1995). Psychotherapy as liberation: Toward specific skills and strategies in multicultural counseling and therapy. In J. G. Ponterotto, J. M. Casas, L. A. Suzuki, & C. M. Alexander (Eds.), *Handbook of multicultural counseling* (pp. 53–72). Thousand Oaks, CA: Sage.

Ivey, A. E., & Authier, J. (1978). *Microcounseling: Innovations in interviewing, counseling, psychotherapy, and psychoeducation.* Springfield, IL: Charles C Thomas.

Ivey, A. E., D'Andrea, M., Ivey, M. B., & Simek-Morgan, L. (2001). *Theories of counseling and psychotherapy: A multicultural perspective* (5th ed). New York: Allyn & Bacon.

Ivey, A. E., & Ivey, M. B. (2007). *Intentional interviewing and counseling: Facilitating client development in a multicultural society* (6th ed.). Belmont, CA: Wadsworth.

Ivey, A. E., Ivey, M. B., Meyers, J., & Sweeney, T. (2004). *Developmental counseling and therapy: Promoting wellness over the lifespan.* Mahwah, NJ: Lawrence Erlbaum.

Ivey, A. E., & Simek-Downing, L. (1980). *Counseling and psychotherapy: Skills, theories, and practice.* Englewood Cliffs, NJ: Prentice Hall.

Pedersen, P. B., & Ivey, A. E. (1993). *Culture-centered counseling and interviewing skills.* Westport, CT: Praeger.

Sue, D. W., Ivey, A. E., & Pedersen, P. B. (1996). *A theory of multicultural counseling and therapy.* Pacific Grove, CA: Brooks/Cole.

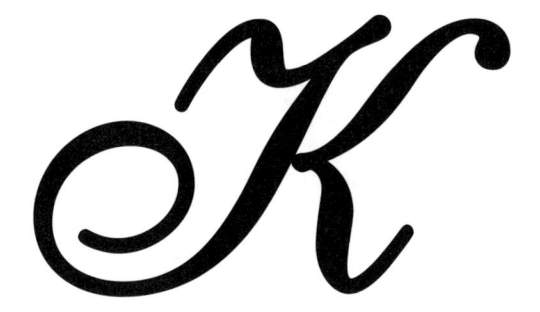

Kwanzaa

Kwanzaa is an African American holiday that was created by Maulana Karenga, an authority on African studies. It was first celebrated from December 26 through January 1, 1967, in Los Angeles, California, and Kwanzaa continues to be celebrated annually at that time of year as a Black holiday embraced by millions of African Americans. Kwanzaa was inspired by the agricultural African people who gathered and celebrated annually at harvest time, but it currently is designed to meet the needs of African Americans living in the United States. It makes a cultural and political statement, providing an alternative to Christmas and the associated commercialism and emphasis on expensive gift giving during that holiday season.

Kwanzaa gives African Americans an opportunity to celebrate themselves and their history with gifts, mainly gifts given to children to acknowledge commitments made and kept. Children have always been at the core of Kwanzaa in light of how they influenced the spelling of the word; the original Swahili word *kwanza* means "first fruits," but adding the extra *a* meant there were seven letters to represent the seven children at the first Kwanzaa program. The result is more than merely a word, allowing Kwanzaa to convey a distinct identity and holiday.

Kwanzaa also was made a 7-day holiday to establish and promote the Nguzo Saba: the seven basic principles that serve as the central focus of Kwanzaa and provide a Black value system. These seven principles are as follows:

1. *Umoja* (Unity)—To strive for and maintain unity in the family, community, nation, and race

2. *Kujichagulia* (Self-determination)—To define ourselves, name ourselves, create for ourselves, and speak for ourselves instead of being defined, named, and created for and spoken for by others

3. *Ujima* (Collective Work and Responsibility)—To build and maintain our community together and make our sisters' and brothers' problems our problems and to solve them together

4. *Ujamaa* (Cooperative Economics)—To build and maintain our own stores and other businesses and to profit from them together

5. *Nia* (Purpose)—To make our collective vocation the building and developing of our community in order to restore our people to their traditional greatness

6. *Kuumba* (Creativity)—To do always as much as we can, in the way we can, to leave our community more beautiful and beneficial than it was when we inherited it

7. *Imani* (Faith)—To believe with all our heart in our people, our parents, our teachers, and our leaders in the righteousness and victory of our struggle

There is no holiday named Kwanzaa that is practiced on the African continent, nor is there one that uses the distinct symbols, practices, or principles associated with Kwanzaa. Instead, Kwanzaa is a distinct African American holiday designed to respond to the social conditions in which African Americans lived in the 1960s, while underscoring the cultural unity among all African descendants. The seven Nguzo Saba principles continue to represent a powerful acknowledgment of and response to the sociopolitical reality in which people of African descent live in the United States. These principles also constitute a paradigm and Africentric worldview upon which mental health professionals may draw when designing culturally relevant and appropriate research and interventions for African Americans.

Barbara C. Wallace

See also African Americans (v3); Afrocentricity/ Afrocentrism (v3); Black Racial Identity Development (v3); Cultural Values (v3); Ethnic Identity (v3); Ethnic Pride (v3); Racial Identity (v3); Racial Pride (v3)

Further Readings

Karenga, M. (1988). Black studies and the problematic paradigm. *Journal of Black Studies, 18,* 395–414.

Karenga, M. (1994). *Maat, the moral ideal in ancient Egypt: A study in classical African ethics.* Los Angeles: University of Southern California.

Karenga, M. R. (1965). *Kwanzaa: Origin, concepts, practice.* Los Angeles: Kawaida.

Karenga, M. R. (1988). *The African American holiday of Kwanzaa.* Los Angeles: University of Sankore Press.

LaFromboise, Teresa Davis (1949–)

Teresa Davis LaFromboise was born in a small southern Indiana town. She is of American Indian (Miami Nation) and European descent and is best known for her work in American Indian adolescent suicide prevention.

LaFromboise began her career as a middle school art and language arts teacher with the Turtle Mountain Band of Chippewa and later the Saginaw Chippewa in Michigan, where she also worked with the Johnson-O'Malley Program. Noticing that 80% of the American Indian students on the Saginaw Chippewa reservation were dropping out of school, she sponsored a group of her students to participate in Suitcase Theatre, a national youth performing arts program that aimed to empower youth and promote respect for cultural diversity. As LaFromboise became more aware of how limited her opportunities were, as a teacher, to impact student issues, she wrote a grant that was funded to provide counseling services for the Saginaw Chippewa middle school students. At that point in her career, her family moved to Norman, Oklahoma, where she worked as a teacher for homebound students and began her graduate studies, focusing on mental health issues among American Indians. LaFromboise began her doctoral education at the University of Oklahoma fully intending to provide clinical services to American Indians. As she became aware of the lack of published research addressing American Indians, her focus shifted to a career in academics and research. LaFromboise received her Ph.D. in counseling psychology from the University of Oklahoma in 1979. She was on the faculty at the University of Nebraska–Lincoln and the University of Wisconsin–Madison before going to Stanford University.

LaFromboise's research topics include interpersonal influence in multicultural counseling, bicultural competence development, and ethnic identity and adolescent health. Her American Indian Life Skills Development is among the promising evidence-based treatments for youth suicide prevention and is used extensively in schools and public health prevention programs. LaFromboise has written extensively about multicultural service delivery. She is currently investigating the effectiveness of a culturally tailored suicide prevention intervention with American Indian youth in school and in home settings. In addition to assessing the impact of this intervention on the reduction of suicidal behavior, LaFromboise is exploring the role of cumulative stress, perceived discrimination, cultural identity, depression, and substance use on suicidal ideation. She teaches seminars titled Adolescent Development and Mentoring in an Urban Context, Racial and Ethnic Identity Development, Social and Emotional Learning in Schools, and Psychology and American Indian Mental Health. LaFromboise's research and published works have gained the respect and notice of academicians worldwide.

In the early 1990s, LaFromboise was appointed to the Office of Technology Assessment Committee to produce the report on adolescent health. Her daughter was an emerging adolescent at the time that LaFromboise served on this committee, which was also examining American Indian adolescent health statistics. During that time she became much more aware of the issues impacting her daughter's current and future health. With an appointment to the National Research Council on the effectiveness of community-based interventions for youth, LaFromboise moved her research and work toward issues of resilience and positive youth development.

Among the honors LaFromboise has received are the Distinguished Career Contribution to Research Award from the American Psychological Association's Society for the Psychological Study of Ethnic Minority Issues, 2002; U.S. Department of Health and Human Services, Substance Abuse and Mental Health Services Administration Excellence Award, 2005; Effective Practices and Models in Communities of Color: Effective Behavioral Health Interventions for Children, Adolescents, and Families of Color from the First Nations Behavioral Health Association, 2005; and Who Made a Difference from the University of Oklahoma College of Education, 2004.

LaFromboise is currently the chair of Native American Studies at Stanford. She has served as president of the American Psychological Association Division 45: Society for the Psychological Study of Ethnic Minority Issues and on the American Psychological Association Council of Representatives.

Jacqueline S. Gray

See also American Indians (v3); Bicultural (v3); Cultural Values (v3); Depression (v2); Discrimination (v3); Discrimination and Oppression (v2); Ethnic Identity (v3); Multicultural Counseling (v3); Physical Health (v2); Resilience (v2); Stress (v2); Stress Management (v2); Substance Abuse and Dependence (v2); Suicide Postvention (v1); Suicide Potential (v2)

Further Readings

Bryant, A., Jr., & LaFromboise, T. D. (2005). The racial identity and cultural orientation of Lumbee American Indian high school students. *Cultural Diversity & Ethnic Minority Psychology, 11*(1), 82–89.

LaFromboise, T. (1996). *American Indian life skills development curriculum.* Madison: University of Wisconsin Press.

LaFromboise, T. (2006). American Indian youth suicide prevention. *Prevention Researcher, 13*(3), 16–18.

LaFromboise, T. D., Hoyt, D. R., & Oliver, L. (2006). Family, community, and school influences on resilience among American Indian adolescents in the upper Midwest. *Journal of Community Psychology, 34*(2), 193–209.

Miranda, J., Bernal, G., Lau, A., Kohn, L., Hwang, W. C., & LaFromboise, T. (2005). State of the science on psychosocial interventions for ethnic minorities. *Annual Review of Clinical Psychology, 1*(1), 113–142.

Yoder, K. A., Whitbeck, L. B., Hoyt, D. R., & LaFromboise, T. D. (2006). Suicide ideation among American Indian youths. *Archives of Suicide Research, 10*(2), 177–190.

LATINOS

The rapidly growing population of Latinos/as in the United States underscores the profound need for counselors to broaden their clinical treatment approaches to attend to specific culture-related concerns. Latinos/as are faced with a number of social, health, and psychological difficulties that affect their need for mental health services. The negative impact of these life circumstances has made Latinos/as susceptible to a variety of mental health problems. However, because of a number of institutional and cultural barriers to treatment, Latinos/as tend not to make use of available mental health services in U.S. society. To increase utilization and effectiveness of treatment, and decrease early termination, the Latino/a population requires counseling services that will meet their needs in ways that are culturally relevant. The more mental health services reflect the culture of the Latino/a client, the more likely the services will be utilized and effective.

Latinos/as are an ethnically diverse group that includes Mexican Americans, Puerto Ricans, Cubans, Dominicans, and Central and South Americans. The cultural roots of each Latino/a country are a distinct mixture of indigenous, European, and African influences, resulting in differences in cultures for each country and differences in racial makeup of the individuals of that country. As a result of this blending of cultures, the term *Hispanics* has often been rejected by groups who believe the term excludes the indigenous and African influences, while others believe that the term *Hispanics* is a generic term imposed on Latinos/as by the U.S. Census to calculate the numbers of a new population group. Consequently, the term *Latinos/as* rather than *Hispanics* is used in this entry to reflect a more inclusive and politically progressive term. Furthermore, because of the differences in ancestry among and within each country, Latinos/as vary greatly in terms of racial makeup, with a blend of Spanish, Native American, Black, and Asian descent.

Therefore, the term *Latinos/as* emerges not only as an inclusive ethnic term, but also as a term that contains a racial component as well, leading others to claim the term is somewhat ambiguous.

Latinos/as make up the largest racial/ethnic group in the United States, comprising an estimated 37.4 million people, which is equivalent to 13.3% of the U.S. population. Projections for comparative growth rates indicate that the Latino/a population will increase at a rate 3 to 5 times faster than the general population with an estimated 100 million by the year 2050, resulting in one in four Americans identifying themselves as Latino/a. Currently, Mexican Americans comprise the majority of Latinos/as in the United States, followed by Central and South Americans, Puerto Ricans, Cubans, and other Latinos/as. The Latino/a population is geographically concentrated, with 87% residing in 10 states: California, Texas, New Mexico, Colorado, New York, Florida, Illinois, New Jersey, Arizona, and Massachusetts.

Because the Latino/a population is a rapidly growing ethnic group, the need for services to address their mental health concerns is tantamount. Latinos/as face a number of sociocultural, physical, and mental health problems, including immigration and acculturation stress, language barriers, disrespect for their culture, discrimination in employment and education, and poverty. This constellation of negative life circumstances makes Latinos/as vulnerable to mental health problems that require specific psychotherapeutic services.

Mental Health Needs of Latinos

For Latinos/as who immigrate to the United States, immigration can be a source of considerable stress. As a result of being transplanted into a foreign culture and away from the familiarity of his or her own culture, the individual can experience a negative impact on his or her mental health. Moreover, some immigrants arrive in the United States as political refugees with the additional psychological distress of the experiences of war and violence in their native countries. Furthermore, many Latinos/as immigrate to this country without family members, resulting in a lack of a social support network and feelings of loss and guilt for the family members they left behind. Additionally, many Latinos/as settle into poverty-stricken neighborhoods, often with dilapidated housing conditions and high crime rates, where illegal drugs and gangs are often present. These are persistent stressors that adversely impact the new immigrants.

In addition to the stress associated with relocation to the United States, immigrants may experience stress caused by the cultural conflict between their own culture and the new culture in the United States; this is termed *acculturative stress*. Stress of acculturation is associated with high levels of depression, anxiety, and physical health problems. Furthermore, the differences in the level of acculturation among Latino/a family members may lead to family discord and stress. The school system allows for children to become more quickly acculturated than their parents, resulting in a form of cultural conflict within the family. Parents are often not able to speak English or feel uncomfortable speaking English, a situation that can lead to their children serving as social and legal mediators for them, giving rise to a power imbalance in the relationship between the children and parents. Children who find themselves in the roles of social and legal mediators experience heightened stress and anxiety due to the increased sense of responsibility and authority in these roles.

Another source of stress experienced by Latinos/as that could account for higher incidences of mental health problems is the discrimination and racism they experience as minorities. Discrimination and racism can take the form of denial of services, difficulty on the job, firing from the job, demeaning insults, or more severe events, such as hate crimes and other violence. Psychological distress, reduced self-esteem, feelings of disempowerment, depression, and poorer physical health are cited frequently as psychological and physical consequences of discrimination and racism.

Poverty is yet another source of stress for Latinos/as. Latinos/as are twice as likely to live below the poverty level as the total U.S. population. In 1999, 23% of Latinos/as lived below the poverty level compared with 8% of European Americans. Additionally, 40% of Latino/a children living in the United States live below the poverty level. There is substantial evidence that psychological disorders are most common and severe among the impoverished and lowest socioeconomic classes. Research has indicated that lower-socioeconomic individuals suffer from a mental illness at a rate of 2 to 3 times higher than those in the higher socioeconomic arena. Some of the adverse psychological affects associated with poverty and a lower-socioeconomic stratum include anxiety, depression, low self-esteem, and loneliness.

Some of the contributory factors to the higher rate of poverty among Latinos/as can be attributed to relocating to the United States, lack of educational attainment, discrepancy in occupation, and disparity in occupational pay. Many Latinos/as leave their native country without any financial means on which to live. Additionally, in some cases, they arrive illegally without an ability to get government support or decent-paying jobs. In addition, Latinos/as have the lowest high school and college completion rates (51.3% and 9.7%, respectively) compared with African Americans (66.7% and 11.5%, respectively), Whites (79.9% and 22.2%, respectively), and Asian Americans (81.8% and 39.1%, respectively). As a result of low educational attainment, Latinos/as tend to procure jobs that are lower paying, less stable, and more hazardous. Furthermore, these jobs tend to have no medical or long-term financial benefits. Among the types of occupations procured by Latinos/as, 52% have labor and craft jobs, whereas only 6% are employed in professional or technical occupations. Latinos/as with the same educational level as European Americans earn less in monthly income. Latinos/as with high school diplomas earn an average of $1,092 per month, whereas European Americans earn $1,405 per month. Additionally, this inconsistency can also be found in Latinos/as with master's degrees (monthly income of $2,840) as compared with European Americans with master's degrees (monthly income of $3,248). As a result of the discrepancy in education, types of occupations, and pay, Latinos/as experience feelings of disempowerment, stress, anxiety, and depression.

Still another area that impacts the needs of mental health services for Latinos/as is the high rates of health-related complications. These health issues may result in a number of negative consequences, such as educational setbacks, unemployment, family problems, and marital discord. Latinas are getting pregnant at a rate of 51% before the age of 20, compared with the national average of 30%. Additionally, Latinas currently have the highest birth rate of all ethnic groups, approximately twice the national average.

Latinos/as are also disproportionately represented among the population in their use of drugs and alcohol. Latino men (31%) have higher rates of alcohol use and dependence than European American men (21%). Furthermore, many substance abuse programs appear to have difficulty recruiting, retaining, and successfully treating minority clients. Consequently, Latinos/as are less likely than other ethnic groups to seek substance abuse treatment and to complete treatment.

Furthermore, Latinos/as are overrepresented in the diagnosis of human immunodeficiency virus (HIV); Latinos/as account for 17% of adult male cases, 20% of adult female cases, and 27% of pediatric cases. For Latinos/as ages 25 through 44, HIV/AIDS infection is the second leading cause of death.

In summary, as the population of Latinos/as increases, so will their need for mental health services. Latinos/as suffer heightened stress related to acculturation, discrimination, poverty, lower-paying occupations, lack of educational attainment, discrepancy in pay, pregnancy, drug use, and HIV/AIDS. To the extent that stress leads to mental health problems, Latinos/as experience unique situations that generate a greater risk of psychological problems and need for mental health services, creating a necessity to find ways to address Latinos/as' unique mental health needs.

Latinos/as and Mental Health Services

Although there is an evidenced association between Latinos/as' experiences and psychological distress, review of the research indicates that Latinos/as tend not to make use of available mental health services. Latinos/as tend to severely underutilize community outpatient services and university counseling centers and overutilize inpatient services. For instance, Latinos/as were less likely (8.4%) than their European American counterparts (16.8%) to visit a mental health professional, and Latinos/as reported greater delays in receiving psychological services than European Americans (22.7% and 10.7%, respectively). Furthermore, Latinos/as tend to drop out of treatment very quickly, with 50% dropping out after the first session compared with 30% for European Americans. Length of treatment is an important factor in mental health treatment: Findings indicate that the longer clients stay in treatment, the more beneficial the outcomes are.

Researchers have attempted to hypothesize explanations for underutilization of mental health services by Latinos/as. Currently, two different theories have been proposed: the institutional barrier theory and the cultural barrier theory. The institutional barrier theory posits that Latinos/as desire services, but factors inherent in the mental health institutional system pose barriers to utilization. The cultural barrier theory assumes that clients want help, but aspects within the Latino/a culture hamper them from seeking out mental health services.

The institutional barrier theory pertains to the barriers found within the institution, or in the structural components of the institution, that provides psychological services. These variables include the geographic location of the mental health service center, cost of treatment, schedule of services, and lack of culturally relevant treatments. The location of the organization is a key factor in serving the Latino/a population. To better serve this population, mental health services need to be located within the Latino/a community, near public transportation, or both. Additionally, the monetary cost of the mental health treatment must not cause a financial burden on the family. With many Latinos/as living at or below the poverty level and being unemployed or having lower-paying jobs and less-stable employment, psychological treatment is considered a luxury. Therefore, consideration of finances must be taken into account when offering psychological services. Mental health services should be offered in the evening and weekends because family members may have difficulty taking time off from work. Additionally, requiring clients to come in on a weekly basis may not be feasible for many Latino/a families. Many Latinos/as are not employed in occupations that have benefits that allow for time off, and child care may be an additional financial issue. Lastly, mental health services should include interventions that are culturally relevant to the Latino/a client by considering Latino/a cultural worldview, beliefs, and values. By providing services that reflect the culture of the Latino/a client, the more likely the services will be effective.

Culturally Relevant Mental Health Services for Latinos/as

Latinos/as comprise persons of various ethnic, racial, and national backgrounds, and yet there are many commonalities among them. Many times, Latino/a cultural beliefs and values are antithetical to the beliefs and values that are found within the traditional Western-based psychotherapies, thus requiring counselors to adapt new ways of approaching therapy. Additionally, providing effective services to the Latino/a population requires counselors to assume roles that are at times different from the traditional counselor role. Counselors must also consider the language of the client when providing mental health services. Lastly, counselors need to be aware of and assess the societal factors impacting the Latino/a client. A therapist's failure to consider these variables can result in early termination and ineffective treatment.

Latinos/as live with a collectivistic worldview in which immediate and extended family, community, and social networks are valued more than the individual and emphasis is on interdependence rather than independence. Traditional psychotherapies share an individualistic worldview, with concentration on the individual and independence in therapy. An intense focus on the individual and independence would be completely foreign to a Latino or Latina client and may cause uneasiness, resulting in early termination and ineffective treatment. In terms of consideration of the collectivistic worldview, a therapist should consider incorporating interdependence as a continued goal and including immediate and extended family members in therapy.

Psychotherapy is not value free, even when the counselor intends to stay neutral. In fact, values play a significant role in counseling, influencing theories of personality and pathology, interventions, goals of treatment, and treatment outcome. As a result, a counselor's value system affects his or her perception of the nature of the client–counselor relationship, as well as the process and outcome of treatment. The client also enters counseling with a value system, which includes beliefs about the appropriateness of counseling, nature of the client–counselor relationship, and expectations for treatment. Therefore, in terms of mental health treatment, if a counselor's value system is opposed to that of the client's value system, then these differences in value system may lead to the counselor labeling a client as "pathological" or "resistant to treatment," and/or the client prematurely terminating treatment and/or receiving treatment that results in ineffective outcomes. Consequently, it would be in the counselor's best interest to work within the value system of the client. When working with a Latino/a client, one would incorporate the following values that are inherent within the Latino/a culture: *familismo, simpatia, personalismo, respeto, machismo, marianismo*, religiosity, and folk illness beliefs.

Familismo is described as a strong attachment of individuals to their families and strong feelings of loyalty, reciprocity, and solidarity. Latinos/as view the family as the single most important reference group, providing influence on decision making, reinforcement of traditional values and patterns, and emotional security. Culturally relevant therapy would involve asking about family members, including family members in therapy, and interviewing family members. By incorporating the immediate family members in therapy, Latinos/as may be able to work in an environment that most closely relates to their Latino/a values. Additionally, a counselor may also want to include extended family members and kinship ties such as *compadrazgos* (i.e., godparents) in the counseling sessions. In considering the strong attachment to the family, counselors should not focus treatment on independence from the family. In addition, individual family members are seen as a reflection of family functioning. Therefore, any negative personal information discussed is viewed as a reflection of the entire family functioning, and disclosing this information to "outsiders" is unacceptable and offensive. Furthermore, because family members are expected to turn to one another for support, then it may be perceived as an insult to the family if an individual family member relies on an "outsider" for support. When considering the value of familismo in therapy, the counselor needs to be sensitive to the client's ability to openly disclose to an "outsider." This uneasiness with disclosure should not be construed as pathological or resistant to treatment.

Latinos/as strongly adhere to the value of *simpatia,* which includes promoting social relationships that are pleasant and without conflict. As a result, there exists a tendency in Latinos/as to avoid interpersonal conflict and emphasize positive behaviors in agreeable situations. However, mainstream psychotherapy places a value on confronting problems, issues, and/or people. Consequently, when working with Latino/a clients, counselors should consider finding ways to approach conflict situations in a more positive way, for example, having the client approach the issue with the individual from a place of concern for the other person rather than an individualized place. Additionally, lack of confrontation or desire to confront by Latino/a clients should not be viewed as pathological.

Personalismo is defined as a valuing of connectedness with others and basing these connections on trust. There is a personal bond and sharing that exists in all interpersonal relationships, including professional relationships. However, many Western psychotherapies value a detached professional relationship that may seem foreign to Latinos/as that adhere to the value of close interpersonal relationships. Subsequently, when working with Latino/a clients, therapists should consider being less detached and using self-disclosure as a means to making the clients feel more comfortable.

The Latino/a value of *respeto* refers to deference afforded to those individuals with higher authority in the relationship, such as parents, elders, and authority figures (e.g., doctors, religious officials, and those with higher education). To the extent that adherence to the value of respeto mandates respect and credibility for those that are older and/or have a higher educational level, counselors would be highly respected and considered credible. As a result, a Latino/a client may put more value on, and agree more often with, the counselor's suggestions or interpretations in session. Therefore, it is advised that counselors be aware of how the relationship may be strongly influenced by their behaviors.

The Hispanic value of *machismo* is used to describe male roles and attitudes, whereas *marianismo* is used to describe female roles and attitudes. These values are significant factors in which Latinos/as develop a sense of identity. Within the value of machismo, men are granted considerable freedom, whereas women are much more restricted. Moreover, machismo is associated with men having dominance over the affairs of the family and wife, but it also includes courage and protection of the family and wife. This Latino/a value conflicts with the mainstream psychotherapy value of egalitarian relationships; thus, counselors should consider the dominant and protective role of the husband and/or father that may exist when working with a Latino/a individual, couple, or family. Questioning the division of household responsibilities may also help a counselor understand Latino/a gender roles when seeing an individual, couple, or family. In a family that honors Latino/a traditional male and female gender roles, a counselor should consider greeting the male of the family first. In addition, men who adhere to machismo often prefer not to demonstrate or admit to any vulnerability or emotion. Consequently, counselors should not stress the expression of vulnerability and emotion when working with Latino clients. The value of marianismo pertains to the expectation that women aspire to be like the Virgin Mary by acquiring the characteristics of humbleness, self-sacrifice, and other-centeredness. Furthermore, the value of marianismo dictates that women must be willing to endure the suffering that motherhood often requires, live in the shadow of their husbands and children, and support their husbands and children by all means necessary. To work with a Latina client, a counselor needs to be aware that mothers and wives feel an honor in dedicating themselves completely to their family. A culturally sensitive counselor would not propose self-care to a mother who upholds the Latino/a value of marianismo, because self-care would be considered selfish and overindulgent. The recommended way of introducing self-care to a Latina client would be to emphasize that the client would be a better mother and/or wife if she took care of herself. Additionally, a culturally aware counselor should be sensitive to the attitude that some Latina women may feel uncomfortable discussing their own feelings and needs with their spouses or family.

Religiosity plays a significant role in the lives of Latinos/as, including a way of maintaining cultural identity and community connection. For many Latinos/as, social activities center in the church, allowing for social support and feelings of connectedness. Furthermore, the religious official is often a primary confidant to Latino/a patrons. Therefore, a counselor should explore the client's spirituality and connectedness to the church in the assessment process and may consider including the client's religious official as part of a multidisciplinary team in treatment.

Folk illnesses are sets of physical and personal symptoms believed to be caused by supernatural or natural events that are external to the individual. For example, *Mal Puesto* is characterized by severe psychological symptoms, such as hallucinations, mania, and delusions, resulting from a supernatural cause. Furthermore, the belief in folk illness includes a belief in folk healers, such as *Espiritistas* for Puerto Ricans, *Santeros* for Cuban Americans, and *Curanderos* for Mexican Americans. The reason Latinos/as may seek out folk healers may come from the desire to see someone that shares their cultural beliefs about the causes of and cures for mental health problems. This value is also contrary to the mainstream psychotherapy view that psychological problems are seen as residing within the individual and under the control of the individual. Therefore, it might be beneficial for a counselor to consult a spiritual leader, shaman, or medicine man/woman or to include a traditional folk healer reflective of the community culture as part of a multidisciplinary team. Furthermore, some mental health clinics have included traditional activities for their clients, for example, sweat lodges, medicine wheels, talking circles, and so on. Although some Latinos/as may not consult traditional folk healers, they at times continue to subscribe to traditional folk remedies, such as herbs and tonics. A culturally sensitive counselor working with Latinos/as should be aware and accepting of these traditional supplements and, if experienced, may want to recommend some forms of them.

Another factor to consider when providing culturally relevant services to Latinos/as is the type of counselor role taken by the provider. Western-based therapies are often regimented to a role of providing services in an office setting within a specified treatment session time and getting clients to experience insight and/or catharsis; these may be factors that are irrelevant to the life experiences and needs of many Latinos/as. Some Latino/a clients do not have the financial means or time needed to travel to mental health centers; thus, counselors should consider leaving their offices and venturing into the client's environment—into homes, schools, and community centers and programs. Additionally, by entering the client's environment, counselors will then be better able to understand societal factors impacting their Latino/a clients and reach out to those individuals who are underserved. Counselors should also adjust the time in session to meet the needs of the client, including shorter sessions if the client is unable to attend for the traditional 50 minutes. Lastly, counselors should consider engaging in alternative roles to the traditional insight-oriented psychotherapy role, such as advocate, change agent, consultant, and advisor. For example, in the advocate role, counselors may take an active role in contacting bureaucratic organizations, whereas in the advisor role, counselors may advise their clients as to the possibility of difficulties and conflicts they may encounter as they attempt to adjust and live in their new culture.

Yet another element in providing culturally relevant treatment to Latinos/as is inclusion of culturally linguistic appropriate services. It is believed that words expressed in the bilingual's first language may have richer meanings and allow for easier access to emotions. Therefore, having bilingual Latino/a clients talk about events in Spanish fosters them to experience their emotions more fully, whereas the use of English may allow them to use intellectual defenses that assist in distancing themselves from their emotions. Counselors may want to encourage Latino/a clients to switch between languages depending on the desired level of emotional expression. Even if the counselor is not bilingual, the counselor can be attuned to the nonverbal expression as the client speaks in Spanish, while allowing the Latino/a client to experience an emotional release.

Lastly, counselors need to be aware of the specific societal factors that impact their Latino/a clients. Counselors must make a full assessment of the client's experience of political, social, and economic factors affecting his or her ability to adjust and live in the United States. Mental health service providers should then address these factors in the treatment in terms of prevention and remediation.

In conclusion, the growing Latino/a population will continue to be underserved and ineffectively served if mental health providers continue to base their treatment on Western-based, mainstream psychotherapy. It is essential that mental health providers understand the importance of the role of ethnicity in the psychological treatment of Latino/a clients. Subsequently, it is imperative to adjust traditional Western-based psychotherapy goals of treatment, interventions used in treatment, and treatment outcomes to reflect Latino/a cultural worldview, beliefs, and values. Furthermore, because of the increased risk of mental health problems associated with the political, social, and economic factors uniquely impacting the Latino/a population, it is essential that counselors consider these societal factors and address them accordingly in treatment.

Elizabeth D. Fraga

See also Acculturation (v3); Acculturative Stress (v3); Bilingual Counseling (v3); Career Counseling, Immigrants (v4); Career Counseling, Latinos (v4); Collectivism (v3); Communication (v3); Cross-Cultural Psychology (v3); Cross-Cultural Training (v3); Cultural Values (v3); Demographics, United States (v3); Espiritismo (v3); Ethnic Minority (v3); Familismo (v3); Immigrants (v3); Machismo (v3); Marianismo (v3); Multicultural Counseling (v3); Religion/Religious Belief Systems (v3); Spirituality/Religion (v2); Visible Racial/Ethnic Groups (v3)

Further Readings

Arredondo, P., & Perez, P. (2003). Counseling paradigms and Latina/o Americans. In F. Harper & J. McFadden (Eds.), *Culture and counseling: New approaches* (pp. 115–132). Boston: Allyn & Bacon.

Atkinson, D. R., Morten, G., & Sue, D. W. (1998). *Counseling American minorities: A cross cultural perspective* (5th ed.). Dubuque, IA: William C. Brown.

Burnam, M. A., Hough, R. L., Karno, M., Escobar, J., & Telles, A. (1987). Acculturation and lifetime prevalence of psychiatric disorders among Mexican Americans in Los Angeles. *Journal of Health and Social Behavior, 28,* 89–102.

Casas, J. M., & Vasquez, M. J. T. (1996). Counseling the Hispanic: A guiding framework for a diverse population. In P. B. Pedersen, J. G. Drugans, W. J. Lonner, & J. E. Trimble (Eds.), *Counseling across cultures* (4th ed., pp. 146–175). Thousand Oaks, CA: Sage.

Garcia, J. G., & Zea, M. C. (1997). *Psychological interventions and research with Latino populations.* Needham Heights, MA: Allyn & Bacon.

Fraga, E. D. (2003). *The relationship among perceived client-counselor ethnic similarity, perceived client-counselor Hispanic cultural value similarity, and counseling process and outcome variables.* Unpublished doctoral dissertation, University of California, Santa Barbara.

Fraga, E. D., Atkinson, D. R., & Wampold, B. E. (2004). Ethnic group preferences for multicultural counseling competencies. *Cultural Diversity & Ethnic Minority Psychology, 10,* 53–65.

Lopez, S. R., Lopez, A. A., & Fong, K. T. (1991). Mexican-Americans' initial preference for counselors: The role of ethnic factors. *Journal of Counseling Psychology, 38,* 487–496.

Moore, J., & Panchon, H. (1985). *Hispanics in the United States.* Englewood Cliffs, NJ: Prentice Hall.

Paniagua, F. A. (1994). *Assessing and treating culturally diverse clients: A practical guide.* Thousand Oaks, CA: Sage.

Ponterotto, J. G., Casas, J. M., Suzuki, L. A., & Alexander, C. M. (1995). *The handbook of multicultural counseling.* Thousand Oaks, CA: Sage.

Ramos-Sanchez, L., Atkinson, D. R., & Fraga, E. D. (1999). Mexican Americans' bilingual ability, counselor bilingualism cues, counselor ethnicity, and perceived counselor credibility. *Journal of Counseling Psychology, 46,* 125–131.

Santiago-Rivera, A. L., Arredondo, P., & Gallardo-Cooper, M. (2002). *Counseling Latinos and la familia: A practical guide.* Thousand Oaks, CA: Sage.

Sue, D. W., & Sue, D. (1990). *Counseling the culturally different: Theory and practice.* New York: Wiley.

U.S. Census Bureau. (2002). *Statistical abstract of the United States. The national data book.* Washington, DC: Author.

LEARNED HELPLESSNESS

Learned helplessness is a condition that is brought about by repeated exposure to negative stimuli. The result is that the individual learns that there are no options and no possibility for an escape from the negative stimuli. Helplessness exists when an individual's actions have no perceived positive effect on outcomes.

Learned helplessness is when an individual learns the response of resigning oneself passively to aversive conditions rather than taking action to change, escape, or avoid them. This learning occurs through repeated exposure to inescapable or unavoidable aversive events. Research by Martin Seligman has shown that helplessness is prominent in humans and has emotional, cognitive, and motivational consequences. He discovered from his research that prior experience, lack of discriminative control, and the importance of outcomes are three factors that contribute to learned helplessness. The concept has been successful at explaining the response of members of a minority group to the pressures of living in an oppressive cultural milieu.

Applications to Understanding Responses to Oppression

Learned helplessness is an important psychological construct to assist in understanding the experience of a minority member living in an oppressive society. The negative stimuli in this situation are the perpetual onslaughts of the pernicious racism that is present in U.S. culture. It is important to point out that these negative stimuli do not need to be severe (e.g., lynching) to have their effect. It is the omnipresent, repeated exposure to oppression, oftentimes in the form of microaggressions, that can create learned helplessness. The recipient of these repeated assaults eventually comes to accept them and sees no other possible options. Institutionalized racism also influences personal behaviors and decisions made by minorities that lead to learned helplessness. This perceived lack of options makes the current social and economic power structure seem inescapable and unchangeable.

A related concept that contributes to the understanding of the dynamics of racism is the fundamental attribution error. The fundamental attribution, also known as correspondence bias or overattribution effect, is the tendency to explain other people's behavior in dispositional terms, while underemphasizing situational influences. For example, if an African American tells a European American that he or she is unemployed, the European American may view the individual as lazy or unmotivated, ignoring that there may be a high unemployment rate or a lack of economic opportunity for the individual. The sociocultural and economic milieu in which an individual is living may create a state of learned helplessness (the unemployed African American has been denied economic opportunity for so long that he or she may come to accept it as an immutable condition), yet the outside observer explains this individual's behavior in terms of internal causes, such as pathological personality or lack of moral character.

Development of the Concept

In early 1965, Seligman and his colleagues, while studying the relationship between fear and learning, accidentally discovered an unexpected phenomenon while replicating Ivan Pavlov's classical conditioning experiment. Pavlov's 1905 experiment demonstrated that if a ringing bell or tone is repeatedly paired with a presentation of food, a dog will salivate. Later, upon hearing the ringing of the bell without the food, the dog will salivate. In Seligman's experiment, instead of pairing the tone with food, he paired it with harmless shock. The idea was that after the dog learned to associate the tone with the electrical shock, the dog would feel fear on the presentation of a tone and would then run away or attempt to avoid the shock in some way.

This treatment was carried out for many days, and after this conditioning phase, the same dog was placed, unrestrained, in a large box that had a low fence dividing the box into two sections. Seligman and his colleagues made sure that the dog could see the fence and easily jump over the fence to escape his section any time he wished. They then rang the same bell and expected the dog to jump over the fence because he was conditioned to associate this bell with pain from the electrical shock. Instead, they were surprised that the dog did not move! They then decided to subject the conditioned dog to an electrical shock; again there was no response on the part of the dog. Next, they put an unconditioned dog (one that had never experienced inescapable electrical shock) in the same box. This dog immediately jumped over the fence to the other section as soon as the shock occurred. It seems that the conditioned dog, which was repeatedly subjected to pain, learned that trying to escape from the shocks was useless. In other words, the dog learned to be helpless.

Extension of the Concept to Humans

Seligman and his colleagues started a scientific revolution resulting in more focus on cognitive psychology instead of focusing solely on behavioral psychology. His theory of learned helplessness was extended to human behavior. Through experiments with humans, Donald Hiroto and Seligman determined strong support for the theory that helplessness involved learning that one did not have control over events. Seligman led other helplessness researchers to reach the conclusion that the helplessness phenomenon, as produced in animal and human laboratories, was similar to certain failures of human adaptation.

Learned helplessness explained a lot of things, but then researchers began to find exceptions of people who did not get depressed, even after many bad life experiences. Seligman discovered that a depressed person thought about the bad event in more pessimistic ways than a nondepressed person. He called this thinking "explanatory style," borrowing ideas from attribution theory.

Explanatory style is the process by which individuals explain why they are victims to a negative event. There are three components to explanatory style. The first such component is internality. *Internality* refers to the degree with which one feels responsible for the cause of the event or the degree to which one believes that it is someone else's responsibility. The second characteristic is stability. *Stability* refers to whether the event was a one-time occurrence or whether it will continue indefinitely. The third component of explanatory style is globality. *Globality* refers to the extent of the negative event upon the individual. We can see how an individual from a marginalized group could come to feel a low level of internality (the individual's situation is molded by external forces over which he or she has no perceived control), a high level of stability (the oppressive components of the culture are embedded into the bedrock of our society and are not going away), and a high degree of globality (racism impacts every aspect of life for the person of color). An event can impact a minor aspect of the individual's life or affect every aspect.

Symptoms of learned helplessness include lack of motivation, listlessness, cognitive breakdown between actions and outcomes (i.e., inability to link actions to the consequences they bring about or blaming others or external factors for one's situation, condition, and outcomes), boredom, anxiety, frustration, anger, hopelessness, and depression.

Gregory Benson, Paul E. Priester, and Asma Jana-Masri

See also Action Theory (v4); Career Barriers Inventory (v4); Classism (v3); Client Attitudes and Behaviors (v2); Discrimination (v3); Discrimination and Oppression (v2); Fatalism (v3); Person–Environment Interactions (v2); Power and Powerlessness (v3); Prejudice (v3); Racial Microaggressions (v3); Racism (v3); White Privilege (v3)

Further Readings

Hiroto, D. S., & Seligman, M. E. (1975). Generality of learned helplessness in man. *Journal of Personality and Social Psychology, 31,* 311–327.

Jones, E. E., & Harris, V. A. (1967). The attribution of attitudes. *Journal of Experimental Social Psychology, 3,* 1–24.

Seligman, M. E. (1992). *Helplessness: On depression, development, and death.* New York: W. H. Freeman.

Seligman, M. E. (2006). *Learned optimism: How to change your mind and your life.* New York: Random House.

LEONG, FREDERICK T. L. (1957–)

Frederick T. L. Leong is a first-generation Asian American of Chinese descent, who was born and educated in Malaysia. He came to the United States in 1975 on an international student scholarship to study for a B.A. in psychology at Bates College in Lewiston, Maine. He graduated cum laude and Phi Beta Kappa in 1979 with high honors in psychology. His undergraduate honors thesis, "Males' Responses to Female Competence," was published in *Sex Roles* in 1983. He was also the founder and first president of the International Student Club at Bates College. After graduating from Bates, he spent some time working as a psychiatric aid at the Institute of Living in Hartford, Connecticut.

Leong went to the University of Maryland, where he completed graduate studies with a double specialty in counseling and industrial/organizational psychology in 1988. His dissertation was titled "Cross-Cultural Epidemiology of Psychological Disorders: A Comparison of Asian-Americans and White Clients in Hawaii's Mental Health System." During his graduate studies he was also selected as a Minority Fellow of the Minority Fellowship Program, American Psychological Association, from 1984 to 1986. As part of the doctoral program, he completed a 2-year internship at Dartmouth Medical School in Hanover, New Hampshire, where he focused on psychodynamic psychotherapy. Leong's academic appointments include the following: (a) instructor and then assistant professor in the Department of Psychology at Southern Illinois University; (b) associate professor, full professor, and director of training in the Department of Psychology at Ohio State University; (c) full professor and director of the counseling psychology program in the Department of Psychology at the University of Tennessee; and (d) full professor in the Department of Psychology at Michigan State University, where he was hired to lead the Multicultural Initiative and is serving as director of the Center for Multicultural Psychology Research.

Leong has authored or coauthored more than 110 articles and 60 book chapters in psychology. He has coedited 10 books, including *The Psychology Research Handbook: A Guide for Graduate Students and Research Assistants* (1996; second edition 2005, Sage), *Handbook of Racial and Ethnic Minority Psychology* (2003, Sage), *Handbook of Asian American Psychology* (1999; second edition 2006, Sage), and *Suicide Among Racial and Ethnic Groups: Theory, Research, and Practice* (in press, Routledge). He has delivered over 100 presentations at professional meetings and has been invited to lecture, present, or be part of an expert panel at more than 50 events. Leong's other professional contributions and roles include serving on the editorial boards of numerous psychology journals (e.g., *Psychotherapy: Theory, Research, Practice & Training; Journal of Counseling Psychology; Journal of Career Assessment; Cultural Diversity & Ethnic Minority Psychology; Journal of Career Development; Asian Journal of Social Psychology; Asian American & Pacific Islander Journal of Health; The Counseling Psychologist;* and *Psychological Assessment*) and being guest editor of numerous special issues of journals on topics that have focused on ethnic, racial, minority, or international issues (e.g., *Career Development Quarterly, Journal of Vocational Behavior, Psychotherapy: Theory, Research, Practice & Training,* and *Death Studies*). Other editorial positions have included the following: (a) associate editor for International and Cross-Cultural entries in Alan Kazdin's *Encyclopedia of Psychology*, (ii) counseling section editor for Charles Spielberger's *Encyclopedia of Applied Psychology*, and (c) editor for a book series focused on racial and ethnic minority psychology.

Leong is a member of various associations and has been appointed Fellow of the American Psychological Association (APA; Divisions 1, 2, 12, 17, 45, and 52), the Association for Psychological Science, the Asian American Psychological Association, and the International Academy for Intercultural Research. He has also held various offices in professional associations (e.g., chair of the APA Student Affiliate Group of Division 17, treasurer of the Association for Multicultural Counseling and Development, member of the board of directors for the Asian American Psychological Association, president of the Ohio Association for Multicultural Counseling and Development, president of the Asian American Psychological Association, president (and founder) of the Division of Counseling Psychology (Division 16) for the International Association of Applied Psychology, president of the APA Society for the Psychological Study of Ethnic Minority Issues).

As president of the Asian American Psychological Association (AAPA; 2003–2005), Leong continued to improve the structure and functioning of the association by incorporating the following: (a) Several bylaws were changed, and a new membership category of Fellows was established. This recognized the outstanding and distinguished contributors to the AAPA, some of whom have been recipients of the Lifetime Achievement Award and the Distinguished Contributions Award and those who were past presidents of the Association. The second major bylaw change that was passed involved the formation of the Council of Past Presidents (COPP) that would serve as a consultant and support system for the functioning of the Association. The third bylaw change involved the procedures for the formation of new divisions. Since then, new divisions such as the Division of Students (DoS) and the Division of South Asian Americans (DoSAA) have been formed. (b) Additional initiatives have included the formalization of the Association's Policies and Procedures Manual to ensure continuity between administrations. (c) In addition, the *Handbook of Asian American Psychology* was launched, with several members of the AAPA Executive Committee serving as coeditors (Arpana G. Inman, Angela Ebreo, Lawrence Hsin Yang, Lisa M. Kinoshita, and Michi Fu) and with many members as authors of chapters for the *Handbook*. The editorial team decided to donate the royalties from all future proceeds from the *Handbook* to the Association. (d) Leong also initiated the production and distribution of the association's Digital History Project in an effort to prevent the loss of the association's important documents and historical archives. The Digital History Project involved digitizing all of the documents from the Association's historical archives onto CDs for distribution.

Leong has served on many APA committees (e.g., Committee on Employment and Human Resources,

Committee on International Relations in Psychology; Committee on Psychological Test and Assessment; the Implementation Task Force for the Commission on Ethnic Minority Recruitment, Retention, and Training; and the Advisory Committee of the Minority Fellowship Program). In the summer of 2006 he was elected to the Executive Council of the International Test Commission. Leong also serves on the APA Board of Scientific Affairs.

Leong's service and dedication to the field of psychology has also extended to the international arena. He has participated actively in international congresses of psychology and has been invited to organize numerous symposia at these congresses. Examples of these include the Pacific Science Congress in Beijing (1996), the International Congress of Applied Psychology in Singapore (2002), the International Congress of Psychology in Beijing (2004), and the International Congress of Applied Psychology in Athens (2006). He is also working on organizing a symposium on the intersection between personnel psychology and vocational psychology for the International Congress of Psychology in Berlin in 2008.

Leong has consistently supported the development and advancement of psychology in Asia and on Asian issues. On many occasions he has been invited to serve as a discussant at conferences featuring Asian issues. He has served as an external examiner on doctoral dissertations in Pakistan, Singapore, Hong Kong, Bangladesh, and the United Arab Emirates. He has invested time in teaching and researching in the Asia-Pacific region by undertaking visiting professor appointments at the University of Hawai'i, Chinese University of Hong Kong, and National University of Singapore. Other efforts in this area include the development of journals in Asia. For example, he served on the editorial boards of the *Journal of Psychology in Chinese Societies, Asian Journal of Social Psychology,* and *The Asian Psychologist.* He has been involved in several grant-funded projects with Fanny Cheung at the Chinese University of Hong Kong, which has involved regular trips to Asia. While at the Ohio State University, the University of Tennessee, and Michigan State University, Leong has recruited, mentored, and taught numerous international students from Asia and Asian American doctoral students.

Leong has also received numerous awards and nominations. For example, he received the Ralph F. Berdie Memorial Research Award from the American Association for Counseling and Development in 1986. In 1987 he received the Young Investigator Award at the International Congress on Schizophrenia Research held in Clearwater, Florida; the APA Minority Fellowship Program's Achievement Award for Teaching and Training in 1992; the Distinguished Contributions Award from the Asian American Psychological Association in 1998; and the John Holland Award from the APA Division of Counseling Psychology in 1999. Most recently, he received the APA Award for Distinguished Contributions to the International Advancement of Psychology at the 2007 APA convention in San Francisco for all his international work.

Leong's major research interests center on issues of cross-cultural psychotherapy and mental health, especially with Asians and Asian Americans. His organizational psychology interests involve cultural and personality factors related to career choice, work adjustment, and occupational stress. For the past decade Leong has devoted much time and effort toward internationalizing counseling and clinical psychology through his research, scholarly writing, and professional activities. For instance, Leong has served as the coeditor of the International Forum, a section devoted to advancing international perspectives within *The Counseling Psychologist,* where he has authored some of the pioneering papers recommending the internationalization of the field of psychology. He also served as a member of the APA Committee on International Relations in Psychology.

Arpana Gupta

See also Asian American Psychological Association (v3); Asian Americans (v3); Bicultural (v3); Career Counseling, Asian Americans (v4); Cross-Cultural Psychology (v3); Cross-Cultural Training (v3); Discrimination (v3); Discrimination and Oppression (v2); Model Minority Myth (v3); Multicultural Counseling (v3); Multicultural Counseling Competence (v3); Multicultural Psychology (v3); Stereotype (v3); Visible Racial/Ethnic Groups (v3)

Further Readings

Leong, F. T. L. (Ed.). (2006). *Handbook of Asian American psychology* (2nd ed.). Thousand Oaks, CA: Sage.

Leong, F. T. L., & Austin, J. T. (Eds.). (2006). *The psychology research handbook: A guide for graduate students and research assistants.* Thousand Oaks, CA: Sage.

Leong, F. T. L., & Leach, M. M. (in press). *Suicide among racial and ethnic groups: Theory, research, and practice.* London: Routledge.

Locus of Control

Locus of control refers to an individual's overall beliefs regarding whom or what is in control over events that occur in his or her life. People may attribute their chances of success and failure to either external or internal causes. Development of locus of control likely stems from a combination of family background, culture, and past experiences. People with an internal locus of control may come from families that focus on effort and responsibility. On the other hand, those with an external locus of control may come from backgrounds where there is lack of life control. Since the locus of control construct was first introduced, it has undergone considerable explanation, and several theories about locus of control have arisen.

Types

Internal Locus of Control

People with an internal locus of control often believe that they are in control of their own destinies and happenings in their lives. People with an internal locus of control likely see a relationship between the effort they put into an endeavor and the outcome. People with an internal locus of control feel that events that happen to them are a result of their own work and effort. The benefit of an internal locus of control is that people feel in control of their life situations and responsible for what happens to them. Thus, they may be likely to work hard in order to do well in educational and vocational areas.

External Locus of Control

People with an external locus of control are more likely to believe that their fate is determined by chance or outside forces that are beyond their control. People with an external locus of control see environmental causes and situational factors as being more influential than internal ones. These individuals would more often see luck rather than effort as determining whether they succeed or fail. A benefit of this viewpoint is that people with an external locus of control may be better able to cope with failure or trauma because they do not blame themselves for what happens to them. However, an external locus of control may be harmful in that it may lead to feelings of helplessness and loss of personal power.

Explanation of Construct

Multicultural Considerations

From a traditional psychological perspective, an internal locus of control is considered indicative of a healthy, adaptive, and self-determined approach to life. An external locus of control would be associated with apathy, passivity, and pathology. It is important to realize that the locus of control construct was developed within the perspective of a Eurocentric worldview. As a result, the construct assumes that individual control and choice are to be highly valued. The assumption that an internal locus of control is to be preferred to an external locus of control assumes that individualism and self-determination are inherently valuable. Thus, the Eurocentric locus of control construct pathologizes worldviews that de-emphasize individual choice and control. Moreover, the Eurocentric conception of locus of control ignores the role that discrimination and oppression play in undermining opportunities and choices of members of marginalized communities.

Cultures with a collectivistic worldview, as found in some African American, Asian, Latino/a, and Native American cultural groups, may value commitment to relationships above individual concerns and identify with a larger social group more so than do individualistic cultures. For example, in some Asian cultural settings, a family and group orientation is valued above individual needs. From this perspective, cooperation with the goals of family or community would be considered more important than self-determination. Members of such a culture may be likely to endorse an external locus of control, since external forces such as family and societal expectations play a prominent role in their lives. Thus, in this context, an external locus of control would indicate not pathology, but rather a socially sanctioned respect for the influence and expectations of family and society.

It is therefore important to recognize the culture-specific perspective inherent in the traditional conceptualization of locus of control, which views internal locus of control as optimal. For individuals who do not identify with the dominant cultural worldview, it may be inappropriate to apply the traditional use of locus of control as an indicator of psychological health, as attributes that are normal and healthy within the dominant cultural context could be considered indicative of pathology in individuals from a nondominant culture.

For marginalized groups, external locus of control may be a result of a realistic perception of limitations caused by racism, discrimination, or socioeconomic status. For example, for individuals who regularly experience discrimination based on their race, it would be accurate to attribute difficulties they experience to external forces. From the traditional standpoint, such external attributions would indicate a lack of self-determination rather than recognition of discrimination. Consequently, the individual's experience of discrimination would be invalidated, and the external locus of control resulting from such experiences may lead to an assumption of pathology on the part of the individual.

Consideration should be taken when applying locus of control concept to multicultural populations. Locus of control should be understood as a concept that is embedded in a European American cultural worldview, and limitations of applying it with more collectivistic cultures should be recognized. Marginalized individuals might endorse greater levels of external control, not as a result of psychopathology or lack of self-determination, but as a result of actual experiences of discrimination and limitations placed on them by society.

History

Julian Rotter first described the concept of locus of control in the 1950s. Rotter was viewed as one who was able to bridge the gap between behavioral and cognitive psychology when he developed the locus of control construct. Rotter theorized that behavior was significantly directed by the use of reinforcements, such as punishments and rewards. These punishments and rewards subsequently shaped the way people interpret the results of their own actions. The original locus of control formulation classified generalized beliefs concerning who or what influences things along a bipolar dimension of control between internal and external.

Other theorists, including Hanna Levenson, developed alternative theories of locus of control. Whereas Rotter explains locus of control as being bipolar, Levenson's model asserts that there are three dimensions: internality, chance, and powerful others. Internality is similar to Rotter's internal locus of control, in which people believe that they are in control over events that happen to them. Those who endorse chance would attribute events to luck. And those who consider control to be in the hands of powerful others would attribute events to others who have more power and control. According to Levenson, one can endorse each of these dimensions of locus of control independently and at the same time.

Related Perspectives

Expectancy, which concerns future events, is a critical aspect of locus of control. Locus of control is grounded in expectancy-value theory, which describes human behavior as determined by the perceived likelihood of an event or outcome occurring and the value placed on that event or outcome. Expectancy-value theory states that if individuals value a particular outcome and believe that taking a certain action will produce that outcome, then they are more likely to take that action.

Self-efficacy is a concept introduced by Albert Bandura and refers to an individual's belief in his or her ability to perform a certain task at a given time. Self-efficacy and locus of control are related; people may believe that they are in control of how some future events turn out, and they may or may not believe in their own ability to perform a certain task. For example, athletes may believe that they have control over how well they perform (internal locus of control), but they may not have the belief that they are capable of putting in the training to succeed (low self-efficacy).

Attributions are explanations that people give to explain why some event has occurred. Like locus of control, attributions can be classified—among other ways—as either internal or external. Attribution theory has been utilized to explain the difference between highly motivated individuals and low achievers. Attribution theory explains high achievers as being willing to take risks to succeed and low achievers as avoiding success because they believe it is based on luck and will not happen again.

Terri L. Jashinsky and Joshua Scherer

See also Allocentrism (v3); Barriers to Cross-Cultural Counseling (v3); Collectivism (v3); Cross-Cultural Training (v3); Cultural Values (v3); Decision Making (v4); Empowerment (v3); Fatalism (v3); Individualism (v3); Meaning, Creation of (v2); Multiculturalism (v3); Self-Efficacy/Perceived Competence (v2); Self-Esteem (v2); Self-Esteem, Assessment of (v2); Worldview (v3)

Further Readings

Lefcourt, H. M. (Ed.). (1981). *Research with the locus of control construct.* New York: Academic Press.

Lefcourt, H. M. (1982). *Locus of control: Current trends in theory and research.* Hillsdale, NJ: Lawrence Erlbaum.

Levenson, H. (1974). Activism and powerful others: Distinctions within the concept of internal-external control. *Journal of Personality Assessment, 38,* 377–383.

Marks, L. I. (1998). Deconstructing locus of control: Implications for practitioners. *Journal of Counseling & Development, 76*(3), 251–260.

Rotter, J. B. (1966). *Generalized expectancies for internal versus external locus of control of reinforcement.* Washington, DC: American Psychological Association.

Rotter, J. B. (1982). *The development and applications of social learning theory.* New York: Praeger.

Sue, D. W., & Sue, D. (2003). *Counseling the culturally diverse: Theory and practice* (4th ed.). New York: Wiley.

LOSS OF FACE

Loss of face expresses loss of social status, a matter of social ostracism, in Asian collective cultures that esteem fulfilling social obligations. One's face shows to others one's identity and integrity. Thus face is personal *and* interpersonal, individual *and* social, both at once. Face represents social confidence and communal esteem in a person's integrity, social respectability a person deserves, and one's self-respect in meeting obligations, communal, and unwritten. Loss of face is serious, for fulfilling the social requirements is essential to one's status and prestige in a society, and to lose face amounts to being branded "immoral" in public.

Asian individuals develop subtle and intricate communications to maintain face against its "loss," which damages one's social standing. To lose face is to lose social status and prestige, in embarrassment, shame, anger, and self-blame for being ostracized from social intercourse. Loss of face carries intense emotions due to three factors: one's deep shame, the importance of others' opinions, and high values a person holds of the Asian tradition. For example, senior and traditional Asians may feel more disturbed at losing face than young ones do.

Loss of face may be due to oneself, friends, or family members to whom one's reputation is tied, or when someone *else,* whoever it is, violates one's standards and jeopardizes one's reputation. One may lose face in three situations: when one fails to meet social expectations, when others do not treat one with respect that one deserves, and when one's ingroup members fail to fulfill their social roles and responsibilities.

Those who have experienced loss of face may resort to three sorts of behaviors to redress the loss. First, when one has violated social expectations, *compensation* is taken to restore one's face. Second, when others have violated social expectations to cause one to lose face, one could cut relations with them in *retaliation*. Third, when neither compensatory nor retaliatory actions are feasible or acceptable, one may *defend oneself* by devaluing the opponents or de-emphasizing the seriousness of losing face in "this specific" instance.

Loss of face has relevance to cross-cultural counseling. The implications of loss of face for Asians are subtle, critical, and negative. Asians use the term *loss of face* to express their embarrassment, humiliation, and disappointment. With knowledge about loss of face, cross-cultural practitioners and theorists will better grasp Asian people's emotions related to loss of face.

Moreover, loss of face applies to every culture in which individual dignity counts. People's appropriate comportment to appropriate persons is so essential to human decency and integrity that racial prejudices and personal partiality cause psychological injuries. The seriousness of woes of refugee camps, for example, can be explained as brutal loss of face.

Loss of face is an issue of utmost importance to human mental health, worthy of careful sensitive attention by all counselors in all fields. Counselors do well to watch how Asian people restore the loss of face, to become the fourth Western way (besides the three mentioned earlier), of recovering the loss of face.

*Ruth Chao, Heather Knox,
Francis L. Stevens, and Rebecca Wagner*

See also Asian Americans (v3); Bicultural (v3); Career Counseling, Asian Americans (v4); Collectivism (v3); Confucianism (v3); Cross-Cultural Psychology (v3); Cross-Cultural Training (v3); Cultural Values (v3); Culture (v3); Filial Piety (v3); Identity (v3); Multicultural Counseling (v3); Social Identity Theory (v3)

Further Readings

Bedford, O. A. (2004). The individual experience of guilt and shame in Chinese culture. *Culture and Psychology, 10,* 29–52.

Ho, D. Y.-F., Fu, W., & Ng, S. M. (2004). Guilt, shame and embarrassment: Revelations of face and self. *Culture and Psychology, 10,* 64–84.

Kim, J. Y., & Nam, S. H. (1998). The concept and dynamics of face: Implications for organizational behavior in Asia. *Organization Science, 9,* 522–534.

Low-Context Communication

Anthropologist Edward T. Hall introduced the construct of low-context communication to describe the degree to which people rely on contextual factors rather than the explicit and transmitted part of the message to derive meaning in communication. In low-context (LC) communication, people attend to the explicit, communicated speech to gather information. LC communicators place less emphasis on the context that surrounds the communication event than on the communication itself. LC communication may be adaptive when transactions occur in dynamic contexts that are rapidly changing. LC communication involves messages that tend to be direct, precise, and open. LC communicators tend to openly exchange information so that they can better predict each other's behaviors. Finally, LC persons may be direct and open about disagreement.

Hall proposed that the nervous system has developed an information-processing mechanism whereby it can effectively cope with the information overload through a culturally determined process called *contexting*. This process posits that individuals need only to select a portion of the total information available in an event to create meaning. The information that is not selected for processing but needed to create meaning is filled in by context. According to Hall, as contexting decreases in a communication event, more information is needed from the explicit code to create meaning.

Culture shapes the contexting process by socializing individuals to organize their past experiences according to a prescribed system of symbolic representations. This pattern of symbolic representations determines the cultural norms, rules, and expectations that guide how people communicate with one another.

LC communication occurs to different degrees in all cultures but may predominate in certain cultures. LC predominance is found in the North American (i.e., U.S.), Australian, German, Swiss, Scandinavian, and other Northern European cultures. Individuals within these cultures tend to compartmentalize their personal and work relationships.

When a client says to the counselor, "You've been really helpful, but I don't think I will need any more counseling," an LC communicator may take the expression at face value and form an impression that the client benefited from counseling and is now ready to terminate. LC may be particularly beneficial in aspects of counseling that place importance on accurate and precise information, such as when conducting risk assessment, recording notes, and reporting diagnostic information to insurance companies.

Yong S. Park and Bryan S. K. Kim

See also Barriers to Cross-Cultural Counseling (v3); Bilingual Counseling (v3); Bilingualism (v3); Communication (v3); Counseling Skills Training (v2); Cross-Cultural Training (v3); Culture (v3); E-Counseling (v1); High-Context Communication (v3); Meaning, Creation of (v2); Multicultural Counseling (v3); Translation Methods (v3)

Further Readings

Gudykunst, W. B., & Ting-Toomey, S. (1988). *Culture and interpersonal communication*. Newbury Park, CA: Sage.

Hall, E. T. (1976). *Beyond culture*. Garden City, NY: Anchor Press.

Hall, E. T., & Hall, M. R. (1990). *Understanding cultural differences*. Yarmouth, ME: Intercultural Press.

Machismo

Historically, the term *machismo* is a derivative of the Spanish word *macho*. Although the term *machismo* is Mexican in origin, the construct of machismo is an international phenomenon. *Macho* is a term that describes a male animal or specific types of tools related to husbandry. The term was translated by European Americans to describe a concept for Latino men and Latino male behavior. Ultimately, the universal term *machismo* came to describe a negative set of hypermasculine behaviors among Latino men. Machismo is countered by the traditional Latino/a standard of femininity, *marianismo* (a construct defined by the Virgin Mary's feminine virtue) and *hembrismo*. *Marianismo* describes women as spiritually superior to men, capable of enduring great suffering, whereas *hembrismo* describes women's strength and perseverance. However, for the Mexican people, and for many Latinos/as, solely viewing machismo from the negative or antisocial derivative of the term is debatable. A more culturally relevant and sensitive perspective includes both positive and negative aspects of the term.

Currently, the one-sided negative historical perspective has been substituted with an expanded, dialectical perspective that assumes a more gender-positive stance without minimizing negative characteristics associated with the term. This dialectical perspective defines *machismo* within a social, political, and cultural context as both progressive and reactionary to the historically and socioeconomic realities of society. As a result of these variables, the masculine ideology of the term *machismo* is prevalent in the United States and is not solely a characteristic of Latino/a Americans. Studies have shown that next to Latinos/as, White Americans are the second highest ethnic group in their value of traditional masculinity. A significant difference between the masculine construct valued by White Americans and the Latino/a machismo is the social acceptance of these concepts by one group over another. For example, when masculine ideologies such as toughness, competition, and assertiveness are associated with White males, the terms are more socially accepted than when applied to Latino males. Machismo or the idea of masculinity varies within the cultural, social, and economic groups that comprise that society. If machismo is examined from this more expanded perspective, the term becomes more complicated but also prevents the formation of a reductionistic perspective that permeates Western society and assumes that all Latinos/as, and all racial/cultural groups, manifest machismo in similar ways.

Latino/a American machismo has been socially misconstrued as synonymous with negative terminology such as *chauvinism, exaggerated aggressiveness, emotionally restrictive, controlling,* and *homophobic*. While machismo is multidimensional, consisting of both positive and negative elements, the positive elements have been neglected in the Western interpretation. The positive dimensions are, in reality, the most central components of machismo. They include honor, respect, bravery, dignity, and family responsibility. These virtues are of tremendous importance and a source of great strength for the Latino/a community. Examining machismo from this more dialectical perspective, which includes both the positive and negative aspects, allows for increased flexibility and utility within a therapeutic or counseling setting when working with clients.

A counselor may emphasize these positive values with the Latino/a client—encouraging the client to utilize these resources to facilitate adaptive behaviors and personal growth. In addition, challenges may also arise in counseling a client who values machismo. Potential barriers include the client's discomfort with expressing emotional vulnerability, resistance to disclosure in the counseling setting, and avoidance of counseling altogether. This is troubling because reluctance to discuss personal issues has been shown to result in depression and a limited ability to cope with traumatic life events. Therapeutic encounters such as these may be seen as degrading and antimasculine for men who place emphasis on a traditional machista value system. Additionally, it is debatable whether or not a male therapist is seen as a more viable option for machista men than a female therapist.

Regardless of the client's issue, the culturally responsive counselor must consider each individual client's unique worldview. Machismo, although widely valued by the Latino/a community, varies on an individual and social basis. Likewise, an understanding of machismo can be extended across all cultures to better counsel individuals who value similar ideologies. Cultural responsiveness requires the unbiased knowledge of cultural constructs, such as machismo, as well as the recognition of each individual's uniqueness. With this awareness, a counselor can optimize therapy by watching for potential obstacles and compensating for these challenges with unlimited wealth of individual and cultural strengths.

Miguel E. Gallardo and Shannon Curry

See also Career Counseling, Latinos (v4); Cross-Cultural Training (v3); Cultural Values (v3); Culture (v3); Latinos (v3); Marianismo (v3)

Further Readings

Fragoso, J. M., & Kashubeck, S. (2000). Machismo, gender role conflict, and mental health in Mexican American men. *Psychology of Men & Masculinity, 1*(2), 87–97.

Gonzalez, R. (Ed.). (1996). *Muy macho: Latino men confront their manhood.* New York: Doubleday Press.

Torres, J. B., Solberg, S. V., & Carlstrom, A. H. (2002). The myth of sameness among Latino men and their machismo. *American Journal of Orthopsychiatry, 72*(2), 163–181.

Marianismo

Marianismo is a term first proposed in the literature in the 1970s as a way to describe a set of values and norms associated with being a woman in Latin American culture. It was initially conceptualized as a response to the term *machismo,* suggesting that marianismo occurs in the context of machismo. Marianismo generally refers to the cultural expectation that a woman be passive and submissive along with being sexually pure. These traits respond to those prescribed by machismo, which expects a man to be active, aggressive, and sexually experienced.

Marianismo traces its roots to the Spanish colonization of Latin America. One of the biggest legacies of the Spanish conquest was their religious beliefs. Roman Catholicism holds in high regard the figure of *la Virgen María* (Spanish for "the Virgin Mary"). Only the purest of women could be chosen by God to be the mother of His son. Mary lived the ultimate sacrifice in giving herself up to God's will: a life of self-denial, purity (e.g., virginity), and devotion to motherhood that was duly rewarded with eternal salvation and the privilege of giving birth to Jesus.

Marianismo stems from these ideals. The term refers to the expectation that women live as the Virgin Mary did. Women are expected to be submissive to men and meet their every need in a passive and unassertive manner. They are loving, caring, and docile—completely devoted to their roles as wives, mothers, and life bearers. To accomplish this, women must renounce their own needs, acting in a spiritual and immaculate manner.

Marianismo prescribes a set of norms that encourages women to maintain and promote cultural values at their own expense or face public scrutiny as an alternative. Women are held in high regard by others if they have children and are caring mothers. Single mothers and divorcées are frowned upon, as they have acted in a self-serving and egotistical manner by disrespecting the sanctity of matrimony and placing their own needs before those of the family. These values are passed down from generation to generation. Caring mothers teach their young men to be wary of sensual, manipulative, and possessive girls who see sex for anything other than procreating. (These "bad" women are thought of as loose and deceitful or as whores.)

Marianismo will impact the way counselors work with and conceptualize clients. Help-seeking behavior is discouraged, and women may have a difficult time committing or engaging in therapy. They may present with concerns related to gender-role strain and may be more prone to accept problems as "part of being female." Gender-inconsistent behaviors (e.g., substance abuse, aggressiveness) may increase a sense of worthlessness. Confrontation is often avoided. Sexuality and other intimate concerns may be brought up with much shame—if at all. Infidelity is tolerated only if it comes from men. Men may also view assertive women as "problematic" and may sabotage self-promotion efforts of women who "argue all the time." Both men and women may initially see female therapists as caretakers, more capable than male therapists of solving problems in a fair and unselfish manner.

Culturally competent counselors who want to appropriately work with marianismo in therapy will need to increase their level of comfort with, and knowledge of, traditional gender norms. They may need to determine the level of acculturation of their clients to assess how engrained these cultural values are. Interpersonal conflict may surface between men who ascribe to traditional machismo cultural values and women who denounce marianismo (and vice versa). Exploring family relationships will also help counselors to understand the extent to which marianismo values are present. Women may choose male partners haphazardly and may stay in potentially abusive relationships longer for the sake of their children. Marianismo has also been associated with poorer physical and mental health in women.

As the definitions of *marianismo* have developed, so have the terms associated with it. One such term is *hembrismo*. Hembrismo seizes on the more positive traits of marianismo to redefine the role of women in Latin American culture. Aligned with the power that the Virgin Mary demonstrated in helping shape Catholicism by giving birth to Jesus, hembrismo conceptualizes women as strong, proactive players who shape lives—their own as well as those of others. They are morally and spiritually superior to men. They also carry the strength to help keep families together, transmitting norms and cultural values in their roles as single parents, mothers, breadwinners, and heads of households. Hembrismo is therefore not quite the counterpart or response to machismo that marianismo is but rather an additional and more affirming way to conceptualize Latinas.

Luis A. Rivas

See also Acculturation (v3); Career Counseling, Latinos (v4); Colonialism (v3); Cross-Cultural Training (v3); Cultural Values (v3); Culture (v3); Latinos (v3); Machismo (v3); Sexism (v3)

Further Readings

Gil, R. M., & Vázquez, C. I. (1996). *The María paradox: How Latinas can merge old world traditions with new world self-esteem.* New York: Putnam.

Stevens, E. P. (1973). Marianismo: The other face of machismo in Latin America. In A. Pescatello (Ed.), *Female and male in Latin America* (pp. 90–101). Pittsburgh, PA: University of Pittsburgh Press.

MARSELLA, ANTHONY J. (1940–)

Anthony J. Marsella, Emeritus Professor of Psychology, University of Hawai'i, Honolulu, is a pioneer in the study of cultural determinants of psychopathology and therapies. He has also been a major contributor to cross-cultural psychology and global and international psychology. Many of his writings are considered essential reading for students and scholars in psychology, psychiatry, and the social sciences. During his career he has been a leader in the field, challenging the ethnocentricity and inherent cultural and racial biases of Western psychology and psychiatry assumptions and practices. In an article published in 1998, he voiced the need for a new and expanded cross-cultural emphasis in psychology for the global era, calling for psychology to recognize and reconsider its cultural/racial biases and to acknowledge the validity and value of the traditional healing psychologies used in different cultures. In this publication and related publications on internationalizing the psychology curriculum, Marsella proposed changes in the training of psychologists to prepare them to participate in a global era filled with the complex challenges of poverty, war, migration, terrorism, urbanization, and population growth. His more recent writings have focused on these global problems and proposed solutions, calling for peace and social justice and for better understanding of terrorism through the use of cultural psychology approaches.

Marsella was born in Cleveland, Ohio, on September 12, 1940, into a first- and second-generation Sicilian family that maintained the rich cultural traditions of their ancestral heritage. The large family dinners, gender role distinctions, expressive emotions, the centrality of children, and religious and superstitious practices were part of everyday life. He spoke Sicilian with his grandmother, other relatives, and his stepfather, with whom he had a nurturing caring relationship. Marsella claims that even in these early years he had become acutely aware of the complexities of cultural differences and the power of one's ethnic culture to shape one's identity and worldview. This was especially true when he entered school and encountered the contrasting values and expectations of the dominant culture of the day. His adjustment to school was initially quite difficult, and he, like so many others from immigrant families, often found himself embarrassed about his Sicilian heritage. This was to change later in his life when he began to grasp the nuances and abuses of cultural power, marginalization, and privilege. Indeed, in 2004, in collaboration with Elizabeth Messina, he organized the Italian-American Psychology Assembly, to promote studies and collegiality among psychologists interested in Italian culture and history.

At an early age, the nascent educational and psychological testing program at his school suggested he had exceptional intellectual skills. This was puzzling to his teachers, as his family was essentially poor and uneducated. Thus, how could he speak and write so fluently? Nonetheless, because of his test performance, he soon became a subject for psychometric demonstrations at nearby universities, colleges, and clinics. He remembers the audience's applause and laughter when, at 8 years old, he successfully answered a question about the meaning of the term *apocalypse* in a demonstration session. He never told the audience that he had heard the priest use the term the previous Sunday in a sermon.

During high school years at John Adams High School, a large public inner-city school in Cleveland, Anthony emerged as a school leader (e.g., president of the Student Council and president of the senior class) and also participated in athletics and community activities. His academic and extracurricular record resulted in his selection as Teenager of the Year in 1958 in a citywide contest sponsored by the *Cleveland Press* leading to a 4-year General Motors Scholarship to Baldwin-Wallace College in Berea, Ohio. It was here that he fell in love with psychology and subsequently graduated with honors in psychology. During his undergraduate years, he was a volunteer at local mental hospitals where he interacted with severely disturbed clients, stimulating a lifelong interest in schizophrenia, mood disorders, and trauma, that subsequently became the topic of his doctoral dissertation in clinical psychology at Pennsylvania State University.

It was at Baldwin-Wallace College that Anthony met his wife of 43 years, Joy Ann Marsella, Professor Emeritus, Department of English, University of Hawai'i. They were married in 1963 and together survived the peregrinations of graduate school, fieldwork, and the development of professional careers.

In 1964, Marsella entered the Ph.D. program in clinical psychology at Pennsylvania State University. It was here that his long interests in cultural variations in behavior were nurtured and sustained as he began to work with George Guthrie, an established cross-cultural psychologist who pioneered studies of Filipino child development. From Penn State, he went on to Worcester State Hospital for his internship. There he was mentored further in cross-cultural studies by Juris Draguns, a notable figure in the field of culture and mental health. Following a Fulbright Research scholar award to the Philippines in 1967, and a stint as field director of a psychiatric epidemiology project in Sarawak, Malaysia, that examined rates of mental disorder among Iban tribes people, he received an appointment as a National Institute of Mental Health Culture and Mental Health Fellow at the University of Hawai'i in 1968.

Marsella remained at the University of Hawai'i, rising to the rank of full professor of psychology until his retirement in 2003. At the University of Hawai'i, he began a career-long research effort studying ethnocultural variations in psychopathology and psychology among Chinese American, Hawaiian American, Filipino American, and Japanese American populations. His publications in these projects called attention to basic differences in the expression and rates of mental illness and in normal patterns of behavior. In a bold study, he explored variations in the sensory patterns and sense uses of different ethnic groups. In 1978, he was appointed the director of the World Health Organization Psychiatric Research Center in Honolulu, one of twelve centers around the world engaged in international studies of psychosis. It is noteworthy that he was the only psychologist to serve in this capacity across the World Health Organization centers.

Throughout his 35-year career, Marsella supported the fusion of personal and professional goals. He proposed a Transcultural Mental Health Code that calls for professionals and scholars to adopt a total lifestyle characterized by advocacy and a commitment to progressive ideas to advance the field, including the use of factor-analytic stress-resource interactional and ecological models. He also has been pivotal in introducing indigenous terms and concepts into the field to ensure epidemiological accuracy, as well as increasing the use of qualitative methods as a source of insight into the cultural construction of reality. Another major contribution in advancing the field was Marsella's recognition and application of multiple culturally responsive healing principles in therapies rather than adherence to single approaches (e.g., cognitive-behavioral therapy, psychoanalysis). His work in promoting issues in cross-cultural psychology, internationalizing the field, and doing psychological practice and research from a comprehensive framework that incorporates the ecological, social, political, and economic context has been pivotal in advancing the field.

As of 2007, Marsella has published 14 edited volumes, most in the area of cultural and international psychology, and 160 book chapters, journal articles, and technical reports in a wide range of areas, such as depression and disorders across cultures, culture and conflict, culture and mental health, social justice, global psychology, traditional healing, culture and psychopathology, internationalizing mental health, cross-cultural imagery, schizophrenia across cultures, and intercultural relations. He also served as a senior editor for the *Wiley Encyclopedia of Psychology* and the *Oxford-American Psychological Association Encyclopedia of Psychology*. Many of his 96 graduate students went on to become highly published major contributors to cultural and international psychology, including Pamela Hays (Professor, Antioch University), Howard Higginbotham (Professor, Newcastle University, Australia), Hwang Kwang Kuo (Professor, National Taiwan University), Velma Kameoka (Professor, University of Hawai'i), Junko Tanaka-Matsumi (Professor, Gakshuin University, Japan), and Anne Marie Yamada (Professor, University of Southern California). But perhaps more importantly, his graduate students include more than 30 international and ethnic minority students. Marsella now lives in Atlanta, Georgia, where he continues to write and lecture and also to cook, read, travel, and ponder the vicissitudes of life.

Fred Bemak

See also Bicultural (v3); Counseling Skills Training (v2); Cross-Cultural Psychology (v3); Cultural Values (v3); Multicultural Counseling (v3); Multiculturalism (v3); Multicultural Psychology (v3); Poverty (v3); Social Justice (v3)

Further Readings

Carr, S. C., Marsella, A. J., & Purcell, I. P. (2002). Researching intercultural relations: Towards a middle way? *Asian Psychologist, 3,* 58–64.

Marsella, A. J. (1998). Toward a "global-community psychology": Meeting the needs of a changing world. *American Psychologist, 53,* 1282–1291.

Marsella, A. J. (2006). Justice in a global age: Becoming counselors to the world. *Counseling Psychology Quarterly, 19,* 121–132.

Marsella, A. J., & Pedersen, P. (2004). Internationalizing the counseling psychology curriculum: Toward new values, competencies, and directions. *Counseling Psychology Quarterly, 17,* 413–423.

Marsella, A. J., & Quijano, W. Y. (1974). A comparison of vividness of mental imagery across different sensory modalities in Filipinos and Caucasian-Americans. *Journal of Cross-Cultural Psychology, 5,* 451–464.

Marsella, A. J., & Yamada, A. M. (2002). Culture and mental health: An introduction and overview of foundations, concepts and issues. In I. Cuéllar & F. A. Paniagua (Eds.), *Handbook of multicultural mental health: Assessment and treatment of diverse populations* (pp. 3–24). San Diego, CA: Academic Press.

Moghaddam, F. M., & Marsella, A. J. (Eds.). (2004). *Understanding terrorism: Psychosocial roots, consequences, and interventions.* Washington, DC: American Psychological Association.

Shizuru, L. S., & Marsella, A. J. (1981). The sensory processes of Japanese-American and Caucasian-American students. *Journal of Social Psychology, 114,* 147–158.

MODEL MINORITY MYTH

The model minority myth refers to a set of stereotypes that are composed of several positive qualities purportedly unique to all Asian Americans. Asian Americans represent a very diverse population in the United States, with approximately 29 distinct ethnic groups differing in languages, religions, and customs. However, the model minority myth tends to generalize more toward East and Southeast relative to all Asian American groups. The model minority myth generally characterizes this group as intelligent, academically conscientious, educationally achieving, skilled in math and science, respectful, obedient, well-behaved, well-assimilated, self-disciplined, serious, hardworking, affluent, and professionally successful, particularly in business, science, and technology.

History of Asian American Stereotypes

Although the current and most common stereotype of Asian Americans that exists in the United States is the model minority myth, stereotypes about this population have evolved through numerous changes since the first wave of Asian immigrants in the mid-1800s. These stereotyped images have included the "pollutant," the "coolie" (i.e., an unskilled Asian laborer), the "deviant," the "yellow peril," the "gook" (i.e., used to describe North Vietnamese soldiers during the Vietnam War), as well as the model minority.

Political and economic issues have largely influenced the evolution of Asian American stereotypes. Asian immigrants were often portrayed in the media as the pollutant, coolie, and deviant during the 1800s and 1900s. These Asian stereotypes originally evolved from White Americans' feelings of threat and invasion by Chinese immigrants during the unstable and depressed economy between the 1870s and 1890s. Because of their willingness to work for lower wages, Chinese immigrants were used as scapegoats, often facing attacks for sending money made in the United States back to their families in China and becoming work competitors with small American farmers and workers. Eventually, the *yellow peril* terminology was coined by journalists to warn White Americans that the Chinese and Japanese were going to take over the United States and destroy their civilization; thus, the press depicted Asians as irrational, dark, and inassimilable.

The yellow peril stereotype was extended to other Asian groups as the wars with Japan, Korea, and Vietnam evolved. At the same time, the restrictions on the immigration of Asian women and the bans on miscegenation contributed to the image of "asexual" Asian men. Therefore, Asian men were often depicted as either hypermasculine and dangerous or as impotent and sexually undesirable in popular fiction and movies. During the wars, the use of comfort women by the Japanese military in Asia contributed to the stereotypes of Asian women as exotic and promiscuous. The U.S. media also sexualized Asian women and depicted them as submissive, quiet, mysterious, or untrustworthy. Asian women also were portrayed to fall in love with White men rather than Asian men.

During the civil rights movement and Black Power movement in the 1960s, and possibly in reaction to these movements, the model minority stereotype first appeared in popular media in *U.S. News and World Report* in 1966; this was followed by similar articles in *Newsweek* in 1984 and *Time* magazine in 1987. Asian Americans were described as a racial minority group that had overcome hardship and discrimination through hard work and determination and were, therefore, set as an example for other ethnic minority groups to follow. Many have argued that the characterization of Asian Americans as a model minority was developed as a political propaganda against other racial minority groups by creating a racial triangulation between White Americans, Asian Americans, and African Americans, such that Asian Americans are triangulated as alien to White Americans but superior to African Americans. More specifically, it was used to place the blame of racism and social inequality in the United States onto the minorities themselves, suggesting that African Americans and Latinos/as did not have the intelligence or discipline for success that Asian Americans possessed and that other minority groups should try to be as well-behaved and obedient as Asian Americans. This marked the beginning of the model minority myth that would come to dominate the image of Asian Americans in the United States.

The Model Minority Myth Today

An abundance of evidence suggests that the model minority myth is still alive and well today. For example, current media primarily depict Asian Americans as successful, affluent, intelligent, wise, technologically skilled, industrious, altruistic, and highly driven to achieve academic excellence and professional accomplishments. Research has demonstrated that White American students hold the model minority myth about Asian Americans, such as perceiving Asian Americans as being more successful in technical careers than social careers and characterizing Asian Americans as hardworking, intelligent, self-controlled, cautious, obedient, and being loyal and committed to family. Also, studies have shown that the model minority myth has been accepted by other ethnic and racial groups and internalized by Asian Americans.

Although the model minority myth often emphasizes positive stereotyped traits, it is important to note that some negative stereotypes have continued to exist about Asian Americans. For example, stereotypes that describe Asian Americans as quiet, shy, and overly compliant remain commonplace. Women of Asian descent continue to be depicted as exotic and subservient, whereas Asian men are often portrayed as asexual, submissive, and nerdy.

Impact on Asian American Populations

The prevalence of the model minority myth, as well as its acceptance in U.S. society, has raised some concerns about the influence of these racial stereotypes on Asian Americans. Specifically, demographic profiles seem to suggest that Asian Americans have greater purchasing power, obtain higher education degrees, have higher standardized test scores, earn a greater median income, own more homes, and save more earnings than other ethnic groups in the United States. Although these demographic profiles continue to fuel the model minority myth, a closer examination of these statistics demonstrates that Asian Americans receive lower incomes given their higher levels of education. Also, studies have found that Asian American college students are not as academically successful (i.e., having a lower grade point average, higher dropout rates due to medical reasons, greater risk of academic probation, and lower placement on the Dean's list) as the stereotype would suggest when compared with their White counterparts. Furthermore, Asians who are high academic achievers and seem to fit the model minority myth actually consist of a very selective sample (i.e., some but not all Asian Indians, Chinese, Taiwanese, Korean, and Japanese), while many of the underprivileged and less-successful Asian groups (i.e., Cambodian, Indonesian, Malaysian, and Hmong) are often neglected. This bias is also reflected in the media portrayal of model minority Asian Americans, with East Asian Americans most visibly displayed in U.S. advertisements, South and Southeast Asian Americans less visibly displayed, and several other Asian groups almost never portrayed in the media (i.e., Afghanis, Bangladeshis, Pakistanis, Malaysians, and Indonesians). Although the model minority myth may describe some Asian Americans, existing evidence suggests that this stereotype certainly does not accurately represent all Asian Americans, and within-group differences (e.g., ethnicity, socioeconomic status) are often ignored.

In addition, recent research has demonstrated that the highly positive generalizations of the model minority myth may have negative implications. For example, Asian Americans have commonly been excluded from universities' affirmative action policies because of the misperception that, unlike other ethnic minority groups, Asian Americans will succeed academically without any additional assistance. Research has focused on the negative impact of the model minority myth and on the popular stereotype that Asian American students do not need academic or personal help and are more psychologically adjusted than other groups. The underutilization of mental health services by Asian Americans, in general, also led to the erred belief that Asian Americans do not need psychological services, which has contributed to the lack of attention to the physical and mental health of Asian Americans and a dearth of culturally sensitive services for this population. In fact, preliminary research suggests that the additional pressure to maintain and live up to the model minority image may contribute to negative psychological adjustment for Asian Americans (e.g., depression), especially given Asian parents' awareness of their minority status in the United States and fear of downward mobility, as well as the cultural value placed on education by Asian American families. In particular, Asian Americans who may not have the talent or motivation for a career in mathematics or sciences may suffer from stress and feelings of inadequacy and failure.

Future Directions

Because the model minority myth is generally used to portray select Asian American groups, future research needs to be conducted to identify the needs of less-visible Asian American groups. Results from such research can help better identify Asian American groups that may be in need of, and benefit from, affirmative action and other forms of academic and emotional support on U.S. colleges and universities campuses. More qualitative research should also be conducted to better understand the differential impact that the model minority myth may have across various Asian American groups. Furthermore, more research is needed to explore and determine the effects that internalizing the model minority myth may have on Asian Americans' career choices, experiences of academic pressure and stress, and physical and psychological health. This type of knowledge may be particularly helpful not only for college administrators who are concerned about the success and well-being of their student body, but also for mental health professionals in better understanding the experiences of Asian American clients and identifying more culturally relevant resources. As Asian Americans tend to underutilize psychological services, university counseling centers need to develop more culturally appropriate outreach interventions for Asian American students to reduce the stigma of seeking counseling and provide culturally sensitive counseling services to better meet the needs of Asian American students. Counselors working with Asian American clients should examine their own stereotypes against, and assumptions about, Asian Americans; evaluate the impact of the model minority myth and internalizations of these stereotypes on clients' career development; and assess potential anxiety and stress related to expectations or pressures of maintaining the model minority image.

Yu-Wei Wang and Frances C. Shen

See also Academic Achievement (v2); Asian Americans (v3); Bias (v3); Career Counseling, Asian Americans (v4); Cultural Paranoia (v3); Identity (v3); Multicultural Counseling Competence (v3); Racism (v3); School Counseling (v1); Social Discrimination (v4); Stereotype (v3)

Further Readings

Espiritu, Y. L. (1997). *Asian American women and men: Labors, laws, and love.* Thousand Oaks, CA: Sage.

Kawai, Y. (2005). Stereotyping Asian Americans: The dialectic of the model minority and the yellow peril. *The Howard Journal of Communications, 16,* 109–130.

Lee, S. J. (1994). Behind the model-minority stereotype: Voices of high- and low-achieving Asian American students. *Anthropology & Education Quarterly, 25,* 413–429.

Success story of one minority group. (1966, December). *U.S. News & World Report, 61,* 73–76.

Sue, S., & Kitano, H. H. (1973). Stereotypes as a measure of success. *Journal of Social Issues, 29,* 83–98.

Toupin, E., & Son, L. (1991). Preliminary findings on Asian Americans: The model minority in a small private east coast college. *Journal of Cross-Cultural Psychology, 22,* 403–417.

Yee, A. H. (1992). Asians as stereotypes and students: Misperceptions that persist. *Educational Psychology Review, 4,* 95–132.

MONOCULTURAL

The term *monocultural* is used in several fields to refer to a single homogeneous culture that de-emphasizes diversity. In the United States, a Western or White hegemonic culture has been emphasized. Under this monocultural perspective, dominant American cultural values, expectations, behaviors, and definitions are presumed to be superior to values of other cultures. Thus, to the degree that minority groups internalize the monocultural worldview of the dominant group (i.e., assimilate), those groups come to see themselves through the perspective of the dominant group.

In counseling psychology, the dominant monoculture used to describe the processes of individual and group counseling has been that of a European American perspective. Underlying this Eurocentric ideology is the assumption that people from minority and marginalized groups ought to assimilate their behaviors, attitudes, beliefs, values, language, and perceptions to the dominant's group culture (i.e., European Americans) in order to attain uniformity and unity. Implied in this paradigm is that there is something inadequate about the minority groups' culture and behavior.

As a field, counseling psychology was shaped by this Eurocentric paradigm, which assumes that existing Eurocentric theories are generalizable despite differences among groups. In fact, all traditional counseling theories, assessments, diagnoses, and treatments are embedded in the Eurocentric paradigm. Hence, the training of counseling psychologist historically was rooted in this same paradigm. Based on their training and the dominant practices of the field, counseling psychologists were likely to ignore alternate interpretations of reality and culturally grounded healing methods that might be utilized by different cultural or racial groups. This oversight—and the adherence to the Eurocentric ideology—has resulted in the misdiagnosis, mistreatment, and victimization of persons from minority and marginalized groups who have sought psychological help. Furthermore, the inaccuracies and mistruths about minority and marginalized groups perpetrated by the unquestioned use of the Eurocentric paradigm have created a stigma toward psychological help within these communities, resulting in their underutilization of psychological services (even in the face of great need).

Monocultural views have been challenged for their exclusionary principles by those who want to include and value the experiences of human diversity. Specifically, the ideology of multiculturalism shifts the perspective to illuminating the experiences and voices of all human beings by focusing on issues of race, ethnicity, sexual orientation, age, gender, education, religion, disability, and socioeconomic status. Multiculturalism challenges the implicit assumptions of Eurocentric bias embedded in dominant monoculture. Hegemony and assimilation are rejected; instead, the various cultures, traditions, and values of different groups in the United States are celebrated and valued.

For years, multiculturalists have affirmed the need to diversify psychology. Issues of justice, fairness, and ethical practice, for instance, have been at the backdrop of multicultural counseling. Most importantly, multicultural counseling advocates use culturally appropriate and sensitive theories, assessment, and treatment modalities in hopes of increased utilization of psychological services and positive counseling outcomes for persons from minority and marginalized groups. Currently, the progressive development of multicultural competence is becoming the model to guide practitioners, researchers, and educators and is changing the face of the counseling psychology field. Several efforts—including the creation of multicultural guidelines for education, teaching, research, and practice for psychologists and the infusion of multicultural courses into programs and departments—reflect the transformation of psychology. The field has expanded its view of what it means to be a competent practitioner in today's heterogeneous American society. In making the necessary transition from a monocultural to a multicultural paradigm, the field recognizes the need to improve training, research, and practice.

Brenda X. Mejia and Rachel L. Navarro

See also Assimilation (v3); Bicultural (v3); Cross-Cultural Training (v3); Cultural Encapsulation (v3); Cultural Values (v3); Culture (v3); Deficit Hypothesis (v3); Ethnocentrism (v3); Eurocentrism (v3); Multicultural Career Assessment Models (v4); Multicultural Counseling Competence (v3); Multiculturalism (v3); Worldview (v3)

Further Readings

Constantine, M. G., & Sue, D. W. (2005). *Strategies for building multicultural competence in mental health and educational settings.* Hoboken, NJ: Wiley.

Kramer, E. M. (2003). *The emerging monoculture: Assimilation and the "model minority."* Westport, CT: Praeger.

Mio, J. S., Barker-Hackett, L., & Tumambing, J. (2005). *Multicultural psychology: Understanding diversity in America.* Boston: McGraw-Hill.

Schlesinger, A. (1998). *The disuniting of America: Reflections on a multicultural society.* New York: W. W. Norton.

MULTICULTURAL COUNSELING

Multicultural counseling is one of the major theoretical forces in psychology. It emerged as a necessary backlash to traditional psychological theories that assumed that Eurocentric/White and middle-class values are societal norms. Competence in multicultural counseling is crucial in societies with multiple representations of cultural groups whose social power and privilege statuses are differentiated based on visible (e.g., race, gender) and invisible (e.g., homosexual/bisexual/transgendered orientation, language) attributes.

Minority Worldviews, Therapist Biases, and Relationship Dynamics

Multicultural counseling is best understood in relation to competence guidelines published and enforced by professional counseling and psychology associations in multicultural countries (e.g., United States). A tripartite model presented by Derald Wing Sue and his colleagues in 1992 provided a conceptual basis to delineate three key components of multicultural counseling competency: (1) knowledge of cultural minority groups, (2) awareness of therapist's own worldview and cultural biases, and (3) application of culturally appropriate skills to intervene with client's presenting concerns as well as therapist biases.

Cultural Knowledge

In the past, multicultural counseling has focused on knowledge of cultural characteristics (e.g., Asians are collectivistic) and culture-specific tactics purported to be preferred by minority clients (e.g., Asians prefer a directive counseling approach). Stanley Sue and Nolan Zane have argued that knowledge of this kind, however, is distal to positive treatment goals as it perpetuates cultural stereotypes and ignores the individual differences within the respective minority groups. What is more important is therapist knowledge of the within-group differences in minority clients' cultural identity development. Some minority group members aspire to or internalize majority values, some embrace their cultural roots and reject the majority culture, and some attempt to appreciate and integrate both majority culture and cultural roots toward developing a bicultural identity. Theories of racial identity development, including the work of Janet E. Helms and her colleagues, and lesbian/gay/bisexual identity development, including the work of Reynolds and Hanjorgiris, have delineated the identity confusion and conflicts between self-acceptance and self-rejection among cultural minorities during the process of developing awareness of and confronting oppression and marginalization. As such, multicultural counseling competence entails therapist empathic understanding of the catalytic impact of majority oppression on the identity development and coping of minority clients.

Recognizing that both clients and therapists are products of cultural socialization that assigns them a majority or minority status, multicultural counseling emphasizes therapist knowledge of how cultural upbringing and ascribed status shaped their own worldview. Along with micro-knowledge of cultural group characteristics and macro-knowledge of societal forces that perpetuate and exacerbate client's counseling concerns, multicultural counseling emphasizes therapists' knowledge of their own attitudes and biases toward other cultural groups, especially therapists who are members of the majority group. Rather than developed through the lens of a single theorist, multicultural counseling is rooted in a culture-centered tradition, recognizing the therapists and the mainstream theoretical approaches they are trained to use are also culture bound. In a multicultural counseling relationship, therapist credibility is reflected by competence to discern and curb the therapist's own biases that may result in discriminatory, oppressive, or racist practice throughout the assessment, diagnostic, and intervention process.

Minority Group

Multicultural counseling is concerned with the psychological development and psychosocial (mal)adjustment of clients who are ascribed a power-disadvantaged societal status due to their cultural group membership. Regardless of their numerical representation in a given society, these cultural groups are considered minorities in sociopolitical power. Consequently, they are subjected to experiences of discrimination, racism, or oppression. Multicultural counseling literature has focused on women, non-White Americans in predominantly White societies (e.g., Asians, Blacks, Latino/as in the United States), and people with homosexual/bisexual/transgendered orientations.

Majority Group

Of equal if not more significance, multicultural counseling examines and delineates the psychosocial impact of oppression caused by people who internalized the power afforded by virtue of their cultural group membership. These people represent the majority group as the imbued sociopolitical power enables them to maintain and consolidate their privileged status at the expense of other minority groups. Sexism, racism, and heterosexism have been associated with the majority groups of men, Whites (e.g., White Americans), and heterosexual people in multicultural societies.

Counseling Process and Intervention

To address the common problems of premature termination and attrition by minority clients in psychotherapy, therapist competence to establish credibility is considered essential to positive treatment outcome. *Credibility* refers to the client's perception of the therapist as effective and trustworthy. Minority clients' underutilization of and attrition from psychotherapy have been attributed to their perception that psychotherapy is a tool to conform them to the majority worldview. In other words, therapists and psychotherapy lose credibility when minority clients do not have trust and faith that their counseling concerns will be understood from their cultural belief system. Therapist credibility can be ascribed, achieved, or both. *Ascribed credibility* refers to the position or status assigned to the therapist by the minority client. Therapist race, gender, and age are some of the determining factors. Such status may be afforded independently of the therapist skills. For example, a Black client who had repeated experiences with White racism may ascribe low credibility to a White therapist. A female therapist may be perceived as more credible than a male therapist by a female client who is a victim of rape. Regardless of the therapist skills, ascribed credibility is somewhat beyond the therapist's control. *Achieved credibility* refers more directly to skills demonstrated during the therapeutic encounter. Credibility is achieved when therapist actions lead a skeptical and guarded client to trust the therapist and stay in counseling. Achieved credibility is related to therapist skills to offer conceptualization that is congruent with the minority client's belief system, as well as provide intervention strategies that are appropriate and acceptable within the client's cultural system.

In a cross-cultural dyad, a minority client may ascribe initial credibility based on a particular therapist attribute (e.g., racial match in which a Black client believes a Black therapist would understand experiences of racism). Yet when a therapist fails to consider the client's cultural system and minority status (e.g., a Black therapist who denies existence of societal racism) in the assessment, conceptualization, and intervention process, the therapist loses achieved credibility. Despite the initial ascribed credibility, low achieved credibility may result in client distrust of the therapist, nondisclosing behaviors, and attrition from therapy. On the other hand, a minority client may ascribe low credibility due to a particular therapist status attribute (e.g., cross-racial dyad in which therapist race triggers client's feelings of racism). Yet, therapist ability to depersonalize, contextualize, and empathize with the client's initial guardedness and skepticism may enhance the therapist's achieved credibility, thereby decreasing client defensiveness and facilitating client retention in therapy.

Beyond credibility, social justice is the ultimate concern for which therapists and the profession of psychotherapy enable and empower minority clients. Multicultural counseling, therefore, focuses on therapist knowledge of the intricate factors that facilitate and impede the counseling relationship and dynamics between a therapist and client from different cultural groups.

In clinical practice, multicultural counseling positions and conceptualizes clients' presenting concerns within the context of societal discrimination, racism, or oppression. It seeks to help clients whose counseling concerns are rooted in their minority status to re-attribute sources of distress to contextual rather than personal causes. In training and supervision, multicultural counseling delineates and analyzes if the power differential due to counselor and client's majority–minority group statuses adversely affects the quality of the therapeutic relationship, such as premature termination or conforming minority clients to majority values. As such, effective intervention focuses not only on the minority client, but also on the therapist cultural biases, as well as the interplay of majority–minority values in the therapeutic relationship. Recognizing the catalytic impact of majority oppression, multicultural counseling intervenes at both the individual and the systemic level. Beyond individual psychotherapy, multicultural counseling engages in advocacy for, and empowerment of, minority clients to achieve social justice.

In sum, multicultural counseling entails therapist competence in the following three domains: (1) empathic knowledge of the impact of societal oppression on the identity development and conflicts of clients who are ascribed a minority status by virtue of cultural characteristics, (2) recognition and confrontation of the therapist's own cultural biases and internalized worldview of the majority group, and (3) skill to discern and apply cultural knowledge to instill trust and credibility in the cross-cultural therapeutic relationship. Beyond individual psychotherapy, therapists also intervene in social advocacy and empowerment of minority clients for the cause.

Kwong-Liem Karl Kwan

See also Acculturative Stress (v3); Barriers to Cross-Cultural Counseling (v3); Bilingual Counseling (v3); Cross-Cultural Psychology (v3); Cultural Accommodation and Negotiation (v3); Discrimination (v3); Ethnocentrism (v3); Eurocentrism (v3); Multicultural Counseling Competence (v3); Multiculturalism (v3); Multicultural Psychology (v3); Oppression (v3); Social Justice (v3); Sue, Derald Wing: Contributions to Multicultural Psychology and Counseling (v3); Therapist Techniques/Behaviors (v2)

Further Readings

American Psychological Association. (2002). *Guidelines on multicultural education, training, research, practice, and organizational change for psychologists.* Washington, DC: Author.

Helms, J. E., & Cook, D. A. (1999). *Using race and culture in counseling and psychotherapy: Theory and process.* Needham, MA: Allyn & Bacon.

Reynolds, A. L., & Hanjorgiris, W. F. (1999). Coming out: Lesbian, gay, and bisexual identity development. In R. M. Perez, K. A. Debord, & K. J. Bieschke (Eds.), *Handbook of counseling and psychotherapy with lesbian, gay, and bisexual clients* (pp. 35–56). Washington, DC: American Psychological Association.

Sue, D. W., Arredondo, P., & McDavis, R. J. (1992). Multicultural counseling competencies and standards: A call to the profession. *Journal of Counseling & Development, 70,* 477–483.

Sue, S., & Zane, N. (1987). The role of culture and cultural techniques in psychotherapy: A critique and reformulation. *American Psychologist, 42,* 37–45.

MULTICULTURAL COUNSELING COMPETENCE

Multicultural counseling competence—the intentional consideration and utilization of culture to facilitate therapeutic change—has become one of the most critical forces guiding the discipline of counseling psychology. In response to both the diversifying of the population of the United States and the civil rights, women's rights, and gay and lesbian rights movements of the 1960s and 1970s, pioneers in the counseling profession instigated changes in their theories and practices. One of the enduring changes is the profession's deploring of racist, ethnocentric, sexist, and heterosexist practices, which were found to be ubiquitous in the mental health system. Although the deplorable practices sometimes were unintentionally motivated, the consequences for consumers, nevertheless, were deleterious. Among the more formidable initiatives were attempts to make counseling more accessible to members of disenfranchised groups and also the development of new competencies to shape and guide counseling practice.

Counseling psychologists, led by visionaries such as Derald Wing Sue, Patricia Arredondo, Stanley Sue, William Cross, Joseph Ponterotto, Janet Helms, Gargi Roysircar, Teresa LaFromboise, Michael D'Andrea, Thomas Parham, Paul Pedersen, Allen Ivey, Donald Atkinson, Madonna Constantine, Donald Pope-Davis, Hardin Coleman, and others, drew formal critiques of a mental health system that had been steeped in racist practices for nearly a century. The findings and conclusions of their careful analyses were disturbing. Traditional theories of counseling and psychotherapy were developed primarily by European White middle-class men without consideration of the cultural zeitgeist in which their theories were rooted. Training followed from these theories and reinforced European ideas about normalcy and pathology. Racial and ethnic minority clients often were underserved, more likely provided with substandard care from inexperienced therapists, and more likely to terminate prematurely than were White clients. A call for systemic-wide change was heeded.

D. W. Sue and his colleagues have been among the most influential counseling psychologists to respond to the call for change. In 1982 the team of scholars published a groundbreaking article titled "Position Paper: Cross-Cultural Counseling Competencies." The position paper provided a general description of three competencies: attitudes and beliefs, knowledge, and skills. Attitudes and beliefs pertain to counselors' self-awareness as cultural beings and their sensitivity to, and respect of, cultural differences with their clients. Knowledge is having a good understanding of sociopolitical systems, particular client populations, generic characteristics of counseling, and institutional barriers for minority clients. A broad range of skills are deemed necessary, covering verbal and nonverbal communications and also institutional interventions. In 1992 D. W. Sue and another group of scholars expanded on the tripartite model in an article titled "Multicultural Counseling Competencies/Standards: A Call to the Profession." Intending to provide a new lens through which counseling could be conceptualized and practiced, the Standards offered important initial perspectives for the field. The Standards were organized in a 3 (characteristics) × 3 (dimensions) matrix format in which the characteristics (i.e., counselor awareness of own assumptions, values, and biases) were each grounded along the three dimensions of beliefs and attitudes, knowledge, and skills. The Standards implored counselors to develop a more nuanced understanding of their own cultural identities, as well as those of their clients, and to best use this understanding to help develop therapy strategies and interventions.

In addition, the authors made two other assertions. They argued for the broad inclusion of multicultural perspectives in the areas of assessment, practice, training, and research. They advocated the adoption of these standards by the American Association of

Counseling and Development, which later was renamed the American Counseling Association.

The publication of the Standards and the resulting discourse were pivotal in the multicultural counseling competence movement. They heightened awareness of the need for better training and practice, and they stimulated discourse on the topic not only among counseling psychologists but in the larger professional organizations as well. Professional codes of ethics were revised to include multicultural considerations, and the field enjoyed a proliferation of conference presentations, trainings, symposia, and extensive publications. One important publication was commissioned by the Association for Multicultural Counseling and Development. Titled "Operationalization of Multicultural Counseling Competencies," the 1996 article was authored by Arredondo and colleagues. Extending the scholarship of Sue and colleagues, these authors organized the multicultural counseling competencies into three domains: counselor awareness of own cultural values and biases, counselor awareness of client's worldview, and culturally appropriate intervention strategies. Overall, 31 competency statements and 119 explanatory statements were described in the article. Another influential publication, *Guidelines on Multicultural Education, Training, Research, Practice, and Organizational Change for Psychologists,* was published in 2003 and approved as policy of the American Psychological Association. These guidelines, cochaired by Nadya Fouad and Arredondo, build on the aforementioned documents related to multicultural counseling competencies.

Although the Standards were pivotal in advancing the movement, they are not without criticisms. Doubt was cast on the adequacy of the Standards to reflect the multifaceted nature of multicultural counseling competence. For instance, researchers noted that the therapeutic relationship was not reflected in the Standards even though the relationship is widely acknowledged as a critical component in therapeutic change. Compelling research by a leading multicultural scholar substantiated the criticism. Additional debate arose about whether the construct of multicultural counseling competence should be limited to conversations about race and ethnicity or whether *culture* ought to be defined more broadly to include considerations of individuals from a wide array of disenfranchised and often-overlooked groups (e.g., women; gay, lesbian, bisexual, and transgendered people; people with disabilities). The Standards led to the development of several self-report measures intended to capture the complex construct of multicultural counseling competence. The three best known of these measures are the Multicultural Awareness/Knowledge/Skills Survey, the Multicultural Counseling Inventory, and the Multicultural Counseling Knowledge and Awareness Scale. While the field generally regarded these instruments as positive first steps, their publication actually posed several additional challenges to the profession. Problems with the instruments themselves soon became apparent. Because the instruments were self-report, they introduced a social desirability confound. They also failed to capture the complex experiences of clients in therapy.

As the movement continues to advance, difficult questions remain. Is counseling competence the same as multicultural counseling competence? Can the multicultural counseling competencies be construed as being synonymous with cultural competence? Is multicultural counseling inclusive or exclusive? The following propositions are set forth to answer these questions. First, multicultural counseling competence and counseling competence are synonymous. Therefore, a competent counselor should be able to attend to cultural considerations in counseling. Second, the unequivocal purpose of multicultural competence is the facilitation of therapeutic change. The achievement of this purpose hinges largely on counselors' attention to cultural considerations. Third, multicultural counseling competencies are subsets of multicultural counseling competence. Therefore, the competencies must be coordinated and integrated in a fashion that achieves the purpose of the construct. Fourth, the multicultural counseling competencies must be defined prescriptively. Their prescriptions should guide counselors in *how* to intervene with clients, not simply describe *what* they should do. Fifth, multiculturally competent counselors can facilitate therapeutic change, regardless of their, or their clients', backgrounds. This places a greater emphasis on the process nature of the construct as opposed to requiring counselors to have an in-depth knowledge of various cultural groups.

The literature on the construct has yielded stimulating discussions that fall into five general categories: (1) asserting the importance of multicultural competence; (2) characteristics, features, dimensions, and parameters of multicultural competence; (3) training and supervision; (4) assessing cultural competence; and (5) specialized applications. In each of these categories, a number of important issues are raised. The emergence of a number of models of multicultural competence is particularly noteworthy. Examination of these models reveals the intense thinking that has taken place and complexity inherent in multicultural competence.

In retrospect, multicultural competence has moved from obscurity to the periphery and then to the center of counseling training, research, and practice. Its central role now is unmistakable. In looking to the future, much more needs to be accomplished if the profession is to explicate exactly what it means to be multiculturally competent. To provide all clients with the type of care they rightly deserve, the profession cannot rest on the achievements of the past.

Charles R. Ridley and Debra Mollen

See also Acculturation (v3); Barriers to Cross-Cultural Counseling (v3); Bilingual Counseling (v3); Counseling Skills Training (v2); Cross-Cultural Training (v3); Cultural Accommodation and Negotiation (v3); Ethnocentrism (v3); Eurocentrism (v3); International Developments, Counseling (v1); Multicultural Counseling (v3); Multiculturalism (v3); Multicultural Psychology (v3); Sue, Derald Wing: Contributions to Multicultural Psychology and Counseling (v3); Therapist Techniques/Behaviors (v2)

Further Readings

American Psychological Association. (2003). Guidelines on multicultural education, training, research, practice, and organizational change for psychologists. *American Psychologist, 58*, 377–402.

Arredondo, P., Toporek, R., Brown, S. B., Jones, J., Locke, D. C., Sanchez, J., & Stadler, H. (1996). Operationalization of multicultural counseling competencies. *Journal of Multicultural Counseling and Development, 24*, 42–78.

Constantine, M. G., & Ladany, N. (2001). New visions for defining and assessing multicultural counseling competence. In C. M. Alexander, J. M. Casas, J. G. Ponterotto, & L. A. Suzuki (Eds.), *Handbook of multicultural counseling* (2nd ed., pp. 482–498). Thousand Oaks, CA: Sage.

D'Andrea, M., & Daniels, J. (2001). Expanding our thinking about White racism: Facing the challenge of multicultural counseling in the 21st century. In C. M. Alexander, J. M. Casas, J. G. Ponterotto, & L. A. Suzuki (Eds.), *Handbook of multicultural counseling* (2nd ed., pp. 289–310). Thousand Oaks, CA: Sage.

Ponterotto, J. G., & Casas, J. M. (1991). Value systems in counseling: A racial/ethnic minority perspective. In J. G. Ponterotto & J. M. Casas (Eds.), *Handbook of racial/ethnic minority counseling research* (pp. 49–66). Springfield, IL: Charles C Thomas.

Pope-Davis, D. B., Coleman, H. L. K., Liu, W. M., & Toporek, R. L. (Eds.). (2003). *Handbook of multicultural competencies in counseling and psychology.* Thousand Oaks, CA: Sage.

Ridley, C. R. (2005). *Overcoming unintentional racism in counseling and psychotherapy: A practitioner's guide to intentional intervention* (2nd ed.). Thousand Oaks, CA: Sage.

Roysircar, G., Sandhu, D. S., & Bibbins, V. E. (Eds.). (2003). *Multicultural counseling competencies: A guidebook of practices.* Alexandria, VA: Association for Multicultural Counseling and Development.

Sue, D. W., Arredondo, P., & McDavis, R. J. (1992). Multicultural competencies/standards: A call to the profession. *Journal of Multicultural Counseling and Development, 20*, 64–68.

Sue, D. W., Bernier, J. B., Duran, M., Feinberg, L., Pedersen, P., Smith, E., et al. (1982). Position paper: Cross-cultural counseling competencies. *The Counseling Psychologist, 10*, 45–52.

Sue, D. W. & Sue, D. (2003). *Counseling the culturally diverse. Theory and practice* (4th ed.). New York: Wiley.

Multiculturalism

The term *multiculturalism* refers to a perspective in which diversity in backgrounds and experiences related to race, ethnicity, gender, sexual orientation, age, religion, disability, education status, and socioeconomic class is recognized. In the United States, multiculturalism has been described as a social movement that celebrates and values *pluralism,* or differences between individuals and groups. From a political stance, pluralism ensures that *all* citizens of society are affirmed and that the fundamental principles of democracy are honored. Multiculturalism advances the view that the cultural heritages and experiences of different racial and ethnic groups are legitimate and enrich society at all levels. As a movement, multiculturalism values the dignity, human rights, and diversity of people.

Historical Considerations

Concern for multiculturalism evolved out of sociopolitical movements and educational approaches. Historically, multiculturalism became integrated into official government policies following the civil rights movements of the latter 20th century, which sought to terminate racism, sexism, and segregation. The efforts of many African Americans and other people of color, such as Latinos/as and American Indians, who organized and demonstrated for equal rights throughout the 1900s, led to milestone changes in racial and ethnic discriminatory practices. The civil rights struggles of these various racial/ethnic groups and their allies granted all citizens in the United States, regardless of their racial or ethnic group membership, access to many aspects of mainstream society, including education, employment, and housing, as well as ensuring voting rights. Major legislation changes in the latter 20th century abolished discrimination on the basis of religion, race, sex, handicap, or national origin. In sum, the civil rights movements in the 20th century contributed significantly to the protection and justice of people of color by implementing social justice policies that protected and represented the human rights of all Americans.

Unfortunately, despite these critical civil rights victories, many people of color today continue to face overt and covert forms of racism and discrimination as well as a double standard regarding their abilities and skills. For example, many people of color continue to be systematically excluded from important positions in schools and other institutions. And when people of color hold positions of power, they may be viewed as "token" representatives or as "experts" on minority issues (e.g., Black and Latino/a professors may be expected to teach the multicultural courses even if they are unprepared to do so).

Furthermore, the propagation of racial stigmatization continues to play a central role in maintaining racial and ethnic inequality in the United States. Empirically unfounded ideas about biological inferiority and cultural pathology of various racial/ethnic groups, for instance, continue to be propagated by various institutions and in some educational settings. Backlash movements against multiculturalism in employment and academic settings have emphasized the rights of majority workers and students to continued access to critical funding. Moreover, other recent movements attempting to install an "Academic Bill of Rights" for students have apparently targeted scholars who promote multiculturalist perspectives, and increasing hostility toward immigrants and their children is, at the same time, being promoted in some legislatures. In sum, as the 21st century begins, civil rights victories that characterized the previous century seem imperiled, and multiculturalism has lost ground within the sociopolitical and educational structures that once supported it. However, many multicultural scholars continue their work in education and psychology, continuing to call for research, training, and practice in competencies necessary to work with various racial/ethnic groups.

Multiculturalism in Education

Educational settings have always been important to multiculturalism. Throughout the 19th century and well into the 20th century, state laws existed that systematically excluded or separated children and adolescents of African American, Latino/a (particularly Mexican), and American Indian heritage from mainstream schools. Not only were these students segregated, school systems that served these children often were hostile to their cultural values, customs, and native languages.

A seminal historical event in the education of all Americans was the 1954 case of *Brown v. Board of Education of Topeka,* which dismantled racially segregated schools. This judicial decision was an important turning point in equal access to education for all. The decision also had implications for the field of psychology, marking the first time psychological research was used in a court decision. Similarly, the enactment of the Civil Rights Act in 1964 paved the way for additional legislation that prevented discrimination based on race, color, religion, or national origin. Additionally, the Bilingual Education Act of 1968, and later 1974, passed under Title VII of the Elementary and Secondary Education Act, granting equal access to curriculum for language minority children and providing funding for programs for students with limited English proficiency. Unfortunately, controversy has always surrounded the inclusion of multicultural perspectives in education, a topic that is discussed more fully in a later section of this entry.

Multiculturalism in Psychology

In addition to education, multiculturalism also has been a major force in psychology. Multiculturalism in psychology reflects a comprehensive paradigm in which the knowledge and skills needed for the profession have evolved out of the historical and sociopolitical changes in society. The movement toward multicultural counseling, for instance, occurred in tangent with the civil rights movement, the advocacy work of counselors and psychologists in the early 1970s, and the subsequent establishment of several racially/culturally based professional associations (e.g., the Association of Black Psychologists, the Association of Psychologists Por La Raza, and the Asian American Psychological Association).

In the 1973 American Psychological Association (APA) Vail conference, psychologists began to focus on the significance of race and culture in theory, research, and practice. For example, the recommendation and implementation of subsequent training in cultural diversity for doctoral students evolved out of this conference. In addition, the establishment of the Office of Ethnic Minority Affairs, followed by the Board of Ethnic Minority Affairs and the Division of Ethnic Minority Affairs, represents concrete efforts by the APA to promote and encourage competent and ethical practices and fair treatment of psychologists and their potential clients, research participants, and trainees. Throughout the years, the initiatives of these offices have expanded participation of psychologists of color in the APA, who still represent less than 10% of all psychologists. These entities also help to recruit and retain ethnic minority students and prepare all psychologists for an increasingly diverse society. In addition, these offices have recognized and supported policies and programs that encourage pluralism and multiculturalism in the United States. For example, under the recommendation of the Board of Ethnic Minority Affairs, the APA approved a resolution against an English-only initiative in 1990.

A number of subsequent APA publications also have highlighted the need to prepare psychologists to work effectively with diverse populations. These include the *APA Accreditation Handbook;* the *Guidelines for Providers of Psychological Services to Ethnic, Linguistic, and Culturally Diverse Populations;* the *Guidelines and Principles for Accreditation of Programs of Professional Psychology;* and, most recently, the *Guidelines on Multicultural Education, Training, Research, Practice, and Organizational Change for Psychologists.*

Today psychologists work and interact with individuals from all walks of life, and thus they are encouraged to be cognizant of issues related to all of the dimensions of multiculturalism in their education, training, research, and practice. In counseling psychology, in particular, multiculturalism emphasizes respect for the life experiences and cultural values of diverse individuals and groups as a fundamental principle of competent assessment, diagnosis, and treatment. As cultural beings, multicultural psychologists also are aware of their beliefs, attitudes, and impact on individuals with whom they work.

Debates About Multiculturalism

Multiculturalism in the United States is not without controversy. A central debate is the universal versus relative nature of multiculturalism. On the universal side is the argument that there is only one race—the human race. In other words, because all human beings are members of the human race, they share common aspects, such as life experiences (e.g., birth, death, and happiness), similar biological makeup, and the capacity to use language and symbols. The underlying assumption of universalism is that all people are essentially alike, and this should be the primary emphasis of educational and psychological interventions.

Conversely, the relativism argument states that each culture possesses values, norms, and ideals, and social practices unique to that group. Membership in a particular culture shapes and influences individuals and group members. Through the process of socialization, individuals acquire the knowledge, belief systems, cultural patterns, and values needed to function in their group. The underlying assumption of relativism is that people are not alike. As a result, mainstream practices are deemed inappropriate when they exclude unique culture and life experiences. Instead, treatment should include differences to most effectively work with people.

Multicultural Education

Among the controversies surrounding multiculturalism is a general debate about multicultural education. Proponents of multicultural education argue strongly that a multicultural curriculum and multiculturally trained teachers ensure that *all* students have an equal educational opportunity according to their needs, values, and learning styles. Thus, multicultural pedagogy necessitates that teachers alter their instruction to meet the needs of diverse students, as based on race-culture, linguistic diversity, gender, socioeconomic class, religion, sexual orientation, and disability.

Moreover, advocates of multicultural education challenge the Anglo-Eurocentric perspectives that underlie the curricula of most U.S. school systems; these curricula are viewed as unresponsive and ineffective for culturally diverse students. Multiculturalists argue that when educators teach solely from a Eurocentric view, they lose non-White students because they are taught that they are not part of the story. The exclusion from historical events, coupled with various types of cultural incongruencies in curricula, is viewed as a significant factor explaining why many students of color disengage from academics. The strong disconnection in the curricula between the students' culture and school culture has been referred to as "cultural imperialism" to describe how the dominant's group experience and culture have been established as the norm in educational systems.

Multiculturalists note that it is fallacious to conclude that the numerical majority in the United States should be considered the dominant group whose worldview is assumed to be superior and the basis of universality. The previous ideal of assimilation into an Anglo-American model where immigrant students, for example, were expected to get rid of their cultural traits in order to be taught "American" values and behavior also is rejected because it perpetuates the eradication of many cultures and the inferiority of other groups and their traditions. In addition, cultural dispositions associated with autonomy, competition, individualism, and internal locus of control place some children (e.g., low socioeconomic status) at a disadvantage because they are not equipped with the skills rewarded in the school environment that are predominantly operated by middle-class White European American teachers and administrators.

Multicultural education is anchored in the principles of inclusiveness, diversity, and unity. Far from being a source of divisiveness, many advocates assert, multicultural education helps to unify a divided nation. They recognize that the multicultural education model is beneficial for everybody, not just racially/culturally diverse students of color, because it prepares all students to understand multiple perspectives and to function in an increasingly multicultural society. More importantly, supporters contend that a multicultural curriculum fosters the development of cognitive abilities by teaching students to become critical thinkers and innovators and to function as humane citizens.

Critics, on the other hand, argue that multicultural education departs from conventional studies of Western civilization in the direction of a more "revisionist history" by rewriting history from a different point of view to misrepresent facts or events. Opponents contend that multicultural education opposes Western traditions because it aims to recognize and empower historically oppressed groups. Thus, critics confound multiculturalism with an anti-Western stance by contorting it as an attempt to change or rewrite history rather than provide a more holistic framework. Other critics believe that multicultural education is simply an entitlement curriculum for students of color and a mechanism for providing therapy to females and culturally and linguistically diverse students, objectives deemed inappropriate for education and for which teachers should not be held responsible.

Another major criticism of multiculturalism is that it is destructive of the values that unite Americans. This view stems from the suggestion that multiculturalism disparages the *unum* and venerates *pluribus* by discarding the ideals of assimilation and integration and instead calling attention to specific ethnic, cultural, and gender experiences. Thus, some critics believe that multiculturalism takes attention away from unifying experiences of being "American."

Bilingual Education

Underlying controversies about multiculturalism are issues of language and culture. Bilingual education and programs for diverse language learners illustrate one example of this ongoing debate. Historically, bilingual abilities have been viewed as a handicap rather than an asset to the learning environment. Indeed for much of the 20th century, many educators believed that being bilingual actually slowed learning and diminished intelligence rather than increased performance and cognitive complexity. Unfortunately, most studies between the late 1800s and the 1960s yielded findings linking bilingualism with lower academic performance. However, recent reviews of this research reveal many of these studies were flawed in their methodologies, including their definitions of *intelligence* and their sampling techniques.

Biases toward bilingualism also have been reflected in public policies affecting school systems that serve bilingual students. For example, a landmark and progressive 1976 law passed in California enabling education programs for limited-English-proficient students framed the issue as a "language problem" to be solved by transitioning students from their native language into English, with an unfortunate outcome of prejudicing these students against their own languages. In short, the legislated goals of bilingual education programs were to dispense with native languages as quickly as possible, in order that English might be learned.

Although bilingual education continues in many public schools, legislation in more recent years has reflected increasingly hostile attitudes toward providing funding for school learning in any other language but English. The ongoing debate regarding bilingualism in the United States has been summarized by educators Kenji Hakuta and Eugene García in this way: "Is bilingualism strictly the knowledge and usage of two linguistic systems, or does it involve the social dimensions encompassed by the languages?" (1989, p. 374).

Anti–bilingual education perspectives view this form of education as a barrier to learning English and detrimental to student academic achievement. This view holds that English should be the only form of instruction because of the importance of developing content knowledge and literacy in English. The use of the primary language in the classroom and at home is believed by some to cause a cycle of dependence. In the English-only model, teachers alter their instruction for English language learners with the goal of transitioning students after 1 year of intensive English instruction. In addition, proponents of English-only education contend that only English proficiency prepares students to function in U.S. society and does not harm their self-esteem as has been suggested. In several states, such as California, Arizona, and Massachusetts, English-only initiatives have been adopted.

Opponents of English-only education state that bilingual education is more effective because this approach results in biliteracy; for example, instruction is delivered in the students' primary language and in English, sending the message that being bilingual is important. Furthermore, these opponents' suggestion that bilingual education creates dependency is simply unfounded and, instead, represents English-only proponents' deep lack of appreciation for linguistically and culturally diverse students.

In the face of strong criticism regarding the need for more effective programs targeting bilingual students, scholars today emphasize the potential positive impact of dual language learning. Recent research indicates that learning in a second language may actually facilitate cognitive functioning, particularly cognitive flexibility and metalinguistic awareness. More sophisticated research has revealed that language learning, whether first- or second-language, uses the same basic cognitive processes. As Hakuta and García note, learning dual languages "share[s] and build[s] upon a common underlying base rather than compete[s] for limited [cognitive] resources" (p. 375).

Proponents of bilingual education also argue that bilingualism serves as a bridge between the school and home to strengthen learning. To require students to speak only English at home and school, they contend, is to deprive an equal opportunity to learn. Moreover, advocates for bilingual education have argued that it takes longer than 1 year for students to obtain the language skills needed to perform complex abstract tasks. Also, cultural identity is critical to self-esteem, and language is significant in the formation of identity. Banning students from speaking their native language, critics maintain, can be demoralizing and result in lower self-esteem of English learners.

Clearly, the controversy around bilingual education is complex with differing views about the best way to educate diverse language learners. These differing views have had important implications for legal and policy legislations. Indeed, the passage of Proposition 227 in California is illustrative of legislation of an English-only ideology (this legislation also reverses the previously mentioned legislation from the 1970s) and illustrates the continuing debate of multicultural education in the United States.

Affirmative Action

Another multicultural policy implemented to advance historically racial/ethnic groups in the United States is affirmative action. Initiated in 1965 by President Lyndon Johnson to correct discrimination on the basis of race, ethnicity, and gender, affirmative action has been a highly contentious issue. Opposition to affirmative action began after the popular Allan Bakke case in 1978, in which Bakke claimed reverse discrimination because he was rejected from medical school for 2 consecutive years. Bakke argued that he was rejected because the school admitted less-qualified minority applicants under a special admissions program designed to help minority students. Since then, terms such as *preferential treatment* and *reverse discrimination* have been used to express opposition to affirmative action. Affirmative action opponents have attempted, and continue to attempt, to advocate policies that dismantle equal opportunity in higher education and employment.

Conversely, affirmative action advocates counter that the history of slavery in the United States coupled with racial discrimination continues to put several racial/ethnic groups, such as African Americans, Latinos/as, and American Indians, at political and economic disadvantages. Affirmative action, they assert, is justified reparation for social and historical inequality. The reality today, these advocates uphold, is that Whites continue to hold the power, privilege, and wealth in the United States. Thus, affirmative action programs promote critical opportunities for access and advancement to historically oppressed individuals and groups.

Affirmative action programs have been implemented in learning institutions to foster educational diversity for students and faculty. In higher education institutions, affirmative action policies are utilized as a strategy to enroll ethnically and racially diverse students. Advocates maintain that multiculturalism and affirmative action practices in universities promote racial unity and expand the discourse to multiple perspectives. In a major victory for the University of Michigan in the early 2000s, the Supreme Court upheld the right of educational institutions to sustain affirmative action policies that consider race as one of the various factors in the admission process. Among the most compelling evidence cited in favor of this decision were the educational benefits (e.g., intellectual improvements) obtained from participating in ethnically and culturally diverse classrooms.

Implications for Clinical Practice

Given the increasing diversity of the population of the United States, competent and racially/ethnically diverse educators, practitioners, and researchers within the field of psychology are in great demand. In particular, psychologists must be prepared to meet the needs and demands of multicultural clients. Historically, however, issues of race, ethnicity, and culture, along with other important dimensions of diversity (e.g., gender, socioeconomic status, and sexual orientation), have been ignored in the field of psychology. For example, conventional models of psychological theories and treatment are encapsulated by Eurocentric perspectives; nonetheless, they have been assumed to be appropriate for non-White clients in the same way that Eurocentric curricula have been viewed as appropriate for culturally and linguistically diverse students.

Western theories of psychology were conceptualized under a culturally universal perspective (*etic*), which defines concepts of normality and abnormality as similar across cultures. Furthermore, the etiology, course, and manifestation of disorders are presumed to be the same across individuals despite their culture. As noted earlier, multiculturalists propose that a solely universalist assumption may be oppressive for diverse clients. Consequently, when practitioners operate from an etic perspective, they may be perpetuating monocultural and ethnocentric biases.

On the other hand, when practitioners operate from a culturally specific perspective (*emic*), they are aware that culture and life experiences affect the origin and expression of disorders. As a result, they are more likely to use culture-specific strategies for counseling and therapy. The challenge for psychologists, researchers, and educators is to revise existing major theories and incorporate multicultural perspectives to improve understanding and interventions for diverse clients. Moreover, multiculturalism compels psychologists to reevaluate their personal beliefs and perspectives.

Multicultural Competency

Competency models of multicultural counseling have been developed to improve the quality and effectiveness of psychotherapy services for multicultural individuals. Derald Wing Sue first outlined the characteristics of culturally competent psychologists in three areas: (1) awareness of personal values and beliefs around issues of race and ethnicity toward culturally diverse clients; (2) knowledge of diverse cultures, worldviews, and experiences; and (3) utilization of effective skills or techniques when working with clients of color. This tripartite model was later expanded and refined to include specific characteristics of multicultural counselors: awareness of their personal biases, understanding their client's worldview, and developing culturally suitable intervention strategies.

Following the refined tripartite model, Patricia Arredondo and her colleagues delineated specific behavioral expressions of the awareness, knowledge, and skills areas of competencies in an attempt to clearly define the constructs. D. W. Sue and colleagues also developed a comprehensive that delineated multicultural counseling competencies for counselors and organizations. In this body of literature, the role of psychologists in working to ameliorate the effects of racism and advocating for clients is emphasized.

Respect for individual and group differences is a major principle of multiculturalism. When this standard is extended to psychology, it applies to the role of psychologists and their knowledge, awareness, and skills. As professionals working with diverse people, psychologists must have an honest desire to learn about and explore different cultures and backgrounds. They must become aware of how their attitudes, feelings, and perceptions are likely to influence the therapeutic process and outcomes. Without a willingness to unlearn perceptions and judgments of prejudice, racism, ageism, and heterosexism, for example, multicultural competence becomes difficult to attain.

Finally, a glance at the population of the United States clearly indicates the steadily increasing numbers of racially and ethnically diverse people in all aspects of society. If educators, psychologists, and other professionals hope to meet the mission of promoting psychological well-being, multicultural concerns must be examined. In sum, multicultural perspectives have the power to promote human well-being and the potential to enrich and transform members of society through the exploration and understanding of human diversity.

Brenda X. Mejia and Marie L. Miville

See also Acculturation (v3); Affirmative Action (v3); Bicultural (v3); Bilingual Counseling (v3); Bilingualism (v3); Cultural Accommodation and Negotiation (v3); Cultural Encapsulation (v3); Cultural Equivalence (v3); Cultural Relativism (v3); Cultural Values (v3); Culture (v3); Diversity (v3); Ethnocentrism (v3); Eurocentrism (v3); Multicultural Counseling (v3); Multicultural Counseling Competence (v3); Multicultural Psychology (v3); Pluralism (v3); Universalism (v3)

Further Readings

Abreu, J. M., Chung Gim, R. H., & Atkinson, D. R. (2000). Multicultural counseling training: Past, present, and future directions. *The Counseling Psychologist, 28*(5), 641–656.

American Psychological Association. (1993). Guidelines for providers of psychological services to ethnic, linguistic, and culturally diverse populations. *American Psychologist, 48,* 45–48.

American Psychological Association. (2003). Guidelines on multicultural education, training, research, practice, and organizational change for psychologists. *American Psychologist, 58*(5), 377–402.

Arredondo, P., Toporek, R., Brown, S. P., Jones, J., Locke, D. C., Sanchez, J., et al. (1996). Operationalization of multicultural counseling competencies. *Journal of Multicultural Counseling and Development, 24,* 42–78.

Constantine, M. G., & Sue, D. W. (2005). *Strategies for building multicultural competence in mental health and educational settings.* Hoboken, NJ: Wiley.

Crawford, J. (1997). *Best evidence: Research foundations of the Bilingual Education Act.* Washington, DC: National Clearinghouse for Bilingual Education.

Curry, G. E., & West, C. (1996). *The affirmative action debate.* Cambridge, MA: Perseus.

Ezorsky, G. (1991). *Racism and justice: The case for affirmative action.* Ithaca, NY: Cornell University Press.

Hakuta, K., & García, E. E. (1989). Bilingualism and education. *American Psychologist, 44,* 374–379.

Sue, D. W., Arredondo, P., & McDavis, R. J. (1992). Multicultural counseling competencies/standards: A call to the profession. *Journal of Multicultural Counseling and Development, 20,* 64–88.

Sue, D. W., Carter, R. T., Casas, J. M., Fouad, N. A., Ivey, A. E., Jensen, M., et al. (1998). *Multicultural counseling competencies: Individual and organizational development.* Thousand Oaks, CA: Sage.

Taylor, C. (1994). *Multiculturalism: Examining the politics of recognition.* Princeton, NJ: Princeton University Press.

MULTICULTURAL PERSONALITY

The multicultural personality refers to a constellation of traits, attitudes, and behaviors that predispose individuals to adapt successfully to culturally diverse environments. The conceptual roots of the multicultural personality can be traced to work in clinical psychology and counseling psychology in the United States and personnel psychology in the Netherlands. Manuel Ramirez, working in the southwest region of the United States, discussed the multicultural personality as a synthesis of the resources learned from different cultures that enable people to develop cultural flexibility in navigating their environments. Ramirez is a clinical psychologist, and his work focuses on helping clients develop bicultural coping and adaptation skills.

Writing from a counseling and positive psychology perspective, Joseph G. Ponterotto and colleagues discussed the multicultural personality in terms of its relationship to psychological well-being. Working with the general population, these authors hypothesized that given the rapidly changing demographic landscape of the United States, which is becoming an increasingly multicultural, multilingual society, those individuals who exhibited multicultural personality dispositions would adapt more successfully and embrace more fully the diverse components of society and therefore would experience a higher quality of life.

While counseling and clinical psychologists in the United States were developing the construct of the multicultural personality, two researchers in the Netherlands, Karen Van der Zee and Peter Van Oudenhoven, working from the specialties of personnel and organizational psychology, were also conceptualizing a version of the construct. These researchers were interested in studying personality variables of corporate expatriates that predicted success (personal life satisfaction and work productivity) while living and working in a new country.

After an extensive review of the theory and research that possibly related to the multicultural personality, Ponterotto and his colleagues presented an integrated and comprehensive working definition of the construct. They defined the construct as multidimensional and inclusive of the following traits: emotionally stable, secure in one's multiple identities (e.g., racial, gender, religious, ethnic), intellectually curious regarding novel cultures, culturally empathic, feeling centered with regard to spirituality, cognitively flexible, introspective, and committed to social justice.

Though a relatively recent construct, the multicultural personality appears to be correlated to a number of variables central to the work of counselors, namely, life satisfaction, work success, and quality of life. Research on the construct, however, is still in its early stages, and additional studies are needed before counselors can make any definitive conclusions regarding the importance of the construct or even its uniqueness relative to more global personality traits. At present, the most comprehensive assessment of the construct is the 91-item Multicultural Personality Questionnaire developed in the Netherlands by Van der Zee and Van Oudenhoven. If ongoing research continues to find that the multicultural personality is related to important life variables, then counselors and other mental health professionals will want to work toward assessing and then increasing their clients' levels of multicultural personality development. The construct holds great promise for theory and research in counseling.

Joseph G. Ponterotto

See also Acculturation (v3); Bicultural (v3); Change Agent (v3); Cultural Accommodation and Negotiation (v3); Ethnic Identity (v3); Identity Development (v3); Multicultural Psychology (v3); Personality Assessment and Careers (v4); Personality Theories (v2); Personality Theories, Traits (v2); Racial Identity (v3)

Further Readings

Ponterotto, J. G., Utsey, S. O., & Pedersen, P. B. (2006). *Preventing prejudice: A guide for counselors, educators, and parents* (2nd ed.). Thousand Oaks, CA: Sage.

Ramirez, M., III. (1999). *Multicultural psychotherapy: An approach to individual and cultural differences* (2nd ed.). New York: Pergamon Press.

Van der Zee, K. I., & Van Oudenhoven, J. P. (2000). The Multicultural Personality Questionnaire: A multidimensional instrument of multicultural effectiveness. *European Journal of Personality, 14,* 291–309.

MULTICULTURAL PSYCHOLOGY

Multiculturalism has been called the "fourth force" of psychology by Paul B. Pedersen, Pius K. Essandoh, and others (following psychoanalysis, behaviorism, and humanism as schools of thought). Multicultural psychology is a major influence in contemporary psychology and includes such broad topic areas as racial identity development, acculturation, prejudice and stereotyping, and multicultural competence. Research focused on multicultural psychology differs from other schools of thought in psychology because, in addition to a focus on individual and intrapsychic factors, the cultural context is considered an important aspect of the lives of individuals and groups. Some important questions in multicultural psychology are the following: How do factors in the cultural context impact individual differences, and how do psychological phenomena vary across cultures?

Although the terms *multicultural* and *cross-cultural* are often used interchangeably, they differ slightly in meaning. Multicultural psychology considers the influence of contextual variables (e.g., race or ethnicity) on human functioning in diverse societies. Cross-cultural psychology focuses on relationships between individuals and/or groups from different cultures. Cross-cultural psychology also focuses on comparisons between cultural groups (e.g., contrasting cultural values, practices, etc.).

History

The history of multicultural psychology is best understood within the context of sociopolitical oppression in the United States. According to the American Psychological Association (APA), psychologists' explicit involvement in controversies related to cultural issues began with *Brown v. the Board of Education of Topeka* in 1954. In this case, psychologists provided significant information regarding the detrimental effects of segregated education for children of color, empirically challenging the notion of "separate but equal." This case also was the first time that psychological research was incorporated in a Supreme Court decision. Political movements and subsequent legislation and policies, such as the Civil Rights Act of 1964, exerted an influence on psychologists' integration of multicultural issues in research and practice. In 1971, the National Institute of Mental Health Office of Minority Research was founded, making funding available specifically for research with racial and ethnic minorities.

Although psychologists have addressed racial and cultural issues in their professional work for more than a century, culture was not explicitly considered an important variable in professional practice until the Vail Conference of Graduate Educators in Psychology in 1973. Recommendations from the conference included the integration of cultural diversity training in psychology graduate programs. Since that time, there has been an explosion of research on multicultural training and competence.

In addition to racism and other forms of cultural oppression as a driving force of multicultural psychology, recent demographic changes have been at the center of discussions about the importance of multicultural competence in psychological research and practice. According to the 2000 U.S. Census, the ratio of racial/ethnic minorities to White people is increasing dramatically. In some parts of the country, such as some areas of California and Texas, people of color (e.g., African Americans, Latinos/as, Asian Americans) are no longer a minority, and many population experts believe that current racial/ethnic minority groups will become the numerical majority in the United States by the middle of the 21st century. Multicultural psychologists such as Derald Wing Sue and Pedersen state that there is an ethical imperative to practice culturally competent psychology. Moreover, demographic trends in the country have led many psychologists to understand the value of incorporating cultural issues into research and practice, minimally because of the increasing likelihood that they will encounter racial/ethnic minority people in their work. Indeed, in 1997 Christine C. Iijima Hall stated that mainstream psychology was becoming obsolete in the face of these demographic changes.

Prejudice and Stereotypes

Research on prejudice and stereotyping in social psychology has contributed to understanding the links between individual cognition, prejudice (i.e., negative social attitudes), and discriminatory behaviors toward various groups, providing an essential cornerstone to multicultural psychology. John F. Dovidio, Ana Validzic, and Samuel L. Gaertner cite research on the "contact hypothesis" in understanding prejudice between groups. The contact hypothesis purports that prejudice arises from limited contact with groups other than one's own, and increasing contact with another group is one way to reduce bias. However, it is not simply the contact but also the conditions under which the contact occurs that lead to decreased intergroup biases (e.g., cooperative interactions between the groups).

In addition, social psychologists have explored the consequences of belonging to a stigmatized group. For example, Claude M. Steele and Joshua Aronson defined the term *stereotype threat* to reflect the impact that negative stereotypes about stigmatized groups (e.g., women and African Americans) can cause individuals from these groups to experience anxiety that may lead to a negative impact on performance. This anxiety arises from fear of being reduced to generalizations made about members of a socially stigmatized group. Their research has been extended to other stigmatized groups, such as people of low socioeconomic status, although more recent research indicates the stereotype threat can occur to most individuals regarding any social group membership, such as being male or being White. However, given the continued underrepresentation of certain groups in several settings (e.g., people of color and women in math and sciences), it is these individuals who are at higher risk of suffering negative social consequences associated with stereotype threat.

Other researchers have proposed complex hypotheses about intergroup relations to help explain prejudice and stereotypes. One example is Marilynn B. Brewer's optimal distinctiveness theory. According to Brewer, individuals do not simply value their own group (ingroup) and devalue other groups (outgroups). Instead, they strive for a balance between fitting in or belonging to a group, in conjunction with standing out or being distinctive from that group. The optimal distinctiveness theory suggests that although understanding ingroup experiences is important, ingroup attraction does not by itself imply outgroup repulsion. Instead, Brewer suggests, there are specific phenomena (e.g., attitudes of moral superiority, perceived threat) that may link ingroup loyalty with prejudice against outgroups.

Racial/Ethnic Identity Development Models

In *Counseling the Culturally Diverse,* D. W. Sue and David Sue review both racial-cultural minority and White racial identity development as these apply to the work of psychologists and counselors. Such models address individual differences within racial/ethnic groups, going beyond demographic or phenotypic definitions of race and ethnicity to address the psychological meaning of racial/ethnic group membership. Various identity models pertaining to racial/ethnic minorities have been proposed by others, including William E. Cross's Nigrescence model; Janet E. Helms's model of Black racial identity development; and Donald R. Atkinson, George Morten, and D. W. Sue's minority identity development model. These models share in common the articulation of developmental processes whereby people of color (a) initially value the dominant group and devalue their own group, (b) then value their own group and devalue the dominant group, and (c) finally move beyond these conflicts to value both groups. Although most scholars no longer ascribe to invariant stage models, these racial/ethnic identity models provide a framework for understanding the psychological impact that racial/ethnic group membership has on identity development and social constructions of the self.

Helms also developed a model of White racial identity development. Central to this model is the influence of racism on White identity. In the White racial identity development model, the first three levels, or statuses, incorporate racism as a core feature of development, ranging from a lack of awareness about race and racism to beliefs in White superiority. The last three statuses involve the development of a non-racist White identity and include the painful realization that racism does exist that may lead to overidentification with people of color in a way that actually perpetuates racism; focusing on the meaning of Whiteness and White privilege; and the development of awareness regarding White privilege, along with decreased feelings of guilt and a commitment to antiracism.

Understanding the racial/ethnic identity statuses of clients can help mental health professionals to focus on systemic issues that play a role in presenting problems. Studies have found relationships between various psychological variables and racial/ethnic identity statuses. For people of color, less "mature" or sophisticated identity statuses (i.e., pre-encounter, encounter) have been linked to high anxiety, low self-esteem, depression, and psychological distress. However, other studies have yielded different results, such as positive relationships between less-mature or sophisticated statuses and low anxiety. This may be attributed to variations in the expression of racial/ethnic identity status. For example, William Cross and Beverly Vandiver suggest that it is possible for some individuals to have racial/ethnic identity statuses marked by less-mature strategies yet have healthy personality profiles because race may be of low salience to their identities. Janet Helms and Donelda A. Cook describe in depth some of this research as well as important applications of racial identity to various psychological services, including individual therapy, group counseling, and supervision.

Psychologists focusing on multiracial and biracial people have suggested that traditional racial/ethnic identity development models may not be adequate or appropriate for understanding mixed-race people. Though monoracial identity development models have been used with multiracial populations, other theorists have proposed separate models of identity development for biracial/multiracial people. W. S. Carlos Poston proposed the first of these models in 1990. Incorporating the concept of "reference group orientation" (as opposed to personal identity) cited in previous racial identity development models, Poston described five stages of biracial identity development: personal identity, choice of group categorization (pressure to choose one group), enmeshment/denial (conflicted feelings regarding choice of group), appreciation (of multiple identities), and integration (experience of wholeness, valuing all ethnic and racial identities).

Similar to earlier monoracial identity development models, Poston's model is a stage model ranging from immature to mature identity resolutions. Others who focus on multiracial identity, such as Maria P. P. Root, have questioned the idea that there is a single process of identity development that applies to multiracial people, or to people in general. She instead proposes an ecological approach to understanding multiracial identity, emphasizing various contextual factors that influence the way in which multiracial people see themselves. Unlike Poston, she does not believe that integration of ethnic identities is a necessary identity resolution. Multiracial people can identify with one group or the other, change their identity based on context, identify with multiple groups, or develop a new and independent identity as multiracial.

In a review of the literature on both racial/ethnic identity development and psychological functioning of biracial people in 2005, Marie L. Miville pointed to the need for research that captures the fluidity of biracial and multiracial identity. Qualitative studies conducted by psychologists such as Root and Miville and colleagues have begun to capture themes not addressed by traditional identity development models thus far (e.g., simultaneous identification as both a monoracial and a multiracial person).

Other multicultural psychologists have focused on ethnic identity. For example, Jean S. Phinney uses the term *ethnicity* to encompass both race and culture, noting disagreement within psychology over what "race" really means. Similar to psychologists who focus on racial identity rather than race as a descriptive or demographic variable, Phinney suggests that it is important to understand the meaning of ethnicity, including the subjective meaning and experience of people from different ethnic groups and the various labels that people use to describe their own ethnicity. In her 1996 article on American ethnic groups, Phinney states that "ethnic identity is a complex cluster of factors that define the extent and type of involvement with one's ethnic group" (p. 923). Her multigroup ethnic identity model has several components that address the complexity of ethnic identification, including self-identification (chosen ethnic group label), ethnic behaviors and practices, affirmation and belonging, positive evaluation, preference for the group, and ethnic interest and knowledge. Phinney developed an oft-used scale based on the multigroup ethnic identity model that contains 14 Likert-type items on the components of ethnic identity (listed in the previous sentence) and six items on "other" group identity. The subscales have been adequately reliable, with higher reliability among college students than high school students, suggesting that ethnic identity might become more stable with development. Studies have found that self-esteem is positively correlated with ethnic identity and that ethnic identity is usually more strongly endorsed among people of color than among White people.

Acculturation and Biculturalism

Considering the increasing diversity of the United States and most other modern societies, acculturation is an important topic in multicultural psychology. Acculturation is a process of individual and group change that occurs when cultural groups come into contact. Understanding the process of acculturation is important when working with immigrant clients because they are adjusting to the dominant culture. Moreover, other racial/ethnic groups undergo an acculturation process because the dominant culture does not include the multiple racial and ethnic groups that are a part of the United States. For example, many African Americans experience an acculturation process when growing up in Black communities and then attending schools or working in predominantly White settings. John W. Berry describes various acculturation strategies, including assimilation and marginalization. Acculturation can lead to *acculturative stress* as individuals navigate multiple cultural norms and try to meet group expectations that often conflict. However, as with racial and ethnic identity development, acculturation is not a linear process that occurs in the same ways or directions for all people and groups. Research on acculturation has shown that in some contexts, acculturation to the dominant culture can have positive psychological effects, but in many others, acculturation to the dominant culture is detrimental to development as individuals and groups lose support from their culture and communities of origin.

Psychologists such as Theresa LaFromboise and her colleagues have challenged the assumption that individuals from nondominant cultural groups are necessarily "marginal people." LaFromboise and colleagues critiqued several models of second-culture acquisition as inadequate because they traditionally relegated racial/ethnic minority cultures to an inferior status. These researchers then presented a theory of bicultural competence that states that, although racial and ethnic minorities will experience discrimination and hardships in an oppressive culture, the experience of living in two cultures does not necessarily predict dysfunction. In fact, the experience of being bicultural may be positive because individuals living in more than one culture have access to multiple resources and ways of being that can result in both cognitive and emotional flexibility. The strength of both individual (ego) identity and cultural identity is an important factor in coping with biculturalism. LaFromboise and colleagues proposed six dimensions of bicultural competence: knowledge of cultural beliefs and values, positive attitudes toward majority and minority groups, bicultural efficacy, communication ability, role repertoire, and a sense of being grounded. They further suggest that individuals living in more than one culture can experience multiple adaptive processes, not simply assimilation to the dominant culture or its antithesis, withdrawal from the dominant culture. Indeed, individuals may make conscious choices regarding their level of biculturalism in certain settings (e.g., high school).

Multicultural Competence

In August 2002, the APA adopted the *Guidelines on Multicultural Education, Training, Research, Practice, and Organizational Change for Psychologists.* These guidelines were an important step in a long history of work on multicultural counseling competencies. This work began in 1982 when D. W. Sue and others in the Society of Counseling Psychology (APA Division 17) proposed the Cross-Cultural Counseling Competencies. The purpose of the APA guidelines is to provide a rationale for the need to address multiculturalism and diversity, specifically those involving racial/ethnic interactions, in addition to reviewing relevant research and providing standards for integrating cultural concerns into the varied work of psychologists.

The APA multicultural guidelines are divided into six categories: commitment to cultural awareness and knowledge of self, commitment to cultural awareness and knowledge of others, education, research, practice, and organizational change and policy development. The influence of years of research on multicultural competence in counseling is evident in the document. The competencies focus first and foremost on psychologists' awareness of their own culture, attitudes, and so on. Psychologists' awareness, knowledge, and skills in working with people from various cultures are central to multicultural counseling competence. The literature also focuses on psychologists' understanding of their clients' cultural values and worldview from a nonjudgmental standpoint.

In addition to the three dimensions of multicultural competence (attitudes and beliefs, knowledge, and skills), multicultural psychologists have proposed three characteristics of multiculturally competent practitioners. The characteristics are a commitment to actively engaging in a process of understanding one's own attitudes, including values and biases; a commitment to understanding the worldview of clients who are culturally different; and a commitment to developing intervention strategies that are appropriate and relevant for each client based on his or her cultural experiences. There are specific competencies related to each dimension for each of the characteristics.

Although measurement of multicultural competence is complicated because of self-report bias and the various instruments available, multicultural competence and training have been linked to positive outcomes for both counselors and clients. For example, multicultural competence and exposure to multicultural training have been linked with counselor empathy, White racial consciousness, White racial identity attitudes, and interracial comfort. In addition, multicultural case conceptualization ability has been linked to multicultural competence.

Some studies also have focused on the multicultural competence of supervisors. In a recent study by Arpana G. Inman, supervisor multicultural competence was related to the working alliance between supervisor and supervisee and to supervisee satisfaction with supervision. In addition, the working alliance served as a mediator between supervisor multicultural competence and satisfaction with supervision.

Multicultural Training

To facilitate the development of multicultural competence in counseling and other forms of applied psychology, multicultural psychologists such as D. Sue have focused on effective multicultural training. D. Sue reviewed various models of multicultural training, including a generic approach that assumes traditional techniques are applicable to all cultures; the etic approach, which seeks to understand the universal aspects of human experiences that go beyond cultural differences; and the emic, or culture-specific, approach. Although each approach has its shortcomings, some multicultural psychologists, such as D. W. Sue, have argued that it is crucial to simultaneously attend to individual, group, and human (universal) characteristics in counseling. It is important to note that traditionally, professional psychologists have focused much more on individual and etic ("universal") approaches than on those that take group differences into account.

D. Sue also described the various ways in which multicultural training may be implemented into the counseling curriculum. He identified four approaches: the single course approach, multicultural counseling as an area of concentration, the interdisciplinary model, and the integration model. In the integration model, material regarding cultural differences is a part of each and every course in a training program. Although this may be the ideal approach, many programs continue to use the single course approach. In addition, most multicultural training programs today are more successful in addressing attitudes-beliefs and knowledge than in addressing skills.

Recently, Timothy B. Smith, Madonna G. Constantine, and colleagues conducted a meta-analysis on multicultural education in mental health graduate programs. This study, focused on outcomes of multicultural training programs, showed that multicultural education had an overall positive effect on factors such as multicultural competence, racial prejudice, and the client–counselor relationship. This study provides further support for D. Sue's and others' call for psychology training programs to integrate multicultural issues throughout their curricula.

Focus of Multicultural Psychology

Although great strides have been made regarding the acceptance of multicultural issues in psychology, there is still debate regarding the definition and focus of the term *multicultural*. According to D. Sue, some scholars define multicultural psychology broadly, stating that every interpersonal encounter is multicultural because all individuals are cultural beings. This approach considers multiple dimensions of diversity to be a part of the purview of multicultural psychology (e.g., religion, gender, sexual orientation, age, and social class). This definition also considers the cultural experiences of the majority group to be a part of multicultural psychology. At a minimum, some scholars argue that racial/cultural contexts of these other dimensions should be a focus of both research and practice in multicultural psychology.

Other multicultural psychologists take a more specific approach to the definition and focus of multicultural psychology, arguing that integrating aspects other than race and ethnicity into multicultural psychology overly broadens the field, thereby minimizing the true effects of these two variables. In addition, some scholars who support this perspective argue that although social identities other than race and ethnicity may be important, multicultural competence and multicultural research as they stand today do not necessarily apply to gender and other cultural experiences.

Although the majority of research in multicultural psychology has focused on race and ethnicity, recent work by feminist multicultural psychologists such as Louise B. Silverstein has begun to incorporate gender and other identity experiences. In addition, several APA divisions, such as those that founded the National Multicultural Conference and Summit (Society for the Psychology of Women; Society for the Psychological Study of Ethnic Minority Issues; Society of Counseling Psychology; and Society for the Psychological Study of Lesbian, Gay, and Bisexual Issues), have called for their members to develop practice guidelines and to conduct research regarding multiple demographic identities. A common theme of multicultural psychology today is understanding multiple processes of oppression, as highlighted by the title of the 2007 National Multicultural Summit: "The Psychology of Multiple Identities: Finding Empowerment in the Face of Oppression."

LeLaina Romero and Marie L. Miville

See also Acculturation (v3); Bicultural (v3); Cross-Cultural Psychology (v3); Cross-Cultural Training (v3); Culture (v3); Diversity (v3); Ethnic Identity (v3); Ethnicity (v3); Identity Development (v3); Multicultural Counseling (v3); Multicultural Counseling Competence (v3); Multiculturalism (v3); Pluralism (v3); Prejudice (v3); Race (v3); Racial Identity (v3); Social Identity Theory (v3); Stereotype (v3)

Further Readings

American Psychological Association. (2003). Guidelines on multicultural education, training, research, practice, and organizational change for psychologists. *American Psychologist, 58,* 377–402.

Brewer, M. B. (1999). The psychology of prejudice: Ingroup love or outgroup hate? *Journal of Social Issues, 55,* 429–444.

Cross, W. E., Jr., & Vandiver, B. J. (2001). Nigrescence theory and measurement: Introducing the Cross Racial Identity Scale (CRIS). In J. G. Ponterotto, J. M. Casas, L. M. Suzuki, & C. M. Alexander (Eds.), *Handbook of multicultural counseling* (2nd ed., pp. 371–393). Thousand Oaks, CA: Sage.

Dovidio, J. F., Validzic, A., & Gaertner, S. L. (1998). Intergroup bias: Status, differentiation, and a common in-group identity. *Journal of Personality and Social Psychology, 75,* 109–120.

Essandoh, P. K. (1996). Multicultural counseling as the "fourth force": A call to arms. *The Counseling Psychologist, 24,* 126–137.

Helms, J. E., & Cook, D. A. (1999). *Using race and culture in counseling and psychotherapy: Theory and process.* Needham Heights, MA: Allyn & Bacon.

LaFromboise, Teresa, Coleman, H. L. K., & Gerton, J. (1993). Psychological impact of biculturalism: Evidence and theory. *Psychological Bulletin, 114,* 395–412.

Miville, M. L. (2005). Psychological functioning and identity development of biracial people: A review of current theory and research. In R. T. Carter (Ed.), *Handbook of racial-cultural psychology and counseling* (Vol. 1, pp. 295–319). New York: Wiley.

Pedersen, P. B., Draguns, J. G., Lonner, W. J., & Trimble, J. E. (2002). *Counseling across cultures* (5th ed.). Thousand Oaks, CA: Sage.

Phinney, J. S. (1996). When we talk about American ethnic groups, what do we mean? *American Psychologist, 51,* 918–927.

Root, M. P. P. (1999). The biracial baby boom: Understanding ecological constructions of racial identity in the 21st century. In R. Hernandez-Sheets & E. R. Hollins (Eds.), *Racial and ethnic identity in school practices: Aspects of human development* (pp. 67–90). Mahwah, NJ: Lawrence Erlbaum.

Silverstein, L. B. (2006). Integrating feminism and multiculturalism: Scientific fact or science fiction? *Professional Psychology: Research and Practice, 37,* 21–288.

Smith, T. B., Constantine, M. G., Dunn, T. W., Dinehart, J. M., & Montoya, J. A. (2006). Multicultural education in the mental health professions: A meta-analytic review. *Journal of Counseling Psychology, 53,* 132–145.

Steele, C. M. (1997). A threat in the air: How stereotypes shape intellectual identity and performance. *American Psychologist, 52,* 613–629.

Sue, D. (1997). Multicultural training. *International Journal of Intercultural Relations, 21,* 175–193.

Sue, D. W., & Sue, D. (2003). *Counseling the culturally diverse: Theory and practice* (4th ed.). New York: Wiley.

Multiracial Families

As the numbers of both transracial adoptions and interracial relationships have increased, the notion of family has expanded in recent decades beyond the traditional monoracial nuclear family. Changes in both of these factors have influenced family compositions and resulted in a larger number of immediate families (i.e., parents and their children) comprising more than one race and, subsequently, individuals and families who identify with multiple races. As this population increases, it is critical for mental health professionals to develop greater knowledge of, and competence in, working with multiracial families.

Definition

Multiracial families are those consisting of parents of different races and their biracial/multiracial offspring. Within the realm of the interracial family literature, however, there has been disagreement as to the meaning of the term *multiracial*. Some theorists assert that the term should be used only to describe a family composed of more than one race (e.g., a multiracial family), stating that offspring of interracial marriages have only two racial heritages (i.e., they are biracial). Others have used it to describe both families and individuals, asserting that children of a monoracial parent and a biracial parent or of two biracial parents may identify with more than two races and, therefore, would consider themselves to be multiracial. Furthermore, parents of the same race who adopt a child outside of their race also comprise multiracial families. It is important to note that multiracial families are determined by the race, not the ethnicities, of their members.

Historical Perspective

Political and federal policy changes have caused an increase in the number of interracial unions and, thereby, multiracial families, in the United States. Before 1967, 16 states still deemed it unlawful to marry outside one's racial group. Following the Supreme Court ruling of the case *Loving v. Virginia*, which overturned the last antimiscegenation law, the prevalence of interracial marriages increased substantially. Approximately 13% of marriages in the United States include persons of different races, and interracial marriage rates for Asians and Latinos/as are nearly 3 times that of Blacks and 5 times that of Whites. In fact, by the late 1990s, more than 30% of Asian or Latino/a individuals had spouses of another race (most often White). Such changes have caused a considerable increase in the population of biracial children and multiracial families in the United States.

According to the 2000 Census, there are nearly 7 million self-identified biracial and multiracial people. Of those responders who reported a multiracial background, 93% reported two races, 6% reported three races, and 1% reported three or more races. Overall, approximately 1 in 40 persons identify as multiracial, and by the year 2050, it is estimated that 1 in 5 people will identify as multiracial.

Policy changes throughout the past several decades also have changed the face of adoption, permitting more in-country transracial and international transracial adoptions and increasing the number of multiracial families in the United States. Large numbers of interracial adoption placements began in the 1940s with a growing prevalence of international adoptions. Adoptions of Black children by White parents were not as prevalent during the 1940s and 1950s, but they grew in number during the 1960s and peaked in 1971 with approximately 2,500 Black/White transracial adoptions. In the 1970s the numbers of transracial adoptions with Asian and Latino/a children steadily rose. Because of the disproportionate number of children of color in the foster care system and the prevalence of White parents looking to adopt, legislation was passed in 1994 to encourage the practice of transracial adoption. The Multiethnic Placement Act stated that placement agencies could not delay an adoption based solely on racial factors. When agencies still did not follow this act, it was reinforced in 1996 with the Removal of Barriers to Interethnic Adoption Act and then in 1997 with the Adoption and Safe Families Act. Since that time, the number of multiracial families formed by transracial adoptions has increased.

Extant Literature

A substantial amount of research has addressed racial identity development in people of color and White individuals of monoracial families, yet there is a distinct void in empirical literature pertaining to the racial identity development of individuals living in multiracial families. Moreover, the literature on multiracial families is predominantly conceptual and theoretical in nature and tends to focus on models of identity development.

Identity Models

Multiracial identity may be more complex than monoracial identity in that multiracial individuals have a choice of how they identify racially: with the race of either one of their parents or with the race of both parents. Society generally has held the false notion that a "solid" sense of identity is one in which an individual identifies exclusively with one race, but multiracial individuals are confronted with a more complicated process in terms of understanding their racial identity. Rather than exploring the meaning of this complexity and the fluidity inherent in the identity of multiracial individuals, some people have deemed multiracial identity as a precursor to feelings of confusion, uncertainty, and marginalization. In response to these assumptions, scholars have sought to better understand the experience of multiracial individuals by developing racial identity models specifically for this population. They purport that multiracial identity development is a qualitatively different experience from monoracial identity development and that several important issues need to be considered in the context of multiracial identity development. These issues include, but are not limited to, a lack of multiracial role models representing various multiple racial group backgrounds, conflicting racial identifications imposed by others, and feelings of rejection from members of the racial groups that comprise the background of biracial or multiracial individuals.

Identity development models pertaining to transracially adoptive families are even sparser than those developed for other multiracial families. One model, the cultural-racial identity model, describes 16 possible cultural-racial identities for transracially adopted youth. These identities are determined by four axes: the adoptee's birth culture, the adoptive parents' culture, the adoptee's race, and the adoptive parents' race. The model is intended to illustrate the complexity of racial identity for transracially adopted individuals, as well as to depict how various contextual situations and familial beliefs can affect transracially adopted individuals' understanding of themselves.

Psychological Outcomes

Findings on psychological adjustment outcomes for individuals of multiracial families are inconsistent across studies and indicate that, although there are differences inherent in multiracial families as compared with monoracial families, these differences are not necessarily risk factors for poor developmental outcomes. Such discrepancies in the research point to important methodological aspects (e.g., use of monoracial measures on multiracial populations) that can make results inconclusive or misleading.

Implications for Counseling

American society continues to place a negative connotation on the processes that result in multiracial families (i.e., interracial unions and transracial adoptions). Individuals in multiracial families often are expected to justify who they are and how they see themselves. Racial/ethnic background inquiries faced by many multiracial individuals convey a message from society that there is something wrong with identifying with more than one race; this message can contribute to feelings of isolation and low self-esteem among many multiracial individuals. These feelings of isolation often manifest within multiracial family dynamics when parents fail to understand or support the complexities associated with having a mixed racial heritage (e.g., biracial or multiracial children) or a race different from that of both parents (e.g., transracial adoptees).

If parents of multiracial or biracial children have not resolved some of their own racial identity issues, they might expect their children to choose one race over the other(s). Adoptive parents of transracial adoptees may purport a monoracial family identity, expecting their child to identify primarily with the family's race rather than embracing a multiracial family identity. Given the influence of others' (particularly parents') perceptions on the salience of race for multiracial individuals and transracial adoptees, exploration into the impact of parents' racial identities may further inform counselors' understanding of multiracial families. As such, family therapy may be a particularly useful and appropriate mode of counseling for individuals of multiracial families. Counselors working with these families should not assume that their presenting problems are specifically racially or culturally based. However, it is imperative they consider how the family's presenting problems are intertwined with the social and psychological implications of being multiracial.

*Rebecca M. Redington
and Madonna G. Constantine*

See also Biracial (v3); Ethnic Identity (v3); Family Counseling (v1); Identity Development (v3); Interracial Comfort (v3); Interracial Marriage (v3); Parent–Adolescent Relations (v1); Race (v3); Racial Identity (v3); Racism (v3); Transracial Adoption (v3)

Further Readings

Cooney, T. M., & Radina, M. E. (2000). Adjustment problems in adolescence: Are multiracial children at risk? *American Journal of Orthopsychiatry, 70,* 433–444.

DeBerry, K. M., Scarr, S., & Weinberg, R. (1996). Family racial socialization and ecological competence: Longitudinal assessments of African-American transracial adoptees. *Child Development, 67,* 2375–2399.

Javier, R. A., Baden, A. L., Biafora, F. A., & Camacho-Gingerich, A. (Eds.). (2007). *Handbook of adoption: Implications for researchers, practitioners, and families.* Thousand Oaks, CA: Sage.

Milan, S., & Keiley, M. K. (2000). Biracial youth and families in therapy: Issues and interventions. *Journal of Marital and Family Therapy, 26,* 305–315.

Miville, M. L., Constantine, M. G., Baysden, M. F., & So-Loyd, G. (2005). Chameleon changes: An exploration of racial identity themes of multiracial people. *Journal of Counseling Psychology, 52,* 507–516.

Radina, M. E., & Cooney, T. M. (2000). Relationship quality between multiracial adolescents and their biological parents. *American Journal of Orthopsychiatry, 70,* 445–454.

Vonk, E. M., & Angaran, R. (2001). A pilot study of training adoptive parents for cultural competence. *Adoption Quarterly, 4,* 5–18.

NATIONAL ASSOCIATION FOR THE ADVANCEMENT OF COLORED PEOPLE

The National Association for the Advancement of Colored People (NAACP) is the premiere civil rights organization in the United States with the largest membership and longest record of combating racism and discrimination. As a democratic, independent, grassroots organization, the NAACP played a vital role in every major civil rights struggle in the 20th century. The NAACP pioneered the combined use of litigation, lobbying, political action, education, and social action within a national social reform movement spanning decades. The organization is renowned for obtaining equal access to integrated education, the right to vote, residential housing, and public accommodations for Black Americans, in particular, radically improving their lives.

The official founding of the NAACP is February 12, 1909, the 100th anniversary birthday of former President Abraham Lincoln. However, the conference planned for that date was held May 31 to June 1, 1909; at that conference, the National Negro Committee was formed. When the committee met again, in May 1910, the name National Association for the Advancement of Colored People (NAACP) was adopted, with incorporation in 1911.

Why Was the NAACP Needed?

The 14th Amendment (1868) to the Constitution guaranteed Blacks (freed from slavery in 1865) the same freedoms and rights as Whites. The 15th Amendment (1870) guaranteed the right to vote, regardless of race. However, equality for Blacks remained elusive, at the dawning of the 20th century, as an epidemic of race riots reigned; Whites entered Blacks' homes, lynched occupants of all ages, and burned down homes and businesses. Also common were false accusations of Blacks raping White women, insulting Whites, or committing other crimes; mobs removed Black suspects from jail and lynched them.

With formation of the NAACP, a solution arose involving lawyers traveling across states to defend the accused; legal scholars devising strategies for the enforcement of the 14th and 15th Amendments and all existing laws and enactment of new laws to secure civil rights; activist social workers garnering public sympathy; diverse religious leaders lending moral imperative to reform; and journalists educating the public on the racial discrimination, constitutional rights, and lawful action to secure exercise of those rights. The official monthly NAACP publication, *The Crisis,* provided such education, building grassroots support for reform. Hence, the NAACP filled a void, mobilizing resources and people of all races and religions for a social reform movement.

Branches, Membership, and Key Historical Developments

The NAACP has over 2,000 branches across the United States, including youth, college, and international chapters. With membership in the hundreds of thousands, most members have been women. Membership peaked in 1963, the year of the March on Washington, with 535,000 dues-paying members.

The NAACP has roots in what began in 1905 as the Niagara movement—a group of influential African Americans that first met in Canada under the leadership of the Black Harvard scholar William Edward Burghardt Du Bois. In 1906, three Whites became members—activist social workers Mary White Ovington and Henry Moskowitz and prominent journalist William English Walling. A 1908 race riot in Springfield, Illinois, the hometown of former President Lincoln, underscored the crisis of violence against Blacks. Walling wrote an article, calling of others to take a stand. Prominent White reformers responded, meeting in May 1909 with Du Bois, Niagara movement members, and the antilynching crusader and journalist Ida B. Wells-Barnett. They formed the National Negro Committee, renamed the National Association for the Advancement of Colored People (NAACP) at their 1910 conference. Initially, most elected officials were White, including first president Moorefield Storey. The only Black official, Du Bois was director of publicity and research (1910–1934) and editor of *The Crisis.* Jewish leadership was prominent, including the first chairman of the legal committee, Arthur B. Springard.

An integrated team of lawyers won three important Supreme Court decisions within 15 years, helping secure the right to vote, regardless of race; striking down racial restrictions on access to residential housing; and making courts an effective weapon in the fight for full citizenship. Other citizenship rights and racial discrimination cases were chronicled in *The Crisis,* highlighting injustice suffered by real people and motivating many to become NAACP members and activists—building a grassroots and financial base. Also, across the first three decades, an unsuccessful campaign for an antilynching bill was led by James Weldon Johnson—the African American chief executive officer (CEO) from 1920 to 1930. Johnson initiated NAACP field staff positions, expanding organizational reach.

Walter White, an African American with features allowing him to pass for White when traveling to investigate cases, became CEO in 1931. During his tenure, White utilized state conferences, regional meetings, and annual national convention workshops to prepare members for changes to come with litigation. In 1939, the NAACP organized the NAACP Legal Defense and Educational Fund, Inc. (known as the LDF)—permitting collection of tax-deductible contributions as a 501(c)3 to support expanding litigation.

Across the 1940s, the NAACP created regional offices to support distant branches. Annual campaigns increased membership and funds. Cases focused on practices to bar Blacks from equal access to residential housing; Thurgood Marshall successfully argued they were unconstitutional and unenforceable. Other cases involved White primaries and educational discrimination in the South. The main architect of NAACP legal strategy was Charles Hamilton Houston. Houston selected Marshall to assist him.

After the death of Houston in 1950, Marshall was assisted by Robert L. Carter. The legal team included White and Jewish lawyers, including Jack Greenberg. Some cases challenged unfair voter registration laws. By 1951, Wilkins and Clarence Mitchell, Jr. formed powerful coalitions with labor unions and Jewish organizations—both central to lobbying. The 1954 Supreme Court decision *Brown v. Board of Education of Topeka* led to school desegregation, the most important victory won by the NAACP. In legal arguments, the use of social psychological evidence provided by Kenneth Clark was pioneered.

Another strategy involved coalition building (e.g., with the Southern Christian Leadership Conference, Congress on Racial Equality, and Student Nonviolent Coordinating Committee), as well as activism via marches, sit-ins to desegregate lunch counters, and boycotts. The NAACP supported the 1955–1956 Montgomery bus boycott, triggered by lifetime NAACP member Rosa Parks's refusal to give up her seat on a bus for a White passenger. Coalitions also brought tension. Becoming executive secretary in 1955, Wilkins frequently disagreed with Martin Luther King, Jr., over strategy: King's nonviolent mass protests versus the NAACP's litigation and lobbying. Mitchell, head of the NAACP Washington Bureau, was heralded as the leading lobbyist of his era, working closely with Wilkins and helping to secure the 1964 Civil Rights Act, followed by the Voting Rights Act of 1965. The historic 1963 March on Washington was another victory the NAACP helped to coordinate through coalitions.

In the 1970s, cases covered violation of Blacks' voting rights. Across the 1970s and 1980s, Jack Greenberg provided leadership for the Legal Defense Fund for cases on school integration, equal employment, fair housing, and voter registration. Some cases covered enforcement of the new civil rights legislation of the 1960s, including public accommodations and health care. Campaigns were started on prisoners' rights and against capital punishment. Also, in 1982, the NAACP registered more than 850,000 voters—a milestone. In 1982, the Supreme Court upheld the argument of William T. Coleman, LDF board chair, against granting tax exemptions to religious schools that discriminate.

The LDF assisted in passage of the Civil Rights Act of 1991, restoring protections against job bias. In 1993, the NAACP endorsed and participated in the march by gays and lesbians in Washington, D.C. Controversy and financial scandal led to the 1994 ouster of the Reverend Benjamin Chavis as CEO. Revitalizing leadership followed: Myrlie Evers-Williams became chair of the board of directors in 1995; Democratic congressman and head of the Congressional Black Caucus, Kweisi Mfume, became president and CEO in 1996; Julian Bond became board chair in 1998; and, after Mfume's resignation, the business executive, Bruce S. Gordon, became president and CEO in 2005. Also, in the past decade or so, the NAACP (a) launched an economic reciprocity program in response to anti–affirmative action legislation springing up around the country, (b) launched a campaign against an increase in youth violence, and (c) negotiated agreements to increase diversity in television and film. Thus, up to the present day, the NAACP continues to be a vital organization.

Barbara C. Wallace

See also Affirmative Action (v3); African Americans (v3); Civil Rights (v3); Discrimination (v3); Racism (v3); Stereotype (v3)

Further Readings

Berg, M. (2005). *"The ticket to freedom": The NAACP and the struggle for Black political integration.* Gainesville: University Press of Florida.
Greenberg, J. (1994). *Crusaders in the courts: How a dedicated band of lawyers fought for the civil rights.* New York: Basic Books.
Jonas, G. (2005). *Freedom's sword: The NAACP and the struggle against racism in America, 1909–1969.* New York: Routledge.
Wedin, C. (1998). *Inheritors of the spirit: Mary White Ovington and the founding of the NAACP.* New York: Wiley.
Wilson, S. K. (Ed.). (1999). *The* Crisis *reader: Stories, poetry, and essays from the N.A.A.C.P.'s Crisis magazine.* New York: Random House.

Wilson, S. K. (1999). *In search of democracy; The NAACP writings of James Weldon, Walter White, and Roy Wilkins (1920–1977).* New York: Oxford University Press.

NATIONALISM

Nationalism is a sociopolitical ideology that defines the solidarity, history, and destiny of a human population based on a nation or national origin. Nationalism is either the consequence or the basis for establishing nation-states throughout the world, usually distinguished by borders confining a nation to a certain territory or homeland. Today, most of the world's population lives in nation-states, which have a national identity typified by a common language, a flag, and other national emblems. However, because of the diversity of many nations, various social movements (e.g., Black Nationalism) use the term *nationalism* to distinguish their cultural identity from the dominant national identity of the nation in which they live.

Origins and Historical Development

Nationalists, historians, and political theorists debate whether nations created nationalism or nationalism created nations. Most staunch nationalists contend that preexisting nations, dating back thousands of years, provide a foundation for every human to fit within a world category that has a unique identity. In contrast, modernist theorists argue that local and religious loyalties were the dominant ideological influences until only about 200 years ago when European states endeavored to modernize their societies and establish a basis for armies and taxation. Most theorists agree that nationalism is based on a powerful ideology that is rooted in real, imagined, and invented memories of conflict, a homeland, traditions, mythology, and customs.

Non-Eurocentric accounts of the origins of nationalism are scant in the literature. Most theories of nationalism indicate that the European nation-states marked the beginnings of nationalism. In the late 18th and early 19th centuries, nationalist movements advanced throughout European societies. Some of the movements were formed in opposition to monarchies and religious empires, whereas others sought to unify fragmented territories into larger nations. The movements generally opposed autocratic regimes and royal families. Nationalist movements also sought to define their territory and competed for borders. By the late 19th century, most of Europe was organized into nations. However, the nations spawned from the American Revolution, the South American independence struggles, and the Haitian Revolution predate most European nationalist movements.

Because of modernization and colonialism, by the early 20th century, nationalism was essential to the survival of most of the human populace. Populations with local loyalties were dominated by vast armies representing large nations. Some colonized populations successfully adapted a national identity in order to defeat tyrant nations (e.g., India's nationalist struggle to end British rule). Other populations (e.g., Native Americans and Australian aborigines) who never, or only recently, claimed a national identity were ruled, displaced, and oppressed by organized nations for centuries.

Nationalism also became linked to racial divisions, as many nations began to use race, or ethnic origin, to enlighten their national identity. By the beginning of the 20th century, race became the basis for most nations—an ideology that posed challenges for multiethnic nations. In the United States, President Woodrow Wilson influenced the worldview on nations through his "Fourteen Points," which challenged the legitimacy of multiethnic empires, such as the Ottoman Empire and the Austro-Hungarian Empire. In addition, Wilson's domestic policies fueled Black and White nationalist separatist movements in the United States. The Ku Klux Klan's primary propaganda tool, the film *The Birth of the Nation*, opens with a quote from Wilson hailing the Klan as "a veritable empire of the South, to protect the Southern Country." Black Nationalism, largely influenced by Marcus Garvey, also originated during this period, as a result of the United States's open bigotry and what many African Americans perceived as the betrayal of the Republican Party.

Abroad, nationalism based on racist extremism emerged during the period between World War I and World War II. State leaders such as Adolf Hitler and Benito Mussolini used extreme versions of nationalism such as fascism and Nazism, which held that race and national identity superseded individual rights. After gross human rights violations, including the Holocaust, fascism and Nazism lost popular support after World War II, but they remain the dominant ideology of modern White supremacists and other White nationalist organizations worldwide.

By the mid-20th century the largest wave of nationalism came from African colonies achieving independence. Many native Africans found it necessary to adopt the language and borders drafted by their European colonists in order to build the national identity necessary to fight for independence. After violent and peaceful anticolonialist movements succeeded, Africa transformed from a collection of European colonies to a continent of nation-states. However, borders drafted by European explorers encompassed many very distinct languages, cultural identities, and localized loyalties to ruling "tribes." Many tribal wars were amplified by European and Western powers arming factions that supported their economic interests. Pan-Africanist movements, such as the African National Congress, are Africa's most successful nationalist movements in unifying large numbers of native Africans for the purpose of creating a viable African state.

Nationalism Within Nations

Amplified nationalism usually emerges during international competitions, such as the Olympics, when people worldwide don their nations' emblems and cheer for national heroes. Elevated nationalism is also usually necessary for a nation's government to launch a far-reaching agenda. Arguably, the high levels of nationalism that took place in the United States after 9/11 softened opposition to the subsequent wars in Iraq and Afghanistan and stimulated new domestic surveillance methods.

Today, because most nation-states are firmly established, nationalism is more commonly used to describe various social and political movements within nations that seek to define and unify a group with social, economic, or ethnic traits that are distinctive enough to distinguish it from others within the same nation. Within nations, nationalist movements have sought to strengthen national unity, especially during times of crisis (e.g., flag campaigns after the attack on the World Trade Center in 2001); reject foreign influences and limit immigration, sometimes motivated by cultural conservatism and xenophobia; and affirm the distinct identity, culture, and struggles of a marginalized population (e.g., Black Power movements in the United States).

Nationalist movements within nations almost inherently attract controversy. In the past, nationalism in national politics has often emerged as a pretext to war. In some extreme cases, nationalism has promoted ethnic cleansing and genocide, such as in Nazi Germany, the Balkans, and Rwanda. Secession is a less extreme but still controversial consequence of nationalism and includes both successful and unsuccessful attempts to completely withdraw from a nation and create a new nation. Secession often leads to civil wars, such as those experienced in the United States and Sudan.

In contrast, many empowerment organizations that promote social, political, and economic equality through social reform and tactical resistance consider themselves nationalists. Many such nationalist movements are not seeking to secede or overthrow the government of their nation. However, they are often heavily scrutinized and covertly targeted by national governments. In the United States, for example, during the 1960s, the Federal Bureau of Investigation (FBI) targeted Black civil rights organizations, Puerto Rican nationalists, Native American organizations, and the New Left/antiwar movements through COINTELPRO (Counter Intelligence Program). Post-Watergate congressional hearings revealed that the FBI opened more than 500,000 files on more than 1 million Americans during the COINTELPRO era to investigate subversion and dissent. Some believe that overzealous nationalism promoted by the government, such as the former House Committee on Un-American Activities, leave nations vulnerable to the type of abuse in power experienced during COINTELPRO.

Criticisms and Critiques

The scope and complexion of nationalism has changed throughout the centuries. Originally, nationalists sought to create nations. Today, nationalists strive primarily to redefine nations and assert national identity. Nationalism—and the geopolitical mandate that all nations be organized into separate states—dominates world culture. National governments and nationalist movements within nations are often in conflict with governments promoting a national identity. The recent emergence of multinational agendas (e.g., the European Union) and globalism have added to the complexity of nationalism as a political force.

Far-reaching claims, divisiveness, militarism, radical agendas, and cultural conservatism have led to widespread criticisms and critiques of nationalism. Liberals and pacifists argue that nationalism traditionally leads to intolerance and causes conflict and war between world populations. Liberal ideology generally de-emphasizes national identity and focuses on individual liberties. By contrast, many groups who are not liberal in the traditional sense (e.g., the Nation of Islam and Puerto Rican independence movements) combat national governments with nationalism. Antiracists campaign against nationalist attitudes that promote chauvinism and xenophobia, but they do not necessarily challenge the existence of nation-states. Most liberals and antiracists are usually neutral toward, or supportive of, nationalist organizations that form in opposition to unjust national policies.

While most antinationalists target negative attitudes, such as xenophobia, and consequences, such as war, of nationalism, some ideologies challenge the legitimacy of nation-states. Marxist revolutionaries have called for a world revolution to end nation-states and engender a global state unrestricted by borders. Cosmopolitanism also supports a world state but de-emphasizes common struggles or resistance to power among the majority social class. By contrast, cosmopolitanists promote cooperation among nations through international laws. Many nationalists and antiglobalists are suspicious of cosmopolitan ideas.

Implications for Counseling

Nationalism can invoke strong emotions that can weaken one's ability to be impartial, a quality most believe is essential for counseling. Some nationalists are genuinely motivated by their desire to improve conditions for a marginalized group. Other nationalists have extremist views that are influenced by bigotry. On a macro level, state-sponsored nationalism may have the intended or unintended effect of promoting cultural conservatism and reducing general acceptance of foreign citizens.

Therefore, while striving to understand the impact of nationalism on their clientele, counselors must recognize their own thoughts and biases regarding nationalism and how nationalism may influence their subjective worldview. Like the world's populace, the vast majority of counselors live in a nation-state dominated by a national agenda, usually promoted by the government. At various times, particularly during times of national crisis, a counselor's allegiance to, or dissonance with, his or her government's agenda may lead to close-mindedness, conflict, and confusion. Overall, counselors working within nations or with people influenced by nationalism must be both open-minded and sensitive to the needs of marginalized populations and keenly aware of paranoia, xenophobia, political cults, and other thought problems associated with extreme nationalism.

Ivory A. Toldson

See also Colonialism (v3); Cultural Values (v3); Culture (v3); Ethnic Identity (v3); Ethnocentrism (v3); Eurocentrism (v3); Immigrants (v3); Racial Identity (v3); Worldview (v3); Xenophobia (v3)

Further Readings

Bellier, I., & Wilson, T. M. (2000). *An anthropology of the European Union: Building, imagining and experiencing the new Europe.* Oxford, UK: Berg.

Blackstock, N. (1976). *COINTELPRO: The FBI's secret war on political freedom.* New York: Vintage Books.

Cheah, P., & Robbins, B. (Eds.). (1998). *Cosmopolitics: Thinking and feeling beyond the nation.* Minneapolis: University of Minnesota Press.

Lawrence, P. (2005). *Nationalism: History and theory.* Harlow, UK: Pearson Education.

Maddox, G. (1993). *African nationalism and revolution.* New York: Garland.

May, S., Modood, T., & Squires, J. (2004). *Ethnicity, nationalism, and minority rights.* Cambridge, UK: Cambridge University Press.

Moses, W. J. (1978). *The golden age of Black nationalism, 1850–1925.* Hamden, CT: Archon Books.

NATIONAL LATINA/O PSYCHOLOGICAL ASSOCIATION

The National Latina/o Psychological Association (NLPA) is a national professional psychological organization that represents Hispanic/Latino/a issues in psychology. NLPA was founded in 2002 under the leadership of Patricia Arredondo, who became the founding NLPA president. The mission of NLPA is to generate and advance psychological knowledge and foster its effective application for the benefit of the Hispanic/Latino/a population.

NLPA was a reinvigoration of the National Hispanic Psychological Association (NHPA), which had been founded in 1979 at a conference of Hispanic psychologists convened at Lake Arrowhead, California. The conference was jointly sponsored by the Spanish-Speaking Mental Health Research Center and the National Institute of Mental Health. By 2002 NHPA membership had declined, and it was not possible for the remaining members to sustain momentum for the organization. The last president of NHPA was Maryann Santos de Barona. Despite the decline of NHPA, there was still general interest in the profession in organizing around Latino/a psychology. For example, during the 1990s a series of conferences were held that focused on Latino/a psychology and were highly successful. The transformation of NHPA to NLPA parallels the growth of interest in ethnic/minority psychology and issues of multicultural competence in counseling and psychology during the late 1990s and the early 21st century, as well as the overall growth and migration of the U.S. Latino/a population. Events such as the 1999 and 2001 National Multicultural Summit and Conference, diversity-focused American Counseling Association (ACA) and American Psychological Association (APA) conventions, and the pioneering presidencies of key APA and ACA divisions by Arredondo and Melba Vasquez fueled interest in Latino/a psychology. Therefore the stage was set for the 2002 Rhode Island Latino Psychology Conference where Arredondo led the chartering of NLPA. NLPA membership was, and continues to be, open to individuals committed to the mission of NLPA; being of Latino/a heritage is not a requirement.

NLPA is one of the five groups that the APA recognizes as an Ethnic Minority Psychological Association under the auspices of the Council of National Psychological Associations for the Advancement of Ethnic Minority Interests (CNPAAEMI). The other members of CNPAAEMI are the Asian American Psychological Association, the Association of Black Psychologists, the Society of Indian Psychologists, and Division 45 of the APA—the Society for the Psychological Study of Ethnic Minority Psychology. Although affiliated with the APA, NLPA is an independent organization. In 2006 the Council of Representatives of the APA (the governing body of the APA) invited the presidents of the national Ethnic Minority Psychological Associations to speak to the Council and efforts began to establish a seat on the Council of Representatives for each of the organizations. Although there is a national structure for the organization, NLPA has also been successful in establishing and allying with independent state (e.g., California, Texas, New Jersey) and regional (e.g., Midwest Association of Latino/a Psychologists) Latino/a psychology organizations. While primarily located in the United States, NLPA membership also reflects an international perspective on Latino/a psychology in that NLPA members are found in

Guatemala and Puerto Rico, and the president of the *Sociedad Interamericana de Psicología* was one of the founding members of NLPA.

NLPA membership grew dramatically after the 2002 Latino Psychology Conference in Rhode Island. In October 2004 NLPA held the inaugural NLPA national conference in Scottsdale, Arizona. The president of NLPA at that time was Patricia Arredondo, and the theme for this conference was Advancement in Latino Psychology 2004: Strengthening Psychology Through Latino Family Values. More than 200 psychologists, academics, researchers, graduate students, and undergraduate students were in attendance at this 3-day conference. NLPA conferences were held biannually, and the 2006 conference was held in Milwaukee, Wisconsin, home to the second president of NLPA, Azara Rivera-Santiago. The conference theme was Latina/o Psychology in the 21st Century: New Trends and Challenges in Research and Practice. In 2005 Jose Cervantes was elected as the third president of NLPA followed by Edward Delgado-Romero who was elected in 2007 to be the fourth president.

In addition to the biannual conference, NLPA members meet annually at the APA and ACA conventions. NLPA also maintains a website with a database of resources relating to Latino/a psychology, recent research publications, announcements, and resources for student and professional development. NLPA manages an electronic listserv and a quarterly bilingual newsletter (*El Boletín*/The Bulletin) that highlights member activities and announcements. NLPA also sponsors several professional and student awards that are presented at the biannual NLPA conference, including the Distinguished Professional Career Award, the Distinguished Professional Early Career Award, the Star Vega Distinguished Service Award, the Cynthia de las Fuentes Dissertation Award, and the Distinguished Student Service Award.

The organizational structure of NLPA is similar to that of other ethnic minority associations. The elected positions are as follows: president, secretary, treasurer and membership chair, and student representative. There are also several additional positions and committees within the organization, including newsletter editor and assistant editors, APA liaison, historian, public relations, awards, and student and professional development coordinators. Finally, to facilitate the dissemination of information in both English and Spanish, a large Spanish translation team exists within NLPA. Graduate student involvement and mentorship are integral to NLPA. The graduate student representative is a member of the executive committee who works as an advocate for student issues and concerns an serves as a liaison between professionals and students.

The term *Latina/o* was chosen for two reasons: first, the term *Latino* was chosen over the term *Hispanic,* as the term *Latino/a* was considered more politically progressive and inclusive. Second, although it is grammatically incorrect to list the feminine form of a Spanish word first (*Latina/o* instead of *Latino/a*), the founders of NLPA felt that it was important to both embrace and challenge Latino traditions (e.g., using a Spanish term but challenging potentially sexist linguistic hierarchy).

The membership and visibility of NLPA continues to grow. Current members are professionals, students, institutions, and lifetime founding member contributors, and as of 2006 they totaled more than 500 members. NLPA continues to work toward advancing psychological knowledge and the application of research in the field of Latino/a psychology, promoting the educational and professional advancement of Latino/a psychologists, and fostering an awareness of issues faced by Latino/a mental health professionals in their work.

Edward A. Delgado-Romero
and Lisa M. Edwards

See also Arredondo, Patricia (v3); Asian American Psychological Association (v3), Association of Black Psychologists (v3); Latinos (v3); Society for the Psychological Study of Ethnic Minority Issues (v3); Society of Indian Psychologists (v3)

Web Sites

National Latina/o Psychological Association:
http://www.nlpa.ws

OPPRESSION

The concept of oppression has been written about by scholars and educators in various fields. Oppression has been defined as a system that allows access to the services, rewards, benefits, and privileges of society based on membership in a particular group. Oppression involves the abuse of power whereby a dominant group engages in unjust, harsh, or cruel activities that perpetuate an attitude or belief that is reinforced by society and maintained by a power imbalance. It involves beliefs and actions that impose undesirable labels, experiences, and conditions on individuals by virtue of their cultural identity.

In the counseling and psychology literatures, the term *oppression* is often discussed in relation to privilege. *Privilege* refers to attitudes and behavior that reinforce the notion that one group's beliefs and standards are superior to those of other groups. Systems of privilege and oppression operate in the workplace, education, housing, media, and the legal system, which perpetuate inequities for some and unearned advantages and opportunities for others. Social inequities, cultural imposition of a dominant group on minority groups, and cultural disintegration and re-creation of the oppressed groups characterize systems of oppression. Oppressive systems are manifest in prejudicial attitudes and discrimination in areas such as race, ethnicity, religion, gender, class, and sexual orientation.

Fred Hanna, William Talley, and Mary Guindon describe two modalities of oppression (oppression by force and oppression by deprivation) and three types of oppression (primary, secondary, and tertiary). Primary oppression refers to overt acts of oppression, including oppression by force and oppression by deprivation. Secondary oppression involves individuals benefiting from overt oppressive acts. Individuals involved in secondary oppression do not actively engage in oppressive acts but also do not object to others who do engage in overt oppressive acts and benefit from the aggression. Tertiary oppression, also referred to as internalized oppression, refers to the identification of the dominant message by members of the minority group, often to seek acceptance by the dominant group. Like secondary oppression, tertiary oppression can be passive in nature.

Paulo Freire's writings on oppression have significantly influenced the fields of education and counseling. He is considered a major founder of liberation pedagogy and based his theory on his experiences with teaching peasants and disenfranchised persons in Brazil. In his best-known work, *Pedagogy of the Oppressed,* Freire discussed the "banking" concept of education in which a knowledgeable teacher projects an absolute ignorance onto others, who are passive recipients of information, as an instrument of oppression. Such education attempts to control thinking, promote passivity, and stifle creativity. Oppression is described as any situation in which some individuals prevent others from engaging in the process of inquiry. Human beings are viewed as alienated from their own decision making. In contrast, the revolutionary educator uses problem posing or liberating education in which students become critical coinvestigators who are in dialogue with the teacher. Freire introduced the term *conscientização,* or the process of developing a critical consciousness, advocating for the development of awareness of oneself within one's social context. According to Freire, a crucial component of critical consciousness is helping students understand how they learned to define themselves as their oppressors viewed them.

The study of oppression is prominent in the field of postcolonial studies (see, e.g., the writings of psychiatrist Frantz Fanon). This entails the study of the interactions between European nations and the societies they colonized in the modern period and, more specifically, the deleterious effects of European colonization on various cultures in the world. Research in postcolonial studies is growing, as postcolonial critique allows for a wide-ranging investigation into power relations in various contexts. Topics in the field include the impact of colonization on postcolonial history, economy, science, and culture; the cultural productions of colonized societies; agency for marginalized people; and the state of the postcolony in contemporary economic and cultural contexts.

Feminist scholars have described the complexity of multiple intersecting identities. Depending on the context, one may be an oppressor or be oppressed. For example, a man of color may be the recipient of racism, but he may exploit women. Similarly, a White woman may oppress people of color and simultaneously experience oppression, or sexism, in relationships with men. The work of feminists of color such as Angela Davis and bell hooks has also informed understandings of multiple oppressions. They describe the "double or triple jeopardy" of racial and ethnic minority women who often experience oppression associated with race, class, gender, and sexual orientation. Chicana feminists such as Delores Degaldo Bernal, Chela Sandoval, and Paula Moyahave have discussed the survival skills needed for managing multiple oppressions and experiences of marginalization, such as those associated with language issues, immigration and migration, generation of residence in the United States, and religion.

The writings of such scholars, educators, philosophers, and social justice advocates have influenced the field of counseling and psychology. Psychologists such as Beverly Greene and Lillian Comas-Díaz have discussed the clinical implications of multiple oppressions and intersecting identities. In fact, the fields of counseling and psychology have moved from a focus on intrapsychic factors to an analysis of the interplay between intrapsychic and contextual forces, such as oppression, and its impact on psychological functioning. "Internalized oppression" is a central theme in minority psychology. Internalized oppression is seen as common to many colonized or formerly colonized individuals, and has also been discussed with respect to sexual minority populations. Internalized racism and internalized homophobia are two forms of internalized oppression. *Internalized oppression* refers to a condition in which oppressed individuals and groups come to believe they are inferior to those in power. The oppressed eventually comes to believe an identity that is consistent with the oppressor's stereotyped perceptions of the oppressed. The internalization of oppression leads to a devalued self-worth among the oppressed. Internalized oppression can lead to self-hatred, self-concealment, feelings of inferiority, isolation, and powerlessness. Fanon described the self-doubt and identity confusion in colonized persons that results from the continuous denial of their humanity. Racism is seen as a form of colonialism in which oppressors inscribe a mentality of subordination in the oppressed. Oppression has been linked to a range of psychiatric problems, including depression, anxiety, posttraumatic reactions, identity confusion, substance abuse, domestic violence, and eating disorders, as well as physical ailments such as high blood pressure. The high rates of suicide, alcoholism, and domestic violence among Native Americans have been linked to a history of oppression and its internalization.

Internalized oppression has also been discussed in the counseling and psychology in relation to identity development. The identity development process varies according to specific aspects of identity. Identity development is often characterized as an individual's movement from internalized oppression or privilege, lack of awareness or salience with regard to a particular identity, toward increased awareness of societal oppression and/or privilege, cognitive flexibility, and internal standards of self-definition. Racial and ethnic identity development theorists such as William Cross and Janet Helms have argued that internalized oppression may lead oppressed individuals to highly value the dominant racial and ethnic group and devalue their own. The development of a critical consciousness regarding one's role in perpetuating racism and oppression is a significant aspect of achieving a nonracist White identity. Feminist identity development also involves a recognition and understanding of internalized sexism and its effects.

Application to Counseling

Given the interrelatedness of oppression and privilege, the multidimensional and complex nature of both these constructs, and their relationship to mental health issues, clinicians must be able to identify and understand the complexity of clients' multiple identities and address issues related to the various forms of oppression and privilege. Oppression in the form of racism and discrimination has been identified as a stressor that affects psychological functioning, adjustments, social adaptation, and physical health. Clinicians' misdiagnosis of individuals from oppressed groups is common, as majority norms are often used as the standard against which all clients are compared. In addition, clinicians may mistake trauma-like reactions to oppressive circumstances for intrapsychic pathology. Culturally and contextually influenced expressions of distress may be misunderstood.

The Multicultural Counseling Competencies, a self-assessment form developed by the Association for Multicultural Counseling and Development and endorsed by both the American Counseling Association and the American Psychological Association, offers guidelines for becoming a culturally skilled counselor, which includes a commitment to self-awareness and knowledge of various types of oppression. In addition to the Multicultural Counseling Competencies, there has been an increased focus on social justice and social action related to multicultural counseling. In this context, therapists are not only aware and knowledgeable about oppression but take action against the causes and conditions of oppression. Guidelines for psychotherapy with girls and women; guidelines on multicultural education, training, research, practice, and organizational change; and guidelines for lesbian, gay, bisexual, and transgendered clients continue to be developed.

Educators and therapists as social justice agents must address issues of oppression and privilege at the training level and the practice level. Studies support the importance of exploring oppression and privilege issues within coursework (i.e., facilitation of multicultural counseling competency) and suggest that not addressing these constructs may in fact obstruct the therapeutic process and compromise the client's identity, as well as lead to misunderstanding and misinterpretation of the client's perspective and actions. In fact, social activism has also been viewed as an important aspect of identity development for members of marginalized groups. The literature suggests several strategies for addressing oppression and privilege issues at both training and practice levels. These strategies involve liberating both the oppressor and the oppressed and include awareness of self, establishment of empathy, and building of coalitions. Specifically, educators and therapists encourage students and clients to explore their cultural identities, become knowledgeable about the sociocultural and historical backgrounds of their students and clients, and apply this awareness and knowledge to inform culturally relevant practice.

Future Directions

Conceptualizations of oppression in the counseling literature have evolved over time. More recent perspectives have moved from a dualistic approach and pointed to the complex dynamics of oppression and privilege that vary across contexts. This position considers the impact of multiple social identities and situations.

More recent research has focused on the development of inventories that assess awareness of and attitudes toward oppression and privilege, the effects of multiple oppressions on individuals' mental health, and counseling interventions designed to decrease the deleterious effects of oppression on mental health.

Julie R. Ancis and Catherine Y. Chang

See also Classism (v3); Deficit Hypothesis (v3); Discrimination (v3); Discrimination and Oppression (v2); Multicultural Counseling Competence (v3); Prejudice (v3); Racism (v3); Sexism (v3); Social Class (v4); Social Discrimination (v4); Social Justice (v3); White Privilege (v3)

Further Readings

Ancis, J. R. (Ed.). (2004). *Culturally responsive interventions: Innovative approaches to working with diverse populations.* New York: Brunner-Routledge.

Arredondo, P. (1999). Multicultural counseling competencies as tools to address oppression and racism. *Journal of Counseling & Development, 77,* 102–108.

Freire, P. (1970). *Pedagogy of the oppressed.* New York: Herder & Herder.

Hanna, F. J., Talley, W. B., & Guindon, M. H. (2000). The power of perception: Toward a model of cultural oppression and liberation. *Journal of Counseling & Development, 78,* 430–441.

hooks, bell. (1984). *Feminist theory from margin to center.* Boston: South End Press.

ORGANIZATIONAL DIVERSITY

The workforce of the United States continues to grow more diverse. Employment equity legislation has made organizational diversity an issue of legal, ethical, and strategic interest. Data reported in 2005 by the Equal Employment Opportunity Commission (EEOC) indicate an increase in the percentage of people of color in the private sector from 27% in 1998 to 30% in 2003. In 2005 the Department of Labor reported that while foreign-born workers currently account for 15% of the workforce, up from 11% in 1998, they have also accounted for 46% of the net increase in the labor force since 2000. The percentage of women in the workforce has also risen. In 2004, 59% of all women were in the workforce, up from 43% in 1998, as compared to 75% and 73% of men in the workforce in 2004 and 1998, respectively. Additionally, the Bureau of Labor Statistics projections for 2004–2014 predict the number of workers over 55 years old will grow by 49.1%, outpacing growth in the entire workforce by five times. The number of disabled Americans in the workforce increased from 29% in 1998 to 35% in 2004, according to the National Organization on Disability. These trends indicate that the workforce continues to become more heterogeneous on multiple dimensions.

There are two major perspectives on what characteristics the term *diversity* should encompass in organizational settings. One perspective defines *diversity* based on the demographic characteristics covered in the civil rights legislation enforced by the EEOC. This defines diversity in terms of race/ethnicity, gender, age, national origin, religion, veteran status, and disability. The other perspective is broader, encompassing the EEOC categories as well as other distinguishing characteristics, including sexual orientation, values, abilities, personality characteristics, education, languages spoken, physical appearance, marital status, geographic origin within the United States, tenure with the organization, functional specialization, and economic status. Although a broader definition of diversity may be more inclusive because it encompasses the many ways in which organizational members can differ from one another, it is also problematic in that it ignores the power differences associated with the powerful impact of race, gender, and disability status. The narrower EEOC definition includes only the legally protected categories—groups whose social identities limit their access to societal and organizational resources.

Although it is important to acknowledge that diversity can be constructed across multiple aspects of a person, the impact of different identities is certainly not equal. Segregation in organizations and the demographics of organizational hierarchies reflect American society broadly, which shapes the expectations and experiences of employees. Power, authority, and leadership are allocated disproportionately to certain demographic groups; hence, access to higher-level positions is likely to be difficult for historically disadvantaged groups. Although organizations are more diverse in sheer numbers in the workforce, this diversity is not seen within a given job type or across levels within organizations. Data from the 2000 Census indicate that job segregation by race and gender are common in the workplace. According to EEOC data, although White men make up 37% of the private industry workforce, they comprise 85% of all officials and managers and only 21% of all service positions. Whereas women of color make up 15% of the private industry workforce, they comprise only 6.3% of the officials and managers and 25% of all service positions. Thus, positions of power and authority in the private sector are populated disproportionately by White males. Low-wage sectors continue to be dominated by women and people of color, where they have little access to training or advancement opportunities; such thwarted access is a well-documented source of stress and turnover.

Employee reactions to diversity in organizations as well as concerns about racial and gender segregation in the workforce are often framed as issues of organizational justice. Researchers have found that government-legislated programs, such as affirmative action and elective organizational diversity initiatives, evoke strong feelings from historically advantaged and disadvantaged group members alike. Historically disadvantaged group members are often disappointed at the limited resources devoted to preventing discrimination. Conversely, members of historically advantaged groups may perceive that too many resources are devoted to achieving equity and preventing discrimination. Research has found that members of both groups experience stress over these concerns.

The experience of stress in diverse organizations depends on where an individual is located in the organizational hierarchy. Segregation into work that is not fulfilling or that limits one's career opportunities is an experience shared by many foreign-born workers, female workers, and people of color. Additionally, workers may find they have been hired into a department where they are the only member of a visible minority group and thus face the stress of working in a homogeneous environment. Possibly treated or perceived as "token" members of a group, they may be expected to represent their community, racial/ethnic group, or gender. This situation has been demonstrated to lead to stereotype threat, a situation where an individual is concerned that he or she will confirm a negative stereotype about his or her group. Stereotype threat has been demonstrated to impair performance in these situations and can cause psychological strain. Token members of visible minority groups may also experience the stress of attempting to maintain their cultural identity while adapting to a homogeneous work environment that may not value their cultural identity and may be overtly or subtly racist or sexist. Consequences of this type of stress can include the following: resentment at having to do one's work as well as adapt to social norms that seem arbitrary, exhaustion at the extra effort required to adapt to the norms of the workplace, frustration and anger in response to racism, lowered performance outcomes, reduced organizational commitment, cynicism, turnover, and long-term physical outcomes such as elevated blood pressure. Such workers are likely to need the support of psychological or wellness services that an organization offers, if they feel comfortable using them. Unfortunately, they may then encounter a psychologist or human resource staff person who fails to understand that the homogeneous environment is a source of stress and therefore does not provide real support for the individual, or worse, compounds the experience of social isolation, which leads to further reduced work and negative health outcomes.

There is also research on the stress experienced by historically advantaged group members when they find themselves working in diverse work settings. In a study on the effects of diversity on psychological and behavioral commitment to organizations, researchers found that White men experienced the greatest difficulty in adapting to diverse work units. The impact of having greater gender and racial diversity led to increased absenteeism, lowered organizational commitment, and the increased likelihood of turnover. Possible factors accounting for this stress may include the concerns that many White Americans have about appearing prejudiced. Thus, it might be more stressful for Whites to work with people of color because of the worry that they may appear prejudiced. Status factors have also been found to influence preferences for type of jobs for both men and women, who prefer to work in male-dominated groups because of men's historically advantaged status. Researchers have found that gender affects wages; controlling for all other factors, a manager earns more money when his or her subordinates are predominantly male. This research suggests that diversity can be stressful for all concerned, albeit for different reasons.

Initially, organizations were motivated to address diversity by the need to comply with the EEOC legislation. However, as affirmative action programs have been challenged in court cases, legal compliance has become only one of the reasons that organizations cite for engaging in diversity efforts. Currently, most organizations that are engaged in diversity initiatives describe their interest in diversity as a reflection of the belief that it makes good business sense to do so. The business case for focusing on diversity suggests that to stay competitive, organizations must respond to demographic changes by learning to strategically manage a diverse workforce and appeal to a diverse customer base. Some organizations have responded by hiring according to the demographics of their customers. Unfortunately, this approach can exacerbate job segregation and limited career mobility by channeling women and racial/ethnic minorities into areas where their customer base matches their identity group. The emphasis on the business case may also create the impression that issues of discrimination and inequality are of little importance, thus heightening the sense of cynicism among women and racial/ethnic minorities, for whom these are issues of central psychological importance.

The limitations of this approach have been noted by researchers who suggest that a more optimal way to capitalize on demographic diversity is by focusing on the potential for learning and innovation that a diverse workforce offers. The variety of perspectives that accrue from different cultural or experiential backgrounds can offer an organization new and potentially more flexible, improved ways of working. This requires openness to change and innovation generally, because it invites genuine debate over how to do the work of the organization and who should have the opportunities to do that work. A learning approach could help reduce job segregation. Although research on the benefits of diversity remains mixed, some patterns are emerging. Those organizations that have adapted a learning and innovation approach to diversity and that have been able to create a climate where individuals can truly learn from the diversity of perspectives that exists within their organizations have been financially successful.

The workforce of the United States will continue to become more diverse, providing challenges and opportunities for organizations. In addressing this, organizations have used different definitions of diversity in crafting their responses. The approach that best addresses issues of power and intergroup conflict is one based on the EEOC guidelines, since the guidelines pertain to the groups that have experienced the greatest limitations in the workplace, as well as high levels of stress. However, those who have not historically experienced discrimination are now experiencing stress in adapting to more diverse organizations. Counseling psychologists will play a critical role in helping workers cope with the stress of working in diverse organizational environments. Researchers have identified significant potential for organizations that use diversity proactively, as a source of learning and innovation, rather than in a narrower and more reactive fashion. This is an important area for research in understanding how to leverage diversity for both individuals and organizations.

Brenda K. Johnson and Caryn J. Block

See also Affirmative Action (v3); Assimilation (v3); Career Counseling (v4); Demographics, United States (v3); Diversity (v3); Diversity Issues in Career Development (v4); Interracial Comfort (v3); Multiculturalism (v3); Political Correctness (v3); Racial Identity (v3); Stereotype Threat (v3); Tokenism (v3)

Further Readings

Ely, R. J., & Thomas, D. A. (2001). Cultural diversity at work: The effects of diversity perspectives on work group processes and outcomes. *Administrative Science Quarterly, 46*(2), 229–273.

Jackson, S. E., Joshi, A., & Erhardt, N. L. (2003). Recent research on team and organization diversity: SWOT analysis and implications. *Journal of Management, 29*(6), 801–830.

Kochan, T., Bezrukova, K., Ely, R., Jackson, S., Joshi, A., Jehn, K., et al. (2003). The effects of diversity on business performance: Report of the diversity research network. *Human Resources Management, 42*(1), 3–21.

Linnehan, F., & Konrad, A. M. (1999). Diluting diversity: Implications for intergroup inequality in organizations. *Journal of Management Inquiry, 8*(4), 399–414.

Ragins, B. R., & Gonzalez, J. A. (2003). Understanding diversity in organizations: Getting a grip on a slippery construct. In J. Greenberg (Ed.), *Organizational behavior: The state of the science* (pp. 125–163). Mahwah, NJ: Lawrence Erlbaum.

Stockdale, M. S., & Crosby, F. J. (2004). *The psychology and management of workplace diversity*. Malden, MA: Blackwell.

Orthogonal Cultural Identification Theory

Orthogonal cultural identification theory argues that in a pluralistic environment, individuals may identify with more than one culture without necessarily sacrificing one cultural identity for another. The central element of this theory is that identification with any one culture is independent from identification with other cultures. Cultural identification can be distinguished from ethnic self-labels, or ethnic group categorizations, such as Latino/a, Mexican, American Indian, African American, and European American. Ethnic labels can gloss over the heterogeneity of cultural identification within ethnic groups because not all individuals who use the same label may identify with the culture in the same manner or to the same degree. Ethnic self-labels also may not accurately represent the way in which individuals identify with more than one culture. Generally, cultural identification is dynamic and complex and can be defined as following a culture's way of life (e.g., participation in traditional activities, cultural behaviors, feeling successful within a culture, and/or family involvement in cultural activities). An example of the complexity of cultural identification is that within ethnic groups, individuals vary not only in their range of cultural identification (e.g., from strong to weak to nonexistent) but also in their identification with one culture, multiple cultures, or none. Orthogonal cultural identification theory argues that cultural identification is the result of the interaction between the individual and his or her environment, which may include family cultural identification, ethnic peers, and available traditional activities. Cultural identification is also distinct from cultural/ethnic identity, which can be defined as a social identity that represents the emotional value and significance of belonging to an ethnic group.

Importance

This theory made a significant conceptual contribution to both research and counseling, in that it acknowledged the influence of a pluralistic environment and normalized experiences of identification with multiple cultures. Previous acculturation theories assumed that developing a dominant majority cultural identification would result in loss of the ethnic minority culture. Thus, a significant advance of this theory is the conceptualization of biculturalism as a dual identification with more than one culture without any necessary loss of either culture.

Moreover, the improved quantitative assessment of cultural identification that resulted from this theory advanced the study of ethnic identity and acculturation beyond simple categorizations of individuals to capture more of the complexity inherent in cultural identification. As such, the theory reflects the dynamic and fluid nature of cultural identification of individuals within pluralistic societies by representing a wide range of combinations of cultural identifications. Identification with any one culture can range from "low" to "high" along a continuous dimension and is not necessarily dependent on identification with other cultures.

Eugene Oetting and Fred Beauvais developed an instrument that has been used frequently in the literature, wherein survey questions are phrased in this way: "Are you a success in the ... (culture identified) ... way of life?" Responses range from "a lot" to "not at all" in this instrument. Each set of questions is asked separately for different cultures. Typically, six items are used in this scale and include family way of life, personal way of life, family success, personal success, family cultural traditions, and personal cultural traditions. A total score can be created for each culture separately and then combined or used separately. Additionally, orthogonal cultural identification theory advanced the state of the study of cultural change by making the measurement more inclusive for both majority and minority cultures, whereas previous measures were specific only to certain ethnic minority groups.

Research

The prevalent "melting pot" analogy of the immigrant experience in the United States assumed that immigrants would "melt" or assimilate into the U.S. dominant culture by leaving behind their native culture. Researchers argued that living in an environment with more than one culture may be difficult due to negotiating more than one set of values, norms, and identities; thus, it was presumed that such individuals would experience more stress and often feel marginalized. Based on this model, it was assumed assimilation would result in the best mental health and adaptation because of the inherent stress in negotiating more than one culture. However, the reality of immigrants as well as native groups has been that individuals maintain aspects of their original culture while integrating the dominant culture. Researchers are continuing to find that maintenance of one's culture of origin is not pathological; rather, it can be an adaptive approach that promotes mental health and well-being. Additionally, the orthogonal cultural identification theory demonstrates that maintaining one's culture does not impede adaptation to the dominant culture, as had been assumed in melting pot theories.

Current cultural identification and acculturation models are based on the "cultural stew" analogy. In this analogy, individuals, like the vegetables or meats in a stew, contribute to the overall U.S. dominant culture; yet they may also retain their cultural integrity and can be identified separately. As such, individuals may maintain their cultural integrity while contributing to the dominant culture. The orthogonal cultural identification theory has contributed much to the understanding of the complexity of cultural change and cultural identification. Furthermore, this research has helped document that individuals can successfully integrate and maintain more than one culture. This theory is distinctive from other acculturation models in that it allows for change over the life span and more options for cultural identification with more than one culture.

The orthogonal cultural identification theory has improved understanding of biculturalism, where individuals identify with two cultures simultaneously. Teresa LaFromboise and her colleagues have described bicultural individuals as those who are able to use behaviors and language at the appropriate times and contexts because they have experience and knowledge of both cultures. Researchers have argued that biculturalism is the most adaptive outcome for some minority groups, in part because the nature of their environment is bicultural. However, recent work suggests that being bicultural may be stressful and that successful integration of biculturality may be the most significant factor for mental well-being. Research has suggested that to understand how culture impacts mental health, it is important to assess the fit between the individual and the multicultural environment.

The orthogonal cultural identification theory has made significant conceptual and measurement advances in the study of culture at an individual psychological level. The central aspect of this theory is that cultural identification is separate and independent when there is more than one culture. This theory more accurately reflects the pluralistic nature of culture. Additionally, it portrays individuals as active social agents who have the power to determine their own cultural identification with more than one culture. Multicultural individuals can be defined as those who identify with more than one culture simultaneously. This theory identified not only that assimilation to U.S. culture did not automatically indicate loss of ethnic culture but also that maintenance of ethnic culture may be a positive adaptive strategy for minority ethnic groups in the United States.

Implications for Counseling

Maintenance of a positive ethnic identity may be beneficial for minority and immigrant mental well-being. Counselors should be aware that biculturalism may be adaptive in certain settings; however, bicultural environments may also create stressful experiences for some individuals and successful integration for different identities may be necessary. The alternation model of acculturation may be helpful in understanding how bicultural individuals can switch between cultural frameworks based on situational cues and their bicultural competency. Counselors may integrate multicultural self-assessments into their practice to assist individuals in understanding how cultural context influences their personal histories as well as their current behaviors. Increasing awareness of cultural identities and resolving related cultural context stressors may be integral to improved therapeutic outcomes for some individuals. An example of bicultural identification is a Mexican American student who is successful in higher education (e.g., a task that may entail internalized aspects of cultural values characteristic of dominant U.S. worldviews) while at the same time successful in maintaining strong family ties (e.g., a value that may reflect Mexican ways of endorsing familismo). This individual would feel equally successful in both the U.S. and Mexican ways of life. Additionally, this example demonstrates that being successful in the U.S. way of life does not necessarily mean that one is not successful in the Mexican way of life. However, as noted by Manuel Ramirez, the potential conflict, contradictions, and stress that some individuals experience in negotiating more than one cultural way of life may be addressed within a counseling setting.

Andrea J. Romero

See also Acculturation (v3); Acculturative Stress (v3); Assimilation (v3); Bicultural (v3); Cultural Accommodation and Negotiation (v3); Cultural Equivalence (v3); Cultural Values (v3); Culture (v3); Enculturation (v3); Ethnic Identity (v3); Identity Development (v3); Second Culture Acquisition (v3); Stress (v2)

Further Readings

LaFromboise, T., Coleman, H., & Gerton, J. (1993). Psychological impact of biculturalism: Evidence and theory. *Psychological Bulletin, 114,* 395–412.

Oetting, E. R., & Beauvais, F. (1990–1991). Orthogonal cultural identification theory: The cultural identification of minority adolescents. *International Journal of the Addictions, 25,* 655–685.

Phinney, J. S. (1990). Ethnic identity in adolescents and adults: Review of research. *Psychological Bulletin, 108,* 499–514.

Ramirez, M., III. (1998). *Multicultural/multiracial psychology.* Northvale, NJ: Jason Aronson.

Romero, A., & Roberts, R. E. (2003). Stress within a bicultural context for adolescents of Mexican descent. *Cultural Diversity & Ethnic Minority Psychology, 9,* 171–814.

Pacific Islanders

Pacific Islanders refers to the indigenous people of the Polynesian, Micronesian, and Melanesian islands. *Polynesia* refers to the islands settled by Polynesians, which includes (but is not limited to) Tahiti, Hawai'i, American and Western Samoa, Tonga, Rapanui (Easter Island), the Cook Islands, and French Polynesia. *Micronesia* refers to the islands in the Western Pacific with its main islands being the Carolina Islands (including Federated States of Micronesia and Palau), the Gilbert Islands, and the Mariana Islands (including Guam). The Chamorros are native to Guam and the Northern Marianas. The islands of Melanesia consist of Papua New Guinea, Solomon Islands, Vanuatu, New Caledonia, and Fiji. The history of the three divisions of the Pacific Islands is tied to the colonization process of the Pacific (also referred to as Oceania) and is related to the geographic locations of these islands rather than commonalities of culture and language. However, two areas of commonalities exist across these island cultures: (1) commitment to cultural values such as the emphasis on family, interdependence, holism, and harmony with nature; and (2) historical trauma due to colonization and the current challenges facing many Pacific cultures to maintain their cultural identity, lands, and traditions. To be consistent with the language of the U.S. Census, *Pacific Islander* will be referred to as a racial category.

In the field of counseling, there is some debate in terms of the distinction between race, ethnicity, and culture, yet no conclusion has been made indicating whether *Pacific Islander* is a racial or ethnic category. Each island has unique cultural aspects that may be similar to or different from those of other nearby islands; therefore, generalizations about chains of islands should be interpreted with caution given the heterogeneity within the Pacific Islands' cultures and their respective native inhabitants.

The 2000 U.S. Census was the first census to have *Pacific Islander* as a distinct racial category separate from *Asian* for all 50 states. The 2000 Census included three specific Pacific Islander groups—Native Hawaiian, Samoan, and Guamanian or Chamorro—as well as a separate Other Pacific Islander response category for people to write in their Pacific ancestry. Other Pacific Islander groups living in the United States are Tahitian, Tokelauan, Mariana Islander, Saipanese, Palauan, Carolinian, Kosraean, Pohnpeian, Chuukese, Yapese, Marshallese, I-Kiribati, Fijian, Papua New Guinean, Solomon Islander, and Ni-Vanuatu. In the 2000 U.S. Census, the total number of individuals who identified as fully or partially Pacific Islander was 874,414 people (0.3% of the total U.S. population), with 398,835 reporting solely as Pacific Islander and 475,579 as Pacific Islander in combination with one or more races. The increase in Pacific Islanders (who indicated only one racial category) living in the United States was 9% from 1990 to 2000, while the increase of Pacific Islanders who indicated one or more races increased 140% within this same time period. The Pacific Islander racial category consists of more than 20 different groups with the 4 largest accounting for slightly over three fourths (76%) of this racial group: Hawaiians (n = 401,162; 45.9%) constituted the largest cluster of Pacific Islanders, followed by the Samoans (n = 133,281; 15.2%), the Chamorros or Guamanians (n = 92,611; 10.6%), and the Tongans (n = 36,840; 4.2%). The other Pacific Islander ethnicity categories ranged from a total of 18 (Ni-Vanuatu) to 12,581 (Fijian) people living in the United States.

Pacific Islanders also reported the highest concentration of individuals who recorded as being of more than one race in comparison with all other races in the United States and the only race that had a higher number of people indicating multiple racial categories than a sole racial category. Pacific Islanders are becoming increasingly a multiracial and multiethnic population. Pacific Islanders live throughout the United States, with nearly three quarters (73%) living on the West Coast of the continental United States and Hawai'i.

History of Pacific Islanders and the United States

The United States is the colonial landlord of more than 2,300 islands in the Pacific (excluding Hawai'i). The only Pacific island that officially became a state of the United States was Hawai'i, in 1959. Guam, American Samoa, and Northern Mariana Islands are U.S. territories, and the Republic of the Marshall Islands, Federated States of Micronesia, and the Republic of Palau are considered freely associated states. Guam is considered an unincorporated territory of the United States because not all provisions of the U.S. Constitution apply to this territory; however, the government was organized based on the U.S. Constitution, including an elected representative to Congress.

Status of Pacific Islanders in the United States

Pacific Islanders, in general, have lower median earnings (for both men and women), have lower family income, and are less likely to hold management and professional positions in comparison with the total U.S. population. In addition, Pacific Islanders have higher rates of poverty (17.7%) in comparison with Caucasians (11.5%) and Asian Americans (9.4%). Pacific Islanders have a high prevalence rate of high school graduates: 78% (compared with 90% for Caucasians and Asian Americans) but are concentrated in the lower percentage of persons having completed a bachelor's degree (14% compared with 24% of the total U.S. population) and graduate degrees (4% for Pacific Islanders and 10% for Caucasian Americans).

Pacific Islanders have higher prevalence rates of smoking, alcohol consumption, and obesity, while having a lower survival rate for cancer, in comparison with Caucasians and other racial and ethnic groups. Unfortunately, knowledge about the prevalence rates of mental health issues and the needs of Pacific Islanders is limited given the low numbers of Pacific Islander participants in epidemiological studies. However, studies on Native Hawaiians have found Pacific Islanders to be at risk for depression, anxiety, substance abuse disorders, and suicide. Many indigenous populations in the Pacific are facing similar challenges and health risk factors.

Research on Pacific Islanders

The proliferation of empirical research on counseling, treatment, and mental health issues among Asian Americans in the past 25 years has masked the paucity of research among Pacific Islanders. Furthermore, research on cultural values, norms, beliefs, attitudes, and family dynamics in Pacific Islander cultures have been advanced through ethnography and anthropology investigations leaving psychological theories and interventions without a solid culturally appropriate foundation upon which to build a body of knowledge. The emergence of stereotypes from ethnographic research of Pacific Islander cultures has resulted in appropriate concern about the value of extant knowledge in guiding psychology and clinical interventions. Without overdramatizing the limitations of past anthropological studies, an example may be found in the classic work of Margaret Mead, who portrayed Samoans as warm, easygoing, pleasant, happy people with playful and open sexual relationships living in a society lacking competition, aggression, and hierarchy. Results from ethnographic studies were used as evidence to support the stereotype of the Pacific Islander as lazy, promiscuous, happy, easygoing, and nonassertive. These stereotypes have been further perpetuated and maintained by the tourism industry and the media. Further research has found Pacific Islanders and their respective cultures to be much more complex than these initial anthropological studies demonstrated, with heterogeneity within and between cultural groups within the Pacific Islander community. Generalizations need to be interpreted with caution given the varying degree of Western contact and influence, interracial relationships, migration, and heterogeneity among the various peoples and cultures of the Pacific Islands.

Cultural Values

Pacific Islander communities have come together to reclaim their identity, their land, their cultural values, and their spiritual beliefs to strengthen themselves and their families after years of colonization. The movement of "indigenous ways of knowing" and re-embracing cultural strengths to help heal past historical injustices can be seen in multiple Pacific Islander communities, including the Native Hawaiians, Tongans, and the aboriginal peoples of Australia and New Zealand. This cultural renaissance of ethnic beliefs, values, customs, expectations, and practices has also created a sense of pride and strength to help empower indigenous groups to create their own empirical investigations about their own people.

At the center of Pacific Islander culture is the family system, that is, the network of interpersonal relationships that shape the processes by which cultural practices and values are transmitted, maintained, and affirmed. The network of relationships is at the *piko* (Hawaiian for "center") of health and healing processes and can be a strong source of support and identity in Pacific Islander culture. A person's family can consist of extended family and informal relationships such as friends and family members of friends. The Pacific Islander's concept of self is tied to the view that the individual, society, and nature are inseparable and key to psychological and physical health. Such relational and emotional bonds that shape the individual, family, and community have implications for psychological functioning and well-being.

Mental health symptoms may be related to disharmony or dysfunction within the family or collective unit. A conflict within this network of social relationships can lead to mental illness such as depression, substance abuse, anxiety, alienation, and isolation. The etiology of mental illnesses and its respective symptoms can be seen as related to disharmony or discord within social relationships. Therefore, treatment of mental health issues using indigenous health practices may focus on treating social relationships rather than the individual.

Another critical component to understanding Pacific Islanders is the concept of a sense of place in connection to one's identity. Place is the source of one's worldview, genealogy, and existential foundation. The connection to a place or land is also embedded with responsibility and obligation to the land, the place itself, and one's kin. Space in contrast to place refers to where a person is living or dwelling; however, it may not be the origin of one's identity. A person's space may be dictated by circumstances in his or her life, such as living on the continental United States for educational or work opportunities.

One of the most common misunderstandings about Pacific Islanders is the assumption that by either living away from one's island or being born elsewhere somehow means that person is less "native" or "indigenous" to the islands. Mental health professionals may make an erroneous claim that if Pacific Islanders are not living in their "place," they have forfeited their identity as indigenous or native Pacific Islanders. However, this need to "legitimize" or "authenticate" a Pacific Islander's identity and cultural heritage can feel like negating this person's sense of identity and the essence of his or her *mana* (Hawaiian for "life force"). Another misconception about Pacific Islanders is the idea of migration as being one way toward another place, such as the continental United States, rather than circular migration. Circular migration occurs when people may live away from the islands but return home for long visits or move back in later stages of their lives (e.g., after having children or after retiring).

Another similar feature among Pacific Islanders is the emphasis and importance placed on one's cultural identity. The importance of knowing one's ancestral heritage and its respective connection to the land can be viewed as a key element in developing a coherent sense of self. There are terms within the language such as *Fa'a Samoan* ("the Samoan way of life" or "the Samoan way") or *anga fakatonga* ("the Tongan way") that indicate this connection between one's culture, heritage, the land, and cultural identity. However, this importance placed on cultural identity and the influence of Western individualism and capitalism has had an effect of the definition and development of Pacific Islanders' cultural identity.

Psychological Issues Facing Pacific Islanders

The issues facing Pacific Islanders are also embedded in the events in history and similar challenges faced by other groups of color living in the United States. These issues include acculturation, ethnic identity, the effects of colonization and annexation, and the effects of racism, discrimination, and oppression. Charles Darwin indicated that "wherever the European has trod, death seems to pursue the aboriginal." One issue that Native

Hawaiians and Chamorros have had to face is the cultural genocide of the indigenous peoples of the islands. Explorers who came to the Pacific Islands brought with them many foreign diseases for which the native populations had no immunity; the results were death and infertility among the native people. In addition, contact with foreigners also led to warfare, thus increasing the death toll of the indigenous peoples of the islands. The colonization process and cultural genocide of Pacific Islanders, such as Native Hawaiians, has been noted as a major contributor to the prevalence of depression, anxiety, and despair among these indigenous people. Missionaries in the 1820s came to the Pacific Islands to help save souls of the native inhabitants. Along with Christian doctrine, Western cultural norms were also transmitted as the ideal to these indigenous cultures. The result was the emphasis on native people to conform and assimilate to Western values. This included Western notions of economic and sociopolitical development, such as private ownership of land and the restructuring of hierarchy and privilege based on wealth rather than on genealogy. These radical shifts and changes in the social, political, economic, and religious structures within these indigenous communities resulted at times in ethnocide, that is, the destruction of the Pacific Islanders' way of life.

The study of the psychological impact of Western contact resulting in colonization and annexation of Pacific Islanders is in the early stages of development in research. Models and theories have indicated that the accumulation of losses—including land, language, culture, ancestors, and kin—can lead to depression, anxiety, drug and alcohol abuse, deviant behavior, and suicide. The stressors associated with colonization can include historical trauma and the effects of the multiple losses and the ripple effects throughout indigenous peoples' daily lives and significant life events. The need to perpetuate one's culture after such significant loss is a responsibility felt by many indigenous peoples; this need can influence life decisions such as choice in a partner or spouse, where to live, the pursuit of higher education, career choice, and child-rearing practices.

Decolonization has been greatly discussed in Pacific Islander communities politically, economically, and psychologically. Decolonization refers to the process where a colonized group of people develop a consciousness based on the remnants of the traditional culture and redefine and reassert their identity and unique qualities that historically guided their existence. This may entail sovereignty, the reacquisition of land, and the rediscovering and reaffirming of indigenous epistemology to guide one's life in understanding the past, present, and future. An example of this renewed identity is the reemergence of traditional and indigenous healing practices, which is being researched by mental health professionals. Indigenous healing practices can be helpful in treating symptoms of psychological distress while also empowering Pacific Islanders in maintaining traditional customs and practices. The colonization process associated with the acquisition of Pacific Islands was accompanied by the institutionalization of ethnic categories as formal social entities used to dictate rights and privileges within a society. This socialization process has raised the importance of cultural identity to a new level. Not only is cultural identity important to the well-being of the Pacific Islanders, but it has been empowered to be a critical source of political power and economic influence.

These latent issues, which have both historical and current influence on the psychological and social well-being of the Pacific Islander peoples, ultimately shape their cultural identity. The postcolonization struggles, including the need to maintain their cultural identity, are a prevalent theme across many Pacific Islander communities, including Samoan, Tongan, Chamorro, Hawaiian, and aboriginal Australian communities. Pacific Islander literature reflects this struggle in stories of indigenous people living on the margins in order to express their identity finishing their lives in isolation, madness, and suicide. These stories demonstrate that the Western notion of "functioning" may in fact be inherently pathological for Pacific Islanders.

A testimony of resilience of Pacific Islanders is the circular migration pattern of indigenous peoples returning to their homelands, revitalizing their native cultures, affirming their sense of place and cultural identity, and utilizing their "Western" knowledge to help their communities to become self-sufficient and to heal from the detrimental effects of previous colonization. The efforts to maintain one's language, spirituality, cultural healing practices, and customs have resulted in feelings of pride, strength, renewal of spirit, and hope for the future of Pacific Islanders. The reclaiming of one's culture, land, and identity can be empowering and healing. The social process in Western communities to quantify and essentialize racial groups in order for those groups to receive benefits from the government (e.g., land acquisition by blood quantum) has implications for Pacific Islander communities. The Western socialization process of legitimizing or authenticating who is to be considered "native" to the islands has led to fractions within Pacific Islander communities. It has also created a social class system within Pacific Islander groups with a social elite class defining who is "native" or "indigenous" and who has access to resources such as education, land acquisition, and economic opportunities.

Counseling Pacific Islanders

As a group, Pacific Islanders have not received much attention in studies of racial and ethnic groups in counseling. One of the main reasons for this lack of attention is the trend of combining Asian American and Pacific Islander groups together, which has led to a paucity of counseling literature focused on this racial group as a separate entity. This aggregation of the data for Asian American and Pacific Islanders has led to Pacific Islanders being invisible or misrepresented in public policy and the mental health field. The ramifications of this collapsing of these racial/ethnic groups have been the failure to understand the health needs of Pacific Islanders, the impact of social history on assessment of mental health factors, undercounting of Pacific Islanders in general, and a limited awareness of the poverty, discrimination, and the adjustment of these indigenous groups in the United States. Also, by combining Pacific Islanders with Asian Americans, there has been a lack of knowledge by clinicians and mental health professionals about the historical similarities of these indigenous groups in the Pacific to other Native Americans living in the United States.

It is important to note that the social norms found in Western models of counseling—such as individualism and the need to separate from one's family of origin after a certain age—may not be applicable to Pacific Islanders. In fact, these Western norms may be viewed by Pacific Islanders as pathological and detrimental to their social network. In addition, symptoms of distress, such as depression, anxiety, or suicidal ideation, should be viewed within the historical context of the Pacific Islander and understood that it may be a reflection of an unhealthy society rather than a problem that lies within the individual.

Asian Americans and Pacific Islanders have limited availability and access to mental health services and tend to underutilize counseling services. Possible explanations for this underutilization are the lack of trained healthcare professionals who are fluent in Pacific Islander languages and lack of understanding of Pacific Islanders' history and worldviews. Counselors that have been trained in working with culturally diverse clients may be applying Asian American values that do not fit for Pacific Islanders, which may lead to early termination. For example, despite assertions that Asian Americans and Pacific Islanders express more somatic symptoms and that shame and stigma may be related to the lack of utilization of mental health services, there is no empirical research to support this claim with Pacific Islander samples. In addition, given that 17% of Pacific Islanders are below the poverty level, they may lack health insurance to pay for mental health services. Access to mental health providers and their respective services may also be problematic because of the remote and rural locations where Pacific Islanders reside.

With the emphasis on family as the social unit and the need to maintain harmony within one's extended kin, family therapy based on the values of the Pacific Islander group may be an effective invention that is culturally congruent with the values and beliefs of this population. For example, *ho'opono'pono,* a Native Hawaiian indigenous healing practice, focuses on "setting right" family issues or conflict to maintain harmony with one's family, community, and ancestors in the spiritual world. Similarities within this practice exist when compared with other Western family therapy models, but its uniqueness lies in (a) the goals of the *ho'opono'pono* (seeking family harmony through confession and the seeking of forgiveness within the group rather than within oneself), and (b) the spiritual focus (including prayer and seeking help from the spiritual world, for example, from a higher power or ancestors that have passed on) of the sessions.

Given the paucity of research about the mental health needs of Pacific Islanders within the United States, more research is needed focusing on Pacific Islanders and the groups within this racial category. Future research of Pacific Islanders should include (a) the prevalence rates of mental health issues; (b) the availability, accessibility, and utilization of counseling services within this population; (c) culturally competent therapies, prevention, and intervention strategies; (d) cultural factors that help promote well-being and protect against mental illnesses; and (e) help-seeking behavior, including indigenous health practices and Western models of therapy.

The literature on indigenous communities reveals links between sovereignty issues and health, with economic and political freedom being key to the well-being of native peoples. It has been proposed that the restoration of the rights and privileges of these communities—including self-governance, the freedom to cultivate and practice the cultural traditions of ancestors, and having a relationship with the environment—will help promote the psychological well-being of Pacific Islanders. In light of the history of colonization and oppression of Pacific Islanders, it is understandable that political factors such as self-governance would be linked with the promotion of physical and mental health.

Predictably, Pacific Islanders have a place in counseling and psychology in spite of the limitations of extant research. Pacific Islanders have a history of being invisible or marginalized within the field of psychology, and this is being remedied accordingly. Yet the indigenous people of these islands have been a part of social changes and resurgence of their cultures, the migration of cultures, and the adaptation of their people. With the importance of multicultural competence in counseling, researchers have taken on the challenge of understanding these unique populations of people and their mental health needs. Future research on Pacific Islanders and counseling should be designed to improve upon the ability to serve these populations with full understanding of their histories and the strengths and resilience of their cultures.

Laurie D. McCubbin

See also Acculturation (v3); Colonialism (v3); Cultural Values (v3); Culture (v3); Espiritismo (v3); Ethnicity (v3); Familismo (v3); Multiculturalism (v3); Nationalism (v3); Poverty (v3); Race (v3)

Further Readings

Andrade, N. N., Hishinuma, E. S., McDermott, J. F., Johnson, R. C., Goebert, D. A., Makini, G. K., et al. (2006). The National Center on Indigenous Hawaiian Behavioral Health study of prevalence of psychiatric disorders in native Hawaiian adolescents. *Journal of the American Academy of Child and Adolescent Psychiatry, 45*(1), 26–36.

Grieco, E. M. (2001, December). *The Native Hawaiian and Other U.S. Pacific Islander population: 2000* (Census 2000 Brief No. C2KBR/01-14). U.S. Census Bureau. Retrieved May 13, 2006, from http://www.census.gov/prod/2001pubs/c2kbr01-14.pdf

McCubbin, H., & McCubbin, L. (1997). Hawaiian American families. In M. K. DeGenova (Ed.), *Families in a cultural context*. Mountain View, CA: Mayfield.

Office of Minority Health. (2006). [Native Hawaiian/Other Pacific Islander profile]. Retrieved May 21, 2006, from http://www.omhrc.gov/templates/browse.aspx?lvl=2&lvlID=71

U.S. Department of Health and Human Services. (2001). *Mental health: Culture, race, and ethnicity: A supplement to mental health: A report of the surgeon general*. Rockville, MD: U.S. Department of Health and Human Services, Substance Abuse and Mental Health Services Administration, Center for Mental Health Services.

PEDERSEN, PAUL BODHOLDT (1936–)

Paul Bodholdt Pedersen, considered by most psychologists to be the founder and major contributor to multicultural psychology and cross-cultural counseling and psychotherapy, was born on May 19, 1936, in Ringsted, Iowa. Located in a rural farming community in northern Iowa near the Minnesota border, the tiny community of Ringsted provided Pedersen with a strong, stable set of values that encouraged hard work, kindness, spirituality, generosity, compassion, and a respect for all living things. His family and community members were deeply religious; thus, many of his cherished childhood memories mirrored his experiences in the local Danish church. Pedersen traced his deep respect and appreciation for humanistic-spiritual perspectives to his family and community members of Danish, Norwegian, and Swedish ancestry. Much of his youth was spent working on the family farm in a secure family-centered environment. Pedersen's parents were avid collectors of books and placed a high premium on reading and music. Although his father and sister were accomplished musicians, Pedersen struggled to master the violin. After 7 years of lessons, he put the violin aside and turned his interests to reading as many books as he could find.

After graduating high school, Pedersen enrolled in Grand View Junior College in Des Moines, Iowa, and completed his Associate of Arts degree in 1956. He transferred to the University of Minnesota and graduated in 1958 with a concentration in history and philosophy; in 1959, he earned a Master of Arts degree in American Studies at Minnesota. Following his interests in religious studies, Pedersen received a Master of Theology degree in 1962 from the Lutheran School of Theology in Chicago. Then, in 1966, Pedersen earned a Master of Science degree in counseling and student personnel psychology from the University of Minnesota. In 1968 Pedersen received his Ph.D. in Asian Studies, with a concentration in the fields of counseling, cultural history, comparative religion, and political theory, from Claremont Graduate School in Claremont, California. His doctoral dissertation was titled *Religion as the Basis of Social Change Among the Bataks of North Sumatra*, adapting the 500-item Church Youth Research Inventory to Chinese and Malay/Indonesian languages.

Pedersen's abiding interests and commitment to promoting the importance of culture in psychology were sparked by his early travels hitchhiking across Europe and his academic appointments, beginning in 1962 as a visiting lecturer in ethics and philosophy and the chaplain at Nommensen University in Medan, Sumatra, Indonesia. He studied Mandarin Chinese full-time in 1968 in Taiwan. From 1969 to 1971, Pedersen was a part-time visiting lecturer in the Faculty of Education at the University of Malaya; also, he was the youth research director for the Lutheran Church of Malaysia and Singapore. While in Indonesia and Malaysia, Pedersen quickly realized that what he had learned about conventional counseling approaches at the University of Minnesota and Claremont Graduate School did not accommodate the worldviews of Malaysians, Chinese, and Indonesians. The daily dose of rich deep cultural experiences combined with the challenges associated with understanding culturally unique life-ways and thought-ways quietly planted the seeds for his plans to develop, advocate, and promote the value and significance of considering cultural differences in the counseling and clinical psychology professions.

In 1971, Pedersen accepted the position of assistant professor in the Department of Psycho-educational Studies at the University of Minnesota in Minneapolis; he also held a joint appointment as an international student advisor in the International Student Office. Drawing mainly on his experiences in Indonesia, Malaysia, and Taiwan and his daily counseling sessions with international students at Minnesota, Pedersen's growing concern for the relevance of conventional counseling approaches led him to consider more culturally sensitive counseling strategies. As an alternative to the use of conventional counseling education approaches, Pedersen devised and implemented his well-known and well-respected triad training model. Pedersen describes triad training as a self-supervision model where the counselor processes the positive and negative messages a client is thinking but not saying in counseling. Articulating these hidden messages and checking out their validity helps the counselor (a) see the problem from the client's viewpoint, (b) identify specific sources of resistance, (c) diminish the client's need for defensiveness, and (d) help the client develop recovery skills for getting out of trouble.

In 1975, Pedersen accepted an appointment as a Senior Fellow at the Culture Learning Institute at the East-West Center in Honolulu, Hawai'i. From 1978 to 1981, he was director of a large, predoctoral training grant from the U.S. National Institute of Mental Health titled Developing Interculturally Skilled Counselors. With eight predoctoral trainees, Pedersen conducted training programs that emphasized cross-cultural counseling approaches primarily through use of the triad training model; the programs brought together counselors from several Asian countries, North America, and countries in Oceania to learn the fundamentals of the then-emerging field of cross-cultural counseling. Pedersen closely maintained his Hawaiian appointments and ties for the rest of his illustrious career by serving as a visiting professor of psychology at the University of Hawai'i at Mānoa and as a Fellow at the East-West Center.

In 1982, Pedersen accepted an appointment at Syracuse University as professor and chair of the Department of Counselor Education. In 1995, he received the professor emeritus title at Syracuse and subsequently accepted an appointment as a professor in the Department of Human Studies at the University of Alabama at Birmingham. In 2001, after a year as Senior Fulbright Scholar at Taiwan National University and after marrying Doris H. F. Chang, Pedersen formally retired from academic life and moved back to his much beloved Hawai'i to continue his writing, traveling, and scholarly interests. He retained his appointment as a visiting professor in the Department of Psychology at the University of Hawai'i at Mānoa. Pedersen has three married children and five grandchildren in Minnesota.

Pedersen's remarkable career includes the publication of more than 40 books and more than 150 book chapters and journal articles; the concept of culture is the common thread that runs through all of them. In reviewing Pedersen's extraordinary accomplishments, one quickly realizes that he is imaginative and farsighted. Among many of his significant initiatives, in 1973 Pedersen organized and chaired the first symposium dealing with cross-cultural counseling and presented it at the American Psychological Association's annual convention in Montreal, Canada. Symposium panelists, together with other authors, contributed to the first major book in the field of cross-cultural counseling; Pedersen was the senior editor and was assisted by Walter J. Lonner and Juris Draguns, and later by Joseph E. Trimble. Titled *Counseling Across Cultures,* the book is now in its sixth edition in an expanded version that is almost twice the length of the first edition.

Most scholars in the counseling and psychotherapy fields consider Pedersen's edited book published in 1999 titled *Multiculturalism as a Fourth Force* to be a milestone in the history of psychology. The book surveyed the prospect of moving toward a universal theory of multiculturalism that recognizes the psychological consequences of each cultural context. Pedersen and his colleagues argued that the fourth force supplements the three forces of humanism, behaviorism, and psychodynamism for psychology.

Along with his commendable scholarly accomplishments, Pedersen has been actively involved in research activities, many of which received external funding. He was codirector of an intercultural communication laboratory for 60 Japanese/U.S. intercultural communication experts at Nihonmatsu, Japan, funded by the Lily Foundation; director of U.S. Department of Education–funded research on sex-role stereotypes in higher education; director of a 3-year National Institute of Mental Health mental health training program; and director of a 2-year Harvard Institute for International Development project in Indonesia to evaluate and upgrade training at Bank Rakyat Training Centers. Pedersen was awarded many grants, including a 6-year grant from the National Science Foundation to study the re-entry adjustment of engineers returning to Taiwan after study abroad; a National Institute of Education grant to develop a measure of cross-cultural counseling skill; a State of New York Department of Social Services grant to develop mental health training materials geared toward treating unaccompanied refugee minors; and an Asian Foundation grant to co-organize a conference in Penang, Malaysia, on constructive conflict management in a cultural context.

Because service to the professional community is an important value for Pedersen, he has found time to serve on numerous boards and committees. His activities have included 3 years as president of the Society for Intercultural Education Training and Research (SIETAR); series editor for Sage Publications' *Multicultural Aspects of Counseling* (MAC) Series; and advising editor for a Greenwood Press book series in education and psychology. Additionally Pedersen is a board member of the Micronesian Institute located in Washington, D.C., and an external examiner for Universiti Putra Malaysia, University Kebangsaan, and Universiti Malaysia Sabah in psychology. From 1999 to the present, Pedersen was a Senior Fulbright Scholar teaching at National Taiwan University. Within the American Psychological Association Pedersen was a member of the Committee for International Relations in Psychology (CIRP) from 2001 to 2003 and was invited to give a master lecture at the American Psychological Association Convention in Los Angeles in August 1994. Pedersen also is a Fellow of Divisions 9, 17, 45, and 52 of the American Psychological Association.

By all professional and personal standards, Pedersen is a visionary as he has contributed significantly to the emergence of multiculturalism in psychology and in related disciplines. Pedersen's commitment to multiculturalism extends well beyond the mental health professions. In thinking about the future of multicultural counseling and social justice, Pedersen firmly believes that the multicultural perspective will evolve into a perspective that acknowledges how people may share the same common ground expectations, positive intentions, and constructive values even though they express those expectations and positive intentions through different and seemingly unacceptable behaviors. He also maintains that counselors and psychologists must generate a balanced perspective, wherein both similarities and differences of people are valued, and at the same time avoid partisan quarreling and get on with the important task of finding social justice across cultures.

Joseph E. Trimble

See also Cross-Cultural Psychology (v3); Cross-Cultural Training (v3); Culture (v3); Multicultural Counseling (v3); Multicultural Counseling Competence (v3); Multiculturalism (v3); Multicultural Psychology (v3); Universalism (v3)

Further Readings

Connerley, M. L., & Pedersen, P. B. (2005). *Leading in a multicultural environment: Developing awareness, knowledge, and skills.* Thousand Oaks, CA: Sage.

Marsella, A., & Pedersen, P. (Eds.). (1981). *Cross-cultural counseling and psychotherapy.* New York: Pergamon Press.

Pedersen, P. (Ed.). (1999). *Multiculturalism as a fourth force.* Philadelphia: Brunner/Mazel.

Pedersen, P. (2000). *Handbook for developing multicultural awareness* (3rd ed.). Alexandria, VA: American Counseling Association.

Pedersen, P. (2000). *Hidden messages in culture-centered counseling: A triad training model.* Thousand Oaks, CA: Sage.

Pedersen, P. (2004). *One hundred and ten experiences for multicultural learning.* Washington, DC: American Psychological Association Press.

Pedersen, P., & Carey, J. (2003). *Multicultural counseling in schools* (2nd ed.). Needham, MA: Allyn & Bacon.

Pedersen, P., Draguns, J. G., Lonner, W. J., & Trimble, J. E. (Eds.). (2007). *Counseling across cultures* (6th ed.). Thousand Oaks, CA: Sage.

Pedersen, P., Marsella, A., & Sartorius, N. (Eds.). (1984). *Mental health services: The cross-cultural context.* Beverly Hills, CA: Sage.

Ponterotto, J. G., & Pedersen, P. B. (1993). *Prejudice prevention: A developmental counseling perspective.* Beverly Hills, CA: Sage.

Personal Space

Personal space can be described as the amount of space around individuals that allows them to feel comfortable. People's expectations and needs for personal space may differ based on race, ethnicity, gender, and/or social class. For some people, this may mean keeping others at arm's length, whereas for others it may entail moving in very closely when they communicate. From a cultural point of view, different cultures have different ideas about appropriate personal space, and personal space holds different meanings when one considers the variables of social class and gender. People have their own individual ideas about what is comfortable to them and what is not comfortable in terms of personal space.

The world of business has brought the idea of personal space into the forefront as a vital consideration. For example, when conducting business, it is important and considered proper to maintain appropriate personal space based on what the host or majority culture considers to be personal space. Within dominant White American cultures, this may mean a firm handshake, staying about 3 feet away from other people during interactions, and not touching them in any way other than a handshake. However, in, Japan, a bow between two people, placed 2 to 3 feet apart, is a standard greeting and a sign of respect; further, the extent of the bow may differ across social and professional contexts.

Personal space is a form of nonverbal communication. For human beings, ideas and expectations about personal space may differ depending on whether interactions are occurring with strangers, family members, or intimate partners. Furthermore, in some cultural contexts, norms and expectations about personal space may be directly related to the social standing or class of the people involved. For example, in some cultures, people from higher social standings or classes tend to be more formal and maintain larger distances in personal space, whereas those who are from lower social standings or classes tend to have smaller distances of personal space. Moreover, gender differences can play an important role in personal space, as men, in general, find it more difficult to touch or be touched than do women.

In a counseling situation, maintaining appropriate personal space while trying to develop a therapeutic and empathic relationship can be a challenge. Personal space is an important aspect of therapy and when misused, it can be seen as threatening; further, when cultural norms are not respected or are violated, lapses in the working alliance may ensue. In cross-cultural counseling dyads, personal space may be a valuable means of communicating cultural respect. For example, if a client who identifies with a culture that endorses greater physical expression of care and support shares a personal, emotional story, the client may be expecting a hug or gentle touch on the arm from her or his counselor. However, if the counselor does not ascribe to those norms and does not express her or his empathy through such physical displays, the client may feel unheard or disrespected. On the other hand, if the counselor wants to offer a hug or gentle touch and the client has distinct ideas about personal space and boundaries, the client may feel threatened by the touch. It is very important for counselors to remember that their own racial/cultural worldview may differ from their client's worldview, and that will, in turn, have an impact on the therapeutic relationship that they are able to develop.

Janice E. Jones

See also Barriers to Cross-Cultural Counseling (v3); Communication (v3); Cultural Values (v3); Culture (v3); Worldview (v3)

Further Readings

Hall, E. T. (1966). *The hidden dimension*. Garden City, NY: Doubleday.

PLURALISM

In its general sense, pluralism refers to the existence and validity of a variety of beliefs, values, realities, and identities. Pluralism has been used to describe the variety of beliefs and values that exist within a society (e.g., political pluralism), a discipline (e.g., scientific pluralism), or culture (e.g., cultural pluralism). In the multicultural counseling literature, pluralism refers to the existence and inclusion of all aspects of diversity (e.g., individual diversity, group diversity) within a society or culture (cultural pluralism). Pluralism carries the inherent belief that the inclusion, validation, and affirmation of multiple aspects of diversity are intrinsically valuable to the overall well-being of a group or community.

Philosophical and Sociological Perspectives

The origins of pluralism as a philosophical thought can be traced to Western philosophy, with roots in early Greek philosophy. Developed in the 5th century B.C. by philosophers Empedocles and Anaxagoras, pluralistic philosophy sought to provide a different explanation for the natural world. Natural world phenomena were previously defined by the Ionian philosophers as based in a single element; pluralistic philosophy challenged this notion and posited that natural world phenomena were based in multiple elements. From this philosophical basis comes the contemporary view of pluralism that posits the existence of multiple realities. Neither of these views of pluralism accounts for a complete explanation of total reality.

From this background, sociological aspects of pluralism were developed. Within sociological theory, pluralism is the social condition that accepts, embraces, validates, and celebrates the multiple cultures and the many beliefs and values that exist in a society. The strength and health of such a society is predicated upon the belief that such a diverse collection of cultures and beliefs is a valuable and integral component to the welfare of that society.

Counseling and Pluralism

In 1990, Paul Pedersen dubbed multiculturalism as the "fourth force" in counseling, which would shift the existing paradigms of counseling and therapy to integrate the cultural experiences and identities of clients. Multiculturalism was seen as the next wave in counseling that would promote the value of a culture-centered approach in working with clients and promote the value of a pluralistic society. Since Pedersen's naming of this fourth force in counseling, the multicultural movement within counseling has grown, and with it has grown the increasing recognition of the value of pluralism in society.

The foundation for multicultural counseling is the inherent assumption and valuing of pluralism. Pluralism, in this sense, was initially seen as the collection of various racial or ethnic cultures and worldviews. Pluralism and culture-centric counseling attempted to then define culture and its constructs (e.g., identity) from etic and emic perspectives. As pluralism and multiculturalism continued to grow and to be explored within the counseling literature, the definition of *culture* also grew to encompass other aspects of personal and social identity, including, for example, socioeconomic status, gender, sexual orientation, spirituality and religion, physical ability, and numerous other personal and social variables, both seen and unseen. From this, the term *cultural pluralism* was then used to reflect the multifaceted and multidimensional nature of culture and identity.

Pluralism and multiculturalism are intimately tied together within the counseling profession. Although both terms may be used interchangeably, *pluralism* connotes the broader philosophical principle whose roots are in ancient Greek philosophy whereas *multiculturalism* is used to refer to the inclusion of various cultural and racial groups and identities. More recently, *multiculturalism* has been used to refer to the broad spectrum of individual and group diversity to include sexual orientation, physical ability status, spirituality and religion, and socioeconomic status, among the variety of individual and group differences.

The Growth of Pluralism in Counseling

For the greater part of the 20th century, the counseling profession has relied on theories and practices of counseling with clients that have been based on Western, Eurocentric teachings, perspectives, and values. For the most part, the majority of mainstream counseling theories have reflected this Western ethnocentric approach to working with clients, which has neglected the role of cultural and individual differences in identity and values formation. Only within the latter part of the 20th century did pluralism and cultural pluralism gain ground within the counseling profession.

The increasing presence of pluralism in counseling can be directly evidenced in the increase of publications, the development of educational curricula, and the establishment of organizational policies and statements that affirm pluralism. Since Pedersen's claim that multiculturalism is the fourth force in counseling, there have been numerous publications that address issues of cultural pluralism within the counseling profession. Landmark publications in this area include *Counseling the Culturally Diverse: Theory and Practice*; *Counseling and Psychotherapy: A Multicultural Perspective;* and the *Handbook of Multicultural Counseling*.

A number of graduate programs in counseling have recognized the need to prepare graduates for counseling in a pluralistic society. Graduate programs in counseling have been developed to reflect training and education in the principles of multicultural counseling. Though graduate programs have gradually made the shift to an inclusion of multicultural issues within their curricula, full integration of multiculturalism that reflects the basic tenets of inclusion in pluralistic philosophy is still needed.

Professional counseling and psychological associations have pioneered a variety of publications, guidelines, policies, and resolutions proclaiming the importance of multiculturalism and the value of a pluralistic society. Organizations such as the American Counseling Association and the American Psychological Association have developed guidelines and standards that endorse the importance of a pluralistic society and the development of multicultural awareness, knowledge, and skills in the work of the counselor. While these and other organizations have professed the importance of multiculturalism and pluralism in counseling clients and in counselor development, continued work is necessary to promote and integrate these guidelines and pronouncements within the greater counseling profession.

Social Justice and Pluralism

The counseling profession has recently attended to the concept of social justice within its theory and practice. However, the idea of social justice has existed within other disciplines (e.g., theology) before it gained the attention of the counseling profession. Social justice has as its foundation the core values and philosophical tenets of pluralism; that is, social justice strives to advocate for, and to bring justice to, those individuals, peoples, groups, and cultures that suffer from oppression and social stigma. Social justice is, then, an action that promotes the values of pluralism within societies and organizations.

Within the counseling profession, pluralism and social justice embrace the notion of counselors as agents of prosocial change. Social justice and pluralism recognize the role of the counselor in advocating for the needs and rights of clients who experience social oppression. Beyond that, social justice and pluralism also recognize the role of the counselor as an active member within the community to work toward advancing the work of social justice and pluralism within the community in ways that promote social welfare and cultural pluralism.

Ruperto M. (Toti) Perez

See also Bicultural (v3); Cultural Relativism (v3); Culture (v3); Diversity (v3); Ethnocentrism (v3); Idiocentrism (v3); Multiculturalism (v3); Pedersen, Paul Bodholdt (v3); Social Justice (v3); Universalism (v3); Worldview (v3)

Further Readings

Ivey, A. E., D'Andrea, M., Ivey, M. B., & Simek-Morgan, L. (2007). *Counseling and psychotherapy: A multicultural perspective* (6th ed.). Boston: Allyn & Bacon.

Ponterotto, J. G., Casas, J. M., Suzuki, L. A., & Alexander, C. M. (Eds.). (2001). *Handbook of multicultural counseling* (2nd ed.). Thousand Oaks, CA: Sage.

Sue, D. W., & Sue, D. (2008). *Counseling the culturally diverse: Theory and practice* (5th ed.). New York: Wiley.

POLITICAL CORRECTNESS

A little more than a decade after the demands for Black, Latino/a, and women studies on college campuses across the nation in the late 1960s, universities witnessed a new articulation of inclusion. With the rise of hate speech and racially motivated incidents on campuses in the 1980s and 1990s, universities began to find ways to help create a learning environment in which all students felt respected, valued, and free to actively participate in the community life of these institutions. Universities implemented speech codes as one method of creating a more inclusive learning environment; these codes were later ruled unconstitutional because they were considered to be too vague to be administered fairly. Books that critiqued efforts to establish a multicultural curriculum were published on the coat tails of these cases, including Dinesh D'Souza's oft-referenced treatise *Illiberal Education: The Politics of Race and Sex on Campus*. The tension between those fighting for antisexist, antiracist, and multicultural education on campus and those, such as D'Souza, who wanted to maintain the status quo fueled the rise of the "political correctness" debate in and outside of the academy.

Political correctness (PC) is a hotly contested term with different meanings across ideological stances. Although the term *PC* reportedly dates back centuries and, some would argue, has more modern-day usage as early as the 1930s with the Frankfurt School, the term is most identified with public discourse about inclusive language, behaviors, and policies over the past 2 decades. PC as a concept was created and legitimized by conservatives, or the political right. Neoconservatives alleged that policies designed to prevent the use of offensive language to a wide range of social groups (e.g., racial/ethnic minorities, lesbian/gay, bisexual/queer/transgendered individuals, persons with disabilities, women) were politically repressive and infringed on freedom of speech. From this perspective, being "PC" silenced viewpoints that countered multicultural and inclusive agendas, including the perspectives that race is biological and reparative therapy can "cure" gay and lesbian individuals. In essence, it has been argued that being PC limits the terms of debate negatively and punishes those with more conservative viewpoints.

On the other hand, progressives and radicals argue against the existence of PC as a concept. From this perspective, political correctness is conceptualized as a rhetorical argument arranged by the political right to dismiss efforts to create safe public spaces in which various marginalized social groups are protected from the use of slurs and epithets and have the right to name, define, and study their own lived experiences. Many adopting this perspective view the term *PC* as pejorative. Feminist scholar Sara Mills argued for antisexism (antiracism, heterosexism, oppression, etc.) because it simultaneously adopts a stance against social group oppression while questioning the validity of claims about "correctness." By using more descriptive terms, one locates the problem as one of oppression (e.g., racism) as opposed to one of control (e.g., political correctness).

The field of counseling has been indirectly influenced by the PC debates. The movement for multicultural counseling competencies emerged in the 1980s, during a time in which other disciplines were also reconstructing their curriculum to become more inclusive. Training programs have struggled with finding ways to provide a curriculum supporting the development of multicultural counseling competencies with students who oppose interrogating their own core beliefs and assumptions. Some students argue that they should not be pressured to explore their (negative) beliefs about certain social groups (e.g., lesbian, gay, bisexual, and transgendered individuals); in essence, these students assert that political correctness in the field has infringed on their personal and/or religious beliefs.

Helen A. Neville

See also Bias (v3); Color-Blind Racial Ideology (v3); Discrimination (v3); Diversity (v3); Classism (v3); Multicultural Counseling Competence (v3); Multiculturalism (v3); Organizational Diversity (v3); Racism (v3); Sexism (v3)

Further Readings

Brace, C. L. (1995). Race and political correctness. *American Psychologist*, pp. 725–726.

Dong, D. (2006). Free speech and multiculturalism in and out of the academy. *Political Psychology, 27*, 29–54.

Ladany, N., Friedlander, M. L., & Nelson, M. L. (2005). Heightening multicultural awareness: It's never been about political correctness. In N. Ladany, M. L. Friedlander, & M. Lee (Eds.), *Critical events in psychotherapy supervision: An interpersonal approach* (pp. 53–77). Washington, DC: American Psychological Association.

Mills, S. (2003). Caught between sexism, anti-sexism and "political correctness": Feminist women's negotiations with naming practices. *Diversity & Society, 14*, 87–110.

POVERTY

Poverty is a global problem. Using the U.S. dollar as a hallmark for living standards, approximately

2.8 billion people live on less than 2 dollars a day, and almost 1.2 billion live on less than 1 dollar a day. Given the differing living standards across nations, a dollar has different weight depending on context. But in the United States, how much does it cost to live adequately? That is, what is the minimum one should expect to have to provide for adequate housing, food, health care, and transportation for instance? And more importantly, what measure should one use to indicate when an individual or family has fallen below these standards of acceptable living? To understand poverty in the United States, it is important to address (a) the consequences of poverty, (b) the definitions of poverty, and (c) counseling and psychology's understandings of poverty and social class and classism in relation to poverty and future research and practice.

Consequences of Poverty

Poverty's effect on individuals, families, and communities is a growing and deleterious problem. For instance, U.S. Census Bureau data show that in 2002, 8% of Whites were in poverty, unchanged since 2001. Among African Americans, 24.1% were in poverty, which was higher than the 22.7% reported in 2001. For Asian Americans, the poverty rate was 10.1%, unchanged from 2001. And for Latinos/as, the poverty rate remained unchanged from 2001 to 2002 at 21.8%. For children, the percentage in poverty remained unchanged at 16.7% from 2001 to 2002. The poverty rate for families rose from 4.9% to 5.3%, and the percentage of female households remained unchanged at 26.5%.

Factors that contribute to the rise in poverty include the decrease in real wages earned by lower-educated workers and the increase in single-parent families. Real wages may be considered the actual worth of income an individual receives after inflation and other adjustments are considered; unadjusted wages, for instance, may seem to be high, but considering the actual worth of the wage in relation to inflation, the unadjusted wage may be an erroneous figure. Furthermore, those with 12 or fewer years of schooling experienced the greatest decrease in their earning power. This group of the working poor, or those with regular employment but living in near-poor or poverty conditions, has increased by 35% from 1990 to 1998. For many families, limited income restricts their ability to invest in their children's education and future, thereby limiting children's future social class mobility and furthering the intergenerational transmission of poverty.

Research also suggests that poverty is overrepresented among recent immigrants; African, Latino/a, and Native American communities; women and single mothers; and children. The research shows overwhelmingly that transient and persistent (chronic) experiences of poverty have the most serious consequences for children and adolescents. Essentially, poverty creates an environment wherein risk factors converge. For instance, for children and adolescents in an unsafe or violent and crime-prone environment, options for exercise and outdoor play are limited. Consequently, children's health behaviors are affected, and outcomes may be increasing rates of sedentary behaviors, childhood obesity, and diabetes. Poverty also increases the exposure to other toxicities, such as lead poisoning and pesticides, and to low birth-weight—all related to later intellectual and social functioning. Other effects of poverty on children and their development may be evidenced in IQ scores, graduation rates, or adequate educational environments. Children who have experienced poverty may also exhibit higher aggression and conduct problems than children who have not experienced poverty, psychophysiological stress, and developmental delays. Additionally, experiencing poverty in preschool and early years decreases the probability that these children will graduate from high school when compared to experiencing poverty later in their education. Finally, for many children, there are deleterious effects of poverty on their mental health and emotional life. For instance, children who live in families experiencing financial stress also may have lower social competence.

Poverty creates situations where toxicities converge and limit the developmental potential of children and adolescents. For adults and children, poverty also creates situations of psychological strain and stress, which are related to poor health. For example, in one study, nuns, who in their adult life shared similar diet, health care, housing, and lifestyles, had patterns of disease and incidences of dementia that were related to their socioeconomic status almost 50 years earlier before becoming nuns. The results suggested the long-range effects of poverty in a person's life. Furthermore, if access to health care is held constant, those living in poverty tended to have poorer health than those in higher social class groups. Therefore, chronic psychological stress related to living in poverty has a greater effect on an individual's health than structural and societal safety nets such as adequate healthcare services. Because those in poverty or who are poor often have the worst mental health prognoses, there is little doubt that a mental health gradient exists. For those living in poverty, the prospect of experiencing psychological stress and limited access to mental health care is high; whereas for those individuals living in higher social classes, their psychological outlook is better as well as their access to mental health care. Those in poor and impoverished environments may experience psychological stress and, consequently, have higher rates of mental illness.

Two main theories have been posited to explain this mental health gradient. In the social causation theory, it is posited that individuals are made vulnerable to psychological stress as a result of living in poverty. In the social selection theory, individuals experiencing mental health problems are likely to be from economically disadvantaged settings and/or have a downward social mobility resulting from problems in their social and occupational life. Some research suggests that evidence supports both theories and that the evidence is generally mixed. Yet the overwhelming evidence supports the social causation theory, that is, poverty makes people vulnerable to mental health problems. In one example of a natural experiment, 1,420 rural children ages 9 to 13 were given annual psychiatric assessments for 8 years (1993–2000). Approximately 25% of the children were Native American and the rest were predominantly White. About halfway through the study, an Indian casino opened on the reservation and increased family incomes through a supplement. Of the Native American families, 14% moved out of poverty (ex-poor), 53% remained poor (persistently poor), and 32% were never considered poor. Results showed ex-poor children's psychiatric problems dropped to the never-poor level, while those who were persistently poor remained high in rates of psychiatric problems. But the results for the ex-poor were symptom specific such that conduct and oppositional-defiant disorders decreased, but anxiety and depression were unaffected.

Although research into impoverishment, deprivation, and poverty shows a relationship with poor physical health, mental health, and educational outcomes, it is still unclear what constitutes poverty. Typically, the U.S. Census Bureau definitions are used, but the research also varies in operationalizing poverty from author to author. It is important to understand how poverty is generally conceptualized and used in the extant literature in a way inclusive of multiple definitions of poverty.

Definitions of Poverty

Poverty, as a term, has been used to both denote (signify literally) and connote (signify indirectly) situations of deprivation. Poverty may be a transient situation, a persistent state, an abstract demarcation between rich and poor, or an indicator of insufficiency. Often, what is considered poverty varies by study. Variations in the definitions of poverty have allowed for a nuanced understanding of the contexts in which poverty can be salient and for which comparisons can be difficult to make. For instance, using one definition of poverty to understand urban versus rural poverty is difficult given differing living standards, the composition of people of color, and context-specific stressors such as access to health care, violence and crime, and the monetary value of governmental subsidies.

In the United States, the standard definition for poverty comes from the Census Bureau and the Department of Commerce, which identify monetary income as the sole criteria for determining a poverty threshold. In 2002 for example, the poverty threshold, pre-tax income, for a family of four, consisting of two parents and two children, was $18,244. Monetary income does not include any capital gains or non-cash benefits such as public housing, food stamps, or Medicaid.

The poverty thresholds offer one measure to understand who may be considered poor in the United States, but it should not be used as the sole criterion. If a family's income is above the poverty threshold, the family is not considered to be in poverty even though actual monetary benefits from their "above-poverty income" may be slight and, in fact, they are still poor. To illustrate, a family of five has a poverty threshold of $22,509. Even if their total family income was $25,000, they would not be considered "in poverty" given the current criteria. Although they would be considered "near poverty or near poor," they still are above the official poverty threshold.

The Census Bureau calculates three categories of poverty based on an income-to-poverty ratio. This ratio is calculated by dividing the family's income by their poverty threshold. Given the previous example of the five-member family whose income was $25,000 and a poverty threshold of $22,509, their ratio would be 1.14. In this example, this family is above 1.0, which is the threshold for a family of their size, but below 1.25, which is considered near poor. Families who are below 1.0 or below .50 are considered either at poverty or in severe poverty, respectively.

The poverty threshold was originally developed in 1963 and 1964 by Mollie Orshansky. Orshansky did not develop the poverty threshold as a standard budget for a family. That is, Orshansky did not determine the list of goods and services needed for a family of a particular size to exist at a determined level. Except for food stuffs, there was no standard, and there still is no standard, for minimum consumption needs for a family. Instead, what could be determined were food expenditures in a family, and Orshansky determined the minimum income needed to afford basic food stuffs and then multiplied that amount by three. The multiple of three was derived from a 1955 Department of Agriculture's Household Food Consumption Survey that found families typically used one third of their household-budget, after-tax income, on food. The problem for many families under this definition is that this amount did not consider other needs, such as housing, clothing, medical costs, and transportation.

Several criticisms of the criteria for the current poverty threshold have been presented. First, although the poverty threshold is updated annually for inflation, the poverty threshold does not consider actual growth in consumption. That is, the food expenses do not reflect rising living standards and other consumption; instead the current poverty threshold reflects today's dollar. The problem with this is that the living standard was set 30 years ago. The poverty thresholds do not consider the cost of fuel, child care, technology, health care, and housing, to name a few. Second, the poverty threshold is a standard, regardless of geography. Therefore, the poverty threshold is the same for someone living in rural areas as it is in an urban setting wherein living standards and costs of living may vary greatly.

Recommendations have been made to the Census Bureau and the Office of Management and Budget to revise their calculations. In 1995, a National Academy of Sciences (NAS) panel recommended new ways to measure income, families' needs, and other aspects related to measuring poverty. The NAS panel recognized that official poverty indices did not account for the effect of taxes and medical expenses on those in poverty and did not account for the relative change in costs of food in relation to housing, clothing, and medical costs. The NAS panel developed six alternative measures, each accounting for different and related family income and expenses such as food stamps or housing subsidies, and each estimate is adjusted for family size. Each of the different measures produces varying levels of poverty depending on the criterion used. For example, even though the official poverty rate in 2003 was 12.7%, the Census Bureau reports poverty rates ranging from 8.3%, which used a comprehensive definition of income, to 19.4% using a definition of poverty excluding governmental payments.

Yet, regardless of what metric is used to assess poverty, the condition of poverty and its physical, psychological, and societal consequences need to be addressed and rectified. Poverty is clearly a social justice concern and a social inequity with consequences across all spectra of society. One potential direction to better understand poverty in psychology is to connect it with the study of social class and classism.

Poverty, Social Class, and Classism

Poverty is one outcome of sociostructural (e.g., legal, education, and economic systems) forces that marginalize and oppress individuals, creating inequities (injustice and unfairness) and inequalities (social and economic disparities). Poverty intersects with race and racism, and the aggregate effects on people of color are deleterious. Consequently, one outcome for many people of color is limited access to adequate and necessary health care. Those in poverty or poor conditions may have access to health care, but it may be in the form of emergency room visits rather than preventive care or regular health visits. Additionally, those in poverty may experience truncated, ineffective, or poor care when they are seen by physicians and psychologists. Another problem is the increased exposure to environmental racism. Environmental racism is an example of settings wherein toxicities—such as lead contamination, electromagnetic radiation, and refuse and waste management facilities—are generally isolated to poor and/or racial and ethnic communities.

Although poverty is easily identified, it is not well understood by counselors and psychologists. In part, the vagueness of poverty is linked to counseling and psychology's poor conceptualization of social class and classism. One study of counseling journals and counseling psychology journals found more than 450 different terms used to discuss social class and socioeconomic status. In this review of 20 years of journals, the term *poverty* was used in the following ways:

economic pressures of poverty, high-risk poverty, live in poverty, poverty, poverty level, poverty line, poverty rate, economic poverty, and poverty level incomes. Similar to poor conceptualizations of social class and classism, psychology's limited understanding of poverty may contribute to the limited theoretical and empirical literature.

For counselors, psychologists, and other mental health care workers, poverty is not only a static monetary demarcation (i.e., the poverty line) but also a representation of varying levels of deprivation and marginalization. The poor, near poor, and working poor may all experience the deleterious effects of poverty, for example, exposure to environmental toxins (e.g., lead), poor schools, inadequate food, lack of transportation, and violence, to name a few. Poverty is a context that creates the conditions wherein various physical and psychological problems may arise. There is no singular causal link, but psychologists should consider a constellation of problems. For instance, counselors and psychologists should be aware of job demands and environments in which many people who are poor find themselves. High levels of stress, lack of autonomy and independence, and lack of decision-making ability are related to poor physical health indicators, such as cardiovascular disease, depressed mood, and cognitive deterioration. Additionally, the additive effect of living in impoverished neighborhoods and working in stressful and demanding jobs may also affect people's worldview and perception of others.

For instance, people in lower social class groups tend to describe their world as hostile, dominating, and unfriendly. Furthermore, these same individuals are likely to anticipate less-friendly interactions with others. It may be that these individuals are constantly reminded of their low status and that this, in turn, reinforces their perception of a hostile world. For counselors and psychologists, awareness and sensitivity to interactions with clients and the covert and subtle ways in which status is communicated are important considerations. Additionally, developing a strong working alliance and therapy relationship may entail additional effort to prove oneself as credible and trustworthy. Counselors and psychologists may also find themselves challenging clients' "paranoia" about hostile climates and interactions. Sensitivity to clients' setting and predicament is important; dismissing and denying their hypersensitivity to interpersonal "slights" may be counterproductive in psychotherapy.

Poverty, much like social class and classism, needs to be conceptualized within a coherent theory that encompasses causes and consequences. In developing a theoretical model to conceptualize social class, classism needs to be an integral function. Much like race and racism, social class and classism are co-constructed; that is, social status differences cannot materialize without social and individual forces that exclude and marginalize certain groups and individuals. Similarly, by conceptualizing social class and classism as a worldview wherein an individual attempts to maintain his or her social class standing through classist behaviors and attitudes, poverty research may also benefit from connecting the environment to a person's psychological understanding, perception, or coping. Examining the psychological function of poverty does not diminish or minimize the sociostructural oppression experienced by those in poverty, but it may provide researchers and clinicians with more tools for prevention and intervention within these communities.

William Ming Liu

See also Abuse (v2); Classism (v3); Deficit Hypothesis (v3); Oppression (v3); Physical Health (v2); Racism (v3); Social Class (v4); Socioeconomic Status (v3); Substance Abuse and Dependence (v2)

Further Readings

Costello, E. J., Compton, S. N., Keeler, G., & Angold, A. (2003). Relationships between poverty and psychopathology: A natural experiment. *Journal of the American Medical Association, 290,* 2023–2029.

Evans, G. W. (2004). The environment of childhood poverty. *American Psychologist, 59,* 77–92.

Fisher, G. M. (1992). The development and history of the poverty thresholds. *Social Security Bulletin, 55*(4), 3–14.

Gallo, L. C., Smith, T. W., & Cox, C. M. (2006). Socioeconomic status, psychosocial processes, and perceived health: An interpersonal perspective. *Annals of Behavioral Medicine, 31,* 109–119.

Geronimus, A. T., Bound, J., Waidmann, T. A., Hillemeier, M. M., & Burns, P. B. (1996). Excess mortality among Blacks and Whites in the United States. *New England Journal of Medicine, 355,* 1552–1558.

Liu, W. M., Ali, S. R., Soleck, G., Hopps, J., Dunston, K., & Pickett, T., Jr. (2004). Using social class in counseling psychology research. *Journal of Counseling Psychology, 51,* 3–18.

Orshansky, M. (1988). Counting the poor: Another look at the poverty profile. *Social Security Bulletin, 51*(10), 25–51.

Sapolsky, R. (2005, December). Sick of poverty. *Scientific American, 293*(6), 92–99.

Short, K. S., & Garner, T. I. (2002, July). *A decade of experimental poverty thresholds: 1990–2000.* Paper presented at the annual meeting of the Western Economic Association, Seattle, Washington.

U.S. Census Bureau. (2003). Poverty in the United States: 2002. *Current Population Reports, P60-222.* Washington, DC: U.S. Department of Commerce.

Wood, D. (2003). Effect of child and family poverty on child health in the United States. *Pediatrics, 112,* 707–711.

POWER AND POWERLESSNESS

Power is a broad concept that is used in many contexts, including sociological and psychological realms. The term *power* has become so expanded and widely used that some believe it has lost strength in its use and value. Diverse conceptualizations of the power construct exist, which are based on the differing theories and philosophies that are present in research and literature. Power may be described as the ability or practice of exerting control over others or as the capability to influence others. Power is also presented as an innate ability to take action to make changes in one's life or in a community, nation, or the world.

Three identified types of power include force, influence, and authority. *Force* may be put forth through physical power, psychological power, or social power. *Influence* suggests the exercise of personal power, and *authority* includes traditional authority, legal or rational authority, and authority based on a person's disposition. Power has further been described as being a strong influence in the exercise of oppression; that is, those who are in power are able to oppress those with less power. Conceptualizations of power are also demonstrated in self-efficacy, as power may influence the extent to which an individual believes he or she is able to carry out a particular task or goal. Power is viewed by some as an object and a possession to which some have ownership of and others do not. Others view power not as an object but rather as a position in a relationship or social milieu. Power may be viewed in various contexts as either real or perceived, and it can be described as either a fixed construct or a variable aspect of a social relationship.

The opposite of power is powerlessness. Powerlessness refers to the expectancy that people's behaviors cannot determine the outcomes or reinforcements that they seek. Powerlessness may further be explained as the lack of strength or the absence of power. People experiencing powerlessness may feel out of control and have no solution to regain control. Subsequent to feeling out of control comes the lack of capability to be in command of most aspects of one's life. Powerlessness also can be considered as the absence of complete authority or status to affect how others will act toward others. It is viewed by some that, when confronting powerlessness, individuals may be able to affect or change the negative behaviors (e.g., compulsions and addictions) of either themselves or others. Confronting and addressing powerlessness is believed by some to be what helps people to change past events that have had a negative impact on people's current lives, or to help people change things that they may have attempted to change in the past with little success. People may experience feelings of powerlessness when considering areas where they feel a lack of strength, competence, or skills to overcome realities in life that have no solution or answer. For example, people may feel powerlessness when considering persistent problems facing society that are not currently solvable, such as widespread violence and war or a cure for AIDS or cancer.

Powerlessness can be a learned feeling or response that occurs when individuals are kept in powerless positions repeatedly and over long periods of time by others who are in positions of power. These powerful others are able to exercise their power via money, social position, or physical strength. Power may also be exerted over others through legal status or military force. Powerlessness may further be felt by individuals who are targets of racism or ethnic discrimination. When individuals feel powerlessness, they may feel hesitant, afraid, or unwilling to express their feelings, fearful that what little they have will be taken from them.

The externally imposed powerlessness of racial, class, and gender oppression may be enforced through various means including economic, social, or physical ways. People in positions of power may have control over others in determining, for example, who gets jobs, who is given opportunities in education, and how help is given to those with financial needs. When those in powerful positions are exercising control over less-powerful groups, collective power and direct action may be used to facilitate empowerment and overcome the feelings of powerlessness. Collective power refers to the power generated by an organized group. An example of collective power would be the formation of a union. An example of direct action to address powerlessness would be the development of a lawsuit or the arrangement of a strike. A powerful formula for effective action against powerful others would be one that combines the collective power with direct action, such as the formation of a workforce union that works together (collective power) and coordinates a strike effort (direct action).

People may also experience feelings of powerlessness if they have been abused. When powerlessness becomes a chronic and repeated occurrence, these continuous, persistent feelings of powerlessness may lead people to become afraid to feel and express their needs. This may result in people becoming immobilized or developing feelings of helplessness. People may unwittingly become immune to the feeling of powerlessness, possibly leading them to experience hindered growth and development. When powerlessness is learned, people may feel that they are responsible for their powerlessness. People with whom powerlessness is learned may remain in powerless positions, even when the external forces of power have decreased or diminished. These continuous feelings of powerlessness may lead one to then enter into situations that repeat experiences of powerlessness, such as engaging in a relationship with an abusive person. Powerlessness may also become internalized and lead people to self-abusive behaviors, compulsive behaviors, or depression. It has been suggested that one of the most harmful forms of powerlessness occurs when external forms of powerlessness are combined with the learned feelings of powerlessness, which may lead individuals without power to a position in which they feel insecure or unable to assert their rights.

Power in Counseling Relationships

Therapists and counselors are equipped with an array of skills to work effectively with clients. In counseling, it is not unusual for imbalances of power to surface. The historical view of therapy is similar to the medical model of illness, in which those seeking mental health services are seen with regard to symptom presentation and are subsequently prescribed a treatment to reduce those symptoms. This view of mental health focuses on mental health disorders as illnesses that require a cure to solve the presenting problems. Thus, with regard to power, this traditional medical model and approach to mental health treatment puts the therapist in a dominant role of a healer, with the client in a position of needing to be fixed or cured. From this traditional perspective, power differences may present in the relationship between the counselor and the client because of the perceived roles of the counselor and client. Additional imbalance of power between the counselor and the client may occur due to characteristics of either the counselor or client, such as racial, gender, age, and education differences. Some theorists believe that a power imbalance may be beneficial in a counseling relationship, suggesting that a counselor's power and perception of expertise lead to less resistance and more engagement from the client. Furthermore, some imbalance of power may be viewed as unavoidable. Because some imbalance of power may be inevitable and is considered by some as beneficial to therapeutic change, counselors ought to practice caution and awareness when exploring the dynamics of their relationships with clients. This may be accomplished by working to address and confront power positions and possible feelings of powerlessness, both outside of the counseling relationship as well as between the counselor and the client. This is particularly critical when the counseling relationship includes a cross-racial or cross-gender dyad.

Most theories of counseling often present information as being appropriate for all populations, suggesting that it is fitting to treat all clients of various racial, cultural, or ethnic backgrounds the same. This biased approach attempts to universalize the experience and social context of the White middle class. In clinical settings, psychological conditions may be better understood when issues of power, such as powerlessness or helplessness, are considered. The tendency of those in privileged positions to ignore, disregard, or pathologize the experiences of marginalized people can have damaging effects on the counselor–client relationship. In counseling, therapists may work to focus on patient's strengths, which can be a way of knowing and problem solving that relates to modification of this tendency to pathologize targeted people. For example, expression of resistance can be identified and validated, the resilience that clients use to manage oppression can be acknowledged, and the ethical implications of the client's struggles can be identified. Counselors may work with clients to address power imbalances. Working with clients to recognize and address feelings of powerlessness—within and beyond the counseling session—may possibly lead clients to experience thoughts of empowerment.

History and Development

Several theorists describe various thoughts regarding the concept of power. Friedrich Nietzsche is commonly viewed as a contemporary theorist with reference to the power construct. Nietzsche coined the concept of "will of power," which refers to the domination over others and over environments. From a social and political perspective, Keith Dowding's explanation of power differentiates between outcome power and social power. Dowding describes outcome power as the ability of individuals or groups to bring about change, and social power is referred to as the ability of groups or individuals to change the structures of other individuals or groups in order to bring about change.

Michel Foucault and others have argued that power should not and cannot be interpreted as a possession, an entity, or an object; rather, Foucault suggests that power is present only from its exercise within the structure of society or a particular point in time. Foucault contends that power is available to everyone but has different effects depending on who is acting and the context of that action. From Foucault's perspective, control and resistance to power can occur at any time and in any place. Foucault critiques the concept of oppressor and oppressed and instead offers the idea of power as stemming from relationships that are always dynamically changing. Foucault's contention was that people in power roles, such as psychologists, use their positions to oppress individuals who diverge from the norm. This is demonstrated throughout historical conceptualizations of mental health, in which psychologists are regarded as authorities in defining and reinforcing standards of normalcy and aberrance, thus exercising control and power through their positions.

In literature, multiple forms of power are presented. In sociological literature, power comes in two forms: as coercive and as choice. In its coercive form, power is the capacity to act in a manner that influences the behavior of others even against their wishes, possibly with the use of force. This type of power is also known as primary power and is considered the most destructive form of power in society today. Power as choice refers to the capacity to act in a manner that influences the behavior of others without violating free moral choice. To practice this form of power is described as the height of self-control. Other literature describes several types of power that are manifested in the following five forms: coercive power, reward power, legitimate power, expert power, and referent power. As described in the previous paragraph, coercive power refers to the type of power in which a punishment exists. The second type of power, reward power, involves the power one has to provide rewards. Legitimate power is the power that is gained via legitimate means, such as a law enforcement position. Expert power refers to the type of power that is gained through educational or experiential endeavors. Lastly, referent power refers to the power gained by an individual due to respect.

Examples

Race and Power

Dominant groups have a tendency to disregard injustice or fail to recognize the persistent systems of inequality that exist in their societies. *Dominant discourse* is a term that refers to the recognition process that people often encounter when they begin to explore ways in which they have disregarded issues of oppression. Dominant discourse describes the manner in which dominant groups may begin to acknowledge their previous failures to recognize that oppression exists. Dominant discourse occurs as people start questioning what would ordinarily be regarded as unbiased. People then search to explore the underlying values embedded within their perceived cultural norms. The analysis that occurs through dominant discourse shifts attention to the specific contexts that shape culturally appropriate beliefs.

The subtle approval of certain arrangements of racial privilege and power is an especially important implication. The biases embedded within dominant discourse are hidden by their exceeding normalcy, and this sense of order allows this subtle approval to persist in society and communities without questioning. The construct of dominant discourse can be used to investigate how unrecognized cultural assumptions surround counseling theory and the practice of therapy. People's examination of their own biased realities and practices influences the shaping of larger social contexts and the underlying values of those individuals. The understanding of this concept is critical to the professional development of counselors and counselors in training, particularly those who are from dominant cultures in society, such as White counselors. Multicultural awareness that results from deconstructive inquiry and analysis may create knowledge and understanding that help future therapists look beyond their own learned views and beliefs.

Addictions and Power

Individuals with addiction concerns are often drawn to particular kinds of mood changes or highs. There are specific addiction highs to which individuals are attracted, such as arousal, satiation, and fantasy. Arousal causes sensations of strong, unchecked power and gives the individual feelings of being all-powerful and untouchable. This arousal often comes in the form of taking substances such as amphetamines, cocaine, and ecstasy, and from gambling, sexually acting out, spending, stealing, and behaving in other risky or unsafe ways. Arousal gives those with addictions the sensation of omnipotence and overcoming any feelings of powerlessness. Yet people with addictions may eventually lose all feelings of power, and to get additional power they may return to the object or behavior that provided the arousal, ultimately becoming dependent upon it. People who are addicted to arousal become engulfed by fear, as they fear their loss of power and that others will discover how powerless they are.

Alcoholics Anonymous (AA) and the other 12-step programs based on AA principles teach that individuals with addictions are powerless over alcohol or drugs and that recovery necessitates acceptance of powerlessness. Some argue that this may be a convenient paradigm for some people, such as those who have been given to believe that they are responsible for controlling the world and everything in it, namely White, mainstream, heterosexual men. Promoting a sense of powerlessness may aid in easing the discomfort regarding areas over which they may have little or no control. However, other individuals utilize 12-step programs, namely, individuals from varying socioeconomic classes, women, racial and ethnic minorities, individuals from various sexual orientations, and other populations. Feminist theorists, in particular, have described the endorsement of powerlessness among women in various contexts as a confinement method meant to make certain that women remain depoliticized and as a part of a pattern of degradation of women. Some have argued that the theory of addiction, which asserts individual responsibility, is harmful to women because the theory denies the political, social, and economic realities that organize women's lives.

Disability and Power

The history of counseling people with disabilities originated following World War I after the vast demand for services for veterans with acquired disabilities. The beginning of services for people with disabilities included the development of post–World War I rehabilitation and social agencies for people in need of assistance. The industrialized economy garnered the creation of a select number of adaptive devices that were of significant help to people with disabilities who were capable of work. Today, people with disabilities may experience societal barriers of independent living. Societal barriers may include governmental policy, minimal accommodation, negative attitudes, or discrimination. People with disabilities may feel that the barriers and negative attitudes toward them serve to augment their disabilities, decrease their independence, and enlarge their sense of powerlessness. Thus, the dimension surrounding power and disability may put people in positions of needing help while also feeling resistant to accept help from others. Counselors working with people with disabilities may work toward empowerment of people with disabilities, advocacy, and assisting people with disabilities in areas of accommodations and work.

Sex/Gender and Power

There is general agreement that men and women differ in the degree to which they hold powerful positions in certain fields. Although various cultures may value the different kinds of power differently, male heterosexual power is almost universally respected. Males typically have more power than woman in the public arena outside the home and in leadership positions. Men usually control powerful institutions that sustain the social hierarchy, such as the government, military, and law. Women typically have far more responsibilities in the home than do men, often in daily caretaking activities. Though women may have more power in the home than men may have, this power is not analogous to public power. Although the distribution of power between men and women in the United States has changed over the past few decades, men continue to hold distinct power over women. Westernized culture has traditionally linked women's economic and social power with appearance. Within current gender-power relations, women's access to power is connected to their acceptance of mainstream beauty ideals.

In some racial/ethnic groups, gender roles are clearly defined. For example, in traditional Latino/a families, males are considered to be in superior roles within a well-defined family hierarchy. The male is the head of the household who sets the rules within the family. A macho concept of the exaggerated importance of being male is instilled in male children from a very early age. Marianismo, sometimes viewed as the submissive and obedient female, permeates the conventional role of wife imparted upon the Latina.

Age and Power

Age is one domain in which power differs across groups. In general, children have less control over their lives and the lives of others than do adults. Various cultures differ in how they distinguish age-related obligations and power, yet most cultures do make a distinction between the power of adults and the power of children. Some societies have a strong focus on the hierarchies related to age, specifically that older individuals have more control and power. In certain racial/ethnic minority groups, older-age individuals are often given a significant amount of respect and authority. Cultural values play a major role in the treatment of the elderly. In the Native American culture, elders are respected for their knowledge and experience, and they are considered to be invaluable community resources. Elders traditionally hold positions of power in their communities and are valued for their experience and wisdom. In traditional Latino/a culture, older adults are generally given great deference. The Latino/a elderly continue to hold a central role in the family and are treated with respect, status, and authority. The elderly are thought to have an inner strength so they can be a resource for the younger generations and are links to the past. In many Asian cultures, age is associated with many positive features, as age often denotes wisdom, authority, and the freedom to be flexible and creative. A conventional Japanese ritual is the *kankrei*, which acknowledges the release of the older person from the responsibilities of middle age and recognizes new freedoms and capabilities. In a majority of African societies, old age is believed to be a sign of divine blessing, and in some of African languages the elder is the "big person."

With regard to age as it relates to gender, researchers have demonstrated a shift in the perception of interpersonal power of women with age. In these studies, power included both the personal characteristics of self-respect and empowerment and the interpersonal component of influence over others. The disparity in power between men and women appears to shift over the life span. Studies have documented an increase in the perceived strength, confidence, and interpersonal power of women later in life. Likewise, studies have also demonstrated a decrease in the perceived power of men in older age groups. In many African societies, women who reach middle age experience the elimination of restrictions in an often gender-typed society. As women reach middle and older age, their power is approximately the same as that of men.

Multicultural Considerations

The question of how to address inequality is often presented, especially when considering this issue with people of privilege and those in controlling positions. The concept of power becomes a part of this question. Differences in power are less apparent to people in privileged positions, because people in privileged situations are more willing to accept a view of American society as classless and color-blind—supporting what literature describes as the myth of a level playing field. However, this viewpoint ignores the experience of marginalized groups and people in less-privileged positions. This view would discount issues such as discrimination and injustice that marginalized groups frequently face. The social differences can become extremely relevant to some, while remaining obscured to those who view the world as equal.

When power differences are not addressed, the likely disconnection between oppressed and privileged groups remains. Through educational and training opportunities, along with experience, people may begin to recognize and acknowledge their cultural biases. Acknowledgment of cultural biases leads people to become more aware of their endorsement of Eurocentric attitudes and behaviors. These attitudes and behaviors could be represented in styles of communication, nonverbal behaviors, and beliefs and values about society, family, and individuals. A deconstructive examination of one's own views can help one to move beyond a one-sided description, such as a "them" and "us" viewpoint, and more toward a dialogue in which one's cultural assumptions are questioned.

This may lead to self-awareness, multicultural competence, and personal and professional growth.

Terri L. Jashinsky and Melissa K. Smothers

See also Barriers to Cross-Cultural Counseling (v3); Classism (v3); Counseling Process/Outcome (v2); Discrimination (v3); Empowerment (v3); Hope (v2); Learned Helplessness (v3); Multicultural Counseling (v3); Multiculturalism (v3); Oppression (v3); Positive Psychology (v2); Prejudice (v3); Racism (v3); Relationships With Clients (v2); Self-Efficacy/Perceived Competence (v2); Self-Esteem (v2); Sexism (v3); Social Justice (v3); White Privilege (v3); Worldview (v3)

Further Readings

Albee, G. W., Joffe, J. M., & Dusenbury, L. A. (1988). *Prevention, powerlessness, and politics: Readings on social change.* Newbury Park, CA: Sage.

Dowding, K. M. (1996). *Power.* Minneapolis: University of Minnesota Press.

Friedman, A., Tzukerman, Y., Wienberg, H., & Todd, J. (1992). The shift in power with age: Changes in perception of the power of women and men over the life cycle. *Psychology of Women Quarterly, 16,* 513–525.

Friedman, D. (1987). Getting powerful with age: Changes in women over the life cycle. *Israel Social Science Research, 5,* 76–86.

Griscom, J. (1992). Women and power: Definition, dualism, and difference. *Psychology of Women Quarterly, 16,* 389–414.

Haines, E. L., & Kray, L. J. (2005). Self-power associations: The possession of power impacts women's self-concepts. *European Journal of Social Psychology, 35,* 643–662.

Holmes, E. R., & Holmes, L. D. (1995). *Other cultures, elder years.* Thousand Oaks, CA: Sage.

Krestan, J. (Ed.). (2000). *Bridges to recovery: Addiction, family therapy, and multicultural treatment.* New York: Free Press.

Lips, H. M. (1991). *Women, men, and power.* Mountain View, CA: Mayfield.

Maroda, K. (2004). A relational perspective on women and power. *Psychoanalytic Psychology, 21,* 428–435.

Twerski, A., & Nakken, C. (1997). *Addictive thinking and the addictive personality.* New York: MJF Books.

PREJUDICE

Prejudice has been defined as a preformed adverse judgment or opinion that is not grounded in knowledge, or an irrational suspicion or hatred of a particular group, race, or religion. In legal terms, prejudice has been defined as an irrational hostile attitude directed against an individual, a group, a race, or their supposed characteristics. Prejudicial behavior is responsible for a significant amount of anguish, psychological and emotional pain, and abuse of the target in cross-cultural and intergroup encounters. Examples of prejudicial behaviors include everyday life events of racism, sexism, and classism that can heighten subjective experiences of stress. Similarly, stresses experienced by women; intersexual, gay, lesbian, and transgendered people; religious minorities; and Arabs, Muslims, and Pakistanis (considered "villains" by some after September 11, 2001) may have their origins in personal and social prejudices.

Prejudices are defended strongly, as early cultural socialization experiences mold beliefs about people across ways of life. Prejudices can be embedded in worldviews (e.g., beliefs, values, and assumptions) and are integrated in individuals' expectations of others. Given the different definitions of prejudice, most theorists agree that it involves some kind of a negative assessment or evaluation of the "other."

Theorists have stated that prejudices are attitudes that involve negative feelings such as loathing, hatred, or contempt. Discrimination, on the other hand, refers to behaviors, often motivated by prejudices, wherein people are treated differently (e.g., negatively), based on group membership (e.g., culture, religion, gender, complexion, ethnicity, sexual orientation). Prejudice degrades the human experience and can motivate people to behave in destructive ways.

Prejudiced beliefs are often related to stereotypes. Stereotyping involves the inaccurate categorizing of people. Stereotyping ascribes negative characteristics to people on the basis of their group membership or other visible characteristics. Some theorists consider stereotypes pictures that people carry about others which are usually flawed and lead to assumptions. Prejudice, discrimination, and stereotyping are interrelated and tend to feed on each other. Such attitudes and behaviors may affect the self-actualization of stigmatized people negatively and result in significant human suffering. Counseling psychologists have argued that bearing prejudices has deleterious consequences. At a minimum, prejudice and discrimination can contribute to identity crises for the target populations and members of distinct cultural groups as they struggle with negative evaluations and projections.

All cultural groups display prejudice toward others, regardless of their status (i.e., dominant or nondominant group membership). People born and raised in racist, sexist, ageist, heterosexist, and otherwise oppressive systems tend to operate from internalized beliefs that are informed by these hierarchies. Though processes involving "unlearning" the socialization reinforce prejudices, individuals may begin to address how holding on to prejudices influences their appraisals of themselves and others. Moreover, being the target of prejudices may become a significant part of cultural socialization experiences, thus shaping how individuals respond toward members of other groups. When individuals are confronted with something or someone different from themselves, they may view the new object negatively if they themselves have been targets of prejudice and discrimination.

Why Does Prejudice Occur?

Early theorists constructed prejudice as a survival response to the extent that categorical thinking served to identify enemies and threatening situations. Knowing and recognizing members of one's ingroup (e.g., family, clan, community) was imperative if one was to survive; outgroup members often fought for ownership and access to vital resources, including land, wealth, and power. Although recent literature has attended to emotional, social, economic, and historic dimensions of prejudice, psychologists also have proposed that prejudice is partly a result of normal human functioning.

Categorical thinking intrinsic to prejudice is employed when people distinguish ingroup from outgroup members, and it informs the perception of greater similarity within a group and dissimilarity between groups than actually exists. In other words, individuals may perceive members of their own groups as more similar to them than they are in reality, and outgroup members are perceived to be more homogenous, such that they also are seen as interchangeable and expendable. Biases toward others are strengthened not out of hatred toward others but rather from positive perceptions of, and favoritism for, the ingroup (i.e., ingroup bias). Diverse races and cultures have ingroup biases; further, positive cultural identity development factors include positive emotions and self-appraisal as a member of a given cultural group.

According to social dominance theory, people feel more positively about themselves when they denigrate others. This creates a false sense of superiority, although it may have no basis in reality. It is further noted that the mechanism fueling prejudicial behavior is a desire to disparage others to ensure the perception of superiority and goodness. It has been suggested that prejudice and discrimination serve to maintain institutional oppression and affirm a sense of superiority among dominant groups across social locations (e.g., race, gender, and class). For example, it can be argued that within the present social structure, White males who are identified as middle and/or upper class (i.e., owning class) may hold prejudices that serve to maintain their status as dominant. Several studies have linked social dominance to anti-Black and anti-Arab prejudice, sexism, nationalism, opposition to gay rights, and other attitudes concerning social hierarchies.

Historical Perspective

Psychology started focusing on prejudice in the 1920s, when the emphasis was on American and European race theories that were developed to support the belief that Whites were the superior race. The emphasis started to shift in the 1930s and 1940s with progress in civil rights, challenges to colonialism, and a growing concern about antisemitism. Following the Holocaust, theories concerning personality variables that created a predisposition to prejudice became a focus of study. The most influential proposition was that underlying prejudicial behavior was an authoritarian personality.

The authoritarian personality was described as cognitively rigid and dichotomous, deferential to authority, and strictly adherent to social rules and hierarchies. Within this personality style, prejudices were thought to maintain categories and rules that were defended. Although this hypothesis had been met with criticism for lacking empirical support, later research supported the claims that related authoritarianism to political conservatism, hierarchical worldviews and endorsement of social dominance orientations, and categorical thinking.

The original expressions of prejudices tended to be blatant, open, and direct, indicating a person's attitude and behavior in one simultaneous act (e.g., lynching, restriction of voting rights). Given the protests of stigmatized people and the changes in laws and understanding of the oppression caused by such prejudices, racism, sexism, classism, and all other types of prejudice have been moved into a new domain called modern and aversive racism, sexism, and classism. Recent changes in legal and social norms have curtailed overt discrimination, but they also have fueled the emergence of more subtle forms of oppressions. For example, modern racism is characterized by the acknowledgment that racism exists alongside denial and attempts to address and resolve persistent inequities in today's society, under the claim that specific racial and cultural groups make unfair demands. Similarly, an example of modern sexism is endorsing the statement that it is not acceptable to consider women unintelligent compared with men while not endorsing measures to equal employment and wage disparities that women face. In effect, prejudices are said to evidence more subtly in current society.

Cross-Cultural Counseling

As mentioned, prejudice can be considered a maladaptive response to the anxieties people face or self-generate in response to human differences. It is maintained that this anxiety is exacerbated by the central existential problem of how one should live, what kind of person one should be, and whether that way of being has value. People living with condemnation of their skin color, gender, age, disability, sexual identity and orientation, or all of these, struggle with negative prejudicial behavior and stereotypes imposed upon them. This leaves the work of addressing the identity crisis of stigmatized individuals to psychologists, counselors, and therapists.

Recent research has psychological distress among the target populations, especially as it relates to prejudice, discrimination, and social stigma research. Additional research has documented the influence of experiencing prejudice and discrimination on psychological distress as well as the influence of mediating and moderating factors that can influence the extent to which individuals experience anxiety or stress related to prejudice (e.g., self-esteem). Empirical evidence has been found that people who endorse worldviews that teach tolerance and respect for diversity are resilient to defensive manifestations of intolerance; further, people who endorse such worldviews may actually become more tolerant under ambiguous, anxiety-provoking situations.

Counselors and mental health professionals are encouraged to recognize how their own prejudices may influence counseling processes. Psychologists have asserted that all human encounters are cross-cultural encounters on the basis of differences in gender, race, culture, ethnicity, age, sexual identity and orientation, religion, class, religion, and disability and other social positionalities. As a function of being socialized in hierarchies wherein social groups are ascribed power and members of groups are assumed to be deficient based on differences, counselors are likely to carry prejudices that can influence their assessment treatment of diverse clients. Moreover, given the power of the counseling role, such ascription of prejudices to clients may have implications beyond the scope of the consultation room. For example, some counseling psychologists have argued that foundational theories of psychological normality and abnormality were based in Eurocentric worldviews that reflected favoritism for that ingroup and perceived outgroups (e.g., people of color) and their cultures as deficient. Prejudices may evidence to the degree that values and experiences characteristic of a specified group of people may not be valued or legitimated within Eurocentric or androcentric theories of psychology.

In addition, counselors and mental health professionals may be invested in their prejudices such that they manifest defenses in their work with culturally diverse clients. Counseling psychology literature has presented several defense mechanisms that are believed to emerge in cross-cultural and cross-racial counseling, specifically when the counselor is White and the client is a visible racial/ethnic group member; these defense mechanisms include color-blind racial attitudes, color consciousness, cultural transference and counter-transference, cultural ambivalence, and pseudo-transference. Color-blindness is a lack of consideration of race, whereas color-consciousness overemphasizes the sociopolitical construct of race. Cultural transference and counter-transference refer to the exchange of racial and cultural projections between counselors and clients, as informed by each party's personal experiences with members of the other parties' racial-cultural group. Cultural ambivalence refers to counselors' preoccupation with their own issues as they confront race, including White guilt for historical atrocities and focusing on their personal racial privileges rather than the clients' experiences. Pseudo-transference refers to the refusal to take responsibility for one's prejudices and discrimination, such that clients are blamed for breakdowns in the relationship. Defense mechanisms identified for counselors of color are overidentification with clients' perceived issues and identification with the oppressor in their role as counselor. Across these counselor-specific defenses, counselors' prejudices may be operative to the extent that counselors may struggle to acknowledge their own biases or the realities of oppression (i.e., color-blindness), project racial assumptions on to their clients (i.e., counter-transference), or disown their roles in racial dynamics in the dyad (e.g., pseudo-transference or identifying with the oppressor).

Addressing Prejudices in Counselor Training

Several techniques and educational strategies are now being employed to educate counselors and psychologists to reduce the learned prejudices and biases that are a result of growing up in a racist, sexist, and classist society. Cross-cultural or multicultural counseling techniques and strategies are a part of curricula in nearly all counseling training programs; further, the existence of competencies and guidelines by the major counseling and psychology associations have encouraged increased sensitivity, awareness, knowledge, and skills in both educators and counselors. It is recommended that education and training focus on teaching the ability to navigate among foundational theories of counseling (e.g., psychodynamic, cognitive-behavioral) to inform culturally relevant treatment approaches for clients. In addition, it is encouraged for counselors and mental health professionals to move away from deficit models to recognizing clients' strengths based on biculturality, multi-culturality, or both. To the extent that counselors' endorsement of cultural identity attitudes has been related empirically to multicultural counseling competence, training programs may employ measures of racial identity attitudes, acculturation, gender identity attitudes, and worldview in evaluating the efficacy of multicultural counseling training curricula.

It is recommended that counselors and counseling trainees examine the extent to which they have internalized a Western bias toward compartmentalizing cultural variables that are embedded in counseling theories. Namely, counseling theories tend to examine gender, race, sexual orientation, and class separately, rather than the interplay among them. Thus, the lives of people with multiple stigmatized identities are compartmentalized into fragmented cultural categories that do not mirror real life. Consequently, Eurocentric and multicultural perspectives share a limitation in that the complex manner in which multiple stigmas operate in the lives of individuals is largely unexamined. More specifically, the degree to which counselors may hold prejudices related to multiple cultural identities (e.g., stereotypes related to women of color or lesbian, gay, bisexual, transgendered people of color) may go unapproached without addressing the realities of the intersections of social locations.

Farah A. Ibrahim and Carmen B. Williams

See also Antisemitism (v3); Bias (v3); Classism (v3); Discrimination (v3); Discrimination and Oppression (v2); Oppression (v3); Racism (v3); Sexism (v3); Stereotype (v3)

Further Readings

Allport, G. (1982). *The nature of prejudice* (4th ed.). Reading, MA: Addison-Wesley.

Croteau, J. M., Talbot, D. M., Lance, T. S., & Evans, N. J. (2002). A qualitative study of the interplay between privilege and oppression. *Journal of Multicultural Counseling and Development, 30,* 239–258.

Duckitt, J. H. (1992). Psychology and prejudice: A historical analysis and integrative framework. *American Psychologist, 47,* 1182–1193.

Fiske, S. T. (1998). Prejudice, stereotyping, and discrimination. In D. T. Gilbert, S. T. Fiske, & G. Lindzey (Eds.), *Handbook of social psychology* (4th ed., pp. 357–411). New York: McGraw-Hill.

Jones, J. M. (1997). *Prejudice and racism* (2nd ed.). New York: McGraw-Hill.

Levin, J. (1982). *The functions of prejudice.* New York: Harper & Row.

Nelson, T. D. (2002). *The psychology of prejudice.* Boston: Allyn & Bacon.

Neville, H. A., Worthington, R. L., & Spanierman, L. B. (2001). Race, power and multicultural counseling psychology. In J. G. Ponterotto, J. M. Casas, & C. M. Alexander (Eds.), *Handbook of multicultural counseling* (2nd ed., pp. 257–288). Thousand Oaks, CA: Sage.

Plous, S. (2003). The psychology of prejudice, stereotyping, and discrimination: An overview. In S. Plous (Ed.), *Understanding prejudice and discrimination* (pp. 3–48). New York: McGraw-Hill.

Sidanius, J., & Pratto, F. (1999). *Social dominance: An intergroup theory of social hierarchy and oppression.* Cambridge, UK: Cambridge University Press.

RACE

Race refers to a label that is commonly ascribed to individuals in certain societies based on their affiliation with a group of people. Members of racial groups typically share common characteristics in physical appearance or phenotype, but more significantly, they share a common stature within a given society. Although not widely regarded as such, many societies are hierarchically arranged by race, with the sociopolitically dominant group being composed of Whites and other racial groups variously (and frequently interchangeably) arrayed at lower rungs. Convention suggests that racial classification is a reflection of an objective scheme about biogenetic differences among humans (the presumption of "natural race"); however, such a conclusion is irrefutably false. According to the American Anthropological Association, race is a social construction whose origins can be traced to an ideology that associates observable physical qualities of people that serve as markers of race, with presumptions about the person's personality, morality, temperament, or "deservedness" of prized resources in a society. These resources include entry into political and judicial arenas, access to valued academic institutions, and opportunities to enter and be promoted in various occupational settings. That biogenetic differences are found in human groups appears to relate not to race, but rather to such factors as regional differences, group sensitivity to ultraviolet light, and resistance to disease.

Race is distinguished from ethnicity in that the former evolved out of a history of racial oppression. Determining which people constituted what racial group was influenced in part by ethnicity; yet the evolution of race appears to relate closely with the sociopolitical circumstances that surrounded the people in a society. Indeed, racial groups encompass people from different ethnicities. For example, in the United States, the White racial group category can include the multiple European ethnic groups that migrated to the country, just as the Asian/Pacific Islander American racial group includes people with ethnic origins in Cambodia, Japan, Korea, the Philippines, and the various inevitable admixtures. The other racial groups that have been constructed in the United States are African or Black American, Hispanic or Latino/a American, and Native/Alaskan/Aleutian American. People from historically marginalized racial groups can form pan-ethnic (or pan-tribal) allegiances because of the oppression they have endured. People who are visibly descended from ethnic groups often come to associate themselves as White people and, as such, become associated with the benefactor of racial entitlements in that society.

Race as a phenomenon is linked to European conquest that stems from thousands of years ago, but it began to take on greater virulence about 400 years ago. It continues to influence people's worldviews through a process of socialization. According to Diane Hughes and her colleagues, racial socialization occurs not only from direct teachings about issues of race that are conveyed by parents to children, but also through media, formal education, discourse that is considered acceptable according to societal norms, and politically resistant efforts, as in the establishment of learning settings that promote racial awareness and understanding. Over time, ideas can shift about who constitutes what race, as in far-gone delineations of

Africans that included distinguishing those of "mixed" race (labeled mulattoes or octoroons) from those with more African appearance in skin color, nose shape, and texture of hair.

As an illustration of the questions regarding the suggestion that determinations of race are objective, *hypodescent* is a practice that originated in the earlier years of racial formation in the United States and is characterized by the automatic assignment of the children of racially different couples to a less privileged group. Another illustration of race as a social construction is the experience of a person being designated one racial group in one setting and another in another setting. Persons of mixed Black–White parentage with discernible African features most likely would be classified as Black or biracial in the United States but potentially as White in some Caribbean countries.

A more elaborate history of the origins of race follows.

Historical Context

Shared phenotypic qualities have historically been the basis for a distinction between racial groups, and those in power have used race as a justification to identify some groups as inferior and thus to justify their mistreatment of such groups. What developed in this construction of race was an ideology of differential human worth that could be linked to observable phenotypic features. Several scholars, including J. L. Graves, presented documented evidence of how White scientists attempted to prove such a connection using an assortment of "scientific" measures and tests. Certain intrinsic qualities, such as intellectual abilities, moral fiber, aesthetic tastes, personalities, and physical abilities were "proven" to be associated with racial group membership. Positive human qualities were associated with Europeans, who labeled themselves as racially White, whereas various non-White populations throughout the world were considered to possess negative qualities.

Notably, scholars describe the emergence of a new identity among Whites in North America that paralleled the evolving construction of race. Many Whites saw themselves as having superiority in worth and being the deserving heirs of the territories inhabited by non-Whites. They viewed the colonized and exploited as inferior and deserving of their fate. In the United States, an ideology of race became reproduced over time, catalyzed by forces such as shifts in the nation's demography—shifts that resulted not only from increases in the population of enslaved Africans and immigrants but also from factors such as the preponderance of "mixed" racial parentages, fluctuations in the economy that were linked intricately to racial and ethnic competition in the labor force, and legal issues surrounding definitions of who constituted what race.

Also developing over time were responses to racial oppression by non-Whites. Depending on the extent of violence or, threat of violence, non-White racial groups often built alliances across ethnicities to form kinships, or, rather, networks of support and endurance. Yet another response by many oppressed racial groups was to align themselves with their White oppressors to decrease the severity of their conditions. As history has shown repeatedly that violence can breed further violence, we know from documented accounts that multiple conflicts have existed between racial groups, for example, between non-Whites and Whites during uprisings for liberation, and among similarly marginalized racial groups, as in Black cowboys' participation in Native American massacres. The spawning of divisions within racial groups can be attributed in part to racial oppression, as well as to the confluence of other forces that pertain to unfair systems of stratification, like class exploitation and sexism.

From History to Contemporary Contexts

Racism is perpetuated when people are unable to resolve the dehumanization that underlies its existence. A crucial step in this resolution is the need for a wider acknowledgment of its existence and the understanding of the varied meanings that people attach to race. Evidence shows that people of all walks of life are hampered by the erroneous belief that racial groupings can be associated reliably with biogenetic variation or other differences in traits presumed to be immutable. For counseling professionals, it is especially troubling that behavioral scientists seemingly carry this belief when they examine racial issues. A base of knowledge that could inform mental health practitioners about the relevance of race to psychological functioning is compromised by a preponderance of research studies in which self-identified race is used to speculate about research outcomes. A more direct approach would be to investigate the meaning that people ascribe to race as related to these outcomes. J. E. Helms, M. Jerrigan, and M. Mascher recommend methodological strategies for studying race that can best inform mental health practice.

In the absence of forceful efforts to abrupt societal racism, there is the continued threat that racism's reach will extend to various parts of the world. C. E. Thompson, J. A. Annan, S. S. Auma-Okumu, and A. Qureshi contend that the spread of racist ideology has had an impact on *all* episodes of genocide and ethnic cleansing in the past century and in current-day Sudan. The American Anthropological Association links the adoption of an ideology of race to the extermination of 11 million "inferior" people in Nazi Germany.

Although some propose that an obliteration of "race" as a human label is necessary to this goal of the elimination of racism, most scholars seem to agree that this charge can be viewed as a manifestation of *color-blindness,* that is, the desire to ignore race for the expressed purpose of seeing people "merely as people." The problem with color-blindness ideology is that it assumes that racism can be tackled easily by an insistence that the person is not noticing something that probably, for most people, is impossible *not* to notice. In other words, people who uphold an ideology of color-blindness assume that the perceptual erasure of race is possible; yet recent studies by J. Dovidio and his colleagues show that racial cues often spark implicit biases in Whites that contradict their nonracist, verbal messages. An erasure of labels, though a laudable aspiration in view of their association with a loathsome past, would also detract from non-Whites' pride in the resiliency of their groups. Moreover, because racism is a construction that is multiply layered and given to imperceptibility, resolving its pathological manifestations would require systemic efforts and the engagement of the varied racial groups that comprise the society. Learning to acknowledge rather than deny the experiences of different racial groups can be seen as a healthy start to these strategies.

Relevant to the discussion on ways to resolve problems over, and confusions about, race is the proliferation of labels that better reflect the amalgamation of people across races and regions of the world. Terms like *Afro-Cuban, biracial* or *multiracial, Black-Indian,* and so forth, challenge ideas about the more commonly used racial categories that were indicated earlier. These labels, which are internally defined as opposed to other racial labels that were externally imposed, help identify people's multiple heritages. They therefore complicate the notion of racial classification and could very well urge people to consider the taken-for-granted nature of established racial labels. With improved lines of research and further study on race and racism, science and theory can help better determine the extent to which the varied uses of these labels—whether for the purpose of asserting one's desire to break free of racial labels, denoting one's loyalty to certain or varied family members, building alliances with similarly labeled people, or a combination of these and/or other factors—can operate to extinguish racial pathologies.

Implications for Counseling

In promoting positive mental health, counselors and therapists conduct assessments of individuals, groups, and families to determine client needs and strengths and the obstacles that hinder such promotion. Incorporating an understanding of race, as well as an understanding of its meaning to the client, can be helpful to the counseling process and outcome. How does this occur with so little research to guide professionals? Racial identity theory is a conceptualization in which the cognitive and affective processes associated with people's response to racism are viewed as patterned. Whites and people of color experience these patterns differently, yet they share some commonalities: People develop racial identity as they are increasingly exposed to racial stimuli, and when their abilities to cope with these stimuli are depleted, particularly with exposure to the contradictions in reality and their proneness to moral reasoning, they then are compelled to seek out newer, more complex ways to cope. Racial identity theory is a valuable template for thinking about and working through issues of race and racism in counseling. The theory can be used as a means to make assessments about a client, about the counselor-self relative to his or her understanding of racial issues in counseling, and as a road map for facilitating advanced development. Advanced racial identity development refers to characteristics about a client's way of behaving and viewing the world that include risk-taking behaviors (to move the person to more enlightened perspectives about racism and other forms of oppression) and greater complexity in thinking about others *and* the self. Racial identity theory does not concern itself with racial labels, but it may elicit information about labels to achieve a rich understanding of how the individual perceives the self and others within the racism-hierarchical scheme.

There are many cues to determine how or if matters of race are relevant to counseling. C. E. Thompson and R. T. Carter recommend that practitioners help create a climate in which the client can assume that these matters are viewed as permissible in counseling and, therefore, *can* be relevant to counseling. Such deliberate engineering is important in view of the suppression that surrounds racial discourse. One way to create this climate is to briefly point out the racial designation the client indicated on an intake form, or simply ask him or her directly.

As noted earlier, racial socialization refers to a process of learning about racial issues. Racial identity theory more specifically examines how people come to view their worth relative to others in racialized societies. These appraisals of worth are influenced by stereotypes about racial groups, such as the stereotype of lazy Latinos/as or low-intelligent Black people. Stereotypes reduce the complexity of humans by conveying ideas about individuals based on their visible group affiliation. Stereotypes contain kernels of truth about people, yet the propensity of societal institutions to downplay and distort historical conditions of oppression, as well as continued experiences of racial discrimination in various spheres of public life, helps crystallize notions about "the way people are." It is essential that the counselor be aware of the cognitive and affective processes that can distort his or her view about people and, especially, the view of certain groups as possessing less worth than others.

In trying to glean the meaning that clients make about race, counselors need to develop skills in inquiring about a topic that is considered fairly off-limits in polite society. Complicating matters, it is not uncommon for some people to express an indifference or rejection to race labeling, as in "I don't refer to myself racially," and showing some annoyance in the counselor raising issues of race during these interactions. White clients may express this racelessness as a means to express their indifference to race or deflect any embarrassment they might have about their affiliation with other Whites. Consistent with racial identity theory, responses to how clients react to racial cues will differ according to their understanding and degree of comfort with these stimuli.

The following two scenarios are presented to offer some glimpse of some of the meanings that people can ascribe to racism, notably the question: "What is your racial group?" On a preemptive note: How clients respond to racial stimuli offers useful information about the client's worldview; however, it would be unwise to conclude anything based on very brief responses. Determining the relevance of race of a particular client requires systematic exploration. As illustrated below, racial discourse characterized by the counselor's attempts to determine how race and racism have been incorporated into a client's worldview also reveals knowledge of how the person currently understands him- or herself in general, and as a person socialized in a structurally unequal and unfair world. As people talk about racial matters, a skillful assessment can help glean positive and negative ideas about the self. Constructions of race are closely linked to constructions of others; consequently, when clients in therapy share their feelings of fragility and low self-worth, the counselor potentially has clues about how their clients might relate or see others by comparison. People who need to be seen as distinct from a different group may have carved out ideas about who they want to be affiliated with as well as which group they do not want to be affiliated with.

In the first illustration is a person whose race is ambiguous and who is asked by the counselor, "Racially, how do you identify yourself?" With the response "biracial," the counselor notices that the client exhibits discomfort. These observations are marked by the client's rapid eye-blinking and twists of her body. The counselor may take these nonverbal cues as indications of the client's annoyance at being asked the question. For people who appear racially ambiguous, there is some wariness to such questions because of the sense that inquirers seem to *need* to know to settle their own intolerance for the ambiguity. The skilled therapist should take note of the detected physical reactions, perhaps even explain that this is a question he asks all of his clients and that he suspects that she is bothered by it because she's been asked many times and perhaps by those for whom the intent is not entirely known but suspected. As the client listens, she may appear to become more relaxed as she infers that the counselor's desire to know her race is different from the others she has encountered. Over time, the client explains that her parents, one of whom is Black and the other White, raised her in a loving home in which matters of racism were addressed openly. Her family also honored their different racial and ethnic heritages—Irish, African, Chinese, and Polish—and made special efforts to celebrate the rich heritage of her African ancestors because these ancestors, and others descended from them, are seen as the "undesirables" of American society. The counselor learns, still over the course of some time, that opportunities to interact with Black people have always been and continue to be plentiful, as with people from other backgrounds. As a result of her family, the client recognizes that deliberate efforts have to be made to relinquish negative ideas about her heritage as a marginalized member of society and that getting to know people from a range of backgrounds in ways that honor them as people is something that she constantly strives for, not only because of race but also because of how she has to come to know the host of forces that create divisions among humans in society.

Based on this information and the evolving relationship, the counselor is able to learn some important information about the client's psychological makeup. He learns that there is open communication in the family about a very difficult subject as well as deliberate efforts to go about their lives that counter mainstream ideals. He also learns that the person exudes confidence in a manner that is unapologetic. Her relationship with diverse groups of people suggests that she can traverse many situations socially and that she seeks rather than avoids close relationships with people without the barrier of stereotyping or skillful avoidance accompanied by deft justifications. What one can surmise from this client is that she functions in psychologically healthy ways in many areas of her life. With someone so advanced in racial identity, Helms noted, the race of the counselor may not matter so much as when the client's development is less advanced.

Consider this next example of a client, who appears White, and when asked about his race, quickly responds "Caucasian," then proceeds to shifting the topic to the "real" issue at hand. He may harbor some questions about why the question was even asked but is so smooth with his indifference to race that the slightly annoyed mood barely registers. As sessions proceed, he makes certain subtle yet disjointed remarks about his admiration of Native American people whom he believes "have suffered *so* much." He may even start dropping hints of his new relationships with Native Americans. His therapist is Native American, which is discerned by name, appearance, and dress in a town with a critical mass of Native Americans. The stimulus of race (i.e., the perceived race of the therapist) invokes the notion not only of difference but also of the disparities that exist between Whites and Native Americans within a society in terms of resources, living conditions, and so forth. Race also signals different experiences between groups, whereby non-Whites face everyday racism, exoticism, and discrimination, while Whites encounter privilege, often unrecognized. The client's reference to "Caucasian" signals perhaps the notion that this term sounds official and less embarrassing than "White." What the counselor learns, at least in a tentative manner, is that the client is open to making inroads with people whom he may have formerly been indifferent to or whom he has relegated as inferior to him. But those overtures are indirect and suggestive of a lack of maturity in racial identity development. He also may have a lack of meaningful social supports to make these connections more constructive. The client may be impelled to unresolved problems related to race because he is experiencing a positive relationship with his counselor and would like the counselor to approve of him. A more authentic relationship would yield not only more mature strategies for connecting with the counselor but also an ability of the client to discover a more genuine interest in Native American people. Stated another way, the client may be restricted to viewing the therapist and other Native American people as objects that are important in helping him diminish feelings of self-worth. In promoting psychological health, the counselor would need to better assess the extent to which the client's objectification serves to feed a fictitious image of himself as good and help replace these strategies with those that reflect more genuine engagement in people in general.

Both illustrations reveal how racism establishes a *yoked* existence among individuals in society. In contrast to the interdependence that exists in creating functioning societies, racism and other unfair systems of stratification impose a twisted interdependence that thwarts the realization of these societies. According to Thompson and her colleagues, the yoke is experienced when people in racialized societies collude in belief systems about human superiority. Because of the lack of "working through" the generations-long challenges inherent in racial oppression, people invoke the yoke when they come to believe that human worth is achieved in ascending these constructed hierarchies. In some societies like Brazil, racial ascendancy can be characterized by the marriage of non-Whites to Whites or by the acquisition of wealth. Racial ascendancy can be tied to social class, ethnicity, gender, and skin color in many societies. But importantly, a striving for ascension through constructed hierarchies does little to dismantle the hierarchies. The individual ultimately responds in collusion with the distortions about humankind, thus reaffirming bias and distancing.

To break from the construction, people must recognize the need for equity, integrity, and other goals that would foster the creation of human family across stratified groups.

Counselors need to learn to disengage from the yoke and its varied proliferations. To do this, it is recommended that therapists gain an understanding of how race is dramatized locally and nationally and learn to work through it in their own lives and in the counseling process. Furthermore, and because racism is but one form of oppression in an unfortunately lengthy list of oppressive forces, counselors need to learn about the other forces that have an impact on people in conjunction with one another. In view of these forces, the focus of counseling and treatment plans should be not only to remove symptoms but also to foster more liberating worldviews in clients.

Chalmer E. Thompson

See also African Americans (v3); Alaska Natives (v3); American Indians (v3); Asian Americans (v3); Biracial (v3); Black Racial Identity Development (v3); Color-Blind Racial Ideology (v3); Critical Race Theory (v3); Demographics, United States (v3); Diversity (v3); Ethnic Identity (v3); Ethnicity (v3); Latinos (v3); Multiracial Families (v3); Racial Identity (v3); Racism (v3); Reversed Racism (v3); Visible Racial/Ethnic Groups (v3); White Racial Identity Development (v3)

Further Readings

American Anthropological Association. (1998). American Anthropological Association statement on "race." *American Anthropologist, 100,* 3. Retrieved from http://www.aaanet.org/stmts/racepp.htm

Dovidio, J. F., Gaertner, S. L., Kawakami, K., & Hodson, G. (2002). Why can't we just get along? Interpersonal biases and interracial distrust. *Cultural Diversity & Ethnic Minority Psychology, 8,* 88–102.

Graves, J. L., Jr. (2001). *The emperor's new clothes: Biological theories of race at the millennium.* New Brunswick, NJ: Rutgers University Press.

Haney Lopez, I. F. (1996). *White by law: The legal construction of race.* New York: New York University Press.

Helms, J. E. (1995). An update of Helms's White and people of color racial identity models. In J. Ponterotto, J. M. Casas, L. A. Suzuki, & C. M. Alexander (Eds.), *Handbook of multicultural counseling* (pp. 181–198). Thousand Oaks, CA: Sage.

Helms, J. E., Jerrigan, M., & Mascher, J. (2005). The meaning of race in psychology and how to change it: A methodological perspective. *American Psychologist, 60,* 27–36.

Hughes, D., Rodriguez, J., Smith, E. P., Johnson, D. J., Stevenson, H. C., & Spicer, P. (2006). Parents' ethnic-racial socialization practices: A review of research and directions for future study. *Developmental Psychology, 42,* 747–770.

Miville, M. L. (2005). Psychological functioning and identity development of biracial people: A review of current theory and research. In R. T. Carter (Ed.), *Handbook of racial-cultural psychology and counseling: Theory and research* (Vol. 1, pp. 295–319). Hoboken, NJ: Wiley.

Root, M. P. P. (2001). Negotiating the margins. In J. G. Ponterotto, J. M. Casas, L. A. Suzuki, & C. M. Alexander (Eds.), *Handbook of multicultural counseling* (2nd ed., pp. 113–121). Thousand Oaks, CA: Sage.

Smedley, A. (1993). *Race in North America: Origin and evolution of a world view.* Boulder, CO: Westview Press.

Thompson, C. E., Annan, J. A., Auma-Okumu, S. S., & Qureshi, A. (in press). Building cultures of peace in postcolonial Africa: A case in point. In C. E. Thompson & R. T. Carter (Eds.), *Racial identity theory: Applications to individual, group, and organizational interventions* (2nd ed.). Mahwah, NJ: Lawrence Erlbaum.

Thompson, C. E., & Carter, R. T. (1997). *Racial identity theory: Applications to individual, group, and organizational interventions.* Mahwah, NJ: Lawrence Erlbaum.

Thompson, C. E., & Neville, N. A. (1999). Racism, mental health, and mental health practice. *The Counseling Psychologist, 27,* 155–223.

Trimble, J. E. (2005). An inquiry into the measurement of ethnic and racial identity. In R. T. Carter (Ed.), *Handbook of racial-cultural psychology and counseling: Theory and research* (Vol. 1, pp. 320–359). Hoboken, NJ: Wiley.

Racial Identity

Racial identity is a dynamic sociopolitical construction and assists in the understanding of within-group differences of people of different races. Racial identity development is relevant to all racial groups and incorporates perspectives of a person's view of self with regard to his or her own racial group and other racial groups. Racial identity is an important construct because it is a more meaningful concept, and likely a better predictor of behavior, than racial group membership alone. In addition, the experiences of people of color are not homogeneous and have resulted in different meanings and attributions about being a part of a specific racial group.

Definition of Racial Identity

A number of theorists and researchers have attempted to define racial identity. Janet E. Helms described the construct as a sense of collective identity that is based on a perceived common heritage with a racial group. Helms integrated perceptions of self and others in her definition of racial identity. Robert T. Carter stated that racial identity development is a lifelong process that involves how a person interprets messages about racial groups. Additionally, racial identity has been described as the significance and meaning of race in one's life.

Independent researchers have identified various aspects of racial identity, but no one has combined them to form one single definition of the term incorporating a developmental perspective, perspectives of both dominant and minority groups, and qualitative meaning of group membership. In combination, the racial identity literature has shown that racial identity is a multifaceted construct that refers to (a) the qualitative meaning one ascribes to one's own racial group, (b) meaning attributed to other racial groups, (c) sense of group identification with one's own racial group, (d) salience of race in defining one's self-concept, and (e) perspectives regarding race over time.

Ethnic Identity Versus Racial Identity

To understand the distinctions between racial identity and ethnic identity, it is important to distinguish the concepts of race and ethnicity. In the United States, *race* is a social construct that refers to factors such as skin color and physical features, while ethnicity refers to one's national or religious origin. *Racial identity* is comprehensively defined as the qualitative meaning and salience one ascribes to one's own and other racial groups, whereas *ethnic identity* is a dynamic construct that refers to one's sense of self as a member of an ethnic group. At their core, both constructs reflect an individual's sense of self as a member of a group; however, racial identity integrates the impact of race and related factors, while ethnic identity is focused on ethnic and cultural factors. Some authors suggest that ethnic identity development is an individual's movement toward a more conscious identification with his or her own cultural values, behaviors, beliefs, and traditions, whereas others note that theories of racial identity tap into racial psychological development rather than ethnic development.

History of Racial Identity Models

African American/Black Racial Identity

The concept of racial identity in the psychological literature has existed since the 1970s and was developed in response to the civil rights movement. The first models of racial identity were focused on Black American racial identity. For example, Clemmont Eyvind Vontress proposed that there were different personality types for Black Americans: Colored, Negro, and Black. This theory emphasized societal stereotypes and suggested that the personalities of these individuals were static. William E. Cross, Jr.'s Nigrescence theory was another early Black racial identity theory. The most recent version of this theory incorporates six different issues, including the structure of Black self-concept (i.e., the integration of aspects of personal and reference group orientation), the variety of Black identities, identity socialization from infancy to early adulthood, adult resocialization experiences, continued identity development and enrichment across the life span, and identity functions that incorporate the variety of Black identities that are displayed within and across situations. These and other stage models (e.g., Dizzard, 1971; Gibbs, 1974; Jackson, 1975; Milliones, 1980; Thomas, 1970; Toldson and Pasteur, 1975) suggest that individuals progress from holding negative views of themselves based on internalized racism to having a more positive view of their own and other racial groups.

White Racial Identity

White racial identity models have been proposed by a number of researchers. Rita Hardiman proposed a five-stage developmental model (no social consciousness, acceptance, resistance, redefinition, and internalization) of racial identity development for Whites born in America. Helms also described different components of White racial identity, including Phase I (abandonment of a racist identity: contact, disintegration, and reintegration) and Phase II (establishment of a nonracist White identity: pseudo-independence, immersion/emersion, and autonomy). In the contact status, people are satisfied with the racial status quo, are unaware of continuing subtle racism, and believe that everyone has an equal chance of success. In the disintegration status, the White person may become conflicted over unresolvable racial moral dilemmas and obliviousness about the impact of race begins to break down. In the reintegration status, the White person might regress to basic beliefs about White superiority and minority inferiority; there may be an idealization of the White European American group and denigration of other minority groups in this status. In the pseudo-independence status, a person is propelled into this status by a painful or insightful encounter that jars him or her from the reintegration status and may lead him or her to identify with the plight of persons of color. There is an intellectual understanding of racial issues in this status. In the immersion/emersion status, the White person continues a personal exploration of him- or herself as a racial being, and questions focus on the meaning of Whiteness; personal meaning of racism is explored. In the autonomy status, there is an increased awareness of one's own Whiteness and reduced feelings of guilt. There is also an acceptance of one's role in perpetuating racism and a renewed determination to abandon White entitlement.

Helms noted that ego status (differentiated by a person's understanding of the concept of race) has been integrated into the concept of racial identity because the use of stages may not adequately describe attitudes, beliefs, and emotions that are exhibited from more than one stage. In addition, *stage* is a static term, and racial identity theory and measurement do not support the idea that stages are mutually exclusive or temporally stable. It has been noted that racial identity attitudes change and develop based on environmental and temporal influences, and change in identity does not necessarily imply a developmental process. In addition, stage models have been critiqued, and alternative conceptualizations such as White racial consciousness have been proposed.

General Racial Identity

Models of racial identity have been applied to people of color in general in the United States. One example is Donald R. Atkinson, George Morten, and Derald Wing Sue's racial/cultural identity development model for people of color. This model was first introduced as the minority identity development model and was expanded in later years. In this model, people of color are posited to progress through different stages, including conformity, dissonance, resistance and immersion, introspection, and integrative awareness. Each of these stages takes into account a person's attitudes toward self, others of the same and different racial groups, and the dominant racial group. Similar to the Helms's model, in the conformity stage, people of color depend on White society for definition and approval. In the dissonance stage, there may be feelings of confusion and conflict about the meaning of one's race. The person of color may encounter information or experiences that are inconsistent with culturally held beliefs and attitudes. In the resistance and immersion phase, the person of color may endorse minority-held views completely and reject dominant values. In the introspection phase, the person of color may experience feelings of discontent and discomfort with previously held rigid group views. In the integrative awareness stage, people of color develop an inner sense of security and can own and appreciate unique aspects of their own group as well as the dominant group.

Extending Helms's model, Julie R. Ancis and Nicholas Ladany's heuristic model of nonoppressive interpersonal development can be applied to a variety of demographic variables (e.g., gender, sexual orientation, socioeconomic status), including race, for which an individual is either in a position of privilege (socially privileged group [SPG]) or oppressed (socially oppressed group [SOG]). In this model of means of interpersonal functioning there are four stages. The first stage, adaptation, is reflective of complacency and conformity regarding a socially oppressive environment for both SOG and SPG members. In the second stage, incongruence, there is some dissonance or internal conflict about oppression. This stage is followed by the exploration stage in which members of SOG and SPG evaluate and explore the meaning of membership to their respective group. The last stage, integration, includes awareness of oppressive environments and situations, multicultural integrity, and commitment to advocacy for oppressed groups. This model is unique in that stages of development can be applied to both members of privileged and oppressed groups. Similar to other models of identity development, people may go through different phases in specific situations or with respect to certain demographic characteristics.

Interactional models of racial identity suggest that one's level of racial identity development impacts one's interactions with others. These models have been applied to counseling and supervision to compare the racial identity development of clients to that of their counselors, as well as trainees compared to their supervisors. For example, in parallel-high relationships, both individuals are in later stages or statuses (i.e., Phase II) of identity development. In parallel-low relationships, both individuals have lower levels of identity development (i.e., Phase I). Progressive relationships involve either the supervisor or counselor being in Phase II, while in regressive relationships they are both in Phase I. The racial identity level of supervisors and counselors can impact the course and depth of discussions of racial issues, the formation of an authentic working relationship, and feelings of cultural trust and rapport in counseling or supervision.

Measurement and Research

African American/Black Racial Identity

Racial identity has been one of the most heavily researched areas in the psychological experiences of African Americans. One of the most widely used measures of Black racial identity is the Black Racial Identity Attitudes Scale (RIAS-B) from Thomas A. Parham and Helms. The original RIAS (Short Form A) is a 30-item self-report measure designed to assess four of the five stages of racial identity proposed by Cross's Nigrescence model: pre-encounter, encounter, immersion/emersion, and internalization. The fifth stage, internalization/commitment, was not included in the RIAS because it was conceptualized as a style of behaving with respect to identity issues that might be present in other stages.

RIAS items were developed to measure stages of Black awareness development. The RIAS was revised into two forms: Short Form B, which also consists of 30 items, and the RIAS-Long Form, which was developed to increase the subscales' reliabilities and contains 20 additional items. RIAS items are rated on a 5-point Likert scale ranging from 1 (*strongly disagree*) to 5 (*strongly agree*). Item scores on each subscale are averaged, with higher scores indicating the presence of that type of racial identity attitude.

The RIAS has been shown to be a reliable scale overall, meaning that it measures the construct of racial identity in a consistent, stable, and uniform manner over repeated measurements. However, some researchers have found low reliabilities for the subscales of the various versions of the RIAS, especially the Encounter subscale. In addition, given the low test–retest reliability estimates for the subscales, some researchers have concluded that the attitudes measured by the RIAS-B should be considered state rather than stable trait variables. Evidence shows that the RIAS is a valid measure of the construct of racial identity because the relationships between the subscale scores and measures of other related constructs are consistent with racial identity theory.

Research using the various forms of the RIAS is extensive. It has been used to study the relationship between racial identity and other constructs, such as psychological distress and self-esteem, Minnesota Multiphasic Personality Inventory-2 scores, counselor demographic preference, and career choices. Strengths of this measure include its frequent use in published literature, the availability of both short and long forms, and strong support for its construct validity. However, the low reliability coefficients found by several authors suggest the measure requires additional psychometric investigation and improvements. Also, the measure has not been significantly updated since Cross's was revised and is therefore not consistent with the changes to the theory.

The Cross Racial Identity Scale (CRIS; Vandiver et al., 2001) was designed to measure the theoretical constructs proposed in the updated version of the Nigrescence theory. The CRIS was developed to measure six of the seven identity clusters described in the revised theory: assimilation and anti-Black (pre-encounter), intense Black involvement and anti-White (immersion/emersion), Black nationalist and multiculturalist (encounter). The CRIS is a 40-item scale that uses a 7-point Likert scale ranging from 1 (*strongly disagree*) to 7 (*strongly agree*). A pool of 250 items was developed by the authors and later reduced to 126 items which were evaluated by expert judges knowledgeable about the revised Nigrescence theory. Validity of the measure has been demonstrated through its relationships with other measures of Black racial identity and measures of self-esteem and social desirability. Statistical analysis indicates that the CRIS can be used to measure either the six individual identity clusters in the model or two general stages that are conceptualized as pre-discovery and discovery.

The CRIS has not been utilized extensively in published literature beyond studies of its psychometric properties. In one study, Afrocentric cultural values and a positive ethnic identity were found to be negatively related to a racialized identity, as measured by the Immersion-Emersion Anti-White subscale of the

CRIS. In another study it was found that racial identity attitudes were related to internalized racism. While the evidence supporting the CRIS is strong thus far, additional research is needed to further investigate its contribution to racial identity literature.

Robert M. Sellers, Stephanie A. Rowley, and colleagues developed the Multidimensional Inventory of Black Identity (MIBI; Sellers et al., 1998) to operationalize the concepts proposed in their multidimensional model of racial identity. Items were developed by combining items from previous scales on African American racial identity, ethnic identity, and social identity with original items created by the authors. The MIBI contains 56 items rated on a 7-point Likert scale ranging from 1 (*strongly disagree*) to 7 (*strongly agree*). It comprises three scales (Centrality, Ideology, and Regard), as well as subscales (i.e., Nationalist, Assimilation, Minority, Humanist, Private Regard, and Public Regard). Studies have indicated that the MIBI is an adequately reliable, valid measure of three distinct factors: centrality, ideology, and regard.

The MIBI has been used to investigate the relationship between racial identity and perceived discrimination and distress, academic performance, and personal self-esteem. Strengths of the MIBI include its potential ability to capture the multidimensional aspects of African American racial identity and be used as a complement to other stage-based measures. Additional research is needed to further validate this instrument and explore its contribution to racial identity literature.

White Racial Identity

Several researchers have attempted to operationalize and measure White racial identity. Helms and Carter developed the White Racial Identity Attitude Scale (WRIAS), a 50-item inventory that includes five subscales designed to measure the extent to which a person uses the race-related schemas (i.e., Contact, Disintegration, Reintegration, Pseudo-Independence, and Autonomy) through which one interprets racial cues. Items were developed based on Helms's model of White racial identity development and are assessed on a 5-point Likert scale ranging from 1 (*strongly disagree*) to 5 (*strongly agree*). Studies of the WRIAS have suggested it is adequately reliable, while the relationship of its subscales to measures of personality constructs has indicated that it is a valid measure of White racial identity.

The WRIAS has been used extensively in research on White identity. White identity has been found to be related to cultural values, preference for counselor race, self-reported multicultural counseling competencies, self-actualization, and cross-cultural education. Several researchers have criticized the validity and reliability of the WRIAS; others have argued that it does not measure the five distinct aspects of racial identity it was designed to measure. To address the latter issue, some researchers have used the WRIAS to measure two theoretically proposed *phases* of racial identity (i.e., Phase I and Phase II) instead of five *stages*.

Sandra Choney and John Behrens developed the Oklahoma Racial Attitude Scale-Preliminary Form to measure the types of racial attitudes White individuals hold regarding their own and other racial groups. White racial consciousness has been defined as the characteristic attitudes regarding the salience of being White and the implications of this on interactions with those from other racial groups. The 50-item scale measures whether White people have achieved White racial consciousness and includes four basic *achieved* attitudes (dominative, conflictive, integrative, and reactive) and three *unachieved* attitudes (avoidant, dissonant, and dependent). Items were developed to measure the attitudes proposed in their model and are rated on a 5-point Likert scale with responses ranging from 1 (*strongly disagree*) to 5 (*strongly agree*). Scores that differ the most from the mean indicate which type of racial attitude best characterizes the individual's outlook.

N. Kenneth LaFleur, Wayne Rowe, and Mark M. Leach developed the 35-item revised Oklahoma Racial Attitudes Scale (ORAS) following initial studies of its reliability and validity and theory revisions. Investigations of the measure have suggested that the items measure their predicted factors and support the measure's reliability. Although limited, published research using the measure has found White racial consciousness to be predictive of racial prejudice. While this measure has promise as a tool to assess White racial identity, it requires additional psychometric and empirical investigation.

People of Color Racial Identity

Black and White racial identity attitudes have been assessed more often in research than the racial identity attitudes of other racial groups. While some researchers have suggested that ethnic or cultural identity may be more salient than racial identity for people of color, others argue that measures of racial identity are appropriate for people of color. In an attempt to operationalize the statuses described in her people of color racial identity model, Helms created the People of Color Racial Identity Attitudes Scale (POCRIAS). The POCRIAS contains 50 items with four subscales measuring the conformity, dissonance, immersion/emersion, and internalization/integrative awareness statuses. Items are measured on a Likert scale ranging from 1 (*strongly agree*) to 5 (*strongly disagree*), with higher scores on each subscale indicating greater levels of that racial identity attitude. Studies have supported the reliability of the measure, although published empirical support for its validity is limited. Therefore, while one of its strengths is that it is one of the only scales available to assess the racial identity of people of color in addition to that of African Americans, this measure is limited by its lack of empirical support and utilization in published literature. The limited psychometric support for this measure has led some researchers to use African American racial identity measures (e.g., the RIAS) to examine the racial identity of other individuals of color.

Although limited, empirical research on racial identity for racial groups other than White and Black individuals has been conducted. For example, Asian American racial identity has been found to be related to gender role conflict and psychological symptoms, gender role conflict and male norm roles, psychosocial development, and levels of racial adjustment. For Latinos/as, racial identity has been found to be related to gender role conflict and psychological symptoms, ego identity, and psychosocial development. Psychometric research on the POCRIAS with Native Americans suggests it is appropriate for investigating the racial identity attitudes of this group. While one study found that Native Americans endorse high internalization identity attitudes, additional research is needed on the racial identity of this population.

Future Directions

Racial identity is one of the most extensively investigated constructs in counseling psychology and has important implications for research and practice. With the addition of recent theories and measures, racial identity is likely to continue to be widely studied. One of the largest gaps in the racial identity literature is the application of the construct to individuals of color other than African Americans. Additional research on the measurement of racial identity is needed for these groups, as well as for biracial and multiracial individuals. More research is also needed on the psychometric properties of the measures used to operationalize racial identity. Further, practical applications of racial identity theory need to be investigated more fully.

Anju Kaduvettoor, Aimee-Nicole Adams, and Nicholas Ladany

See also Black Racial Identity Development (v3); Cross, William E., Jr. (v3); Ethnic Identity (v3); Ethnicity (v3); Helms, Janet E. (v3); Identity (v3); Identity Development (v3); Multicultural Counseling Competence (v3); Sue, Derald Wing: Contributions to Multicultural Psychology and Counseling (v3); Visible Racial/Ethnic Groups (v3); White Americans (v3); White Racial Identity Development (v3)

Further Readings

Ancis, J. R., & Ladany, N. (2001). A multicultural framework for counselor supervision. In L. J. Bradley & N. Ladany (Eds.), *Counselor supervision: Principles, process, and practice* (3rd ed., pp. 63–90). New York: Brunner-Routledge.

Atkinson, D. R., Morten, G., & Sue, D. W. (1998). *Counseling American minorities: A cross-cultural perspective* (5th ed.). Dubuque, IA: William C. Brown.

Carter, R. T. (1995). *The influence of race and racial identity in psychotherapy: Toward a racially inclusive model.* Oxford, UK: Wiley.

Cross, W. E., Jr., & Vandiver, B. J. (2001). Nigrescence theory: Current status and challenges for the future. *Journal of Multicultural Counseling and Development, 29*, 201–213.

Hardiman, R. (1994). White racial identity development in the United States. In E. P. Salett & D. R. Koslow (Eds.), *Race, ethnicity and self: Identity in multicultural perspective* (pp. 117–140). Washington, DC: NMCI.

Helms, J. E. (1984). Toward a theoretical explanation of the effects of race on counseling: A Black and White model. *The Counseling Psychologist, 12*, 153–165.

Helms, J. E. (1995). An update of Helms's White and people of color racial identity models. In J. G. Ponterotto, M. J. Casas, L. A. Suzuki, & C. M. Alexander (Eds.), *Handbook of multicultural counseling* (pp. 181–198). Thousand Oaks, CA: Sage.

LaFleur, N. K., Rowe, W., & Leach, M. M. (2002). Reconceptualizing White racial consciousness. *Journal of Multicultural Counseling and Development, 30*, 148–152.

Parham, T. A., & Helms, J. E. (1981). The influence of Black students' racial identity attitudes on preferences for counselors' race. *Journal of Counseling Psychology, 28,* 250–257.

Ponterotto, J. G. (1988). Racial consciousness development among White counselor trainees: A stage model. *Journal of Multicultural Counseling and Development, 16,* 146–156.

Pope-Davis, D. B., Vandiver, B. J., & Stone, G. L. (1999). White racial identity attitude development: A psychometric examination of two instruments. *Journal of Counseling Psychology, 46,* 70–79.

Rowe, W., Bennett, S. K., & Atkinson, D. R. (1994). White racial identity models: A critique and alternative proposal. *The Counseling Psychologist, 22,* 129–146.

Sellers, R. M., Smith, M. A., Shelton, J. N., Rowley, S. A., & Chavous, T. M. (1998). Multidimensional model of racial identity: A reconceptualization of African American racial identity. *Personality and Social Psychology Review, 2,* 18–39.

Sue, D. W., & Sue, S. (2008). *Counseling the culturally diverse* (5th ed.). New York: Wiley.

Vandiver, B. J., Fhagen-Smith, P. E., Cokley, K. O., Cross, W. E., Jr., & Worrell, F. C. (2001). Cross's Nigrescence model: From theory to scale to theory. *Journal of Multicultural Counseling and Development, 29,* 174–200.

Racial Microaggressions

Racial microaggressions are subtle and commonplace exchanges or indignities (both conscious and unconscious) that somehow convey demeaning messages to people of color. These racial slights can be verbal, behavioral, or even environmental. The exchanges often are viewed by perpetrators as harmless and inoffensive, but racial microaggressions can be a cause of psychological distress and drain spiritual energy for people of color who experience them.

A taxonomy of racial microaggressions was proposed by Derald Wing Sue and his colleagues, and their taxonomy classified racial microaggressions into three forms: microassaults, microinsults, and microinvalidations. *Microassaults* are explicit and conscious derogatory racist epithets that are purposefully meant to hurt people of color. *Microinsults* and *microinvalidations* are the unconscious and unintentional demeaning slights made toward people of color. An example of a microinsult would be a White man telling a person of color who is interviewing for a job, "The person who is most qualified will get this job."

Historical Perspective

The term *microaggressions* was first introduced by Chester Pierce in 1970. According to Pierce's definition, microaggressions are interracial interactions that convey contempt, disregard, and/or ambivalence that often reflect racial slights toward people of color. They are subtle racial behaviors that act as reminders of the societally inferior racial status of people of color in the United States. Because racial microaggressions are so unpredictable and occur intermittently, they force people of color to react and remain vigilant to preserve their self-respect. In the late 1980s, Peggy C. Davis defined *racial microaggressions* as stunning automatic acts of disregard that come from unconscious attitudes of White superiority and reveal a verification of Black inferiority. Therefore, racial microaggressions have evolved over time to reflect subtle and unconscious forms of racism.

Contemporary Views of Racial Microaggressions

Implications for Counseling and Supervision

Existing research and literature today focus on different aspects of microaggressions, particularly the contexts in which they occur. Microaggressions not only occur in daily interracial interactions for people of color, but they also occur in counseling and supervision relationships.

In a therapeutic relationship, where therapists are in positions of power and clients are more likely to view their therapists in positions of authority, clients who experience racial microaggressions from their therapists are more likely to question themselves than their therapist. For example, if a client shares an experience that she or he perceived as racist and wanted to process this experience with her or his therapist, the therapist may respond by saying, "I think that you are being paranoid," thus completely invalidating the client's experience. Well-intentioned White therapists also may claim that they understand racial oppression completely in an attempt to identify with or make a connection with their clients of color. However, such an intervention could further demean clients' experiences of racism and invalidate their identification as a person of color who experiences unique racial oppression.

Racial microaggressions also have been found to occur in cross-racial supervisory relationships involving White supervisors and Black supervisees. For example, Black supervisees have reported that White supervisors have blamed clients of color for problems stemming from oppression, made stereotypic assumptions about these supervisees and clients of color, offered culturally insensitive treatment recommendations to these supervisees, and been reluctant to give performance feedback to them for fear of being viewed as racist. These experiences have been found to be detrimental to Black supervisees and, indirectly, to the clients they serve.

Implications for Counseling

Mental health practitioners must be aware of the detrimental effects that racial microaggressions have on people of color. The literature reveals that this experience of everyday racism for people of color has an effect on their intrapsychic structure. Racial microaggressions perpetuate and promote feelings of invisibility, unworthiness, and anguish among people of color. Because racial microaggressions can be so subtle, yet so powerful, people of color usually are left with feelings of disbelief about their occurrence and, in turn, question themselves as to what really happened in a microaggressive situation. It is imperative that counselors are sensitive to and aware of experiences of racial microaggressions when they are shared in a therapeutic context so that these experiences are not disregarded or invalidated through minimization.

Madonna G. Constantine and Cristina Dorazio

See also Bias (v3); Communication (v3); Constantine, Madonna G. (v3); Discrimination (v3); Discrimination and Oppression (v2); Oppression (v3); Prejudice (v3); Racism (v3); Stereotype (v3); Sue, Derald Wing: Contributions to Multicultural Psychology and Counseling (v3)

Further Readings

Constantine, M. G. (2007). Racial microaggressions against African American clients in cross-racial counseling relationships. *Journal of Counseling Psychology, 54,* 1–16.

Constantine, M. G., & Sue, D. W. (2007). Perceptions of racial microaggressions among Black supervisees in cross-racial dyads. *Journal of Counseling Psychology, 54,* 142–153.

Franklin, A. J., & Boyd-Franklin, N. (2000). Invisibility syndrome: A clinical model of the effects of racism on African-American males. *American Journal of Orthopsychiatry, 70,* 33–41.

Harrell, S. P. (2000). A multidimensional conceptualization of racism-related stress: Implications for the well-being of people of color. *American Journal of Orthopsychiatry, 70,* 42–57.

Sue, D. W., Capodilupo, C. M., Torino, G. C., Bucceri, J. M., Holder, A. M. B., Nadal, K. L., et al. (2007). Racial microaggressions in everyday life. *American Psychologist, 62,* 271–286.

RACIAL PRIDE

Racial pride is an attitude signifying a preference for cultural representations of one's racial group. Much of the conceptualization and research regarding racial pride has focused on the socialization experiences of African Americans, an ethnic group within the Black population. Information about racial pride among other racial groups remains relatively unknown. The definition of racial pride evolved to denote both a racial socialization message promoting heritage and culture to children and adolescents and an attitude endorsing positive racial identity among adults. Currently, racial pride contributes to furthering the multidimensional conceptualization and measurement of socialization processes and racial identity among Blacks and, potentially, other racial groups.

Conceptualization and Measurement of Racial Pride

Conceptualization and measurement of racial pride evolved following decades of researchers attempting to understand the racial preferences of Black children under the reactionary premise that Blacks were an inferior and devalued group in the United States. In the 1930s, studies finding African American children's preference for White over Black dolls produced a prevailing yet flawed belief in Black self-hatred, low self-esteem, and low racial pride that endured until Black self-esteem studies in the 1960s suggested the contrary. Marked by the pro-Black, proactive stance of that time, positive racial identity theories in the 1970s, followed by affirmative racial socialization theories in the 1980s, began to appear in the psychology literature with inclusion of the racial pride concept.

Racial Identity Factor

Racial pride is one of multiple racial identity attitudinal factors that describe how Blacks identify with their racial group. Conceptually, racial pride is the endorsement of a positive Black identity and an attitude of interest or involvement in activities related to the culture. Empirically, measures of racial pride are subsumed in racial identity scales such as the Black Racial Identity Attitudes Scale and brief scales to measure collectivism, religiosity, racial pride, and time orientation. Racial identity research based on racial pride attitudes consistently support its conceptual assumptions, and associate more positive pride attitudes with fewer general psychological distress symptoms and improvement in health-related behaviors, such as breast cancer–related knowledge and mammography screening. Conversely, racial pride's contribution to racial socialization research is more complex.

Racial Socialization Factor

As a construct in the multidimensional conceptualization of racial socialization, racial pride refers to one of the messages parents convey to their children regarding the meaning of being Black. Theoretically, like other socialization messages, racial pride is transmitted intentionally and unintentionally from parents to children in tacit and explicit ways to aid in their psychological adjustment, especially in dealing with racism and discrimination in society. Empirically based racial pride measures emerged out of qualitative data from the landmark National Study of Black Americans and subsequent racial socialization measures, such as the Cultural Pride Reinforcement subscale of the Scale of Racial Socialization; this subscale measures knowledge about African American history and culture and positive feelings about the cultural group. Growing evidence supports greater racial pride socialization among girls than boys, whereas boys are more likely to receive socialization messages related to racial barriers such as discrimination. Moreover, racial pride differentially contributes to psychological outcomes such as depression, anger, and aggression for boys and girls. Among adolescents, racial pride has been positively associated with self-esteem, kinship social support, knowledge about one's racial group, and favorable ingroup attitudes. However, some evidence suggests negative relationships between racial pride and academic curiosity and grade point average outcomes, raising questions about whether the pride socialization comes before or after the poor academic indicators. The complex findings surrounding racial pride provide impetus for future directions of the research.

Future Directions

For more than two thirds of a century, racial pride has helped explain a portion of how Blacks identify with their own racial group. Subsumed within racial identity research, positive pride attitudes are consistently associated with fewer general psychological distress symptoms and improvement in health-related behaviors. Yet complex correlational relationships with attitudinal and behavioral factors along with gender differences among females and males exist. Future research exploring the relationships among racial pride, racial identity, and racial socialization for Blacks, Asians, Hispanics, and other racial group members will aid in formulating multidimensional conceptualizations of racial issues in cross-cultural counseling theory. Longitudinal studies will help explain the directional associations between racial pride and its identity and socialization factors. Future research that examines the interactions among racial pride, gender, other demographic variables, racism and discrimination experiences, health, and educational outcomes will provide a more accurate understanding of the multiple factors that contribute to how individuals are socialized and how they identify with their racial group.

Ma'at E. Lewis-Coles

See also African Americans (v3); Afrocenticity/Afrocentrism (v3); Black Racial Identity Development (v3); Cultural Values (v3); Ethnic Pride (v3); Racial Identity (v3)

Further Readings

Constantine, M. G., & Blackmon, S. (2002). Black adolescents' racial socialization experiences: Their relations to home, school, and peer self-esteem. *Journal of Black Studies, 32,* 233–335.

Kreuter, M. W., & Haughton, L. T. (2006). Integrating culture into health information for African American women. *American Behavioral Scientist, 49*(6), 794–811.

Neblett, E. W., Philip, C. L., Cogburn, C. D., & Sellers, R. M. (2006). African American adolescents' discrimination experiences and academic achievement: Racial socialization as a cultural compensatory and protective factor. *Journal of Black Psychology, 32*(2), 199–218.

Neville, H. A., & Lily, R. (2000). The relationship between racial identity cluster profiles and psychological distress among African American college students. *Journal of Multicultural Counseling and Development, 28*(4), 194–207.

Stevenson, H. C. (1994). Validation of the scale of racial socialization for African American adolescents: Steps toward multidimensionality. *Journal of Black Psychology, 20*(4), 445–468.

Stevenson, H. C., McNeil, J. D., Herrero-Taylor, T., & Davis, G. Y. (2005). Influence of perceived neighborhood diversity and racism experience on the racial socialization of Black youth. *Journal of Black Psychology, 31,* 273–290.

RACISM

Racial categorization is a central construct within American society and, as such, has had an enduring impact on all levels of social relations. Given the hierarchical social structure within the United States, racism has emerged as a logical outcome of a society based on and structured around race. A growing appreciation of the social and psychological costs associated with racism has led to racism being viewed as an important area of inquiry and intervention for counselors and psychologists.

Racism, a term coined in the 1930s, is centered on the belief that persons can be separated into categories based on physical attributes. Racism is understood to have three fundamental components. First, it is rooted in the belief that perceived group differences can be attributed to fundamental differences in biology (stereotypes); second, racism involves the negative evaluations one has of another racial group relative to one's own (prejudice); and third, racism reflects the unequal treatment of groups (discrimination). Fundamentally, racism involves the presumption that one race is superior over others in areas of aptitude, abilities, intelligence, physical prowess, and/or virtues, and it is exhibited through acts of discrimination and harassment.

Various types of racism include individual, institutional or structural, and cultural or ideological. *Individual racism* is characterized by one person's treatment toward another based on race, for example, an employer not hiring a qualified individual or a sales clerk not helping a customer. *Ideological racism* is a perception or worldview that may formulate into a personal theory about individuals belonging to a particular race (e.g., the assumption that all African Americans have inferior intelligence or the assumed superiority of European art forms over other racial groups' artistic expressions). *Institutional* or *structural racism* is located within political and economic systems and social institutions such as education and law enforcement. Institutional racism is thought to involve unfair distribution of resources and unequal participation in the above-mentioned systems based on racial categorization. Such discrimination can be seen in a financial institution's practice of consistently providing loans at higher rates of interest to persons of color.

Racism in Historical Context

Racism as a social phenomenon and psychological reality is built entirely on the concept of race. A historical review of the word *race* indicates that from its inception, race has been associated with classification. The Latin derivative of the word *race, razza,* was first applied to the classification of animals into species. With the advent of European exploration and the convergence of economic, political, religious, and scientific forces in the colonialist age, the word *race* began to be applied to groups of people. This development culminated in the establishment of a racial hierarchy, with peoples of European origin forming the top of the hierarchy and people of African origin being at the base. It is easily understood then how certain groups of people began to be viewed as inherently inferior, a belief which the then scientific community supported by means of Social Darwinism and the Eugenics movement. Current thinking, largely led by anthropologists and supported by genetic research, indicates that race, as a biological construct, is in fact nonexistent. Genetic data consistently yields evidence of greater variability within so-called racial groups than across them. However, race as a social construct continues to hold much sway with unstated views of inferiority/superiority being reinforced by the existence of significant social inequalities across racial lines.

A review of various socioeconomic indicators in contemporary U.S. society reveals that, proportionately, White Americans tend to accumulate the greatest amount of wealth and have more consistent access to educational opportunities and health care than do their non-White counterparts. In the corporate world, Whites disproportionately hold the greatest percentages of managerial and executive positions, and in the political arena, Whites have been singularly represented in the positions of president, vice president, and Speaker of the House of Representatives. Furthermore, racial disparities that exist in the areas of health and health care, as well as the disproportionately higher rates of incarceration among Blacks and Latinos/as, serve to reinforce stereotypical notions of the racial hierarchy as well as provide further evidence of the institutional and structural nature of racism. Many observers have concluded that even though race is in and of itself inherently meaningless, the significance that is attached to race has made it a real and enduring concept. Perhaps the most powerful and damaging aspect of race is simply the belief that physical differences are representative of differences in traits, abilities, and aptitude, a belief that provides the core ideological foundation for the persistence of racism.

Privilege

An important correlate of racism is the notion of privilege, also referred to as unearned advantage or conferred dominance. Essentially privilege is viewed as the accruement of social power based on historical inequities. Given the history of race within the United States, the accepted understanding is that Whites currently are the racial group to whom concept of privilege most accurately applies. Before and during the time of slavery, Whites inherited certain privileges that were denied to non-White persons. These privileges included receiving an education, working for wages, having the right to vote, and having the right to own property. As a racial group, Whites continue to benefit from these types of "privileges." It is this system of unearned advantages, irrespective of individual knowledge or intent, that forms the basis of institutional and structural racism. When this system is accompanied by a personal belief in the notion of racial superiority, individual racism is the result.

Psychological Models of Racism

Although racism is viewed primarily as a sociological phenomenon, it is also understood to have distinct psychological components.

Theoretical Foundations

Prejudice is viewed as a core aspect of individual racism and racial discrimination. G. E. Allport was one of the first scholars to offer a psychological model of prejudice. Allport viewed prejudice as an inflexible attitude, defined by generalizations based on inaccurate information, that could be directed toward a group or an individual of that group. Although evolutionary psychologists have suggested that prejudice is embedded in the genetic makeup of humans, social psychological theory proposes that prejudicial attitudes are habitual and learned, either through imitation of others or in the ways in which we construct our psychological reality. While initially thinking that prejudice was in fact a type of personality, Allport eventually introduced an integrated theoretical model of prejudice, which focused on the various causes of prejudice, including historical, sociocultural, situational, personality-type, phenomenological, and individual factors. In addition to concepts outlined in Allport's model, social psychologists have also viewed prejudice to be embedded in the human need for self-justification, status, and power. People's unfair treatment of others is justified if they assign derogative labels such as "inferior," "unworthy," "stupid," or "subhuman" to others who are different from themselves. The notion of prejudice is thought to be a foundational element of the larger phenomenon of racism.

Current Psychological Models of Racism

Aversive Racism and Racial Microaggressions

S. Gaertner and J. Dovidio have described aversive racism as a subtle process whereby White Americans, while holding on to egalitarian beliefs, continue to feel discomfort and negative feelings in relation to people who are racially different. Given the positive developments in race relations over the past few decades (e.g., civil rights legislation), the notion of aversive racism is now viewed as having replaced the overt racism of the Jim Crow era. For Black

Americans and other people of color, the Jim Crow era was marked by legalized racial segregation, consistent threat to their physical well-being, intimidation practices such as cross burning, and the ubiquitous loss of property and personal rights. Although these intentional and overt acts of hostility and discrimination are now disavowed, the more unintentional behaviors consistent with avoidance and minimization of racially different others continues to provide racism with a ubiquitous hold on American society.

A correlate of aversive racism is the phenomenon of racially based *microaggressions*—a term introduced by Chester Pierce. Racial microaggressions are thought to be the day-to-day demeaning and insulting messages directed toward people of color, both directly and indirectly. One type of microaggression is the experience of invisibility among African American men. The "invisibility syndrome," as described by A. J. Franklin, is thought to be a phenomenon whereby, irrespective of accomplishments, Black men continue to be interacted with based on stereotypical notions of inferior intelligence, criminality, and danger. Hence, their individual self is lost to the stereotypical view of who they are, and a feeling of invisibility ensues. The consistent exposure to racial microaggressions is understood to have a detrimental effect on well-being.

Racism as a Type of Stressor

Racism has become appreciated as representing a significant aspect of psychological stress for people of color. R. Clark and colleagues and S. Harrell have provided important theoretical frameworks from which the individual impact of racism can be understood. Although primarily focusing on the African American experience, their frameworks have applicability for individuals from all racial groups who are exposed to racism within the United States. Both models view racism and its effects as an interaction between the individual and his or her environment. Accordingly, various forms of racism-related stress have been identified, namely, racism-related life events, vicarious racism experiences, daily racism microstressors, chronic contextual stress, collective experience of racism, and transgenerational transmission of group traumas. Racism-related stress, therefore, can be understood as a combination of episodic stress, daily hassles, and chronic strain. How an individual evaluates or perceives the experience of racism is considered to be a central determinant of the manner in which the individual will be impacted by the experience of racism. If an environmental stimulus is perceived as racism, an individual will employ various coping responses. The coping response in turn determines the physical or psychological outcome of the environmental stimulus, possibly leading to adverse psychological and physiological stress.

Racism as a Type of Mental Illness

There is debate as to whether White racism is a type of mental illness. James E. Dobbins and Judith H. Skillings have argued that the dynamics of White racism are similar to those dynamics seen among individuals who experience addictions. Accordingly, it is argued that individual racism includes a specific set of behaviors and symptoms, such as a reduced racial sensitivity marked by increasing tolerance of racist behavior, denial of the presence of racism (both individual and socially), withdrawal and isolation from people of color, persistent maladaptive behavior designed to maintain distance between self and the racial other, and persistence of maladaptive behaviors irrespective of consequences. As such, it is thought that racism can be arrested through interventions such as the restructuring of distorted cognitions, the use of self-help groups to engage in antiracist dialogue, and the implementation of a 12-step model with the goal being a change in ideas, attitudes, and behaviors.

Expanded Psychological Definitions of Racism

Psychologists have begun to call for an expanded understanding of the manner in which racism impacts people of color. Included in this call is a need to rethink the definition of *racism*. One approach is to parcel out aspects of racism in relation to racial discrimination (withholding) and racial harassment (acts of hostility). In making this distinction it is thought that the psychological and emotional impact of racism could be more efficiently explored. Additionally, preliminary evidence indicates that those individuals who report experiences consistent with racial harassment are more likely to report increased levels of psychological distress such as depression, anxiety, and intrusive thoughts. In relation to racism-related stress, researchers have commented on the significant differences in rates of posttraumatic stress disorder (PTSD) between Whites and people of color. The offered explanation is that people of color, possibly due to chronic exposure to racism, might have a lower stress threshold when encountering traumatic events. Subsequently, it is argued that current understandings of traumatic stress might not capture the type of stress induced by consistent exposure to, and involvement with, racism. For people of color it is thought that generic or general life stress most likely includes aspects of stress that are inherently associated with living in a society structured on race and defined by racism.

Psychological Correlates of Race and Racism

Mental Health

Racism has long been viewed as having important psychological aspects. Early scholars such as Frantz Fanon spoke in terms of racism leading to alienation—alienation from self, from significant others, from one's culture and history, and from self-determination and access to various forms of social power. In the 1950s A. Kardiner and L. Ovesey introduced the notion that a defining characteristic of the "Negro personality" was the belief in their inferiority. Kenneth and Mamie Clark provided some of the first empirical evidence of the harmful psychological impact of racism when their study showed that Black children displayed a preference for White dolls over Black dolls. The notion of racism as an intrapsychic process whereby the targets of racism accept the inferior view of their racial group and, by extension, an inferior view of themselves, is referred to as *internalized racism*. More recently, Shawn Utsey and Mark Bolden have suggested that acute reactions to racism might include racism-related trauma, racism-related fatigue, anticipatory racism reaction, race-related distress, racism-related frustration, and racism-related confusion. A growing body of research indicates that experiences of racism are linked to psychological distress, decreased quality of life, and specific physiological disorders such as hypertension. With regard to psychological distress, racism is associated with experiences of depression, anxiety, increased feelings of hostility, and higher levels of paranoia. Currently, the accepted understanding is that racism is generally associated with poorer health status and that the association is the strongest for mental health.

Finally, there is a growing appreciation of the manner in which racism functions at the psychological level within the dominant racial group. Research suggests that for Whites, the psychological correlates of racism include a distorted sense of self and personal accomplishments, an irrational sense of superiority, a fear of those who are racially different, and a predominant sense of guilt.

Racial Identity

The construct of racial identity is an important psychological correlate of racism. Racial identity theorists such as William E. Cross, Jr. and Janet E. Helms have been at the forefront of increasing the understanding of race as a psychological variable as exhibited by racial identity statuses and attitudes. Racial identity is understood to be an aspect of personality that reflects an individual's identity in relation to his or her racial group membership. Additionally, racial identity is believed to influence the manner in which an individual processes racial stimuli and experiences of racism and is understood to encompass affective, cognitive, and behavioral functions. Racial identity theory posits varied maturational statuses in relation to how an individual processes racial stimuli and therefore is an important construct to consider when exploring the individual impact of racism. The statuses that are viewed as more immature for people of color are pre-encounter and encounter and for Whites are contact, disintegration, and reintegration. Essentially, the immature racial identity statuses are defined by a denial of race and racism and confusion in relation to self as a racial being and racism as social reality. For Whites, the more mature statuses are re-integration, pseudo-independence, and autonomy while for people of color, the more mature statuses include immersion/emersion, internalization, and integrative awareness. These statuses are defined by a recognition and appreciation of the presence of race and racism and the acceptance of self and others as racial beings. Research has indicated that more mature racial identity statuses tend to be associated with greater degrees of psychological well-being and that racial identity statuses have a direct impact on the perception and appraisal of race-related events. Finally, there is preliminary evidence for a potentially moderating role of racial identity in relation to racism-related stress and psychological functioning. Scholars have posited that the more mature racial identity status might act as a buffer, protecting individuals against the more harmful psychological effects of racism.

Racial Socialization

Socialization is understood to be a process by which individuals learn the beliefs, values, and behaviors that are considered to be normative within their specific reference groups—racial, ethnic, religious, and so forth. In relation to racism, racial socialization is viewed as an important element influencing how individuals both anticipate and respond to experiences of racism and discrimination. Given that people of color within the United States are raised in a negative and, at times, hostile environment, racial socialization practices are instrumental in facilitating a healthy self-concept. Through implicit and explicit messages, children are taught to value those beliefs, behaviors, and values that are specifically associated with their racial group membership. As with racial identity, racial socialization is considered to be an important construct in the development of resiliency and can also be viewed as potentially protective for individuals and groups who are consistently exposed to experiences of racism.

Racism and Mental Health Practice

The importance of racism in mental health practice is understood in relation to the nature of a client's presenting concerns, the impact of race and racism on the quality of the therapeutic relationship, and factors associated with coping and resilience.

Cultural Mistrust

Perceived racism is the subjective experience of racism and discrimination. Symptoms that tend to be associated with paranoia (i.e., suspiciousness, feelings of ill will, beliefs in external control) are viewed as effects of perceived racism. However, in populations that have been consistently exposed to racism, perceived racism has been associated with a type of "cultural paranoia." Contrasted to clinical paranoia, cultural paranoia is initiated by the experience of being a racial minority in a socially hostile environment. Within counseling and psychotherapeutic services, the notion of cultural paranoia is often labeled "cultural mistrust," a distrust and attitudinal response that people of color might have toward the dominant majority, brought on by years of social and economic oppression as well as continued everyday experiences of perceived racism, prejudice, and/or discrimination. Cultural mistrust is demonstrated in the counseling relationship, especially between a racial minority client and dominant racial majority counselor. Trust on behalf of the client toward the counselor must be established for the counseling to be effective. The client must trust that the counselor has his or her best interests in mind during treatment. Importantly, a person of color who pursues counseling wants to be ensured that the counselor is also understanding of issues related to race and racism. Hesitance to engage in the counseling process due to the notion that the counselor lacks the understanding of how one's culture plays a part in the presenting problem is often a result of cultural mistrust. Although the impact of racial similarity in counselor pairing has not yet been empirically settled, there is research to suggest racially similar dyads might have an important influence on the counseling process. For example, Black clients have been noted to report lower levels of rapport with White counselors and greater counseling satisfaction with racially similar counselors, a finding considered largely due to an increased perception of trust. More often than not, if trust is not established, there is risk for premature termination, lower amounts of self-disclosure, and increased negative attitudes about seeking help.

Cultural-Specific Coping

Using a culture-specific framework, James M. Jones developed a model that describes the manner in which peoples of African descent are able to cope with racism. Jones argues that racism is a cultural legacy that has been embedded in the psychological consciousness. Subsequently a person or group's ability to cope with racial oppression is dependent on their psychological resiliency. He theorized that one's coping strategy is heavily dependent on one's racial identity and the subscription to the cultural foundation of one's cultural African legacy. Jones's model, TRIOS—which stands for time, rhythm, improvisation, orality, and spirituality—is thought to capture the cultural resources available to, and utilized by, Black Americans. Although prejudicial attitudes from the dominant group remain, the marginalized or minority group has gained the ability to cope with prejudice by detecting and protecting themselves from racism, eliminating self-defeating perceptions, and enhancing self-worth. Models such as these might shed light on how individuals and groups who experience racism consistently report high levels of subjective well-being and how they have developed resilience. For the mental health practitioner, an appreciation of cultural-specific coping styles, such as relying on religion and spirituality, culture-specific behaviors and rituals, is an essential requirement when working with populations who regularly experience discrimination. Finally the role of cultural enclaves (i.e., living in racially similar communities) has also been recognized as potentially providing a buffer against those negative psychological reactions experienced by individuals and groups when faced with racist incidents.

Implications of Racism for Counselor Practice

The phenomenon of racism impacts counselor practice on multiple levels. Counselors are involved in assisting individual perpetrators of racism in gaining a healthier sense of self and accordingly shifting away from dysfunctional ways of perceiving racial difference. Counselors also work with individuals or groups who have experienced racism in order to facilitate the employment of more effective coping patterns as well as the development of self-efficacy and personal power. On a more systemic level, counselors work to challenge racist structures that lead to differential rates of mental illness and disproportionate access to adequate health care. Counselors work to have increased racial representation among mental health professionals. Counselors work to legitimize practices of indigenous healing that might be questioned by the dominant racial majority as being unscientific. Finally, counselors and counseling psychologists seek to challenge dominant psychotherapeutic theories that view psychological functioning from an individualistic perspective, which could be less helpful to people of color who tend to value communal ways of being and incorporate spirituality as an essential aspect of well-being.

A recent development within counseling and counseling psychology has been the focus on social justice as a core aspect of who counselors are and what counselors do. Antiracism training is therefore a critical aspect of counselor training and preparation. Effective counselors recognize that they too are products of socialization experiences and cultural upbringing. Living in a society structured around race, counselors have also been influenced by various aspects of individual and structural racism. Counselors therefore seek to maintain an active awareness about the ways in which they participate and contribute to the maintenance of racism as a system of oppression. Antiracist attitudes and behaviors have been incorporated within the rubric of multicultural competence and therefore represent one of the baseline qualities needed for competent and effective counselor practice.

Alex L. Pieterse and Kilynda V. Ray

See also Affirmative Action (v3); Antisemitism (v3); Bias (v3); Color-Blind Racial Ideology (v3); Cultural Mistrust (v3); Cultural Paranoia (v3); Discrimination (v3); Discrimination and Oppression (v2); Multicultural Counseling Competence (v3); Oppression (v3); Prejudice (v3); Race (v3); Racial Identity (v3); Sexism (v3); Social Justice (v3); Stereotype (v3)

Further Readings

Allport, G. (1954). *The nature of prejudice.* Boston: Beacon Press.

Carter, R. T. (1995). *The influence of race and racial identity in psychotherapy: Toward a racially inclusive approach.* New York: Wiley.

Carter, R. T., & Pieterse, A. L. (2005). Race: A social and psychological analysis of the term and its meaning. In R. T. Carter (Ed.), *Handbook of racial-cultural psychology and counseling* (Vol. 1, pp. 41–65). Hoboken, NJ: Wiley.

Clark, R., Anderson, N., Clark, V. R., & Williams, D. R. (1999). Racism as a stressor for African Americans: A biopsychosocial model. *American Psychologist, 54,* 805–816.

Dobbins, J. E., & Skillings, J. H. (2005). White racism and mental health: Treating the individual racist. In R. T. Carter (Ed.), *Handbook of racial-cultural psychology and counseling* (Vol. 2, pp. 427–446). Hoboken, NJ: Wiley.

Feagin, J. R. (2001). *Racist America: Roots, current realities and future reparations.* New York: Routledge.

Franklin, A. J. (1999). Invisibility syndrome and racial identity development in psychotherapy and counseling African American men. *Counseling Psychologist, 27,* 761–793.

Gaertner, S. L., & Dovidio, J. F. (1986). The aversive form of racism. In J. F. Dovidio & S. L. Gaertner (Eds.), *Prejudice, discrimination, and racism* (pp. 61–90). San Diego, CA: Academic Press.

Harrell, S. P. (2000). A multidimensional conceptualization of racism-related stress: Implications for the well-being of people of color. *American Journal of Orthopsychiatry, 70,* 42–57.

Jones, J. (1997). *Prejudice and racism* (2nd ed.). New York: McGraw-Hill.

Robinson, T. L., & Ginter, E. J. (Eds.). (1999). Racism: Healing its effects [Special issue]. *Journal of Counseling & Development, 77*(1).

Smedley, A., & Smedley, B. D. (2005). Race as biology is fiction, racism as a social problem is real. *American Psychologist, 60,* 16–26.

Sue, D. W. (2003). *Overcoming our racism: The journey to liberation.* San Francisco: Jossey-Bass.

Tatum, B. D. (1997). *"Why are all the Black kids sitting together in the cafeteria?" and other conversations about race.* New York: Basic Books.

Thompson, C. E., & Neville, H. A. (1999). Racism, mental health, and mental health practice. *The Counseling Psychologist, 27,* 155–223.

REFUGEES

Refugees are people who flee their native countries to seek sanctuary in another country as a means of escaping persecution or oppression. Typically, refugee populations are especially active in times of war, though many also leave their countries of origin to escape an oppressive government. The traditional countries that accept refugees are Australia, Canada, Denmark, Finland, the Netherlands, New Zealand, Norway, Sweden, and the United States. In certain political eras in history, the criteria for receiving refugee status and the countries that the United States aided by accepting refugees fluctuated. During World War II, when thousands of people were fleeing violence and persecution, the United States and many other countries turned away refugees because their numbers were much higher than the immigration quotas instituted at the time. The U.S. Department of State refused to increase the quotas and to relax the limits on immigration. In response to the overall failure of countries to respond to the needs of World War II refugees, the United Nations High Commissioner for Refugees (UNHCR) was created, and the 1951 Convention Relating to the Status of Refugees delineated the international obligation, which the United States accepted, to shelter people who faced death and persecution in their own countries.

In contrast to the response to refugees during World War II, during the cold war, people from Southeast Asia, the Soviet Union, and Cuba were accepted into the United States as refugees although they did not meet the criteria for being a refugee. This illustrates how the political atmosphere—in this case, the need to "liberate" people from communism—influences which nationality groups of refugees are allowed into the country. More recently, the United States has focused on smaller refugee groups, such as Sudanese refugees, who have been victims of repression in Egypt, Ethiopia, and Kenya, and refugees from Bosnia and Kosovo who were fleeing religious persecution.

The United States traditionally has accepted more refugees than the other countries of resettlement combined. However, after the terrorist attacks on September 11, the number of refugees admitted has declined. For persons to be declared refugees in the United States, they are generally interviewed by an officer from the UNHCR and an officer of the U.S. Citizenship and Immigration Services to assess if the person is considered a refugee under U.S. law. Despite these procedures, there are still ways to allow refugees into the country who do not fit the profile of a refugee. For example, under the Widows and Orphans Act, (a) women who fear they will be harmed because of their sex and (b) children under 18 whose parents cannot provide adequate care can be admitted into the United States as refugees. Although the United States does not admit as many refugees as in the past, there is still a significant refugee population in the United States that continues to grow.

Refugees are known to suffer extensive psychological distress as a result of war experiences, flight from their native country, residence or incarceration in foreign refugee camps, and their involuntary immigration to a host country. At present, posttraumatic stress disorder (PTSD) and major affective disorders are known to be common symptom patterns within refugee populations, and there has recently been a rise in the prevalence of PTSD. However, despite the known association between refugee status and the likelihood of mental illness, diagnoses may go undetected due, in part, to culture-related presentations (e.g., somatization) and assessment biases of mental health practitioners. Thus, the combination of cultural factors in mental health presentations and new refugee groups in the United States demonstrates a need for research to better understand the problems of refugee populations and to propose effective treatment that is culturally sensitive.

Mental Health Interventions

The task of mental health providers has been to develop programs that refugees can access and utilize, as well as receive in their own language. Kenneth E. Miller discussed an intervention approach with an ecological perspective. He suggested identifying and training community members, who are obviously familiar with local beliefs and practices, to assist as mental health paraprofessionals and with prevention services. It is important that mental health practitioners expand the range of settings in which mental health is practiced from traditional clinic-based approaches to community-based approaches, including psychoeducation, that allow for an expansion of consumers and a network of interdisciplinary collaboration among psychiatrists, psychologists, social workers, translators, teachers, medical doctors, and stakeholders from within the community. In political persecution, perpetrators aim to destroy people's sense of belonging and their community ties. Thus, interventions for refugees should be embedded in communities. Community outreach projects serve to bring communities and families together in some collaborative effort.

Gargi Roysircar reported on specific guidelines for working with refugee populations. First, counselors should attend to refugees' immediate and concrete needs; this provides the opportunity to build rapport with refugees. Some guidelines to increase effectiveness in developing a working relationship with refugees include (a) treating them with respect and dignity, (b) determining beforehand the appropriate means of greeting in the refugee's culture, (c) finding out where the refugee can obtain food appropriate for his or her culture, (d) arranging for an interpreter, (e) locating a religious community appropriate for the refugee's faith, and (f) connecting new arrivals with other members of their ethnic community. Finally, counselors' ability to listen to the refugees will be key in the facilitation of a trusting relationship.

Roysircar also suggested several community outreach services appropriate for refugee populations. First, she advocates for the establishment of a life skills group. This educational group should be structured to teach refugees about American society. Topics of a life skills group could include using public transportation, writing a résumé, applying for benefits, understanding the school system, and learning how to enroll in English as a Second Language (ESL) classes. Another community outreach program could focus on nutrition classes. The idea behind this service is that it will teach refugees how to prepare nutritious and inexpensive meals. Another possible outreach service could be to offer a stress management class. An example of this type of class might include Tai Chi, deep breathing, and relaxation exercises. In such a class, refugees can begin to understand trauma and its deleterious effects rather than remaining confused about PTSD or stigmatizing it. In addition, an acculturation class can relate life problems of employment difficulties, legal issues, absence of primary support group, lack of American education, housing issues, economic issues, access to health care, and social functioning problems in the challenging process of acquiring a second culture. Other types of groups include men's and women's support groups, ESL classes, and community outreach projects (e.g., a gardening project, organizing a cultural festival). Community outreach projects also can serve to bring communities and families together in some collaborative effort.

Gargi Roysircar and Emily Pimpinella

See also Acculturation (v3); Acculturative Stress (v3); Adaptation (v3); Assimilation (v3); Bicultural (v3); Bilingual Counseling (v3); Career Counseling, Immigrants (v4); Cultural Accommodation and Negotiation (v3); Culture Shock (v3); Help-Seeking Behavior (v3); Immigrants (v3); Multicultural Counseling Competence (v3); Oppression (v3); Posttraumatic Stress Disorder (v2); Second Culture Acquisition (v3)

Further Readings

Barnett, D. (2006, December). A new era of refugee resettlement. *Center for Immigration Studies.* Retrieved February 2, 2007, from http://www.cis.org/articles/2006/back1006.html

Huynh, U., & Roysircar, G. (2006). Community health promotion curriculum: A case study of Southeast Asian refugees. In R. L. Toporek, L. H. Gerstein, N. A. Fouad, G. Roysircar, & T. Israel (Eds.), *Handbook for social justice in counseling psychology* (pp. 338–357). Thousand Oaks, CA: Sage.

Miller, K. E. (1999). Rethinking a familiar model: Psychotherapy and the mental health of refugees. *Journal of Contemporary Psychotherapy, 29,* 283–306.

Refugees. In *Holocaust encyclopedia.* U.S. Holocaust Memorial Museum. Retrieved February 2, 2007, from http://www.ushmm.org/wlc/article.php?lang=en&ModuleId=10005139

Roysircar, G. (2007). *Disaster recovery: Counseling interventions.* Alexandria, VA: American Counseling Association.

Religion/Religious Belief Systems

The term *religion* comes from the Latin *religare*, which means "to bind together or to express concern." In modern times, religion has become a visible institution that provides an organizational structure for faith in the divine, sacred, or supernatural. In addition, there frequently are moral codes, ritual practices, worship, and celebrations associated with each religion or religious belief system.

Religion and spirituality are two constructs that have become inextricably and inappropriately linked in the professional literature, despite their differences. Although religion and spirituality are not necessarily mutually exclusive, they remain separate and distinct constructs. For example, one may express her or his spirituality through religion, whereas another may feel that religion inhibits the full expression of individual spirituality. Hence, some people will find religion and spirituality to be mutually exclusive. It is important to note that there is no consensus on the definitions of the terms *spirituality* and *religion*, and many scholars continue to merge the two erroneously. People may generally have a similar lack of precision regarding their religious and spiritual self-perceptions; this presentation is most likely a reflection of their personal experiences with, and understanding of, religion and spirituality in their lives.

In the United States, there are approximately 12 major religions represented, with an unknown number of lesser-known groups as well. Of the major organized religions in the United States, the overwhelming majority of the population (77%) is Christian. The remaining major groups, with the percentage of the population in parentheses, are Judaism (2%), Islam (2%), Buddhism (1%), and Hinduism (0.5%). The rest of the 12 major American groups include Unitarian Universalist, Wiccan/Pagan/Druid, Spiritualist, and Native American religion, as well as secularism, atheism, and agnosticism; each represents less than 0.5%, except secularism (i.e., nonreligious persons), which represents 13%. It is important to note that these figures are estimates of the religious composition of the current U.S. population; the government no longer assesses religion as part of its annual census. It also bears attention that religious diversity tends to be greater near large metropolitan areas, and religious minorities tend to cluster as communities in specific demographic areas (e.g., East Coast and West Coast).

The religions in the United States are somewhat comparable to those in the world, with a few noted exceptions. The largest world religions include Christianity (2.1 billion), Islam (1.3 billion), secularism/atheism/agnosticism (1.1 billion), Hinduism (900 million), Chinese traditional religion (394 million), and Buddhism (376 million). Recent trends include the rapid rise of Islam in the United States and worldwide, as well as a significant increase in the numbers of Buddhists and Hindus in the United States.

Worldview

Like culture, religion provides its members with a unifying sense of identity and feeling of belonging. In addition, religious groups often espouse certain worldviews and expect that their congregations will hold similar, if not identical, views. Said another way, religion provides people with a lens through which to view the world. Related to this, religious traditions also prescribe attitudes about specific issues and behaviors related to observance. For example, there are five foundational principles of Islam: (1) the belief in monotheism and Muhammad as the final prophet, (2) prayer 5 times per day, (3) giving charity, (4) fasting and abstaining from sexual activity from sunrise to sunset during Ramadan, and (5) making a pilgrimage to Mecca.

Hinduism provides another worldview example. Hindus believe in the repetitious reincarnation of the soul after death into another body, a process called *Samsara*. *Karma*, which is essentially a tallying of one's good and bad deeds, determines whether a Hindu will be reborn at a higher or lower level in her or his next life. Hindus can escape *Samsara* by becoming enlightened. In pursuit of enlightenment, Hindus structure their lives around the four aims of Hinduism: (1) dharma (righteousness in one's religious life), (2) artha (economic success), (3) kama (sensual, sexual, and psychological enjoyment), and (4) moksa (becoming enlightened and thus liberated from *Samsara*). Of course, the degree of adherence to religious doctrine will likely guide the degree of adherence to the espoused worldview (and associated attitudes and behaviors) of the particular group. Judaism is a good example, with a variety of denominations that reflect varying degrees of adherence to traditional Jewish law.

Family and Marriage

Religious doctrine often includes specific guidelines for families, including marriage, sexuality, roles of family members, and divorce. For example, many religions discourage intermarriages among different religious groups, and some may require conversion of one partner before the marriage can be sanctioned by the religious body. Choosing which religious rituals and customs to observe may be difficult within mixed marriages, particularly when children are involved. Within a marriage, the specific roles and rights of male and female partners may be prescribed, though the degree to which these roles are followed may depend on the couple's level of religiosity. In some religions, the children's relationship with their parents is also prescribed. In Islam and Buddhism, for example, adult children are obligated to provide care for their elderly parents. Most Western religions prohibit sexual activity outside of marriage, though the degree of adherence to this clearly varies. A recent issue of debate within both Eastern and Western religious groups is the degree to which same-sex relationships can be recognized and accepted. This has resulted in a range of responses, from ordination of gay clergy in some Protestant denominations and Reform and Reconstructionist Judaism, to varying levels of tolerance in Buddhist traditions, to expressions of stern disapproval by fundamentalist Protestants, the Roman Catholic Church, Orthodox Jews, and Islam. Once a marriage has been sanctioned by a religious body, most religions strongly discourage divorce. In some cases, such as in Roman Catholicism and Orthodox Judaism, a marriage must be dissolved by a religious body in addition to a civil divorce proceeding, before the individuals may remarry.

Career

An emerging area for career counseling is the role of religion in career decision making. While understanding an individual's work-related values is a recognized component of career counseling, some individuals may feel called to a career by a higher power. Such a calling may arise from Christian or Muslim religious values, such as service to the poor, or from the Jewish concept of *Tikkun Olam*, which is a call to heal the world. In such cases, a client might be encouraged to go beyond traditional career choice methods, such as interest and skills inventories, and engage in a process of "discernment," which is derived from the process used to assist individuals contemplating religious vocations.

Counseling Implications

Because religion may affect a wide range of personal issues, counselors must consider that their clients' religious value systems may affect the presenting issues. When counseling couples and families, counselors are commonly called to resolve value conflicts, which may occur within, as well as across, religious groups and across generations. Just as importantly, counselors should seek to explore and understand the effect of their own religious values on their own lives and on their clinical judgments. Counseling is not a value-free process, but responsible counseling may be achieved if counselors are attentive to the interaction of their own values with their personal and professional lives.

Everett L. Worthington put forth a model that examines level of religious commitment as a predictor for client behavior as it relates to counseling. For example, clients with higher levels of religious commitment are more likely to want counselors with similar values. Assessing clients' level of religious commitment can also assist counselors with understanding how clients may respond to challenges in session and generally how clients will perceive the counselor. Hence, counselors may want to assess both religious identity and religious commitment in their clients. In fact, getting the identity without understanding the degree of adherence and commitment to the religion will limit the counselor to operating from stereotypes of the particular religious tradition.

There is tremendous within-group variability in all religious groups. Hence, counseling experience with a member of a particular religious group may not necessarily translate to applied work with another person from the same faith. Counseling professionals need to educate themselves about the religions of their clients yet, at the same time, allow their clients to define what religion means for them or how religion affects their lives.

Lewis Z. Schlosser and Pamela F. Foley

See also American Jews (v3); Espiritismo (v3); Indigenous Healing (v3); Spirituality (v3); Spirituality/Religion (v2); Worldview (v3)

Further Readings

Matthews, W. (2004). *World religions.* Belmont, CA: Wadsworth.

Richards, P. S., & Bergin, A. E. (Eds.). (2000). *Handbook of psychotherapy and religious diversity.* Washington, DC: American Psychological Association.

Schlosser, L. Z. (2003). Christian privilege: Breaking a sacred taboo. *Journal of Multicultural Counseling and Development, 31,* 44–51.

Worthington, E. L. (1988). Understanding the values of religious clients: A model and its application to counseling. *Journal of Counseling Psychology, 35,* 166–174.

Worthington, E. L., Kurusu, T. A., McCullough, M. E., & Sandage, S. J. (1996). Empirical research on religion and counseling: A ten-year update and prospectus. *Psychological Bulletin, 119,* 448–487.

REVERSED RACISM

Reversed racism is a controversial contention in which members of a dominant racial group allege racism and discrimination targeted toward them by, or on behalf of, a subordinate or minority racial group. That is, members of a dominant racial group contend that they are being victimized on the basis of their race. Reversed racism can be considered to be a subclass of reversed discrimination, in which members of any majority group feel discriminated against by a minority group, as in, for example, reversed sexism or reversed ageism. As with other forms of reversed discrimination, individuals, groups, or governments can practice reversed racism. In the history of the United States the dominant racial group has been White people. The concept of reversed racism entails White people alleging that they are discriminated against by virtue of being White. For example, a White individual may feel that African Americans are given preferential treatment in hiring or admission criteria and thus allege that those preferences constitute reversed racism.

The concept of reversed racism has been highly controversial, with some scholars debating the validity of the construct. For some, a key component of the definition of racism entails the recognition of the socioeconomic power to put racist beliefs into action in a systemic way. This definition of racism explicitly focuses on the power differential between Whites and racial minorities. Although persons of color may hold prejudices, they lack political, economic, and societal power, and consequently, according to this definition racial minorities, on the whole, lack the power to be racist. Further undermining the concept of reversed racism is the fact that many question the construct of race itself. For example, some scholars contend that race is a social construction that lacks a scientific basis and exists primarily to preserve power and privilege. Therefore, if racism is a social construction, then under a social constructionist definition, reversed racism is also a social construction that ultimately serves to protect and preserve the power of the dominant racial group. Often underlying the issue of race in the United States is the concept of racial salience—the belief that race is an essential part of identity of racial minorities and a nonessential, optional, and unspoken part of the identity of Whites. As a result, when racial minorities seek to overtly address the issue of racism, they are often labeled racist or as practicing reversed racism or labeled as "race baiters."

While some may question the legitimacy and basis of reversed racism, the term seems to have prominently entered the public discourse in many arenas. For example, to address past racial discrimination and current systemic inequities in health, education, and employment, there may be a need to provide access to health care, jobs, and education previously denied to racial minorities. Such attempts to "level the playing field" mitigate the inherent advantages and privileges of White people. Systemic attempts to provide access and opportunity to racial minorities are often targeted on a systemic level yet may be perceived on an individual level by an individual White person who feels he or she personally has been denied a position or opportunity given to racial minority. Consequently, the individual may present a challenge based on the allegation of reversed racism, frequently seeking a legal remedy. An issue that is often overlooked is that the allegation of reversed racism may emanate from racist beliefs. That is, some White individuals may (consciously or not) endorse racist beliefs in the inherent superiority of Whites and resulting inferiority of other racial groups and therefore may interpret the success of racial minorities as possible *only* through means of reverse racism. This type of circular reasoning is self-reinforcing.

Federal affirmative action programs and university admissions have often been the flashpoints for allegations of reversed racism. Implemented in 1965 under the Johnson administration, affirmative action programs were created to ensure that qualified women and racial minorities had opportunities of which they had historically been denied and that they were given equal access to educational and employment opportunities. The legislation has been criticized and incorrectly interpreted as a program that maintains a strict quota system and provides racial minorities with preferential treatment to employment, education, and housing opportunities, while excluding or preventing Whites from achieving such positions. Federal Equal Employment Opportunity laws have also been challenged in a similar manner. These allegations and the resulting litigation popularized the notion of reversed racism. Although the debate over affirmative action and Equal Employment Opportunity legislation has been cast in terms of reversed racism, often overlooked is the fact that the main beneficiaries of such programs have been White women.

Education is another arena against which the allegations of reversed racism have been leveled. Admissions policies and race-based scholarships, in particular, have come under fire. Courts have made it clear that quotas cannot be used in selecting applicants, and increasingly the courts have ruled against race as the determining factor in admissions. The University of Michigan was in the national spotlight in 1997 when it had to defend its admissions policy. Rather than defend the presence of racial minorities as a remedy to past discrimination, Michigan successfully made the case that diversity was in the best interest of all students and necessary for optimal learning. Race-based scholarships and programs have also been challenged, with several states having to disband programs or scholarships or open them to all applicants, regardless of race. Although many focus solely on the negative impact of the allegation of reversed racism (e.g., drastically lowered racial minority enrollments in higher education in California), there may have been some positive impact as well. By having to defend admissions policies and commitment to diversity, colleges and universities may have been forced to consider the essential need for diversity rather than rely on programs that may have inadvertently created an atmosphere of tokenism. In addition, a positive impact has been the focus on rural and economically disadvantaged Whites as a group in need of attention from colleges and universities.

Concerns over reversed racism are not confined to the educational and employment arenas; often the media are criticized for practicing reversed racism. For example, the National Council of La Raza and Latino/as protesting U.S. immigration policies has been accused by some in the media of practicing reversed racism in their advocacy of undocumented Latinos/as. Often in the media, attempts by racial minorities to display racial pride are interpreted as reversed racism or equated to overt White racism such as the Ku Klux Klan.

Counselors may deal with the allegations of reversed racism as part of their work with marginalized or oppressed groups in the larger community, or they may encounter statements endorsing reversed racism in individual and group therapy. Counselors may need to keep in mind that a belief in reversed racism may be indicative of a level of racial identity development in an individual. For White clients a stated belief in reversed racism may be indicative of early stages (also termed *statuses* to reflect the dynamic and fluid nature of identity) of racial identity development (e.g., contact and reintegration) in which the client endorses a belief that race is not important and that U.S. society is fair or neutral on the subject of race. Consequently, the client may be willing to equate acts or statements about racism as having equal impact regardless of the race of the people involved. Some White clients may have experienced or perceived racism or discrimination targeted toward them and, as a result, may have considerable anger and become entrenched in racist beliefs as a matter of self-protection. The counselor's challenge is to help the White client move toward a higher level of racial identity. Likewise, a racial minority client may also endorse a belief in reversed racism, and this may also be indicative of his or her racial identity development. A necessary prerequisite for helping clients to advance their racial identity is for the counselor to have first advanced his or her own racial identity. Janet Helms has stated that a progressive relationship (in which the counselor's racial identity is more advanced than the client's) is optimal for growth in therapy.

It is also important to explore clients' experiences of reversed racism, because ineffective coping strategies and faulty beliefs could interfere with the counseling process and goal attainment. The notion of reversed racism may be very applicable for White clients who present for educational or career counseling. Reversed racism is perpetuated by the belief that for one group to advance, another must suffer. In the United States, racial minority groups today attain higher levels of education, higher incomes, and are promoted to upper management jobs more than ever before in American history. Those who support reversed racism claim that individuals of the dominant culture unjustly suffer at the expense of advancing racial minorities. Thus a client may perceive himself or herself as a victim without acknowledging the privilege he or she has been afforded. Beyond helping clients move to a higher level of racial identity, integrating race and ethnicity with educational and career counseling can help White clients locate schools or programs and career choices that will best meet their educational and employment needs.

Edward A. Delgado-Romero and Kimber L. Shelton

See also Affirmative Action (v3); Bias (v3); Color-Blind Racial Ideology (v3); Discrimination (v3); Discrimination and Oppression (v2); Oppression (v3); Prejudice (v3); Race (v3); Racial Identity (v3); Racism (v3); Sexism (v3); Social Justice (v3); Stereotype (v3)

Further Readings

Carter, R. T., Helms, J. E., & Judy, H. L. (2004). The relationship between racism and racist identity for White Americans: A profile study. *Journal of Multicultural Counseling and Development, 32,* 2–17.

Helms, J. E. (1990). *Black and White racial identity: Theory, research, and practice.* Westport, CT: Greenwood Press.

Stubblefield, A. (1995). Racial identity and non-essentialism about race. *Social Theory and Practice, 21,* 346–368.

Santería

Santería, also known as Lukumí, Regla de Ocha, or "the way of the saints," is an Afro-Cuban and earth-centered religion transmitted primarily in oral fashion. Its main objective is to find solutions to human problems in a world that is simultaneously physical and spiritual. Its origins can be traced to the 19th century or earlier, when the Yoruba (*Yorùbá* in Spanish) people of West Africa were brought as slaves to Cuba. They are also known as Lukumí people. *Lukumí* means "friends" in the Yoruba language. The term also applies to Yoruba slaves' descendants, their music and dance, and their dialect.

Santería is now practiced throughout the Caribbean, Mexico, Argentina, Colombia, Venezuela, and the United States. The religion was brought to the United States by Cuban exiles. Santería has been observed in Miami, Tampa, New York City, Newark, Detroit, Chicago, Atlanta, Gary (Indiana), Savannah (Georgia), and several other urban locations. Storefront botánicas provide Santería figures, incense, and herbs for nearly a million adherents.

During the colonization of Cuba, Brazil, Haiti, and Trinidad, thousands of Yoruba natives were transported there as slaves. These slaves wanted to remain attached to their religious practices and African traditions but were forced to adjust to the New World. They faced widespread persecution by slave masters who prohibited the practice of African religions within their Roman Catholic society. Thus, the religion was practiced in secret, and its survival was due primarily to the convergence of Yoruba's religiosity and Catholicism. Many elements from the Catholic religion and their symbols are often present in Santería rites.

Santería devotees believe in a creator who is called Olodumare ("owner of the heavens"; also known as Olorun, Oluwa Orun, or Eleda). His power, called Ashe, is the cosmic energy present in everything in the world. He created the universe and the Orishas. According to Santería devotees, everyone receives a destiny from Olodumare, which can be fulfilled with the aid and energy of the Orishas. The Orishas govern over nature. They are powerful but not immortal. Their human limitations help them understand and assist humans. For these reasons, devotees strive to establish a personal relationship with them.

Because the Orishas need food, animal sacrifice is a principal form of worship. In exchange, the deities protect and visit the houses of devotees, empowering them and dignifying their living conditions. Sacrifices are performed at birth, marriage, initiation of new members and priests, and other major celebrations, as well as for the cure of the sick and for death rites. Sacrificial animals include chickens, pigeons, doves, ducks, guinea pigs, goats, sheep, and turtles. The sacrificed animal is cooked and eaten, except after healing and death rituals.

Each Orisha has an associated Catholic saint, principle, important number, special color, favorite food, dance posture, and emblem. The following 16 Orishas are recognized in Cuba (their corresponding Catholic saint and principles are added in parenthesis): Agayu (Christopher, fatherhood), Babaluaye (Lazarus, illness), Esu/Elegbara/Eleggua/Elegua (Anthony of Padua, fate), Ibeji (twins Cosmus and Damien, children), Inle (Rafael, medicine), Obatala/Orunmila/Ifa (Mercedes, clarity), Ogun/Gun (Peter, labor), Olokun (Regla, profundity), Orula (Francis, wisdom, destiny), Osanyin (Joseph, herbs), Oshosi (Norbert, justice), Oshun/Ochun (Caridad, love), Oya/Yasan (Therese, adversity), Shango/Chango/Obakoso (Barbara, passion), Yemoja/Yemaya (Regla, womanhood). The religion does not have a devil figure.

Priests are known as Santeros or Santeras, the high priest as Babalawo, and the second highest priest as Italero. Under the priests' guidance, initiates to the priesthood have to commit to memory the songs, incantations, laws, pharmacopoeia, and actions of all Santería rituals. Their rituals include the following:

Divination. This ritual is used to deal with everyday problems. Santería believers go to Santeros to get advice and to seek solutions for their problems of friendship, health, love, money, or work. Santeros manipulate coconuts, seashells, or other devices to get the Orisha to reveal the believers' needs and to provide solutions to the problem. Santeros use verses, myths, folktales, prayers, and songs to find a suitable prescription for the client's problem.

Sacrifices and Offering. These rituals are used to respond, express gratitude and praise, and supplicate Orishas to continue their positive work on behalf of people. Specific food offerings are recognized as appropriate for each Orisha. For example, a devotee will offer a rooster to Chango and yellow hen to Oshun.

The practice of animal sacrifice is seen by followers of Santería as a necessary part of their relationship with their Orishas; it is sometimes seen by others as abhorrent. Legal action to stop the practice of this religion in the United States failed. In 1993, the U.S. Supreme Court ruled in *Church of Lukumi Babalu Aye v. City of Hialeah* that animal cruelty laws targeted specifically at Lukumí were unconstitutional. The court indicated that religious beliefs are protected by the First Amendment even if they are not acceptable or comprehensible to others. Furthermore, the historical association between animal sacrifice and religious worship suggests that animal sacrifice is an integral part of their religion that cannot be deemed bizarre or incredible.

Drum and Dance Festivals. These festivals, also known as bembe, are held in the Santero's house. The purpose of these rituals is to honor those Orishas that are important in the lives of the participants. A specific drum rhythm and dance posture are associated with each Orisha. For example, the dances for Ochosi, the Orisha of the hunt, include shouts of a hunter and the actions of using a bow and arrow. The drum rhythms and the dance postures bring participants to a sacred state of consciousness, manifested as a spirit possession. The spirit possession is wanted because it opens the channels of Ashe as the dancers merge with the deity. In addition, during this state the Orisha can give other attendants advice, warnings, and admonitions through the devotee.

Implications for Counseling

Given the number of Latinos/as and others who adhere to Santería, counselors would benefit by becoming familiar with these beliefs. Multiculturally competent counselors are aware of the spiritual perspectives they bring to counseling and of the importance of the role religious beliefs play in the lives of their clients. The explanations clients from culturally diverse backgrounds give when explaining the causes of their psychological concerns provide insights about their worldviews and their belief systems, which affect how they relate to their personal problems and to their counselors. Exploring the spiritual beliefs of clients during intake can facilitate rather than hinder the counseling process.

Furthermore, it is important to note the varied levels of belief in Santería. Some Latinos/as may have an altar at home dedicated to a specific deity, whereas others may attend Santería ceremonies and seek guidance from a Santero. Some clients may be seeking help from a Santero while in counseling. They may discuss work-related issues with their counselor but choose to discuss family-related issues with their Santero. For this reason, it is important that the counselor assess the importance of the Santería belief for their clients as well as their level of participation. It is recommended that counselors inquire about the client's spiritual beliefs instead of introducing elements of Santería. The counselor should let the client bring up the subject of Santería; not all Latinos/as or Cubans embrace such beliefs, and some (e.g., Evangelicals) find them abhorrent or diabolical. If the client reveals his or her beliefs, then the counselor can let the client know that he or she is familiar with Santería beliefs. This may help the client feel understood and feel more comfortable in therapy.

In addition, it is also important for the counselor to explore the client's religious interpretations of his or her current problems and not to dismiss the client's interpretations. The counselor can explore within the sessions the client's visions, dreams, and religious experiences using a culturally sensitive approach instead of prejudging them as psychopathological symptoms.

Clients who believe in Santería usually have strong spiritual beliefs and expect that their counselor will treat their beliefs with respect. Some counselors may tailor their counseling to include their client's spiritual belief as a support system and may invite the Santero to collaborate in the treatment on behalf of the client (if agreeable to the client). Many Santeros are knowledgeable about mental disorders and frequently advise clients to seek more conventional mental health treatments.

Carlos P. Zalaquett

See also Espiritismo (v3); Latinos (v3); Multicultural Counseling Competence (v3); Religion/Religious Belief Systems (v3); Spirituality (v3); Spirituality/Religion (v2); Worldview (v3)

Further Readings

De La Torre, M. A. (2004). *Santería: The beliefs and rituals of a growing religion in America*. Grand Rapids, MI: Eerdmans.

Drinan, R. F., & Huffman, J. I. (1993). Religious freedom and the *Oregon v. Smith* and *Hialeah* cases. *Journal of Church & State, 35,* 19–36.

Eliade, M. (Ed.). (1987). *The encyclopedia of religion*. London: Macmillan.

Lefever, H. G. (1996). When the saints go riding in: Santería in Cuba and the United States. *Journal for the Scientific Study of Religion, 35,* 318–330.

Wedel, J. (2004). *Santería healing: A journey into the Afro-Cuban world of divinities, spirits, and sorcerers*. Gainesville: University of Florida Press.

SECOND CULTURE ACQUISITION

Second culture acquisition, an integral aspect of the acculturation process, is the adjustment of the immigrant to the dominant culture. In the new culture, immigrants must navigate through situations in which they have no experience, often without a grasp of the language. Immigrants must deal with changes such as alterations in diet, climate change, different customs and social practices, unfamiliar clothing, new employment, and different family composition, as the majority of their family may reside in their country of origin or in another host country. Several different models have been constructed to explain the methods immigrants use to adapt to the new culture and to highlight reasons for adaptation difficulty. All these factors must be taken into consideration when counseling an immigrant client.

Models of Adaptation

Unilinear Model

Unilinear acculturation considers adaptation to the second culture as a function of time. Individuals appear to become more acculturated the longer they are exposed to the new culture. The rate of acculturation varies depending on another aspect of time: the age of the immigrant at the time of entry. Children aged 12 and younger often become accustomed to the new culture faster than those who immigrate at an older age.

Bilinear Model

Berry postulated that immigrants grapple with two questions: Is it valuable to maintain cultural identity and characteristics (enculturation)? and Is it valuable to maintain relationships with other groups (acculturation)? Although the answers to these questions are independent of each other, they interact, leading to four qualitatively different responses to the second culture: integration, assimilation, separation, and marginalization.

In the integration mode of adaptation, also known as biculturalism, individuals value both the original culture and the host culture and are able to balance the retention of cultural identity and relationships within the dominant society. This strategy is considered the most psychologically healthy strategy for a person to use. A person's development of a bicultural identity is highly individualized and dependent on characteristics such as age, gender, personality, and socioeconomic status.

There are several aspects of biculturalism that positively influence mental health. The first is that the individual maintains positive attitudes toward both cultural groups. In this way, the individual is able to interact with, and gain support from, both groups (groundedness). For example, Kim and Omizo found in their study that Asian American participants who engage with the majority culture both perceive themselves as being able to cope with different cultural situations and feel that people from the majority culture view the Asian American group favorably. They also expressed more cognitive flexibility and general self-efficacy. Similarly, Kosic found that immigrants who favored the integration strategy were more socioculturally adapted than those who used the separation and marginalization strategies. Engaging with the original culture is important as well because enculturation behaviors are associated with the membership dimension of collective self-esteem (the worth placed on one's cultural group).

Another factor that comes into play is bicultural efficacy, which is the sense that the person can live in the two groups without compromising his or her identity. This factor also influences personal relationships with both cultural groups in that people can interact with others without fear that they are betraying their identities. Another crucial part of biculturalism is the person's ability to communicate well in both cultures. Without this ability, it is difficult to have a positive relationship with both groups and to believe that one can function well in each of them. Another facet of biculturalism is role repertoire, in which the individual has developed a range of roles and behaviors that can differ based on situational factors. This flexibility and knowledge of roles helps the individual navigate through both cultures in appropriate ways. Kosic asserts that being able to function well in both cultures helps an individual to be more psychologically adapted, exhibiting less emotional distress and psychosomatic symptoms.

In the assimilation strategy, individuals relinquish their original cultural identity and interact only with the dominant group. People who choose the assimilation strategy of acculturation may experience psychological stress caused by the weakening of ties and support to their original culture and the new and tenuous relationship with the new culture. In this mode, there is the possibility that the person will be rejected by both their original culture and the mainstream culture. It is also difficult to learn new cultural behavior and to completely immerse oneself in another cultural way of thinking and being. Unfortunately, many immigrants feel that they must reject their cultural values and adopt the values of the mainstream to be successful. Though assimilation can have some negative effects on individuals, in some ways it is healthier than the separation and marginalization modes of adaptation. For example, Kosic found that assimilated participants were more socioculturally adapted, had lower levels of emotional disorders, and had lower levels of psychosomatic symptoms than did participants who favored either separation or marginalization strategies.

In the separation mode, the opposite of assimilation, individuals value the original culture and avoid contact with the dominant culture. Kosic talks about how people who choose this strategy have been shown to have the lowest level of sociocultural adaptation when compared to all the other strategies, as well as higher levels of emotional disorder and psychosomatic symptoms when compared to assimilated and integrated participants.

In the marginalization mode, individuals have low connection with both cultures. Kim and Omizo speculated that marginalization may be the most psychologically harmful adaptive strategy because people who employ this strategy may feel isolated, as if they don't belong anywhere. According to Kosic, those who employ this strategy exhibit low levels of sociocultural adaptation and higher levels of emotional disorder and psychosomatic symptoms.

Ample research, such as research done by Berry, points to integration as being the best alternative for immigrants; however, integration can be achieved only in a society that values multiculturalism. Societal multiculturalism requires low degrees of discrimination and prejudice, acknowledgment of the rights of any group to live in a culturally different manner within the larger group, positive attitudes between groups, an attachment to the greater society among all groups, and recognition of cultural diversity as an asset. Program development grounded in research on acculturation and intergroup relations can help immigrants and host cultures avoid unnecessary acculturative stress and intergroup conflict and can promote positive adaptation and mutual accommodation.

Nonlinear Model

Roysircar proposed an adaptation of Berry's model that is bilinear but contextual, which makes it a nonlinear model. Essentially, individuals will move across Berry's four acculturation modes depending on the nature of the situation. This model takes into account varied human experiences; no one acts the same way consistently, and context plays a large role in behavior. A case in point is illustrated by a foreign-born female immigrant from India who has lived in the United States for 27 years. The prejudice and racism she has experienced in the United States may influence her to lean toward the separation mode of adaptation to make herself resilient, while her identification with gender roles as a successful professional leads her to assimilate a feminist orientation of the dominant culture. However, she is very conscious that she is a feminist of color with different priorities, which sets her apart from many White American feminists. As a result, she cannot relate completely to either her original Asian Indian culture or the White dominant culture when dealing with gender issues, so she falls into the marginalization mode of adaptation. In addition, most of the time, she is able to reach out and interact with the dominant culture while still retaining her cultural identity, which shows integration. So, depending on the situation, all four acculturation modes are functional adaptations for this Indian woman. The idea of multiple options and solutions in immigrant adaptation is important in therapy, as the therapist needs to know the adaptation strategies immigrant clients use most frequently or less so, when they use these, and why. Consciously giving up the stereotyped notion that "one size fits all," the therapist seeks from clients their cultural reasonings, while probing into aspects of the second culture that they are struggling with, as well as aspects of the old culture they wish to retain or leave behind.

Second Culture Acquisition and Mental Health

Second culture acquisition is a stressful process. Acculturative stress is exhibited in the reduction of health status for those trying to navigate through new cultural experiences and it occurs when the individual has insufficient resources to adapt to the new culture. Berry found that the groups under the most stress were those who were the least similar to, but still had some contact with, the dominant group and who preferred the separation mode of adaptation.

Adapting to a new culture can also be stressful for immigrants because it may negatively impact existing mental health problems in an individual. For example, immigration can exacerbate existing posttraumatic stress disorder in political refugees because of the added stress of the person being in an unfamiliar place, feeling alienated because of prejudicial and discriminatory treatment in the host culture, feeling isolated because no one wants to listen to their story of pain and horror or even knows about their sociopolitical history, and being separated from their own culture and kinship. As a result, therapists must treat the multiple complex stressors in the psychopathology of immigrant clients. In addition, the culturally competent therapist serves as a cultural broker and bridge for immigrant clients, advocating their access to resources and mental health care, as well as showing them how to use these resources.

Bicultural Stress

Bicultural stress refers to the stress that U.S.-born second generation (and later) immigrants experience while trying to negotiate between their two inherited cultures. For example, a second-generation Asian American immigrant would be born into an Asian family and be pressured to adhere to Asian traditions while simultaneously being pressured to adopt American values and practices. This stress may cause tension in a family where the parents and children have very different strategies in dealing with the dominant culture. An example of this is if the children identify primarily with the dominant culture and favor more of an assimilation approach and the parents struggle to maintain their original cultural identity and favor an approach closer to separation. Bicultural skills are extremely important in promoting the mental health of U.S.-born second and later generation immigrants and the lack, or perceived lack, of these skills causes stress for the individual. Sodowsky and Lai described two dimensions involved in bicultural stress: the interpersonal and the intrapersonal dimensions. The interpersonal dimension, which deals with intercultural competency, is exemplified by having cultural conflicts with one's own cultural group and/or the dominant culture. The intrapersonal dimension deals with acculturative distress such as that initiated by identity crisis, sense of inferiority in one's cultural group, feeling marginalized by one or both cultures, and anger toward either group.

As implied, bicultural stress is important to consider in counseling. Therapists are cautioned against invalidating the impact of bicultural stressors, such as the stress of becoming proficient in two languages, and the incongruence between home culture and the dominant culture. For example, when a counselor says "keep your own culture," as well as "adopt a second culture," it leads to mixed messages for a psychologically impaired mental health client, which may lead to an unclear understanding of the counseling relationship and unpleasant feelings toward mental health care on the part of a minority client. Because immigrant children and adults are less likely to use mental health services and have higher rates of counseling dropout compared with White clients, it becomes paramount for counselors to carefully address and consider all of a minority client's motives for seeking mental health assistance. Therefore, it is important for therapists to determine if bicultural, bilingual, and familial stressors are too great (with the potential to lead to more serious issues such as depression, suicide, substance abuse, violence, running away) before reframing contextual multiplicity as positive challenges universal for immigrants.

Factors That Facilitate Second Culture Acquisition

Several different factors can make second culture acquisition easier and reduce acculturative stress. The first and perhaps most obvious factor is English proficiency. The immigrant will find it much easier to utilize services and to function in the dominant culture if he or she is able to communicate with the people in the dominant society. People of a higher socioeconomic status also have an easier time with second culture acquisition and less acculturative stress because they have more access to resources because of their financial status. Individuals' motivation for immigration also makes a difference in the stress experienced; people who immigrate voluntarily fare better than people who are forced to relocate to escape persecution or international students making only temporary contact. These factors are important to consider in therapy to determine what coping resources the individual has at his or her disposal, and knowing these factors can help the counselor better predict how the individual will adapt.

The positive complement to bicultural stress is bicultural skills. Living in and balancing two or more cultures is worthy of praise, admiration, and acknowledgment and can be demonstrative of resiliency, which in turn can assist with reducing the effects of acculturative stress. Simultaneously functioning in two distinct cultures also can help build skills that immigrant youngsters can use in the future for adjusting and thriving in a variety of systems (e.g., jobs/careers, personal relationships, new communities, college/university, etc.). For example, Feliciano studied the academic success of immigrant Asian and Latino/a students as measured by their likelihood of dropping out of high school. She found that bicultural students, those that had not abandoned their native culture and language while accepting their need to succeed in mainstream society, were more successful in school and were more positive about their future. She indicated that it was these youngsters' skills at finding support in both cultures that led them to be better adjusted than those who were polarized toward the native culture or mainstream society. Other researchers have reported that bicultural youths demonstrate fewer conduct disorders and also less depression than their peers who are fully assimilated into mainstream society. In addition, bicultural youth may display more effective methods for functioning in various sociocultural situations than their fully assimilated peers.

Second Culture Acquisition and Counseling

Second culture acquisition is a complex and often stressful process for immigrants of all ages. Therefore, it is important for the therapist to be aware of the trials and confusion an individual faces while struggling to integrate two value systems and ways of living that may be strikingly different from each other. It is also important that mental health professionals not fail to validate the cultural conflicts immigrant families may encounter at home as a result of parents who wish their children to adhere to traditional values, experiences at school or work where these immigrants may feel pressure from teachers and employers to acculturate to U.S. customs, or in social settings (e.g., after-school programs, social functions, organized sports, community activities) where peers may harass them for "being different" or "not talking right." Therefore, it is recommended that counselors implement individual and group counseling goals centered on increasing the awareness and reframing of immigrants' bicultural skills and using bicultural skills in various academic, employment, and social settings to cope with cultural conflicts.

In addition, counselors, therapists, and psychology trainers are encouraged to highlight the personal-social and cognitive skills (e.g., speaking two languages, managing different sets of nonverbal cues, understanding how cultures can coexist even if they differ on certain values and beliefs, etc.) necessary for someone to balance practices and values of two cultures. Counselors may also elect to focus on the strength and resilience of their clients in the face of juggling a traditional culture at home as well as a new and developing American culture in their schools and jobs. For example, children can help parents understand that they are learning how to balance both their home culture and their American culture, which is more desirable in today's economy, or they may be encouraged to share with teachers and peers how their bicultural perspectives frame their views of history or even fashion trends.

Gargi Roysircar and Emily Pimpinella

See also Acculturation (v3); Acculturative Stress (v3); Adaptation (v3); Assimilation (v3); Bicultural (v3); Cultural Accommodation and Negotiation (v3); Immigrants (v3); Multicultural Counseling Competence (v3); Multiculturalism (v3); Orthogonal Cultural Identification Theory (v3); Refugees (v3)

Further Readings

Berry, J. (2001). A psychology of immigration. *Journal of Social Issues, 57,* 615–631.

Feliciano, C. (2001). The benefits of biculturalism: Exposure to immigrant culture and dropping out of school among Asian and Latino youth. *Social Science Quarterly, 82,* 865–879.

Kim, B. S. K., & Omizo, M. M. (2006). Behavioral acculturation and enculturation and psychological functioning among Asian American college students. *Cultural Diversity & Ethnic Minority Psychology, 12,* 245–258.

Kosic, A. (2002). Acculturation attitudes, need for cognitive closure, and adaptation of immigrants. *Journal of Social Psychology, 142,* 179–201.

Roysircar, G. (2004). Counseling and psychotherapy for acculturation and ethnic identity concerns with immigrant and international student clients. In T. B. Smith (Ed.), *Practicing multiculturalism: Affirming diversity in counseling and psychology* (pp. 255–275). Boston: Pearson.

Sodowsky, G. R., & Lai, E. W. M. (1997). Asian immigrant variables and structural models of cross-cultural distress. In A. Booth, A. C. Crouter, & N. Landale (Eds.), *Immigration and the family: Research and policy on U.S. immigrants* (pp. 211–237). Mahwah, NJ: Lawrence Erlbaum.

SEXISM

It has been called the world's oldest oppression: sexism. Sexism is the name given to the systematic oppression of women. In its most obvious forms, sexism includes conscious, deliberate, and overt discrimination against women, such as denying women the right to vote or own property, as was the practice in the United States in the early 19th century and is still seen in other parts of the world. At the other end of the continuum, it also includes subtle behaviors and attitudes that might go unnoticed in everyday life; sexism is operating anytime a woman is expected (or expects herself) to diet to extreme thinness, maintain a youthful appearance in perpetuity, downplay her own competence, accept verbal or physical mistreatment, or otherwise "know her place." Although the conceptual isolation of sexism is useful for the purposes of discussion, it is important to note that sexism is just one part of an interlocking system of oppression that also includes racism, heterosexism, and classism, among others. So although some overarching themes can be explored with regard to sexism, these themes play out differently in the lives of women of color, lesbians, bisexual women, transgendered people, and poor and working-class women.

Sexism, Patriarchy, and Feminism

Understanding sexism begins with understanding patriarchy, the context in which sexism occurs. In *The Gender Knot,* Allan Johnson explained that a patriarchal society is one whose power structures, values, norms, and institutions are specifically male-identified. In other words, positions of power and authority tend to be occupied by men, important resources are generally controlled by men, values tend to reflect stereotypically masculine strengths and characteristics, norms are shaped around the ways that men live their lives, and institutions and their procedures tend to advance and promote the needs and success of men. In a patriarchy, the privileged status of men is rooted deep in society's subconscious, so that well-intentioned men and women who would oppose outright gender discrimination often unintentionally hold and perpetuate sexist stereotypes. American society's continuing patriarchal nature can be seen in such realities as the nearly all-male makeup of the nation's chief executive officers (CEOs) and legislators, as well as the vast gap between the amounts of income and wealth accruing to men and women. Patriarchy places men at the center of American cultural expression, whether in music, literature, or the movies; important contributions by women film directors or composers are often singled out as being noteworthy on that basis alone. Patriarchy explains the fact that, whereas assaults against individuals on the basis of most group memberships merit special designation and prosecution as "hate crimes," violence against women does not capture people's attention in the same way.

The movement to end sexism is called feminism. Feminism is frequently characterized as having evolved in three "waves." The first wave took shape in the late 1800s and focused on securing fundamental legal rights for women, culminating in the right to vote for women in 1920. Second-wave feminists moved beyond these basics in the 1960s and 1970s to work for broader personal, political, social, economic, and sexual equity among men and women. The objectives that second-wave feminists took on were, therefore, not only conceptually more complex but also more controversial: Whereas the double standard involved in disenfranchising half the American adult population was relatively clear-cut, the deconstruction of deeply held beliefs about conventional gender roles and relationships presented a much more complex challenge to mainstream understanding. Second-wave feminists elucidated and confronted sexism as manifested in such important issues as sexual harassment, images of women in the media, violence against women, pay inequities between men and women, limits on women's reproductive freedom, and the oppressive underpinnings of conventional heterosexuality.

Even this second wave of the women's movement, however, had thus far failed to address issues of race, class, and sexual orientation as they intersect with sexism, resulting in a feminism that spoke primarily to the experiences of White heterosexual middle-class women. Influential African American feminist authors such as Audre Lorde, bell hooks, and Angela Davis were among the scholars whose work helped to illuminate the intersections of multiple oppressions within patriarchy. In 1983, Alice Walker introduced the term *womanism* to refer to Black feminism and the feminism of women of color. Placing the experiences of women of color at its center, Walker defined womanism as emphasizing wholeness, spirit, strength, and community, a valuing of African American heritage, and a cherishing of other women of color.

The second wave of feminism, then, inspired important legal, medical, and social protections for women. It also spurred an emotionally charged, contentious response from some corners that resulted in what has been called the "backlash" against feminism in the 1980s and 1990s. As part of this regressive trend, the word *feminism* itself was cast in a negative light; even many women who affirmed their disapproval of sexist discrimination now wished to disassociate themselves from the feminist movement. Beginning in the 1990s, however, a generation of women young enough to have benefited from feminist accomplishments all their lives advanced a third wave of feminism, which emphasized the intersectionality of sexism with other aspects of identity, broadening feminist discourse to incorporate queer theory, women-of-color feminism, and postcolonialism.

Sexism in the United States

The Wage Gap

The wage gap is one of the most obvious and enduring examples of the continuing presence of sexism in American culture. Despite the passing of the Equal Pay Act in 1963, which outlawed sex discrimination regarding pay, the U.S. Census Bureau reported in 2005 that for every dollar that a man earns, a woman earns 77 cents. The same report demonstrated that women are 40% more likely to live in poverty than are men. The National Committee on Pay Equity, a coalition of legal, educational, professional, and civil rights organizations, explained in 2005 that women workers are concentrated in low-wage paying occupations such as clerical, service, and sales positions; furthermore, as women workers become more prevalent in an occupational segment, income levels there decrease. A 2003 U.S. General Accounting Office report found that even when differences in work-related factors such as occupation, job tenure, and experience are accounted for, an unexplained 20% wage gap remains; this gap is attributable to discrimination. Intersections with racism mean that the wage gap for women of color is even more severe. In 2000, African American women's average weekly wages were 64% of the wages of White men, while Latinas earned just 52% of that amount.

The Glass Ceiling

One of the reasons that women workers tend to be found at the lower end of the pay scale is that corporate hierarchies do not advance women at the same rates as men, often promoting them only as far as the so-called glass ceiling. First labeled as such by the *Wall Street Journal* in 1986, the U.S. Department of Labor convened the Glass Ceiling Commission in 1991 to study this phenomenon, defining it as an artificial, bias-related barrier that prevented qualified employees from advancing into management-level positions. In 1995, the Commission's final report documented the unquestionable presence of the glass ceiling with regard to women and people of color, finding that although women held more than 45% of the nation's jobs, 95% of senior managers were men. Furthermore, those women who were managers earned only 68% of what men made in similar positions. Ten years later, Catalyst, a research firm that tracks women's experiences in a wide range of workplaces reported that 50.3% of all professional and management positions and 1.4% of Fortune 500 CEOs were women. Six of these seven women were White; Andrea Jung, CEO of cosmetics maker Avon Products, is Asian American. In their 2005 study of corporate leaders titled "Men 'Take Charge' and Women 'Take Care,'" Catalyst researchers found that both men and women considered women to be more supportive but less leaderful than men and that men (but not women) believed that women are not good problem solvers.

Business is, of course, not the only workplace setting in which a glass ceiling is operational. In 2006, the *New York Times* reported that although law schools have been graduating equal numbers of men and women for roughly 2 decades, and although firms have been hiring graduates in comparable numbers, the percentage of women dwindles drastically in terms of who is promoted to the higher tiers of the firm: Approximately 17% of the partners at major law firms nationwide were women in 2005. Inadequate mentoring of women by predominantly male partners was cited as a factor, as was the fact that much of the networking and development opportunities that can advance a law career tend to take place in stereotypically male environments, such as football games or the golf course. Similarly, the American Association of Medical Colleges reported in 2001 that although 45% of medical students were women, there was an average of 21 women full professors per academic medical center, compared with 161 men at that rank. As for senior administrative positions, just 7.5% of medical department chairs nationwide were women. Women comprise one third of American journalists, according to Indiana University's 2003 American Journalist Survey, yet a 2001 study by Annenberg Public Policy Center found that, among top media executives, women occupy only 13% of those positions.

Sexual Harassment

Another expression of sexism that can occur in a woman's place of work is sexual harassment. The U.S. Equal Employment Opportunity Commission (EEOC) describes sexual harassment as unwelcome sexual advances, requests for sexual favors, and other verbal or physical conduct of a sexual nature that explicitly or implicitly affects employment, interferes with work performance, or creates an intimidating, hostile, or offensive work environment. In 1979, feminist legal scholar Catharine MacKinnon pioneered the analysis of this issue in her book *The Sexual Harassment of Working Women*. Before MacKinnon's analysis was published, sexual harassment was often considered to be a normal, biologically based instance of "boys being boys"; MacKinnon was instrumental in explicating it as a discriminatory misuse of power within workplace culture. Today, many businesses actively educate employees about this form of discrimination, and the EEOC reports that 12,679 reports of sexual harassment were filed in 2005, as compared to a high of 15,889 in 1997.

Women's Physical Health

A nonsexist framework for understanding the prevalence of certain disorders among women locates them within a patriarchal context, bringing a focus to such issues as body image, eating disorders, sexual health, reproductive freedom, and the pathologizing of women's experiences through conventional mental health diagnostic practices. Throughout history, women's behaviors and feelings have been given various explanations and diagnostic labels by male-dominated society. Hippocrates warned that women who remained virgins for longer than was appropriate would find that their menstrual periods brought on visions, murderous rage, and a longing for death; women whose behavior did not conform to conventional expectations were hunted as witches for centuries. In the 19th century, medical textbooks portrayed women as the puppets of their ovaries and uterus, organs which were considered to be responsible for myriad mental and physical complaints as well as for the generally flighty nature and immature judgment seen as hallmarks of the feminine character.

In fact, the favorite diagnostic label for women of the late 19th century (which can still be heard today), *hysteria,* is derived from the Greek word for uterus.

Other forms of oppression also impact women's health, as evidenced by statistical data regarding the well-being of women of color. In 2002, the National Institute of Health released a report documenting the shorter life expectancies of women of color as compared with White women. Elevated risk factors were heart disease, cancer (especially African American women), diabetes (all women of color), cerebrovascular diseases (especially Native Americans), unintentional injuries, and HIV/AIDS (especially African American women). Eighty percent of all new cases of HIV/AIDS in women occurred among African American women and Latinas. Women of color were also at greater risk to give birth to low-birth-weight babies, to report unmet mental health needs, to be obese, and to be without health insurance. The cumulative impact of sexism and racism, compounded by the overrepresentation of both women and people of color among the nation's poor, leaves women of color the most vulnerable of all Americans in terms of basic health care.

Contraceptives are an important form of health care for women, enabling them to make basic decisions regarding their own fertility and sexual health. In December 2000, the EEOC moved to protect women from sexist deterrents to sexual health when it ruled that an employer's exclusion of contraceptives from its health insurance plan constituted impermissible sex discrimination. Protection of these rights has not always been consistent, however; in 2005, the Center for Reproductive Rights sued the U.S. Food and Drug Administration for violating its own procedures and statutes as it failed to approve the emergency contraceptive product Plan B for over-the-counter status. Emergency contraception, also known as "the morning after pill," reduces the risk of pregnancy when it is taken within 72 hours of unprotected intercourse. As of 2006, the federal government completed 3 years of its delay in providing a ruling on the distribution of Plan B. In a 2006 statement titled "The War on Women," Planned Parenthood explained its view that restricted access to contraceptives, the funding of medically unsound abstinence-only sex education programs, and the resulting reduction in access to family planning represented critical human rights violations regarding the health and empowerment of women.

In 1973, the Supreme Court established constitutional protection of a woman's right to choose abortion in the well-known case *Roe v. Wade.* This ruling was in accord with advocates of women's rights and nonsexist reforms of women's health care, who pointed out that preventing a woman from exercising fundamental freedoms regarding her own body, including the rights to regulate fertility and terminate an unwanted or dangerous pregnancy, constituted a particularly overt demonstration of gender discrimination. Simultaneously, this ruling inspired the growth of the anti–reproductive rights movement, and the National Organization for Women estimates that the backlash to *Roe v. Wade* began in earnest when the Supreme Court upheld a Connecticut ban on public funding for abortion in 1977. Since 2000, the federal government has moved to limit women's reproductive freedom through such acts as the so-called Partial Birth Abortion Ban, which does not include an exception to preserve a woman's health. Most recently, the governor of the State of South Dakota signed a bill banning all abortions outright except in cases where the woman would otherwise die; survivors of rape or incest or women whose health or fertility were at risk were not protected. The citizens of South Dakota subsequently rejected the bill by a margin of 55% to 45%.

Women's Emotional Health

Feminist analysis has examined the ways that conventional psychological theory and psychopathological nomenclature are themselves derived from patriarchal constructions of femininity. Hope Landrine's work demonstrated that stereotypical assumptions about women's behavior form the basis for such personality disorders (PDs) as histrionic PD and dependent PD. In *Women and Madness,* Phyllis Chesler elaborated on this issue, explaining the double bind that women are placed in as a result: While both men and women who show these personality characteristics are considered ill, women will also be labeled as deviant if they *fail* to enact them to some degree. Along these lines, feminist psychologist and scholar Laura Brown has suggested that conceptions of mental illness derived from dominant culture norms have limited utility for understanding the difficulties experienced by members of subordinated groups, many of which might be more properly understood as "oppression artifact disorders."

Working as they do from gender-biased representations of mental health and disorder, it is not surprising that counselors' attitudes toward women clients can be compromised by sexist stereotyping. Beginning with the work of I. K. Broverman in the 1970s, findings have demonstrated that clinicians have different standards and conceptions regarding the mental health of men and women, with typical adult women conceptualized as having characteristics incompatible with mentally healthy functioning more frequently than are typical adult men. Based on these analyses, feminist psychologists began in the 1960s to describe the ways that traditional approaches to psychotherapeutic practice were misapplied, and even oppressive, with regard to women clients. Women's experiences of living in connection to others were often pathologized by therapists schooled in the patriarchal belief that autonomy should represent the pinnacle of emotional development, and the power-over configuration of the conventional psychodynamic therapist–client dyad was shown to reproduce the subordinate position that women occupied in the larger society. Feminist counseling approaches were conceptualized to affirm the lived experiences of women, to encompass the oppression-related components of women's stories and struggles, and to facilitate empowerment within a collaborative working relationship. An example of one such approach is relational-cultural therapy, which originated with the work of Jean Baker Miller and continues to be elaborated by psychologists at Wellesley College's Stone Center. Taking women's experiences at the crossroads of multiple oppressions as a point of departure, relational-cultural theory posits that psychological connection, rather than separation, is most crucial to understanding optimal human growth and development. The counseling relationship, then, is reframed with an emphasis on mutuality, empathic connection, and power sharing.

Cultural Representations of Women

Representations of women in the media, particularly in advertising, have been analyzed over the years for their sexist depictions of women. Contemporary popular culture features women in a much wider variety of roles than were seen decades ago, yet whether they are doctors, lawyers, housewives, detectives, or psychics, women are still portrayed as overwhelmingly young, thin, beautiful, White, and dressed in the latest fashions. Patriarchal emphasis on women as objects of men's attentions, combined with the bottom-line motivations of the billion-dollar fashion and cosmetics industries, compels women to conform to this culturally prescribed feminine ideal; as Susan Brownmiller explained in her 1984 book *Femininity,* to fall short in one's achievement of "the feminine difference" is to appear not to care about men, to risk the loss of their attention and approval, and to thereby relinquish one's core identity as defined within a patriarchal context.

Culturally constructed ideals of female beauty are frequently used to sell products featured in advertisements, and the toxic environment that this creates for women has been explored by media analysts such as Jean Kilbourne, author of *Deadly Persuasion: Why Women and Girls Must Fight the Addictive Power of Advertising.* Commercial images are increasingly more unrealistic, thanks to the development of digital photo–enhancement technology, and frequently depict thin, young, partially nude White women posed in sensual or sexual contexts. Older women, when depicted at all, are also presented in ways that reinforce the predominant commercial image: Most often they appear uncommonly youthful and are selling cosmetics, drugs, or surgeries promising to offer the same. Women of color and larger-sized women are, for the most part, invisible or relegated to specific niche markets. Such images create anxiety for women, regarding the appearance of their own normal, healthy bodies, and are a factor in the development of eating disorders, body dysmorphic syndromes, and the abuse of diet regimes and medications. With regard to women of color in particular, these images simultaneously enforce a White beauty ideal, paving the way for sales of hair straighteners, skin bleaches, and colored contact lenses.

Problems with body image and eating illustrate the relationship between cultural messages to women regarding their appearance and the ways that women care for their own bodies. Susie Orbach, author of the 1978 book *Fat Is a Feminist Issue,* explored the idea that, in a patriarchal context, weight gain can be seen as a form of rebellion against these often-impossible standards. In 1991, Naomi Wolf elaborated on this theme in *The Beauty Myth,* relating the cultural obsession with smaller-sized women to a patriarchal enforcement of their diminished status in society. Pointing to a cultural backlash against feminism, Wolf demonstrated that the more equity women have achieved, the more harshly cultural prescriptions for beauty have constrained them, as seen in the upsurge in anorexia, bulimia, cosmetic surgery, and diet pills and products.

Violence Against Women

Patriarchal oppression has life-threatening consequences when it is expressed through violence against women. Many women have experienced everyday forms of violence, such as sexual comments on the street, acquaintance rape, obscene phone calls, or sexual harassment at work, aggressions that society often sanctions by blaming the woman herself: She "asked for it," her attire was too provocative, she has no sense of humor, and so forth. Unfortunately, significant numbers of women also face more serious threats to their safety and health. The National Organization for Women reported in 2005 that one in six women will experience rape. Half of women who report rape are under the age of 18, and 22% are under the age of 12. Estimates are that domestic violence affects from 2 to 4 million women each year, with at least 170,000 of those attacks being serious enough to require emergency room care. According to the United Nations Commission on Human Rights, pornography also represents a form of violence against women, in that it legitimizes the degradation and maltreatment of women and asserts their subordinate function with regard to men.

Internalized Oppression

Sexism, like other forms of oppression, is learned by both dominant and subordinate members of society, with the result that women themselves, intentionally or not, participate in the enforcement of oppressive restrictions in their own lives and on other women. When women take oppressive, patriarchal definitions of femininity into the deepest levels of their own identity, it is called *internalized oppression*. In other words, when women believe in their own inadequacy, when they feel that they cannot be seen without makeup on their faces, when their speech is characterized by expressions of tentativeness and uncertainty, when they attempt to conceal their intelligence, when they disparage other women who speak up, when they wear comfortable clothing, or when they otherwise defy conventional stereotypes, they are revealing the extent to which they have internalized their own oppression. In her 2003 book *Women's Inhumanity to Women*, Phyllis Chesler explored the ways that women wound themselves and each other by gossiping and scapegoating other women, allowing their relationships with women to be competitive and transient as they prioritize obtaining the attentions of men. Women's reluctance to associate themselves with movements of women can be seen as part of this trend, reminiscent of the old Groucho Marx line, "I wouldn't join any club that would have me as a member." bell hooks has described the paradoxical phenomenon that is created by this reluctance: modern women who have benefited throughout their lives from feminist-generated social reforms yet go to great lengths to insist that they are not feminists.

Women of color and queer women internalize double and triple doses of oppression. In her book *Homophobia: A Weapon of Sexism*, Suzanne Pharr elucidated the linkages between homophobia, heterosexism, and sexism. Attacks and discrimination against lesbians and gay men serve to enforce the traditional heterosexual power structure, in that adults who break ranks by defying conventional sex role behaviors—women who are not dependent on men, men who do not structure their identities around difference from and dominance of women—are ostracized. To identify as a lesbian, then, is to be stigmatized as the ultimate outsider within a patriarchal context. In her book *Sister Outsider*, Audre Lorde explored the anger, suffering, and self-rejection that racism, heterosexism, and patriarchy create, dividing women of color from themselves and each other.

Transcending Sexism

Feminists are sometimes speciously dismissed as advocating something like a reversal of dominant-subordinate sex roles as the alternative to sexism. In fact, a world beyond sexism is envisioned as one in which both men and women are free to live, learn, work, and love without the confinement, the posturing, and the damage imposed by patriarchal sex role requirements. As bell hooks explained in her book of the same title, feminism is for everybody.

Laura Smith

See also Bias (v3); Discrimination (v3); Discrimination and Oppression (v2); Empowerment (v3); Feminist Therapy (v1); Marianismo (v3); Oppression (v3); Pay Equity (v4); Prejudice (v3); Racism (v3); Sexual Harassment (v4); Sexual Violence and Coercion (v1); Social Justice (v3); Stereotype (v3)

Further Readings

Albelda, R., & Tilly, C. (2005). *Glass ceilings and bottomless pits: Women's work, women's poverty*. Boston: South End Press.

Chesler, P. (2005). *Women and madness* (Rev. ed.). New York: Palgrave Macmillan.

Faludi, S. (1992). *Backlash: The undeclared war against American women* (Reprinted ed.). New York: Anchor Press.

Hernandez, D., & Rehman, B. (Eds.). (2002). *Colonize this! Young women of color on today's feminism*. Emeryville, CA: Seal Press.

hooks, b. (2000). *Feminism is for everybody*. Boston: South End Press.

Johnson, A. (1997). *The gender knot: Unraveling our patriarchal legacy*. Philadelphia: Temple University Press.

Lorde, A. (1984). *Sister outsider*. Berkeley, CA: Crossing Press.

MacKinnon, C. A. (2005). *Women's lives, men's laws*. Cambridge, MA: Belknap Press.

Miller, J. B. (1987). *Toward a new psychology of women* (2nd ed.). Boston: Beacon Press.

Moraga, C. (1984). *This bridge called my back*. New York: Kitchen Table—Women of Color Press.

Pharr, S. (1997). *Homophobia: A weapon of sexism* (Reprinted ed.). New York: Chardon Press.

Walker, A. (2003). *In search of our mothers' gardens: Womanist prose* (Reprinted ed.). New York: Harvest.

Wolf, N. (2002). *The beauty myth* (Reprinted ed.). New York: Harper.

SOCIAL IDENTITY THEORY

Originally developed by Henri Tajfel and John Turner to understand the psychological bases of intergroup discrimination, social identity theory seeks to explain the psychological and social bases for intergroup behavior and has more recently been used to also understand intragroup processes. Social identity theory can be used in the contexts of multicultural counseling, research, and practice to understand the processes by which individuals develop and maintain social identities and groups. The theory includes three core elements: social categorization, social identification, and social comparison. Social identity theory proposes that individuals engage in a natural process of categorizing their social world into "us" and "them." Individuals strive for a positive self-concept and maintain and enhance their self-esteem through their memberships in social groups. Individuals derive positive valuation from their ingroup (i.e., members of the group to which they belong) through engaging in social comparison of their group with other groups. To enhance their self-concept, individuals view their social groups as unique and of higher status than other groups.

Social Categorization

Individuals naturally categorize their social environment into those in their ingroup and those in outgroups. Tajfel and Turner suggest that this simple categorization is sufficient to trigger ingroup favoritism and outgroup discrimination. That is to say, individuals need only be aware that an outgroup (i.e., those with whom they do not share group membership) exists for them to engage in intergroup competition with those whom they perceive are part of their outgroup.

Individuals engage in categorization because it helps to simplify the social environment. Therefore, individuals will categorize people according to how similar and different they are to each other. Furthermore, individuals will accentuate these perceived differences in a stereotyped fashion, viewing people as more similar to or more different from them than they actually are.

Social Identity

Individuals are thought to have multiple levels of identity that define who they are. On the most basic level, individuals define themselves according to individual personality traits and interpersonal relationships, and this is referred to as *personal identity*. Through social categorization, individuals also understand themselves as members of social groups and derive social identity from these group memberships. Specifically, social identity includes those aspects of a person's self-concept that are based on their perceived membership in social groups (e.g., Black, Catholic, university student).

Social Comparison and Positive Distinctiveness

To have a positive self-concept and social identity, individuals engage in social comparison with other groups and view themselves as better than and different from members of other groups (i.e., with positive distinctiveness). The dimensions along which individuals of one group differentiate themselves from other groups depend on the social context. For example, race is a salient attribute with which ingroup and outgroup members are defined in the United States, whereas it may not be a relevant attribute in other countries. For social comparison to take place, outgroups must be seen as similar enough to the ingroup to make social distinctions relevant, and all groups must agree that the attribute of distinction is of importance.

It has been argued that regarding one's ingroup with positive distinctiveness is essentially a form of intergroup competition because the goal of such a comparison is to assert the group's superiority over an outgroup. As such, social identity theory has been widely used to understand intergroup discrimination and conflict, as well as social changes that involve an individual's desire for mobility into a more positively regarded social group or a group's efforts to assert positive distinctiveness.

Implications

Social identity theory aids in our understanding of intergroup social phenomena, such as stereotyping and discrimination, as well as intragroup social phenomena, such as differentiation of members within the group and within-group effects on individual attitude change.

Intergroup Processes

Stereotypes and Discrimination. When social identity is salient, an individual perceives his or her group to be normative and holds attitudes and behaviors consistent with perceived group norms. Self-enhancement results in individuals viewing their group favorably while holding negative stereotypes about the outgroup. Intergroup behavior can thus be understood as the collective action of individuals of an ingroup who behave similarly and treat outgroup members similarly, viewing them as stereotypically homogeneous.

Social groups organize into status hierarchies as a result of social comparison. According to social identity theory, when individuals do not derive a positive social identity from a particular group membership, they will strive to leave this group and/or act to make their group more positively distinct.

Individuals who strive for upward social mobility try to dissociate from members of the ingroup that they perceive as lower in the status hierarchy and display preferences for members of a higher-status group. An example of this phenomenon is internalized racial oppression, involving self-hate among racial minorities and their desire to emulate mainstream White Americans. Mobility out of a lower-status group is considered an individual rather than a group endeavor, and while possibly changing the status of an individual, such individual mobility does not change the status of the groups.

Rather than attempting to leave their existing groups, some members of lower-status groups may instead try to make their group more positively distinct. They can do this by redefining how their group is being compared with others. For example, lower-status groups may attempt to emphasize another dimension for social comparison, one that casts a more positive light on them. Lower-status groups may also change the values of attributes assigned to their group from negative to positive. For example, whereas being African American was perceived to be negative, the Black nationalism movement in the 1960s and 1970s, proclaiming that "Black is beautiful," redefined being Black as positive. In addition, lower-status groups may select a different outgroup as a comparative frame of reference. This usually involves selecting a comparison group that is perceived to be of lower status than the group. These processes by which members of lower-status groups attempt to make their group more positively distinct are collective actions that attempt to change the status of the group as a whole.

Another way that an ingroup may assert their positive distinctiveness is by attempting to change the status position of their group along the valued dimension of comparison. For example, the civil rights movement was an attempt by minorities to change their status position in the United States through fighting for more rights. The result of social competition changes the status hierarchy as a whole. When competition occurs over scarce resources, social competition will lead to conflict between higher-status groups, who wish to retain their resources and social position, and lower-status groups.

Intragroup Processes

More recently, social identity theory has been applied to better understand how individuals organize themselves within groups. When individuals define themselves with a social identity, they construct and conform to the ingroup norms. However, few groups exist where all members are entirely homogeneous. According to social identity theory, differentiation among members of an ingroup may be allowed, with the nature of such differentiation dependent on the social context in which group norms are agreed. Members of a group may agree that heterogeneous roles among members are allowed or even necessary for the group to enhance its positive distinctiveness. Individuals are allowed a level of optimal distinctiveness, or the freedom to balance the desire to be part of a group while maintaining individuality, so long as there remains a greater perceived difference between, rather than within, groups. For example, a basketball team comprises players who all identify as members of the same team, but each player contributes to help the team win games.

Attitude change is internalized by individuals through their self-categorization as group members. For example, Jim Sidanius and his colleagues have found that ethnic minority college students' membership in ethnic organizations increases not only their sense of ethnic identity but also their perceptions of discrimination.

Social identity theory informs our broad understanding of the complex social processes through which individuals interact with others as individuals and as group members. This perspective is shaped entirely by the sociocultural context in which individuals and groups reside.

Anne Saw and Sumie Okazaki

See also Bias (v3); Black Racial Identity Development (v3); Discrimination (v3); Ethnic Identity (v3); Identity (v3); Identity Development (v3); Prejudice (v3); Stereotype (v3); White Racial Identity Development (v3)

Further Readings

Capozza, D., & Brown, R. (Eds.). (2000). *Social identity processes: Trends in theory and research.* Thousand Oaks, CA: Sage.

Hogg, M. A., & Abrams, D. (1988). *Social identifications: A social psychology of intergroup relations and group processes.* New York: Routledge.

Robinson, W. P. (Ed.). (1996). *Social groups and identities: Developing the legacy of Henri Tajfel.* Oxford, UK: Butterworth-Heinemann.

Sidanius, J., Van Laar, C., Levin, S., & Sinclair, S. (2004). Ethnic enclaves and the dynamics of social identity on college campuses: The good, the bad, and the ugly. *Journal of Personality and Social Psychology, 87,* 96–110.

Tajfel, H., & Turner, J. (1986). The social identity theory of intergroup behavior. In S. Worchel & W. G. Austin (Eds.), *Psychology of intergroup relations* (2nd ed., pp. 7–24). Chicago: Nelson-Hall.

SOCIAL JUSTICE

Social justice refers to the promotion of full and equal participation of all individuals and groups, allowing their needs to be met equally. Most societies around the world have fallen short of creating conditions of social justice. This is evidenced by the existence of marginalization in many societies, as evidenced by the fact that many groups do not have full participation or share equal power in society because of race, ethnicity, age, socioeconomic status, religion, disability, or sexual orientation. Because inequities exist based on these cultural differences, societies that strive for social justice often have attempted to identify and rectify the existence of oppressive structural barriers embedded in the social, economic, and political systems. Historical examples within the United States are the women's suffrage movement that led to the federal right for women to vote in 1920 and the civil rights movement in the 1960s, which was aimed at abolishing racial discrimination against African Americans.

The negative psychological effects of social injustice are numerous and include the development of symptoms such as depression and anxiety. Within the field of psychology, it has been argued that the reality of oppression and social injustices must be incorporated into the treatment plans of individuals who are members of marginalized groups (e.g., women, people of color). A failure to acknowledge the adverse effects of social injustice on individuals' mental health and functioning can be problematic for many reasons. For example, a recent immigrant who is having difficulty finding a job may benefit from having a counselor with whom to process his or her frustrations, but therapeutic processing alone may not be sufficient in helping the client understand the full range of reasons he or she has had difficulty finding work. A counselor who is not aware of the potential of societal oppression might even attribute the client's difficulty in finding work solely to individual factors (e.g., an underlying personality issue), rather than the possibility that the client is also facing workplace discrimination. As a result, the client may end up feeling as misunderstood in therapy as he or she does in other facets of life.

Because the genesis of some mental health problems can include experiences of social injustice, it has been argued that mental health professionals should expand their roles beyond that of traditional counseling.

Although the counselor can provide a place to process emotions related to oppression, of equal importance is the counselor's role as an agent of social change. Rather than changing people only through individual empowerment, a social justice framework within the mental health field encourages counselors to change the contextual variables that contribute to social inequity and oppression. Numerous scholars have suggested that client advocacy and public policy work can be infused into the skills of counselors.

Advocating for social justice requires that mental health counselors become more knowledgeable about oppression and societal inequities and how they are experienced by individuals and groups. For example, a counselor may benefit from visiting the neighborhood in which a client resides so as to learn more about the client's everyday experience. When counselors learn more about their clients' communities, they are better able to assist clients in accessing their indigenous support networks, such as religious leaders, community leaders, friendship networks, and family. Counselors must also personally reflect on issues of oppression and privilege in their own lives. An important part of being a social justice–oriented counselor is to critically examine one's experience as an oppressor, the oppressed, or both. To think critically about these experiences may influence the ways one conceptualizes and interacts with clients.

In addition to increasing knowledge of oppressive forces and gaining self-awareness regarding power and privilege, it is important that counselors strive to actively engage in the work of social justice on behalf of their clients. For example, counselors can implement and evaluate both remedial and preventive mental health intervention programs to assist marginalized populations. Preventive mental health interventions can serve as a unique way to effect change within a community. Rather than waiting until a problem occurs, prevention programs provide the possibility of protecting their stakeholders from the negative outcomes of social inequity. Counselors can become more involved in community organizations that confront social injustice as a way to not only assist the community but also extend the scope of their reach beyond individual client. Thus, a commitment to social justice requires more than becoming aware of inequity; it requires a commitment to working to end inequity.

Professionals in the field of counseling have unique insight into the detrimental effects of oppression and social injustice on individual health and well-being. It is incumbent upon such professionals to advocate for marginalized groups to help alleviate oppression. In addition to implementing outreach and prevention programs that are aimed to alleviate the detrimental effects of oppression, counselors can also play an important role as advocates for political policies that seek to end the injustices that plague marginalized communities. This has implications for training mental health professionals to become competent with members of historically marginalized groups.

Educators must not only train counseling students to develop multicultural competence (i.e., the ability to work effectively with diverse and marginalized populations) but also encourage students to act individually and in groups to become agents of social change. In addition to teaching these important skills and encouraging discussions of political and social issues, counselor educators should encourage trainees to get involved in out-of-class activities on campus and in the surrounding community. This could include the addition of real-world experiences as a component of courses that focus on topics of oppression, prevention, outreach, and/or advocacy. Such real-world experiences might include facilitating students' creation of an action research project that examines social issues within the campus, or organizing and participating in a service project that benefits local underserved populations. Through such outreach and service activities, counseling students will develop a greater understanding of the diverse experience of others and be exposed to broader social issues.

In addition to infusing social justice teachings into counselor training programs, counselor educators must enact a combination of advocacy research and social action designed to support the oppressed rather than the powerful. Research aimed at social justice should focus, in particular, on how institutions serve to promote or sometimes prevent social changes and on how individuals and groups can overcome the consequences of an oppressive system. In addition, action-oriented research would assess the need for, or impact of, social policies within marginalized groups and communities (i.e., needs assessments or outcome studies). The delivery of research findings to policy makers through direct presentations to community members and leaders who can get involved at the policy level is imperative. A link between social justice research and its intended beneficiaries must be maintained for the field of counseling to continue to serve as an active agent of social justice.

Laura Dick, Kimberly Bena, and Elizabeth M. Vera

See also Bias (v3); Classism (v3); Discrimination (v3); Discrimination and Oppression (v2); Multicultural Counseling Competence (v3); Oppression (v3); Power and Powerlessness (v3); Racism (v3); Sexism (v3); Social Class (v4); Socioeconomic Status (v3); Stereotype (v3); White Privilege (v3)

Further Readings

Constantine, M. G., Hage, S. M., Kindaichi, M. M., & Bryant, R. M. (2007). Social justice and multicultural issues: Implications for the practice and training of counselors and counseling psychologists. *Journal of Counseling & Development, 85,* 24–29.

Prilleltensky, I., & Nelson, G. (1997). Community psychology: Reclaiming social justice. In D. R. Fox & I. Prilleltensky (Eds.), *Critical psychology: An introduction* (pp. 166–184). Thousand Oaks, CA: Sage.

Vera, E. M., & Speight, S. L. (2003). Multicultural competence, social justice, and counseling psychology. *The Counseling Psychologist, 31,* 253–272.

SOCIETY FOR THE PSYCHOLOGICAL STUDY OF ETHNIC MINORITY ISSUES

The American Psychological Association (APA) is organized with divisions that focus on specialty and interest areas within psychology. As one of the 56 divisions of APA to date, the Society for the Psychological Study of Ethnic Minority Issues (also known as Division 45) has its own governance structure elected by its members.

The Society for the Psychological Study of Ethnic Minority Issues serves as a means to promote the development of knowledge and understanding of ethnic minority psychology; the application of psychological principles specific to ethnic minorities; consideration of how social concerns impact ethnic minority populations; and the incorporation of the importance of cultural diversity in society. The purpose of this organization, as noted in the Division 45 bylaws, is to advance the contributions of psychology as a discipline in the understanding of issues related to people of color through research, including the development of appropriate research paradigms; to promote the education and training of psychologists in matters regarding people of color, including the special issues relevant to the service delivery issues relevant to ethnic minority populations; and to inform the general public of research, education and training, and service delivery issues relevant to ethnic minority populations.

The formation of Division 45 can be traced to a long history of efforts by many individuals and organizations through the years, and a good account of this history can be found in an article by Lillian Comas Diaz in the division's journal, *Cultural Diversity & Ethnic Minority Psychology.* In addition, a list of Division 45 founders is provided on Division 45's Web site. The Council of Representatives of APA voted to establish Division 45 at the August 1986 annual APA meeting. An interim president and executive committee were selected to set up the organization and establish bylaws and procedures. Elections were held in 1987, and the first elected executive committee of Division 45 was formed. Division members elect representatives to the APA Council of Representatives, which is the governing body of the APA, and set policies and direction for the organizations and the field of ethnic minority psychology. Division 45 also has provided leadership in generating many policy changes within APA, as well as in contributing to the knowledge base of the field of psychology. In particular, significant inroads have been made to effect the representation of ethnic minority psychologists within the governance structure of the APA.

Division 45's journal, *Cultural Diversity & Ethnic Minority Psychology,* is regarded as one of the top APA journals in terms of utilization rate, hit rates on computerized searches, and subscriptions. The division's newsletter, *Focus,* is published twice a year and provides information about Division 45's activities and provides articles of interest to the membership of the division. Members of Division 45 have been very active in many other APA divisions and have advocated for the inclusion of multicultural issues within the field of psychology at large. This advocacy fostered the development of the *APA Multicultural Guidelines,* which were approved by the APA Council of Representatives in 2002. This document described cultural competencies for psychologists and the expected approaches for incorporating ethnic minority issues in research, teaching, psychology training, and practice. The *APA Multicultural Guidelines* represent a central guiding source for evaluating psychologists for licensing, ethical practices, training and education, and professional advancement in colleges and universities.

Division 45 also has collaborated on various other projects with APA divisions to enhance cultural diversity training and to bring resources to a broader audience, such as state psychological associations, practitioners via online continuing education training, and conferences, to examine various issues and evidence-based practices for ethnic minority groups. For example, several APA divisions have collaborated and cosponsored a biannual Multicultural Summit conference that focuses on ways to advance the field of psychology through multiculturally sensitive and competent efforts. Other such conferences have emerged or are being planned with similar collaborations on topics such as the impact of immigration, the effect of violence in diverse communities, and evidence-based practices with ethnic minorities.

Eduardo Morales

See also Asian American Psychological Association (v3); Association of Black Psychologists (v3); Ethnic Minority (v3); National Latina/o Psychological Association (v3); Society of Indian Psychologists (v3)

Further Readings

Comas Diaz, L. (in press). Changing psychology: History and legacy of the Society for the Psychological Study of Ethnic Minority Issues. *Cultural Diversity & Ethnic Minority Psychology.*

Web Sites

Division 45: http://www.apa.org/divisions/div45

SOCIETY OF INDIAN PSYCHOLOGISTS

The Society of Indian Psychologists (SIP) is a formal professional organization of American Indian, Alaskan Native, and non-Native psychologists, as well as other affiliated professionals, whose purpose is to promote and improve the psychological health and well-being of the indigenous peoples of the Americas. Additionally, SIP advocates for the development and application of culturally competent and relevant psychological theory, research, education, and clinical practice with American Indian and Alaskan Native peoples.

Through biannual meetings, Internet listservs, and other venues, the society provides a forum for professionals who share these collective concerns to consult with one another. SIP also serves as a network for American Indian and Alaskan Native professionals. This network provides opportunities for professional development, advisement, mentorship, and sharing of knowledge, experience, and skills for American Indian and Alaskan Native psychological professionals and others who work with indigenous communities.

Beginnings

The precursor to SIP was an informal group of newsletter subscribers, persons interested in sharing information about psychological services then available in indigenous communities. The newsletter, called *Network of Indian Psychologists,* was founded in 1970 and solely administered by Carolyn Attneave (Delaware/Lenni Lenape), an internationally renowned American Indian psychologist. Five years later, SIP was formally established as a professional organization for American Indian and Alaskan Native psychologists. Today, with a membership of more than 300 professionals, SIP continues to honor Attneave's revolutionary work through sponsoring a memorial scholarship fund in her name.

Policy Making

SIP is one of five national ethnic minority psychological associations; other such organizations include the Association of Black Psychologists, Asian American Psychological Association, National Latina/o Psychological Association, and the Society for the Psychological Study of Ethnic Minority Issues (Division 45) of the American Psychological Association. Together, these organizations constitute the Council of National Psychological Associations for the Advancement of Ethnic Minority Interests.

In 1999, SIP proposed a resolution that supported the retirement of all Indian mascots, personalities, images, and other symbols in use within schools, colleges, universities, and athletic teams in the United States. In 2005, the highest governing body of the American Psychological Association, the Council of Representatives, adopted a similar resolution that recommended immediate retirement of American Indian mascots within educational institutions, athletic teams, and organizations. Both resolutions were based on concerns about the ethical practice of psychology within these contexts as well as psychological research that had demonstrated harmful and negative effects of the use of Indian mascots and other symbols on American Indian children, communities, and students.

Jill S. Hill and María R. Scharrón-del Río

See also Alaska Natives (v3); American Indians (v3); Asian American Psychological Association (v3); Association of Black Psychologists (v3); Bureau of Indian Affairs (v3); Indian Health Service (v3); National Latina/o Psychological Association (v3); Society for the Psychological Study of Ethnic Minority Issues (v3)

Future Readings

Fryberg, S. (2001). *Really! You don't look like an American Indian.* Unpublished doctoral dissertation, Stanford University, Palo Alto, CA.

LaFromboise, T. D., & Trimble, J. E. (1996). Obituary: Carolyn Lewis Attneave (1920–1992). *American Psychologist, 51,* 549.

Peregoy, J. J., & Gloria, A. M. (2007). American Indians and Alaskan Native populations. In M. G. Constantine (Ed.), *Clinical practice with people of color: A guide to becoming culturally competent* (pp. 61–84). New York: Teachers College Press.

Web Sites

Society of Indian Psychologists: http://www.okstate.edu/osu_orgs/sip/

SOCIOECONOMIC STATUS

Socioeconomic status (SES) typically refers to a person's position and esteem in society based on economic and other resources. The most commonly cited indicators of SES are income, occupation, and education. In social science research, SES is often used interchangeably with the term *social class.* However, some would argue that these are different terms and that social class is determined both by the quantifiable amount of resources someone has and their relative standing in relation to others. For example, the terms *lower class, middle class,* and *upper class* can be thought of as income demarcations and are often used as such in census data, but others look at these terms as descriptors of job prestige (e.g., both a college professor and a lawyer may fit into the "upper class" category though their incomes differ greatly). N. Krieger, D. R. Williams, and N. E. Moss, in their paper on measuring social class in public health research, stated that "socioeconomic position" consists of both actual resources and status (i.e., qualities related to prestige and rank). The confounding between the terms *SES* and *social class* reflects the lack of clarity of these concepts in society due to the "myth of the classless society," which is the idea that ability and effort alone are responsible for one's class standing. Oppression by those with material and power and privilege also contributes to the confusion of these terms. This entry focuses on SES but integrates social class concepts as they are relevant to counseling psychology.

SES Indicators and Disparities

Income and Wealth

Income is defined as money received (e.g., from wages, interest, child support, Temporary Assistance to Needy Families), whereas *wealth* consists of assets accumulated. Another way to define wealth is net worth, or assets (e.g., home ownership, stocks, cars, leftover income after expenses) minus debts. Typically, when talking about SES in the United States, the media focus on income. However, wealth statistics paint a more accurate picture of SES and inequality. In addition, income cutoffs for federal programs such as food stamps do not accurately portray the amount of money actually needed for U.S. families to meet basic needs.

According to the U.S. Census Bureau, the median income of families in the United States in 2004 was $44,389. There are significant income disparities based on race. In 2004, the median household income was $48,977 for non-Hispanic Whites, $30,134 for Blacks, $57,518 for Asians, and $34,241 for Hispanics. These figures are estimates and often omit working undocumented immigrants and intergroup differences, such as the status of Southeast Asian refugees.

There are also disparities in income between men and women. The median income for men with earnings in 2004 was $40,798, and for women with earnings it was $31,223. According to this estimate, women are making almost 77 cents on the dollar compared with men. Other estimates claim that the pay gap is decreasing, and women are making about 80 cents for every dollar of men's earnings. However, part of this narrowing is due to the fall of wages for working-class men rather than increases in wages for women.

In 2004, 12.7% of the U.S. population lived below the poverty line. That year, the Department of Health and Human Services defined the poverty threshold as an income of $18,850 for a family of four. However, many economists and social scientists question the formula used to calculate this figure. The threshold is calculated using a formula that was developed in the 1960s, based on the cost of food for a family multiplied by three. This formula fails to incorporate rising housing and healthcare costs, not to mention the need for child care in most American families. Several economists have proposed new formulas for calculating the income that families need to meet their basic needs, and the results of these formulas suggest that families in the United States need an average of 2 times the federal poverty threshold to simply survive. In some regions of the country, the difference is even greater.

Continuing to use the Department of Health and Human Services definition of poverty, glaring differences based on race are apparent. The poverty rate (percentage of the population living under the federal poverty threshold) in 2004 was 8.6% for non-Hispanic Whites, 24.7% for Blacks, 9.8% for Asians, and 21.9% for Hispanics. Two-year average poverty rates (2003–2004) were calculated for American Indians/Alaska Natives and Native Hawaiian/Pacific Islanders, respectively: 24.4% and 12.9%. There are also disparities based on citizenship status. The poverty rate for U.S.-born citizens was 12.1%, compared with 9.8% for foreign-born naturalized citizens and 21.6% for noncitizens. Female-headed households are much more likely to experience poverty. The poverty rate for female households with no husband present was 28.4%. For male households with no wife present it was 13.5%, and for married couple households it was 5.5%.

Wealth disparities are even more staggering. The median net worth (i.e., assets minus debts) for White households in 2001 was $121,000. For Black households, the median was $19,000, and for Latino/a households the median was $11,500. Even as the gap in income between races decreases very slowly, wealth disparities have stayed the same or increased.

Some economists and social scientists, such as Chuck Collins and Felice Yeskel, the authors of *Economic Apartheid in America* with United for a Fair Economy and Class Action, argue that inequality is a critical social problem even if the standard of living has improved for Americans overall. They discuss inequality between racial and ethnic groups, men and women, and wealthy and poor (and, increasingly, between wealthy and middle-income people). Salaries of chief executive officers (CEOs) and other executives have increased exponentially, while workers' wages are stagnant or even decreasing. In addition, CEOs' salaries are positively correlated with downsizing, so as more and more working and middle-income people lose their jobs, the wealth of executives increases. In 2003, the average CEO made as much money as 301 workers. According to the U.S. Census Bureau in 2004, income for families in the top 5% of the population grew by 75% between 1979 and 2003, and for those in the middle 20%, income grew by only 15% during the same period. In 2001, 10% of the population owned 70% of all wealth, and 90% of the population owned 30% of all wealth. Collins and Yeskel reviewed several studies regarding inequality and public health and found that the regional gap between the rich and the poor predicts health better than poverty rates do. In the United States in particular, most working people are working longer hours and earning less; struggling to afford health insurance, higher education, and retirement; going into more debt to pay for everyday expenses; saving less; and working more temporary jobs with no security or benefits.

Occupation

Occupation is another indicator of SES used in social science research. Some researchers simply distinguish between the employed and unemployed, and others use various job categorization schemes. Nancy Lynn Baker noted that the current terms for distinguishing between social classes (e.g., *working class, professional class*) are simply job descriptions and do not capture important distinctions between occupations, such as personal control and level of danger.

Occupations are sometimes grouped by income, but most schemes rely on categories based on prestige, skill, or education required. The U.S. Census groups occupations into 23 major groups, some of which are management; legal; education, training, and library; protective services; building and grounds;

cleaning and maintenance; sales and related; office and administrative support; construction and extraction; and transportation and material moving. According to the U.S. Department of Labor, in May 2005, the occupational group with the highest mean annual wage was management ($88,450), and the occupational group with the lowest mean annual wage was food preparation and serving ($17,840). However, understanding SES by these categories is not particularly meaningful, as management occupations include, for example, CEOs and social and community service managers, and food preparation and service-related occupations include both chefs and dishwashers. In both cases, these occupations differ greatly in terms of income, education required, prestige, and personal control over one's workday. Prestige and power are associated with such categories, as captured by the Occupation Score of the Hollingshead Index of Social Position. The original Hollingshead Two-Factor Index grouped occupations from highest prestige (which could be called business management and professionals) to lowest prestige (unskilled employees). Industrialized nations seem to have similar conceptions of occupational prestige. Michael Argyle reviewed studies of occupational prestige across various countries and found that professionals are usually held in highest esteem, whereas unskilled service workers, farmers, and farm laborers are usually regarded in lowest esteem.

In his book *The Working Class Majority: America's Best Kept Secret,* economist Michael Zweig defined social class in terms of the power workers have in different occupations. He discussed three types of power important in determining one's social class: economic power (based on earnings and wealth, and power over the means of production, including other workers), political power (the power to influence policy), and cultural power (power over the processing of information, such as the media and education). Though someone could have one type of power and not another, all three types generally reinforce one another. He divided occupations into three major classes based on the amount of power each class has: the capitalist class (which includes the ruling class), the middle class, and the working class.

The capitalist class consists of business owners, particularly owners of corporations or "big businesses." Many small business owners fit into Zweig's definition of the middle class. The distinction is that members of the capitalist class do not come into much contact with workers or the process of production, though they have great control over the workforce through middle management. The ruling class consists of a small percentage of the capitalist class who serve on the boards of several corporations, affording them access to political and cultural leaders. Zweig defines the middle class as small business owners; supervisors and managers; and professionals, such as doctors, professors, and computer programmers. He described the middle class as caught between the competing interests of the working and capitalist classes: On the one hand, they have an interest in maintaining their privileges by limiting the power of working-class people, but on the other, they are losing control over their jobs (e.g., designing curricula, HMO policies) to the capitalist class. The working class is the largest class according to Zweig's analysis (about 60% of the U.S. workforce) and is quite diverse. Working-class people are those with the least amount of power and control in their occupations. In the U.S. Census categories, they are typically found in sales, administrative support services, production, and technical occupations. Zweig estimates that 75% of the unemployed are working-class people actively looking for jobs.

Education

Education is often used as a descriptive indicator of SES, distinguishing between those who have not completed high school, those who have completed high school or have obtained a general equivalency diploma, those who have 2-year or vocational degrees, and so on. Education is considered a major vehicle of upward social mobility, as higher education is tied to occupations with higher incomes and prestige. However, the education and income of one's family of origin are highly predictive of future educational opportunities. Income, occupation, and education appear to be intertwined and mutually reinforcing. In the United States in 2003, the median annual income for non–high school graduates was $15,610. This figure was $30,936 for those with associate degrees, $40,588 for those with bachelor's degrees, $51,116 for those with master's degrees, $70,985 for those with doctorate degrees, and $81,833 for those with professional degrees.

In the United States, there are stark racial/ethnic disparities in education. According to the U.S. Census Bureau in 2004, 89.2% of non-Hispanic Whites ages 18 and older had a high school diploma or more, compared with 79.5% of Blacks, 86.8% of Asians, and 58.9% of Hispanics. More striking disparities are found in higher education. Twenty-eight percent (28.2%) of non-Hispanic Whites age 18 and older had a bachelor's degree or higher, compared with 15.6% of Blacks, 45.6% of Asians, and only 10.3% of Hispanics. Note that data were not available for American Indians, Alaska Natives, or Native Hawaiians and other Pacific Islanders, who typically fare worse than other groups on SES indicators.

Classification Schemes Based on Prestige

Two of the most popular classification schemes for SES are August B. Hollingshead's Index of Social Status and Otis Dudley Duncan's Socioeconomic Index. Both of these methods rank occupational categories based on prestige. These methods are based on census data from 1970 and 1950, respectively, and are thus outdated. The Hollingshead Index combines education, occupation, gender, and marital status into one social status score. The Duncan Socioeconomic Index classifies occupational prestige based on the income of, and education required for, the occupation. Another classification method is the Nam-Powers Socioeconomic Status Score, which uses a definition of occupational status based on median income and education of those employed in that occupation, combined with educational level and family income. Problems with these measures include few studies on validity and reliability, the combination of highly intercorrelated SES indicators into one measure, and equating socioeconomic resources with prestige.

SES and Health

SES and Physical Health

There is a clear relationship between SES and health, as indicated by studies that have found evidence of a gradient where low SES is correlated with most (but not all) diseases, and the likelihood of contracting or experiencing disease decreases as SES increases. Relationships between various socioeconomic indicators and physical diseases have been found, including cardiovascular disease, hypertension, and certain types of cancer. Level of education alone has been cited as a predictor of mortality and morbidity in the United States and other countries.

SES is highly correlated with physical health for various reasons. Access to health care, safe workplace conditions, and supportive social networks contribute to the health of those with higher SES. In addition, lower SES is associated with a greater likelihood to engage in risky behaviors, such as smoking and alcohol consumption. Individuals coping with the stress of a low SES environment are also less likely to engage in healthy behaviors such as exercise. The physical environment of low SES neighborhoods can also directly impact health. Impoverished neighborhoods are often exposed to pathogens, carcinogens, and environmental hazards. People in poor communities are also more likely to be exposed to, or experience, violence and may have less social support than people living in higher SES communities.

Nancy E. Adler, Elissa S. Epel, Grace Castellazzo, and Jeannette R. Ickovics conducted a study in which they found strong correlations between subjective SES and health, by asking 157 healthy White women to rank their social status on a 10-rung ladder. Significant negative correlations were found between subjective SES indicators of poor health (e.g., body mass index). The researchers also measured psychological health and found significant negative correlations between subjective SES and negative affectivity, chronic stress, subjective stress, pessimism, and passive coping. Significant positive correlations were found between subjective SES and control over life and active coping. This is one of several studies demonstrating relationships between SES and both physical and mental health.

SES and Mental Health

People living in low SES communities face multiple stressors and often do not have the material or social resources to cope with the resulting stress. Aside from severe financial crises that poor families face (hunger, threats of eviction, etc.), they face more hassles in their daily living than do families in higher SES communities. Those of higher SES have more access to high-quality housing, shops, banks, health care, and transportation. These resources alone can be buffers against stress.

Citing national epidemiological studies, Yan Yu and David R. Williams stated that in 1994, individuals who did not complete high school were almost two times more likely to be diagnosed with a major affective disorder than individuals who had a college education or more. In addition, people of low SES were almost

2 times more likely to suffer from a substance abuse disorder than people in the highest SES group. Though these disparities may be the result of the stressors described above, it is possible that classism, racism, and other forms of oppression affect rates of diagnosis in people of low SES. Considering the SES disparities between races in the United States, it is clear that racial/ethnic minorities are more likely to be diagnosed with a psychiatric illness than are White individuals.

Depression has been linked consistently with poverty in adults and children. According to Deborah Belle and Joanne Doucet, adults in poverty are at double the risk for experiencing a new episode of major depression than are other adults. This compounds children's risk for depression and other mental health problems. Poor household economic conditions increase the risk for childhood depression and the poor physical health correlates of depression. Other risk factors for childhood depression that are linked to SES are living in a single-parent home, parental unemployment, and low educational attainment by parents. A recent meta-analysis by Vincent Lorant and colleagues concluded that there is a moderate to strong relationship between SES and depression, and this is especially true for persistent depression.

SES and Counseling

Classism and Counseling Psychology

Bernice Lott and Laura Smith have called attention to the classism that exists in psychological research and practice. Classism, like other forms of oppression, results from those with unearned class privilege exerting their power over others. Lott discussed notions of class superiority and inferiority that result in psychologists and others distancing themselves from poor people through cognitive means such as stereotyping; exclusion of low SES individuals from institutions such as education, housing, and politics; and interpersonal means such as blatant discrimination and invalidation.

Smith traced the history of psychotherapy's treatment of the poor, including the political backlash against community mental health centers and therapists' expectations of clients based on White middle-class norms. Current therapeutic models are most likely not addressing the needs of those from lower SES groups, as evidenced by higher treatment dropout rates. An example of an attitudinal barrier is counselors seeing their interventions as less significant because poor clients are facing multiple stressors. As the multicultural counseling competencies have helped to address counselors' attitudes regarding race and ethnicity, identification of attitudinal barriers to working with low SES clients will begin to increase counselors' competence to work across socioeconomic groups.

The Social Class Worldview Model

William M. Liu developed the Social Class Worldview Model (SCWM) to address the definitional problems surrounding class and SES and to analyze the complexity of within-group differences (i.e., not all people within a certain class or SES are assumed to share the same characteristics). This model specifically addresses the subjective experience of SES most often known as social class. This has important implications for counseling, as clients' and counselors' perceptions of both their own and the others' SES impact the counseling relationship and process.

Liu chose a worldview model because the underlying construct he is describing reflects people's subjective experience of belonging to a specific group. The subjective context of the SCWM is one's perceived class and status position. This influences saliency, consciousness, and attitudes toward social class issues, which interact with referent groups, material objects, lifestyle, and behaviors. Though all aspects of the SCWM influence one another, saliency, consciousness, and attitudes are placed at the center of the model. *Perceived class and status position* is a person's answer to the question, "What is your social class background?" *Saliency* indicates a level of awareness of an SES system in which there are differential opportunities for people in different classes. *Consciousness* refers to the level of awareness an individual has about belonging to, and being influenced by, a social class system. *Attitudes* refer to feelings, beliefs, attributions, and values about social class. Social class attitudes are shaped by one's early socialization experiences.

Referent groups are groups that inform one's socialization experiences. They influence the development of the SCWM and one's behaviors. The three referent groups that Liu names are the *group of origination* (e.g., caretakers, relatives, early peers), *cohort group* (those with whom one spends the most time and are most similar to him or her in their own worldview and behavior), and *group of aspiration* (the group that one would like to belong to). *Material objects, lifestyle,* and *behavior* can be considered "performance" variables, as they are the visible indicators of class and status. Liu discussed the objective SES measures of income, occupation, and education as limits on one's SCWM. One's class aspirations may not match one's resources.

Because of the paucity of research on the subjective experience of social class, this is a preliminary model that has not been validated. The SCWM places a person's subjective interpretations of social class in ecological context by considering cultural values, social comparison groups, and other important systemic variables. It is a promising paradigm for understanding how people make sense of social class.

Lott, Smith, and Liu each have made significant contributions to the understanding of the relevance of SES to counseling. In U.S. society, the ideology of the "American dream" reinforces a cultural myth that there is no class stratification and that anyone can climb the social class ladder with effort. An understanding of class-based oppression is crucial for counselors who may be working with individuals from different SES groups. More often than not, counselors hold a relatively high SES in U.S. society because of their education and occupational prestige. It is crucial for counselors to examine their SES and social class biases, in addition to examining biases based on race, gender, and other social identities. Liu's model offers a helpful framework for counselors to ask themselves questions about their SES-related beliefs, attitudes, and behaviors. It also provides a model for understanding how social class may be related to clients' presenting concerns. Because social class and SES are complex and often misunderstood constructs, models such as the SCWM can provide structure to the examination of these issues.

Future Directions

SES and social class are inadequately defined in social science research, including counseling research. Socioeconomic indicators such as income, wealth, occupation and occupational prestige, and education have clear implications for health and mental health and will benefit from further research. In addition, counseling psychologists have begun to address the subjective meaning of social class and how it plays out in their lives, including in counseling relationships. An important aspect of this research will focus on understanding discrimination and oppression based on SES and how it affects the work of counselors and psychologists.

LeLaina Romero

See also Academic Achievement (v2); Classism (v3); Part-Time Work (v4); Physical Health (v2); Poverty (v3); Social Class (v4); Third World (v3); Vocational Identity (v4); Worldview (v3);

Further Readings

Adler, N. E., Boyce, T., Chesney, M. A., Cohen, S., Folkman, S., Kahn, R. L., et al. (1994). Socioeconomic status and health: The challenge of the gradient. *American Psychologist, 49,* 15–24.

Adler, N. E., Epel, E. S., Castellazzo, G., & Ickovics, J. R. (2000). Relationship of subjective and objective social status with psychological and physiological functioning: Preliminary data in healthy White women. *Health Psychology, 19,* 586–592.

Argyle, M. (1994). *The psychology of social class.* London: Routledge.

Baker, N. L. (1996). Class as a construct in a "classless" society. In M. Hill & E. D. Rothblum (Eds.), *Classism and feminist therapy: Counting costs* (pp. 13–23). New York: Haworth.

Belle, D., & Doucet, J. (2003). Poverty, inequality, and discrimination as sources of depression among U.S. women. *Psychology of Women Quarterly, 27,* 101–113.

Boushey, H., Brocht, C., Gundersen, B., & Bernstein, J. (2001). *Hardships in America: The real story of working class families.* Washington, DC: Economic Policy Institute.

Collins, C., & Yeskel, F., with United for a Fair Economy and Class Action. (2005). *Economic apartheid in America: A primer on economic inequality & insecurity.* New York: New Press.

Krieger, N., Williams, D. R., & Moss, N. E. (1997). Measuring social class in U.S. public health research: Concepts, methodologies, and guidelines. *Annual Review of Public Health, 18,* 341–378.

Liu, W. M. (2001). Expanding our understanding of multiculturalism: Developing a social class worldview model. In D. B. Pope-Davis & H. L. K. Coleman (Eds.), *The intersection of race, class, and gender in multicultural counseling* (pp. 127–170). Thousand Oaks, CA: Sage.

Liu, W. M., Ali, S. R., Soleck, G., Hopps, J., Dunston, K., & Pickett, T., Jr. (2004). Using social class in counseling psychology research. *Journal of Counseling Psychology, 51,* 3–18.

Lott, B. (2002). Cognitive and behavioral distancing from the poor. *American Psychologist, 57,* 100–110.

Smith, L. (2005). Psychotherapy, classism, and the poor: Conspicuous by their absence. *American Psychologist, 60,* 687–696.

Taylor, S. E., Repetti, R. L., & Seeman, T. (1999). What is an unhealthy environment and how does it get under the skin? In I. Kawachi, B. P. Kennedy, & R. G. Wilkinson (Eds.), *The society and population health reader: Vol. 1. Income inequality and health* (pp. 351–378). New York: New Press.

Yu, Y., & Williams, D. R. (1999). Socioeconomic status and mental health. In C. S. Aneshensel & J. C. Phelan (Eds.), *Handbook of the sociology of mental health* (pp. 151–166). New York: Kluwer Academic/Plenum.

Zweig, M. (2000). *The working class majority: America's best kept secret.* Ithaca, NY: ILR Press.

SOJOURNER

A sojourner is a person who resides in a country other than his or her country of origin for an extended time. Sojourners leave their home country for a specific purpose (e.g., teaching, studying, working, military service, humanitarian aide) but have no intentions of applying for citizenship or moving permanently to the host country. International students, peace corps volunteers, military personal, missionaries, and people who temporarily work overseas are all examples of sojourners. Usually this temporary move is purely by choice; however, in certain cases, like that of military personnel, their service may be voluntary but their requirement to move may be a demand of their service and thereby not totally of their own accord. Sojourning has become increasingly popular as technology and communication have advanced to create a global economy.

Sojourning can be considered a major life stressor and individuals may see a counselor for assistance in adjusting to their relocation. Cognitive, behavioral, and emotional adjustment will be necessary. Upon arrival in their host country, many sojourners describe a variety of symptoms such as fatigue, isolation, numbness, irritability, confusion, a sense of loss and/or violation, frustration, anger, exhaustion, depression, and reduced confidence. These tend to be most prevalent upon their arrival in the host country and dissipate over time. A failure to recover from the transition into another culture may result in an early return to their native country, difficulties performing their duties in the host country, and prolonged distress. This failure to adjust may have long-term effects on their career path and interpersonal relationships. Counselors can assist their clients by helping them adjust to their new environment and normalizing their feelings. Counselors must be respectful of their unique worldview and not suggest they change to fit in with the culture of the new country. It is important to understand what the sojourner's expectation is for counseling and how counseling is viewed in his or her country of origin. This will be critical in determining the client's expectations of the counselor. Sojourners may present many challenges to the counselor, such as less fluency in the host culture language, different nonverbal behaviors, and different customs. It is necessary for counselors to familiarize themselves with the customs of their culture of origin to facilitate a multiculturally sensitive approach to treatment.

If sojourners are able to negotiate the adjustment into their host culture, they may return to their native country having gained a new understanding of international relations and an increased appreciation for both their native country and their host country.

Jennifer L. Lemkuil

See also Acculturation (v3); Acculturative Stress (v3); Adaptation (v3); Assimilation (v3); Cultural Values (v3); Culture (v3); Culture Shock (v3); Enculturation (v3); Occupational Stress (v1); Second Culture Acquisition (v3); Stress Management (v2)

Further Readings

Sussman, N. M. (2000). The dynamic nature of cultural identity throughout cultural transitions: Why home is not so sweet. *Personality and Social Psychology Review, 4*(4), 355–373.

Ward, C. (1996). Acculturation. In D. Landis & R. S. Bhafat (Eds.), *Handbook of intercultural training* (Vol. 2, pp. 124–147). Thousand Oaks, CA: Sage.

Ward, C., Bochner, S., & Furnham, A. (2001). *The psychology of culture shock* (2nd ed.). Philadelphia: Taylor & Francis.

SPIRITUALITY

Spirituality, from the Latin *spiritus,* refers to a sense of, or belief in, something bigger than, beyond, or outside oneself. Individual spirituality is often seen as a connection among oneself, others, and that which is beyond oneself and others. In addition, some scholars have referred to spirituality as a holistic connection with the divine or the breath that animates life. Some see spirituality in terms of people's attempts to understand the ultimate nature of things in the universe; in this way, spirituality shares commonalities with some philosophies. Finally, others relate spirituality to psychological health; that is, the person on a spiritual path is also seeking psychological balance and well-being.

Spirituality is often combined and/or confused with religion. There is a lack of consensus among professionals regarding the similarities and differences where spirituality and religion are concerned, which has resulted in a frequent merging of the two constructs. There are, however, some agreed-upon ways to articulate the differences between spirituality and religion. For example, spirituality has been seen as encompassing religion; that is, religion is a form of spirituality. In addition, spirituality is typically seen as a construct that resides within an individual and connotes a personal relationship with a higher power. In contrast, religion is a social institution, with rules and hierarchies for salvation. As a result of this difference, religions tend to proscribe a path to enlightenment or nirvana, while the spiritual person would suggest that there are many ways to achieve the desired goals regarding psychological and spiritual well-being.

Manifestations of Personal Spirituality

There is no one "right" way to be spiritual. To that end, spirituality can be demonstrated in a variety of ways. Some examples of personal manifestations of spirituality include prayer, meditation, yoga, physical exercise, laughter, breathing exercises, worship, rituals, fasting, imagery creation, Bible/Qur'an/Talmud study, pastoral counseling, and quoting sacred texts. It is important to note that this list is not meant to be exhaustive.

Spirituality in the Counseling Process

Like many things in a counseling relationship, the spirituality of the counselor and client can significantly impact the therapeutic process. The spiritual beliefs of both the therapist and the client should be viewed as important characteristics that may affect counseling.

For clients, their spirituality should be considered as important to the therapeutic process as any other salient variable, especially clients for whom spirituality is central to their identity or cultural self-description. For some clients, spirituality provides a lens or worldview with which they see and interact with others in their environment. For highly spiritual clients, then, counselors should be sure to attend to the client's spiritual orientation, as it is likely to facilitate the client's exploration of the problem(s) that brought him or her to counseling. In addition, counseling professionals will obtain a more complete understanding of their clients by attending to the client's spirituality. Of course, some clients might not feel comfortable talking about spirituality with their counselor because they might assume that spirituality is a taboo topic in counseling.

For counselors, there are two conditions in which spirituality affects the counseling process. First, the counselor can facilitate the client's disclosure by welcoming, and perhaps even inquiring about, the client's spirituality in session. In this way, the counselor must provide a safe environment for the client to discuss his or her personal spirituality. Honoring the client's spirituality can be as effective as being empathic and sensitive to the client's other aspects of identity, such as race, ethnicity, gender, sexuality, religion, and socioeconomic status.

Second, the personal spirituality of the counselor can also assist in the development and strengthening of the counseling relationship. For example, many counselors endorse having spiritual beliefs that serve as guiding principles for their lives. This view of self and others can be facilitative with regard to the counselor's understanding and conceptualization of the client's behavior, history, and worldview. The counselor who understands the role of spirituality in his or her own life, even if that means no spirituality, will be better prepared to attend to the client's personal spirituality as it might emerge in the counseling process.

Effectively discussing spirituality between the counselor and client has the potential to establish a sound working alliance, especially where there is some shared perceptions regarding spirituality. Through the counselor's welcoming of spirituality into the treatment room, the client may feel more comfortable in disclosing those aspects of him- or herself, especially as they relate to the presenting problem(s). At the minimum, counselors should attend to the client's spirituality if and when the client raises that issue as part of the counseling process. To ignore a client's sense of spirituality is to deny what could be a vital, if not central, aspect of the client's identity. In sum, clients will be better served by counseling professionals who attend to spirituality in their clients and who have sought to understand what role, if any, spirituality plays in their own lives.

Spirituality in the Lives of People of Color

It is important to attend to spiritual concerns in all clients; however, with clients of color it may be even more critical to understand the role that spirituality plays in their lives. Continuous experiences with social intolerance (i.e., prejudice, racism, discrimination, and oppression) have been primary forces causing a deepened level of spirituality for many people of color. These forces, both powerful and harmful, often have negative psychological impacts; some examples include heightened levels of anxiety, frustration, depression, and identity confusion. As a result, people of color seek refuge from this intolerance through spirituality; this is done to comfortably connect their internal selves with the surrounding world and a self-defined higher power or higher being. Through personal spirituality, people of color find ways of transcending difficult social situations and recognizing the positive aspects of unfortunate circumstances. Hence, spirituality plays an integral part in the lives of people of color by empowering them with renewed hope and strength to endure despite daily personal and social struggles.

Spirituality as a Coping Mechanism

Spiritual practices and beliefs are relevant across all racial and cultural groups, providing coping mechanisms for a variety of stressors. The use of spiritual techniques may help people view difficult or challenging situations in a more positive light by identifying personal meaning in the face of adversity. This could, in turn, lead to acceptance and possibly appreciation of negative experiences. Belief in a higher power may also serve as a powerful resource for clients in terms of feeling supported in the face of struggles. In sum, embracing spirituality can be a powerful tool for building personal strength and enhancing resiliency for the challenges of daily living.

Lewis Z. Schlosser, Raymond D. Brock-Murray, and Tonisha Hamilton

See also Coping (v2); Espiritismo (v3); Multicultural Counseling Competence (v3); Religion/Religious Belief Systems (v3); Spirituality/Religion (v2); Worldview (v3)

Further Readings

Cashwell, C. S., & Young, J. S. (Eds.). (2005). *Integrating spirituality and religion into counseling: A guide to competent practice.* Alexandria, VA: American Counseling Association.

Cervantes, J. M., & Parham, T. A. (2005). Toward a meaningful spirituality for people of color: Lessons for the counseling practitioner. *Cultural Diversity & Ethnic Minority Psychology, 11,* 69–81.

Curtis, R. C., & Glass, J. S. (2002). Spirituality and counseling class: A teaching model. *Counseling and Values, 47,* 3–12.

Fukuyama, M. A., & Sevig, T. D. (1999). *Integrating spirituality into multicultural counseling.* Thousand Oaks, CA: Sage.

Griffith, J. L., & Griffith, M. E. (2002). *Encountering the sacred in psychotherapy: How to talk with people about their spiritual lives.* New York: Guilford Press.

Richards, P. S., & Bergin, A. E. (Eds.). (2000). *Handbook of psychotherapy and religious diversity.* Washington, DC: American Psychological Association.

Richards, P. S., & Bergin, A. E. (2005). *A spiritual strategy for counseling and psychotherapy* (2nd ed.). Washington, DC: American Psychological Association.

STEREOTYPE

Stereotype is generally defined as a consciously or unconsciously held rigid belief or expectation about a group that does not easily permit exceptions. Stereotyped beliefs are held by a group (commonly called the ingroup) and involve an agenda that benefits the ingroup at the expense of the stereotyped group (commonly called the outgroup or target group). Stereotypes help the ingroup members feel good about their group and themselves relative to the target group. A stereotype often concerns a trait that is important to the ingroup's identity and emphasizes the distinctness and inferiority of the outgroup. Relatedly, stereotypes maintain sociopolitical hierarchies in society. They can serve as a justification for believing that certain groups are superior to others and as a rationale for oppressing target groups.

While the phenomenon of stereotyping has been defined and explored primarily in social and cognitive psychology, it has many implications for counseling and has been taken up and discussed by many scholars in counseling psychology. These discussions often focus on the sociopolitical aspects of stereotypes, including the relevance of stereotypes to prejudice and to counseling training, competence, and process.

History of the Term

The term *stereotype* comes from two Greek words meaning "solid" and "a model." In English, it first meant a metal printing plate. The term evolved to become associated with the act of stamping out the same image or text over and over; by the beginning of the 20th century, it connoted rigid, repetitive behavior. Soon thereafter it was applied to cognitive processes of categorization that were consistent and predictable. Early discussions of categorizing objects asserted that stereotypes were useful but also resulted in a certain number of errors. When applied to the social domain in the 1930s, *stereotype* came to denote the misattributions commonly applied to ethnic groups (e.g., Germans are scientific minded; Turks are cruel). Thus, stereotypes became linked to prejudice and discrimination and were often considered negative. At this time stereotypes ceased to involve exclusively errors in cognition and became a social phenomenon resulting more from cultural influences than from individual experience.

In the latter 1970s and the 1980s scholars began exploring the cognitive processes of stereotyping, relating stereotypes to cognitive schemata or theories. Using general principles of cognitive processing to illuminate how stereotyping occurs, the discussion at times ignored the sociopolitical context of the phenomenon. In contrast, when the field of counseling took up the term in examining the impact of prejudice and ethnocentrism on counseling process and training, scholars consistently focused on the sociopolitical underpinnings of stereotyping.

Perspectives on Stereotyping

In discussing stereotyping, counseling scholars often draw heavily on conceptualizations generated by other fields. A discussion of these perspectives can flesh out the phenomenon's meaning for counseling.

Stereotyping as a Social-Cognitive Phenomenon

Stereotypes have been explored a great deal in terms of the cognitive processes of attending to, organizing, and interpreting social information or stimuli encountered in everyday life. Social psychologists have done the majority of this work, applying principles of cognitive psychology to social stereotyping. The premise is that people do not have the capacity or resources to consider and analyze every new stimulus as if it were the first piece of information ever received. To process all incoming stimuli efficiently and effectively, people create sorting mechanisms, expectations, and assumptions, often called *cognitive schemata*. Schemata are systems that help people make sense of the complex sets of stimuli that constantly confront them. Schemata are organizing principles that prioritize what to focus on and that categorize and organize the information for interpretation. For example, we have a schema that helps us efficiently differentiate a table from a chair based on multiple expectations about the attributes of each of these objects. From a social-cognitive perspective, stereotypes are a type of schema—rules and expectations we have about people from different groups.

Schemata often become automatic and unconscious. Thus, stereotype holders are not often aware of the expectations and assumptions that influence their thinking, emotions, and behavior. When asked explicitly, they deny holding these stereotypes, but the stereotypes manifest their influence in implicit ways.

Often, the experiences that give rise to stereotyped beliefs are also implicit and embedded in a society's culture. Implicit messages that give rise to stereotypes are broadcast by societal institutions. For example, the media do not explicitly state that Whites or men are superior to people of color or women, but they present a preponderance of heroic characters that are White men, while presenting people of color and women in secondary and supporting roles. This imbalance in portrayals communicates stereotypes about racial and gender hierarchy, including that White men have greater abilities and are more important than people of color and women. As a result, many members of the society unconsciously hold such stereotypes.

To understand stereotypes, social-cognitive scholars have drawn on rules for how unconscious cognitive sorting and organizing processes function. For instance, based on rules of human cognition, groups that stand out (e.g., groups who are in the minority and are judged to be different from the majority) and traits that stand out (e.g., traits that are not often seen in mainstream experience) are often paired to form stereotypes. In the example, Blacks stand out as a minority group visibly distinguishable from Whites, and criminality stands out as an infrequent, deviant trait, so the two can be connected easily in the White person's mind. Even though the connection does not exist in reality, the distinctiveness of both the group and the trait creates fertile ground for them to be paired in a stereotype.

Of course, stereotyping is a social as well as a cognitive process. The culture, characteristics, and views of the ingroup are important in the development of stereotypes. Fertile ground for a stereotype is increased if the target group is viewed as deviating from the ingroup on the trait in question. It is also increased when the trait is one that the ingroup deems important to its identity. To most Whites, not being a criminal means that one has the favor and help of society's institutions (e.g., the police), and thus one has more value and power in society. Thus, the stereotype that Black and Latino males are criminals can serve to make Whites feel more valuable and powerful by creating a false contrast on an attribute or status that is important in White culture.

Stereotypes also have an emotional component. If an ingroup has strong negative feelings about a trait they perceive in a target group, a stereotype is likely to develop. The in-group's emotions about the target group also come into play: Greater negative feelings toward the group can result in more negative stereotypes about the group. In fact, simply putting people in a bad mood has been shown to elicit more stereotyped judgments of others.

This emotional component of stereotyping contributes to a vicious cycle. When ingroup members experience what they perceive as a negative encounter with target group members, they develop negative feelings about the target group and what they perceive as its undesirable traits. This gives rise to increased negative feelings and expectations (stereotypes), which influence their interpretation of and reaction to future encounters, resulting in further affirmation of the stereotype.

The social-cognitive approach also helps explain why stereotypes are rigid and hard to change. People are more likely to process accurately and remember information that is consistent with stereotypes they hold. Many studies have shown that stereotype-consistent information is easily remembered and readily accepted without question. People also tend to remember (but with a different purpose) information that is contrary to the stereotypes they hold. They pay very close attention primarily to figure out how to explain or interpret the information so that their stereotype remains unchallenged. The new information may be distorted or misperceived to fit the stereotype.

Of course, new information can cause a person to modify or even abandon a stereotype, but this happens only rarely. From a cognitive perspective, people tend to see what fits with what they expect, and they often misperceive what is there, to fit their expectations. This happens in categorizing or characterizing objects as well as people. When this cognitive tendency is added to the emotional component of stereotypes and to the individual and group dividends gained by maintaining a stereotype, it is clear why contrary information often does not produce a change in a stereotype.

One way in which evidence contrary to a stereotype is absorbed without threatening the hold of the belief involves the process of subtyping. People create a slightly different subcategory of the larger target group to hold an individual member of the group who presents with traits that are inconsistent with the stereotype. For example, to absorb the fact that many Blacks are successful and law-abiding, Whites create subtypes (Black businessperson, educated Black), while maintaining the general negative stereotype that Blacks are criminals.

Contrary information may also be processed as extreme: The perceiver may tend to exaggerate the level of the unexpected trait or behavior. Thus, a woman who is competitive or ambitious is seen as extremely (and negatively) so, whereas a man with the same level of these traits is seen as normal. Similarly, stereotypes may create what is called a *shifting standard* for judging the behavior of individuals from different groups. For example, if a teacher who holds the stereotyped expectation that Blacks are less intelligent than Whites sees the same test score from a Black and a White student, the Black student may be perceived as highly intelligent and the White student as of average intelligence. Due to the stereotype, the teacher maintains a lower standard for considering a Black student intelligent than for considering a White student intelligent. The Black student will be perceived as very smart *for a Black person.*

The social-cognitive perspective helps counselors understand the functioning and even some of the motivation behind stereotypes, but it is also limited because it more or less views stereotyping in a political vacuum, as if no power hierarchy of social groups existed. Stereotypes play a role in rationalizing and maintaining this hierarchy, and the hierarchy influences the nature of stereotypes.

Stereotyping as a Sociopolitical Phenomenon

Counselors draw upon the social-cognitive approach to stereotypes but often integrate it into a larger context. Sociopolitical factors and cognitive factors interact in both developing and maintaining stereotypes. Stereotypes emerge from the sociocultural context and are driven by power differentials between groups. As noted earlier, the distinctions between groups that are inherent in stereotyping can make the ingroup feel better about itself. To push further on this point, counseling has tended to look at the role of stereotypes in reinforcing power hierarchies between reference groups.

From the sociopolitical perspective, stereotypes grow out of a need to rationalize oppression and subjugation rather than simply out of cognitive processes and errors. For example, in the service of enslavement and genocide, stereotypes emerged that Blacks were childlike and Native Americans savage. Thus, sociopolitical expediencies influence the traits misattributed to a group.

Sociopolitical influence is illustrated by the change in stereotypes held about Blacks before and after slavery was abolished. Before abolition, Blacks were stereotyped as docile, dependent, and incapable of independent thought or action, that is, a group seen as benefiting from enslavement. After slavery was abolished, however, the Whites' stereotype of Blacks tended toward aggressive, dangerous, wild, and uncontrollable. The belief in these traits played a role in justifying brutal treatment of Blacks by Whites both by law (e.g., Jim Crow statutes) and outside the law (e.g., lynching). Thus, the existence and nature of stereotypes can change based on the ingroup's requisites for protecting its privilege and access to power and resources.

Such change suggests that stereotypes may not originate in experience. An initial negative encounter with a target group may not be necessary for a stereotype to develop. Some argue that sociopolitical forces give rise to stereotypes first, and then social-cognitive processes come into play, contributing to their maintenance and rigidity. Power differentials between groups, and the need to rationalize them, may be the starting point for the vicious cycle discussed earlier.

Implications for Counseling

Impact of Stereotypes on the Counseling Process

Among other things, counseling involves evaluating clients and their experiences, to gain an empathic understanding and choose appropriate interventions. Stereotypes have a deleterious effect on this process in several ways. First, they set expectations that limit the counselor's openness to who clients are and what they are experiencing. If a counselor expects a female client to be weak and submissive, the counselor is more likely to ignore or misinterpret information suggesting the opposite. The counselor will misunderstand the client and impose this expectation on her. Such a response can invalidate the client's experience and even negatively influence her sense of who she is. If, due to a counselor's stereotype, a certain trait or experience of a client is always ignored, while evidence of another trait is always emphasized and focused on, the client may start to believe and behave as if the stereotype were true. Counseling scholars have noted that this is a form of oppression and must be avoided in counseling practice.

Even when counselors recognize information contrary to a stereotype, they may distort the information and the relationship. A counselor who holds stereotypes about female gender roles (that women are "feminine" by nature) and encounters "masculine" traits in a female client may perceive those traits as exaggerated, resulting in a distorted view of the client. Or a counselor may not take seriously a successful Black client's vocational concerns if the counselor perceives that the client has achieved great success *for a Black person*. Holding this lower standard for certain groups has broad implications in areas within the counseling realm. At the individual level a school counselor may not encourage a Black student to pursue college, and at the institutional level, the allocation of resources to these groups will match the low standard of performance expected from them.

Stereotyping can lead to nongenuine and condescending relations between counselor and client. Because it is socially unacceptable to stereotype openly, White guidance counselors may evaluate the performance of Black students less critically in an attempt to avoid being perceived as stereotyping. Although this behavior may even come out of a desire to counteract racism (though it may also arise out of a motivation not to *appear* prejudiced), in essence it perpetuates prejudice and the stereotype by implying that the target group should be held to a lower standard.

Most people are not aware of the stereotypes they hold. Because stereotypes are unconscious, a counselor will perceive the aforementioned evaluations of clients as objective and perhaps not even linked to group membership. Thus, communication of the stereotype from counselor to client may be implicit and highly subtle, making it hard for either party to identify and counter. In fact, stereotypes often set off subtle, unconscious interactive patterns between the stereotype holder (counselor) and the target (client). The counselor's expectations create both a cognitive and an emotional disposition toward the client that may be subtly communicated to the client through nonverbal and other behavior. The client may well respond to these cues in ways that the counselor interprets negatively according to the stereotype. The counselor, unaware of the impact the stereotype has already had on the client's behavior, concludes that the client's behavior represents clear evidence for the truth of the stereotype. Again, the vicious cycle ensues.

Stereotypes and Multicultural Counseling Competence

The multicultural counseling competencies specifically mandate that counselors be aware of the stereotypes that they hold and the impact these beliefs have on their work with clients. This implies that most, if not all, counselors hold stereotypes and must become aware of them and avoid their negative effects.

Some counseling scholars note that counselors must eliminate the negative effects of stereotypes to become culturally sensitive, an attribute mandated by the American Counseling Association's code of ethics. The inverse relationship between cultural sensitivity and stereotyping can be seen when one considers stereotypes as a type of cognitive schema.

Schemata can be seen in two ways. On the one hand, they are flexible hypotheses that can be influenced by information coming in. For instance, when a piece of information is not accounted for by an existing schema, the schema may change and adapt to incorporate the new information. If a schema for chair is flexible, a newly encountered bean bag may be considered a chair. Scholars assert that flexible schemata about social groups characterize cultural sensitivity.

On the other hand, schemata can be rigid expectations that influence what is perceived and how it is interpreted. They can impose a selective focus on incoming stimuli and prioritize information that poses no threat to the schema. Such schemata also affect how stimuli are interpreted, so even contradictory information may be interpreted in a way that supports the schemata, and the meaning of the information is distorted. Counseling scholars note that such rigid information processing is the basis of stereotyping.

Some counseling scholars state that, if counselors apply any stereotype of a particular group to all its individuals, the counselors are likely to misperceive and misunderstand the clients and fail to be culturally sensitive. Stereotypes block interpersonal communication and rapport; they can lead clients to early termination, alienation from the counseling process, and cultural oppression. To avoid these errors and outcomes, scholars suggest that counselors work to become more conscious of their information processing in client encounters and treat expectations as hypotheses whose fit with the particular client must always be evaluated. Such caution should be exercised even when counselor and client are members of the same group, as within-group variance may make automatic expectations erroneous.

In overcoming the negative impact of stereotypes on the counseling process, and promoting culturally sensitive counseling, counselors critically need self-awareness of their own cultural and group memberships and their influences on their expectations. Self-analysis should include exploring the origins of, and possible motivations behind, each expectation, bringing these to consciousness. Only then can they be held as hypotheses to understand others' experiences and behaviors rather than rigid stereotypes kept in place by unknown agendas.

A self-aware counselor can be purposive and active in applying schemata to work with clients. An unexamined, passive, automatic application of schemata is likely to result in stereotyping the client. Counselors must actively explore and intentionally direct what stimuli they attend to, how they interpret the information, and what they do based on the information. Because many counselors have been socialized not to attend to group membership issues, inattention is the default. Inattention allows unexamined stereotypes to hold sway over what is acknowledged and how it is responded to.

Some counseling scholars, noting that stereotyping provides the ingroup with a self-definition distinct from and superior to that of the target group, assert that asking counselors to stop their stereotyping behavior is akin to asking them to give up a source of positive self-regard. They suggest that such work must be done in a safe environment and must include help in breaking down the connection between anti–target group sentiment and beliefs and positive self-construal.

Impact of Stereotypes on the Target Group: Stereotype Threat

Another effect of stereotyping on the counseling process is the impact on targets. Counselors must be aware of how stereotyping affects the ways both counselors and their clients present. Such understanding can help counselors develop interventions, especially at the programmatic level, that can mitigate the negative impact of stereotypes.

One impact that has been extensively explored is the phenomenon of stereotype threat. Stereotype threat is a situationally triggered phenomenon in which a target group member's efforts to avoid confirming a stereotype lead to performance deficits. Stereotype threat can arise when a target group member approaches a task for which a stereotype expects poor performance by the target group. The individual tends to experience pressure to disconfirm the stereotype. Cognitive resources are marshaled to deal with this pressure, so they are not available for completing the task, and this negatively impacts performance. For example, when a female science student takes a biology exam she may be hampered by pressure to disconfirm the stereotype that women are not good in science.

The negative effect of the stereotype goes beyond the poor performance. It can cause target individuals to avoid domains in which a stereotype exists and their behavior may be evaluated. This can cause targets to avoid certain majors or fields, or even avoid speaking in class.

Thus, simply by their existence, stereotypes can produce the behaviors that they predict in target group members. An ingroup member need not react to a target based on a stereotype for the target to experience a negative effect. To mitigate these negative effects, counselors must do more than simply be aware of the stereotypes they hold and limit the negative effects of those on counseling. Scholars suggest that programs and interventions must reduce the stereotype threat experienced by targets. First, counselors must avoid ascribing clients' difficulties exclusively to internal processes such as the internalization of stereotypes by targets. Modification of contextual and situational factors must also be considered important avenues for intervention. Second, programs and interventions must avoid being a source of stereotype threat themselves. Threat can occur when a program or intervention is presented as remedial, suggesting that those who need this intervention are inferior. Targets may often be identified as having a problem and be referred to programs created to help them. Participation in the program can then be seen as a confirmation of a stereotype. One suggestion is that programs and interventions be modified to challenge participants sensitively, rather than lowering the expected standard. Participation, too, must be reframed as an earned privilege, showing that the client is up for the challenge, rather than a punishment for poor performance. Such programs and interventions actively counter the stereotypes in the air and create an environment where participants can feel proud of both their group membership and their efforts in the domain of their choice. Pride can create a positive linking of these two in the perception of all, countering stereotypes as well as their negative impact.

Noah M. Collins

See also Antisemitism (v3); Bias (v3); Classism (v3); Cross-Cultural Training (v3); Discrimination (v3); Discrimination and Oppression (v2); Model Minority Myth (v3); Multicultural Counseling Competence (v3); Oppression (v3); Prejudice (v3); Racism (v3); Sexism (v3); Social Class (v4); Social Discrimination (v4); Social Identity Theory (v3); Stereotype Threat (v3)

Further Readings

American Counseling Association. (1995). *Code of ethics and standards of practice.* Alexandria, VA: Author.

American Psychological Association. (2003). Guidelines on multicultural education, training, research, practice, and organizational change for psychologists. *American Psychologist, 58,* 377–402.

Arredondo, P. (1999). Multicultural counseling competencies as tools to address oppression and racism. *Journal of Counseling & Development, 77,* 102–108.

Biernat, M. (2003). Toward a broader view of social stereotyping. *American Psychologist, 58,* 1019–1027.

Davies, P. G., Spencer, S. J., & Steele, C. M. (2005). Clearing the air: Identity safety moderates the effects of stereotype threat on women's leadership aspirations. *Journal of Personality and Social Psychology, 88,* 276–287.

Dovidio, J. F., & Gaertner, S. L. (1999). Reducing prejudice: Combating intergroup biases. *Current Directions in Psychological Research, 8,* 101–105.

Jones, J. M. (1997). *Prejudice and racism* (2nd ed.). New York: McGraw-Hill.

Ridley, C. R., Mendoza, D. W., Kanitz, B. E., Angermeier, L., & Zenk, R. (1994). Cultural sensitivity in multicultural counseling: A perceptual schema model. *Journal of Counseling Psychology, 41,* 125–136.

Schneider, D. J. (2004). *The psychology of stereotyping.* New York: Guilford Press.

Smedley, A. (1999). *Race in North America: Origin and evolution of a world view* (2nd ed.). Boulder, CO: Westview Press.

Steele, C. M. (1997). A threat in the air: How stereotypes shape intellectual identity and performance. *American Psychologist, 52,* 613–629.

Sue, D. W., Carter, R. T., Casas, J. M., Fouad, N. A., Ivey, A. E., Jensen, M., et al. (1998). *Multicultural counseling competencies: Individual and organizational development.* Thousand Oaks, CA: Sage.

Thompson, C. E., & Neville, H. A. (1999). Racism, mental health, and mental health practice. *Counseling Psychologist, 27,* 155–223.

Stereotype Threat

In 1995, Claude M. Steele and Joshua Aronson coined the term *stereotype threat.* The cornerstone of the phenomenon of stereotype threat is the pressure to not conform to a given expectation of poor performance. This results in an activation of negative and internalized stereotypes. In other words, the pressure to not conform to a known negative stereotype about the group with which one identifies can result in compromised performance on a said task.

Steele and Aronson first examined stereotype threat among African Americans. One negative stereotype toward African Americans is low intelligence; when intelligence is defined as fixed, it creates a belief that innate or biological limitations may be to blame for poor performance. Unfortunately, these stereotypes have been applied wrongly to explain the achievement gap between African Americans and Caucasians on standardized test scores. Steele and Aronson's 1995 study created a scenario characterized by stereotype threat, where this stereotype was made salient by telling the treatment group that the test they were taking measured intelligence. The control group was told that the test was a measure to study problem solving. When stereotype threat was absent, the scores of the African American students only differed to the degree that would be expected on the basis of their prior Scholastic Aptitude Test (SAT) scores. When stereotype threat was present, the African American students performed worse than the Caucasian students. The difference was beyond what prior SAT scores would predict for individual differences in skill level. Stereotype threat was shown to be a condition where negative stereotypes about a group identity are evoked and individuals are in a situation where they could conform to that stereotype. In the previous example, the suggestion that the test was a measure of intelligence invoked the stereotype that African Americans have lower intelligence for the African American students and under the pressure of the possibility of confirming this stereotype, they actually performed worse than would have been expected. The stereotyped group does not have to believe the stereotype for this effect to materialize.

Generality

Stereotype threat can be generalized to populations where stereotypes are present. Numerous studies have confirmed the presence of stereotype threat among diverse racial groups, ethnicities, genders, socioeconomic statuses, and age groups. In an article published in 1999, Aronson, Michael Lustina, Catherine Good, and Kelli Keough demonstrated that stereotype threat can be present in groups that do not have a history of stigmatization or internalized feelings of inferiority. Their study found that White males performed worse on a math test than their control group counterparts when it was suggested that Asians are better at math. It seems reasonable that all groups have a negative stereotype that can be made salient in circumstances where there is pressure to perform.

Much of the research focuses on test performance; however, there have been studies confirming that stereotype threat could be induced in other domains as well. For example, a 2005 study done by Paul Davies, Steven Spencer, and Steele confirmed that exposure to gender stereotypes about leadership affected female participants' interest in taking on a leadership role. Women who had been exposed to the negative stereotypes about women's abilities in leadership were less interested in assuming a position of leadership on the task.

Consequences

Consequences of stereotype threat are numerous. It can create a setting where a socially constructed concept can interfere with the measurement of constructs such as intelligence. Currently, high-stakes testing is used as a gatekeeper to many educational opportunities. Stereotype threat may have a role in lower test scores, which in turn may function to keep people from gaining access to opportunities. Although the concept of stereotype threat has been studied most in the area of academic achievement and the achievement gap, stereotype threat may evidence in other contexts such as work performance. Second, this concept demonstrates how powerful stereotypes are and what the impact of internalized negative stereotypes is. Stereotype threat may create a scenario where there is now a vicious cycle. For example, a person knows of a stereotype for his or her group and, feeling pressured to not conform to a negative expectation for this reference group, the person's performance on a given task suffers: The person may be denied entrance to the school of his or her choice, or the person may miss other opportunities like jobs or community leadership roles. This denied opportunity can contribute to social inequities, including the achievement and wage gaps. In essence, this concept is critical to understanding the complex effects of stereotyping on performance. There are also effects on self-esteem and confidence for those who perform under their expectations. Many people may not be aware of stereotype threat and may begin to believe that their lower performance was a result of personal characteristics.

Mediators

Aronson and Steele published a chapter in 2005 that explored potential mediators of stereotype threat on test performance. Anxiety has been found to be a mediator as negative stereotypes are posited to create more anxiety. The knowledge of a negative stereotype can produce anxiety, which can hinder performance. Stereotype threat can be enacted most powerfully by individuals who care strongly about doing well in a particular domain. Stereotype threat poses a particular jeopardy because it seems to be present even in situations where the student is actually motivated and interested. For example, a female student who wants to attend the best university to study math can do poorly on the math section of an entrance exam because of stereotype threat (i.e., the negative expectation that is operative is that women are not adept at math).

Individuals who have a strong identification with their group are more likely to be aware of the stereotypes about their group. Thus, research has found that people who are the most identified with their group are more affected by stereotype threat. For example, a Latino/a who is highly identified with his or her ethnic group is affected more by stereotype threat than a Latino/a student who does not identify highly with the group. However, that same student may identify highly with being lesbian or female, and therefore stereotype threat may be more salient for the stereotypes about lesbians or females.

In the context of competition among reference groups, stereotype threat can be induced in individuals who believe they are good at the particular exercise. For example, Steele and Aronson showed that stereotype threat can be evoked for White males if they are being compared to a group, such as Asian Americans, who are stereotyped to excel at math. See Aronson and Steele (2005) for a comprehensive review of some of the research results that led to these conclusions.

Relevance to Cross-Cultural Counseling

The phenomenon of stereotype threat is relevant to cross-cultural and multicultural counseling in several ways. First counselors need to be aware of the stereotype threat and how it works, as they may evoke stereotype threat through subtle words and/or behaviors when administering tests or during the actual process of counseling. Also, counselors may be in a position to educate those that they come in contact with about the phenomenon so that steps can be taken to reduce the likelihood of stereotype threat occurring.

Jennifer L. Lemkuil

See also Academic Achievement (v2); Academic Achievement, Nature and Use of (v4); Achievement, Aptitude, and Ability Tests (v4); Achievement Gap (v3); Bias (v3); Cross-Cultural Training (v3); Discrimination (v3); Ethnic Identity (v3); Intelligence Tests (v3); Multicultural Counseling Competence (v3); Racial Identity (v3); Stereotype (v3)

Further Readings

Aronson, J., Lustina, M. J., Good, C., Keough, K., Steele, C., & Brown, J. (1999). When White men can't do math: Necessary and sufficient factors in stereotype threat. *Journal of Experimental Social Psychology, 53,* 39–46.

Aronson, J., & Steele, C. M. (2005). Stereotypes and the fragility of academic competence, motivation, and self-concept. In A. J. Elliot & C. S. Dweck (Eds.), *Handbook of competence and motivation* (pp. 436–456). New York: Guilford Press.

Davies, P. G., Spencer, S. J., & Steele, C. M. (2005). Clearing the air: Identity safety moderates the effects of stereotype threat on women's leadership aspirations. *Journal of Personality and Social Psychology, 88*(2), 276–287.

Martens, A., Johns, M., Greenberg, J., & Schimel, J. (2006). Combating stereotype threat: The effect of self-affirmation on women's intellectual performance. *Journal of Experimental Social Psychology, 42,* 236–243.

Steele, C. M., & Aronson, J. (1995). Stereotype threat and the intellectual test performance of African Americans. *Journal of Personality and Social Psychology, 69*(5), 797–811.

Steele, C. M., & Aronson, J. (1998). Stereotype threat and the test performance of academically successful African Americans. In C. Jencks & M. Phillips (Eds.), *The Black-White test score gap* (pp. 401–427). Washington, DC: Brookings Institution.

SUE, DERALD WING (1942–): CONTRIBUTIONS TO MULTICULTURAL PSYCHOLOGY AND COUNSELING

Derald Wing Sue is a pioneer and leader of multicultural psychology, counseling, and therapy. He is professor of psychology and education at Teachers College, Columbia University, and contributes extensively to the field through his teaching, publications, research, consultation, and organizational work.

Sue graduated with a Bachelor of Science degree in psychology from Oregon State University in 1965 and received his Ph.D. in counseling psychology from the University of Oregon in 1969. He was formerly professor at California State University East Bay (then California State University Hayward) and at Alliant International University (then California School for Professional Psychology).

Sue's extensive body of work has been pivotal in transforming psychology to be inclusive of cultural considerations in multiple domains, including theory, research, education, training, and practice. Sue has been honored numerous times for his contributions and work on multiculturalism and cultural diversity, and he has received awards from many organizations, including the American Psychological Association, the Association for Multicultural Counseling and Development, the Asian American Psychological Association, the Society for the Psychological Study of Ethnic Minority Issues, the American Counseling Association, and the American Academy of Counseling Psychology. In addition, Sue is a Fellow of the American Psychological Society, the American Association of Applied and Preventive Psychology, and the American Psychological Association (Divisions 1, 17, and 45), as well as a member of the American Counseling Association.

Research and Teaching

Sue's research and writings on multicultural issues in psychology have led and challenged the field of psychology to examine and critique the Eurocentric basis and assumptions of its fundamental theories, concepts, frameworks, and practices. Before the early 1970s, cultural variables were generally ignored in the field of psychology, and there was scarce research on Asian American psychology. During this time, Sue was a pioneer in the study of Asian American mental health when he collaborated with other researchers to study different aspects of Asian American psychology.

Sue's research efforts span his earliest work in Asian American psychology, to his contributions to multicultural competencies and multicultural theory, and, most recently, his research on racial microaggressions (i.e., the brief and everyday exchanges that send denigrating messages to people of color because of their racial minority status). Sue argues that racial microaggressions sap the spiritual and psychological energies of people of color and create disparities in education, health care, and employment.

Sue also has been a trailblazer in the arena of multicultural counseling teaching and training. As a young professor in the early 1970s, he developed multicultural counseling courses and infused multicultural content into other counseling courses. These courses were initially met with heavy opposition at multiple levels but have now become standard requirements in graduate clinical and counseling psychology training programs.

Sue's teaching contributions are not limited to academia, as he has provided cultural diversity training and consulted for many organizations, from Fortune 500 companies to nonprofit mental health agencies all over the world. Most notably, Sue served as a consultant and invited panelist on President Clinton's Race Advisory Board on the National Dialogue on Race in 1997, in which he called for individual, institutional, and societal efforts to confront and address racism, injustice, and discrimination. Sue also participated in a congressional briefing on the psychology of racism in 1995.

Writing and Publications

In 1981, Sue wrote and published the seminal textbook, *Counseling the Culturally Diverse*; his brother David Sue joined him as coauthor of subsequent editions. Initially criticized for its sociopolitical content, the book has become a classic in the field and is the textbook of choice for almost 50% of graduate counseling psychology programs. Now in its fifth edition, the book also has the distinction of being one of the most frequently cited references in multicultural counseling and therapy. Sue also has authored and coauthored many articles and books that have been the impetus for the field of psychology to adopt the multicultural competencies as guidelines. These books include *A Theory of Multicultural Counseling and Therapy* (cowritten with Allen Ivey and Paul Pedersen in 1996) and *Multicultural Counseling Competencies: Individual, Professional and Organizational Development* (coauthored with members of the Division 17 and Division 45 multicultural committees in 1998). Sue's 2003 book *Overcoming Our Racism: The Journey to Liberation*—a trenchant and hard-hitting call to Whites to acknowledge and take responsibility for their racism—was the direct result of his testimony before President Clinton's Race Advisory Board.

Sue also has written 13 textbooks on personality theory, introductory psychology, racism, and abnormal behavior. These textbooks are distinctive in presenting the subject of psychology through a multicultural framework. Most notably, Sue has challenged prevailing notions of universals of mental health, instead advocating for an understanding of cultural variables in the conceptualization, assessment, and treatment of mental illness. His work also has been featured in other media formats; for example, he has produced several videotapes on racism and psychology, including *The Psychology of Racism: Where Have We Gone Wrong?*; *What Does It Mean to Be White? The Invisible Whiteness of Being;* and *Overcoming Our Racism: What Can I Do?*

Contributions to Professional Organizations

Sue has played an active role in the leadership of many professional organizations, including serving as president for the Society for the Psychological Study of Ethnic Minority Issues (Division 45) from 1998 to 1999 and the Society of Counseling Psychology (Division 17) of the American Psychological Association) from 2003 to 2004. With his brother Stanley Sue, Sue cofounded and became the first president of the Asian American Psychological Association (AAPA) in 1972. AAPA's mission was to promote the study of Asian American mental health and culturally appropriate interventions and to support the training and education of Asian American mental health professionals. Since its inception in 1972, AAPA has grown into a sizeable organization with more than 400 members.

In the 1980s and 1990s, Sue chaired two committees working to develop multicultural competencies for the counseling field. The work of these two committees was published in 1982 and 1998, and the competencies generated by these committees formed the foundation for the adoption of multicultural guidelines by the American Psychological Association in 2002. The concept of multicultural counseling competencies has been profoundly influential in shaping the training, education, and accreditation of counselors, therapists, and psychologists. As a result of these competencies, graduate psychology training programs have been revamped to include multicultural counseling courses in their curricula and to infuse cultural considerations into existing coursework.

In addition to his leadership contributions to various professional organizations, Sue also has held numerous editorial posts, including serving as the first Asian and non-White editor of the *Personnel and Guidance Journal* (now the *Journal of Counseling & Development*). As the editor for the *Personnel and Guidance Journal,* he was innovative in his efforts to include articles that were culturally inclusive, systemically oriented, and prevention focused. These unprecedented efforts were met with tremendous support from some groups and deep resistance from others.

Sue also played a key role in the collaborative effort to organize the National Multicultural Summit in 1999, a conference focused on issues of multiculturalism and diversity. The creation of the summit was one of Sue's presidential initiatives when he was elected president of the Society for the Psychological Study of Ethnic Minority Issues (i.e., Division 45 of the American Psychological Association) in 1998. This was a historic moment in the history of psychology because Sue was one of four people of color that year elected to leadership positions within the American Psychological Association. (Sue was elected as president of Division 45, Rosie P. Bingham was elected president of Division 17, Melba J. T. Vasquez was elected president of Division 35, and Richard Suinn was elected president of the American Psychological Association.) Sue, Bingham, Vasquez, and Suinn acted on the momentum of this historic occasion by deciding to create a national multicultural summit as a celebration of their combined presidencies. Now a biennial event, the National Multicultural Summit has been attended by as many as 1,000 participants and is an important venue for the discussion and dissemination of multicultural research.

Anne Chan

See also Asian American Psychological Association (v3); Asian Americans (v3); Cross-Cultural Psychology (v3); Cross-Cultural Training (v3); Culture (v3); Multicultural Counseling Competence (v3); Multiculturalism (v3); Racial Microaggressions (v3); Society for the Psychological Study of Ethnic Minority Issues (v3); Sue, Derald Wing (v1); Sue, Stanley (v3)

Further Readings

Sue, D. W. (1998). A personal look at psychology in my life. In L. T. Hoshmand (Ed.), *Knowledge, creativity, and moral vision* (pp. 106–125). Thousand Oaks, CA: Sage.

Sue, D. W. (2005). The continuing journey to multicultural competence. In R. K. Conyne & F. Bemak (Eds.), *Journeys to professional excellence: Lessons from leading counselor educators and practitioners* (pp. 73–84). Alexandria, VA: American Counseling Association.

Sue, D. W., Arredondo, P., & McDavis, R. J. (1992). Multicultural counseling competencies and standards: A call to the profession. *Journal of Multicultural Counseling and Development, 20,* 64–88.

Sue, D. W., Carter, R. T., Casas, J. M., Fouad, N. A., Ivey, A. E., Jensen, M., et al. (1998). *Multicultural counseling competencies: Individual, professional and organizational development.* Thousand Oaks, CA: Sage.

Sue, D. W., Ivey, A. E., & Pedersen, P. B. (1996). *A theory of multicultural counseling and therapy.* Pacific Grove, CA: Brooks/Cole.

Sue, D. W., & Sue, D. (2008). *Counseling the culturally diverse: Theory and practice* (5th ed.). Hoboken, NJ: Wiley.

SUE, STANLEY (1944–)

Stanley Sue is a pioneering scholar in the field of Asian American psychology and ethnic minority psychology. He was born in 1944 in Portland, Oregon, as the third son of Chinese immigrant parents. He received his Bachelor of Science degree from the University of Oregon in 1966 and his doctoral degree in clinical psychology from the University of California, Los Angeles (UCLA) in 1971. He completed his dissertation research on cognitive dissonance under Bertram Raven's guidance but soon turned his scholarly attention to mental health issues facing ethnic minorities.

Sue was an assistant professor and associate professor of psychology at the University of Washington between 1971 and 1981, professor of psychology at UCLA between 1981 and 1996, and since 1996 has been professor of psychology and Asian American Studies at the University of California, Davis. In addition to his faculty appointments in psychology, Sue has served as associate dean of the graduate division at UCLA and as the director of the Asian American Studies Program at University of California, Davis. Sue's influence on Asian American psychology and ethnic minority psychology spans a wide range with respect to scholarship, service, and public policy.

Scholarship

Sue has made significant theoretical and empirical contributions in the areas of ethnicity and mental health, cultural competency, and effective delivery of mental health services. His first major contribution was to document treatment disparities in mental health services for ethnic minorities. In his early collaboration with Herman McKinney in the 1970s, Sue analyzed the utilization patterns of nearly 14,000 clients seen in 17 community mental health agencies serving King County in the state of Washington. They found that ethnic minority clients tended to drop out from treatment at a higher rate and to have fewer average number of sessions than White clients. Based on this research, as well as on the consensus of other Asian American mental health providers, Sue made several policy recommendations to improve services for ethnic minorities, such as training therapists to be more knowledgeable about cultural bases of mental health, to recruit and hire more ethnic minority psychologists, to develop ethnic-specific mental health service centers, and to create new therapies and services that better meet the needs of ethnic minorities. These recommendations became fundamental building blocks for increasing cultural competence in mental health service delivery.

Sue's groundbreaking studies, which suggested that inadequate services were being provided to ethnic minorities, were initially challenged by the Washington State Department of Social and Health Services and Sue was asked to testify before the Washington State Senate subcommittee on mental health. After his successful defense of the scientific basis for the findings, many of Sue's policy recommendations were implemented in many areas of the country. In fact, Sue directed the training for the National Asian American Psychology Training Center in San Francisco in 1980, which was established specifically to train service providers in culturally competent practice with Asian Americans.

The early work documenting treatment disparities led Sue to pursue research on culturally competent services. In a 1987 paper, Sue and Nolan Zane proposed a theoretical model for treatment outcome based on various forms of match between therapists and clients. Sue and Zane contended that ethnic match between therapists and clients is important because ethnically matched therapists tend to have higher ascribed credibility with clients, but other factors (e.g., therapist–client match on problem conceptualization and goals, therapist behavior during the first session) contribute to achieved credibility that lead to better retention in treatment and more positive outcomes. In his 1998 paper, Sue articulated his hypotheses about three essential ingredients of cultural competency. In this paper, he argued that although *culture-specific knowledge* (e.g., making direct eye contact with an elder person would be considered disrespectful in a Chinese culture) was a necessary component, a culturally competent clinician must also demonstrate *scientific mindedness* (i.e., to treat such cultural-specific knowledge as a hypothesis rather than as a given in a particular client) and practice *dynamic sizing* (i.e., to know when to apply or not apply a particular culture-specific knowledge to assess and treat a particular client).

Finally, Sue has played a critical role in fostering cutting-edge research in Asian American psychology. He directed the National Research Center on Asian American Mental Health, a research center funded by the National Institute of Mental Health, between 1988 and 2001. Sue and his collaborators at the research center produced some of the major empirical work in Asian American mental health. For example, Sue was critically involved in the first large-scale psychiatric epidemiological study of Asian Americans in the United States, which was headed by David Takeuchi and conducted out of the National Research Center on Asian American Mental Health in Los Angeles. This study documented population estimates for the prevalence of major mental disorders among Chinese Americans.

Service and Advocacy

As a pioneer in the field of Asian American psychology, Sue was instrumental in creating a professional organization to provide scholarly network and public advocacy for the needs of this population. Together with his psychologist brother Derald Wing Sue and other Asian American mental health professionals in the San Francisco Bay Area, Sue founded the Asian American Psychological Association (AAPA) in 1972. In the formative years of the AAPA, Sue and other leaders sought to advocate nationally on behalf of Asian American mental health issues through the American Psychological Association (APA) boards and standing committees that were sympathetic to concerns of Asian Americans and ethnic minorities. Sue and other AAPA leaders also formed coalitions with the leading ethnic minority psychologists of the time to push the APA to move toward more diversification and inclusion.

With encouragement from Patrick Okura, the then executive assistant to the director of the National Institute of Mental Health (NIMH), Sue wrote a conference grant proposal to the NIMH to convene a national conference on the training of mental health service providers to serve Asian American communities. After 2 years of planning, the National Asian American Psychology Training Conference was held in Long Beach, California, in the summer of 1976. This historic conference was critical to the grassroots movement for Asian American psychology in gaining the momentum toward visibility and influence.

Sue's research on mental health of ethnic minorities has impacted public policy on a national scale as well. Sue has served as a task panel member for the President Carter Commission on Mental Health in 1978, planning board member for the Surgeon General's Report on Mental Health in 1999, participant in the White House Conference on Mental Health in 1999, and science editor of *Mental Health: Culture, Race, and Ethnicity* in 2001—a supplement volume to the 1999 Surgeon General's Report on Mental Health.

In recognition of his work and achievements, Sue has won numerous awards and recognitions in all areas of his work. Of note, he has received three major awards from the APA, making him one of a handful of psychologists to be awarded multiple times by the organization. Among the many prestigious awards he has garnered are the APA Distinguished Contributions to Psychology in the Public Interest Award in 1986; the APA Distinguished Contributions to Research in Public Policy, the Distinguished Contributions to Research in Ethnic Minority Psychology from the Society for the Psychological Study of Ethnic Minority Issues (APA Division 45), and the Distinguished Contribution Award from the AAPA in 1990; the Janet E. Helms Award for Mentoring and Scholarship in Psychology from Teachers College, Columbia University, in 1993; the Distinguished Contributions to the Psychological Study of Diversity from the American Association of Applied and Preventive Psychology in 1995; the Dalmas A. Taylor Award for Pioneering Leadership, Scholarship, and Aggressive Advocacy for Ethnic Minorities at the National Multicultural Summit and Conference in 1999; the APA Distinguished Contributions to Applied Research and the Society of Clinical Psychology's (APA Division 12) Stanley Sue Award—which was established to recognize a psychologist who has made distinguished contributions to the understanding of human diversity—both in 2003; the Distinguished Research Contributions to Ethnic Minorities from Section IV of the Society of Clinical Psychology (APA Division 12); and the Davis Prize for Teaching and Scholarship from the University of California, Davis, in 2005.

Sumie Okazaki

See also Asian American Psychological Association (v3); Asian Americans (v3); Cross-Cultural Psychology (v3); Cross-Cultural Training (v3); Cultural Values (v3); Culture (v3); Multicultural Counseling Competence (v3); Multiculturalism (v3); Sue, Derald Wing (v1)

Further Readings

Sue, S. (1998). In search of cultural competence in psychotherapy and counseling. *American Psychologist, 53,* 440–448.

Sue, S., & McKinney, H. (1975). Asian-Americans in the community mental health care system. *American Journal of Orthopsychiatry, 45,* 111–118.

Sue, S., & Zane, N. (1987). The role of culture and cultural techniques in psychotherapy: A critique and reformulation. *American Psychologist, 42,* 37–45.

Takeuchi, D. T., Chung, R. C., Lin, K. M., Shen, H., Kurasaki, K., Chun, C., et al. (1998). Lifetime and twelve-month prevalence rates of major depressive episodes and dysthymia among Chinese Americans in Los Angeles. *American Journal of Psychiatry, 155,* 1407–1414.

U.S. Surgeon General. (2001). *Mental health: Culture, race, and ethnicity. A supplement to Mental health: A report of the Surgeon General.* Rockville, MD: U.S. Department of Health and Human Services.

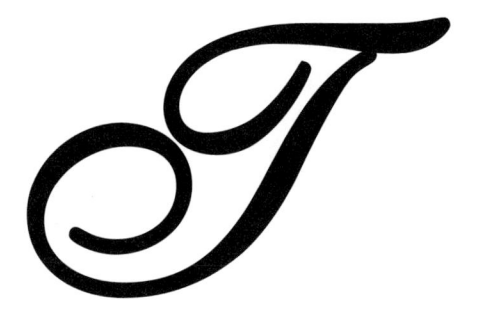

THIRD WORLD

Many authors concur that the *third world* is a term used to describe countries and nations who are poor, in political crisis, contending with pollution, and in debt. Berger believes these differences between developed and underdeveloped nations have also been described as a North–South conflict wherein the developed nations are the North and the underdeveloped are the South. It is assumed that the third world represents a stable set of countries, nations, and territories, but the geographic boundaries between first, second, and third world countries is vague. The *third world*, as a term, has also been used in political movements. Blauner suggests that during the anti–Vietnam War and civil rights movements, a number of organizations used *Third World* to identify themselves as liberation oriented, anticapitalist, and anticolonialist or postimperialist. Because there are many uses and connotations for the term *Third World*, this chapter attempts to clarify the origin of the term and identify how psychologists may better understand its function among individuals.

Origination of the Third World

In 1952, Alfred Sauvy, a French sociologist and demographer, coined the term *Third World*. Originally, the term was *tiers monde*, and was used to describe the "third estate" of commoners who aspired to be similar to the first estate, or society's wealthy and elite. Hobsbawm posits that the notion of a third estate was later used to describe nations that did not belong to either the capitalist and postcolonial nations representing the first world or the socialist and communist nations comprising the second world. More specifically, Sachs shows that the first world represented countries that were either already industrialized as of 1945 or newly industrialized. These countries are generally described as capitalist or proto-capitalist. For instance, the representatives of the G8 (United States, England, Germany, Italy, France, Russia, Japan, and Canada) are considered the first world. The second world are either current or former communist and socialist countries and are characterized by state ownership of production, central planning, one-party rule, and economic connections with other second world countries.

In 1955, the Bandung Conference in Indonesia created the Non-Aligned Movement. During this conference, the term *Third World* became widely accepted to describe the members of the Non-Aligned Movement. The participants in the conference represented nations who considered themselves non-aligned with either the first or second world. These countries opposed colonialism and neocolonialism and were often newly emancipated from colonial powers. Representatives from countries such as China, India, Vietnam, Egypt, and Ghana agreed that they would develop economically through partnerships with each other, would nurture their own industries and infrastructure, protect and subsidize their businesses, refuse aid from foreign multinationals and countries, and limit international trade.

Although the original intent of these non-aligned countries was to become independent from first and second world hegemony, this vision of autonomy quickly evaporated. First, starting around the 1940s, global decreases in mortality rates due to such things as the use of DDT and pharmaceutical advances contributed to a population explosion in some countries. Historically, in some countries, high fertility rates were countered by high mortality rates; but as mortality rates decreased, birth rates did not decrease. Additionally, Hobsbawm shows that the population increases were often not matched with economic development in some third world countries.

Second, Sachs argues that by isolating themselves to global developments in technology, industry, and trade, some third world countries were unable to sustain themselves economically. To help their economies, some countries turned to assistance from the first and second world nations. As third world countries became less aligned and committed to each other, they became more reliant on political and economic assistance from first and second world nations. Consequently, third world countries became politically polarized and economically dependent. Chomsky shows that first and second world nations used third world countries as political proxies and sometimes increased political instability to meet political, economic, and military goals. A coup d'état, for instance, came to symbolize political instability in many third world countries, and Latin American governments were often derogatorily referred to as "Banana Republics." Additionally, many third world countries started to borrow monies, thereby increasing their foreign debt. Consequently, foreign debt came to be the single largest economic problem for many third world countries.

Third world development was often treated differently from European or Japanese postwar development. Rather than provide grants, as the Marshall Plan did for post–World War II Europe, many third world nations were given loans. The United States learned that European debt after World War I created a financial crisis that contributed to the Great Depression and indirectly to the rise of fascism and eventually World War II. But this lesson was not applied to the economic situation in many third world countries. Instead, loans were given to some third world governments that were corrupt and/or inept, and these countries incurred debts that were impossibly high and could never be repaid. For many countries, the only solutions are debt relief or forgiveness, combined with better free-trade agreements.

The Third World and Mental Health

For psychologists and other mental health care providers, the *Third World* is often used to describe conditions and settings of abject poverty or other settings of extreme deprivation. The term may be used to connote, even within the United States, situations of severe poverty, poor health conditions, and economic inequality. The term has moved away from describing nation-states, as originally coined. In current use, it communicates about people and situations with dire need and intervention by mental health care providers.

For mental health care providers, multiculturalists, and those interested in social justice, the Third World represents countries and those individuals who have experienced extreme deprivation. Along with economic inequalities, many of these individuals may have experienced poor treatments by these governments, such as jailing, torture, and other traumas. Comas-Diaz and Padilla believe that individuals from many Third World countries may have comorbid posttraumatic stress related to their experiences in their country of origin. Because many of these individuals are immigrants from other countries, mental health care providers need to be aware of the aggregate affects of migration, trauma, and poverty on the migrant or refugee. When working with these communities and individuals, acculturative stress related to the lack of psychological and economic resources may be especially acute. Along with being attuned to adjustment disorders, mental health care providers need to be conscious of other possible sequelae of migration from the Third World such as depression, anxiety, and posttraumatic stress.

William Ming Liu

See also Career Counseling, Immigrants (v4); Classism (v3); Colonialism (v3); Cross-Cultural Psychology (v3); Immigrants (v3); Multicultural Counseling Competence (v3); Multiculturalism (v3); Poverty (v3); Refugees (v3); Social Class (v4)

Further Readings

Berger, M. T. (2004). After the third world? History, destiny and the fate of third worldism. *Third World Quarterly,* 25(1), 9–39.

Blauner, R. (1987). Colonized and immigrant minorities. In R. Takaki (Ed.), *From different shores: Perspectives on race and ethnicity in America* (pp. 149–160). New York: Oxford University Press.

Chomsky, N. (1991). *Deterring democracy.* New York: Hill & Wang.

Colburn, F. D. (2006, Spring). Good-bye to the "third world." *Dissent,* 38–41.

Comas-Diaz, L., & Padilla, A. (1990). Countertransference in working with victims of political repression. *American Journal of Orthopsychiatry, 60,* 125–134.

Dornbusch, R., & Fischer, S. (1986). Third world debt. *Science, 234,* 836–841.

Hobsbawm, E. (1994). *The age of extremes: A history of the world, 1914–1991.* New York: Pantheon.

Irogbe, K. (2005). Globalization and the development of underdevelopment of the third world. *Journal of Third World Studies, 22*(1), 41–68.

Randall, V. (2004). Using and abusing the concept of the third world: Geopolitics and the comparative political study of development and underdevelopment. *Third World Quarterly, 25*(1), 41–53.

Sachs, J. D. (2005). *The end of poverty: Economic possibilities for our time.* New York: Penguin.

Wiarda, H. J. (1990). The politics of third world debt. *Political Science and Politics, 23,* 411–418.

TOKENISM

Tokenism involves the symbolic involvement of a person in an organization due only to a specified or salient characteristic (e.g., gender, race/ethnicity, disability, age). It refers to a policy or practice of limited inclusion of members of a minority, underrepresented, or disadvantaged group. The presence of people placed in the role of token often leads to a misleading outward appearance of inclusive practices. The term *token* is derived from the Old English word *taken,* which means "to show." Thus tokenism exists because inclusion of the person or group is required or expected, not because of inherent value.

Psychological research suggests that tokenism may occur when members of the underrepresented group comprise less than 15% of the total environmental organizational context they are a part of. Furthermore, when there is only a single representative of a given group in an organizational environment, he or she is considered to have what is termed *solo status.*

Historically psychological research has focused on the experiences of (White) women as they tried to achieve full participation in the workplace. However, in recent years racial and ethnic minorities, people with disabilities, gay men, lesbians, and the elderly have been increasingly the focus of research regarding the effects of tokenism in the workplace. Tokenism, or the role of one as a token, does not necessarily indicate mistreatment or injustice. However, as a result of unfair and inequitable practices, tokenism is associated with several negative outcomes.

Consequences

Tokenism has both individual and organizational impacts. On the individual level a person in the role of a token may feel dehumanized, stereotyped, marginalized, and depersonalized. Quality of life, mental and physical health, and potential for success in the organization may be compromised. For example, this person may begin to question his or her qualifications or abilities, and negative outcomes may result, such as pressure to conform, feelings of isolation, lowered morale, or depression. A person in the role of a token may experience a "glass ceiling" in the organization; that is, his or her success or ability to advance is limited by unseen forces because they are symbolic rather than full participants in the organization.

Token status is more likely to have negative consequences for members of groups that are lower in status or are more culturally stigmatized. Research has indicated that people who feel like tokens may experience challenges as underrepresented members of their specific social context. Three of these challenges are visibility, role encapsulation, and contrast. Visibility entails the perception that others pay a disproportionate amount of attention to people who feel like tokens and are hypervigilant concerning their actions and behaviors. Consequently, those who are in the position of token may feel they are constantly being examined or evaluated. Persons who feel like tokens in an organization may feel intensely self-conscious about how they react to their environment because of the expected and/or internalized pressure to represent their entire minority group.

Role encapsulation entails the group dynamic where a person is forced to play a role based on stereotypes of their group. For example, a racial/ethnic minority psychology faculty member may be expected to only teach classes related to multiculturalism, regardless of their area of expertise. Token status may produce negative consequences for members of traditionally underrepresented and stigmatized groups by increasing feelings of distinctiveness based on group membership, which can increase the salience of negative stereotypes or stereotypical expectancies.

The third challenge, contrast, emphasizes the majority group's established differences between themselves and the people who are tokens that lead to unclear and inauthentic boundaries among the groups. These boundaries, although aimed to protect the majority group members, end up causing the identified tokens in the groups to isolate themselves as a means of protection from mistreatment or expectations of mistreatment by majority members (e.g., being perceived as intelligent when other group members are perceived as uneducated).

For the organization, tokenism may negatively impact morale, lead to high rates of turnover of people from underrepresented groups, and, most pointedly, tokenism eventually may deprive the organization of the full contribution (i.e., diversity) that the individuals in the role of token might have made to the organization. Thus tokenism itself is limiting and can potentially inhibit an organization from developing and competing in a diverse and global marketplace. Of course it should be noted that practices such as tokenism are intended to prevent change from occurring and to preserve the status quo.

Implications for Psychologists

Psychologists are specifically directed toward knowledge of tokenism to facilitate multicultural organizational development in the 2002 American Psychological Association *Guidelines on Multicultural Education, Training, Research and Organizational Change for Psychologists*. Psychologists have an ethical imperative to combat tokenism on the individual and organizational level. On the individual level psychologists can help empower clients who feel like tokens in their environments by helping the client adopt a systemic perspective on tokenism. A full range of options (leaving the organization, attempting to change the organization, adapting to the organization) can be explored. Special care should be taken so as not blame clients for their feelings (in essence, blaming the victim).

On the organization level, psychologists can serve in the role of change agents, consultants, and/or advocates. With knowledge of multicultural organizational development, psychologists can aid organizations in making substantive change. First, the psychologist can help motivate the organization to desire change based on both the benefits of change and a comprehensive evaluation of current and past discriminatory practices. Psychologists can help organizations recognize that a single individual should not be expected to represent an entire population group. Because of the increasing diversity in the population and culturally diverse backgrounds represented in today's workforce, organizational culture may need to change to become inclusive at all levels and to be competitive in a diverse marketplace.

The development of innovative strategies that would incorporate the ideas and beliefs of all members of the group will help to ensure equality and a more inclusive environment for all involved. Although the identified tokens may overcome these negative experiences and the stereotypical beliefs of majority group members, the process can be slow.

The organization can reduce tokenism by avoiding assumptions (stereotypes) associated with the minority group. Combating stereotypes may include implementing advocacy and outreach education into institutional practices. Additionally, working to reduce the difficulties associated with token or solo status requires there be a diverse representation in the power structure of any group. Also, organizations can ensure that underrepresented groups are represented beyond a demographic or symbolic level. Beyond the issues of representation, true organizational change includes the issue of equity in outcomes (salaries, promotions, leadership opportunities).

*Edward A. Delgado-Romero
and Eliza M. Wells*

See also Affirmative Action (v3); Change Agent (v3); Discrimination (v3); Diversity (v3); Diversity Issues in Career Development (v4); Ethnicity (v3); Multicultural Coulseling Competence (v3); Organizational Diversity (v3); Prejudice (v3); Race (v3); Stereotype (v3)

Further Readings

Niemann, Y. F. (1999). The making of a token: A case study of stereotype threat and racism in academia. *Frontiers: A Journal of Women Studies, 20,* 111–135.

Niemann, Y. F. (2003). The psychology of tokenism: Psychosocial realities of faculty of color. *Handbook of racial and ethnic minority psychology* (pp. 100–118). Thousand Oaks, CA: Sage.

TRANSLATION METHODS

The language barrier is one of the biggest obstacles to effective cross-cultural research, testing, and counseling. Translation methods are specialized procedures designed to make possible the communication between people who speak or read different languages. Four translation methods have been identified. The first two are oral methods: (1) simultaneous oral translation, also known as interpretation, and (2) language switching. The other two are written methods: (3) written translation, and (4) back translation. These methods are implemented in three main contexts in the field of counseling. First, translation methods are utilized to communicate with clients in the context of a clinical counseling relationship. To communicate verbally with non-English-speaking clients during intakes, assessment interviews, and early interventions, the most efficient method is the use of trained interpreters who use a simultaneous translation method also known as interpretation. For treatments, a common method utilized in an ongoing clinical situation is the oral translation method known as language switching. Second, translation methods are utilized to turn research and testing material originally conceived in one language into another language. The most researched translation method for research and testing is the method known as back translation. Third, translation methods are utilized in counseling agencies and other institutions to translate written materials from one language into another. The consensus is that institutional forms, such as informed consent, HIPAA (Health Insurance Portability and Accountability Act), and other written materials, need to be translated by a professional translator.

Historical Background

Translation methods grew out of the intercultural and cross-cultural communication needs that expanded toward the second half of the 20th century in the United States. The services of professional translators and interpreters became common in a variety of settings, including business, industry, health care, law, and education. In the clinical counseling field, translation and interpreting was incorporated as immigration from Asia, Latin America, and Eastern European countries increased the number of clients requesting help at counseling agencies. Increases in demand for non-English-speaking counseling in the United States, coupled with a shortage of non-English-speaking counselors, have forced organizations to become responsible for offering interpreters and translators as part of their intake, assessment interviewing, and short-term intervention services. The high expense of hiring professional interpreters has led to the need to incorporate the utilization of paraprofessional foreign language interpreters. The increased need of translators continues to pose challenges. Few counseling organizations hire certified interpreters, and many erroneously utilize the services of bilingual staff not trained in translation methods or mental health, or the relatives of the clients requesting services. The American Counseling Association's ethical guidelines of 2005 include the new recommendation of providing interpreters or translators for non-English-speaking clients.

The initial attention paid to the role of language and translation in long-term clinical counseling comes from the psychodynamic tradition. In the 1970s, authors argued that accessing certain material is more difficult for people who have had an early encoding in a different language and that bilingual clients have different experiences of self according to which language they use. Recent contributions to the psychodynamic literature posit that bilinguals may have two different language codes and that each language system may be related to different experiences of the self. Treatment proposals include analyzing the dual experience of language by utilizing a translation method called language switching.

The method of back translation used in research and testing has its origins in the fields of health and nursing, which, in turn, influenced the field of psychiatry. Most assessment and research instruments were developed originally in English. Researchers and practitioners in other parts of the world who wish to use certain instruments use the back translation method. In 1990, the National Institutes of Health in the United States enacted a policy requiring the inclusion of minorities in study populations, which prompted translation of research instruments. Though there continue to be challenges in the attempts to standardize back translation principles for tests, questionnaires, and assessment instruments, translation of instruments from one language to another for cross-cultural use has become a widespread activity.

Interpretation

Bilingual capabilities are not sufficient for providing interpreting services. The ability to speak a second language is sometimes confused with the ability to interpret. However, when language match cannot be ensured, the services of an interpreter are required. Simultaneous translation, also known as interpretation, is a professional activity. In the counseling field, both professional and paraprofessional interpreters are used in a variety of clinical situations, including psychiatric, substance abuse, forensic, and other assessments and in short-term interventions. According to scant literature on the subject, working with foreign language interpreters is an acceptable, beneficial, and common use of bilingual paraprofessionals who can be trained to deliver appropriate, ethical services provided that each party in this three-way communication process can agree on some basic procedures. When counselors are trained to work with an interpreter, they learn how to ask one question at a time, speak in short sentences, and wait for the interpreter to finish sentences. When interpreters are trained in the field of counseling, they learn to be the transparent mediator between the client and the counselor. The interpreter's role needs to be inconspicuous and provide a direct and simultaneous translation of counselor's and client's words, without analyzing, summarizing, or explaining but rather directly and literally translating utterances. The interpreter, thus, needs to be able to translate what has been heard, without correcting, improving, or changing the client's words. It is recommended that the interpreter use first person when translating, as if he or she were speaking for him- or herself, instead of in third person.

Counselors need to develop alliances with interpreters and learn to communicate effectively with an interpreter in the room. For example, clients and counselors can be encouraged to speak directly to each other, engaging in direct eye contact with each other. For optimal effectiveness in the use of interpreters, time should be allowed for pre-session orientation between the counselor, the interpreter, and the client to clarify the roles in the process, to orient the client, and to answer any questions the clients may have regarding confidentiality or any other aspect of the process of engaging in a session with the presence of an interpreter.

With non–mental health paraprofessionals used as interpreters or with professional interpreters who do not have the clinical mental health background, prior meetings between the counselor and the interpreter are needed to discuss areas of possible difficulty, identify specialized vocabulary that might be needed during the session, and voice ethical concerns.

Language Switching

With few exceptions, long-term counseling relationships between non-English-speaking clients and English-only-speaking counselors is difficult, if not impossible, to sustain. It is possible, however, for the monolingual counselor to work with bilingual clients provided that they have the capabilities to engage in an intimate conversation in English. It is in these treatment situations that the method of language switching has been proposed as a form of oral translation. Clients who have had encoding in more than one language often have different ways of accessing affective reactions depending on which language they are using. Researchers recommend assessing the language acquisition history and current usage to find out what experiences are associated when each language is encoded and how the languages are currently used. Language switching is a method whereby a client can be encouraged to say something in English first and then switch to say the same thing in the language in which the experience was encoded, even if the counselor cannot understand it. The counselor can then ask about affect, memory, or other differences that are elicited by the use of two languages. Bilingual clients' language switching can serve to disclose traumatic or emotionally charged content that may not be accessible otherwise. Also, language switching offers the opportunity to explore clients' different sense of self in both languages and the different cognitive and affective components of each.

Written Translation

Written translation is a professional occupation that requires native written fluency in the target language and the ability to render a cultural adaptation of the original text into a new version that is coherent, well written, and culturally accurate. Bilingual capabilities are not sufficient credentials for providing written translation services, and oral proficiency in one language does not guarantee written proficiency. Professional translators are writers who can effectively render the message of the original text with accurate style and terminology. Bilingual individuals may speak two languages fluently but may not necessarily know how to move information between the two in writing. When counseling organizations do not use professional translators for their written material, translation mistakes can ensue that may be costly, embarrassing, and disrespectful.

Back Translation

Back translation is used when researchers use testing instruments with populations in non-English-speaking countries or with linguistic or cultural groups that differ from the population used to develop the instruments. Back translation methods are also used to translate instruments into American Sign Language. The goal of the back translation method is to ensure that the original and the translated versions of the instrument are semantically and culturally equivalent. The translation of concepts across cultures poses challenges to the researcher interested in adapting instruments for use in languages other than the original. There is evidence that suggests that an inadequate translation and cultural adaptation of an instrument can result in one that is less reliable or valid than the original version. The most widely used translation model in research consists of a series of repeated forward translation and back translation exercises conducted by a team of bilingual translators blind to the previous translations. This process continues until the back translation is considered to reflect congruence of meaning between the original version and the translated one. A challenge to the researcher is to ensure that the assessment tools are equivalent across groups, that the questions capture the same constructs, and that the instruments are culturally equivalent in both languages. Care needs to be taken to ensure that a systematic method of translation renders content and conceptual equivalency, in addition to semantic equivalency. To achieve cross-cultural adaptation more fully, researchers may also rely on committees of expert panels, field testing, and pilot studies, in addition to back translation.

Sara Schwarzbaum

See also Barriers to Cross-Cultural Counseling (v3); Bicultural (v3); Bilingual Counseling (v3); Bilingualism (v3); Career Counseling, Immigrants (v4); Communication (v3); Cross-Cultural Training (v3); Cultural Equivalence (v3); High-Context Communication (v3); Immigrants (v3); Low-Context Communication (v3); Multicultural Counseling Competence (v3); Second Culture Acquisition (v3)

Further Readings

American Translators Association. (n.d.). *Translation: Getting it right.* Retrieved March 22, 2007, from http://www.atanet.org/docs/Getting_it_right.pdf

Amodeo, M., Grigg-Saito, D., & Robb, N. (1997). Working with foreign language interpreters: Guidelines for substance abuse clinicians and human service practitioners. *Alcoholism Treatment Quarterly, 15*(4), 75–87.

Bradford, D. T., & Munoz, A. (1993). Translation in bilingual psychotherapy. *Professional Psychology: Research and Practice, 24,* 52–61.

Marcos, L. R., & Urcuyo, L. (1979). Dynamic psychotherapy with the bilingual patient. *American Journal of Psychotherapy, 33*(3), 331–338.

Matias-Carrelo, L. E., Chavez, L. M., Negron, G., Canino, G., Aguilar-Gaxiola, S., & Hoppe, S. (2003). The Spanish translation and cultural adaptation of five mental health outcome measures. *Culture, Medicine and Psychiatry, 27,* 291–313.

Perez-Foster, R. (1998). *The power of language in the clinical process: Assessing and treating the bilingual client.* Northvale, NJ: Jason Aronson.

Santiago-Rivera, A. L. (1995). Developing a culturally sensitive treatment modality for bilingual Spanish-speaking clients: Incorporating language and culture in counseling. *Journal of Counseling & Development, 74,* 12–17.

TRANSRACIAL ADOPTION

Transracial adoption refers to the placement of children with parents who are racially and ethnically different from the children. The practice of transracial adoption has a long and complex history. Throughout the history of transracial adoption, it has been referred to as *interracial adoption* or *cross-cultural adoption*. Traditionally, the term *transracial adoption* referred to the adoption of Black children by White parents in the United States. However, over time, all transracial placements where the adoptive parents and children were racially different were included in this terminology. Thus, various forms of domestic and international adoption (also referred to as *intercountry adoption*) can result in transracial adoption when the children and parents differ racially and ethnically (e.g., Korean children adopted by White parents). Transracial adoption is the most visible form of adoption due to the phenotypic or visible differences between the adoptive parents and children. In the United States and abroad, the vast majority of transracial adoptions have consisted of White parents adopting children of color or children who are racial/ethnic minorities in the United States. Some estimates suggest that approximately 8% of all adoptions are transracial in nature.

History

Transracial adoption has a long and complex history. Poverty, war, oppression, cultural practices, and social taboos have frequently been core explanations for the rise of both domestic and international adoptions. Although world history may have a sparse sprinkling of stories of transracial placements, transracial adoption was not formally practiced on a large scale until after World War II, and those transracial adoptions were primarily international in nature. Despite the common adoption strategy of matching (e.g., religion, race, appearance) used in adoption practice at that time, domestic transracial adoption began to serve as an option for couples looking to adopt during the 1960s.

Domestic Transracial Adoption

The earliest recorded transracial adoption took place in 1948 in Minnesota. Transracial adoptions on a larger scale took place later; some of the earliest cases of domestic transracial adoption placed American Indian children into White families as a result of the Indian Adoption Project that took place between 1958 and 1967. This project was intended to place these children with families from the dominant culture and away from Indian reservations, and it led to 395 American Indian children being placed in what were both domestic and international transracial placements. Criticisms of this practice ensued, resulting in the 1978 passage of the Indian Child Welfare Act, which made adoption by non-native Americans very difficult.

To begin to move the large numbers of orphaned African American children out of institutional settings (i.e., orphanages), domestic transracial adoption was instituted, challenging a widespread belief that race-matching was vital to the formation of family bonds. However, the extreme difficulty in placing African American children in adoptive homes prior to transracial adoption led to the designation of African American children available for adoption as meeting the criteria for "special needs" at that time. The Open Door Society, "Operation Brown Baby" in Oregon, Minnesota's Parents to Adopt Minority Children, and the Council on Adoptable Children advocated for transracial placements, and more than 2,500 domestic transracial placements of African American children with Caucasian families took place in 1970. Within a few years, however, criticisms of transracial adoption were levied by prominent adoption advocates. In 1972, the National Association of Black Social Workers predicted poor psychological adjustment and problematic racial identity for transracially adopted children as results of this practice that opponents referred to as "cultural genocide." In response to their criticisms, the Child Welfare League of America reversed the changes it had made to the adoption standards and supported the perspective that same-race placements were preferable for orphaned children.

To attend to the concerns of opponents to transracial adoption, empirical research studies were conducted to assess the psychological adjustment and racial identity development of the children who had been transracially adopted. Using Black, transracially adopted children and comparing them to their nonadopted peers, the first studies (as well as many subsequent studies) used combinations of measures, interviews, parent reports, and teacher reports to conclude that the transracially adopted children were generally adjusting as well as their nonadopted peers. Estimates suggest that 70% to 80% of transracial adoptees were adjusting as well as their nonadopted peers. These findings were complicated by reports of increased referral rates and disproportionate ratios of adopted persons in psychiatric treatment. More recent research explains the higher rates of psychological problems among adoptees in comparison with their nonadopted peers as due to a skewed distribution where the majority of adoptees were adjusting well and in the middle of the distribution, but at the extremes, there were substantially higher rates of adoptees than nonadoptees.

After a series of studies was conducted to disprove the criticisms of transracial adoptions, legislation was passed that allowed resurgence in transracial adoption placements (e.g., the Multiethnic Placement Act of 1994). Subsequent research has worked to clarify these concerns, and legislation (e.g., Interethnic Placement Act of 1996) has prevented restrictions in adoptive placements based on these concerns. The Multiethnic Placement Act of 1994, sponsored by Senator Howard Metzenbaum (D–Ohio), banned agencies that received federal funding from denying or delaying transracial placements of orphans on the basis of race alone. However, this act did allow the use of race as one of several factors that could be considered in foster and adoptive placements. In 1996, this law was revised in the Interethnic Placement Act. This law prohibited the consideration of race in any way when federally funded agencies made placement decisions.

International Transracial Adoption

International adoption was utilized to care for orphans from war-torn Europe after World War II, but the Korean War in the 1950s led to a more widespread and visible form of international adoption. In practice, South Korean orphans were placed with White American adoptive parents, thus constituting some of the earliest transracial placements. Since that time, international adoptions have taken place from a wide array of countries. In 2005, 7,906 visas were issued to orphans adopted from China to the United States. Other countries from which children have been adopted by U.S. citizens include Guatemala, South Korea, Kazakhstan, Ethiopia, India, Haiti, and Colombia. International adoption has also faced criticism and opposition with references to it serving as a clear example of American imperialism and as a result of colonialism. Despite these criticisms and changes in the availability of children and policies for international adoption, international transracial adoption continues to be an increasingly popular option for couples seeking infants for adoption. Historically, as the availability of White infants in the United States decreased due to the increased social acceptability of single-parenthood and pregnancy out of wedlock, families seeking to adopt have turned to international adoption. Poverty, wars, political crises, population control policies, and social taboos in countries around the world have continued to provide children for adoption. In 2005, 21,968 children were adopted internationally and the vast majority of those adoptions would also be considered transracial in nature.

Transracial Adoption and Counseling

Transracial adoption and counseling have a brief and inconsistent history. Recent issues of *The Counseling Psychologist* have given brief attention to counseling issues for transracial adoptees, but no systematic study of clinical issues, counseling skills or techniques, or counseling process has focused on transracial adoptees. Adoption advocates and more counselors and psychologists have drawn attention to the need for "adoption sensitive" or "adoption competent" counseling skills. Nationally, several U.S. states (e.g., Oregon, New Jersey, Connecticut, New York, and Washington) have developed certificate programs in therapy with adoptive families. Despite the dearth of studies on the counseling process with adoptive families, research, anecdotal reports, and case studies reflect that common concerns for transracial adoptees tend to center on racial and ethnic identity.

Identity Development for Transracial Adoptees

Given that one of the chief concerns of opponents to transracial adoption is racial/ethnic identity, identity issues among transracial adoptees must be explored. The research studies that examined racial/ethnic identity for transracial adoptees have generally concluded that they identify with their racial/ethnic group differently than do nonadopted individuals from their same racial/ethnic background. However, that different identification has not been systematically or empirically demonstrated to be associated with psychological maladjustment or self-esteem difficulties.

One model to address these issues was created by Amanda L. Baden and Robbie J. Steward and is called the cultural-racial identity model. The cultural-racial identity model serves as a framework for understanding and attending to racial and cultural differences among parents and children and by considering the impact that the experiences and the attitudes of parents, peers, extended family, social support networks, and the larger community have on identity development. This model accounts for transracial adoptees' shifting affiliation or connection with their adoptive parents' culture (e.g., often White, American, middle-class culture), their birth culture (e.g., the culture into which they were born), people from their parents' racial group (e.g., often White Americans), and people from their own racial/ethnic background. Transracial adoptees navigate the cultures and racial/ethnic groups with which they are familiar and those with which they want to become more familiar, adept, and at ease. In essence, the process of developing an identity around culture and race is often a primary task for transracial adoptees throughout their lives.

Amanda L. Baden

See also Acculturation (v3); Acculturative Stress (v3); Black Racial Identity Development (v3); Ethnic Identity (v3); Family Counseling (v1); Identity (v3); Identity Development (v3); Multiracial Families (v3);

Parent–Adolescent Relations (v1); Parenting (v1); Racial Identity (v3)

Further Readings

Baden, A. L., & Steward, R. J. (2000). A framework for use with racially and culturally integrated families: The cultural-racial identity model as applied to transracial adoption. *Journal of Social Distress & the Homeless, 9*(4), 309–337.

Hollingsworth, L. D. (1997). Effect of transracial/transethnic adoption on children's racial and ethnic identity and self-esteem: A meta-analytic review. *Marriage & Family Review, 25*(1), 99–130.

Javier, R. A., Baden, A. L., Biafora, F. A., & Camacho-Gingerich, A. (Eds.). (2007). *The handbook of adoption: Implications for researchers, practitioners, and families.* Thousand Oaks, CA: Sage.

Lee, R. M. (2003). The transracial adoption paradox: History, research, and counseling implications of cultural socialization. *The Counseling Psychologist, 31*(6), 711–744.

McRoy, R. G., & Freeman, E. M. (1986). Racial-identity issues among mixed-race children. *Social Work in Education, 8*(3), 164–174.

Miller, B. C., Fan, X., Christensen, M., Grotevant, H. D., & van Dulmen, M. (2000). Comparisons of adopted and nonadopted adolescents in a large, nationally representative sample. *Child Development, 71*(5), 1458–1473.

TRIMBLE, JOSEPH E. (1938–)

Joseph E. Trimble is a pioneer and distinguished psychologist widely known for his work in cultural diversity, multicultural counseling, and issues related to culture and psychology. He has published extensively in peer review journals, books, and technical reports and has an extensive list of presentations at professional conferences. His contributions to service are extensive, and he is heavily sought out for his expertise and eloquence as a speaker. He has received numerous awards and citations for his career achievements and contributions.

Trimble is a social psychologist who is located at the Center for Cross-Cultural Research, Department of Psychology, at Western Washington University in Bellingham, Washington. He is also a research associate at the University of Colorado Health Sciences Center and the National Center for American Indian and Alaska Native Mental Health Research. He is a scholar and adjunct professor of psychology at the Tri-Ethnic Center for Prevention Research at Colorado State University. Trimble received his B.A. degree from Waynesburg College in 1961, with concentrations in psychology, natural science, English literature, and French. He obtained an M.A. in general psychology from the University of New Hampshire in 1965, and in 1969, he received his Ph.D. in social psychology at the University of Oklahoma. His concentration was in interdisciplinary studies in psychology and sociology at the Institute of Group Relations.

Awards

Trimble's extensive list of awards, honors, and fellowships include the Allen L. Edwards Lecturer Fellowship at the University of Washington; Radcliffe Fellow at Radcliffe Institute for Advanced Study at Harvard University; Peace and Social Justice Award given by the American Psychological Association's (APA) Division of Peace Psychology; Distinguished Psychologist Award in 2002, awarded by the Washington State Psychological Association; Janet E. Helms Award for Mentoring and Scholarship in Professional Psychology at Teachers College, Columbia University; Paul J. Olscamp Outstanding Faculty Research Award, Western Washington University; Lifetime Achievement Award from Division 45 (Society for the Psychological Study of Ethnic Minority Issues) of the APA; Excellence in Teaching Award from the Western Washington University; election to Fellow status from the APA; and Fellow of the National Science Foundation. These awards were based on Trimble's scholarly contributions together with his extensive service contributions within psychological associations, university settings, and committees that set policy in, and direction for, the field of psychology.

Service

Among his numerous service contributions, Trimble served as president of Division 45 of the APA; chaired the Committee on Ethnic Minority Recruitment, Retention and Training Task Force Textbook Guidelines Initiative of the APA; served as a member of the APA Council of Representatives; and chaired numerous committees of the APA related to ethnic minority issues and Native Americans. As a university professor, Trimble has served on various committees of governance and issues related to ethnic minorities, and he has taught courses in psychology, human services, and occasionally in curriculum theory and instruction. To date, he has chaired over 30 master's theses and several doctoral dissertations, and he has served on more than 30 additional master's-level thesis and doctoral-level dissertation committees.

Publications

Trimble has written 91 peer-reviewed journal articles, chapters, and monographs; 15 authored or coauthored books; and 75 technical reports. He has given more than 130 professional presentations. He has been associated with 23 different journals throughout his career as an associate editor, editorial board member, reviewer, and consulting editor. Besides his professional contributions, Trimble's personal journey in achieving these accomplishments has shaped his thinking and perspectives.

Personal Journey

Trimble's formal training, career achievements, and significant contributions did not let Trimble sway from understanding and appreciating his cultural, ethnic, and familial roots. In a chapter he wrote for the second edition of the *Handbook of Multicultural Counseling*, he describes his personal journey as a psychologist in training and in the profession. The struggle of managing two or more cultures with polarizing perspectives is similar to that of many minority psychologists of that time and even today. On the one hand he was raised with a perspective about life that is seen as more holistic, that emphasizes cooperation and collaboration, and that integrates the interrelationships, commonalities, and interconnectedness of all factors that influence behavior. On the other hand, the field of the social sciences and the mainstream U.S. culture tend to emphasize competition over cooperation, to prefer methods of thinking that reduce factors to a few variables of importance over the interrelatedness of factors, and to view unexplainable phenomena, such as culture and social influences, as extraneous factors of minimal importance.

The opposing perspectives in psychology generated a determination to seek out others who had similar concerns about linking culture and psychology. With the support of an Arapaho elder and his grandfather, these conflicts only motivated him to provide the scholarship and research that was missing in the field demonstrating the connection and the importance of examining context that includes culture and ethnicity. As a true pioneer, Trimble has paved the way for others to join and build the body of knowledge, while at the same time advocate for the perspectives of appreciating diversity and integrating culture and ethnicity within the field of psychology.

Eduardo Morales

See also American Indians (v3); Bureau of Indian Affairs (v3); Cross-Cultural Psychology (v3); Cross-Cultural Training (v3); Indian Health Services (v3); Multicultural Counseling Competence (v3); Multicultural Psychology (v3); Racism (v3); Society for the Psychological Study of Ethnic Minority Issues (v3); Society of Indian Psychologists (v3)

Further Readings

Bernal, G., Trimble, J., Burlew, K., & Leong, F. (Eds.). (2002). *Handbook of racial and ethnic minority psychology.* Thousand Oaks, CA: Sage.

Pedersen, P., Draguns, J., Lonner, W., & Trimble, J. E. (Eds.). (2002). *Counseling across cultures* (5th ed.). Thousand Oaks, CA: Sage.

Trimble, J. E. (2001). A quest for discovering ethnocultural themes in psychology. In J. G. Ponterotto, J. M. Casas, L. A. Suzaki, & C. M. Alexander (Eds.), *Handbook of multicultural counseling* (2nd ed., pp. 3–21). Thousand Oaks, CA: Sage.

Trimble, J. E., & Fisher, C. (2006). *Handbook of ethical considerations in conducting research with ethnocultural populations and communities.* Thousand Oaks, CA: Sage.

Trimble, J. E., Stevenson, M. R., & Worell, J. P. (2003). *Toward an inclusive psychology: Infusing the introductory psychology textbook with diversity content.* Washington, DC: American Psychological Association.

Universalism

Universalism is defined as the principle that a given value, behavior, theory, or treatment will be the same across all groups independent of culture, race, ethnicity, gender, and other social identities. This principle has been a core philosophical assumption within the fields of counseling, psychology, medicine, and many other social sciences. This foundational tenet has maintained a stronghold on theories, research, and practice within the counseling profession. In addition to being a core belief within counseling, universalism has also become one of the central philosophical perspectives in defining multiculturalism.

Core Belief Within the Counseling Field

Historically, the dominant view within counseling has been that theories and practices are to be viewed as universal hypotheses that require empirical examination to test their veracity, meaningfulness, and effectiveness. Developmental theories examining moral and cognitive development as well as counseling theories such as behaviorism and Gestalt are just a few examples of theories that purport to address the concerns and realities of all individuals. Even though attention to individual differences has always been a core belief within the counseling profession, the universal assumptions within many of these theories were not rigorously challenged until multicultural scholars identified them as being culturally insensitive and not inclusive of alternative worldviews. This etic point of view suggests that it is possible and productive to fully understand all aspects of psychology, and even a particular culture, from a universal standpoint. Examples of such universal assumptions include how we define what is "normal," what is "effective" counseling, and who is a "good" client. Another universal assumption is the belief that all disorders occur in all cultures and present in similar ways.

Fields such as counseling, psychiatry, and assessment have all experienced the effects of universal assumptions and biases that have led to discussions, sometimes controversial, about their effects on theories, diagnosis, norm groups, and standardized testing. The ultimate effect of universalism on theories and practice can be ethnocentric, androcentric, and even counterproductive when human complexity and diversity are not actively incorporated.

Cultural relativism is an alternative approach to understanding the behaviors, beliefs, and perspectives of others. Rather than presume that the experiences, beliefs, and developmental processes are the same for all others, examining specific cultural and individual realities help to inform this alternative perspective. This belief does not presume that having a global understanding has no value but rather that universal and cultural realities can be mutually considered and applied to bridge cultural, political, and other group differences and further our understanding of human behavior.

Universalism and Cultural Differences Within Multicultural Counseling

Within multicultural counseling, various philosophical assumptions about multicultural perspectives in counseling have been used to organize the assumptions and strategies used for multicultural counseling and training. Descriptions of those diverse perspectives vary depending on an author's point of view. A universalistic or etic definition of multiculturalism encourages a transcendental perspective that is grounded in human commonalities. This universal approach tends to emphasize within-group differences as being greater than between-group differences. In other words, differences within groups (like unique aspects of American Indians) are more significant than differences between groups (like African Americans and Latino/a Americans). Some proponents of the universal perspective have expressed concern that focusing on cultural differences can lead to stereotyping, overgeneralization of group perspectives, or a type of cultural determinism that takes away both individually unique and universal aspects of a person. Universalism within the multicultural movement has a different perspective than the universal perspective present in the larger field of psychology. Individuals within the multicultural movement who embrace universalism do not deny culture but rather choose to focus on the human bond that connects all individuals. They believe many aspects of psychology, such as emotion, may be universally present in all cultures, but they manifest differently across cultures.

Most other perspectives could be classified within the cultural differences point of view, which is typically viewed as an alternative to universalism. The cultural difference approach, whether it focuses specifically on race or a broader understanding of difference (e.g., gender, sexual orientation), typically emphasizes incorporating the ideographic experiences of a particular cultural group as the basis for interpreting their behavior and offering psychological services. This emic point of view suggests that a culture's perspective is best understood from within that culture. Individuals who embrace the cultural difference perspective suggest that the universal point of view ignores the crucial realities of racism and other forms of oppression and their impact on the sociopolitical histories, power dynamics, and identity of various cultural groups. Issues of cultural bias and avoidance of cultural realities may be more likely to occur in a perspective that does not specifically value and embrace cultural differences as core. The cultural difference point of view does not deny that there are universal realities that connect individuals but rather chooses to view such universal connection as less central to understanding individuals who have been historically underserved and misunderstood by the counseling profession.

Future Directions

The universal versus cultural difference discussion is inevitably dichotomous. Although these diverse perspectives acknowledge and embrace some aspects of the other beliefs, they approach the issue of human difference from unique standpoints. Within the multicultural field there has been some discussion of the need to reconceptualize such dualistic thinking away from either/or perspectives and embrace a more unifying dialectic point of view.

Many multicultural scholars articulate the need to combine the universal and cultural relativistic perspectives to counteract their weaknesses and accentuate their strengths. The possibility of integrating a universal and inclusive perspective that honors the various social identities experienced by all (e.g., gender, social class, sexual orientation, religion) with a race-based approach that honors the unique history of race and racism in the United States would be an alternative approach that moves beyond the either/or dichotomy of universal versus culture specific. Discussions about universal and cultural relativism represent an important and ongoing conversation that is occurring within the multicultural counseling field.

Universalism will continue to be a core belief within psychology as a whole and within the specific field of multicultural counseling as counselors struggle to fully understand and explain human beings and their behaviors. However, the continued existence of cultural differences as well as cultural biases will create the need for a cultural differences perspective. Undoubtedly, such definitions will evolve as counselors attempt to appreciate and integrate the complexity of individual, cultural, and universal perspectives, and it is likely that universalism and the similarities that link human beings will remain a significant point of view.

Amy L. Reynolds

See also Cross-Cultural Psychology (v3); Cross-Cultural Training (v3); Cultural Accommodation and Negotiation (v3); Cultural Encapsulation (v3); Cultural Equivalence (v3); Cultural Mistrust (v3); Cultural Paranoia (v3); Cultural Relativism (v3); Cultural Values (v3); Culture (v3); Etic–Emic Distinction (v3); Multicultural Psychology (v3); Pluralism (v3); Worldview (v3)

Further Readings

Carter, R. T., & Qureshi, A. (1995). A typology of philosophical assumptions in multicultural counseling and training. In J. G. Ponterotto, J. M. Casas, L. A. Suzuki, & C. M. Alexander (Eds.), *Handbook of multicultural counseling* (pp. 239–262). Thousand Oaks, CA: Sage.

Draguns, J. G. (2002). Universal and cultural aspects of counseling and psychotherapy. In P. B. Pedersen, J. G. Draguns, W. J. Lonner, & J. E. Trimble (Eds.), *Counseling across cultures* (5th ed., pp. 29–50). Thousand Oaks, CA: Sage.

Fukuyama, M. (1990). Taking a universal approach to multicultural counseling. *Counselor Education and Supervision, 30,* 6–17.

Schwartz, S. H. (1994). Are there universal aspects in the structure and contents of human values? *Journal of Social Issues, 50,* 19–45.

Speight, S. L., Myers, L. J., Cox, C. I., & Highlen, P. S. (1991). A redefinition of multicultural counseling. *Journal of Counseling & Development, 70,* 29–36.

White, D., & Wang, A. (1995). Universalism, humanism, and postmodernism. *American Psychologist, 50,* 392–393.

Visible Racial/Ethnic Groups

Visible racial/ethnic groups is a euphemism for racial/ethnic classification in the counseling profession when discussing American racial/ethnic groups that are non-Caucasian or not of European descent. This terminology, coined by Janet E. Helms and Donelda A. Cook, for African, Latino/a, Asian and Pacific Islander, and Native/Indigenous Americans, is an alternative to the term *racial/ethnic minority groups*. Identifying visible racial/ethnic groups as "minorities" in research and counseling implicitly compares these groups to Caucasians/European Americans as the standard, thereby disempowering them. Additionally, the term *minorities* connotes subordinate social status. The use of the terms *minority* for visible racial/ethnic groups and *majority* for Caucasian/European Americans reinforces the existing racial power differences in societal relations in the United States.

The term *visible racial/ethnic groups* signifies two aspects of American racial socialization of peoples of African, Asian, Latin, and Indigenous North American descent. The first aspect focuses on common cultural characteristics, norms, values, attitudes, and behaviors that stem from cultures of origin and are transmitted across generations. For example, cultures of Africa, Asia, Latin America, and Indigenous North America typically stress the importance of the collective society, emphasizing interdependence and connectedness. Secondly, the term *visible racial/ethnic groups* recognizes the ways in which the aforementioned groups have been subject to unequal social, economic, legal, and political power in American society, based on visible racial characteristics, such as skin color, facial features, and native language.

Implications of Racial/Ethnic Labels

Professional Mandate

The *Publication Manual of the American Psychological Association, Fifth Edition,* calls for the appropriate identification of research participants and clientele by specifying major demographic characteristics such as sex, age, and race/ethnicity. Language for racial/ethnic designations changes over time, and members of designated racial/ethnic groups perceive some terms negatively. It is recommended that racial/ethnic designations reflect the preferred nomenclature of the groups discussed. It is important to use terminology that empowers racial/ethnic groups in their collective social identities, as well as in their psychological well-being.

Historical Evolution of Racial/Ethnic Labeling

During the early 20th century, psychological research (i.e., intelligence research) and counseling practice recognized racial differences by comparing Caucasians with non-Caucasians (typically Black Americans) and interpreting any differences between groups against Caucasians as the standard or normative group. Thus, non-Caucasian groups were labeled deviant or deficient when found to differ from Caucasians as research participants and as counseling clientele.

As the representation of visible racial/ethnic group counselors and psychologists increased in the 1960s, they began to confront the deficit models of diversity in the profession, moving toward affirming diversity in racial/cultural identity. That is, research and practice began to examine cultural characteristics of African, Asian, Latin, and Indigenous Americans, to develop normative standards common to each racial/ethnic group. Research of within-group differences rather than between-group differences was promoted. The positive aspects of each racial/cultural group were affirmed by within-racial-group research.

In the 1970s, the social and psychological influences of racial oppression on members of visible racial/ethnic groups came to the forefront in counseling research and practice. The influence of racial socialization on the counseling process examined White counselor–Black client relationships and expectations for counseling. William Cross's theory of psychological Nigrescence introduced the role of oppression as a critical factor in shaping the stages of Black racial identity, emphasizing the impact of Blacks' encounters with the White normative standard in the development of Blacks' sense of their social and psychological identities. In the 1980s and 1990s racial identity theory in research and practice was expanded to all racial/ethnic groups. Racial identity theories are concerned with how individuals abandon the effects of oppression (as either oppressed or the oppressor) and develop respectful and equitable attitudes toward their own racial group and other racial groups.

Research in the 21st century recognizes race/ethnicity in the United States as a social construction rather than a biological entity, with racial/ethnic designations reflecting how society perceives individuals and how individuals come to perceive themselves due to racial socialization. Racial classifications are not precise measures: Self-designations of race or racial designations by others (i.e., researchers, counselors) are based on societally defined categories and societal racial positive and negative stereotypes.

The term *visible racial/ethnic groups* is an attempt to recognize the differential societal status of the socio-racial classifications for Blacks/African Americans, Asian and Pacific Islanders, Latinos/as, and Native/Indigenous Americans. This terminology also retains the cultural heritage transmissions of the respective ethnic groups.

Donelda A. Cook

See also African Americans (v3); American Indians (v3); Asian Americans (v3); Ethnic Identity (v3); Ethnicity (v3); Ethnic Minority (v3); Helms, Janet E. (v3); Latinos (v3); Pacific Islanders (v3); Race (v3)

Further Readings

American Psychological Association. (2001). *Publication manual of the American Psychological Association* (5th ed.). Washington, DC: Author.

Cook, D. A., & Helms, J. E. (1988). Visible racial/ethnic group supervisees' satisfaction with cross-cultural supervision as predicted by relationship characteristics. *Journal of Counseling Psychology, 35,* 268–273.

Cross, W. (1971). The Negro to Black conversion experience. *Black World, 20,* 13–27.

Cross, W. (1978). The Thomas and Cross models of psychological Nigrescence: A review. *Journal of Black Psychology, 5,* 13–31.

Helms, J. E. (1990). *Black and White racial identity theory: Theory, research, and practice.* Westport, CT: Greenwood Press.

Helms, J. E., & Cook, D. A. (1999). *Using race and culture in counseling and psychotherapy: Theory and process.* Boston: Allyn & Bacon.

Helms, J. E., Jernigan, M., & Mascher, J. (2005). The meaning of race in psychology and how to change it: A methodological perspective. *American Psychologist, 60,* 27–36.

Helms, J. E., & Talleyrand, R. M. (1997). Race is not ethnicity. *American Psychologist, 52,* 1246–1247.

Sue, S. (1991). Ethnicity and culture in psychological research and practice. In J. Goodchilds (Ed.), *Psychological perspectives on human diversity in America* (pp. 51–85). Washington, DC: American Psychological Association.

Trickett, E. J., Watts, R. J., & Birman, D. (Eds.). (1994). *Human diversity: Perspectives on people in context.* San Francisco: Jossey-Bass.

Yee, A. H., Fairchild, H. H., Weizmann, F., & Wyatt, G. E. (1993). Addressing psychology's problem with race. *American Psychologist, 48,* 1132–1140.

VONTRESS, CLEMMONT EYVIND (1929–)

Clemmont Eyvind Vontress, American counselor educator and psychologist, is recognized generally as a pioneer in cross-cultural counseling. He first used the concept of cross-cultural counseling in a speech at the University of Virginia in 1968. He has contributed to the literature on the impact of culture on counseling, existential psychotherapy, and traditional healing in Africa for nearly 5 decades. Early in his career, he focused his attention on problems that Anglo-Americans encountered in counseling Black Americans. After researching the national culture and its subsystems in the United States, Vontress examined how cultural differences affect the entire counseling process, regardless of the client's background. Today, he is considered one of the leading writers on culture and counseling. During the past 2 decades, Vontress has contributed significantly to the literature on traditional healing in Africa and its implications for counseling culturally different clients in the West. Living and learning in a primarily racially segregated society in the first half of the 20th century, he was influenced significantly by the ethos of the civil rights movement in the United States. His strong feelings about human rights and the equality of people were evident in his writings during the latter half of the 20th century. His concerns about counseling Blacks in segregated and integrated school systems culminated in *Counseling Negroes*, the first book to explore the topic. By the 1970s, race and culture were dominant themes in the counseling field. Vontress was in the forefront of the increasing number of counselor educators who wrote and spoke often at national, state, and local professional conventions about cultural, ethnic, and racial differences as barriers in the counseling enterprise. It was in the late 1970s, 1980s, and the 1990s that Vontress began to explicate existentialism, the philosophy underpinning his personal approach to counseling. In 1979 he outlined his philosophical approach to counseling in the article "Cross-Cultural Counseling: An Existential Approach." In writing and speaking about how existential philosophy can be used as a therapeutic modality, Vontress established himself in the counseling field as a leading advocate of existential philosophy in counseling in general and cross-cultural counseling in particular. After several research and study trips to West Africa where he met with traditional healers and some of their clients, he began to explain in his writings and discourses how spirituality is necessarily a part of the counseling process. He came to respect the efficacy of traditional healing and viewed African healers as partners in the helping profession and in helping people, especially those in developing countries. Starting in the 1990s, his keen interest in and respect for traditional healing have been reflected in his writings.

Background

Vontress was born in Alvaton, Kentucky, in 1929, the year the stock market crashed and the Great Depression began. After graduating from high school in Bowling Green, Kentucky, he attended and graduated in 1952 from Kentucky State University with a B.A. in French and English. Shortly after enrolling in graduate school at the University of Iowa, he was drafted into the U.S. Army and spent a tour of duty in Hammelburg, Germany. While there, he made several trips to Paris. On one of these occasions, he saw and heard Jean-Paul Sartre and Simone de Beauvoir holding forth in a brasserie. This was his first exposure to existentialism. Later, he would read *Existentialism: With or Without God*, by Catholic priest Francis J. Lescoe. He indicated that one of his graduate students, Morris L. Jackson, steered him in the direction of existentialism by recommending Lescoe's book.

Having grown up in legally segregated Kentucky, in Europe he was astonished to see the racial harmony there and wondered why it could not exist in the United States. His experiences abroad would change his outlook on the human condition. He became increasingly focused and filled with new meaning in life and was more optimistic about his future. He was determined to achieve in spite of the social conditions that hindered his development and that of his fellows. He completed the M.S. degree in 1956 and the Ph.D. in 1965 in counseling at Indiana University in Bloomington, Indiana. As a graduate student, he studied the counseling theories of Carl Rogers and E. G. Williamson, well-known counseling theorists at the time. It was while working on his Ph.D. that Vontress had the opportunity to engage Carl Rogers in a question-and-answer dialogue. The study of counseling and human behavior was, in part, due to the influence of his mother from whom he learned by example empathy, striving for perfection, perseverance, quietude, stoic endurance, and unselfishness. The experiences in Europe changed his outlook on life from pessimism to progressive optimism, which manifested itself as an inner driving force that spurred him to achieve. People who entered into his life space recognized that life seemed to have a mission for him. Upon listening to one of his Ph.D. professors' lectures about people being culturally deprived, culturally disadvantaged, or disadvantaged, he decided to focus aspects of his writing on culture and its impact on counseling. Throughout his professional career, Vontress has been an English teacher, high school counselor, counselor educator, and psychologist.

Cross-Cultural Counseling

Culture as an important factor in the counseling relationship always has been a centerpiece of Vontress's writings. He considered culture to be the sum total of a people's belief and procedures for negotiating environments sustaining and affecting their existence. He maintains that it is simultaneously visible and invisible, conscious and unconscious, cognitive and affective. A major shift in his understanding of culture took place when he espoused existential philosophy. Within this philosophical framework, he viewed culture as encompassing five concentric and intersecting cultures: (1) universal, (2) ecological, (3) national, (4) regional, and (5) racio-ethnic. He posited that the universal culture was the most foundational because it influenced all others.

People are more alike than they are different and are similar and dissimilar at the same time. Vontress views cross-cultural counseling as a human-to-human encounter. Therefore, culture, per se, is not necessarily an impediment in a counseling relationship. The key factor contributing to an effective counseling relationship is the ability of the counselor to accept the client as a co-equal human being. The essential therapeutic ingredient is the humanness of the counselor and his or her ability to connect with others in need of help. Vontress recommends that counselors resist the temptation to focus on cultural differences and focus instead on human similarities. In the human-to-human encounter, counselors need to understand their own humanness and that of their clients who have come to them for understanding and resolution of concerns.

Cross-cultural counseling has been the primary focus of Vontress's life work. It was in the late 1960s at an American Personnel and Guidance (now the American Counseling Association) meeting that he presented a paper titled "Cultural Barriers in the Counseling Relationship." It was later published under the same title. In it, Vontress introduced the concept "cross-cultural counseling." Counseling becomes cross-cultural whenever the counselor is unable to understand the humanness of the client and tries to engage from a culturally different perspective. Cultural, racial, ethnic, and other visible differences become impediments to effective intervention. Because differences are perceived as well as real, a cross-cultural dyad may consist of almost any two individuals who fail to recognize their common humanity.

Existential Cross-Cultural Counseling

Existentialism is a philosophy that advocates that people recognize the reality of human existence. Basic to this reality is the continuous movement toward death. Frequent national and international travel caused Vontress to develop a global perspective of humankind. It also contributed to his development of an existential approach to cross-cultural counseling. According to him, existentialism develops and enhances our relationships with ourselves, others, nature, and spirituality. He recommends that counselors use the Socratic dialogue as the basic technique in cross-cultural counseling. Vontress's existential cross-cultural counseling approach was influenced and inspired by Ludwig Binswanger. Central to existential cross-cultural counseling is an understanding of the existential concepts Umwelt (physical world), Mitwelt (public world), Eigenwelt (private world), and Uberwelt (spiritual world). It is also important to understand that ideally the worlds interact harmoniously to ensure a balanced existence for human beings. Vontress's existential cross-cultural counseling approach requires the individual to fully grasp the concepts of existentialism and his or her significance at different stages in the counseling relationship.

Traditional Healing

Vontress's study of traditional healing in Africa was simultaneously a study of his historical roots. The visits to Africa provided a deeper understanding of himself and his own humanity. The paradigm shift in his worldview was made evident by his interest to document in writing his newly found understanding of humanity. It was in 1991 that he wrote his first article on Africa. Vontress continues to write about existential cross-cultural counseling and traditional healing in Africa, and he nurtures his understanding of humanity by interacting authentically with colleagues and by mentoring countless students, many of whom come from Africa.

Morris L. Jackson

See also Cross-Cultural Psychology (v3); Cross-Cultural Training (v3); Cultural Relativism (v3); Indigenous Healing (v3); Multicultural Counseling (v3); Multicultural Counseling Competence (v3); Universalism (v3); Worldview (v3)

Further Readings

Binswanger, L. (1962). *Existential analysis and psychotherapy.* New York: Dutton.

Binswanger, L. (1975). *Being-in-the-world: Selected papers of Ludwig Binswanger* (J. Needleman, Trans.). London: Souvenir Press.

Binswanger, L. (1991). Existential analysis and psychotherapy. In J. Ehrenwals (Ed.), *The history of psychotherapy* (pp. 374–379). Northvale, NJ: Aronson.

Lescoe, F. J. (1974). *Existentialism: With or without God.* New York: Alba House.

Vontress, C. E. (1969). Cultural barriers in the counseling relationship. *Personnel and Guidance Journal, 48,* 11–17.

Vontress, C. E. (1971). *Counseling Negroes.* Boston: Houghton Mifflin.

Vontress, C. E. (1973, August 27). *Racial and ethnic barriers.* Paper presented at the 81st annual convention of the American Psychological Association, Montreal, Canada.

Vontress, C. E. (1979). Cross-cultural counseling: An existential approach. *Personnel and Guidance Journal, 58,* 117–122.

Vontress, C. E. (2003). On becoming an existential cross-cultural counselor. In F. D. Harper & J. McFadden (Eds.), *Culture and counseling* (pp. 20–30). Boston: Allyn & Bacon.

Vontress, C. E. (2005). Animism: Foundation of traditional healing in sub-Saharan Africa. In R. Moodley & W. West (Eds.), *Integrating traditional healing practices into counseling and psychotherapy* (pp. 124–137). Thousand Oaks, CA: Sage.

Vontress, C. E., Epp, L. R., & Johnson, J. A. (1999). *Cross-cultural counseling: A case book.* Alexandria, VA: American Counseling Association.

White, Joseph L. (1932–)

Joseph L. White, born in 1932 in Lincoln, Nebraska, is a well-known African American professor, psychologist, activist, scholar, researcher, consultant, educator, and mentor who revolutionized traditional European American psychology by setting the stage and foundation for what is now known as cross-cultural psychology and multicultural counseling. White received his undergraduate and master's degrees in psychology in 1954 and 1958 from San Francisco State University and graduated with a Ph.D. in clinical psychology and developmental psychology in 1961 from Michigan State University. White has held positions of psychologist, dean, director, assistant vice chancellor, and professor at institutions such as Washington University; California State University, Long Beach; San Francisco State University; and most recently the University of California, Irvine (professor emeritus of psychology and psychiatry). As a luminary in the cross-cultural psychology field, White—respectfully and endearingly known as "Joe," "The Godfather," and the "Father of Black Psychology"—has been challenging theories of psychology, academics, clinical agencies, organizations such as the American Psychological Association (APA), and numerous university and psychology boards for more than 40 years.

White graduated during the groundswell of the 1960s civil rights movement and quickly emerged as a leader of social justice, diversity, and equality in psychology and in the community. White's formal education, talent, intellect, and social and political connectedness brought him into the company of individuals such as Malcolm X, Stokely Carmichael, Eldridge Cleaver, and other members of the Black Panthers and brought him appointments to work with California Governor Edmund G. Brown, San Francisco Mayor Willie Brown, and presidential candidate Robert F. Kennedy.

In September 1968, White and a small group of African American psychologists founded the Association of Black Psychologists (ABPsi) at the San Francisco meeting of the APA. White's initial steps to revolutionize psychology began in 1968 when he and other members of the fledgling ABPsi confronted members of the APA and the convention planning committee regarding the absence of Black programming in psychology. Their truth was reality—that the struggles, strengths, science, practice, and psychology of Black Americans were not reflected in the largest organization of scientist-practitioners educating America on psychology, research, and therapy. Disheartened, angry, and driven by scholarship, White was determined to shift the paradigm of thinking on how psychology defines ethnic minority individuals. Until the 1960s, Black and other minority individuals were conceptualized according to European American and Western standards of living and psychology. In 1970, White published his seminal and groundbreaking article "Toward a Black Psychology" in *Ebony* magazine. His article provided validation to African Americans and ethnic minorities from a Black American perspective and inspired individuals to question psychology and ask questions such as "How does traditional psychology address the mental health needs of ethnic minority individuals?"

White's pioneering work propelled individuals, such as Derald Wing Sue and Stanley Sue, to form other ethnic psychological organizations such as the Asian American Psychological Association, the National Latina/o Psychological Association, and the Society of Indian Psychologists in the following years. ABPsi served as the forerunner of more ethnic organizations and of the creation of Division 45 (Society for the Psychological Study of Ethnic Minority Issues). White's trailblazing actions gave support to others committed to social justice who also went on to become prominent leaders in the field of multicultural psychology (Wade Nobles, Allen Ivey, Stanley Sue, Derald Wing Sue, Thomas Parham, and William Parham to name a few).

White continued to expand traditional American psychology toward a cross-cultural psychology as evident in his commitment to improving the mental health treatment for people of color. Again, his scholarship flourished in his writing and cowriting of several editions of *The Psychology of Blacks: An African American Perspective, The Troubled Adolescent, Black Man Emerging: Facing the Past and Seizing a Future in America,* and, most recently, *Black Fathers: An Invisible Presence in America,* all of which have been instrumental in the creation and current discourse of cross-cultural psychology and the fourth force of multicultural psychology. Underlying White's contributions to psychology are concepts including the historical realities of people enduring the physical and psychological pains of racism, discrimination, and prejudice. He has taught that throughout history in psychology, the poor, the minority, and the non-White have endured the emotional pains resulting from being compared with their European American/White counterparts and being conceptualized as inferior. White's writings and teachings clearly shifted the paradigm of thinking in bringing awareness to counseling and in the application of differing cultural conceptualizations needed into a psychology developed and normed primarily for middle-class European Americans. Furthermore, the core of and development of Black psychology and much of White's theoretical and practical concepts have focused on human strengths, highlighting resilience, "healing in the broken places," and recognizing the positive aspects of one's life course rather than the dysfunction and pathology that one has experienced. Thus, Black psychology needs to be acknowledged as a psychology originally rooted as a psychology of strengths and positive psychology in its theoretical underpinnings and practical application.

White's contributions to cross-cultural psychology and multicultural psychology are not limited solely to his writings and activism. Over the past 4 decades, he has taught, inspired, advised, guided, mentored, and spiritually touched hundreds of individuals, encouraging them to be change agents, to seek social justice, and to make a difference for one individual, which, in turn, will make the larger society a smaller, more manageable place. White truly believes if people make a difference in one person's life and they then make a difference in five people's lives, then this world will be a better place. White's consummate mentoring has been witnessed and experienced by many and has earned him the status of "The Conductor of the Freedom Train," a supportive pipeline for undergraduates in the tracks of aspiring to earn a Ph.D. in psychology. White created opportunities for minority and ethnic students and other students alike to experience the mentorship from beginning to end, as undergraduates to doctoral graduates in psychology. He carefully crafted such opportunities to ensure success and support in pursuit of graduate school in psychology. His pipeline and "Freedom Train" started at the California State and University of California systems and has continued for decades now with students earning Ph.D.s from reputable institutions including Southern Illinois University, Carbondale; University of Maryland, College Park; University of Missouri, Columbia; Washington State University, Pullman; and more. White's teaching abilities, his presence at conferences, his ability to connect with diverse people, and his genuine care to increase the numbers of ethnic minorities who pursue Ph.D.s in psychology are precisely why it has been believed that White has mentored more Ph.D. students in psychology than any other individual in the field, with the majority being individuals from diverse racial-cultural backgrounds.

White has gone beyond making *psychology* a household word and has encouraged individuals to apply their psychology education and diversity knowledge to other fields. Administratively, White worked toward increasing the numbers of ethnic minorities entering college. In addition to mentoring graduate students through counseling/clinical/school/child psychology programs, he was involved in the founding of the Educational Opportunities Program (EOP) at California State University, Long Beach (which led to the development of EOP systemwide). Additionally, White was active in both Head Start and Upward Bound programs in Southern California. In addition to diversifying the educational system, White also was appointed by Governor Brown to serve as chair of the Psychology Examining Committee, State of California, where he fought to integrate and represent the interests of diverse people in the statewide system, in clinical work, supervision, on the Exam for Professional Practice in Psychology, and toward the overall practice of psychology. White has served on numerous committees to create diversity on campuses and has done more than his share in applying his psychological knowledge to diversify the American educational system and psychology. Along the way, he has guided professionals in law, government, business, higher education, political administration, academia, private practice, and medicine with regard to minority mental health. Each generation taught by White continues to advance the field of ethnic minority psychology in some capacity.

Those who know White know of his legacy and pioneering work in the field of Black psychology and multicultural counseling. As reflected in his history, White has had a lifetime of achievements that have advanced the field of ethnic minority psychology. White's several articles and books have served as roots and will continue to serve as the branches to an evolving cross-cultural psychology. White's contributions have been acknowledged through numerous awards, including the 2000 Lifetime Achievement Award from APA Division 45 (Society for the Study of Ethnic Minority Issues), the 2007 Henry Tomes Award for Distinguished Contributions to the Advancement of Ethnic Minority Psychology, and a 2007 honorary doctorate from the University of Minnesota, Twin Cities, for his life contributions to the field of psychology. He was also chosen as one of psychology's senior men of color at the National Multicultural Conference and Summit in 2001.

As a 75-year-old African American licensed clinical psychologist and professor emeritus in America, White has reached all walks of life, people, races, sexual orientations, and color in leading by example and incorporating cross-cultural psychology in his daily life. White's contributions have, without doubt, advanced ethnic minority and cross-cultural psychology as we know it today; his impact has been profound.

Nita Tewari

See also African Americans (v3); Afrocentricity/ Afrocentrism (v3); Association of Black Psychologists (v3); Black Psychology (v3); Career Counseling, African Americans (v4); Cross-Cultural Psychology (v3); Cross-Cultural Training (v3); Cultural Values (v3); Multicultural Counseling (v3); Multiculturalism (v3); Multicultural Psychology (v3)

Further Readings

Connor, M., & White, J. L. (Eds.). (2006). *Black fathers: An invisible presence in America.* Mahwah, NJ: Lawrence Erlbaum.

White, J. L. (1969). Guidelines for Black psychologists. *The Black Scholar, 1,* 52–57.

White, J. L. (1970, August). Toward a Black psychology. *Ebony, 25,* 44–45, 48–50, 52.

White, J. L. (1984). *The psychology of Blacks: An Afro-American perspective.* Englewood Cliffs, NJ: Prentice Hall.

White, J. L. (1989). *The troubled adolescent.* Elmsford, NY: Pergamon Press.

White, J. L., & Cones, J. H., III. (1999). *Black man emerging: Facing the past and seizing a future in America.* New York: Freeman.

White, J. L., & Parham, T. A. (1990). *The psychology of Blacks: An African-American perspective* (2nd ed.). Englewood Cliffs, NJ: Prentice Hall.

White, J. L., Parham, T. A., & Ajamu, A. (2000). *The psychology of Blacks: An African centered perspective.* Upper Saddle River, NJ: Prentice Hall.

WHITE AMERICANS

The identity of White Americans can be described along a number of dimensions. Perhaps the most basic is the statistical portrait derived from numerical data as compiled by the U.S. Census Bureau; however, a more nuanced understanding of this group emerges from consideration of their history, culture, and social location.

White Americans by the Numbers

White Americans are one of the five racial designations defined by the U.S. government, the others being Black/African American, Asian, Native American/Alaskan Native, Native Hawaiian/Pacific Islander (and Other). Whites are defined by the U.S. government as comprising people of European, Middle Eastern, or North African descent. The U.S. Census conducted in 2000 found that 77.1% of the American population indicated that they were White, alone or in combination with another race, with 75.1%

reporting that they were White only. Whites also had the opportunity to indicate their family ancestry, the most commonly reported being German (with 15.2% of the total population), followed by Irish (10.8%) and English (8.7%). With regard to place of residence, Whites are distributed fairly evenly throughout the United States, with the largest total numbers of Whites living in the South (34%) and the Midwest (25%) relative to the West (21%) and the Northeast (20%). The highest concentrations of Whites can be found, however, in the populations of the Midwest (85%) and the Northeast (79%).

Sociopolitical Location

In terms of their social, political, and economic standing, White Americans are the dominant racial group in the United States. The United States has had White presidents and vice presidents exclusively, and as of the November 2006 elections, Whites held approximately 94% of seats in the U.S. Senate and 83% percent of those in the House of Representatives. With fewer than 10 exceptions throughout history, all elected governors of all 50 states have been White. Whites occupy the overwhelming preponderance of corporate executive positions, serving as chief executive officers at about 495 of the 500 largest corporations as represented by *Fortune Magazine* in 2006. White people are overrepresented in every powerful and highly paid profession: Overwhelmingly, American lawyers, judges, physicians, bankers, college professors, and journalists are White. The vast majority of American wealth resides in White hands, as documented by Meizhu Lui and her colleagues in their 2006 book *The Color of Wealth*. For every dollar of wealth owned by a White family, people of color own less than a dime. Family median net worth (i.e., assets minus debts) provides another way of looking at this disparity. According to the Federal Reserve Bank, the median net worth for White American families in 2001 was $120,900, whereas for people of color it was $17,100. In short, in nearly every walk of life, the lists of the wealthiest, the most powerful, and the most influential feature a preponderance of White Americans.

The Origins of Whiteness

Another way of understanding White Americans involves the origins of Whiteness itself as a collective group identity. Race in general has been declared a biological myth by bodies such as the American Association of Anthropology; rather, racial groupings are understood to be socially constructed, historically contingent identities that arise from a particular confluence of social, cultural, political, and/or economic forces. More specifically, the notion of Whiteness as a meaningful way to categorize human beings is a fairly recent development that did not exist at the time the first European settlers ventured onto this continent. The first colonists, therefore, would likely have called themselves English, Dutch, German, or perhaps Christian rather than White. As described by such historians as Howard Zinn, the socioeconomic forces that initiated the creation of Whiteness in the 1700s derived from the emergence of one of the most important economic engines of the new American nation: the transatlantic slave trade. Not only were the profits to be made from the importation and sales of African people considerable, the developing plantation system relied completely upon slave labor. In response to the necessity of justifying these practices, Whiteness materialized as a new group identity that collectively privileged the new American owning class by establishing a racial hierarchy in which Whites could claim superiority. Whiteness, therefore, provided a rationale for the buying and selling of Africans and their children, their subsequent lifelong enslavement, and the appropriation of all profits from their labor.

Africans were not the only people to find that Whiteness—or more specifically, the occupation of a social location outside and beneath it—bore important consequences in their lives. Conquered people of color throughout Central and South America and the Caribbean lost their land and resources to White colonialists, while Asians in the United States saw their wealth-building opportunities legislated away by White lawmakers. Such legislation had its foundation in the Naturalization Law of 1790, which stated that only "a free White person" was eligible for American citizenship. In the century that followed, Asians of every ethnicity filed suits in state and federal courts claiming that they had the right to be considered White and thus were among those allowed to own property and be protected by law. These included, for example, Takao Ozawa, who emigrated from Japan in the late 1800s, attended the University of California, and raised a family in Hawai'i where he worked for an American company. He appealed the repeated denials of his naturalization requests all the way to the Supreme Court, where, in 1922, he was denied a final time for the stated reason that he was not Caucasian. Finally, in the 1940s, racist laws such as the Chinese Exclusion Act of 1882 and the Alien Land Law of 1913 were repealed.

By law, therefore, Whiteness constituted the legally sanctioned platform for social and economic dominance in America well into the 20th century. White Americans' historical control of political power, property ownership, and wealth creation, in addition to all the other rights of full citizenship, sheds light on the contemporary concentration of wealth and power in White American hands. Moreover, it is from this historical context that Whiteness derives meaning; for this reason, psychologist Ruth Frankenburg has conceptualized Whiteness itself as an artifact of sociocultural dominance production.

The Culture of White Americans

Many White Americans would be surprised by the idea that they have a culture. The notion of culture is often associated in the minds of Whites with people of color and the ways in which their ethnic traditions, food, and music are seen as different or exotic. In fact, White Americans do have cultural traditions and norms, even though they are largely invisible as such to Whites themselves. This invisibility derives from the fact that Whites tend to see White culture not as a culture at all but as "just the way things are"—as the standards, customs, and values that describe the essential human experience. White culture, then, gains power through its invisibility, in that it becomes the standard against which all others are judged.

The terms *White culture* and *Eurocentric culture* have been used to describe the culture of White Americans and the worldview according to how they live and perceive reality. Accordingly, the word *Eurocentrism* refers to the tendency to order and understand reality according to the tenets, beliefs, and values of White/Eurocentric culture. Psychologist Judith Katz has explicated the components of White culture, which begin with the value of individualism, as opposed to prioritizing collective or community well-being. In keeping with this value, the individual is understood to be the primary social unit, autonomy is highly valued, and individuals are expected to master the environment and exercise control over the circumstances of their lives. Closely related is the value placed upon competition: All situations can be understood as win/lose propositions, and winning is all-important. Status is accorded to individuals on an economic basis; money and property ownership are important symbols of status, along with titles and credentials. Communication is characterized by direct eye contact, limited emotional expressiveness, and little physical contact. Whites' sense of time is characterized by a future orientation and delay of gratification; time is viewed as a commodity and strict adherence to schedules is valued. Family structure is typically patriarchal, with the male as the traditional head of the nuclear family unit and the female subordinate to him. Beauty ideals for women are based on White physical characteristics (e.g., light skin, blue eyes, blonde hair) along with a thin body and youthful appearance; men are understood to be attractive primarily on the basis of their economic status and sociopolitical power. Musical and artistic aesthetics are derived from European models, and accepted histories are based on the perspective of Europeans who colonized the North American continent. Christian religion is foundational to White American culture, with most holidays deriving from either Christianity or White accounts of North American history.

Psychologist Derald Wing Sue has written about the culture of White Americans, their worldview, and ethnocentric monoculturalism. Ethnocentric monoculturalism refers to (a) the conviction that one's own culture is superior to any other; (b) a sense of entitlement to promulgate one's own beliefs, values, and traditions at the expense of others; and (c) the sociopolitical power to do so. Cultures are not, in and of themselves, either bad or good, and all cultures tend to privilege their own beliefs over others; therefore, it is the latter of these aspects—power—that is the key to ethnocentric monoculturalism and what makes it harmful to outgroups. In the United States, this means that groups other than White Americans, and those whose cultures and worldviews differ from Whites, are often seen as inferior, deviant, alien, and incapable, even if exotic and interesting. The fact that power resides almost exclusively with White Americans means that this negative evaluation damages the life opportunities and well-being of people of color in a White-dominated culture.

Another construct that helps illuminate the operations of Whiteness and White culture in America is hegemony. Hegemony refers to the capacity for powerful groups to maintain dominance not only through institutional, political, economic, and/or military displays of power but also through their ability to shape cultural norms, ideals, systems of understanding, and conceptions of "common sense" in a way that supports their dominance. According to the Italian political theorist Antonio Gramsci, hegemony functions so that dominant groups exercise power from within subordinated people themselves, in that subordinated people internalize ideas and structures that define the dominant group's power as natural and preordained. The culture of White Americans, then, can be said to be hegemonic in the United States in that many of the tenets of White culture have a natural, "of course" quality to them. Celebrations of the "rugged individual," the symbolic display of personal purchasing power, and beauty pageant contestants of various races whose features correspond to White beauty ideals are unremarkable, taken-for-granted features of American life. Along these lines, author Toni Morrison has noted that the phrase "White Americans" itself has a redundant quality; the word *American* contains notions of Whiteness within it.

White Americans and Privilege

Open commentary by White Americans regarding Whiteness has been infrequent, although Black scholars such as W. E. B. Du Bois have written influentially about Whiteness since before the turn of the 20th century. One of the best-known White expositors of Whiteness and its privileges in recent decades is Peggy McIntosh. In her Wellesley College working paper, first published in the late 1980s, McIntosh explored her identity as a White American and the unconscious privileges associated with it, calling it "an invisible knapsack" of assets and advantages that she carried with her into every situation. For example, McIntosh observed that, as a White woman, she nearly always had the opportunity to be interviewed and evaluated by people of her own race, that history told her that people of her race created civilization as she knew it, and that bandages and other products were made to match her skin tone. McIntosh also explored the personal and moral ramifications of allowing oneself to become aware of White privilege, noting that such awareness had direct implications regarding social justice and meritocracy: If certain people acquire unearned advantages simply by being White, then this is not a society where everyone gets what she or he deserves, and Whites who acknowledge their privilege must also acknowledge that any success that they have enjoyed has been furthered because of it.

Marked White Americans

As mentioned, the hegemonic nature of Whiteness in the United States means that Whiteness is, for the most part, unmarked. In other words, anything that does not correspond to White cultural ideals *is* marked as discrepant—as different, ethnic, foreign, or unusual—but Whiteness itself goes unnamed as the accepted standard according to which "differentness" is judged. One group of White Americans, however, occupies a social location slightly outside the unmarked heart of White American culture and therefore requires a label to indicate their outsider status: poor Whites, variously called White trash, trailer trash, rednecks, or hillbillies. Anthropologist John Hartigan has discussed the meaning inherent in the name-calling directed toward poor White Americans. Specifically, the fact that the "Otherness" of poor Whites requires demarcation points to the classist and racist underpinnings of White American culture. Hartigan also discussed the various shades of meaning among these labels. *Redneck* is a label that poor or rural Whites sometimes embrace, in that it conveys a defiant attitude in the face of mainstream social rejection, whereas *white trash* is an identity that no poor White wants to own, in that it corresponds to the nadir of the class spectrum and conveys the lowest point of social contempt. *Hillbilly,* on the other hand, has more specific regional connotations and encompasses the complexity of the Appalachian mountain experience: an identifiable cultural heritage of music, food, art, and love of the land, experienced within a context of shaming poverty and social isolation.

Antiracist White Americans

One of the ways that White culture maintains its hegemonic dominance is by "erasing" White antiracist thought from history. This silence supports the impression that Whiteness has always been an accepted part of American life; moreover, those White Americans who wish to question or challenge White hegemony are left with no models of how such a thing might be done. In fact, there have always been White Americans who comprehend Whiteness and the corresponding oppression of people who are not White and who oppose the oppression outright. For example, Thomas Paine is widely studied by American schoolchildren who learn about his influential pamphlet *Common Sense,* which advocated the emerging American Revolution against the British. What is not as frequently mentioned is that he was also emphatically opposed to slavery and wrote tracts on the slave trade that were certainly read by influential White slave masters of the day such as Thomas Jefferson and George Washington. Radical pre–Civil War abolitionists such as William Lloyd Garrison receive scant, if any, acknowledgment, while John Brown, who was hanged in 1859 for treason after attempting to instigate antislavery insurrections, is cast by history as a zealot. History instead presents White Americans with Abraham Lincoln as the Great Emancipator, a man who was politically neutral on slavery although personally opposed to it. In a letter to the *New York Tribune* in 1862, Lincoln stated that his priority was saving the Union and if he could save it without freeing any slaves, he would do so. This trend continues to the present day; White antiracists such as Robert Jensen, Judith Katz, Tim Wise, Jeff Hitchcock, and David Roediger are virtually unknown in mainstream White American culture or scholarship.

Changing Demographics: White Americans in the Future

Since the 1990 U.S. Census, the White population has grown more slowly than the population as a whole, having increased by 5.9% as compared with the growth of 13.2% for the U.S. population as a whole. This pattern of slowing growth has led to the widely accepted view that by approximately 2050, Whites will no longer be the single most populous racial group. It remains to be seen how these changing numbers will impact the social location of White Americans or their awareness of it.

Laura Smith

See also Classism (v3); Color-Blind Racial Ideology (v3); Demographics, United States (v3); Ethnocentrism (v3); Eurocentrism (v3); Helms, Janet E. (v3); Power and Powerlessness (v3); Race (v3); Racial Identity (v3); Racial Pride (v3); Racism (v3); Sue, Derald Wing: Contributions to Multicultural Psychology and Counseling (v3); White Privilege (v3); White Racial Identity Development (v3); Worldview (v3)

Further Readings

Bonilla-Silva, E. (2003). *Racism without racists.* Lanham, MD: Rowman & Littlefield.
Doane, A., & Bonilla-Silva, E. (Eds.). (2003). *White out: The continuing significance of racism.* New York: Routledge.
Frankenburg, R. (1993). *White women, race matters: The social construction of race.* Minneapolis: University of Minnesota Press.
Hartigan, J. (2005). *Odd tribes: Toward a cultural analysis of White people.* Durham, NC: Duke University Press.
Jensen, R. (2005). *The heart of Whiteness.* San Francisco: City Lights Books.
Katz, J. (2003). *White awareness.* Norman: University of Oklahoma Press.
Lui, M., Robles, B., Leondar-Ross, B., Brewer, R., & Adamson, R. (2006). *The color of wealth.* New York: New Press.
Roediger, D. R. (1991). *The wages of Whiteness.* New York: Verso.
Sue, D. W. (2003). *Overcoming our racism.* San Francisco: Jossey-Bass.
Zinn, H. (2005). *A people's history of the United States.* New York: Harper Perennial.

WHITE PRIVILEGE

White privilege is the concept that European Americans benefit from specific advantages—denied to people of color—solely because of their nonminority status. These are unearned benefits derived not from merit, and these benefits are often taken for granted, if even acknowledged at all. White privilege generally refers to White, male, Anglo-Saxon, middle to upper class, heterosexual, able-bodied individuals.

The concept of White privilege has been evident in discussions of prejudice for some time, but Peg McIntosh articulated it in a way that was able to reach European American counseling students and scholars of all backgrounds. McIntosh, a feminist author writing in the area of male privilege, began to speculate, not about how she was oppressed as a woman, but whether she herself was privileged due to her status as a White person. She used the analogy of a backpack filled with unearned privileges that White persons are given at birth. Her work was seminal and formed much of the subsequent discussions on this topic.

White privilege is best understood when examined in the context of power and oppression. Individuals as well as groups of people can be the victims of classism, sexism, racism, and other forms of oppression. Multicultural competency, a cornerstone of the contemporary counseling paradigm, involves integrating this understanding into practice. However, to achieve this end, it is important for researchers and practitioners to grasp a firm understanding of the dynamics of oppression and its underlying structural components.

Oppression denotes a feeling of being weighed down and kept down by an unnecessary or unjust use of power: Oppression exists symbiotically with power. For oppression to be present, there has to be a stratified system of power differential among people in a society. That is, one person or one group needs to be on top or in a position of power, while another person or group of people is subjugated or kept in a position without power, or at least in a position without as much power as the other group. An integral aspect in the examination of the dynamics of oppression and White privilege is the often overlooked notion that people benefit from oppression without even realizing they are doing so. Many privileged members of the group with power in society do not want to think that they are living their lives in a manner that is oppressing anyone, yet every day they directly and indirectly benefit from the dynamics of oppression.

These dynamics of oppression continue to exist in society because it is difficult to enact systemic change when people are comfortable where they are in their current state of existence. The transaction of empowerment requires a power reallocation; that is, for change to occur, the people with privilege have to surrender some degree of their power. Historically, examinations of oppression have focused on the victims. However, to best understand White privilege, there needs to be an honest and thorough examination of the people who are benefiting from this power, with an emphasis on how it is highly advantageous for them to maintain their power and privilege.

Tripartite Model

The transformation of this definition of racism can be conceptualized by James Jones's tripartite model of contemporary racism, and this model is quite helpful in illustrating the manifestations of White privilege in society. Three levels of racism (i.e., individual, institutional, cultural) comprise this model. The first level, individual racism, can be defined as any action or attitude—conscious or unconscious, intentional or unintentional—that subordinates a person or group because of their race. While hate crimes and other highly visible overt acts fall into this category, individual racism also includes the beliefs and behaviors of well-intentioned people who are unaware that their attitudes and actions may oppress people of color.

The second level, institutional racism, resides in the organizations and institutions of society. Institutional racism is defined as any organizational practice or policy in business, government, schools, churches, courts, and law enforcement agencies that is enacted to unfairly subjugate persons of color, while allowing other groups to profit from these policies and procedures. The third level of racism in the tripartite model is cultural racism, which is the individual and institutional expression of the superiority of one group's cultural heritage over that of another. Cultural racism can be conceptualized as the superordinate umbrella that influences and permits both the levels of individual and institutional racism to exist and flourish.

Evidenced in each level of this model of contemporary racism, the manifestations of White privilege are often subtle, and their hegemonic nature makes them all the more powerful—and insidious. Rarely (if ever) contested, these seemingly invisible incidents of privilege allow White persons to make unlimited withdrawals from the White Privilege bank account without ever having to make deposits or even balance the checkbook.

Individual Level

White privilege at the individual level manifests itself in many forms. It may be a subtle microaggression, perhaps even an unintentional slight, which benefits a White person at the expense of a person of color. One example, from the perspective of a person of color, is the act of a White person being waited upon first even though he or she has come to the counter last.

If the White waiter takes the opportunity in an ambiguous situation to choose to wait on this White customer before the customer of color, it is difficult to discern intentionality. Perhaps the waiter legitimately didn't see the Black person enter first. Perhaps the waiter was having a bad day. Perhaps the waiter doesn't like Black people or thinks that White patrons tip better. On the other hand, if a White patron were to see another late-arriving patron waited upon first, the race-based explanation would most likely not occur to him.

However, sifting through these explanations causes a person of color to expend cognitive energy on the distinct possibility that the waiter chose to disregard societal conventions of "first come, first serve" in favor of extending an unearned privilege to a White person because of their shared racial group membership.

A microaggression is a subtle insult or small act of racism. A microaggression, such as the one in the previously mentioned example, can cause a person of color to mentally rehearse defensive scripts and actions. If the instance is brought up to a friend, colleague, or perhaps even the waiter, a person of color has to prepare to verbally defend himself against the anticipated minimalization of the experience (e.g., "You're being too sensitive and reading too much into it"). Or the person may have to defend against the flat out denial of such a race-based explanation (e.g., "The '60s are over. People don't think like that any more"). Alternately, the person of color may rehearse a defensive script wherein he directly confronts the waiter about the slight, thus taking the chance that he incorrectly attributed a racially based explanation (e.g., the waiter doesn't like Black people) when a potentially benign explanation was more accurate (e.g., the waiter didn't see the Black person come in first).

Other examples can be seen throughout the culture of the United States. These examples include store detectives specifically following people of color when they enter a store because the store detectives believe people of color shoplift more than White people; automatic denial of loans for automobiles or homes for people of color; or even realtors who do not show homes to people of color that are in predominantly White neighborhoods. Examples such as these contribute to the physiological and psychological distress that people feel. Lack of trust underlies the anxiety and stress people may feel, and anxiety and stress contribute to increased high blood pressure, increased heart disease, and an increase in chronic health problems.

Scenarios like these can cause unnecessary stress and duress for a person of color, whether it is an actual incident occurring or just the prospect that such a situation may occur. This race-related stress can be defined as the race-related transactions between individuals or groups and the environment that emerge from the dynamics of racism. Race-related stress can tax or exceed existing individual and collective resources or threaten well-being. Exposure to race-related stress can have psychological and physiological consequences to a member of a discriminated-against group. The exposure to chronic forms of discrimination has been implicated in the development of several stress-related diseases prevalent in the African American community and among other persons of color.

White privilege at the individual level of racism is the ability to arrive at an explanation—benign or otherwise—to an ambiguous social interaction without legitimately considering a race-related explanation. Thus, White privilege provides White persons with a buffer from the physiological and psychological consequences of race-related stress. This buffer is not readily available to persons of color who, at some level, have to at least contemplate the possibility of a racially based explanation (e.g., skin color contributed to the waiter's decision to wait on the White person first).

Institutional Level

At the institutional level of the tripartite model of racism, White privilege may be even more difficult to discern because the unearned benefits afforded to Whites at this level do not originate in one-on-one interactions. Rather, these privileges are embedded within societal institutions and organizations. Having had these benefits denied to them, persons of color may be acutely aware of this dynamic. However, having been raised on the dominant ideologies of rugged individualism and meritocracy, White persons may have difficulty acknowledging racism as a system that structurally benefits White persons at the expense of persons of color because doing so would threaten long-standing beliefs about society and beliefs about one's own accomplishments.

To illustrate the nature of White privilege at the institutional level, a series of compelling questions are offered here. For example, if a White employee makes an unpopular decision at his job, does he worry that his coworkers or customers will assume that a policy such as affirmative action ensured that other more qualified candidates were passed over because his race obscured an assumed lack of ability or qualifications? Is it perceived that his merit or his skin color is the main contributor to his success (or lack thereof)?

If a White person is a defendant in court, is there a good chance that a jury of his peers shares his values or even his racial characteristics? Do these peers make implicit assumptions about his guilt or innocence based on preconceived stereotypical notions about other people who look like him? Furthermore, are these notions based on a critical mass of real-life interactions with others who look like him, or are these notions instead based on isolated incidents or derived from movies, news reports, and other popular culture representations?

Extending beyond these issues of merit, consider assumptions that are made about the protection afforded by law enforcement agencies. Is there a systemic manner in which law enforcement is provided to members of different races? Does it take police officers a comparatively longer time to respond to 911 calls in Black neighborhoods? When teaching their adolescent son how to drive, how many White parents need to include instructions on keeping his hands in plain sight on the steering wheel in the event that he is pulled over by the police?

In contemplating the answers to these questions, the subtle and subversive nature of White privilege illustrates how institutional policies and practices unfairly subjugate persons of color, while allowing other groups to benefit. An unopened backpack of White privilege ensures that these unearned institutionally based privileges are neither acknowledged nor articulated, thus ensuring their continued receipt.

Research has shown that serious educational, occupational, economic, and health disparities exist between persons of color and White persons. In the counseling domain, there is a high rate of clients of color underutilizing mental health services and not returning for second sessions. Reasons for these include economic constraints, service access barriers, and cultural mistrust attitudes toward White counselors. When clients leave counseling early, this results in an increase in underdiagnosis and misdiagnosis, which, in turn, does not allow clients to get the help they need. In addition, psychological testing has been developed and based on the majority culture and does not always meet the needs of the client, specifically for a person of color. Testing is not always culturally sensitive, culturally appropriate, or adequate for the care of diverse clients.

Further research in the counseling literature acknowledges these disparities and highlights these institutional practices in terms of microaggressions against clients of color. These microaggressions are often perpetuated by well-intentioned White counselors, even those with extensive multicultural training. These subtle exchanges convey demeaning messages to clients of color, causing damage to the therapeutic alliance and the client's psychological well-being. Blaming the victim, dysfunctional helping, and self-righteous assertions of being nonracist are all examples of ways that clients of color can be disserviced and even victimized in therapy by White counselors. To clarify, blaming the victim involves a White counselor employing an intervention wherein the counselor assigns responsibility to the client of color for his presenting concern (e.g., depressive symptoms surrounding current unemployment). This microaggression serves to minimize or ignore the reality of White privilege, perpetuate cultural mistrust, and ignore the role of societal racism as a salient contributing factor in the presenting concern of the client of color.

Institutional practices and policies contribute to these disparities. However, because explicitly racist laws, such as Jim Crow laws, are no longer legal, it is difficult for White persons to acknowledge the systemic nature by which institutions subjugate persons of color. Instead, when disparities are observed, individual attributions are made that are congruent with majority values, and corresponding solutions (e.g., work harder, pull yourself up by the bootstraps, stop feeling sorry for yourself) serve to blame persons of color while effectively absolving institutional policies and practices of any responsibility in the matter. Thus, misattribution and denial allow institutional racism to effectively function without interruption.

Cultural Level

At the cultural level of the tripartite model of racism, examples of White privilege may occur in the form of subtle societal messages that are omnipresent in society and are conveyed through myriad media (e.g., television, radio, newspapers, Internet). These messages perpetuate the belief that White culture is superior and that other cultures are subordinate. A prime example is the societal standard for beauty—blonde hair, blue eyes—that favors predominantly Caucasian characteristics. Those who do not conform to this culturally exclusive standard are not fully represented in media and popular culture and thus do not achieve the same level of beauty.

Furthermore, if an attractive African American woman is acknowledged for her beauty—beauty that deviates from this cultural norm—she may be described as an *attractive Black woman*. On the other hand, an attractive blonde-haired blue-eyed Caucasian woman may be described as an *attractive woman* rather than an *attractive White woman*. This example of asymmetric racial marking sets the beauty of the White woman as the default standard. Her beauty does not require a specific racial designation because it is understood that this beauty (i.e., blonde-haired, blue eyed, *White*) inherently conforms to the dominant cultural standard.

Color-Blind Approach

White privilege can be thought of as the mechanism driving the color-blind approach to race relations. A color-blind approach is the position often endorsed by members of mainstream White society wherein they purport not to see race-based differences in people. Instead, they see everybody as equals and treat them accordingly. At the surface level, this is a socially desirable perspective because it conveys the sense of a progressive belief in only one race, the human race, a belief that aligns with the perspective of encouraging people of different cultures to assimilate.

However, embracing a color-blind approach is difficult because in doing so, one neglects to acknowledge the role of power in society, insinuating that we live in a purely egalitarian society wherein the American dream is equally accessible to all members of the human race, if only they work hard enough. Furthermore, it assumes that everybody has the luxury to choose not to see differences based on color. Ignoring racial group differences can validate assumptions that minority groups share the same values as those in the majority, thus leading to maintenance of the status quo. Perpetuating this societal status quo preserves the hierarchical system of racial stratification prevalent in American society, thus denying the reality of people of color—a reality wherein racism is very real to them, despite contentions to the contrary by White persons who have the power to purport not to treat people differently based on race.

White privilege is exemplified in this ability to deny another person's reality without having to acknowledge the ramifications of doing so. This invalidation can be driven by malice, but more often than not, it is driven by naïveté or even apathy when the ramifications do not appear to directly affect White persons. Power is the benefit acquired from deciding which reality is valid, and mainstream American society affords this unearned privilege of power to White persons at the expense of persons of color.

Although the colorblind strategy may appear noble and egalitarian on the surface, it conceals the reality of contemporary racism. Examples of overt racism represent only the tip of the racist iceberg. These examples may include the internment of people of Japanese descent living in the United States during World War II, forcing African American people to ride in the back of the bus, or dousing blankets with disease to trade to Native American people. An exclusive focus on these visible acts obscures the emergence of racism's insidious modern transformation into the invisible default standard of covert racism. Arguing against the color-blind strategy, Eduardo Bonilla-Silva reports that the United States is a racist country and due to the benefits experienced by White privilege, people continue to support racism by continuing to benefit from privilege. He also reports that seemingly innocent comments such as "I am not racist, but..." are more passive-aggressive in nature and continue to provide people with a forum to make racist remarks.

The use of American Indians as mascots for school and sports teams provides another poignant yet rarely acknowledged example of White privilege at the cultural level. Indian-themed mascots, such as the Cleveland Indians' Chief Wahoo, exhibit distorted versions that do not encapsulate or even accurately represent how real American Indians act or what they look like. In the absence of any (or, at best, limited) contact with real-life American Indians, mascots are the image that drives society's perceptions of who American Indians are.

White privilege is the ability to ignore the perspective of those without power or voice and to honor them on terms other than their own. Furthermore, even in the most optimistic scenario, White privilege is manifest in getting all of the facts together, listening to all relevant perspectives, and receiving overwhelming evidence and reasons to make a change. Yet White privilege grants the power to disregard all of this. White persons can rationalize their actions and prioritize other concerns (e.g., tradition, convenience, money) over the denigration of another group of people, even when the implicit becomes explicit and the hegemony of cultural racism starts to unfold. White privilege thrives in this space between.

Extension to Other Groups

Theorists have extended the concept of group-based privilege beyond race. As stated earlier, the notion was first developed within the context of male privilege and then extended to race. Now it has been used to describe

Christian privilege. An example of Christian privilege would be the ability to assume that an individual will not be required to work on a holiday that is celebrated in your religion. It has also been extended to nondisability privilege. A graphic example of nondisability privilege is the fact that an amniocentesis test showed that you did not have Down's syndrome, so you were allowed to be born, as opposed to some people who may decide to discontinue a pregnancy because of the existence of a disability. In addition, it has been extended to heterosexual privilege. A salient example of heterosexual privilege is the fact that, if you are a heterosexual individual, you are allowed to marry and benefit from all of the legal and social positive aspects of the recognition of such a union.

Jesse A. Steinfeldt, Janice E. Jones, and Paul E. Priester

See also African Americans (v3); American Indians (v3); Barriers to Cross-Cultural Counseling (v3); Color-Blind Racial Ideology (v3); Cultural Mistrust (v3); Discrimination (v3); Diversity (v3); Ethnic Identity (v3); Ethnic Pride (v3); Oppression (v3); Power and Powerlessness (v3); Racial Identity (v3); Racial Pride (v3); Racism (v3); White Americans (v3); White Racial Identity Development (v3); Worldview (v3)

Further Readings

American Psychological Association. (2003). Guidelines on multicultural education, training, research, practice, and organizational change for psychologists. *American Psychologist, 58,* 377–402.

Bonilla-Silva, E. (2006). *Racism without racists: Color-blind racism and the persistence of racial inequality in the United States.* New York: Rowman & Littlefield.

Constantine, M. G. (2007). Racial microaggressions against African American clients in cross-racial counseling relationships. *Journal of Counseling Psychology, 54,* 1–16.

Harrell, S. P. (2000). A multidimensional conceptualization of racism-related stress: Implications for the well-being of people of color. *American Journal of Orthopsychiatry, 70,* 42–57.

Jones, J. M. (1997). *Prejudice and racism* (2nd ed.). New York: McGraw-Hill.

McIntosh, P. (1989). White privilege: Unpacking the invisible knapsack. In P. S. Rothenberg (Ed.), *White privilege* (pp. 97–102). New York: Worth.

Neville, H. A., Worthington, R. L., & Spanierman, L. B. (2001). Race, power, and multicultural counseling psychology: Understanding White privilege and color-blind racial attitudes. In J. G. Ponterotto, J. M. Casas, L. A. Suzuki, & C. M. Alexander (Eds.), *Handbook of multicultural counseling* (2nd ed., pp. 257–288). Thousand Oaks, CA: Sage.

Ridley, C. R. (1995). *Overcoming unintentional racism in counseling and therapy.* Thousand Oaks, CA: Sage.

Sue, D. W. (2001). Multidimensional facets of cultural competence. *The Counseling Psychologist, 29,* 790–821.

Sue, D. W. (2003). *Overcoming our racism: The journey to liberation.* San Francisco: Jossey-Bass.

Sue, D. W. (2005). Racism and the conspiracy of silence. *The Counseling Psychologist, 33,* 100–114.

Sue, D. W., Bingham, R. P., Porche-Burke, L., & Vasquez, M. (1999). The diversification of psychology: The multicultural revolution. *American Psychologist, 54,* 1061–1069.

Tatum, B. D. (1997). *Why are all the Black kids sitting together in the cafeteria? And other conversations about race.* New York: Basic Books.

WHITE RACIAL IDENTITY DEVELOPMENT

White racial identity development (WRID) theory describes how White individuals develop a sense of themselves as racial beings, acknowledge the realities of structural racism and White privilege, and come to accept race as a healthy aspect of themselves and others. *Structural racism* is defined here as the policies and practices in the fabric of U.S. society that disadvantage non-White individuals; *White privilege* refers to the rights, advantages, exemptions, and/or immunities granted to White individuals that non-Whites are not provided. WRID is a specific derivation of the more general cultural/racial identity development theory. It is consistent with cultural/racial identity development theory in that it assumes that (a) people have varying levels of awareness about their group identity, (b) the level of awareness is influenced by sociopolitical factors, and (c) the level of awareness has important implications for counseling practice and training.

Models

William Cross developed a Nigrescence model to explain the process of Black racial identity development. This Nigrescence model was later applied by Judy Katz and Allen Ivey to understand how Whites deny their own race and the existence of structural racism. Cross's model, combined with these early investigations of how Whites understand their own race and racism, led to the development of the first WRID models.

There are several models that have been proposed to explicate WRID, and although these models differ in their description and sequence, they generally progress as follows: a minimization of oneself as a racial being and of racism; dissonance created by cross-racial experiences that challenge this naïveté; a recognition of oneself as a racial being and Whites' perpetuation of racism; and the internalization of an integrated White racial identity and comfort in cross-racial interactions. Historically, WRID models referred to *stages* of racial identity development; this term has been replaced with *statuses* to refer to the more fluid boundaries between different racial identity statuses and the dynamic processes by which individuals progress and regress between racial identity statuses.

Helms's Model

Janet Helms's model of White racial identity development is the most researched and applied of the WRID models. Helms's model has given rise to an assessment instrument, the White Racial Identity Attitude Scale (WRIAS), to measure WRID. Helms's WRID model has received some support from psychometric scrutiny of the WRIAS. Helms's model describes six statuses that may be divided into two meta-processes: (1) abandonment of racism and (2) defining a nonracist White identity.

Lack of awareness of oneself as a racial being and obliviousness to racial issues characterize *contact status*. Here, a White person is naive regarding the sociopolitical implications of race. During *disintegration status*, the minimization of race and racism is challenged by witnessing racial oppression or acknowledging one's own racist thoughts and behaviors. This challenges the naïveté of the previous status and creates dissonance. This dissonance may result in feelings of guilt, sadness, or anxiety and may lead a White person to avoid contact with persons of color. *Reintegration status* is marked by recourse to pro-White, antiminority attitudes to deal with the dissonance of disintegration status. One condones White supremacy and blames minorities for their own problems.

Helms's second process—defining a nonracist White identity—begins with *pseudo-independence status*. When racial oppression and a racist White identity are challenged, White people make an effort to understand racial differences. The motivation for multicultural learning is present, but understanding of diversity is immature, and cross-racial interactions may be paternalistic. In *immersion/emersion status* White people search for a personally meaningful definition of Whiteness. Intentionally learning about one's contribution to racism is an important task for this status. Less emphasis is put on trying to change others as one turns inward to address personal racist beliefs and tendencies. *Autonomy status* represents an individual's acceptance of his or her Whiteness and role in racial oppression. Here, the person's reference group is multiracial and the person selects and nurtures those aspects of White culture that "feel right." Finally, the autonomous individual moves beyond intellectualization of antiracism to take action against racial oppression.

Sue and Sue Model

Derald Wing Sue and David Sue have recently proposed a five-phase WRID model, in which individuals fluidly regress and progress across phases. This model differs from Helms's model in the way in which White individuals are theorized to address the dissonance from acknowledging racial inequality and Whites' role in racial oppression. Rather than a movement forward into a "reintegration" phase, as in Helms's model, individuals recycle back to the beginning "conformity" phase before reaching the later phases of WRID in the Sue and Sue model. The five phases of this model are discussed next.

During the *conformity phase,* a White person is highly ethnocentric, one's self-conception as a racial being is minimal, there is a conscious or unconscious belief that White culture is superior, and one professes a nonracist identity. The *dissonance phase* occurs when an individual experiences incongruence between his or her nonracist self-image and contradictory behavior. One's Whiteness and concomitant bias is acknowledged, and there is a dilemma about how to cope with this incongruence. Here, White people may return to the conformity phase or move into the *resistance and immersion phase*, characterized by a confrontation with one's own racism. In this phase, an individual becomes disillusioned to racial oppression, may reject his or her own Whiteness, and identify strongly with non-White groups. The *introspection phase* is a compromise between the preceding two phases, in which one questions and reformulates what it means to be White. The person accepts his or her Whiteness and role in perpetuating racial oppression but seeks to define a new racial identity. The formation of a nonracist White identity is the hallmark of the *integrative awareness phase*. Now, an individual has an understanding of him- or herself as a racial being, appreciates diversity, is aware of oppression, and actively works to confront it.

Applications for Training and Counseling

Because the majority of counseling practitioners are White, WRID scholarship has focused upon the context of understanding counselors' racial identity status in multicultural counseling and training situations. By contrast, non-White racial identity scholarship has focused upon its implications for clients rather than counselors.

From a training perspective, becoming aware of one's own White identity is an important part of multicultural counseling competency, an imperative for working with non-White client populations. Relatedly, Helms argued that White counselors with a greater degree of WRID have a greater capacity to confront and address structural racism and the racial dynamics and racial identity of their clients. Sue and Sue recommended that graduate programs assess WRID status to tailor multicultural training experiences, with the goal of making Whiteness visible and integrated into trainees' self-concept in a nonracist fashion.

Haresh Sabnani and colleagues articulated a WRID model with concomitant training goals for each racial identity status. This model incorporates aspects of the aforementioned models to create five WRID statuses: (1) pre-exposure/precontact, (2) conflict, (3) prominority/antiracism, (4) retreat into White culture, and (5) redefinition and integration. For each of these statuses, Sabnani prescribed objectives for the development of counselors' beliefs and attitudes, knowledge, and skills, with the overall goal of facilitating the counselors' movement to the next racial identity status. Their hypothesis is that counseling trainees will be differentially primed for multicultural training experiences based on their racial identity status. As Helms also argued, targeting training and educational experiences to racial identity status is critical in facilitating White students' racial identity, their capacity to recognize their own contributions to societal racism, and their capacity to counsel non-White individuals.

WRID also has important applications to counseling. Because WRID appears to influence cross-racial interpersonal relationships, White counselors can consider how their racial identity status may influence therapeutic relationships with non-White clients. Helms advanced a complex dyadic model for this purpose; cross-referencing WRID statuses with Black racial identity statuses. The result is a description of the relational dynamic for every potential White–non-White encounter, according to each individual's racial identity development status. This understanding of dyad combinations can attenuate confusion in clinical work and may motivate White counselors to nurture their racial self-concept to maximize the efficacy of their service to non-White populations.

Research examining the impact of WRID upon aspects of the counseling and supervisory relationship has yielded mixed results. For example, Madonna Constantine found that racial microaggressions, subtly racist messages and/or behavior by White counselors with African American clients, adversely affected the therapeutic alliance in counseling. Shawn Utsey and Carol Gernat found that White trainees with less advanced racial identity statuses relied upon more primitive ego defense mechanisms in racially provocative situations within counseling and supervisory dyads. However, Alan Burkard and colleagues did not find that WRID was associated with the capacity to form a working alliance in counseling by White participants.

Future Directions

Helms's WRID model has had a significant impact upon the understanding of Whites' racial identity development and in conceptualizing its impact upon counseling and supervisory dynamics. Although the WRIAS has been widely used, there has been some debate as to the correspondence between the WRIAS and Helms's White racial identity statuses. However, the Helms model and other models of racial identity development have profoundly influenced the Association for Multicultural Counseling and Development multicultural competencies and culturally informed theories of counseling. Future research could build upon the strong theoretical base of WRID to further clarify the impact of identity status upon the working alliance and other aspects of counseling, supervision, and training.

Matthew A. Diemer and Adam M. Voight

See also Black Racial Identity Development (v3); Cross-Cultural Training (v3); Helms, Janet E. (v3); Identity (v3); Identity Development (v3); Interracial Comfort (v3); Multicultural Counseling (v3); Racial Identity (v3); Sue, Derald Wing (v1); Sue, Derald Wing: Contributions to Multicultural Psychology and Counseling (v3); White Americans (v3); White Privilege (v3)

Further Readings

Behrens, J. T. (1997). Does the White Racial Attitude Scale measure racial identity? *Journal of Counseling Psychology, 44,* 3–12.

Burkard, A. W., Juarez-Huffaker, M., & Ajmere, K. (2003). White racial identity attitudes as a predictor of client perceptions of cross-cultural working alliances. *Journal of Multicultural Counseling and Development, 31,* 226–236.

Constantine, M. G. (2007). Racial microaggressions against African American clients in cross-racial counseling relationships. *Journal of Counseling Psychology, 54*(1), 1–16.

Cross, W. E. (1971). The Negro-to-Black conversion experience. *Black World,* July, 13–27.

Hardiman, R. (1982). White identity development: A process-oriented model for describing the racial consciousness of White Americans. *Dissertation Abstracts International, 43,* 104A.

Helms, J. E. (1984). Toward a theoretical explanation of the effects of race on counseling: A Black and White model. *The Counseling Psychologist, 12,* 153–165.

Helms, J. E., & Carter, R. T. (1990). Development of the White Racial Identity Inventory. In J. E. Helms (Ed.), *Black and White racial identity: Theory, research and practice* (pp. 67–80). Westport, CT: Greenwood Press.

Ivey, A. E., D'Andrea, M., Ivey, M. B., & Simek-Morgan, L. (2007). *Theories of counseling and psychotherapy: A multicultural perspective.* Boston: Pearson Education.

Katz, J. H., & Ivey, A. (1977). White awareness: The frontier of racism awareness training. *Personnel and Guidance Journal, 55,* 485–487.

Pope-Davis, D. B., Vandiver, B. J., & Stone, G. L. (1999). White racial identity attitude development: A psychometric examination of two instruments. *Journal of Counseling Psychology, 46*(1), 70–79.

Roysircar, G., Arredondo, P., Fuertes, J., Ponterotto, J., & Toporek, R. (2003). *Multicultural counseling competencies, 2003: Association for Multicultural Counseling and Development.* Alexandria, VA: American Counseling Association.

Sabnani, H. B., Ponterotto, J. G., & Borodovsky, L. G. (1991). White racial identity development and cross-cultural counselor training. *The Counseling Psychologist, 19,* 76–102.

Sue, D. W., & Sue, D. (2008). *Counseling the culturally diverse: Theory and practice* (5th ed.). New York: Wiley.

Utsey, S. O., & Gernat, C. A. (2002). White racial identity attitudes and the ego defense mechanisms used by White counselor trainees in racially provocative counseling situations. *Journal of Counseling & Development, 80*(4), 475–484.

WORLDVIEW

The human psyche represents a complex constellation of activity that impacts how people perceive and respond to reality. Culture firmly impacts the human experience, and worldview is subsequently one of the most studied constructs in the field of cultural, cross-cultural, and multicultural psychology. Worldview has been defined as a person's perception of his or her relationship with the world. More specifically, worldview is a by-product of the way in which a person is socialized to perceive, think, feel, and experience the world. It attempts to make sense of life experiences that might otherwise be construed as chaotic, random, and meaningless. Worldview articulates the basic philosophical assumptions, values, and beliefs underlying culture and is expressed through its various structural or institutional manifestations. Moreover, worldview is a by-product of culture that affects, and tends to determine, behavior.

Historical Synopsis

The construct of worldview is one of the earliest cultural variables to be integrated into psychological research, theory, and practice. Worldview represents a unifying thread in the psychological literature that suggests practices to guide culturally competent research and psychotherapy with culturally diverse communities. In 1970, J. L. White wrote the first article—"Toward a Black Psychology"—that questioned the utility of applying mainstream psychology toward African Americans. This article, which was published in *Ebony,* argued that it was difficult—if not impossible—to understand the African American experience by using traditional psychological theories that were developed by European American psychologists to explain European American behavior. Implicit in this assertion was the position that worldview differences exist between these two groups and that a psychology that is rooted in Western philosophy could lead to conclusions that could be harmful in the scientific research, clinical diagnosis, and prescribed treatment of African Americans.

This investigation into the implications of worldview differences was advanced more broadly by D. W. Sue and his colleagues. In 1982, they published a position paper in *The Counseling Psychologist.* Ten years later (1992), Sue and his colleagues followed up with a call to the profession, which was published in the *Journal of Counseling & Development.* This body of work represented an initial step toward articulating a set of competencies that each culturally skilled psychologist should be able to wield in psychotherapy. Such competencies were organized along the dimensions of beliefs, knowledge, and skills. For the first time, the implications of worldview differences in psychotherapy were clearly delineated and therapist self-exploration was promoted. Two decades after the original position paper was published, in 2002, the American Psychological Association Council of Representatives adopted a set of guidelines on multicultural education, training, research, practice, and organizational change for psychologists. These guidelines noted that awareness of the research participant's—or client's—worldview is not sufficient to actualize cultural competence in research—or psychotherapy. Psychologists must also be aware of their own worldview and have the skills to work through worldview differences in research, training, and psychotherapy in a culturally sensitive and meaningful manner.

Conceptualization of Worldview

Contemporary debates about the construct of worldview are focused more on how it is conceptualized and less on its utility in the field of psychology. It is widely understood that the construct of worldview can be used to understand interpersonal dynamics in a therapeutic relationship. Furthermore, some counseling psychologists have argued that therapists who work with culturally different clients will increasingly be exposed to clients who exhibit different worldview orientations. To the extent that these views diverge, services may be viewed as unacceptable and unnecessary and may influence the underutilization of psychotherapy by various ethnic groups in our society. Given the mental health–related help-seeking disparities that plague such populations, several counseling psychologists have articulated a need for a comprehensive characterization of worldview that can be applied to psychological assessment and psychotherapy.

Perspectives

To date, there are two primary perspectives that are driving the evolving conceptualization of worldview. The most prominent perspective is an existential approach that is rooted in cultural anthropology. Alternatively, some psychologists have tried to provide a more comprehensive articulation of worldview by investigating the depths of culture through the interrogation of various dimensions of philosophy.

Cultural Anthropology

Traditionally, conceptions of worldview in psychology have been grounded in cultural anthropology. In 1961, F. R. Kluckhohn and F. L. Strodtbeck articulated an anthropological model of value orientations that focused on five existential categories: human nature (what is the character of human nature?), activity orientation (what is the modality of human activity?), social relationships (what is the modality of people's relationships?), person–nature (what is the relationship of people to nature?), and time orientation (what is the temporal focus of human life?). Furthermore, each existential category was thought to vary among three potential options: human nature—bad, good and bad, or good; activity orientation—being, being in becoming, or doing; social relationships—lineal/hierarchical, collateral/mutual, or individualistic; person–nature—harmony, subjugation and control, or power of nature; and time orientation—past, present, or future.

Psychologists have used this model to conceptualize various dimensions of worldview orientations and have hypothesized that the beliefs and values along each dimension are shaped by the individual's cultural context. It is important to note that researchers have also operationalized worldview according to other value dimensions such as justice beliefs, sense of coherence, and cultural attitudes. A value-based conceptualization of worldview was the basis of several assessment instruments, including the Value Orientations Questionnaire (Green & Haymes), the Value Orientations Scale (Szapocznik & colleagues), and the Scale to Assess World View (Ibrahim & Kahn). These scales were designed to be applied to psychological research and to improve cultural competence in psychotherapy. In 1991, R. T. Carter provided a comprehensive summary of worldview studies based on this existential values conceptualization. F. A. Ibrahim, G. Roysircar-Sodowski, and H. Ohnishi later updated this review in 2001. Readers may consult these summaries for more detail.

Philosophy

Conceptions of worldview in psychology have also been grounded in the discipline of philosophy. Psychologists such as W. C. Banks, L. James-Myers, K. K. K. Kambon, and W. A. Nobles argued that cultural phenomena—like worldview—could best be captured through the deep structure of culture. According to this conceptualization, worldview is organized into several philosophical constructs: *cosmology*—nature of the universe, *epistemology*—theory of knowledge, *ontology*—connection of psychological facts with reality, *axiology*—science of values, and *teleology*—theory that things act for an end purpose. This method of conceptualizing worldview encompasses the values-based approach, while adding a layer of complexity by including additional culturally influenced dimensions that have the capacity to deepen the breadth of the worldview literature.

Historically, the aforementioned philosophical constructs have been traced back to KMT (or Ancient Egypt) and the definitions of these constructs have been debated by philosophers such as G. Berkeley, R. Descartes, G. W. F. Hegel, M. Heidegger, D. Hume, I. Kant, J. Locke, K. Marx, and Plato, to name a few. In 2005, L. James-Myers and colleagues advanced the cosmology, epistemology, ontology, axiology, and teleology model for analyzing worldview systems. More specifically, they provided potential questions that could be used to gain insight into a person's worldview orientation. Examples of such questions included (a) How was the universe created? (b) What powers animate life and gives it form? (c) What can be accepted as truth? (d) How is knowledge obtained and transmitted? (e) What is the nature of reality? (f) What exists in reality? (g) What are some values that can be used to guide human interactions? (h) What is the purpose of life?

Several behavioral scientists have used these philosophical dimensions of worldview to conceptualize the notion of *self* and *consciousness* for diverse ethic groups. Additionally, several categorizations have been illustrated to delineate differences and similarities between different ethnic groups along these philosophical dimensions of worldview. A philosophically based conceptualization of worldview was the basis of several assessment instruments, including the Worldview Scale (Baldwin & Hopkins) and the Worldview Analysis Scale (Obasi, Flores, & James-Myers).

Measuring Worldview

Although there is a multitude of psychological literature addressing the implications that worldview differences may have in conducting culturally competent psychotherapy, psychologists have been less adamant in investigating this issue in the domain of research. Within the field of psychology broadly, complex formulations of cultural phenomena often are relegated to race-based stereotypes. Whereas there are various theoretical formulations that conjecture the existence of worldview differences among various ethnic groups, there is a dearth in the amount of empirical evidence to substantiate such claims. In part, this is due to conceptual incarceration where Western science dictates what epistemology and methodology are deemed credible for uncovering such ontological relationships. In light of the imposed etic (cultural universals) methodology that is often inherent in Western science, limitations in researching cultural deep thought become inevitable when epistemological and ontological relationships rooted in various non-Western worldview orientations come into conflict with research methods that are grounded in a Western worldview.

For various reasons, this has bearing on the lack of instruments that can be used to research such theoretical formulations. When race-based instruments represent the closest alternative, researchers interested in cultural phenomena are faced with the alternative of pounding a square construct into a round hole. Research on racial constructs—such as racism, racialism, stereotypes, and race-related stress—is very much needed to address the stimulus value that physical features might have on attitude formulation or well-being. However, a racial paradigm will have little to no utility when the researcher is interested in cultural factors that influence spiritual, psychological, and/or behavioral phenomena.

The measurement of worldview is crucial to advancing psychological theory, research, training, and practice. Specifically, worldview is an important cultural variable that has the capacity to effectively assess between- and within-group differences so that individuals can be understood within a broader ethnocultural context. Scholars also have highlighted the importance of assessing the relationship of cultural factors (e.g., worldview, acculturation, cultural identity) to other psychological variables in research studies. Moreover, investigating the influence of a client's worldview in both process and outcome variables in psychotherapy may provide important data regarding effective modes of psychotherapy for culturally diverse populations.

One characteristic of the culturally competent therapist is awareness of personal assumptions, values, and biases. An important dimension of therapist self-awareness includes understanding one's own worldview and how worldview perspectives are shaped by the processes of enculturation and socialization. A worldview assessment instrument can serve as a tool for training programs in helping graduate students become more aware of the lens through which they perceive and interpret events around them. Furthermore, worldview assessment can help therapists understand the client's perception of her or his presenting concerns. In addition to assisting in conceptualizing and assessing the problem, knowledge of the client's worldview can also aid the therapist in establishing methods and goals for psychotherapy that are consistent with the client's worldview and determining the roles the therapist might serve in the context of the therapeutic relationship.

Finally, worldview assessment is invaluable to psychological research. In 1995, A. J. Marsella and F. T. L. Leong identified several methodological problems that contribute to errors in validity in psychological research. Of importance to worldview assessment is the "error of commission." In summary, this error describes conducting psychological research on diverse ethnic groups without regard of their worldview. Not having a valid worldview assessment tool would force the researcher to make stereotypical interferences (e.g., African Americans are spiritual and communalistic people), which were not assessed in the research study, to inform their results. Moreover, uncovering empirical differences in worldview may serve as a catalyst toward deriving much needed research methods that are obligatory for culturally competent research to be actualized.

As a result of the increased focus within psychology on providing effective services to culturally diverse populations that is informed by the research literature, and the recognition that culturally competent therapists and ethically responsible practice necessitate the assessment of worldview, researchers, trainers, and therapists are in need of measurement tools to assess worldview. To date, there are a few instruments to assess worldview orientation that are used in the psychology literature: Scale to Assess World View (Ibrahim & Kahn), Worldview Scale (Baldwin & Hopkins), and the Worldview Analysis Scale (Obasi, Flores, & James-Myers).

Scale to Assess World View

The Scale to Assess World View consists of 45 items and was developed to assess individual and group beliefs, values, and assumptions regarding (a) views of human nature, (b) interpersonal relationships, (c) nature, (d) time, and (e) activity. Human nature is categorized as being either bad (3 items), good and bad (3 items), or good (3 items). The modality of an individual's relationships is categorized as being lineal-hierarchical (3 items), collateral-mutual (3 items), or individualistic (3 items). The relationship of people to nature is categorized as being in harmony (3 items), subjugation to control (3 items), or power of nature (3 items). The temporal focus of human life is categorized into the past (3 items), present (3 items), or future (3 items). Finally, the modality of human activity is categorized as being (3 items), being-in-becoming (3 items), or doing (3 items). Each item is rated on a 5-point Likert scale ranging from *strongly agree* (5) to *strongly disagree* (1). Responses to each item are trichotomized into "no," "neutral," or "yes." A factor analysis was conducted on the Scale to Assess World View and a four-factor solution was reported. These factors were named Optimistic, Traditional, Here and Now, and Pessimistic.

Worldview Scale

The Worldview Scale (WVS) consists of 37 items assessing three broad philosophical-conceptual orientations of African and European worldview: (1) orientation toward nature, (2) orientation toward the physical and the nonphysical/metaphysical realms, and (3) orientation toward other human beings. Additionally, items are included that assess the six bipolar conceptual components of harmony versus antagonism toward nature, spiritualism versus materialism, collectivism versus individualism, strong versus weak religious orientation, interdependence versus separateness, and humanism versus racism. Part I of the WVS consists of 24 items to which participants respond using a 4-point Likert scale ranging from *strongly agree* (4) to *strongly disagree* (1). In part I, 15 items are positively worded for the African worldview, and 9 items are positively worded for the European worldview. Part II consists of 9 items in a forced-choice format that alternates randomly from an African worldview response set to a European worldview response set. The WVS score is computed based on the total scale score; high scores correspond to an African worldview orientation, and low scores correspond to a European worldview orientation.

Worldview Analysis Scale

The Worldview Analysis Scale is a 55-item questionnaire based on the philosophical dimensions of cosmology, epistemology, ontology, axiology, and teleology. These philosophical dimensions serve as a theoretical framework to operationalize measurable dimensions of worldview, such as perceptions of the universe, spirituality, immortality, communalism, knowledge of self, reality, reason, and indigenous value systems. Individual perceptions of these dimensions exist in the fabric of culture and are believed to influence cognitions, decisions, and behaviors. Factor analysis confirmed a seven-factor structure that included Materialistic Universe, Tangible Realism, Communalism, Indigenous Values, Knowledge of Self, Spiritual Immortality, and Spiritualism. The Worldview Analysis Scale hypothesizes several assumptions with regard to worldview assessment.

1. Worldview is a schema that is used to establish meaning consistent with a person's cultural framework.
2. Each culture possesses both universal and particular dimensions of worldview that are similar to and different from other cultures; thus, the measured dimensions should be able to differentiate between-group and within-group similarities and differences.
3. Cultures are constantly in contact with other cultures. Through these interactions, dimensions of worldview can be either borrowed and transformed in a meaningful fashion or rejected altogether.
4. Worldview is a construct that has the capacity to go beyond superficial race-based models to explore cultural phenomena.

Future Directions

Historically, the majority of people of color (African American, Asian American, Native American, Mexican American, etc.) residing in the United States in need of some type of psychological intervention do not seek professional psychological help for their personal dilemmas. Of those who seek therapeutic assistance, an estimated 50% or more prematurely discontinue treatment after the initial session. Factors cited as reasons for this premature termination include traditional psychological paradigms that reflect the worldview of the dominant culture, diagnosis and treatment by a culturally different therapist, differential expectations between clients and their therapists, and lack of resources and lack of availability of services.

People of color are more likely to rely on traditional support networks (e.g., relatives, spiritual advisors, community organizations, and friends) rather than professional psychological services. This growing body of scientific literature consistently identifies common implications (e.g., diagnosis and treatment of the culturally different, differential expectations, and lack of resources in culturally diverse communities) that the field of psychology must address to improve therapeutic practice with diverse groups. Furthermore, these studies hypothesized that factors such as worldview, values associated with the counseling process, and cultural differences between the counselor and client can negatively impact an individual's willingness to seek professional psychological services.

In addition to the cross-cultural/multicultural discourse, it is imperative to look at the impact that worldview can have on designing empirically supported treatment modalities and training competent service providers to administer such interventions. Specifically, it is important to understand the factors that influence worldview and how differences are manifested between and within ethnic groups. For example, which dimensions of worldview predict counselor preferences, treatment modality preferences, conceptualizations of health, help-seeking attitudes and behaviors, and so on? Are culture-specific treatments needed to address worldview differences, or are adjustments to current treatment modalities sufficient? It is anticipated that the construct of worldview will continue to influence the future of psychotherapy while solid empirical evidence continues to accumulate in this area of research.

Ezemenari M. Obasi, Vivian L. Tamkin, and Taisha L. Caldwell

See also Acculturation (v3); Afrocentricity/Afrocentrism (v3); Collectivism (v3); Cross-Cultural Training (v3); Cultural Relativism (v3); Cultural Values (v3); Culture (v3); Individualism (v3); Locus of Control (v3); Multicultural Counseling (v3); Multicultural Counseling Competence (v3); Multiculturalism (v3); Multicultural Psychology (v3); Religion/Religious Belief Systems (v3); Spirituality (v3); Sue, Derald Wing: Contributions to Multicultural Psychology and Counseling (v3); Universalism (v3); White, Joseph L. (v3)

Further Readings

American Psychological Association. (2002). *Guidelines on multicultural education, training, research, practice, and organizational change for psychologists.* Washington, DC: Author.

Baldwin, J. A., & Hopkins, R. (1990). African-American and European-American cultural differences as assessed by the worldviews paradigm: An empirical analysis. *Western Journal of Black Psychology, 14*(1), 38–52.

Carter, R. T. (1991). Cultural values: A review of empirical research and implications for counseling. *Journal of Counseling & Development, 70*(1), 164–173.

Constantine, G. C., & Sue, D. W. (2005). *Strategies for building multicultural competence in mental health and educational settings.* New York: Wiley.

Dana, R. H. (1993). *Multicultural assessment perspectives for professional psychology.* Boston: Allyn & Bacon.

Ibrahim, F. A., & Kahn, H. (1987). Assessment of world views. *Psychological Reports, 60*(1), 163–176.

Ibrahim, F. A., Roysircar-Sodowski, G., & Ohnishi, H. (2001). Worldview: Recent developments and needed directions. In J. G. Ponterotto, J. M. Casas, L. A. Suzuki, & C. M. Alexander (Eds.), *Handbook of multicultural counseling* (2nd ed.). Thousand Oaks, CA: Sage.

Kluckhohn, F. R., & Strodtbeck, F. L. (1961). *Variations in value orientations.* Evanston, IL: Row Paterson.

Sue, D. W. (1978). World views and counseling. *Personnel and Guidance Journal, 56,* 458–462.

Sue, D. W., Bernier, J. E., Durran, A., Pederson, P., Smith, E. J., & Vasquez-Nuttall, E. (1982). Position paper: Cross-cultural counseling competencies. *The Counseling Psychologist, 10*(2), 45–52.

White, J. L. (1970, August). Toward a Black psychology. *Ebony, 25,* 44–45, 48–50, 52.

Xenophobia

Xenophobia is derived from the terms *phobos* (meaning "fear") and *xenos* ("strangers"). Thus, *xenophobia* is defined as fear of strangers or of the unknown or of anything that is different. The fears are unwarranted and triggered by unfounded beliefs and generalizations. These fears sometimes incite hostile behavior and attitudes toward the unknown target.

Some scholars suggest that xenophobia is at the root of racism such that individuals see themselves as part of a superior racial ingroup of similar individuals and see other people as part of an inferior outgroup. The outgroup members are perceived as physically and psychologically dissimilar. Thus, prejudiced attitudes and discrimination toward the outgroup member are by-products of a xenophobic climate. Expressed preferences for ingroup familiarities are problematic and reinforce intolerance in a supposedly pluralistic society. In most societies, there are individuals who are socially, culturally, or otherwise different from the majority.

Xenophobia can lead to either overt discrimination or subtle exclusion of certain individuals. This exclusion is also problematic. Persons who present an unbiased attitude but act in subtle ways that reflect implicit biases regarding race are characterized an aversive racists. The subtlety is in justifying the racist behavior based on some factor other than race. Beyond racism, xenophobia is believed to underlie heterosexism or homophobia. These irrational and irreconcilable fears of human beings based on sexual behavior and practices are also based on gross overgeneralizations and misunderstanding.

Xenophobia is important in the context of counseling in that practitioners and clients are atypically matched by race, gender, sexual orientation, nationality, or a number of fixed factors. Xenophobia potentially contributes to racial microaggressions, subtle verbal and nonverbal communications that demean others as a function of their membership in some stereotyped group. On an implicit level, subtle behavior negatively affects therapeutic experiences and may contribute to the underuse of professional mental health services by certain groups.

People are believed to naturally categorize themselves, preferring similar others and minimizing those who are different. Although this process allows individuals to reduce complex human characteristics to simplified categories, the side effect is demeaning attitudes and behavior toward underrepresented persons across multiple contexts.

Rheeda L. Walker

See also Cultural Mistrust (v3); Cultural Paranoia (v3); Discrimination (v3); Ethnocentrism (v3); Pluralism (v3); Prejudice (v3); Racism (v3); Stereotype (v3)

Further Readings

Constantine, M. G. (2007). Racial microaggressions against African American clients in cross-racial counseling relationships. *Journal of Counseling Psychology, 54*, 1–16.

Dollard, J. (1938). Hostility and fear in social life. *Social Forces, 17,* 19–38.

Dovidio, J. F., Gaertner, S. L., Kawakami, K., & Hodson, G. (2002). Why can't we just get along? Interpersonal biases and interracial distrust. *Cultural Diversity & Ethnic Minority Psychology, 8,* 88–102.

Jones, J. M. (1997). *Prejudice and racism.* New York: McGraw-Hill.

Tajfel, K. (1969). Cognitive aspects of prejudice. *Journal of Social Issues, 25,* 79–97.